SCHOOLCRAFT COLLEGE LIBRARY

W9-BQK-160

WITHDRAWN

HN
57
.F87
1974

Furnas, J   C

_ _ _t times

DATE DUE

MAR 2 8 1995

BRADNER LIBRARY
SCHOOLCRAFT COLLEGE
LIVONIA, MICHIGAN 48152

GREAT TIMES

An Informal Social History
of the United States
1914–1929

Other Books by J. C. Furnas

Nonfiction

ANATOMY OF PARADISE

VOYAGE TO WINDWARD

GOODBYE TO UNCLE TOM

THE ROAD TO HARPERS FERRY

THE LIFE AND TIMES OF THE LATE DEMON RUM

THE AMERICANS

Novels

THE PROPHET'S CHAMBER

MANY PEOPLE PRIZE IT

THE DEVIL'S RAINBOW

LIGHTFOOT ISLAND

GREAT TIMES

An Informal Social History
of the United States

1914–1929

by J. C. Furnas

G. P. Putnam's Sons,   *New York*

HN
57
.F8724
1974

309.173
F 9879

COPYRIGHT © 1974 BY J. C. FURNAS

All rights reserved. This book, or parts thereof, must not
be reproduced in any form without permission.
Published simultaneously in Canada
by Longman Canada Limited, Toronto.

SBN: 399-11381-9

Library of Congress Catalog
Card Number: 74-79645

PRINTED IN THE UNITED STATES OF AMERICA

*To the no longer conceivable
Man from Mars
for whom this book
was originally intended*

Acknowledgments

The author is deeply indebted first and foremost to the Princeton University Library; then to the New York Society Library and the New York Public Library. Other institutions from whose generosity he has profited include the San Francisco Public Library, the Trenton Public Library, the San Diego Public Library, the Chicago Public Library, the Free Library of Philadelphia, the Library of Teachers College Columbia University, the Flemington Public Library, the Hunterdon County Library, the School of Hotel Administration of Cornell University, Syracuse University, Dartmouth University, the Chicago Historical Society, the Missouri Historical Society, the Museum of Modern Art, the Detroit Institute of Fine Arts, the American Numismatic Society, the Museum of the City of New York, the National Geographic Society, Franklin College, Crawfordsville High School, the Indianapolis *News*, the Chicago *Tribune*, the American Association of University Professors, the National Association for the Advancement of Colored People . . . and many others.

Individuals kindly supplying data or consultation include Ernest Angell, Albert Boni, Hodding Carter, Stuart Chase, John Dos Passos, Doris E. King, Clark Kinnaird, Freeman Lewis, Nathaniel A. Owings, Helen Papashvily, Max Putzel, Francis Russell, Harold Seymour, Charlton W. Tebeau, Calvin Trillin, Edith Wynner, Michael Yatron . . . and many others inadvertently omitted. None of those mentioned has the slightest responsibility for opinions expressed in the text by the author.

He repeats his previously published sentiments about the origin of this book's predecessor, *The Americans*: He is "obliged to Walter Minton of G. P. Putnam's Sons for suggesting this project, which otherwise would never have occurred to him, and to Harvey Ginsberg of the same firm for being so considerate a midwife." He owes Pearl Hanig's conscientious copyreading for the several occasions on which she turned up errors he would have blushed for. He is grateful to Marjorie Lawrence Street for her skilled prowling of the manuscript from the author's side of the court.

Gratitude is also due all those whose courtesies arranged permissions to quote from copyrighted items, as follows: Robert Benchley, from "Joe McGee the Baggageman," reprinted by permission of Mrs. Gertrude D. Benchley.

Stephen Vincent Benét, from "Short Ode," in *Selected Works of Stephen Vincent Benét*, Holt, Rinehart & Winston, Inc. Copyright © 1936 by Stephen Vincent Benét, copyright © 1964 by Stephen Vincent Benét. Reprinted by permission of Brandt & Brandt.

Elmer Davis, from *Show Window*, The John Day Company. Copyright © by Elmer Davis. Reprinted by permission of Robert Lloyd Davis.

John Dos Passos, all by permission of Elizabeth H. Dos Passos:
  From *The Best Times*, copyright © 1966 by John Dos Passos.
    The Big Money, copyright © 1937 by John Dos Passos, renewed copyright © by John Dos Passos 1965.
    Number One, copyright © 1943 by John Dos Passos, renewed copyright © 1971 by John Dos Passos.
    One Man's Initiation, copyright © 1969 by John Dos Passos.
    Three Soldiers, copyright © 1921 by John Dos Passos, renewed copyright © 1949 by John Dos Passos.

Edgar A. Guest, from "The Auto" in *Collected Works of Edgar Guest*, copyright © 1934 by Reilly & Lee Company. Used by permission.

"I Didn't Raise My Boy to Be a Soldier," words by Alfred Bryan, music by Al Piantadosi. Copyright © 1915, renewed copyright © 1943. Leo Feist, Inc., N.Y., N.Y. Used by permission.

Vachel Lindsay, from "The Santa Fe Trail" and "Mae Marsh . . . ," in *Collected Poems*, copyright © 1914; 1917 by Macmillan Publishing Company, Inc., renewed copyright © 1942 by Elizabeth C. Lindsay. Used by permission.

"The coming of archy," copyright © 1927 by Doubleday and Company, Inc., from the book *The lives and times of archy and mehitabel* by Don Marquis. Reprinted by permission of Doubleday and Company, Inc.

Edgar Lee Masters, from *The Spoon River Anthology*, The Macmillan Company, Inc., copyright © 1915 by Edgar Lee Masters. Used by permission of Ellen C. Masters.

Grantland Rice, from "Babe Ruth," reprinted with permission of North American Newspaper Alliance, copyright © 1948 by NANA.

Edward Arlington Robinson, "Miniver Cheevy" from *The Town Down the River*, copyright © 1907, Charles Scribner's Sons. Reprinted by permission of Charles Scribner's Sons.

Carl Sandburg, from "The Contemporary Bunkshooter" in *The Complete Poems of Carl Sandburg*, revised and expanded edition, copyright © 1970 by Harcourt Brace Jovanovich. Used by permission.

Contents

Introduction

MY *The Americans* of several years ago described our countrymen's circumstances and ways-of-doing from the time of the Lost Colony to 1914. It sought to follow Sir George Macaulay Trevelyan's definition of social history as "history with the politics left out." Certain lapses made it clear, however, that, as common sense had already warned, complete adherence to that formula is necessarily impossible.

This successor volume uses the same compass. But the waters to be navigated make it a rather different kind of voyage. It is even harder to keep politics out. Since World War I Americans have had a stronger smell of Aristotle's "political animal" than their forebears had. And personal views are likelier to have crept into this text because the writer was often a spectator of and, in some of the things dealt with, more or less of a participant in his subject matter. That can help a reporter but may also sometimes clog his judgment. Another clog is the time factor. As Heraclitus said, one cannot wade into the same river twice. He might have added that there are two reasons for that: Neither water nor wader is the same.

I

Old Times That Were Before Us

There are two kinds of fools: Those who say "This is new and therefore better," and others who say "This is old and therefore good."

—THE VERY REVEREND WILLIAM RALPH INGE

T HE time span of this book begins on January 1, 1914. The hemispherical scoop for ice cream was replacing the generous conical kind. They were about to break ground for the Lincoln Memorial in Washington and the Panama-Pacific Exposition in San Francisco. The last known specimen of the passenger pigeon—its teeming millions had once been an ornithological marvel—was dying in a cage in Cincinnati.

The United States then contained only half as many Americans,* actual or nominal, as it does now. They occupied only half the room, needed only half the raw materials—indeed far less, for the standard of consumption was far lower—and created on the whole less friction than the 200,000,000-odd now exploiting the same area. Yet that 100,000,000 also made the United States the world's fourth most populous polity after China, India and Russia, and the already immense results of Western technology made it far wealthier per capita.

Backward glances make the nation of 1914 look simple and old-timey. It was still taken for granted that not only factories and retail stores but also banks and offices were open for business at least half of Saturday, the schoolteacher being the only jobholder accustomed to the day off. In a good many sizable towns it was still advisable to boil the drinking water in summer. Yet the time's own observers thought it rich in new and complicated things. Its cities, for instance, were already swathed in chaotic suburbs woven by hit-or-miss real estate schemes. Yet since the automobile had its conquests still to make, such elder suburbs were fairly compact in today's terms. "Only a stone's throw from the station"—the house seller's favorite phrase—meant one expected to walk to the commuting train in most weathers, maybe no farther than a city man to his trolley stop or El station. Some commuters living farther out used trolley cars that ran along Forest Drive or Riverview Avenue to the station of the Boston & Albany or the Putnam Division or the Northwestern or the SP. Hence the "Toonerville

* In this book "American" means "a more or less permanent inhabitant of the United States without regard to birthright-citizenship, naturalization or ethnic origin." Positively: "Anybody whose social presence is an intramural responsibility of the United States." It excludes few except, say, foreign actors, athletes, diplomats, transient businessmen, tourists. . . .

Trolley That Meets All the Trains" of Fontaine Fox's serial newspaper cartoons based on a railroad-feeder service in commuting Westchester County. The rigidity of these trolley routes was one of the things that kept suburbanites of 1914 from settling in patterns as diffuse and extensive as those that the automobile fostered.

The ailment that would almost destroy trolley cars had just struck California—the jitney bus, a private automobile the driver of which picked up persons on the street and for 5 cents (in the slang of the day a "jitney") transported them wherever they wished along a known route. Within a year the industry was large enough to have become jokesmiths' material. Next came licensing of jitneys; then confining them to arbitrary routes; then expanding them into multiseated buses. . . . Commuters affluent enough to eschew jitneys and trolleys might still go to the station horse-drawn with a groom or coachman driving the rig home and fetching it to the station in the evening. The less conservative, though also affluent, might substitute an automobile with chauffeur. (It still made talk when a rich man, even a young one, habitually took the wheel alone.) Otherwise suburbs felt little of the pending gasoline revolution. When listing the technological complications awaiting the modern child of 1914, John and Evelyn Dewey's study of Progressive schools mentioned "railways and steamboats, traction cars . . . telegraphs and telephones . . ." [1] but not automobiles. One-car families were only a small, if growing, minority—the national ratio was still under 100 automobiles per 1,000 families. Installment buying of automobiles, already common for sewing machines and furniture, was popular enough to be deplored in the press. But most people still thought it immoral to go into debt for so costly a consumption item, and the manufacturers had not yet thought of creating their own finance companies to encourage sales. The decent and usual way to acquire a "machine," as 1914 called the automobile, was to save up for its whole cost—little occasion yet for Will Rogers' suggestion that it would greatly relieve traffic congestion if the law barred all cars from the road till they were paid for in full.

The commuter's wife did not drive him to the 7:58 because the automobile was still nothing for a lady to wrangle. Electric self-starters, practical by 1911, were built into only one in three models (usually expensive ones) available in 1914. Few women could crank starterless cars; few had the mechanical savvy to cajole into action a Chalmers or Marmon that, though starter-equipped, lacked automatic choke and spark adjustment. Those suave electric broughams designed with women in mind had a short radius of use, were confined to paved streets—and cost a lot. The first women to drive gasoline cars in significant numbers were gay young things at gilded summer resorts. Their Locomobile or White roadsters usually carried not only starters but also chauffeurs for the roadside repairs that made motoring so exasperating a sport. Otherwise Woman's role in the dawning motor age remained that of backseat driver, and jokes about her genius for it duly proliferated.

Skimming through the Berkshires with a pretty debutante sounds agreeable, but otherwise the lot of the chauffeur, whether coachman turned mechanic or youngster already hooked on gasoline, was hard. Hours were long and irregular, car designers were only beginning to take account of weather with tire chains (first marketed in 1905) and allegedly nonskid tires. The town car or landaulet bodies popular among plutocrats sheltered the boss but left the chauffeur out in rain or snow, or with a mere roof, no side protection, until well into the 1920's. Even expensive runabouts—a term borrowed from carriage makers for cars of sporty flavor—had no tops at all. For the more prosaic roadster (two passenger) and touring car (five or, with jump seats, seven passenger) there were, often at extra cost, folding tops of fabric stretched over struts and braces and anchored to the windshield frame. To rig these contraptions was about as arduous as getting all plain sail on a brig. Against rain, snow or icy air one broke out black rubber side curtains of fiendishly tortuous design.

The obvious remedy was to extend the town car's weatherproof hutch over the whole, integrating upper works and body as in the electric brougham. One version for cold seasons mounted on the touring car a detachable roof-and-windows like a squared-off diving bell. The sales appeal—"Now you can use your car all winter!"—showed what a fair-weather plaything the automobile still was. Sounder design borrowing European ideas—the exotic ancestry of America's cars long remained evident—permanently joined roof and body. This made the touring car a sedan (from the enclosed chair that took fine folks to parties in the days of cocked hats) and the roadster a coupe (French for a two-passenger closed carriage but in the American trade pronounced "coop" as if for poultry).

Such construction made a car cost 30 percent more, increased the nuisance of rattles and squeaks and, since safety glass was far in the future, quadrupled the ghastly hazard presented by a shattering windshield. Touring cars still sold throughout the 1920's, even dominated new sales until 1923, when the Hudson Motor Car Company brought out sedans at only $100 extra. But the handwriting had been on the wall ever since Henry Ford made and prospered with the first Model T sedan, the pun-named Tudor model. With the triumph of the closed car, comfort and workaday utility leached away the dashing-plaything values associated with dust veils, goggles, windburn, open cutouts, the word "joyride" and acetylene headlights. As ownership of cars penetrated lower-income groups to an extent that Europe would not approach for forty years, it shifted away from ostentatious fun toward serious, all-weather, twenty-four-hour economic use. In time it would be the chief means to get to work, buy household supplies, visit one's peers and travel for business and pleasure. Only secondarily would its relative cost, speed and glitter seek for a prestige now often misinterpreted as of erotic content. Those preaching to advertisers that the automobile is a sex symbol of modern provenance are unaware that a hundred years ago the horse owner hung pride and prestige on the speed and sleekness of the animal he rode or drove in very much the same terms.

The automobile was still as rugged as a Mongolian war wagon when its flavor of adventure sent growing numbers of Americans on self-conscious prolonged trips into a roadside world vastly unlike today's. Its advertising was mostly painted on barns and aimed at the farmer—patent medicines, overalls, farm machinery, chewing tobacco. The filling station as such did not exist. Gasoline and oil came from the few garages or the general stores supplying farmers who cut wood and pumped water with gasoline motors. The cross-country motorist carried much extra fuel and oil and spare tires, jacks, pumps, tire patches, spare tubes and the kit of tire irons used to get a flat off the rim. For tires long remained irksomely flimsy, and the readily changed spare wheel, though introduced in 1913, took long to gain acceptance. Wise motorists also shipped a tent, bedding and emergency rations, for motels were unheard of, small-town hotels usually dismal to atrocious and farm households not always willing to lodge and feed strangers even for pay.

The Good Roads movement that bicyclists launched in the 1890's accomplished little until 1916, when the first federal subsidy to improve state highways was appropriated. When road building and maintenance were wholly the work of counties and townships, each petty boundary meant abrupt change, usually for the worse, maybe complete disappearance of the road. In 1914 America had only 750 miles of concrete highway. The waterbound macadam of what decent roads there were disintegrated under increasing motor traffic. A few hours of rain turned the others, often those connecting principal towns, into slithery swamps. Where the soil contained much clay, not even tire chains got through. In dry weather traction was better but dust was smothering. Getting lost was inevitable—not just a few miles of straying but utter bewilderment in a maze of rutted tracks such as underlay the old story about "You can't get there from here." Off most well-beaten ways one relied on the *Automobile Blue Book*. It mentioned no route numbers, for there were none, instead told the motorist to follow this gravel road for 3.2 miles and take the left of the fork beyond a big barn advertising 666 malaria cure; in wet weather choose the right of the fork though that way it's four miles farther to Springtown. . . . Publicity had made the Lincoln Highway, planned as the nation's first coast-to-coast route in 1913, a household word, but west of the Mississippi evidence that it existed consisted of occasional red, white and blue markers along a rutted quagmire that would daunt a modern driver in a Jeep.

Venturesome motorists bragged of their prowess with towropes and fence rails for levers. To show the distances they dared, they flew pennants carrying the names of their hometowns: "They tour from St. Louis, Columbus, Manistee," chanted Vachel Lindsay of the Southwest-bound traffic in Kansas:

> Cars from Concord, Niagara, Boston
> Cars from Topeka, Emporia, and Austin.
> Cars from Alton, Oswego, Toledo . . .
>   While I sit by the milestone
>   And watch the sky,
>   The United States
>   Goes by. . . .[2]

Their route ran along the main line of the Atchison, Topeka & Santa Fe. Its crack trains made far better time than the most powerful automobiles of the period laboring upgrade with radiators steaming. We know now that every ungainly touring car that got through—as most of them did—added a nail to the coffin of the sleek all-Pullman limited. Even in 1916, however, though the number of cars in use neared 6,000,000 and the Panama-California Exposition at San Diego deliberately enticed motorists to try the trip, *Life*—the dominant humor, cartoon and comment weekly of the period— said that automobiles might come in handy during railroad strikes but they could never compete on long hauls.

Among those driving across the continent to the exposition in 1915 was Mrs. Emily Post, not yet arbitress of the nation's social etiquette but already a handsome, middle-aged ornament of New York Society (capitalized) and author of novels about Americans in Europe. For *Collier's* magazine, she, her sister and her son, a Harvard senior and amateur chauffeur eager for greasy, gritty difficulties, set out from Manhattan in the same frame of mind as if they had been following Theodore Roosevelt up the River of Doubt. The automobile clubs could tell them only that going by way of St. Louis was suicide. In some states the open country speed limit was 20 mph, nudged up to 25 mph by most drivers. Nowhere did the state of the roads let their car, which had done well by them in European conditions, go much over 40 mph. Much of the time it was in second or low gear and barely getting through. Via the Raton Pass and Albuquerque bridges were scarce, but the fords were "generally easy" and in any case "at those . . . too sandy or deep, the automobile associations keep teams [of horses] standing on purpose to see you through." [3]

It took four weeks partly because most rainstorms meant waiting for horse-drawn scrapers to reduce the worst of the ruts and turn the mud into navigable surface. All very primitive; but the bit that best brings it home that this was a different motorists' world is Mrs. Post's joy in "seeing our country for the first time! . . . a train window gives one only . . . the ragged outskirts of the town . . . [for motorists] the roads become the best

avenues of the cities and go past the front entrances of farms. . . .
Well-fenced fields under perfect cultivation . . . splendid-looking cows,
horses, houses, barns. . . ." [4] The next year Theodore Dreiser was noting
as advantages of motor travel "the prospect of new and varied roads,
intimate contact with woodland silences . . . change your mind and go by
this route or that according to your mood. . . ." [5] Nothing could be less
like the interstate freeways that consummate what a rueful highway
engineer promised me thirty years ago: "We'll soon have it fixed so you can
drive from Bangor to Miami and never see a traffic light—or anything else."

The other chief private motive power of 1914—the horse, preferred to the
ox in most uses by the mid-1800's—faced eventual displacement by internal
combustion. Twenty years earlier Ransom E. Olds, whose high rank among
early automobile men persists in the trademark Oldsmobile, first in Detroit
to make a profit from making automobiles, described what he was tinkering
with as better than the horse because "It never kicks or bites, never tires on
long runs, and never sweats in hot weather . . . does not require care in the
stable and only eats when on the road." [6] The electric trolley car had
already spared myriads of horses and mules the chore of daylong plodding
between rails. Gasoline-powered as well as electric taxicabs were replacing
horse-drawn hacks. On omnibuses on Fifth Avenue and elsewhere gasoline
was taking over from hay as source of energy.

Yet heavy lags persisted. Horses still drew the Parmelee Transfer buses
that, with such clatter of hooves on cobblestones, shifted rail passengers
among Chicago's scattered terminals. In the country Four Hooves was
resisting Four Wheels with temporary success. Prospering farmers might
now use automobiles to go to town and to church. Power take-offs and
steel-lugged wheels to make an off-and-on tractor of the Model T were
pointed toward gasoline as a farm necessity. But as yet available tractors
were large and costly, specialized for the huge wheat farms of the West and
lumbering, and the cheap, light tractor was only one of Henry Ford's
dreams. The versatility of Prince and Maud—and Jeff and Sukey in the
mule-minded South—kept the horse and mule population rising in the
decade 1910–1920. Children riding in the country in Pop's Reo could still
find enough equine data for the game of White Horse—score one for white,
two for a mule, three for a white mule.

On the farm this lag had ecological virtues. The litter and excreta from
Prince's stall were good fertilizer and humus builders. In cities, however, the
dwindling of the horse population would be an important sanitary
reform—less and less yellow dung blowing dry in the wind, slippery
underfoot in the rain, requiring armies of street cleaners whose efforts to
keep up with the nuisance were as futile as Hera hoped Hercules' task in the
Augean Stables would be. Only in our time would cities learn that they had
exchanged scatological for chemical pollution—and the latter was worse.

The shift was also disastrous for English sparrows, imported exotics that, thriving on horse droppings, had practically taken over the cities.

Strange as it now sounds, the change from horse to automobile meant safer transportation for people. The current rate of motoring fatalities per 100,000,000 miles is less than a tenth of those resulting from kicking, bucking and runaways. From a less anthropocentric view, however, consider what a blessing it was for horses to be so largely exempted from toil and elevated in steadily growing numbers to the status of pampered national pets. The internal-combustion motor did more for draft animals than anything humane societies had done in the previous fifty years. City pavements and heavy loads on steep hills had never suited the way God made horses. Roughshoeing could not keep the ice of Northern winters from repeating the pitiful sight of downed horses terrified and so injuring themselves in struggles to get up that they had to be shot. Well-meant laws backed by zealous amateurs could not keep horses and mules from too often being pointlessly beaten, overworked while underfed, inadequately watered and sheltered, on farms as well as in town. The theory that economic self-interest persuaded human beings not to damage valuable property helped four-footed no better than it had two-footed slaves.

In 1915 a premature historian of the automobile proclaimed: "The day of railroad building is definitely done. . . . It is cheaper to build good roads than railroads." [7] Yet the iron horse too looked deceptively healthy. His numbers snorting along American rails grew until the Depression of the 1930's. New trackage, often double tracking of existing lines for higher capacity, grew to match, and the great locomotives using it, as long and weighing as much as many a square-rigged ship, were among the most majestic artifacts that man ever created. Since the automobiles coming into use as yet seldom went long distances, the number of railroad passengers almost kept pace with growth of population toward 1920. Concomitant improvements in roadbed and schedules were doing well by the passenger deluxe. The Twentieth Century Limited, pride of the New York Central, welcomed powerful bankers with piqué-edged vests and famous actresses, all furs, hothouse violets and velvet toques, midafternoon at New York City's Grand Central Terminal and whisked them to Chicago's La Salle Street Station by late breakfast time. The Pennsylvania Railroad called its Broadway Limited, making an equivalent schedule by way of Philadelphia, "the greatest commercial masterpiece of the ages." [8] Both trains were all steel—splintery, fire-prone wooden cars were being relegated to branch lines—and supplied baths, barbering, stenographer service and bar cars pouring anything from champagne to Jack Rose cocktails. Their dining cars were stiff with white napery, heavy silver and a menu as opulent as those of most hotels. If it did not mention one's heart's desire, the steward could probably turn up nightingales' tongues in the refrigerator attached to the wonder-working galley. Breakfast, as the train howled across the Indiana flatland or sleeked down the left bank of the Hudson, offered turkey hash, finnan haddie, steaks as well as ham and eggs and hot cereals as well as the world's finest toast crossbarred and slightly smoky from being made on a grill. . . .

Schedules beyond Chicago were so pared down that the magnate bound for the Coast from the Northeast could make the trip in four days with a single change at Chicago. Through openings in the snowsheds he could see from the diner the striking scenery among which, only sixty-eight years earlier, the snowbound Donner party of emigrants had dined on frozen human corpses. Once he left the diner, however, luxury dwindled. The dimensions of his elaborately upholstered drawing room at one end of the Pullman sleeping car were not unlike those of a jail cell. Less affluent passengers spent those four days in Pullman "sections"—pewlike facing seats converted at night into lower and upper berths tolerable only by contrast with the spine-racking seats in which coach passengers sat up to sleep. The arts of dressing while lying on the back in a Pullman upper and of getting into it without either waiting for the porter's little ladder or maiming the occupant of the lower are, thank heaven, lost these days. A drawing room had its own washbasin and toilet; the run of passengers competed for one toilet and three basins per sex. The brakeman and conductor in the roomy caboose of the freight trundling past on the eastbound track were better off—and got paid for being there.

The most for the money was the overstuffed revolving chairs of the daytime parlor car with card tables and refreshments available from a deft porter—and by each chair a brass spittoon to recall a less fastidious day. But even this smooth-sliding example of what money could buy was overheated by overzealous steam in winter and necessarily too hot in summer. Those narrow, fine wire screens in the windows were meant to admit breezes, but what chiefly came in was gritty black soot from the smokestack ahead. That was the reason for the porter's welcoming rite—putting the passenger's hat in a paper bag—and for his parting rite—dusting him off, neck to heels, with an obsequious whisk broom. Oil-burning locomotives being still scarce, this nuisance was absent only on the few electrified lines, chiefly the Chicago, Milwaukee, St. Paul & Pacific and the busiest part of the Pennsylvania.

Sides of beef and crates of oranges moving by rail were artificially cooled, but the human passenger in summer had only ice water from a dribbly tank. The envelope-shaped paper cups reflected growing public awareness of disease germs. During the run across the Mojave Desert the first generation of talent using the Santa Fe—the film colony's traditional railroad—wore ice bags on the head hangover-fashion. But nothing about the rails was more archaic than the slowness of their freight trains gently clickety-clicking along where today's hotshot freights hit what was then express-flier speed. This sluggishness carried no economic penalty. Faster freights would have brought higher cost of maintaining the roadbed, and railroad wages were not yet high enough to make savings in ton-miles-per-hour a vital issue. The over-the-road motor truck hardly existed though railroad managements' shortsighted policies were already doing all they could to make it an attractive alternative.

The airplane for passengers, mail or freight was far in the future. Its chief economic use was to draw crowds to fairs and expositions. A few women pilots, Ruth Law the best known, lent a special tingle to such exhibitions. Europe was well ahead of America in use of planes in war. Transatlantic flight by the Newfoundland-Azores stepping-stones route was the objective of the *America* flying boat built by Glenn Curtiss for Rodman Wanamaker, sporty son of Philadelphia's great department-store fortune. A storm broke up the first *America*; then World War I smothered the scheme. Wilbur and Orville Wright had thought of their invention as primarily a weapon. Appropriately it took that cataclysmic war to develop and train enough pilots to put substance into the dream of airmail across the Atlantic and coast to coast.

The cumbrousness of other communications is striking in the telephone of 1914. Long-distance calls between New York City and Chicago were the latest technological miracle. The instrument on which a Wall Street broker spoke to his Boston or Philadelphia branch or estate on Long Island was fittingly clumsy—a mouthpiece on a disk-bottomed stand like a table microphone; its cylindrical receiver was applied to the ear in use, otherwise hung on a cut-off hook, hence the surviving idiom: to hang up. The French phone—ancestor of today's cradle instrument—was known only in the European high life of movies and stage plays. The mere sight of it on a gilt table upstage-left warned that the ensuing drama concerned some lovely woman no better than she should be. Party lines, which still supply neighborly interaction in some rural areas, were then common in cities too. Though primitive dial systems were already in use here and there, the nation in general would place local as well as long-distance calls through a live operator—the Hello Central so dear to Tin Pan Alley. In the country one summoned her by grinding the crank of a gooseneck telephone mounted on a shoulder-high wooden box. Such things are in museums now. To see them there disconcerts us who once took them for granted in daily life.

In most respects the telegraph was the nation's nervous system. It kept salesmen in touch, speculators close to brokers, and relayed prompt quotations on securities and commodities over leased wires wherever such data were badly needed. Daily S. F. B. Morse's dots and dashes sent millions of words to newspapers from their own correspondents and the wire services led by the Associated Press. Nor had cheap long-distance rates yet stifled the ten-word telegram and the fifty-word night letter. The rival companies went to what now seem incredible pains to get the yellow Western Union envelope or blue Postal Telegraph envelope promptly to its addressee. They maintained offices in quite small towns. In even smaller ones the railroad's stationmaster/baggageman/telegrapher accepted private telegrams and saw to delivery of incoming ones telling that Aunt Mabel had passed on or Lester Blodgett wanted $5 train fare wired to Springfield. The uniformed messengers, mostly teen-age boys, who bicycled telegrams to delivery in large towns learned more than befitted tender years about the racier aspects of 1914.

Radio was only a new public tool confined to marine use. Talked up as a potential lifesaver, it sadly disappointed the world when the *Titanic* sank in 1912. Otherwise "communications"—that owlish but fashionable collective —consisted chiefly of newspapers. Today one would learn of a sudden landing of the U.S. Marines in Mexico through a radio or TV bulletin within minutes of the first hint from Washington or flash from Reuters. In April, 1914, America first learned of the landings at Veracruz through a sort of multiple town crier—a scamper of newsboys fanning out through the streets: "Wee-uxtry pay-puh! Read all about it!" It had taken that local paper many, many minutes to work a scare headline and the text of the bulletin into the front page and put an extra edition through. Outlying villages might know nothing of a crisis until Number Seven puffed into the depot in the late afternoon carrying copies. Farm folks might have to wait until the mail edition reached the RFD box at the foot of the lane next day.

America is now so used to broadcasting that nobody under the age of sixty can grasp how little professional entertainment farm folks had in 1914. And their relations to what they did have sound still stranger. A not too small county seat might occasionally see tent-show repertory troupes, but the straitlaced—usually dominant in numbers, always so in influence— stayed away because the the*ay*ter was sinful. Also taboo were the girlie shows of carnivals and the midways of county and state fairs. Springfield might have recently acquired a dime movie house increasingly accessible as farmers got automobiles, showing last year's features once or twice a week. But movies too were immoral as well as newfangled, so attendance per capita was lower than in cities. The one great break in this drought was the summer week when the Chautauqua—show business reassuringly masked as uplift—hit town. Then Model T's and Hupps and Overlands plus newlyweds in buggies and family-filled springwagons rolled dustily in, each occupant with a season ticket for the annual cultural spree.

This queer segment of the performing arts, peripatetic but not at all fly-by-night, was barely ten years old and doomed to die in ten more years, yet in 1914 it sold nearly 25,000,000 of those season tickets. In 1924, the peak and penultimate year, some 35,000,000 made up the total audience, almost a third of the nation drawn into 12,000-odd towns and villages. The name and the thing were descended from Chautauqua, New York, a lake resort where for some decades a vast summer school for pious adult education, stiff with lecturers, had drawn thousands of Americans of the sort who taught Sunday School classes and joined Dry organizations. In emulation gradually sprang up some 200 minor "Chautauquas" at Winona Lake, Indiana, Pacific Grove, California, Lakeside, Ohio, and so on, each with an open-sided lecture hall, streets of cottages or tents to rent to those taking courses and often a miniature mock-up of the Holy Land about the size of a tennis court.

To diversify platform programs, Chautauquas began to book hymn-singing quartets and churchly instrumental groups who were gradually allowed to branch out into an occasional decorous secular selection. Further to enliven morality came the "chalk talker," a gaily glib lecturer who synchronized patter and snatches of song with his swift fingers drawing in colored chalks The Coming Storm or The Little Gray Home in the West about how the boy left home and took to drink and finally returned all dried out and remorseful to pillow his aching head on the grave wherein lay Mother brokenhearted but asleep in Jesus—and there sure enough with three twists of the chalk were the gravestone and the prodigal tottering up the path. In no time, thanks to moral dramatic monologists, sacred accordionists and gospel elocutionists, the fare enjoyed in 1900 by the sweatily corseted lady students and their male counterparts in straw hats and flannel trousers was, though still determinedly uplifting in theory, far more entertaining than it had been in 1880.

In 1903 the long-established Redpath Lyceum Bureau booking lecturers and supplementary talent into the Midwest's Chautauquas was managed by two bright youngsters who tried to increase bookings by stirring up one-week-only, tent Chautauquas in the many towns that lacked the permanent kind. The first season they lost their shirts. The second season, after they had learned what not to do, was wildly profitable. Rapidly they developed a prospering pattern: A local committee was persuaded to guarantee costs and sell enough tickets to cover. On the appointed day a huge brown tent and knockdown seating and a college boy crew to set it up appeared by rail. Each day for a week a different set of lecturers, singers, musicians and so on arrived, did their stuff in the tent and departed to do it all over again in the next town on the circuit. The nation developed scores of bookers organizing and supplying such circuits. Behold a new institution! the Chautauqua that country folks came to expect annually like the Fourth of July and Groundhog Day. Every year its one-sheet advertisements bloomed in store windows and its gay little pennants fluttered on wires strung across Main Street and the season-ticket sellers fanned out through town and countryside to make sure that the guarantors—the banker, the owner of the dry goods store and the three or four canniest local farmers who did a little note shaving on the side—were not left holding the bag.

All for the sake of spiritual and cultural values. Hence the nuclei of Chautauqua programs were lecturers—some nationally known figures, such as William Jennings Bryan, who spent more time lecturing on the Bible and Temperance at Chautauquas than as formal politician. Country folks' latent Populism welcomed those of Progressive bent—Robert M. La Follette, George W. Norris, Albert J. Beveridge found the Chautauqua platform a handy and lucrative avenue to the grass-roots mind; so did downright radicals like Clarence Darrow, Lincoln Steffens, Eugene V. Debs. The typical Chautauqua star, however, was the logorrheic parson preaching the close relation between dollars and virtue in a fashion that would have pleased Max Weber, if not John Calvin. On the fees from 6,000 renditions of his great lecture "Acres of Diamonds," the Reverend Russell H. Conwell founded Temple University in Philadelphia. Its theme was the good man's duty to get rich so that, like Andrew Carnegie and the Rockefellers, he could do good with his money. Conwell and Bryan were the piers of the Chautauqua arch. The keystone was Colonel George W. Bain's triumph of moral spellbinding in a Dixie accent, "If I Could Live Life Over."

A shifting variety of acts that, though clean as a small boy's mouth just washed out with soap, often leaned toward lightmindedness set off such major jewels. A troupe of Swiss yodelers come to America for the St. Louis Exposition of 1904 discovered how well Chautauqua bookings filled in the summer and became fixtures in the brown tents. Also popular were the Mercedes Ladies' String Quartet, Dunbar's Bell Ringing Singers, the Kaffir Boys' Choir of genuine Bantu Africans, dance troupes of Maori from New Zealand and assorted Red Indian, Hawaiian and allegedly Scottish acts featuring the exotic costumes appropriate. "The native land of the Musical Guardsmen was never made quite clear," a Redpath manager recalled, "but to judge from its resplendent uniforms it hailed from either Ruritania or Graustark." [9] The "pre-lude" might consist of a trio of girl cornetists in Dutch costume blatting out "The End of a Perfect Day" or a magician or a ventriloquist—Edgar Bergen and Charlie McCarthy worked Chautauquas in their early days—or one Mae Saltmarsh managing—God knows how—to play trombone and piano at the same time.

Much Chautauqua music, however, particularly in the staider days before 1914, was probably constructive. An instrumental quintet specializing in request numbers found that Beethoven's Minuet in G was most liked; also valued were Mendelssohn's *Spring Song*, Dvorak's *Humoresque*, Handel's Largo from *Xerxes*—from the *What Every Pianist Plays* book, true, but sounder music than their grandfathers had usually known. Chautauqua also greatly eroded Decaturville's prejudice against the the*ay*ter. Quick-change artists and elocutionists doing all the characters in famous novels, then venturing onto literary flavored plays like *Richelieu*, gradually inveigled

Chautauqua audiences into the essentials of drama. By 1914 Redpath's dared book the then-famous Ben Greet Players in their cut-down—and cleaned-up—repertory of Shakespeare. When the heavens failed to fall, Chautauqua slid into tabloid versions of innocent Broadway hits like *Turn to the Right!*—and there was the the*ay*ter full blown under the staidest auspices. Some students of Chautauqua credit it with crucially damaging the ancestral taboo on worldly doings on Sunday. Bookings required Sunday performances if weekdays were to shift smoothly, and though nobody had to come, there was that season ticket and James Whitcomb Riley was to read "That Old Sweetheart of Mine" and "Out to Old Aunt Mary's" and everybody knew Chautauqua was churchgoing respectable and a cultural credit to the town.

In time this new show business might have developed its own popular art forms instead of merely cannibalizing vaudeville, the Lyceum lecture and the lower levels of Actors' Equity. But it looked ominous, though devastatingly logical, when Chautauqua's claim to primarily educational purposes did not exempt it from the federal amusement tax after World War I. Anyway, the rise of movies and radio combined with, some thought, a lower quality of bookings made it wilt and die, suddenly as dead as celluloid collars, in 1925. One could no longer sit on green-painted bleachers in a brown tent, wielding a palm-leaf fan carrying the name of the local undertaker and relishing the watermelonish smell of fresh-trodden grass while the Chicago Methodist Preachers' Quartet tore into "The Little Brown Church in the Wildwood." Strange that a thing succumbing so young should sound old-timey now.

Nor was old-timeyness always so countryfied. The footgear of the Chautauqua committee was ankle-high boots usually laced, sometimes buttoned, but so was that of the chairman of the board of the important bank in Chicago or Philadelphia. Only big-city dudes—a pejorative for what was earlier known as a dandy—supplemented black patent leather low shoes with those archaic devices, white, gray, lavender or fawn spats. Also, all the time he was outdoors practically every man, from the farmer in the furrow to the traveling salesman who sparked his daughter, wore some sort of headgear. "I took my hat and went" was all one word. Boys and lower-bracket breadwinners and upper-bracket sportsmen favored visored caps of woolen textiles. White-collar men wore hats, the stiffer sort the derby—Britain's bowler—but most were committed to the soft felt Fedora with a dint in each side of the crown. The clothes that went with it still survive in the comic panels *They'll Do It Every Time* and *Our Boarding House* in which the men in the office and at Mrs. Hoople's table wear high detachable collars, waistcoats and neckties left on even when jackets are taken off. The last vestiges of those conventions vanished when the GI's came home in 1945–46.

Women were equally hatbound. Take it also for granted that both the ladies with palm-leaf fans in the Chautauqua tent and those with ostrich-feather fans in boxes at the Metropolitan Opera were laced up the back in strong-boned corsets then practically universal for females past the age of fifteen. The upward flare of the thing propped up the breasts, so only the grotesquely overdeveloped needed the brassiere. In the seedier parts of great cities as well as in hayseedy small towns Mrs. Hoople's boardinghouse still flourished for young bachelors, the widowed and young married couples timid about setting up their own vines and fig trees. The landladies depended on carpet sweeper, carpet beater, ceiling mop, broom and dustpan because, though electric vacuum cleaners were available, they were expensive and inefficient, and in any case a modest boardinghouse, even in a sizable city, might well not have installed electricity; gaslight still had a place in dwellings as well as in streetlights. The only electric appliances listed for an enterprising lower-middle-income family in New York City in mid-1915 were, in addition to lighting fixtures, flatiron and vacuum cleaner. No electric toaster, no electric mixer, no electric percolator, no electric refrigerator—a dank, wood-sheathed icebox cooled by ice delivered daily from a horse-drawn wagon did what it could for the butter, eggs, milk and round steak; a numbered card in the front window told the driver how many pounds to bring in today. One version of hide-and-seek that children played after supper was called "Tap on the Icebox." And the iceman, a daily visitor when husband was away at factory or office, naturally found a place in the folklore of bawdy humor.

The "fireless cooker"—a sort of icebox in reverse, an insulated cabinet in which slabs of preheated soapstone cooked all-in-one meals while the housewife did other things—was the culinary breakthrough of the day. Much of the stubborn dirt with which the landlady struggled came of heating with coal, not gas or automatically fired oil. The farm wife was better off with the clean ash of woodburning stoves. In towns of all sizes outside the southernmost states the scrape of the coal scoop on the concrete floor of the cellar was as familiar a domestic sound as the jingle of the bell on the cat's collar. Odd-job blacks made winter livings with routes of twice-a-day calls to stoke furnaces for manless women. In the Northeast, where anthracite coal was widely used, the grime was not as bad as where factories and dwellings alike, along with locomotives and power plants, burned bituminous coal from Appalachian and Midwestern mines. Stone and brick business blocks, courthouses, churches, schoolhouses, warehouses in St. Louis, Cincinnati, Pittsburgh, Chicago looked as if upholstered in dark gray velvet and the same accumulation was well under way on the new steel-and-curtain-wall office buildings and department stores. In 1914 Booth Tarkington described what may have been his own Indianapolis but could just as well have been Cleveland or Louisville:

Far before him Bibbs saw the great smudge upon the horizon, that nest of cloud in which the city strove and panted like an engine shrouded in its own steam . . . then . . . the chimneys and stacks of factories came swimming into view like miles of steamers advancing abreast, every funnel with its vast plume, savage and black, sweeping to the horizon, dripping wealth and dirt and suffocation over league on league already rich and vile with grime . . . a dirty and wonderful city nesting dingily in the fog of its own smoke . . . people went about in it, busy and dirty, thickening their outside and inside linings of coal-tar, asphalt, sulphurous acid . . . highwaymen walked the streets at night and sometimes killed; snatching thieves were busy everywhere in the dusk; while house-breakers were a common apprehension and frequent reality . . . death or mutilation beneath the wheels lay in ambush at every crossing. . . . The car must stop at every crossing while the dark-garbed crowds . . . hurried before it. . . . Trolley-cars . . . clanged and shrieked their way round swarming corners; motor-cars of every kind and shape . . . babbled frightful warnings and frantic demands; hospital ambulances clamored wildly for passage . . . the ground shook to the thunder of gigantic trucks. . . .[10]

The same year the initials "HCofL" had grown as familiar as the figure of John Q. Public in the newspaper cartoons because the High Cost of Living was grimly oppressing the public mind. *American Cookery*, organ of the famous Boston Cooking School (Fanny Farmer's), deplored how:

during the last decade [living costs have] soared to an appalling extent . . . in the provisioning of the family table . . . fortunate indeed is the woman whose family does not regard meat rather than bread as the staff of life . . . meat in some form is expected . . . too often in all of the three meals . . . there was a time . . . when the household economist might take refuge in the . . . "cheaper cuts" . . . it became the fashion to learn how to prepare them temptingly. Then, alas, all too soon did economic forces too complicated to be discussed in a paper of this scope dictate a rising scale not only including our cheaper cuts but every other known foodstuff.[11]

Grimy industrial pollutions. Pedestrians dying under the wheels of congested motor traffic. "Crime in the streets." Upgrading of the average family's gastronomic expectations combining with rising costs of production to force the price of chuck steak up toward that of choice cuts, while they in turn spiral still higher. Somewhere along here 1914 begins to sound less archaic. Indeed a sociological obstetrician's stethoscope might readily have picked up stirrings of the 1920's-to-be, indeed of the 1970's-to-be, in the swelling belly of America in that spring and early summer of sixty years ago. At the time, however, concentration on the amenities and frictions of peacetime allowed few to foresee the cataclysmic shock of war that would bring on premature labor. Most of the forthcoming litter would be, like Macduff, from the mother's womb untimely ripped—and none the healthier for it.

II

All the Little Acorns

The postwar era from the social historian's point of view started some time previous to that fatal afternoon at Sarajevo. . . . Female emancipation, jazz, bright young people . . . all made their first appearance in a world in which any existing war weariness dated from the Boer War.

—OSBERT LANCASTER, *A Cartoon History of Architecture*

AMERICANS going about their business in those early months of 1914, the last before World War I, moved among many things to which, when discussing its cataclysmic consequences, they would refer for contrast.

At first they called it "the European War," then "the Great War," then as its unprecedented scale imposed itself, bringing it nearer actual worldwideness, it was usually contracted into "the War." Not "*the* War" to set it apart from others as unique—which it surely was—but "the *War*" like "the *weather*" and "the *ocean*." Similarly for my grandparents the Civil War was "the *War*." But awareness of the struggle between Blue and Gray probably did not pervade the North—the South, scene of the fighting and straitened by an elementary economy, was another matter—as World War I had pervaded all America by Armistice Day.

The extraordinary scale of official propaganda, widest that America had yet seen, may account for the depth of this awareness, which was probably disproportionate to the actual dislocations. But not to the War itself. That burned away on the other side of the water like a self-consuming sun casting warping shadows, throwing out glare and heat too intense for much except morbid growth, steadily increasing its distorting gravitational pull. There had been ample, even excessive warning that it would bring drastic change. Throughout its fifty-two months all manner of prophets, eminent or obscure, learned or ignorant, careful or rash, native or exotic, bet on a sure thing by promising all within earshot that the post-War world would be sweepingly different. Afterward both professional observers and the public naturally followed those leads and ascribed to the War just about everything changed in American attitudes since 1914. Post-War inevitably meant *post hoc*.

Thus skirts were shorter. Did that come of a falling off of decorum under the strains of War? Or of War-caused shortages of textiles, hence less yardage available per skirt? One way or another the War got the blame. Like the God of certain philosophers it was the postulated source of every new thing under the sun—even the ghastly pandemic of influenza in 1918 that killed more persons than the War had; Edna Ferber called it "A foul breath from the sodden fields of the dead in France." [1]

Certainly marked sequelae were to be looked for from such dislocation, fear and hate, waste and manslaughter. Grave, real results were already visible. Prohibition was foisted on the nation as a War measure. Northern cities had new problems because the War had moved into them many Southern blacks and poor whites. But most alleged instances of War-born change hardly stood scrutiny. Many were misattributions owing to unthinking homage to the unique scale of the War and to men's weakness for *post hoc* reasoning. For actually most of the changes so eloquently deplored or welcomed in 1920 had already been thriving phenomena before any German soldier crossed the Belgian frontier. The War had not initiated them; it had only sped up change already under way—as one hastens a chemical reaction by shaking the test tube in which it has begun to fizz.

For example, in 1919 the newspapers dwelt on shocking cases of girls defying mother and doffing their corsets in the ladies' room because the boys called corseted girls "Old Ironsides" and refused to dance with them. Another way in which the War had damaged morals? Doubtless in the catch-as-catch-can atmosphere of dances to entertain soldiers girls had grown unwontedly free with their partners; a trend away from corsets might be part of that. Besides, new corsets for girls entering the age at which custom required them were scarce because the War Industries Board had stopped manufacture of corset stays to save 8,000 tons of steel a year. The fact was, however, that for five years before Sarajevo the New Woman had been expressing her dislike of conventional restraint and her new sense of hygiene by leaving corsets off. For instance, Margaret Sanger, American focus of the birth control movement, was thus self-liberated. The rich she-Bohemian in Sinclair Lewis' *Our Mr. Wrenn* (1914) went lissomely uncorseted. In Floyd Dell's *The Briary-Bush*, a novel of Chicago's Bohemia of 1912, the girls at the colony's special Italian restaurant were "comfortably uncorseted" and the hero's wife, seeing a sketch of a female nude, proclaims: "I shall never wear corsets again! . . . I'm going to burn mine up now!" [2] and so she does, in the Franklin stove in the studio, saying, "The last of my conventions!" and then considers bobbing her hair.

The War was also blamed for the astonishing rise in cigarette consumption that would go on skyrocketing for the next forty years gratifyingly for tobacco farmers and the Bureau of Internal Revenue. One cause was said to be that notorious Wartime relaxation of morals; another the pandemic of cigarette smoking among soldiers so crucial to morale that not only the military authorities but also the prim Red Cross and the primmer YMCA felt obliged variously to supply smokes for the boys. No doubt the new duty to give the robust young hero-in-uniform a pack of cigarettes helped to erase the pre-War image of the cigarette smoker as a drugstore-corner loafer or a spats-wearing dude. But that was secondary. And the theory of moral relaxation was leaky because the curve of cigarette sales had begun to rise *c.* 1910 and jerked sharply upward in 1915 well before demoralizing effect from the War could be seriously felt—and for that matter two years before the United States began major recruiting of clean-cut young American manhood.

Indeed the rise was already dramatic enough to draw the notice of the militantly ascetic-minded. Tobacco—chewed or smoked in pipes and cigars—had always met with their reprehension. Chewing was responsible for that national disgrace, dwindling but still nasty, of spitting. Smoking fouled up the lace curtains and Papa's breath and implied ashes on the carpet and ashtrays decorated with stinking cigar butts, not to mention inevitably serious fire hazards. But the newly conspicuous cigarette particularly enraged the kind of activist prone to the deploring of alcohol and the installation of fig leaves. Associations were formed and endorsed by eminent people. The outstanding leader was Lucy Page Gaston, a lady who made publicity for the cause out of her claim to look like Abraham Lincoln, which, unfortunately, she did. By 1914 ten states, mostly among those that had already tried Prohibition, had laws banning the sale of cigarettes, very poorly enforced but symptomatically on the books. Vigorous propaganda in schools and the press soon had "coffin nail" as synonym for cigarette embedded in the slang of the ungodly. And previous allegations of its deadly effect on the organism were gloriously bolstered in 1914, when Henry Ford, already a national hero, acting on mistaken information from Thomas A. Edison, his own hero, embarked on the first of his usually ill-advised crusades—denouncing the cigarette because of the morally degenerative and physically disastrous properties of one of the ingredients in the paper it was rolled in. His hysterical pamphlet *The Little White Slaver* became a classic of the antitobacco movement. We know now that he and the others then denouncing cigarettes in those terms were partly right. The factor of ready inhaling does make them a prime menace to national health, specially in deleterious effects on the lungs. But that was not at all established in 1914. The anticigarette movement had been merely going off half-cocked, unaware that fifty years later responsible research would make it look tardily but especiously good.

Students attributed the nation's growing pre-War appetite for cigarettes to the advent of a new tobacco—"bright" alias "Virginia"—mild enough to be more readily inhaled than the kinds used in cigars and pipes, and to new automatic rolling machines making cigarettes cost far less. The first was probably basic, but the second was not negligible, as anybody who ever rolled his own must know. Tailor-mades not only were more convenient, but smoked more evenly. For a few years Bull Durham cigarette tobacco in its little drawstring bag, advertised by a huge Shorthorn bull depicted behind a post-and-rail fence nicely calculated to conceal his privates, also profited from the new enthusiasm for coffin nails. But the Bull Durham tag hanging from the left-hand shirt pocket gradually withdrew like Fundamentalism into the subculture of the Southwest, and by now even west of the Pecos nobody under the age of fifty would know what you were talking about if you said, "Have you got the makin's?"

Obviously to assess what the War did and did not do to America requires close knowledge of what Americans were doing and professing when it came. Archaic as they were in many ways, these forerunners of today's doers and professors often sound unexpectedly familiar. Going back over that ground tempts speculation as to how America would have developed materially and culturally had that War never occurred. I hope to avoid the temptation, though plagued by the suspicion that, War or not, a number of things and flavors would eventually have been much the same.

Some of the most familiar notes vibrating in 1914 came from phonographs. The gutta-percha disc with the whine-drone of a tuneful mosquito had long replaced the wax cylinder. The sound-creating works, no longer visibly feeding a great horn, was now in a wooden cabinet hiding the megaphone behind a cloth-lined grill representing a lyre or pair of crossed trumpets. It was not yet electrified; that came in next year and spread slowly, so the energy that turned the disc came from a hand-cranked spring. The "blooaaaaaaaa" of a phonograph with its motor lagging was among the most dismal sounds of the era, though Robert Paul Smith has been nostalgic about "the pure joy of hearing [Enrico] Caruso turn from a tenor into a bass!" [3] Consistency of rpm was difficult at best. For that and subtler reasons the reproduction of Caruso's voice was not as uncannily true as the advertisements said. Yet it was nearer the original than the hoarse imitation that Thomas A. Edison's firm had been representing as exactly like; and much improvement on what came out of the $5-a-Sunday tenor in the church choir.

Though its place was as firm as that of the hat rack in the hall, however, the phonograph had made no clean sweep. The upright piano was still there with Tin Pan Alley hits on its music rack for the girls to mangle. On it each afternoon one or another child in one or another stage of glum rebellion practiced the scales, exercises and fluffy little pieces called something like "The Daffydillies' Dance" favored by the lady piano teacher down the street as the royal road to music. Canned music often intruded here too in a built-in or attached player-piano device whereby holes punched in rolls of stiff paper afforded unlimited plankety-plank to all able to pedal with both feet. Some models enabled one to apply his own tempo and shading to the "Barcarolle" from *The Tales of Hoffman.* All of them abetted the phonograph in nudging Americans—seldom earnestly musical then, usually impatient with lonesome pursuit of skill—toward the passive listener's approach to music. The national token of the triumph of the phonograph was not the Columbia Record trademark of a garland of musical notes implying performance but Victor's "His Master's Voice"—a fox terrier motionlessly hearkening. Already "Victrola" was replacing "phonograph" for that "important-looking device in a polished mahogany case . . . surrounded [in the advertisements] by a numerous, enthralled-looking family while the ghost of Beethoven simpered above it. . . ." [4] Or the advertisement might show a debutante waltzing in a great ballroom to music visibly pouring out of the Victrola. The copy boasted that Victor dance records were supervised by Mr. and Mrs. Vernon Castle, the greatest missionaries of ballroom dancing ever known.

Though canned music fostered reluctance to learn to play or sing—things helpful in appreciating music—its effects were not all deplorable. To those in remote places with a thirst for music and nothing to slake it but amateur stumblings on piano or violin, the phonograph's recordings afforded at least a rough notion of what symphonies and opera sounded like. No such thing had previously been available outside the score of cities supporting local orchestras or annual visits of great orchestras on tour. Each rise in quality of reproduction—tempting manufacturers to announce perfection attained at last every few years—worked to permeate America with musical traditions previously limited to overgrown urban centers. Equally direct in another line of descent is the high-fi devotee of the shrine of SS. Woofer and Tweeter.

Canned music also freed the member of the party—usually female, seldom prettiest or wittiest—who played the piano while others danced and told her between numbers how wonderfully she performed. Both player piano and phonograph—the latter gradually took over—made a little ballroom of any living room in which the rugs could be rolled back. Such ready access to professional renditions of established ragtime and upcoming jazz, both conducive to close-contact dancing, greatly fostered the notorious Younger Generation. Soon it had the portable phonograph, cultural ancestor of the portable TV, for beach use. Much of this was international, of course. Among the new dances of the American dance craze c. 1912 the bunny hug and the turkey trot seem to have originated in San Francisco, but the equally showy and more stylish tango and maxixe came to us via Paris and London from Spain and South America respectively. And it was an ethnically mixed couple, the Castles, he British-, she American-reared, their first successes scored in Paris, whose nimble two-step and turkey trot and their own Castle Walk did so much to spread close-contact dancing in America. Indeed Mrs. Castle had more to answer for. She was one of the crucial bridges bringing bobbed hair and the boyish form over from Europe to give the imminent Younger Generation two of its trademarks and, according to F. Scott Fitzgerald, an authority to take seriously, thus set off the era of the flapper.*

* Anita Loos says (*A Girl Like I*, 138) that the first thing she did on arriving in New York City in 1914 was to borrow shears from the barber of the Algonquin Hotel and became "one of

Maybe there was something in the notion that a muddled yearning for androgyny somehow led women to take up cigarettes, short hair, the boyish form and militant feminism more or less all at once in the years just before the War. It can hardly be coincidence. Yet the natural history of those fads, whether petty or important, does little for the theory. Well before a cigarette in a woman's face was a token of emancipation, it was an attribute of the Europophile, rather fast wives of millionaires and of very fast actresses shading into courtesans unlikely to want to stray far from the eternal feminine. The clothes of the lady marchers in the great suffrage parades *c.* 1910 remained trailingly, floppily overdraped, as was then thought appropriately feminine. The gist of their case was that the specially feminine attributes of being more sensitive, moral and commonsensical than men made it specifically advisable for society to give them an equal voice in affairs. And the evolution of the boyish form was intimately involved with what would come to be called sex appeal.

Slenderness, as opposed to our elders' "fine figure of a woman," began to come in with the Gibson Girl of the 1890's, strapping but slim. A decade later voluptuary clubmen were smacking their lips over what we now call nymphettes, not yet mature enough to have much bosom or behind. Corset- and dressmaker fused the two concepts into a poured-into-the-gown effect that penalized excess poundage. At much the same time reform of the silhouette was undertaken in lower strata by a self-appointed devotee of the Body Beautiful, Annette Kellerman. Her advertisements in the magazines candidly pictured her photographed in "fleshings"—much like today's body stocking—with a scarf masking the crotch. They made her a national institution. Follow her advice on exercise and diet, and any woman could be so beguilingly round and yet slender: "In childhood I was puny and deformed . . . my unique system. . . . If you are weak, nervous, fat, thin, unshapely. . . ." Miss Kellerman was none of those things. An Australian from a musical family, she had turned to correcting her childhood physical defects by swimming and diving. Presently she was an internationally respected distance swimmer and tank acrobat and progressing into the diaphanous kind of esthetic dancing. Either cheesecloth or the skin-fitting swimsuits that she invented made the most of her elegant lines. A Harvard researcher who measured her early in her lucrative career in American vaudeville pronounced her halfway between the Venus of Melos and the average Wellesley girl—an admirable formula. Her exposure was vastly increased when she starred in a pruriently ballyhooed movie, *Neptune's Daughter*, leading a bevy of shapely girls wearing her swimsuits through bathing and beach scenes shot in Bermuda. Winsomely she and they gamboled in the surf, skipped through amphibious ballets, posed on rocks

the first girls in the century to be 'bobbed.' . . . About the same time . . . Irene Castle . . . happened to cut hers too [in Paris]. . . . Irene told me later, she had never seen a bobbed head, neither had I." But consider Dell's girl in Chicago *c.* 1912 aforesaid.

like seals playing siren. Her advertisements now read: "You will see in my picture, 'Neptune's Daughter,' what my course of Physical Culture has done for me." It was also good advertising when the Chicago police closed the theater showing the film.

Mrs. Castle's elegant spareness was the other reason why 1914 saw publication of the first best seller manual of easy slimming, *Eat and Grow Thin*, preface by Marie Cahill, actress, crediting its wisdom with melting her down to stylish lissomeness. This too had international prestige. Its editor-author, Vance Thompson, a cultivated cosmopolite, recommended its teachings as "tried and tested on both sides of the sea. In Paris, New York . . . innumerable ladies walk to and fro in slim pulchritude. . . ." [5] The method was simple. No sugars, no starches, no avoidable fats, little alcohol; plenty of trimmed meats, fish, green stuff; gluten bread but little of it; milk and milk products rather frowned on. For breakfast only coffee and fruit; water only between meals; if one must have a glass of wine, only thin Rhenish allowed. Walk instead of taking cabs. Don't sleep too much—a regimen of tolerable nutritional quality that would certainly peel the weight off any but metabolic freaks. Indeed many of today's sound reducing diets are very like it.

The immediate effect on the female population was not too marked. This was Fifth Avenue following a transatlantic gleam, and it took time for the gospel to permeate underlying strata. Until well after the War the advertisements and fashion drawings aimed at the basic small-town clubwoman allowed her still to be comfortably substantial. Only in the largest cities did carriage trade grocers stock that coarse, crashily chewy Swedish rye bread that Emily Post's social peers relied on to keep the flab away. But in 1918 a Californian lady expert in public health, Dr. Lulu Hunt Peters, carried the message into most income groups with a War-occasioned best seller irreverently entitled *Diet and Health with Key to the Calories** that emphasized crash diets (nothing but fruit, baked potato and milk) and gave constructive education on the nature and importance of calories. Within a few years the American woman who took her appearance seriously was classifying all foods within her ken as arbitrarily and intolerantly as her grandmother distinguishing between good and bad women. Item A was *fattening*, Item B *nonfattening* and no two ways about it. (Actually radishes and raw celery are about the only two articles of Western diet that a biochemist can call nonfattening as customarily eaten.) However unscientific this dichotomy, the net effect on the national health was probably valuable particularly as the ladies sought to and to some extent succeeded in imposing deprivations on their often rather gluttonous husbands too. That remained true even when matters reached grotesque heights in the late

---

* No publisher valuing his skin today would risk this flippant travesty of the title of the basic Scripture of Christian Science, *Science and Health with Key to the Scriptures*.

1920's as snooty ladies in *Vogue* came to resemble praying mantises and their younger sisters tried, as Ogden Nash said, to "look like somebody's fourteen-year-old brother in the final stages of some obscure disease." [6]

For years the one-piece precursor of today's tank suit was called an Annette Kellerman. Inevitably the police of summer resorts were soon vexed by women imitating Neptune's Daughter, even leaving off the stockings that went with the blouse-and-bloomer beach garb *c.* 1900. Some may have been aware that bare legs were not uncommon on European beaches.* At the same time chorus girls' tights were giving way to bare legs in a running war of attrition with the law incited into sporadic action by staid public opinion. Stage spectacles of alleged Oriental flavor such as *Chu Chin Chow* fielded girls naked to the waist except for conical breastplates brassiere-fashion, a device that the movie vamp soon made familiar to less affluent audiences. In sinful New York City as well as blushing Boston the police sometimes insisted on skin-colored fleshings to give the illusion of bare skin behind footlights. This spared the audience the girls' vaccination marks, it was noted, yet any movement caused disillusioning wrinkles, and the logic was faulty anyway. Suppose deception complete, the effect on morals of seeing what one was able to believe naked skin would be as corrupting as if the lady's midriff were really exposed.

Here too official numbness and public apathy came of repeated violations. Bare thighs, midriffs and backs became commonplace on the Broadway stage. In the early 1920's bare breasts sporadically appeared. But it had been movie screen and beach that set this spiraling process in motion well before the War—not least Waikiki Beach. For the relatively new acquisition of Hawaii was affecting the mainland as centerpiece of the growing cult of the South Seas in show business and publishing. The Samoan Village at the Chicago Columbian Exposition of 1893 and Moors' Picturesque South Sea Islanders at the St. Louis Louisiana Purchase Exposition of 1904 were an early part. In 1910 H. de Vere Stacpoole's *The Blue Lagoon*—what would have resulted had the *Ladies' Home Journal* commissioned a novel from J.-J. Rousseau—was another. But Hawaii was

---

* Editorials in *Life* are useful here: ". . . our water-side police ought to be shipped in a body to Europe to observe . . . women bathers at Ostend, Deauville . . . the western coast of France and Spain. . . . They would learn . . . how much alleviation of costume women bathers can stand without any noticeable crumbling of civilization. . . . The single-piece suits without stockings that women wear in European waters . . . relieve the strain on the imagination by leaving less to it." (Vol. 66, 316). "Women of all ages and of all degrees of respectability go into the water so garbed, and the supposition is that what further covering they need . . . the water itself will afford them. But the custom over there is to dress and undress in portable bath-houses . . . hauled into fairly deep water . . . from which the bathers slip fairly directly into the brine. Parading or lying about on the sands is not encouraged, and probably not allowed, though one hesitates to say what might not be allowed on the shores of France. At any rate, nothing is made of bare legs." (Vol. 74, 366). This was written before beach sunbathing was fashionable, of course.

the source of the whiny, voluptuously rhythmic music performed by plump brown musicians that flourished in Chautauquas as well as vaudeville—one Joe Kikuku and his band seem to have been the first to assail the mainland—because it suited American taste better than the Samoans' rather tuneless wailings and thumpings. And the girl dancer who went with it soon had made "hula" part of the language and revolving haunches and flashes of brown thigh through a grass skirt part of the syndrome.

The final breakthrough was Richard Walton Tully's melodrama *The Bird of Paradise*, stiff with sorcery, missionaryism, scowling idols, lepers, beachcombers, kava, gin, simulated rainbows, a volcanic eruption—and delightfully ornamented by Laurette Taylor playing her first lead, a star thenceforward. The *Bird* did the same for Lenore Ulric, who had her first lead in its road company that toured two years. Both actresses were considerably more attractive, in Western terms anyway, than genuine Polynesian girls. The road company's press agentry supplied the terms in which mainland Americans would think of their varicolored, polygenetic Hawaiian wards. To both sides the idiom was rather poisonous: ". . . the play of a woman's soul . . . Hawaii with its shores girded by lazy waves in languorous moonlight . . . its intermittent volcanoes muttering menaces and blazing signals . . . its laughing, dancing maidens crowned and garlanded with brilliant flowers, maidens casting eyes of witchery on white strangers. . . ." *

By 1914 "Hawaii" was as much the trademark of easy, lush, exotic carnality as "Paris-France" was of perfumes and dirty pictures. Hundreds of women, some young, some older, some with Polynesian genes but mostly not, just handy with brown makeup, smirked winningly while the barker yapped: "Just the way they shake 'em in the Islands, friends! Only a dime, the tenth pottiva dollah, ten cents, to see the ginuwine Hywoyan hula danced without the aid of human feet. *Hur*-ry, *hur*-ry, *hur*-ry. . . ." The miniature guitar with which the accompanying swarthy trio accentuated that throbbing, wailing music leaped into popularity because it was amazingly easy for white hands to play, hardly more exacting than comb and tissue paper. So ukulele chords were duly noted on the two momentous Hawaiian numbers, "Song of the Islands" and "On the Beach at Waikiki," that reached the mainland in 1915 as vigorously as the influenza three years later. Tin Pan Alley rolled on with "Hello, Hawaii, How Are You?" and "They're Wearin' 'Em Higher in Hawaii." All through the War the momentum grew with "Yakahula, Hickydula," "I Lost My Heart in Honolulu." . . . In the mid-1920's "Ukulele Lady" accompanied by the hoarse whackings of her favorite instrument was a national plague on the fraternity-house porch.

This cult of Hawaiiana had several side effects. It kept Dixie from

* Much of this discussion is condensed from my *Anatomy of Paradise* (1948), 412–8.

monopolizing Tin Pan Alley. It was a timely and maybe salutary distraction from the War and its perplexities. It greatly benefited Hawaii's tourist and pineapple industries. And as the core of South Seaism, it did its bit toward the depersonalization, the abstracting of sexuality that Freud and the flapper had already under way.

The "flapper"—a Britishism for culturally precocious girls in use ten years before the War*—was well established by 1914. The *Smart Set* had a whole article about her unblinking fascination with white slavery, venereal disease, painless childbirth, women's rights and other such topics—all with light or heavy erotic overtones—that startled her elders. Her eventual attributes would be bobbed hair, lack of corset, boyish figure, long cigarette holder, stockings rolled below the knees, frankly applied lipstick and powder, skirts of unprecedented shortness, appreciation of her escort's hip flask. After 1910 the American presumption that no nice girl drank alcohol, spirits least of all, steadily retreated as sherry or liqueurs at hotel tea dances led to preprandial cocktails in restaurants. Stocking rolling came of the engineering problem posed by lack of corset. No longer able to anchor stocking tops to its lower edge, the flapper wound the top between calf and knee, twisting in the slack so that the elasticity of the silk—she insisted on silk—checked downward slippage. This skill is now unknown to any below sixty; but that clumsily sound device, the garter belt, was little used until well into the twenties, and the round elastic garter above the knee was never efficient because the human thigh tapers the wrong way. As for skirts, their climb began some years before the War with "rainy daisies" that showed much buttoned boot. The *Smart Set* noted how the flapper liked to show "her very trim and pretty ankles." [7] Boot tops tried to rise to match, but by 1916—well before America's going to War led to conservation of textiles— it was noted that: "The skirt shrinks faster than the boot can climb . . . [it may come to] top-boots and a ruffle round the waist." [8]

The flapper's only unchallengeable originality was her candor about makeup. Lipstick—originally "lip rouge"—and face powder were used by elegant diners-out as well as actresses *c.* 1910, but the intent was a natural, if heightened, effect, whereas the flapper worked up a mouth of red as blatantly unnatural as a Chinese lady's deformed feet. The Gibson Girl and Edith Wharton's ladies applied their cosmetics clandestinely, only at the dressing table. Ten years later the flapper's generic pose was in absorbed use of compact, lipstick and mirror in public. Did this come of self-drama- tizing hoydenism or candor at all costs? Anyway her commitment to lipstick sixteen hours a day doomed her never to taste anything—cognac,

* Said the *Ladies' Home Journal*, October, 1922: "It would be a fine thing for this generation if the word 'flapper' could be abolished. The prewar definition was 'a sprightly and knowing miss in her teens.' " The heroine of *Bunker Bean* (1912) to whom Harry Leon Wilson applied the term had little in common with the subsequent Clara Bow image.

caviar or cornflakes—without a taint of cosmetician's perfume in it and gave laundries new problems in getting red stains off table napkins, pillowslips and his shirt collar.

A need to revise nature also showed itself in the "Boyishform" brassieres already being advertised in 1918 as enforcing the ideal figure. The things were effective, weakening muscle and mashing tissue so well that many a girl was dismayed when bosoms came back into style *c.* 1929. This cult of the boyish form was wildly inconsistent with the flapper's presumed erotic-mindedness—what was taken to be her chief trait at the same time that she sought diligently to suppress secondary sex characteristics. Such a cult of defeminization might have meant a Lesbian bent. Yet that neurotic deviancy was little or no part of her world; indeed many of her probably didn't even know the word. On the other hand the generic flapper's libido, though heterosexual enough, seldom had much latitude. Consider how baffling Fitzgerald's early stories, based on the affluent youth of 1912–1920, must be to today's student readers. However sultry the rhetoric of the narrative, a mere kiss is climax. Thus the heroine of "Winter Dreams" is "proof against cleverness . . . against charm [in men] . . . she would immediately resolve the affair to a physical basis . . . was entertained only by the gratification of her desires." High times in the Venusberg? Not at all; on examination this means merely that she kissed boys avidly. In view of what words mean in 1974, things can be more deceptive. In "Bernice Bobs Her Hair" the local belle's "infallible test" of whether she loves a suitor is "that when she was away from him she forgot him and had affairs with other boys"—meaning only that she went out with them and was kissed and kissed. In "May Day" the heroine gets "kissed once and made love to six times" at a ball. It sounds like Messalina until one discerns that it means only that she "sat out" dances with six youths, each of whom vowed he loved her. Fitzgerald's texts make it clear that this mere lip service to Eros was well established before the War could affect American young folks— strong evidence that Flaming Youth was no more a War baby than the ragtime to which it was born dancing.

Sometimes, true, a flapper carried away by the urges engendered by kissing-plus did, in the jargon of the day, "go all the way." Sociology finds "a sharp increase in pre-marital sex during the 1920's." [9] But her girl peers tended to think such behavior clumsy as well as inadvisable in view of how boys gossiped among themselves. So though Flaming Youth probably did raise the incidence of fornication among girls in most social strata, it can hardly have been as high as headshakers professed to fear. Priapus' widening opportunities came rather through the already lively cult of Dr. Sigmund Freud.

America had had premonitions of Freud's views of the relation between libido and living in the speculations of its own Dr. William Alanson White,

Dr. Morton Prince *et al.* Direct awareness came through Dr. A. A. Brill, Austrian-born, American-trained, recently home from study in Switzerland under Dr. C. G. Jung, Freud's early chief disciple. In 1909 G. Stanley Hall, president of small, new, sharp Clark University at Worcester, Massachusetts, an educationist-psychologist with an Athenian hunger for new things, celebrated Clark's twentieth birthday with a festival of lectures by eminent scientists: anthropologist Franz Boas of Columbia, physicist Albert A. Michelson of the University of Chicago . . . and a complex of exotic psychiatrists, including Dr. Sandor Ferenczi of Budapest, Dr. Ernest Jones of Toronto, Ontario (eventually biographer of Freud), Jung—all already or soon to be deep in the arcana of the great Dr. Freud himself thus coming to America for the first and last time. Crossing in the same ship, Jung, Ferenczi and he diverted themselves with triangular probings of one another's psyches in stateroom séances that may have originated both group therapy and the frictions soon to arise between Freud and Jung. At the time, however, the three harmoniously let Brill show them briefly around New York City; there Freud saw his first movie.

After the sessions at Clark he visited Niagara Falls and went home, having concluded on the basis of two weeks affording him Worcester, a brief look at the Adirondacks and the Falls and experience with the New York Central Railroad that the United States was "a gigantic mistake." [10] More at length Jung told a psychoanalytic congress in Germany the next spring that Americans' "psychological peculiarities . . . point to energetic sexual repressions due to living together with lower races, especially with Negroes." [11] Freud's weak English had obliged him to lecture in German, which may explain the American press' neglect of his startling ideas. The Boston *Transcript*, handmaiden of cultivated Boston, did run a coherent interview sketching some of them. Otherwise coverage played up only his views on the fashionable bugaboos of "race suicide" (meaning the falling birthrate) and the Yellow Peril. His audiences included several well able to follow, however: psychologist-philosopher William James and such eminent psychiatrists as Prince, Dr. Adolf Meyer, Dr. James Jackson Putnam, who, as first president of the American Psychoanalytical Association, became what Freud called "the chief prop of the psychoanalytic movement in his native land." [12]

That was unfair to Brill, who as proselytizer, translator of Freud and founder of the New York Psychoanalytical Association "contributed more than any other single man to the success of psychoanalysis in America," [13] says Nathan G. Hale, Jr.'s recent *Freud and the Americans*. His peculiar contribution was taking the gospel to lay organizations and the nation's best-situated ideamongers. One meets him lecturing on Freud before the social workers of the People's Institute; then giving the New York Child Study Association the Freudian view of masturbation; then explaining Freud to the Authors' League, offering them "a number of 'plots' which frequently come to my attention through patients, but which they had never heard or imagined." [14] His task was easier because so many within his sights were literary by profession or taste, and psychoanalysis has always been the most bookish branch of medicine. Freud said: "[Imaginative writers'] testimony is to be rated very highly . . . they . . . [know] many of the things between heaven and earth . . . not dreamed of in our philosophy . . . draw on sources . . . not yet . . . accessible to science." [15] He often derived labels from and clinched his points by referring to Greek mythology or tags of poetry or the drama—such as the above bit from *Hamlet.* Hence his disciples' occasional flights into treating Shakespeare's characters as if they were actual persons. Dr. Isador Coriat was soon accounting for "the vengefulness of . . . Shylock . . . by anal eroticism. . . . Lady Macbeth was neither degenerate nor criminal; she was a pitiable coward whose outward ambition to be queen compensated for a repressed wish to have a child. . . ." [16] Jung's system relied on the plots and characters of folklore that are the basic structural elements of fiction from the *Odyssey* to Joyce's *Ulysses.* Thus an obstetrician might bolster the case for a new forceps technique by referring to Zeus' headaches and Jonah's whale.

So Brill was lucky when Walter Lippmann, already a renowned liberal journalist, introduced him into what Lincoln Steffens called "the only successful salon I have ever seen in America" [17]—that of the affluent and libidinous Mrs. Mabel Dodge, destined both to write noted autobiography and to be put into novels by such writers as Max Eastman, Carl Van Vechten. . . . Her evenings were frequented by a self-recruiting intelligentsia avid for ideas: Robert Edmond Jones, John Reed (her bedmate for a bit), Hutchins Hapgood, Emma Goldman, William D. Haywood, Alfred Stieglitz and dozens of their admirers and rivals chewing over a chosen topic of the day: birth control, say, centering on Margaret Sanger; the IWW to promote hero worship of Haywood (Mrs. Dodge practically invented "radical chic"); the Armory Show that brought Europe's avantgarde art down on America like a Bay of Fundy tide; nudism; and now, centered on persuasive Dr. Brill, the early patter ("complex," "frustration" and so on) of psychoanalysis splattering just where it was likeliest to get intellectual fashionable acceptance.

In no time the *Forum* ran a piece on "The New Art of Interpreting Dreams"—the aspect of Freud's work first taking public fancy—as not only clinically useful but also "new light upon the proper training of children . . . [leading] to a new theory of sex . . . [and] the detecting of crime." [18] (Apropos, in 1913 the slick-magazine writer Arthur B. Reeve exploited and expounded Freud in a detective story, "The Dream Doctor"; the crucial clue was the heroine's dreaming of a bull that turned into a snake with the face of her former fiancé.) Eastman, who had sent his mother to consult Brill in 1909, handled Freud for *Everybody's* magazine: slips of the tongue, meaning of dreams, and in view of the findings of psychoanalysis, advice to parents: "Don't be afraid to turn your child loose. . . . He wants . . . to get out from under the shadow of your soul." [19] The *Century, McClure's* and half a dozen other magazines were equally receptive.

Meanwhile, sometimes from Freud in Brill's translations, stronger minds gathered notions juicier than readers of the popular prints were vouchsafed, for instance, that the erotic drive (tersely, if illogically, called Sex) was the protean stuff of all emotion and to resist it led to emotional crippling. That suited romantic-minded tossers of caps over windmills as well as early Christianity suited the Roman Empire's slaves.* On the inadvisability of repression, says Frederick J. Hoffman's *Freudianism and the Literary Mind*, "Americans hung all their resentment with the moral world around them . . . relaxed discipline and smoothed the way to seductions . . . [rationalized] family impiety and extramarital indulgence . . . [condemned] fidelity as smug and conventional." [20] Dr. Samuel A. Tannenbaum, a Manhattan psychiatrist, taught that continence was antihygienic and the sexual drive an emanation of the sun and an attribute of God. Also enticing were those cryptic erotic symbols and the game of swapping dreams and surmises of hidden desires across the previous barrier of reticence between sexes. The unreconstructed mother of the heroine of Don Marquis' *Hermione and Her Little Group of Serious Thinkers* protested against the persistence with which they kept "sitting round discussing free love and sex education . . . no matter whether they start with sociology or psychology, they always get around to Sex in the end." "Isn't it funny about pure-minded people?" Hermione commented. "In the generation before this anything that shocked a pure-minded person was sure to be bad. But now it's only the evil-minded people who are shocked at all." [21]

Edward Carpenter's epicene-tinged *Love's Coming of Age* and surreptitious circulation of the works of Havelock Ellis and Baron Richard von Krafft-Ebbing had already been eroding the bars; but Freud accomplished by far the most. Aldous Huxley observed: "To explain every higher activity of the human mind in terms of incest and coprophily came to be regarded as not only truly scientific but . . . somehow virile and courageous." [22] Randolph Bourne, America's liberal gadfly as acute as Huxley, saw it sooner and differently if just as biliously. America had "made [Sex] either sacred or vulgar . . . when these categories no longer worked, we fell under the dubious and perverting magic of the psychoanalysts . . . a deplorable pseudo-scientific jargon that has no more to do with the relevance of sex than the chemical composition of orange paint had to do with the artist's vision." [23] Philistines had vulgar fun with it all, of course. For example, a

---

* It may and maybe should be objected that this is a lamentably thin summary of Freud's teachings. So it is; not least because his insights grew more elaborate and concerned with fresh issues as he explored his chosen subject matter. But my concern here is with how the early Freud affected the attitudes of little groups of serious thinkers soon after 1910.

syndicated newspaper column *c.* 1915 had a perplexed young wife asking her husband what Dr. Freud would make of her having dreamed of a snake with a spike on the end of its tail impaling a dill pickle. With anomalous irreverence the Provincetown Playhouse staged *Suppressed Desires* (its chief authors were Susan Glaspell and George Cram Cook), a farce based on subconscious puns of Freudian tenor. But the popular versions of Freud's teachings were so much what itching minds wanted to hear that they had small difficulty submerging and drowning *lèse majesté.*

The short-term triumph of this lively pre-War transplant was the spectacle of Alice Brady, a fine actress, caressing a lighted candle in a psychotic seizure at the end of William Hurlbut's *Bride of the Lamb* in 1926. The long-term one was the swamping of American psychiatry by psychoanalytic attitudes—and on the lay level, the group gropes of the hippies. To Europe's persisting surprise radical/esthetic America had located the committed capital of Freudianism in the United States—as ancient Rome became the capital of Greek-created Stoicism. But this need have surprised nobody aware that the same sort of thing had happened with phrenology three generations earlier.

Pseudo-science further confused the post-War decade with talk of an inferior New and a superior Old Immigration. A superficial, narcissistic anthropology had created a cult of the so-called Nordic race that might have stayed largely a European vice coaxed into overweeningness by Wagner, Nietzsche, Kipling *et al.* But it bubbled up toward the end of the 1890's, when increased flow and changes in the origins of immigrants to America from westward as well as eastward were rousing uneasiness. It supplied timely pretexts for measures that many reactionaries yearned for and that some WASP * liberals hoped would be healthy. Both worked from grievously poor information. Nothing much better was yet available, however, and before responsible correction could build up, emotional commitments were too stiff to be readily cleared away.

Never mind how it came to pass,† by 1900 speculative anthropology was

---

* This acronym hardly needs explaining = White Anglo-Saxon Protestant, now applied by blacks, "ethnics" and certain liberals as pejorative to those once called Old Americans. Neither label is worth much; the latter is slightly less foolish. WASP retains the use of "Anglo-Saxon" in the sense used in Jack London's eulogy of Kipling: ". . . by Anglo-Saxon is not meant merely the people of that tight little island . . . [it] stands for the English-speaking people of all the world, who, in forms and institutions and traditions, are more peculiarly and definitely English than anything else." ("These Bones Shall Rise Again" in *Revolution*, 224–25.) In that sense the term was indispensable to the movement of the pre-War years nicely epitomized by John Dos Passos' father's book about it, *The Anglo-Saxon Century and the Unification of the English-Speaking Peoples.* It made Anglo-Saxons of Americans of Scotch-Irish, Cornish, Welsh and Scots Highlander descent, an ethnic imperialism that, even in its own terms, rivals that of the Levantine world in calling "Arab" anybody whose first language is Arabic. Yet WASP is a useful word and, being widely accepted, will be used where needed in this text.

† An admirable, if subtly tendentious, summary is available in John G. Higham, *Strangers in the Land.* Probably the most responsible statement of the position from a proponent is William

accustomed to describe wide, easily distinguished variations in racially determined capacity among yellow, red, white and black major divisions of mankind. Of these, it was gravely held, whites were superior in responsible mother wit and such moral qualities as leadership and integrity. Among them further subdivisions were made—Nordic (first called Aryan, essentially Teutonic, soon taken as synonymous with Anglo-Saxon in English-speaking contexts), Alpine, Mediterranean—and genetically determined racial temperaments were considered distinguishable among them by many sober and astute investigators, such as Harvard's eminent psychologist William McDougall. The physical data involved have morphological usefulness. The error lay in allowing that cultural-behavioral traits could "go with" a given physical type. Thus Nordics were presented as not only fairer, larger and stronger than the others but also more reliable and inquisitive—superiorities set forth as if of genetic, not environmental, provenance. And to "mongrelize" the Nordic gene pool by miscegenation with Alpines or Mediterraneans, let alone blacks or yellows, meant a gradual displacement of the irreplaceable Nordic virtues by the inferior traits of—in Kipling's dangerously memorable phrase—"lesser breeds without the law."

By 1894 such ideas were reputable and tempting enough to move certain well-connected, well-informed—and self-impressed—young Bostonians to form an Immigration Restriction League with an important future. Already for some years well-connected Senator Henry Cabot Lodge of Massachusetts had been seeking Congressional action to stem the flow of fresh immigrants. The occasion was a shift after the mid-1880's in the national origins of Europeans settling in America—relatively more from eastern and southern Europe, relatively few from northern and western. That is, more victims of chronically misgoverned and erosion-ravaged Sicily and Southern Italy; from the Romanovs' shaky empire growing numbers of Jews, Poles, Lithuanians, German-flavored Ukrainians; from the Hapsburgs' tottering empire Czechs, Slovaks, Slovenians, Croats, Hungarians, Galician Jews; from the Ottomans' already shattered empire Greeks, Serbs, Armenians, Syrians. Relatively fewer Germans, Irish, Scandinavians, Britons, who, in that descending order, had dominated immigration from 1820 until well after the Civil War. Hence the notion of a New Immigration. Its numbers topped those of the Old in 1896. By 1914 the Old/New ratio was only 1 in 5.

How valid the Old/New concept was depended on use made of it. In one sense the newcomers of 1890 had much the same character as those of 1850. In both groups particular causes of self-exile might in certain national cases include religious frictions, as with Jews, Armenians, Irish, or politico-ethnic frictions, as with Poles, Finns, Hungarians. At bottom, however, between

---

McDougall, *National Welfare and National Decay* (1921), incidental to the case made for eugenics.

Waterloo and the War the prevailing cause was the infiltration of Old World economic and social life by the effects of machine industry on transport, agriculture, social stratification, family solidarity, population growth. That process began in northwestern Europe, so thence came the bulk of the Old Immigration. Gradually it spread southward and eastward across the Slavic and Balkan lands into the Levant, similarly shaking up society and spinning the less well-attached elements off to, among other places, America. Once allow that the cultural potential, in the broadest possible sense, of all national groups is pretty much the same, as is now thought probable—in 1910 this was much more debatable—and óne sees Old and New Immigrations as mere earlier/later halves of a single century-long phenomenon.

Yet our troubled grandfathers were not muttering about nothing at all. To them, more religion-sensitive than most of us, a glaring facet of the second phase was its different religious associations. The midcentury immigration had been mostly Protestant; the Irish were the only large exception. By the end of the century the waxing flood was largely Roman Catholic garnished with Jews, Orthodox Catholics and Armenian and Syrian Christians. The language problem was also more irksome. Irish and Britons, between them a majority of Old Immigrants, already spoke English. Germans' and Scandinavians' mother tongues were nearer English than the New Immigration's Slavic languages varied with Semitic dialects and the idiosyncrasies of Magyar. Other things being equal, it was harder for a Catholic Pole to become at home in America than for the Lutheran German who had been in his shoes fifty years earlier. Among impatient WASP's this slowness fostered prejudice against him and his ethnic likes as not only Catholic—in itself cause for lively suspicion in many such minds—but also stupid, sulky or both.

What attracted most New Immigrants to America was the prospect of hourly wage jobs in industry. In any case few had even the small capital needed to settle on the land. So they huddled in industrial cities, where their insanitary customs, normal in the peasant villages they came from, got them regarded as congenitally filthy. Some European countries encouraged felons to go overseas to save having to keep them in jail; hence hasty Americans' impression that "immigrant" too often meant "criminal." This deepened when the immigrants' offspring reacted to the strains of slum, school and bewildering new values by forming self-aggrandizing gangs. C. 1850 Pat and Mike had been thus stigmatized—NO IRISH NEED APPLY. Now among not only WASP's but also among first- and second-generation Irish and Germans who had got their economic feet under them the pejorative allegations piled up. New Immigrants were dirty, dumb (in the colloquial sense too), lawless, sunk in outlandish religions, had no future but in pick swinging. . . . With no fear of rebuke the loudest voice in America in 1914, that of the Reverend Billy Sunday, king of hot gospel evangelists, shouted that "America has become the backyard in which Europe is dumping its paupers and criminals . . . they settle here and become a carbuncle on the neck of the body politic." [24]

The reproach of undervaluing God's country was added when many New Immigrants went home to retire on their savings instead of taking out citizenship papers and becoming potential Americans. This came of the wageworker's relative footlooseness plus the change from sail to steam in passenger shipping. For Old Immigrants the voyage to the New World in the steerage of sailing packets had meant at least several weeks of extreme misery. The steamers' passages were far shorter, their quarters for immigrants better. Competition brought fares down toward $10 for the voyage. A thrifty Greek could work hard for twelve or fifteen years in Philadelphia and go home to Arcadia with enough money for comfortable retirement there, and because the return voyage was less of an ordeal, he was likelier to do so than a Swedish carpenter or Irish coachman of an earlier day. Between 1902 and 1924 two Italians thus went home for every three coming in. WASP's deploring this as low-grade New Immigrant behavior had a poor case. Many Swedes and Germans did the same as steam made it fast, cheap and endurable. Those nest eggs that returnees took along showed how much sweaty, dirty, gruelingly prolonged work they had done for America. And in any case those decrying New Immigrants as genetic and cultural threats to the Land of the Pilgrims' Pride should have cheered, not growled, when so many had the impudence to decide—this idiom would soon be part of the language—that they didn't like it here, so they went back where they came from.

The Bostonian founders of the Immigration Restriction movement and their likes tended to get all this by the wrong end because they were reared among false historical values. From the elementary school up they were trained to venerate the immigrant ancestors of the Founding Fathers and the poor devils at Valley Forge as heroes crossing the ocean to build a new nation dedicated to the prosperity of their admiring posterity. It was an article of faith that they had been as sober, clean, law-abiding, literate and Bible-religious as oneself. The actual truth—that essentially the bulk of pre-Revolutionary British coming to America had much in common with these Polacks, Hunkies, Dagos, Yids *et al.*—might have diluted their dismay over the New Immigrants. The run of immigrant Colonists had been just as innocent of bathtubs. Relatively few could read or write. Many were paupers or anyway so marginal in Britain's economy that they were willing to risk the often fatal sea voyage and the miseries of temporary slavery under indenture. A sizable minority in a ratio probably as high as that in the New Immigration were convicts forcibly exiled on pain of the gallows if they came back. A substantial number of the women, like Defoe's Moll Flanders, were professionally no better than they should be. America was woven primarily out of Europe's discards, only secondarily of its self-reliant come-outers. Indeed the immigration of the mid-1800's, when the influx of Germans was at its height and that of capable Scandinavians well begun, must have averaged higher in quality of human raw material than what came to the eventual Thirteen Colonies between 1607 and 1770. Even today that is not widely accepted. At the peak of Immigration Restriction few would have believed a word of it.

What did command attention was a geographical association. Old Immigrants came chiefly from countries that the romantic anthropology of the day represented as commendably Nordic; New Immigrants from those dominated by Alpines and Mediterraneans. Given the fashionable belief that Nordics were genetically superior to other whites and that the native American white population was basically Anglo-Saxon = Nordic, it followed that America faced a creeping genetic calamity and that something had better be done about it. Even in those terms the data were shaky. America's pre-Revolutionary stocks were drawn as much or more from the relatively non-Nordic parts of the British Isles and Germany. And those tall, fair, dolichocephalic textbook Nordics, numerous among Scandinavians, by no means dominated among the Germans of the Old Migration and were even scarcer among the Irish peasants and British lower classes of the rest of it. Yet the dubious assumptions that WASP self-esteem preferred were firmly stated, and over the years a sense of impending emergency grew up.

In 1910 came the bulky report of the U.S. Immigration Commission—an *ad hoc* investigative body combining U.S. Senators and Representatives with outside experts. Three years they had worked on what was meant to be a factual and then strategic study of the problem of immigration. The steering experts, always the core of such undertakings, were committed to the Old/New thesis. The conclusions drawn were, as so often happens in these cases, those that entered the hearing room with the experts. The data often failed to support the findings, indeed sometimes contradicted them.* But well-marshaled facts were buried in seventy-odd volumes of detailed testimony. Press, public and legislators depended on the two volumes of summary allegedly based on the hearings—the gist of which was that as index of human quality the Old/New distinction was valid and that in any case, since New meant less readily assimilable, the bulk of recent immigration had been relatively undesirable. The first was probably nonsense, the second had something in it, but the soundness of the conclusion depended on debatable socio-cultural judgment.

Throughout its later history the problem of immigration was inflamed by recurring crises in the West Coast's not exactly unreal but often hysterically exaggerated Yellow Peril. In the mid-1800's Chinese labor flowed into

* In *Race and Nationality in American Life* (77–109) Oscar Handlin has ably analyzed the shortcomings of the summary of the report.

California to build railroads and wash shirts for wages lower than whites required. As potential competitors for other jobs they inevitably roused enmity in good times and heavy political pressures in bad. In 1882 legal entrance was forbidden them. By 1900 heavy backflow to China had minimized their presence except in lurid stories and movies. But the Coast's brittle eagerness to dream of a Yellow Peril, born among San Francisco's proletariat with the workingmen's slogan "The Chinese must go!," busily fanned by the press led by Hearst's papers, already had a new target—Japanese labor taking over where Chinese were thinning out. Many came from newly annexed Hawaii (1893), where they had gone by thousands to work in sugarcane. Soon many others came direct from Japan to prove as frugal and hardworking as the Chinese, as handy as house servants and gardeners and—to equal detriment of relations between them and whites—physically just as conspicuous. After Japan trounced hulking, stumbly Russia in 1904–05 on the other side of California's Pacific Ocean, there was shrill outcry about the potential hazard of several hundred thousand tough subjects of the Mikado well entrenched in the Coast's most intimate areas.

Washington secured from Japan an informal agreement to deny passports to immigrants planning to go to Hawaii, America or Mexico (staging area for illicit entry). But it was still legal for a Japanese in America to send for his wife. The few women the Chinese had brought had been mostly convenience prostitutes. Now America was agog over "picture brides"— Japanese girls chosen at long range from photographs, married by proxy and brought to California to bear their new husbands a prolific progeny. All those chubbykin, California-born Japanese babies were by definition American citizens with the same constitutional place in the sun as little Waitstill Baxter Cabot. Feeling about that was hotter still when the babies' fathers, turned family men, left bachelor employment and became truck and fruit farmers competing against white producers with an efficiency learned in a country of too many people and too few acres. More outcry led to another crude remedy—state laws forbidding aliens "ineligible to citizenship," as federal courts said Orientals were, to own or lease land.

This seemed woundingly invidious to the Japanese government. Its protests caused scare headlines that heated up the Nordic-minded; so did the advent in 1909 of a conspicuously alarmist book, *The Valor of Ignorance*, by Homer Lea, a hunchbacked, paranoid American soldier of fortune high in Chinese military circles who now authoritatively vouched for the genuineness of the Yellow Peril; his next book dealt with colored colonial unrest in the British Empire. In due season followed *Patria*, Hearst's splashy movie about a sinister conspiracy of Japanese and Americans against the United States (1917), and *Her Father's Daughter* (1919), a novel by the best-selling Gene Stratton Porter, Hoosier prophetess of unspoiled nature and clean romance. It depicted California high schools infested with adult Japanese sent by the Mikado to pose as adolescents while learning colloquial English and white-style techniques; one such is so eager to stand first in the senior class that he tries to murder his chief rival, the winsome heroine's boyfriend.

The fecundity of Orientals and of New Immigrants made them the more feared because, as Freud saw at Clark, the Nordic-minded were in a fashionable panic about "race suicide." Says the precociously glib heroine of *Her Father's Daughter*: "We are head and shoulders above other nations in invention, and . . . falling behind in the birth rate . . . [colored races] copy [Nordic-created modern machines] and use them while rearing bigger families." [25] Says a family friend: ". . . our people . . . won't take the trouble or endure the pain to bear and rear children; and we are going to be outnumbered. . . ." [26] "Race suicide" was coined by E. A. Ross, a wrong-headed, if well-meaning, sociologist—he had once been focus of a celebrated academic freedom case at Leland Stanford, Jr., University—and taken up hammer and tongs by Theodore Roosevelt. (The stationary population of notoriously immoral France was a warning often cited in a tone of voice that sounds queer now, when our most responsible elements see rising population as the great menace.) Ross used it to describe the replacement of a dwindling ethnic group by an increasing ethnic group, which clearly applied to the falling proportion of WASP's in America. One reason why certain nonliberals supported Mrs. Sanger's movement to bring birth control to the masses was that WASP's knew how to cut down on childbearing and unless the non-WASP's were taught to do the same, ethnic balances would be upset—and in their view, not for the better.

Amateur anthropology now set this tangle of anxieties wriggling frantically with a conspicuous book, *The Passing of the Great Race* (1916). Its author, Madison Grant, a well-placed Manhattan lawyer and zealous conservationist, held no scientific union card. But as chairman of the trustees of the American Museum of Natural History he was, as John C. Higham says in *Strangers in the Land*: "well supplied with scientific information yet free from a scientist's scruples in interpreting it," [27] and the preface was supplied by the president of the museum, Henry Fairfield Osborn, paleontologist and eminent spokesman for science. The invidious gloom of his endorsement was exceeded only by that of Grant's prophecies of genetic disaster.

The great race that was passing was, of course, the Nordics, "soldiers, sailors, adventurers, and explorers . . . rulers, organizers, and aristocrats in sharp contrast to the essential [Alpine] peasant. . . . The gods of Olympus were almost all described as blond . . . ancient tapestries show a blond earl on horseback and a dark haired churl holding the bridle . . . the dominant class in Europe is everywhere of that blood. . . . Owners . . . of a fair skin have always been . . . objects of keen envy by those whose skins are black, yellow, or red . . . work in the fields . . . enables the Nordic type to thrive, but the cramped factory and cramped city quickly weed him out. . . . In

the south [Nordics] . . . cease to breed. . . ." Picking up speed as the ink
flowed, Grant was airborne into the inflammatory; even "the poorer classes
of Colonial stock . . . will not bring children into the world to compete in
the labor market with the Slovak, the Italian, the Syrian and the Jew. The
native American . . . too proud to mix socially with them . . . is being
crowded out . . . literally being driven off the streets by the swarm of Polish
Jews . . . [who] adopt the language of the native American . . . steal his
name . . . are beginning to take his women, but they seldom adopt his
religion or understand his ideals." [28] And a man of Osborn's qualifications
endorsed those self-contradictions and flat misstatements!

Once the War was over and hatreds resumed normal channels, Grant
returned to the fight, sponsoring another's book of the same tenor with just
as effective a title: *The Rising Tide of Color.* Its author, Lothrop Stoddard,
was no self-educated dabbler in history but no scientist either. A fellow
graduate student at Harvard recalled him as "the most conceited man I ever
met." * [29] Grant's preface assumed, as did Stoddard's text, that the War
dealt a low blow to Nordics by killing them off disproportionately, since
allegedly they furnished "most of the officers . . . the more stolid Alpine
and above all, the little brunet Mediterranean stayed at home or . . . at the
front . . . took fewer chances, and often saved their skins." [30] To justify his
title, Stoddard drew a panicky—and nowadays interesting—picture of
antiwhite ferments in Asia and Africa. But his chief interest was the same as
Grant's, the "migration of lower human types . . . which have worked such
havoc in the United States . . . upset standards, sterilize better stocks,
increase low types. . . ." [31] German-trained Franz Boas, whose career in
American universities made him a prophet of sound science in the matter of
race, called *The Rising Tide* "contradictory to the fundamental teachings of
anthropology," just the latest in "a long series of publications devoted to
the self-admiration of the white race." [32]

But that was in the liberal *Nation,* most readers of which needed no
telling that Nordic-mindedness was nonsense; their sympathies would have
rejected it even had it made sense. With the general public the book
flourished, and popular magazines vied with one another in rewriting and
expanding on it. Maybe the most striking rehash was that for *Physical
Culture* by Albert Edward Wiggam, a glib Chautauqua lecturer-popularizer
of eugenics, who wrote:

> We can have any kind of race we want—beautiful or ugly, wise
> or foolish, strong or weak. . . . The Renaissance wanted beautiful

* Reading to friends from his dissertation, he would comment, "Isn't that wonderful? Isn't
that perfect?" and once when flatly challenged on a historical datum, said: "Is that so? . . .
My, God, could I have been mistaken?" (Perkins, *Yield of the Years,* 28.) His father, John L.
Stoddard, America's best-known lecturer on foreign travel, fell so in love with the Austrian
Tyrol that he retired there and, when the War came, chose to stay and write anti-Allied
pamphlets useful to Germany's propagandists.

women and got them. . . . We want ugly women . . . and we are getting them in millions. Three or four shiploads are landing at Ellis Island every week . . . broad-hipped, short, stout-legged with big feet, broad-backed, flatchested, with necks like a prize-fighter and with faces as expressionless and devoid of beauty as a pumpkin . . . giving us *three* babies where the beautiful women of old American stock are giving us only one.[33]

Picked up in an early *Reader's Digest*, that article roused such persistent popular interest that it was among the first specially reprinted.

Suggestions that Immigration Restriction in the 1920's came of left-over Wartime emotions probably have merit. The War brought sharply to notice the high cohesiveness of the ethnic blocs. Obviously the famous Melting Pot still had much to do, and many Old as well as New Immigrants had apparently failed fully to value the privilege of assimilating. Crude intelligence tests applied to the armed forces had shown IQ's lower among first- and second-generation New Immigrants than among the old.* The high proportion of foreign-born who had not sought citizenship among the job lots of radicals† deported in 1920–21 surprised nobody but did confirm the association Immigrant = Bombthrower for the man in the street. Returning soldiers were harsh about the many aliens, mostly New Immigrants, who being noncitizens, had escaped the draft and worked for high wages while the native-born were shipped off to risk their lives for a dollar a day. The American Legion angrily pointed out that from among 13,000,000-odd aliens only some 155,000, just over 1 percent, had volunteered into uniform even though to do so gave the volunteer immediate citizenship. Nobody pointed out that the proportion of volunteers among the population of 90,000,000-odd citizens had not been much higher.‡ In 1920 intramural trouble among Italian miners in Frankfort, Illinois, so inflamed the native part of the townspeople that it took 500 National Guardsmen to get the town back from the hands of the shooting, burning, stone-throwing mob that had taken it over in order to show them furriners how to behave. . . .

For all that, however, the case for Immigration Restriction had been

* They could also be made to show that Northern blacks did better than whites from several Southern states, but Nordic-minded restrictionists seldom mentioned that. (Furnas, *Goodbye to Uncle Tom*, 368.)

† The definitions (for purposes of this book) of "radical" and the other political terms necessary for discussion of culture-affecting emotions in the years described are contained in the Appendix.

‡ This issue is obviously complicated by the differing proportions of men of military age between the citizen and the alien groups, probably higher among the aliens; by the influence of the draft, which was fairly soon applied, on incidence of citizen volunteering; and by that use of automatic citizenship as recruiting bait. Nevertheless, anybody who wants to do a little elementary arithmetic and make his own reasonable discounts for those factors will come out persuaded that on the whole the aliens' showing was pretty creditable.

building up a commanding head of steam for a generation. Well before the War not only the U.S. Immigration Commission's cooked report but popular magazines had preached the threat to Nordic supremacy. In 1913 *Hearst's* magazine serialized Jack London's *The Mutiny of the Elsinore.* London had almost completed his hate-heavy evolution from hobo Socialist to Jew-baiting anticapitalist to reactionary racist. The narrator, passenger in a Cape Horner, has read the right books and learned how significant it is that the ship's capable, ruthless officers, born leaders and doers, are all blue-eyed and fair-skinned while the degenerate, imbecile or psychotic wharf rats before the mast are nine in ten brunet. His comment, when the mate saves two such from being swept overside: "I knew augustness and pride . . . [because] my eyes were blue, like his . . . my place . . . aft with him . . . in the high place of government and command . . . the dark-pigmented things . . . the mongrel-bloods . . . how could they count?" [34] Reference to post-War stimuli is not needed. The relation of London's and Grant's writings to the restrictive Johnson Act of 1924 is comparable to that of *Uncle Tom's Cabin* to the Thirteenth Amendment that abolished slavery. They did not create but they did sweepingly and apparently authoritatively confirm and deepen urges to *do something* about a matter long gnawing at the public mind and previously only picked at with minor measures that satisfied nobody.

The problem actually posed two separate questions: Was America admitting too many immigrants of unsuitable sorts? Too many immigrants of any sort? Both hinged on assimilation. Fifty years ago it was still largely axiomatic that, as Caroline F. Ware, a most level-headed sociological observer, defined it, "the basis of immigration adjustment should be the sloughing off rather than the reenforcing of alien cultures." * [35] Acquisition of and submergence into American ways and values—pretty much coinciding with those of WASP's—were supposed to be the immigrant's goal, and the nearer he got, the more favorably he was regarded. Nor was this altogether the spontaneous narcissism of a vigorous culture, whether Eskimo or Ashanti, confident that its ways are best. A community's life runs more harmoniously when practically all its component individuals use the same tongue, expect the same foods and styles of clothes and have the same approaches to right, wrong and interaction. An individual encounters less strain when community consensus trains him in advance to know whether it is right, wrong or matter of indifference for him to wear this kind of hat or sleep with that kind of girl. Without such taken-for-granted help he expends far more time, energy and emotional capital than most persons can afford on moral discriminations. And since Danish ways-of-doing have

---

* The definition remains excellent even though the author writes me that if she were treating the subject today, the shifts in attitudes in the intervening forty years would require corresponding changes in her descriptive passages. At the time she was not endorsing this position, merely stating it fairly and accurately.

more in common with American ones than, say, Syrian, the notion that on the whole Danes would come nearer assimilation sooner and with less strain all around was justified. The error that made so much dispute over immigration invidious was the feeling that because assimilation to American ways was desirable, it was therefore a token of innate superiority—or, put the other way, that the more difficulty an immigrant had assimilating, the more inferior must be his racially determined social and intellectual potential.

America's ethnic enclaves*—practically solid clumps of French-Canadians in New England mill towns, Poles in Hamtramck, Michigan, Swedes in some Minnesota counties, Chinese in San Francisco's Chinatown and so on—came of a standard process as old as the Pennsylvania Dutch settlements of the early 1700's. New-landed immigrants of common origin tended to huddle together for the economic and emotional support of neighbors with the same speech and ways-of-doing. As strange ways and opportunities came nibbling at the edges, jobs or schooling for males, schooling or marriage across ethnic lines were the usual solvents. Individuals detached were probably those atypically adaptable or indifferent to ethnic solidarity, traits often coinciding with cleverness or opportunism. The remaining large majorities, thus losing livelier members, tended to become "nucleated, unassimilated culture groups." [35] Already disinclined to acculturating† adventures, they were further insulated when those with an emotional or economic stake in keeping their ethnicity strong—clergy, teachers, politicians, editors of ethnic papers—organized resistance to outside influences. This centripetal huddling leads to bloc voting and the insensitive scorn of WASP's—and other adjacent ethnic groups—with no use for people persisting in outlandish doings. No wonder that, as Miss Ware observed in the mid-1930's, "No immigrant receiving country made up of a diversity of immigrant peoples has as yet successfully solved the problem of mass amalgamation." [35]

Pessimists took this merely to mean that the Melting Pot‡ didn't work. Its

---

* The ethnic/racial troubles of the 1960's set us using "ghetto" to mean a neighborhood consisting chiefly of one ethnic or racial group when, as in some prospering blue-collar Czech or Scandinavian examples, the residents do not feel that living there is disadvantageous. The term is usually too strong for American situations, so in this book "enclave" will replace it. A ghetto in Italy, where the word came from, was, like Russia's Pale of Settlement, an area where Jews had to live, whence they were forbidden to shift. One of the unfortunate effects of an immigrant enclave comes, as the text shows, from outward drain of its abler or more deviant residents. The economic and social pressures that surrounding whites exert on situations such as those of Harlem and Chinatown come nearer to the genuine ghetto situation. Even there, however, the restrictions are, however nasty, informal, sublegal, and in exceptional cases surmountable.

† "Acculturation" is "a situation where borrowing and lending of cultural traits takes place between two societies living in first-hand contact." (Lowell D. Holmes, *Anthropology*, 284.)

‡ Coined in 1908 as title of a successful and conspicuous Broadway play by Israel Zangwill, English-Jewish intellectual, about the strains and rewards of assimilation in New York City's Eastern Jewish enclave. Probably the most striking use of the metaphor occurred in wartime at

neglected aspect is the quantitative. WASPs' snobbish dismay, New Immigrants' resentments, Old Immigrants' scorn for later comers—in New England the Irish despised the French-Canadians in spite of the identity of religions—and pseudo-scientists' nightmares were all primarily in terms of group quality. Immigration Restriction seemed to take into account but actually ignored the question whether America was being asked to absorb just too many immigrants of whatever sort. In the decade before the War 9,000,000-odd newcomers streamed into a nation that had yet to reach a population of 100,000,000. The return flow was large too, but the new arrivals were far more numerous and new to American ways, while the returnees had usually managed some degree of adjustment, so the average level of adjustment steadily sank.

Suppose the 9,000,000 had been Canadians, they would have been mostly Anglo-Saxon = Nordics (in the half-witted terms of the time) and comprising a sounder cross section of a civilized national population than anything any Old World nation sent to the New. The only sizable emigrant groups that ever came to America representing levels of education and social skills as high as or higher than those of the cultures they left were the French Protestants at the end of the 1600's, the German and East European Jews of the period 1830–1914 and the refugees from the Nazis, mostly but not all Jewish, of the 1930's. Even so such a spate of Canadians would have brought staggering problems of economic assimilation and minor-cultural adjustment. Regardless of cultural compatibility, taking it in terms of demographic numbers alone, the United States was the only nation in history ever trying to absorb such a transfusion. That it worked out as well as it did was miraculous, probably confirming the old faith that God looks after women, children, idiots, drunks and the United States of America. That it should go on after the War as freely as ever—maybe piling another million a year on top of the already present millions still to be digested— was a prospect more picturesque than practical. Restrictions brought about by wrongheaded Nordic-mindedness would gravely damage scientific truth and national ideals. But under post-War conditions—particularly since the public was so hot about it—probably any restrictions were better than none.

Few had seen reason—nor was there much—to object to the early and minor restrictions. In the thirty years before Sarajevo entrance was denied convicts, lunatics, idiots and "those liable to become a public charge" (1882); paupers, polygamists, those with "loathsome or contagious diseases" (1891); epileptics, prostitutes, professional beggars, anarchists or

---

the Americanization school set up in Detroit by Henry Ford, which produced a pantomime of "a great melting pot [center stage]. A long column of immigrant students descended into the pot . . . clad in outlandish garb and flaunting signs proclaiming their fatherlands . . . from either side of the pot emerged another stream . . . each prosperously dressed in identical suits of clothes . . . carrying a little American flag." (Higham, *Strangers . . .* , 247.)

those "believing in the overthrow by force or violence of the government of the United States" (1903); imbeciles, tuberculosis cases and those convicted of a crime "involving moral turpitude" (1907).* Most Western nations had similar self-protective rules, some more sweeping, some narrower. But in the mid-1890's pressures rose and common sense faltered. One evidence was a cluster of state laws forbidding the hiring of aliens for public works, reflecting the job shortages of those years. Another was the Immigration Restriction League's proposal of a clever subterfuge promising not only vastly to reduce the gross number admitted but also—this was the major purpose—to favor Old over New Immigrants. This device was the literacy test. Its ostensible virtue was that a newcomer able to read and write his own language would be more useful and adjust more readily than one lacking such skills. Coincidentally, of course, the per capita ratio of literacy was far higher north and west of Vienna than south and east of it.

A law requiring such tests passed Congress in 1895. President Grover Cleveland vetoed it with implications that it was too sneaky. Another passed in 1913; President William H. Taft vetoed it; another in 1915; President Wilson vetoed it; another in 1917; he vetoed it again, but by then pressures were so high that Congress overrode. The lineup of those pressures and of the forces opposing them was a pretty example of strange bedfellows. Against the literacy test, which everybody knew meant substantial reduction of immigration, were most liberals who sympathized with settlement houses about ethnic-coated acculturation; organized pressure groups, including a formal alliance of the National German-American Alliance and the Ancient Order of Hibernians (Irish), for, though a literacy test was likely to be to their relative advantage, they probably sensed its basic xenophobia; Hearst's newspapers because, though he wanted the Yellow Peril heavily restricted, his circulation in Chicago, New York City and Boston hung on the huge German and Irish minorities; and the National Association of Manufacturers actually lined up with the settlement houses! Mass-hiring big industry needed unlimited supply of well-muscled, unskilled, unorganized men and on the whole preferred them illiterate since thus they could not read labor unions' propaganda even when anybody bothered to couch it in their own language. Forces allied for the test were just as anomalous: the reactionary stump shriekers of the South, their race sensitivity recently triggered by conspicuous infiltration of Dixie by Italians and Eastern European Jews; certain liberal sociologists, such as John R. Commons of the University of Wisconsin, unable to discount the strains that the New Immigration entailed; most of organized labor, apprehensive about wage scales; and the mass of WASPdom,

---

* Some of these categories reflect bits of history. The reference to polygamy recalls the peak of the row about the Mormons' peculiar domestic arrangements; to anarchists the claim of Leon Czolgosz, assassin of President McKinley, that he belonged to the anarchist movement; to prostitution the agitation about "white slavery" that led to the Mann Act (1910).

swinging more weight then than now in both numbers and influence, marshaled by organized snobbery such as the Daughters of the American Revolution and magazine articles again rehashing the Immigration Commission.

The literacy test that went into effect in 1917 was largely theoretical, of course. But once civilian shipping resumed on the North Atlantic it proved effective, from the restrictionist's point of view, in reducing the rush from War-ruined Europe to America, and the momentum of the victory that it represented led to a greater victory in 1921—a frankly discriminatory and numbers-limiting law that was strengthened in 1924 and again in 1927 and persisted with some modifications for the next forty years. Its basis was national quotas. The law of 1924 took 1880 as benchmark and allowed immigrants to enter in proportion to the number of their countrymen shown in the census of that year. Since 1880 preceded the New Immigration this meant relatively many admissions for Scandinavians, Germans, Irish, Britons; relatively few from the Eastern European, Balkan, Mediterranean and Levantine peoples whom national sentiment opposed. Yet this criterion was not overtly insulting, as the simultaneous Oriental Exclusion Act of 1924 certainly was. Then, to make sure annual inflow stayed at less indigestible levels, the law set an overall limit of 150,000 immigrants a year, a mere sixth of the pre-War rate, within which proportionate quotas were assigned by simple arithmetic.

The golden door of Emma Lazarus' sonnet on the base of the Statue of Liberty had not exactly clanged shut, but it no longer yawned open on the principle that everything entering democracy's mill was good grist. Whether or not all those various grains would grind into good meal, given time and patience, their sheer volume was thought to be clogging the machinery. "The new Immigration Law is going to shut the door pretty tight," *Life* said. "We won't like it much. The idea of the United States as a refuge . . . helped to make us feel we were of some use in the world. . . . However, in the present state of human affairs it may be important that the United States should not take on a greater load of unattached humanity than it can carry. . . ." [36] In some ways the Johnson Act was a salutary measure taken for the wrong reasons and with some unexpected dividends. ". . . in the long run," says Earl Pomeroy's *The Pacific Slope*, "for all the passion that inspired it at home, for all the resentment it aroused abroad. . . . When the depression came, foreign scapegoats were in short supply." [37]

The Provincetown Playhouse was on Macdougal Street in the fetidly lively center of Greenwich Village. (In summer certain Villagers had made of Provincetown, Massachusetts, a cooler, temporary seacoast of Bohemia; there some of them staged the first productions of the highly significant Provincetown Players, who soon set up shop in Manhattan in winter.) Mrs.

Dodge's fecund apartment was in a once Victorianly staid town house on Fifth Avenue in the affluent fringe of the Village. In the 1850's artists had had cheap studio quarters in the New York University Building on Washington Square. Gradually the prosperous residents of the three- and four-story party-wall dwellings in these twisty streets, so anomalous in the city's gridiron plan, withdrew up the island. In the usual pattern of urban decay daily-wage Irish and then daily-wage Italians, both groups tenaciously clannish, moved first into these one-family houses turned into multiple-family tenements, then into new, taller tenements built for this low-rent population. Even the name of the neighborhood changed. The politically minded Irish forgot "Greenwich Village," if they had ever heard it, and called it the Ninth Ward. As slums went, these were not the worst. But the downhill trend of the area and its problems of acculturation, the consequent swarms of children, stray garbage, makeshift plumbing called for high-minded solicitude, and social workers came in to set up settlement houses. They were omens of the future, for the staffs of such institutions had marked affinity with America's sporadic Bohemias.

For hard-up writers and artists the Ninth Ward's squalor meant low rent—even more attractive than its archaically elegant fanlights and molded plaster ceilings. C. 1900 aspirants still too young to be prosperous or too emancipated to court prosperity—O. Henry, Stephen Crane, Frank Norris, William Vaughn Moody—lived in the old brick houses on the south side of Washington Square and were spilling over toward the Hudson River. In time the area housed so many of the ambitious and gifted that, as Miss Ware's great social study of it says, "Almost any paragraph written or spoken about the Village sounds like a textbook on modern American literature." [38] Dreiser, Steffens, John Reed, Mary Heaton Vorse, Marsden Hartley, Art Young, the Eastmans, John Sloan are just the first pre-War Villagers coming to mind. These newcomers had little to do with their Irish and Italian neighbors but much with one another and with yeasty new ideas about literary techniques, graphic design, the nasty present of society and its potential beautiful future. In *Winesburg, Ohio*, the generic Villager's long, narrow room was always full of "artists of the kind that talk . . . of art and are passionately, almost feverishly in earnest about it. They think it matters much more than it does." [39]

Emboldened by smatterings of Freud, they talked also about Sex and did attention-attracting things about it, too. The public was already inquisitive about the creatively raffish lives that painters were supposed to lead among girls exhibiting themselves naked for hire. Besides, the sizable talents of a good many of the Villagers attracted deserved notice. By the year of the *Titanic*, say, the full-blown Bohemia south of Fourteenth Street was drawing to itself the defiantly creative from all over America. Dell described them and their milieu as "a moral-health resort . . . [for] young people of talent . . . girls did not have to wonder, as back in the home town, whether it was true that losing their virginities would help in the development of their artistic abilities." [40]

For similar reasons smaller, bush-league Bohemias surfaced in New Orleans, Boston, Washington, D.C., Carmel, California. At Carmel George Sterling, who shared with Edwin Markham the dignities of California's laureateship, was chief psychopomp. Mary Austin, Jack London, Sinclair Lewis found the place valid enough—only Lewis eventually saw a seamy side and wrote "The New Light Colony" about it for the *Saturday Evening Post*. Harry Leon Wilson, who married the daughter of a cult-minded lady Carmelite and settled there, described it as "a hot-bed of gossip and all uncharitableness . . . complicated by amateur acting and amateur author-ship, and very, very funny." He'd write a book about it, he said, only "I can get insurance on my house for only about two thirds of its value." [41] Chicago's Bohemia centered on Fifty-seventh Street and Stony Island Avenue in flimsy buildings built to house tourist traps exploiting the Columbian Exposition of 1893. During her year of library training the heroine of *Main Street* attended one of Chicago's "certified [studio parties] with beer, cigarettes, bobbed hair and a Russian Jewess who sang the Internationale," where Freud, Romain Rolland, syndicalism, feminism, Chinese lyrics and nationalization of mines were discussed. Later she was delighted to find Washington, D.C., sitting up nights in 1919 "to talk of . . . European revolution, guild socialism, free verse." [42]

Most such goings-on hoped to be preparation for the big league on Macdougal Street. Once Dell, for example, won his literary spurs, he left Chicago for the Village. Thither Margaret Anderson, blond young midwife of creativity reared in Indianapolis, took her significant *Little Review* from Chicago in 1917. Others, such as George Cram Cook, went direct from Midwestern hometowns (Davenport, Iowa, in his case) as raw but worthy neophytes. *C*. 1914 the Village harbored few native New Yorkers. The United States was the first nation in history to develop a freshwater, corn-fed intelligentsia.

In a backhanded way the conspicuousness, not to say notoriety, of the Village hampered its search for cultural maturity. Word of mouth expanded from whisper to buzz; "colorful" feature stories informed millions about what was alleged to be going on. Well before the War Villager Steffens was dismayed to find "the place where I lived in New York was known [in the Midwest] . . . in romance and caricature." [43] Hangers-on of the arts began to infiltrate the Bohemian infiltrators. Some, like Mrs. Dodge, were affluent, hence valued as sources of subsidy and givers of parties that meant lavish feeding as well as for themselves. Some, though low in pocket, were high in hopes of the free creative life, at least of opportunity to snuff up its heady odors first hand. Much to the cost of the pioneering contingent, this influx led to sharp rises in Village rents. Sagacious investors rehabilitated slummy side-street houses into single-floor apartments for solvent uptowners with a taste for high ceilings, candlelight and batik scarves. As the public read more about picturesque Bohemian hangouts, sightseers trickled downtown to clutter up the cheap Italian restaurants that had been another good reason to settle there. Hence rising prices for the set dinner of antipasto, minestrone, spaghetti, scrawny chicken, a glass of red wine, bisque Tortoni and bitter coffee. Berton Braley, newspaperman with a sideline of light verse, soon complained in *Harper's Weekly*:

> Oh, but it's gay, this Bohemian spot,
> Where the floor-walkers come, but the artists do not,
> Where the hat-buyer stares at the tailor, mayhap,
> And says "There's a truly Bohemian chap." . . .[44]

A different Village cuisine came in "tearooms"—small restaurants, typically in basements, committed to candlelight, usually owned and managed by a span of women—sometimes a Lesbian ménage or, when one or both were married, Lucy Stoners clinging to their maiden names. They purveyed not so much tea as lunch and dinner in a style originally developed for matrons and spinsters in cities and starched summer resorts. The Village tearoom, however, verged on cultivated rakishness. The ladies in charge wore smocks and berets to identify with the dear Quartier Latin, bobbed their hair, let artist patrons decorate the walls with pseudo-Cubist patterns or caricatures of notably creative customers and named the place something like Down the Rabbit Hole or The Mauve Pussy Cat. They stuck candles into wine bottles down which successive increments of melted wax flowed until a fat stalagmite of motley grease was formed; that somehow symbolized creative freedom. Indeed, in view of how seriously the Village took Freud, its cult of the candle rhymed with scandal. Rather scornfully Max Eastman remembered "Little deliberately crazy book and picture shops, Pirate's Den restaurants . . . gipsy-wagonlike tea-joints,* imitation opium-dens . . . deliberate artifice in response to a demand from uptown people." [45]

Tearoom food was usually cheap and, though on the fussy side, often palatable. More important for success than tastiness, however, was the ability to attract known painters, poets or critics of whom less distinguished patrons might whisper, "Over in the corner—corduroy coat and a big bow tie—that's Conrad Armature, the sculptor." Or it might be a couple, he a writer, she a painter, known to be living together unmarried. At least one Village husband and wife found their self-respect so corroded by marriage that they got divorced to keep their love alight by living in sin. Radical politics were *de rigueur*. In 1919 a woman reporter well acquainted in the

* Nothing to do with marijuana.

Village questioned the first twenty Villagers she encountered one day and found sixteen eager for the overthrow of capitalism; the proportion would have been as high five years earlier. W. A. Swanberg deduced from Dreiser's life a "Dreiser's law" that could have been attributed to most such Villagers: "Beliefs held by the multitude, the bourgeois and their leaders are likely to be wrong *per se*," and a cogent corollary: "Beliefs held by unconventionalists which fly in the face of orthodoxy are in all probability right." [46] For by 1914 the affinity between esthetic skills and radicalism, intensifying ever since the Lake Poets, was largely taken for granted. Indeed it had become traditional, a matter of guild conformity, and artists and writers were duly exasperated when exceptions appeared.

Of pre-War Bohemia's "little magazines" the best known issued from the Village's Greenwich Avenue—the *Masses*, a heady cocktail of mordant prose, verse and cartoons meant to rouse the Revolution and *épater les bourgeois*. Its writers, Eastman, Dell *et al.*, were good, its artists better: Sloan, Boardman Robinson, Art Young, presently Robert Minor and William Gropper. Only two editors got any pay. Contributors expected none. They worked in the good cause on the side while wresting a chancy living from bourgeois patrons and the bourgeois press. The chronic deficit was assuaged by frantic appeals to a kind of person already rife in 1914—the affluent admirer shrinking from selling all to give to the poor but salving the conscience by subsidizing militant radicals. Among those thus succoring the *Masses* and the *Liberator*, its successor, in a crisis were E. W. Scripps, founder of a great family newspaper chain; his able sister Ellen; Adolph Lewisohn, copper king and art patron; Samuel Untermyer, corporation lawyer of liberal bent; John Fox, Jr., author of best sellers about hillbillies; Mrs. O. H. P. Belmont, turned snorting feminist after marriage to two successive great fortunes; William Bross Lloyd, avowed collectivist whose affluence came of his grandfather's having been in command of a large piece of the reactionary Chicago *Tribune*. . . .

What moves certain persons with fat bank balances eagerly to draw checks to the order of collectivist radicals is probably largely subconscious, hence matter of mere surmise. Examples have been many since 1900. Mrs. E. D. Rand of Davenport, Iowa, became namesake angel of the Socialists' Rand School in New York City under the influence of the Reverend George Davis Herron, a bearded Congregationalist who had left his family to elope with her daughter. Mrs. Kate Crane Gartz, daughter of the Crane plumbing-fixture fortune, angel of the Upton Sinclairs, filled her Pasadena mansion with radicals. J. G. Phelps Stokes, heir of a Manhattan banking and land fortune, rose high in Socialism and even higher as husband (for a while) of Rose Pastor, fieriest of the Lower East Side's radical sybils. In 1912 Harry Payne Whitney, polo-playing son of the nation's canniest streetcar magnate, bought the *Metropolitan Magazine* and hired a British Fabian Socialist to guide its adroit attacks on the System. None of them had the moral honesty of Charles Garland, who, inheriting a million or so, turned the bulk of it over to an American Fund for Public Service with a reliably radical board of trustees enjoined to give it all away to worthily subversive causes. One of them, Scott Nearing, was disgusted when, thanks to the inflationary 1920's, disposing of its first million left the fund saddled with another million to get rid of.

Also ironical was the name of the *Masses*. It implied concern for the downtrodden and that those who wrote or drew for it were sympathetically intimate with the nation's underprivileged toilers. To judge from the Village where most of them lived, however, they were nothing of the sort. An invisible membrane of nonintercourse separated Bohemia from the Ninth Ward that it interpermeated like antimatter among matter. Those Irish and Italians with dashes of Germans and Latin Americans were masses all right, but the creative Villager habitually looked right through them. Only when their children shot craps too late and too loudly on the front stoop under the streetlight did Bohemia take notice and complain to the police. Quaint tearoom and hangout for Italian street gang existed next door to each other with no hint of mutuality. And where Bohemia was aloof, the Ninth Ward was contemptuous. These interlopers dressed crazy, let their women smoke and bob their hair, get drunk with them—and then did it with the light on without lowering the shades. They were known often to neglect to marry. When they had children, which was scandalously seldom, they cooped them up except for supervised visits to parks and later sent them to standoffish little private schools. Worst of all—anyway likeliest to rouse contempt among Italians—they were stupid about money and bargaining, haggled feebly or not at all with pushcart vendors and paid landlords unnecessarily high rents for the quarters of which their infiltration deprived good Ninth Warders. No doubt the Villagers were well advised not to try to fraternize. Nevertheless, the logotype of the *Masses* was an inadvertent bad joke.

By 1920 Philistines too were deploring studios where nobody painted or drew, where instead mere Bohemia-struck camp followers pumped up one another's illusions and phobias. The real artists and significant writers, it was said, had gone elsewhere, to Croton-on-Hudson or Taos, New Mexico—a new sub-Bohemia the rarefied atmosphere of which included strong gusts of Red Indian—as their incomes rose and their tolerance of amateurs lowered. It was only half true. Many of the old guard kept one foot in the Village. It remained easygoing—its one consistent positive virtue—and some still valued being whispered about on entering Enrico & Paglieri's. Memories of founding spirits who had flitted lingered in whacking rents for the rooms that their previous tenancy had hallowed. In 1927 my bootlegger-landlord (I think pimping was the third string to his bow) on Eighth Street got $75 a month for one gaunt, fifth-floor room with a wheezy gas radiator and a makeshift bathroom—because Martha Ostenso had written therein a well-received but now-forgotten novel, *Wild Geese*.

Edna St. Vincent Millay's having lived in that miniature house on Bedford Street probably doubled the rents of every habitable room on the same block; at least property values there rose 100 to 300 percent between 1920 and 1930.

Complaints grew louder as rents rose without amenities to match. Not that habitability, let alone amenities, was much on the mind of the self-conscious Villager. Given creative atmosphere enough, he as well as his purse readily put up with cockroaches, bedbugs, surrealist plumbing and noise from the dine-and-dance joint across the street where tipsy uptowners explored how artists and models lived and loved. But by the time of the War what genuineness the Village had was dwindling in inverse proportion to its fame. By the time Babe Ruth was a household word the name of the annual revues produced by John Murray Anderson—the *Greenwich Village Follies*—exploited this degeneration. His productions, though less tasteless and rather less lavish than those of Florenz Ziegfeld, Earl Carroll and George White, were nevertheless butter-and-egg commercial, and their road companies prospered. Never mind the Reginald Marsh curtain showing Edmund Wilson, John Peale Bishop, John Dos Passos and Gilbert Seldes crammed into a truck crossing Seventh Avenue and Zelda Fitzgerald diving into the fountain in Washington Square. The name of the show drew in Boston and Pittsburgh for the same sleazy reason that it paid aisle salesmen at the Old Howard Burlesque to assure the customers that these art studies, friends, show girlies just the way you like to see 'm and come straight from Pair-riss-France.

So already before the War the Village wasn't what it had been. Maybe one reason was that it never had. Maybe another, more evident after the Armistice, was that the training camp preferred by many of the new promising talents and their bottle holders was not the left bank of the Hudson but the Left Bank of the Seine, the old original Bohemia created by Henri Murger and petrified by George du Maurier. In his *Dodsworth* phase Sinclair Lewis noted how much the corner site of the Café du Dôme, a chief rendezvous of expatriates in the mid-1920's, had come to resemble the corner of Sixth Avenue and Eighth Street.

This transplantation also had pre-War roots. Among the elder generation Henry James, Logan Pearsall Smith, Gertrude Stein, Edith Wharton; among the younger T. S. Eliot, Ezra Pound, "H.D." (Hilda Doolittle) were voluntary exiles implicitly or articulately shunning the notorious smothering effect of life in America. Mary Cassatt was only the finest of many American artists behaving—and some talking—as if pigment wouldn't stick to canvas west of Bordeaux; only in old age did she come to doubt the advisability of expatriation. Though Pound, Miss Stein and to some extent Eliot were involved with American newcomers, few of these elders were politically radical, and by and large their habits were staider, their resources stabler. What made their identification of the transatlantic good life infectious was their unimpeachable standing as creative people.

Then the Armistice turned loose on Paris the Sorbonne detachment—numerous talented, turbulent youngsters living on U.S. Army education stipends. Among the horse chestnuts of the spring of 1919 they pursued their expectation that, as to the life creative, they ordered those things better in France. Harold Stearns, prophet of that creed, believed that "remotely, somehow, somewhere, even the dumbest American expatriates have been touched by the spiritual forces of French life." [47] The Sorbonne detachees also learned—and sent home word—that the dollar went farther on the Boulevard Montparnasse than on Greenwich Avenue. Prohibition had heightened the appeal, also felt by the noncreative American, of wine, beer, brandy and strangely named *apéritifs* legal and cheap in those delightful sidewalk cafés with marble-topped tables. Ernest Hemingway scorned the gabbling mob at the Café Rotonde as "The scum of Greenwich Village . . . come across the ocean somehow . . . the artists of Paris who are turning out creditable work resent and loathe the Rotonde crowd." [48] But years later, when denying the validity of Miss Stein's durable cliché, "a lost generation," * he recalled more cordially a rather homogeneous group "round the same age who had been through the war and were now writing or composing or whatever." [49]

They were, as Dos Passos said of himself and his playwright crony John Howard Lawson, "groggy with [Parisian] theater and painting and music." [50] They had fruitful contact with Britons, Scandinavians, Italians, Spaniards paying the same homage to the renown of Paris as forcing frame for the arts; some even knew a few French colleagues. Some tried to derive significance from dealings with French whores. Many frequented the quasi-salons of fairly polyglot flavor kept by the affluent Miss Stein and Natalie Barney, Dayton-born granddaughter of the gaudy Cincinnati speculator who built Pike's Opera House; in this context, as in the Village, hospitable, cultivated hostesses without husbands were not unlikely to be Lesbian. Beyond that the typical creative American in Paris *c.* 1921 was about as walled off as he had been from the Irish and Italians in Greenwich Village. The bustling, shabby life of the Quarter touched him only when shopping or paying for the stack of saucers on the café table. Hemingway seems even to have frequented Harry's New York Bar, the Right Bank water hole for Americans homesick for Nebraskan speech; when in funds, the Ritz bar, as did Fitzgerald, so intent on the life splashy.

* Vincent Sheean (*Personal History*, 281) said that Hemingway's use of this as epigraph for *The Sun Also Rises* was "nonsense. His 'lost generation' included few people and even with regard to them . . . he did not seem to understand why they were lost." Malcolm Cowley (*Exile's Return*, 7) thought the phrase still apt when properly applied: ". . . a boast at first, like telling what a hangover one had at a party to which someone else wasn't invited. Afterwards it was used apologetically . . . even became ridiculous; and yet in the beginning, as applied to writers born at the turn of the century, it was as accurate as any tag could be."

The result was unique—a nation undergoing creative, particularly literary rebirth most of the participants in which lived and worked 4,000 miles beyond its boundaries.* Ectopic pregnancy with a vengeance! When a writer moves to Switzerland today at least one purpose probably is to reap the exile's advantages in reduced income tax. Most of these newcomer expatriates had yet to prosper as Hemingway presently did; many never managed it. The tradition of invidious self-exile that they represented had long been taken for granted, fertilized over the years by instances of American talent having to wait for transatlantic applause, sometimes even for first publication. Dreiser's *Sister Carrie*, Sherwood Anderson's *Windy McPherson's Son*, Robert Frost's, Pound's and Dos Passos' maiden work all followed the groove first traced when Baudelaire began beating the drum for Poe. There were exceptions to this faint-hearted colonialism. The Chicago poets of the pre-War decade got printed and canonized without transatlantic midwifery. But after the War the gravitational pull of Europe was far stronger than fitted America's dominance of the Western scene.

Permanent as well as temporary expatriates did much to-and-froing particularly after the innovation of tourist-third class utilized the seagoing cubage no longer filled by hordes of America-bound emigrants. The visiting fireman from the Left Bank probably saw much of the Village while courting publishers or dealers, but the balance of prestige remained heavily with "the other side," particularly Paris. And neither Miss Stein nor Hemingway probably felt it anomalous that a rich woman born in suburban Pittsburgh and a hard-up young newspaperman born in suburban Chicago should choose *la ville lumière* as arena in which to disagree creatively on the merits of a story written in a Parisian café and entitled "Up in Michigan."

The Village-as-theater had great consequences. Its Provincetown Playhouse kept writers of several levels of talent a-tingle, most notably in staging Eugene O'Neill's early one-acters. Its Washington Square Players, another confraternity of stagestruck amateurs of style and energy, not only gave tingly authors another outlet but presently turned into the highly important Theatre Guild. But stimulating scripts and unhackneyed acting on small Manhattan stages did little for the potential Villagers of what H. L. Mencken called "the hinterland" yearning to step into the cultural tides of the day. The Gopher Prairie Opera House saw no road companies of *Bound East for Cardiff*. Books had to be the chief medium of sensitization for the taxi driver's daughter in *The Briary-Bush* who, *c.* 1912, used to go home after her trick at the wheel in a Chicago suburb and "read *Man and*

---

* On a far smaller scale this had precedent. Rome in the mid-1800's had a self-conscious group of American artists, chiefly sculptors, mixed with their counterparts from northern Europe. Stendhal, Ibsen, Byron, Joyce, the Brownings were long in Italy for various reasons. But the balance of cultural weight and prestige always remained back home.

Superman and cry herself to sleep." [51] H. G. Wells, Tolstoy, Upton Sinclair, Romain Rolland, Nexö, Turgenev, Chekhov, Dostoevsky were prophets becoming watchwords. The plays of Ibsen and Maeterlinck as well as George Bernard Shaw were read in the wistful hope—often fulfilled—that the liberating messages would leap from the printed page without the help of actors and lights. *The Wild Duck* might puzzle, but *An Enemy of the People* did not, and Shaw's brilliant prefaces spelled out what his plays meant and a good deal more.

The difficulty was how to come by *Man and Superman.* Such items were scarce in small-town libraries or small college libraries and cost too much to buy. The successive volumes of Shaw sold at $1.25 to 1.50 when that would buy a serviceable pair of lady's oxfords. Samuel Butler's *The Way of All Flesh*, which Dell justly called "an intellectual acid . . . slowly eating through the traditional family sentiments," [52] cost $1.50; the Garnett translations of the Russian novelists piling up on young America's doorstep after 1910 as much or more. The inexpensive reprints of the day were mostly recent best sellers of the Gene Stratton Porter/Harold MacGrath kind of vapidity or Victorian staples now considered insipid.

Rescue was at hand in a suitably Village-born project—the utterly influential Modern Library of good, inexpensive, pocket-size reprints of items of the sort the Village was cutting its teeth on. Its founders were Albert and Charles Boni, whose Washington Square Bookshop intimately juxtaposed with the famous Liberal Club on Macdougal Street was matrix of the Washington Square Players. Albert Boni had previously worked with Harry Scherman, later founder of the Book-of-the-Month Club, in a highly successful series of modern-flavored, inexpensive reprints, the Little Leather Library. The Modern Library, launched in 1917 by the new firm of Boni & Liveright (Horace), was more elaborate—full-length books to sell for 60 cents. The binding was pebbly imitation leather with a wild but not unpleasant odor as of fertilizer strained through warm celluloid. Lasting for years, specially noticeable in damp weather, that smell was the quintessential savor of cultural merit for hundreds of thousands of eager American minds through the 1920's.

The Modern Library's insigne—a figure running with a blazing torch—was well chosen. The series certainly aimed to enlighten in a hurry. The first twenty items presaged the course it would follow under Albert Boni's exquisitely skillful, exotic- and radical-minded steering. Only *Treasure Island,* not yet banished to the juvenile shelf, and Rudyard Kipling's *Soldiers Three* might have been on the shelves of a typical book-broken household in Cleveland, Ohio. The rest were Oscar Wilde's epicene *The Picture of Dorian Gray,* August Strindberg's misogynistic *Married*, three of Ibsen's most jarring plays, two of Nietzsche's paranoid rhapsodies, fiction from Maupassant, Chekhov, Dostoevsky, Schopenhauer's *Studies in Pessimism,* Shaw's *An Unsocial Socialist.* . . . A choice of such quality, said the

Chicago *Daily News*, that "You could stand before . . . these books, shut your eyes and pick the right one every time." [53]

No American item appeared until William Dean Howells' *A Hazard of New Fortunes* (bringing in radical unrest) became No. 25. The list had got to No. 60 before choice of Frank Norris' *McTeague* again recognized that America too had novelists. Soon the publishers' blurb warned buyers not to be too surprised to find titles a century old in a "Modern Library," for Voltaire and Villon were in spirit as modern as Shaw. Of Nos. 1–20 only eight were English, the rest from six different Continental cultures. This reinforced the developing pre-War orientation of cultivated Americans to look beyond the English Channel. Malcolm Cowley later recalled that his bookish cronies in a Pittsburgh high school *c.* 1914 believed "America was beneath the level of great fiction . . . the only authors to admire were foreign." [54] They devoured Wilde and Shaw ("always mentioned together"), Ibsen, Strindberg, Arthur Schnitzler. . . . Though still filially attached to Britain's leading strings, America was now acquiring a polyglot Continental governess whose free and easy ways—some her own innovations, some of long standing—jarred most stimulatingly.

J. G. Huneker had made a career (that young George Jean Nathan emulated entertainingly) of tossing off in print the names of momentous new Continental writers, artists, composers even to spell which correctly was impressive. Many of them actually did exemplify new techniques and attitudes that would once have waited ten to twenty years to reach America through Britain—as had Ibsen, for instance. Now the American was likely to enter into Stravinsky's music or Rolland's pacifism without waiting for the British imprimatur. E. V. Lucas, British essayist-novelist, was amazed to find American bookshops carrying a wealth of translations of European novels and plays, all relentlessly modern, that no British bookshop had ever heard of. "Modern"—the term came into vogue in the early 1800's—was now blanket label for East Indian batik work, the Ballet Russe, the Cubist painting and free verse that were born in France. Restlessly hard to define, it meant "somehow cultivatedly Continental," welling up between Paris and St. Petersburg, Stockholm, and Geneva with connotations that gave the Bonis' list an unmistakable right to it. The flair for it was what led young Hemingway, given the run of Sylvia Beach's highbrow lending library in Paris in 1921, to load himself down with Turgenev, Dostoevsky, D. H. Lawrence. The underlying feeling was admirably expressed by very young Dos Passos in 1916:

> I defy anyone to confine himself for long to purely American books without feeling starved. . . . Our books are like our clothes . . . all the same. . . . No ghosts hover about our fields . . . no nymphs in our fountains . . . no tradition of countless generations tilling and tending to give us reference for these rocks and rills. . . .

Russian literature . . . has so much that our own lacks . . . the
bizarre pains and passions . . . the hot moist steppe-savour. . . .[55]

It jolted such Americans into an esthetic catholicity that they might have
had difficulty learning unaided. Since most of them could read these
seminal works only in translation, however, its effect on American writing
was probably deplorable. Not that the translations were worse than usual;
the Russian items showed no more and no less the stubborn inability of
English-speaking persons to render Russian into English as if it were a
medium of communication among rational persons. But specific textual
virtue, the grain of worthy prose literature as such, is also, as Frost said of
poetry, "what gets left out in translation." And a prevalence of translations
among the books that the Village most absorbed meant that rising
American writers were soaking themselves in necessarily broken-backed,
counterfeit writing. These are the values that explain why the works of
Dreiser and Upton Sinclair cannot suffer in translation. Suppose the
attention of potential painters confined to black-and-white photographs of
the canvases in the Museum of Modern Art without their ever seeing the
originals. Except for a reasonable notion of gross composition, they would
have a miserably erroneous idea of what painting is really like. Immersion
in translations may well handicap budding writers more seriously than that.
Texts that mar connotations, blunt exact meanings and distort pacing even
where downright clumsiness does not intrude coarsen the feel for his
medium—his mother tongue—that the able writer must have.

The Modern Library can be blamed for this only as large-scale accessory.
As Continent-mindedness rose, several brilliant young American publishers
had earnestly fostered it well before the War—B. W. Huebsch, for instance,
with translations of Chekhov, Gorki, Hauptmann, Sudermann, Strindberg.
A transplanted Briton, Mitchell Kennerley, supplied Björkman and Molnar. In 1915 Alfred A. Knopf began to follow this road, soon becoming, in
Eastman's opinion, "the super-aesthetic avant-garde publisher." [56] Yet the
books of these houses were those already shown to cost too much, which
limited the damage, whereas after 1917 only 65 cents bought that youth in
Gopher Prairie anemic and corrupting texts purporting to be *Madame
Bovary* and *Fathers and Sons*.

Many such youngsters might have cared little about such shortcomings
had they been aware of them. Like Europeans going mad about Byron in
translation a hundred years earlier, the typical Modern Library customer
was probably not seeking that delight that some sage has truly said is the
purpose of literature so much as gratification of certain emotional cravings.
From Ibsen and Shaw he wanted wire-edged, card-stacking analysis of the
social order and disregarded the contrast between Shaw's crackling
brilliance of statement and the sogginess of William Archer's translations of
Ibsen. From Dostoevsky and Nietzsche he sought vertiginous tours of

egocentric psyches all visceral within; from Maupassant what then seemed titillatingly explicit treatment of Sex. Henry Miller recently wrote of the debut of Knut Hamsun in English in the early 1920's ". . . to those of my generation [Hamsun] was what Dickens was to the readers of his time. We read everything he wrote and panted for more." The nature of this thirst is clear as he praises the "adorable, incomprehensible anti-hero [of Hamsun's *Mysteries*]" for his "absolute loathing for the bourgeoisie." [57] Given those emotional joys, the text that the translator served up could be as fuzzy and vapid as that of a dime novel—and often was.

Thus to mine literature, mainly novels, for social ideas and misanthropic emotions had been internationally fashionable for a hundred years. Nobel founded his awards on it. In 1917 the chief contrast between the soulfully aspiring boy in Omaha and his counterparts in Ipswich, Périgueux, Heilbronn, Engelholm and Kazan probably was that he could get stimulating cosmopolitan scriptures at less relative expense from the Modern Library. Fair enough, for, being so far from the European sources of their yeasty values, he needed them more.

Yet, timely and influential as it was, the Modern Library did not reach the bulk of the culturally ambitious or peevish. The price—soon inflated by the War to 95 cents—was still high for marginal purses. Most sales were made in bookshops, which were scarce in county seats and industrial suburbs. Soon after the Armistice this wider market was tapped by a bargain-basement Modern Library—the Haldeman-Julius Little Blue Books sold on mail order, often at 5 cents each, same as a pack of chewing gum. Eventual sales of some 300,000,000 items made them a means of self-education vastly outstripping such later entrants as the Harvard Classics and the Great Books program. They also applied moral solvent to critical areas to a degree that only the movies exceeded.

Over the title on the pale-blue paper cover of each 3½- by 5-inch Little Blue Book stood "Edited by E. Haldeman-Julius." The story of that name tells much about him who flourished it with such innocent energy. Emanuel Julius, hard-up son of an immigrant Russian Jewish bookbinder of Philadelphia, read greedily while he scraped a living as a boy. His aggressive agnosticism began when, still in knee pants, he bought in a 10-cent edition and thenceforth revered Edward Fitzgerald's *Rubaiyat of Omar Khayyam*, already the Bible of the cracker-barrel intellectual.* It was always in his pocket along with a 10-cent *Ballad of Reading Gaol* acquired soon afterward. Having learned from Omar that there might not be a God to lend meaning to his name—in Hebrew Emanuel means "God with us"—he began to sign only the letter *E.* To please his feminist-minded

---

* In such contexts as this, of course, the superb literary gorgeousnesses of Fitzgerald's Omar have little to do with its popularity over the last hundred years among sophomoric iconoclasts.

fiancée, he doubled their names Spanish fashion, making Mr. and Mrs. E. Haldeman-Julius the only hyphen-bearing couple in Girard, Kansas, where they founded his remarkable career.

How he got to this county seat in the coal-mining corner of Kansas tells more about him. Early writing for Socialist papers led to a job on the Milwaukee *Leader*, a wide-ranging German Socialist daily; then to the Socialist Chicago *World*; then the Socialist Los Angeles *Western Comrade*; then the Socialist New York *Call*—an educational, though doubtless ill-paid, circuit for a serious, egocentric son of the marked European Jewish traditions of radicalism and taste for knowledge that also produced the Bonis. In 1915 he joined the *Appeal to Reason*, a "militant and basically midwestern" [58] Socialist weekly published in Girard by Julius Augustus Wayland. In 1912, the year of Eugene V. Debs' whirlwind Socialist campaign for the Presidency, its circulation exceeded 700,000—showing how far corn belt Populists had shifted toward Socialism.

The chief bank in Girard belonged to a brother-in-law of Jane Addams, illustrious head of Chicago's Hull House settlement. His daughter, Marcet Haldeman, was working in the bank after a brief flutter seeking a stage career on Broadway. The two exiles from Gotham married. When the strains of the War split the Socialists and tore great gaps in the circulation of the *Appeal*, Marcet lent her new husband the $25,000 to buy it, press and all. They kept the paper on as an organ of opinion, but what made the investment sound was the printed avalanche set off when the new owner fished out of his pocket his beloved *Rubaiyat* and *Reading Gaol* and had them printed up as 25-cent pamphlets to stir other youths as they had him. The two items sold so well that he added others, mostly of agnostic bent, at 5 for $1 advertised by a circular sent to the 175,000 names on the *Appeal*'s mailing list—send $5 and we'll send you 50 little books to whip your intellect into a glow. Five thousand orders brought in $25,000 to set the presses clanking. A display advertisement in the St. Louis *Post-Dispatch* offered an expanded list of 210 Little Blue Books at 10 for 50 cents. That $150 advertisement drew $5,000 in orders. From then on the Little Blue Books were a national institution like Model T Fords.

Clever gauging of similar potential of rather cornier flavor made the content of the early Little Blue Books strikingly like that of the Modern Library—touches of Stevenson and Kipling for entertainment of high repute; Chekov, Andreyev, Tolstoy; outside humorous items, no Americans but Lowell (once), Thoreau (once) and Jack London with several radical or agnostic tracts; Schopenhauer, Wilde. . . . The many Wilde items reflected not only the editor's veneration of *Reading Gaol* but also the widespread impression among the cultivated of that day that his erotic mishaps lent the man special significance. A missionary urge is clear in Haldeman-Julius' early advertisements: "Are We a Nation of Low-Brows? . . . afraid of ideas, disinclined to think, unfriendly to culture?" Send $1.85 plus postage

for twenty-five books dripping with "the great and beautiful things of life
. . . science . . . philosophy . . ." represented by Marcus Aurelius, Plato,
Mill, Goethe, Pascal, Bacon, Haeckel, Darwin. . . . The buyer assimilating
those would be "well on the road to culture . . . not something dry-as-dust
. . . incomprehensible to the average mind—genuine culture . . . to delight
the common as well as the elect."

The next year the copy leaned on Sinclair Lewis: "Are You A Babbitt?
Do intelligent and successful people laugh at you when you leave? . . . Are
you barred from the company of the cultured because you are a Main
Streeter? You must read books . . . before your mind becomes hopelessly
petrified." Forty-five Little Blue Books for $2.48 was "the sure way to
escape the social stigma of Babbittry." It sounded like contemporary
advertisements of Dr. Cheatham's rupture trusses carrying an impressive
picture of the doctor himself. Analogously Haldeman-Julius' advertisements often had a picture of him all high forehead, high collar and high
seriousness, quoting the St. Louis *Post-Dispatch* that he was "a great
businessman and one of the country's greatest editors . . . the American
Northcliffe" and the striking partial truth from the Chicago *Daily News* that
he had made Girard "the literary capital of the United States."

Another headline called the series "A University in Print." Since it was
wholly on the elective system, the editor claimed that the relative sales of its
1,200-odd titles accurately gauged the nation's reading tastes. The low price
lifted economic inhibitions from masses of potential readers, and nobody
bought Little Blue Books to lie impressively on a table or because a
pince-nez lecturer had told a women's club to read them. Actually,
however, this was no cross section. Haldeman-Julius' own figures show that
his clientele was disproportionately young and 70 percent male, whereas in
America women, typically fortyish, had long been the chief book readers
and buyers. As for social background, the advertisements paid off only in
big-city newspapers; the Middletown *Star* seldom pulled enough orders to
cover the lower cost of the space. The best magazine medium was *Liberty*,
the crankish popular weekly sired by Bernarr Macfadden, a flamboyant
physical cultist, though for certain special lists of LBBs staidly literate
Harper's and the *New York Times Book Review* drew well. Say the typical
customer was a recent high school graduate in Fort Wayne, Indiana,
picking up *Liberty* in the barbershop, coming on the "Great Christmas Sale
of the World's Best Books"—one of them, No. 72, was *The Color of Life* by
E. Haldeman-Julius—and surmising that a dollar's worth of them might be
worth sending for.

The loudest notes were agnosticism and eroticism. Prominent, for
instance, were sour agnostic-evolutionist-Populist pamphlets by Clarence
Darrow—a hero-crony of the editor's—and fifteen antireligious polemics
written for the series by Joseph McCabe, author of *My Twelve Years in a
Monastery*, whom the editor had heard lecture on free thought and

recommended to the world as "the greatest scholar now living." Such items appealed to the widespread feeling against preachers, plate-passing bankers and Sunday School vapidities that silver-tongued Colonel Robert G. Ingersoll—No. 56, *The Wisdom of Ingersoll*—exploited in the late 1800's. Conversely the Little Blue Books' public had little truck with selections from the Bible, reverent lives of Christ, Bryan's *The Prince of Peace*; included to confute charges that the series was hideboundly atheistic, these hardly sold enough to pay for warehouse space, whereas there must have been many youths like the founder of the Damned Souls Club (atheist) at the University of Rochester whose early religious bent had reversed after he read fifty-two LBB's.

The approach to erotics began staidly with Mrs. Margaret Sanger's *What Every Girl Should Know*; Mrs. Annie Besant, the radicalish queen of Theosophy, on *Marriage*; and Ellen Key, the Swedish feminist who was also exultant about motherhood, on *The Evolution of Love*. The gruffer sex could buy *Manhood: The Facts of Life* and a series of Should-Knows for Boys, Men, Married Men; and *Man's Sexual Life, Homosexual Life*. . . . How many buying such felt a rational need for information? How many felt the prurient interest of the acne and drugstore corner set? Anyway, much good may have been done in that day of hush-hush by the LBB's (endorsed by the American Medical Association) on venereal disease. There was still higher profit in the other approach: *Love Letters of a Portuguese Nun, Sex Life in Greece and Rome, One of Cleopatra's Nights*. . . . "Though the superficial impulse is to read something racy," Haldeman-Julius explained, "the result of reading about the world's great lovers must indirectly contribute to human welfare and contentment." [59] As the list grew, this genre began to sound like travesty: *Freud on Sleep and Sexual Dreams*; *Follies of Lovers*; *French Love Maxims*; *What Frenchwomen Learned About Love*. . . .

In his detailed but not exactly candid book about his enterprise the editor explained how he hotted up titles to increase sales. A translation of Victor Hugo's *Le Roi s'amuse* sold badly as *The King Enjoys Himself*; it did 65 percent better as *The Lustful King Enjoys Himself*. His wife's *What the Editor's Wife Is Thinking About* lagged, nor did *Intimate Notes on E.H.-J.* help. But when the title became *Marcet Haldeman-Julius' Intimate Notes on Her Husband*, it began to roll. These titles were all cry and very little wool, of course. They got certain LBB's banned in Canada. Responsible officials challenged to examine the texts lifted the ban, admitting that none contained anything to bring the blush of shame to the most modest cheek. Otherwise, as Haldeman-Julius noted, U.S. postal inspectors already would have barred them from the mails. Pity that was not made clear to the farmhand sending $1 for twenty including *French Tales of Passion and Cruelty*.

In spite of the editor's radical leanings only 6 or 7 of the first 250 titles, including William Morris' *Dream of John Ball* for elegance, dealt directly with Socialism—favorably, of course. Most such items withered on the vine, even Kate Richards O'Hare's letters from the federal prison that her anti-War militancy got her into. Maybe explicit Red radicalism was too cerebral for the LBB public of the 1920's. Possibly in unconscious recognition the overall flavor of the list was going limp. Maupassant, Boccaccio and Shaw were still there to cure Babbittry, but the balance had shifted toward learn-at-home texts; hack-written tabloid biographies; how to avoid grammatical errors, make speeches, sing, psychoanalyze oneself; proverbs of France, Arabia, Yugoslavia and points west; Jewish, Scottish, rube, hobo, drunk jokes. The Sex Hygiene section now had twenty-five titles; Women forty-seven including No. 1070, *Phallic (Sex) Symbols in Religion*; Marriage twenty-five, including a bit of Zola, No. 953, *Four Days of Love* and Marcet's No. 1258, *Why I Believe in Companionate Marriage.*

By 1929 LBB's were selling 80,000 a day. Four years earlier the Haldeman-Juliuses driving to the Dayton trial to enjoy its atmosphere of corny agnosticism, overheated press and headline-happy celebrities, had done it in a Cadillac. In spite of his refusal to hide his light under a bushel, however, success had not made the hero of this success story a yearner after metropolitan salons. King in his little Iberian village, he seldom visited New York City . . . Chicago almost as rarely. . . .

Little Blue Books can still be bought on mail order, and though the list is much changed, No. 2, *The Ballad of Reading Gaol,* is still there.

The coziest approach to what 1914 thought of as Higher Things—and some of them were—was the Little Theater, a force in being well before the War. Its roots were several. In 1910, the year after Freud visited Clark, certain Chicagoans, mostly affluent women admirers of the intellectual-creative, founded a National Drama League to "stimulate an interest in the best drama, and to awaken the public to the importance of the Theatre as a social force and to its great educative value if maintained on a high level of art and morals." [60] Its adherents included social workers from Hull House, where amateur theatrics had proved to stir up healthy interaction, and the Wisconsin Dramatic Society, which recruited students of the University of Wisconsin to produce, translate and publish "work . . . of proven significance on the European stage." [61] The league was soon publishing a quarterly with an interesting transatlantic play in each issue and setting up local branches to supply study materials and create local awareness of Dunsany, Ibsen and the joys of staging civic pageants. How fascinating to learn that so many of the most-renowned recent playwrights—Chekhov, Hauptmann, Brieux, Synge, Shaw and so on—owed their early Old World stagings to groups of amateurs slightly stiffened with professionals able to see promise where the commercial theater was blind! Sing hey the Théâtre du Vieux Colombier, the Abbey Theatre, the Freie Bühne!

As rootstock to graft these exotic lessons on, amateur theatricals were well established in America. Young people amused themselves and their own social sets by procuring yellow-backed sentimental comedies from French's in New York City to produce at the Masonic Temple. High schools did senior plays; colleges had dramatic societies. Fusion of the two traditions on the Wisconsin model now began in Boston, Philadelphia, Chicago, where the generic name of the movement originated—"The Little Theater" was what Maurice Browne, a persuasive and studious Briton of professional background, called the small auditorium in Chicago's Fine Arts Building that housed his stagings of forward-looking plays performed by those interested in those Higher Things.

The "Little Theater" soon epidemic coast to coast—in Erie, Pennsylvania, Fargo, North Dakota, Bridgeport, Connecticut, as well as large cities—was best defined by limitations. Its name fitted, for its quarters, improvised from church, warehouse, stable or schoolhouse, were seldom roomy. Its casts were mostly amateurs, its purposes noncommercial and its finances correspondingly shaky. Its ambitions were loftily defined by one of its leaders in 1915:

> . . . a theatre of imagination, of thought. Before . . . the Little Theatre . . . poetic drama went starving; fantasy shivered in the biting wind of neglect. Now poetry, fantasy, grim realism, star-dust pantomime, and tingling satire find place. . . . Brief social preachments have their say. . . . The historic play, the problem play, the play with or without a purpose can all find space on its boards.[62]

Its pet words were "laboratory," "experimental," "workshop" as, maybe conscious of its friability, it borrowed intellectual plumage from science and the crafts.

C. 1914 such specifications deliberately nudged the movement toward exotic dramatists of Modern Library flavor. The existing body of made-in-America drama afforded few items of the required texture particularly as chewy one-acters stageable in narrow quarters with simple sets. Among dramatists staged in 1910–1915 by Philadelphia's Plays & Players only ten in thirty-eight were Americans, mostly local, whereas the Old World supplied Yeats, Sudermann, Chekhov, Schnitzler, Brieux, Shaw and, for museum pieces, Molière and Wilde. The fare that Browne gave Chicago was almost as Higher Thingish: Ibsen, Strindberg, Schnitzler, Yeats, Shaw, Dunsany; the few flights of local dramaturgy included two pieces of Browne's own. New York City's Provincetown Playhouse and Washington Square Players, however, usually and, in view of the above, properly considered to have been Little Theaters, got numbers of their friends in the effervescent Village to write original one-acters. The Provincetown particularly had not only scripts from O'Neill but other actable things from Dell, John Reed, Neith Boyce and so on.

O'Neill and the Washington Square group were only the outstanding example of Little Theater contributing to the Broadway-centered industry. Stuart Walker, professional from some years of stage-managing for David Belasco, took his Portmanteau Theater, with its own props and knockdown scenery and promising amateur actors, from town to town—hence such fine performers as Gregory Kelly and Ruth Gordon and Walker's admirable stock companies in the lower Midwest. George Pierce Baker's famous playwriting course at Harvard (at Yale after 1923) nurtured a surprising number of playwrights with solid professional futures (Sidney Howard, Philip Barry, S. N. Behrman . . .) with live script tryouts utilizing student actors. This example fostered Little Theatrics as universities set up emulative programs in theatrical techniques one aim of which was to give the neighborhood of the campus something less jejune than the dramatic club's *Charley's Aunt*. Some hopeful observers, such as Kenneth Macgowan, foresaw from all this regional theatrical traditions as strong and professional as those in the minor German capitals, giving San Francisco, Houston and Atlanta something far better than the Broadway road companies of which the dwindling of "the road" was depriving them. Though such hopes persisted for decades and still do, most of it failed to happen. Some Little Theaters acquired elaborate buildings and equipment and more and more professional stiffening, sporadically vigorous. But they have remained parochial, not regional and idiosyncratic.

In view of how difficult professional directors and actors find Chekhov and Ibsen it is kinder not to think of what much of the early Little Theater must have been like. Historical evidence survives: After seeing the creative colony of Carmel in the throes of theatricals, Harry Leon Wilson set the *haut ton* of Red Gap choosing for their annual play *Ghosts* billed as "A Drama for Thinking People." Colonel Marmaduke Ruggles thought the script "rather thick," particularly the part of Oswald, "a youth who goes quite dotty at the end for reasons which are better not talked about," [63] and the consequences were such that the town's Lower Element staged to great acclaim *Gloats: A Dram for Drinking People*. Then early in the 1920's George Kelly, whose vaudeville one-acters Little Theaters sometimes staged as a change from Synge and Brieux, lovingly distilled some of his observations into *The Torch-Bearers*,* which launched him as a major Broadway playwright. The first night audience's hysterics began when the amateur leading lady explained to her husband, back from a long business trip unaware that his wife had gone creative, that the affluent local Drama League directress "tells us where to go, you know, on the stage, so we won't

---

* One of the best things I know about the Little Theater is that it made *The Torch-Bearers* a favorite for its own use; indeed fifty years after it was first produced, it is still going strong in those circles.

be running into each other." [64] Later the same background made good lubrication for Philip Barry's *Cock Robin.*

One of the Little Theater's troubles was that too often it was chauffeur-driven, in which respect it was unlike Off Broadway; another, that it was necessarily Sunday painting even though the class might be taught by somebody who had attended the Art Students' League. Yet it left a creditable mark. It persuaded the *femme moyen intellectuelle* that the Theater was art as high as the Parthenon that she had probably never seen, and that doctrine had much to do, however indirectly, with Broadway's lifting its sights. That was good even though the new targets were not necessarily all she might have wished.

Among observers of America's post-War capers that metaphor of the hangover was inescapable. The stiff doses of bellicosity to which the organism was unused; the dizzying effect of self-righteous shouting and economic pseudo-euphoria; the cold gray dawn of the morning after with the euphoria tattered, a whacking bill to pay and the dregs of adrenalin only half-oxydized in the nation's cerebellum.

Disgust with self is a familiar part of hangovers. That tempted the unwary then and since to see such immediate postwar items as Sinclair Lewis' *Main Street* (1920) and Stearns' many-headed godchild *Civilization in the United States* (1922) as caused by postwar trauma and revulsion. Most of Stearns' grave contributors, however, only summarized what pre-War Villagers had long been feeling and often expressing in their native hinterland. Lewis had been tinkering at *Main Street* since 1916 and can have had little trauma from the War—he was never in uniform, and by 1918 his earlier pacifism seems to have subsided. Except for a few peevish pages toward the end, *Main Street* is a consistently pre-War document. Its forebears were E. W. Howe's *Story of a Country Town* (1885), which had played grisly crosslights on the stage scenery of the James Whitcomb Riley kind of farm and county seat; Hamlin Garland's sourly powerful stories (1891, 1910) of what prairie farming did to people; and Garland's account in his autobiography (1917) of how bleak and arthritic small corn belt towns did look after one had been East—in 1916 Lewis was worshiping Garland. But less remote pre-War credit is due. Consider *Spoon River.*

Its ringmaster, Edgar Lee Masters, came from small, corn-fed Lewistown, Illinois. His father was the town deviant—defending the saloon among a Dry-minded citizenry, brazenly frequenting poker games and fairgrounds racetracks. The boy picked up the Populism then rife thereabouts and never lost it, clinging to even the incidental anti-Semitism that let him believe the Jews had somehow caused the Civil War and, through their hold on publishing, driven Vachel Lindsay to emotional disaster. As a maturing lawyer in Chicago he often went to court for streetcar worker and waitress strikers and presently, as a partner of Clarence Darrow—whom he came to despise—ably attacked before the U.S. Supreme Court the federal law under which alien anarchists were deportable. In his autobiography he blamed Darrow for losing the case; in spite of his evident persecution feelings, his dim view of this gallus-snapping chieftain among America's philanthropic lawyers is interesting.

For decades Masters had been turning out conventional verse occasionally printed in newspapers and had published an obscure volume of them and two high-flown closet dramas. Though Chicago was then (c. 1910) boiling with egocentric creativity, his floundering efforts toward the inner circle had come to little. Then he suddenly reached the promised land by way of vers libre. Born of Whitman, French experimenters and prose translations of Oriental poetry, this prosodic novelty now taken for granted by kindergarten pupils was then raising among devoted followers of the arts the same sort of tumult that plagued Marcel Duchamp and his notorious painting "Nude Descending a Staircase." Among Americans attracted to free verse—that translation of vers libre was bound to ensnare the emancipated—one case was backhanded, that of Don Marquis. In 1916 he hatched out for his column in the New York *Sun* an office cockroach named archy who used Marquis' typewriter after hours to hammer out some of the pithiest bits of writing that America ever saw. Too light to depress the shift key, archy was confined to lower case, no capitals possible, an eccentricity fashionable in advanced circles long before e. e. cummings came to fame.

> expression is the need of my soul
> i was once a vers libre bard
> but i died and went into the body of a cockroach
> it has given me a new outlook on life
> i see things from the underside now. . . .[65]

The model is unmistakable. This is travesty of the droopy snuffle of Masters' *Spoon River Anthology,* literary sensation of 1914.

According to a recent study,* this poetic landmark too bore the bar sinister of travesty. Masters, Michael Yatron maintains, began his *Spoon River* series as spoofing of free verse. Ostensibly, of course, it consisted of confessional soliloquies ascribed as epitaphs to imaginary occupants of the graveyard of Spoon River, Illinois (fictitious, but Lewistown is on the Spoon

---

* *America's Literary Revolt,* 68–69. Yatron says that at the time Masters' original intent to parody was known in local writing circles. Max Putzel's recent good biography of Reedy, *The Man in the Mirror,* led me to seek his opinion; he replied: "There was certainly an element of parody in Masters' first epitaphs, but I always suspected he was more than half seriously trying to outdo Sandburg when he began." Further light, not of the clearest, is in *The Bookman* (August, 1922, 574–75). Masters' autobiography, *Across Spoon River,* gives no hint of sardonic intent but ascribes the start of the project to conversations he had with his mother about old times and personal histories back in Lewistown.

River). Early specimens went to William Marion Reedy, editor of *Reedy's Mirror*, a St. Louis gossip weekly with literary trimmings; he maintained his wide reputation for acumen by liking and printing Masters' epitaphs as they continued all through the latter half of 1914. They read rather as if Robert Browning, his ear impaired and most of his skills wearied, were gathering materials for *Peyton Place*; there was even a reference, startling then, to Lesbianism. Soon Reedy's forward-looking public was taking the Spoon Riverites' confessions as not only striking poetry but also deep insight into the American small town.

The joke—if there was one—fell not altogether on them. With practice, as Masters wrote epitaphs for further persons named Willard Fluke, Barney Heinsfeather and Ida Chicken, the average quality improved; in 1948 William Rose Benét still chose as master example of free verse the *Spoon River* handling of Ann Rutledge, Abraham Lincoln's supposititious fiancée. And some of the joke was on Masters, too. Suddenly famous as the grim gray poet who had scored double by using a brilliant new literary form to bare the emptiness and viciousness of grass-roots America, he spent the rest of his life trying to live up to public misapprehension of his powers.

Whatever his relation to it, *Spoon River* did, as Max Putzel's biography of Reedy says, alter "the course of American verse much as *Sister Carrie* had begun to alter the course of our fiction." [66] It was just as important, however, that readers in America and overseas wading through *Spoon River*—a stream often sluggish when the verse runs free, stagnant when it falls into inadvertent iambs—so eagerly welcomed and relied on this allegedly genuine peep into the home folks' private lives in their white clapboard sepulchers. "A Western village hidden beneath the pretty garb of Puritan convention, festering, lustful, murderous," [67] gloated Waldo Frank. Certainly there was seldom a dull moment:

> Where are Elmer, Herman, Bert, Tom and Charley,
> The weak of will, the strong of arm, the clown,
>   the boozer, the fighter?
> All, all, are sleeping on the hill.
> One passed in a fever,
> One was burned in a mine,
> One was killed in a brawl,
> One died in a jail,
> One fell from a bridge toiling for children and wife. . . .

Indeed Spoon River's vital statistics were striking. Of the first 182 men whose dead tongues spoke to Masters 24, say 13 percent, met unseemly ends, largely violent: 15 by accident, 3 of drink, 1 hanged, 1 suicide. Of 54 women interspersed among these accident-prone men 8 died hard: 4 suicides, 1 murdered, 1 succumbing to lockjaw and—which does not fit the time and area that Masters had in mind—only 2 in childbed. Those ratios are obviously sociological nonsense. As for commercial and erotic morals, most of the recorded residents' lives were scandalous or would have been had the data been as open as they were to Masters. I wish I could remember to whom we owe the Spoon River version of Gray's "Elegy":

Each in his narrow cell forever laid
The lewd forefathers of the hamlet sleep.

Those taking it all seriously were usually unaware that, as his autobiography of 1936 shows, Masters hated Lewistown even more than Jews. It had persecuted his father and warped himself; he took a shuddering delight in exposing its ugliness. As for the neighboring residents of the Spoon River bottoms, they were a nightmare crew of white trash that even he suspected were somewhat exceptional. They swarmed into town on Saturday, "Men with sore eyes from syphilis . . . guns or slings in their pockets . . . fouling the sidewalk with tobacco spit; women dressed in faded calicos twisted about their shapeless bodies . . . howled in their insane cups . . . fought with knives and guns and knucks. The streets stank. . . ." [68] But those confessions of personal animus were still twenty years from publication. Meanwhile, the world could and often did take Spoon River as just what one had always suspected everybody's Hometown, USA, was really like.

While Masters thus made himself a name, another Sunday writer was bemusing himself with a thick pile of short stories about a sister town, alias Winesburg, Ohio. Sherwood Anderson was about to become a sort of American Gauguin. Small-town advertising man and factory manager gnawed by artistic urges abruptly abandons family and job and flees to the literary life creative! Actually, as Frederick J. Hoffman has recently shown in *Freudianism and the Literary Mind*, Anderson's flight to a new career, following an episode of severe mental disturbance that required hospital care, was far less abrupt than in the legend that he helped create. And his destination was not the palm-fanned South Sea Islands but Chicago. Nevertheless, it was an environment offering reassuring welcome from the circles led by Dell, Sandburg, Margaret Anderson *et al.*, and they received favorably his first two novels, examples of dilute Dostoevsky.* Then in 1919 the Winesburg stories came out between covers to great acclaim. Their idiom, admittedly prose, was more lyrical than that of *Spoon River*, their

* In *A Story-Teller's Story* (48), Anderson denied that "though accused of being under the Russians' influence," he hadn't read them till later. To an inquiry from Hoffman Dell replied: "The notion . . . at first was that he had been influenced by Dostoevsky; he said that he only read some of him after he heard that." (*Freudianism*, 236 fn.) Neither statement is as clear as might be wished. Yet there is also the possibility that, in view of both his and Dostoevsky's histories of severe emotional derangement, their basic ailments may have been similar enough to produce parallel motifs and attitudes in their otherwise unconnected works.

content of different texture. However crass, randy or cruel, Masters' subjects mostly stayed within the bounds of practicable sanity, and as their doings reflected Spoon River, it was a going concern, whereas Anderson's Winesburgers were mostly touched in the head or drifting toward it. Almost any of them, Hoffman remarked, "could, at a certain stage . . . have walked into an analyst's office and been justified in asking for treatment." [69] There in Winesburg it was usually after dark on a summer evening with a frustrated spinster stripping off her high-yoked nightgown to play leapfrog, actual or maybe metaphorical, over the iron stags on the lawn of her affluent recluse neighbor, who failed to notice her because he was deep in satyriac fantasies. This remained Anderson's genre. Hence Elmer Davis' gratitude for the "healthy merriment" [70] he derived from the Winesburger-ish goings-on in Anderson's later work.

Nobody doubts the writer's privilege to cobble up or cull from reality any episodes suiting his emotional bent. The point here is that Winesburg, like Spoon River, was widely taken as factual datum—as if William Faulkner's novels about Mississippi were equated with John Dollard's *Caste and Class in a Southern Town.* "These separate fragments of mid-American society combine to make a picture of American life which carries the inescapable conviction of reality," [71] wrote Ernest Boyd, whose qualifications for judging the point came of his being an erudite Irishman resident six years in the United States, chiefly in New York City. The next year *Main Street* added to the map of Americana Deserta the spiritual vacuum of Gopher Prairie. Doubtless part of its success came of Lewis' couching his hatred of the kind of town he came from in the form of slick magazine fiction, a method he had profitably learned over the years. But the eagerness of cultivated Americans to mistake it for a great novel must imply sympathy with its destructive distillation of the small town. It was a good money's worth. Gopher Prairie goes in for "cheap motor cars, telephones, ready-made clothes, silos, alfalfa, kodaks, phonographs, leather-upholstered Morris chairs, bridge-prizes, oil-stocks, motion-pictures, land-deals, unread sets of Mark Twain. . . . A savorless people, gulping tasteless food, and sitting afterward, coatless and thoughtless . . . listening to mechanical music . . . viewing themselves as the greatest race in the world." [72] William Allen White and Vachel Lindsay cheered. Sales eventually climbed into millions of copies in America and abroad, for there too this picture was just what readers rejoiced in.

Deems Taylor, Manhattan-born music critic with wide interests, believed that *Main Street* owed much of its success to its offering culturally insecure Americans (like its twitchily aspiring heroine) "a set of consistently contemptible and uncultured characters to whom [they] must feel superior." [73] Lippmann thought it over several years and concluded that Lewis owed the renown of not only *Main Street* but also *Babbitt* and *Elmer Gantry* to an "extraordinary talent for inventing stereotypes . . . substituting new

prejudices for old . . . marketing useful devices . . . used by millions . . .
to express their new, disillusioned sense of America." [74] True enough; but
the many women readers who, as Mark Schorer said, saw themselves in
Carol Kennicott were not likely to discern all that on their own or, suppose
such unfashionable doubts arose, recognize their validity. Instead, they had
their belief that *Main Street* was valid, deepened by praise of Lewis for
reportorial skills that he actually lacked. "I can't think of anybody who has
been so unerringly right in reproducing talk," [75] wrote Heywood Broun, for
instance. Lewis had a parlor and barroom trick of burlesquing Rotarian
speeches, Fundamentalist sermons or academic lectures that was, by all
accounts most amusing. They must have lost much in being written down.
America then had writers with the kind of ear with which Broun credited
him—on three levels of merit, Harry Leon Wilson, Tarkington, Ring
Lardner. But Lewis' rhythms are often wrong, seldom alive, and his grasp of
idiom was dismayingly shaky.* Curious that the man who did most in his
time to tell non-Americans about his country should have had no better
feeling for the language he was reared in and that made several fortunes for
him.

As for Stearns' *Civilization in the United States*, already on the ways when
Main Street appeared, its bulk could have been reduced to that of the
famous chapter on snakes in Iceland: There was no civilization in the
United States. Conformity and mental sag were king and queen of a nation
of persons as interchangeable as the parts of Fords. All Americans donned
straw hats the same week in June; all discarded them on Labor Day. Such
complaints were fashionable before *Civilization*, true. On returning from the
War, John Peale Bishop and Edmund Wilson looked about them: "Our
countrywomen seemed strange creatures after the kind, witty smiles of the
French . . . we could hardly tell them from the men except . . . they were
duller." [76] Gloatingly Jane Heap, No. 2 editor of the *Little Review:* "A
beautiful Russian woman said to me recently: 'How dangerous and horrible
to fall in love with an American man! One could never tell which one it
was—they are all the same.' " [77] American cities, *Civilization* chimed in,
"are only less identical than the trains that ply between them . . . the casts
of almost any two plays, the staffs of almost any two newspapers . . . could
exchange vehicles without the same results that would attend changing
clothes." [80] Van Wyck Brooks cited Samuel Butler: "America is the last
place in which life will be endurable at all for an inspired writer of any
kind." [81]

It could never have occurred to Brooks that Butler knew little about it

---

* *Babbitt* is full of false rhythms. As for idiom, no writer "unerringly right" on American talk
could have made Leora Arrowsmith say: "I never thought I'd have to live up to a man with a
. . . come-to-Jesus collar. Oh, well, I'll tag!" (Should be: "a gates-ajar collar . . . I'll tag
along!") Later: ". . . a scientist who puts his remarkable discoveries right over third base."
Etc. etc.

since all he knew of the United States was the rail journey from Montreal to New York City to board a homebound steamer; or to Stearns that British workers were just as rigid about visored caps and French workmen about blue blouses as Americans about straw hats; that San Francisco, Boston and New Orleans were then far less alike than Birmingham and Manchester seem to the outsider. This is a well-known culture-bound illusion. At first all Japanese look alike to whites, all whites look alike to African Pygmies.* But the small-town banker or schoolteacher or policeman is acutely aware of wide variations among local people seen from within the group. However ludicrous its details, *Spoon River* made that point well. The outsider, however, seeing all the shirt sleeves and straw hats listening to the same old speech at the Fourth of July picnic takes Spoon Riverites to be cravenly identical. Anyway it flattered the self-conscious refugee from Winesburg/Gopher Prairie to find cultivated, hence discerning, European observers on his side of the family squabble. He had always had personal reason to suspect America was no place for genius. Now here was *Samuel Butler*, whose *The Way of All Flesh* showed so clearly how to feel about the old folks at home, putting the weight of his Old World prestige behind the refugee's opinion.

This romantic snobbery did not go unchallenged among the cultivated as well as among Philistines. In 1925 the *Nation* requested comment from creative persons, mostly writers, on "Can an Artist Live in America?" The consensus was: "Yes, provided he can rely on his own integrity." Dreiser said he found America "as satisfactory . . . stimulating . . . as Russia ever was to Tolstoi or Dostoevski, or Germany to Goethe or Schiller, or France to Flaubert or De Maupassant," [82] which was reassuring about the environment that had produced Dreiser and qualified him for such fast company. Miss Millay, Ludwig Lewisohn recalled, had been "intensely charmed by the freedom and variety of experience in Europe" but then told him abruptly that "for creative purposes, life [in Europe] didn't smell right" [83] and she hurried home. Sherwood Anderson said: "The American who tries to escape by running off to live . . . in Europe is putting himself out of it altogether." [84] Sinclair Lewis listed twenty-two American writers of stature who had not felt so oppressed at home that they had gone into self-exile. He named Sandburg, O'Neill, Lardner . . . some others inconsequential now, whereas the obvious counterlist was quite as long and more brilliant. Add to the names of expatriates already cited those of Glenway Wescott, Cowley, Cummings, Gilbert Seldes, Fitzgerald, Djuna Barnes. . . .

* In the early 1920's, for instance, E. V. Lucas, British man of minor letters, visited the United States and wrote: ". . . American men are more alike than the English are. . . . Again and again in the street I have been about to accost strangers to whom I felt sure that I had recently been introduced, discovering just in time that they were merely doubles . . . also American voices are beyond question alike." (*Roving East and Roving West*, 151.)

Civilization assumed throughout, sometimes explicitly, that "civilization" meant cultivated Europeans' relations with the arts, universities, governments and businesses and that the attitudes and institutions already weaving European elements, genetic and cultural, into a new fabric west of the North Atlantic could end only in a bumptious barbarism. By reading the right things, the rich man's daughter from Red Gap learned that "the whole darn country was hideous and corrupting to the finer instincts," escaped to Paris to study art and was soon giving the name of her native state as "Illin-wah." Such refugees were cousins of America's best-carved character since Huckleberry Finn—Edward Arlington Robinson's Miniver Cheevy whose dyspeptic spirit will preside over the more cultivated contexts of this book:

> Miniver Cheevy, child of scorn,
> Grew lean while he assailed the seasons;
> He wept that he was ever born,
> And he had reasons.
>
> Miniver loved the days of old
> When swords were bright and steeds were prancing;
> The vision of a warrior bold
> Would set him dancing.
>
> Miniver sighed for what was not,
> And dreamed and rested from his labors;
> He dreamed of Thebes and Camelot,
> And Priam's neighbors.
>
> Miniver mourned the ripe renown
> That made so many a name so fragrant;
> He mourned Romance, now on the town,
> And Art, a vagrant.
>
> Miniver cursed the commonplace,
> And eyed a khaki suit with loathing;
> He missed the medieval grace
> Of iron clothing.
>
> Miniver scorned the gold he sought,
> But sore annoyed was he without it;
> Miniver thought, and thought and thought,
> And thought about it.
>
> Miniver Cheevy, born too late,
> Scratched his head and kept on thinking;
> Miniver coughed, and called it fate,
> And kept on drinking.

For him across the Atlantic flocked people, printed pages and artifacts overvalued because of a vestigial cultural colonialism still far too strong then, not yet extinguished among us. ". . . some Americans," said Don Marquis in *The Almost Perfect State*, "capitulate without a struggle to poets from England, rugs from Constantinople, song and sausage from Germany, religious enthusiasts from Hindustan. . . ." [85]

Miniver guided the pen for Waldo Frank in *Our America* (1919): "The crassness of the American world is too much for [sensitive poets and novelists]. Unlike the European lands, where all the activities of life and thought are fused into that integer called Culture, cultural life in America is still a secluded . . . thing." [86] In 1923 Kenneth Burke, a reputable critic, told *Vanity Fair*'s readers: "America has become the wonder of the world . . . the purest concentration point for the vices and vulgarities of the world." [87] Harry Crosby, rich-boy dilettante and generous patron of creative people, lived away from America because "in America the stars were all suffocated inside. I do not wish to devote myself to perpetual hypocrisy." [88] Dos Passos was crisper earlier. A Frenchman says to the hero of *One Man's Initiation:* ". . . we never can find out what you think about things," and the hero answers: "I doubt if we Americans do think." [89] Note that these dismaying conclusions were not reluctantly arrived at by observers whom experience gradually forced to admit to themselves that their native land was all hypocrites and complacent imbeciles. The Crosbys and Franks rushed on such findings exultantly, as if such traits reflected merit on them in proportion to the gravity of the faults adduced. It was largely female Minivers, however, who, as dominant readers and attenders of lectures, made it so profitable on through the 1920's for successive crops of transatlantic pundits—Count Hermann Keyserling, André Siegfried, Salvador de Madariaga, whole platoons of Britons—to travel around the country telling Americans how subhuman they were with an insolence that, had they tried the same sort of thing in European countries other than their own, would have got them ignored, deported or mobbed. As it was, on American lecture circuits it got them lunched, and dined too. Madariaga's routine about Americans as baby-faced babblers so committed to gregariousness that they never think will do as reminder of the whole genre:

"[America] appeared to me as an immense up-to-date nursery and boy's school" where the emotional keynote is: "Let us not remain alone . . . The mind is so queer. God knows what it might be up to if we gave it a chance. Why! it might even grow up and *think*. No." [90]

Civilization pretty much ignored the mass-appeal arts already vigorous in America. Americans' wide patronage of jazz, indigenous and destined to great influence, was omitted from Deems Taylor's otherwise useful piece on the emptiness of American music; Miniver learned the importance of *le jazz hot* from solemn Frenchmen. Also omitted were slapstick movies and such new art forms as comic strips and patchwork newspaper columns. The piece on education neglected the persisting efforts of American educationists to apply to the bulk of American schools the "Progressive" innovations that Europe had yet to take beyond the crank-school stratum. Occasionally, of course, some headshaker fell on a valid insight. Louis Raymond Reed wrote that the trouble with the American small town was that "The basis of all its cultural life is social. The intellectual never enters." [91] True; but he did not point out that the same would apply to the Saumur of *Eugénie Grandet* and the Barbie of *The House with the Green Shutters*. "Americans," says Sir Charles P. Snow, "have a special gift, possibly unique, for demonstrating the silliest and ugliest faces of their society." [92]

Miniver's talent for self-reference was too keen to let him see that Gopher Prairie's shortcomings—crassness, smugness, presumptuous confusion of claim with fact and so on—were not uniquely American. He mistook a narcissistic misanthropy, often with radical overtones, for criticism of a specific society, deeper than the usual feud between creative snob and bourgeois as in the intramural Anglophobias of, say, H. G. Wells and Aldous Huxley. Miniver smacked of the hysterical Calvinist's insistence on his—or his group's—being chief of sinners, an emotional habit implying monumental insecurities. It leads to intemperance of statement, savage distortion of the sometimes recognizable shortcomings adduced. The anti-American slaverings that got Ezra Pound accused of treason during World War II amounted to no more, as Bernard De Voto said, than what Greenwich Village had been saying about us for thirty years.

Note the analogy to the hot pacifism of many of the same people in the 1930's. They did not analyze the undeniable unsavorinesses of greedy arms makers or culture-numb Philistines. They merely lay back in self-aggrandizing scorn. Their counterparts in the 1920's were high on patronizing contempt of the social traditions among which they were born and on fatuous hero worship of the presumably preferable European—in the 1930's read Soviet Russian—side of the coin. Late in life John Haynes Holmes, a renowned liberal, went rarely honest about such attitudes:

> I was always on the unpopular side . . . forever "agin the government" and never so happy as when denouncing it . . . by a kind of . . . inner prompting of the spirit. Seldom did I think a question through before taking sides . . . where I belonged . . . always . . . seemed to be with the minority. Are we appointed, so to speak, some of us to act with the many, others of us with the few? Altogether apart from the ideas and convictions which possess us, are we not temperamentally made to conform, or not to conform?" [93]

The come-outer waist-deep in a juicy cause finds such determinism hard to accept. It implies deflatingly that the merits of a given cause are secondary, that if it weren't pacifism, single tax would do; or why not both? It makes nonconformity not so much a bold virtue as an ingrained trait like an allergy to fish. The hemophiliac heart. . . .

In any case keep Holmes' point in mind in order to be fair to him and Margaret Sanger, John Reed *et al.* He was less pharisaical about it than most. Miniver Cheevy vaunted himself on being "not as other men," instead more sensitive, capable of deeper insights, better skilled in the arts of life. The usual end product, however, is the radical-minded cultural parvenu yearning after "All centuries but this and every country but his own." Those phrases from Gilbert and Sullivan's *Patience* come from Britain, of course, for escapist Cheevyism is no exclusively American ailment. Only Americans came nearer than others to creating an entire intellectual-esthetic caste whose shibboleth was national self-despising.

The Minivers whined about it. The Hugo character in Edmund Wilson's *I Thought of Daisy* scolded about it. Mencken bullied about it. In that eventful year of 1914 he and George Jean Nathan, the most silken *arbiter elegantiarum* ever born in Fort Wayne, Indiana, took over the *Smart Set*, a magazine previously coating scandal with gestures at cultivation, and dedicated it to the proposition that America should be shouted and smirked into becoming a place fit for Mencken and Nathan to live in. They obviously thought it unlikely that they or anybody else could bring such a change about, but they vastly enjoyed the effort—and so did their readers. In 1924 the same pair took objective and methods intact over to Knopf to create the even more conspicuous *American Mercury*. Missionarying was less crude though unmistakable in what Frank Crowninshield did on taking over raffish and precarious *Vanity Fair* magazine in 1913. Into the 1930's a minor proportion of its pages made good use of such invaluable talents as those of Miss Millay, Dorothy Parker, Gilbert Seldes and of Corey Ford's astoundingly brilliant travesties which alone would have made the twenties what his autobiography called them, The Age of Laughter. But throughout its two decades the bulk of *Vanity Fair* came of the principle: If it's transatlantic, print it. Even after American writing was widely thought to have grown up, *Vanity Fair*'s first six months in 1929 carried twenty-eight contributions (outside regular departments) from Britons, twelve translated from French, a mere sixteen from Americans. The June issue ran two Americans to eight Europeans. So abject a cultural dependence was like that of Germany on France in the 1700's.

By coincidence just when *Vanity Fair* and the *Smart Set* were going Cheevyite, literary Americans whose Cheevyism had exiled them were wresting the poetry of the English tongue into radically new habits. Not long before the War Ezra Pound, already eminent among innovator poets in London, met T. S. Eliot—a momentous conjunction of prosodic planets. Already before the meeting Eliot had been weaving those hair shirts of disillusion that post-War youth was to take so stimulatingly to its bosom. Their prickliness came not of despair consequent on the War, however, but of the pre-War personal bent of the temperament that had sent Eliot abroad—Randall Jarrell said that Eliot would have written *The Waste Land* about the Garden of Eden.

In that same 1914 Gertrude Stein, expatriate and affluent American tucked snugly into Paris, threw her hat over the syntax windmill with *Tender Buttons*. It was a remarkable few years. Retrospectively Mark Van Doren set 1913 as the point when "poetry in the United States began once more to be generally good" [94]—which accurately placed a literary epoch though it did not identify the implied previous golden age when American or any other poetry had been generally good. Elmer Davis recalled how poetry "had broken out all over the corn belt . . . a poet sat on every fence post, caroling free verse. Pretty good verse, too. . . ." [95] In 1912 was born the chief agent of this corroboree on Parnassus—*Poetry* magazine, founded in Chicago by Harriet Monroe, whom Charles Norman described as "that American phenomenon, the spinster citizen devoted to a cause . . . alive eyes behind pince-nez flashing zeal and strength." [96] Once girlish composer of the conventional rhapsodic ode that opened Chicago's Columbian Exposition in 1893, she had grown new prosodic antennae and welcomed talent no matter how outlandish its shape—whether "The Love-Song of J. Alfred Prufrock" or Sandburg's efforts to do mural painting with loosely heaped-up words. Even Mencken dropped bladder and slapstick to call her "a very intelligent woman [whose] importance grows more manifest . . . has printed the very best of the new poetry and avoided much of the worst." [97]

And in *Chicago*. How that would have confused Miniver Cheevy had he bothered to consider it! And since he certainly never read the *Saturday Evening Post*, neither he nor Chicago's then flourishing No. 2 company of *La Vie de Bohème* would have been aware of the most notable literary event of 1914, also come out of Chicago like good out of Nazareth—Ring Lardner's first bow before a national public. Who could have foreseen that a string of slick-paper fictions by the Chicago *Tribune* sportswriter who covered the White Sox and conducted its "In the Wake of the News" column would, in time, elicit hosannas from Virginia Woolf, the most finicky critic in Britain? Yet that came to pass. The stories were about baseball, a crude setting—letters from a big-league pitcher to a hometown crony. Their semiliterate idiom would have made Miniver shudder, was totally unlike Sandburg's orotund vocabulary and resembled *Spoon River* only in being in the first person. What first drew attention to these "You Know Me, Al" things was their exuberantly entertaining quality and the novelty of seeing a crack ballplayer depicted as a thickheaded egocentric instead of a mastermind or a modest, magnanimous hero. Within a decade, however, as Lardner not only kept on about ballplayers but also branched off into run-of-mine Americans created out of the breath of their own nostrils, a few discerning observers began to tell any who listened—they grew steadily more numerous—that Lardner was the worthiest wielder of the American language since Mark Twain and the deftest caricaturist of America since Finley Peter Dunne's Mr. Dooley.*

A key early Lardnerian was Gilbert Seldes, a name that even Miniver had to respect: "What is the use of Babbitt in five hundred pages if we have Lardner in five hundred words?" [98] With genial exaggeration he cited a single sentence to show that Lardner could do on his thumbnail what James Joyce did on the grand scale in the literary travesties in *Ulysses*. One of Fitzgerald's best contributions to literature was his persuading Charles Scribner's Sons to issue a well-timed collection of Lardner's magazine stories. (Fitzgerald was a generous midwife for others' careers, including Hemingway's.) Then William McFee, able novelist and shrewd reviewer, grumbled that Lardner, "an absolutely original writer . . . a greater realist than Dreiser, a more competent craftsman than W. D. Howells" deserved a Nobel Prize better than most of the "writers of immense trilogies" [99] who got them. That misconceived the purposes of Nobel's bequest but showed that even a Briton-born, like McFee, could savor the burstingly indigenous spontaneity of "Women" and "A Caddy's Diary." This cross-cultural miracle recurred most strikingly when Mrs. Woolf read *You Know Me, Al* and rejoiced in how well hands-across-the-sea worked between her and Comiskey Park, marveling at Lardner's inability to "waste a moment when he writes in thinking whether he is using American slang or Shakespeare's English . . . whether he is proud of being American or ashamed of not being Japanese; all his mind is on the story. Hence . . . he writes the best prose that has come our way." [100]

Yet this was never another case of the Old World anticipating the New as with Faulkner and Sherwood Anderson. Lardner welled up from beneath American letters because his buoyancy was so high, his underwater lines so fine. He disported himself in the native tongue of his birthplace, Niles, Michigan—it could have been anywhere between Pittsburgh and the Missouri—like a sea otter playing in a tide rip.† At the time of his emergence in the *Post* his work with odd bits for his column had taught him to concentrate a short story without attenuating the run of the narrative and

* The comparison with Mr. Dooley even extends to the fact, highly creditable to both, that Bryan brought out the best in them. Lardner, for instance: ". . . they say this was the first time William ever stood up to cheer a speech. They has been many other speeches that he felt like cheering but he was already standing up." (*The Portable Ring Lardner*, 611.)

† Hemingway ("Defense of Dirty Words," *Esquire*, September, 1934) rated only two Lardner stories "fine"—"Some Like Them Cold" and "The Golden Honeymoon"—and went out of his way to belittle his ear for human speech. This is puzzling even in view of Hemingway's bitter competitiveness. His own ear was good enough to have taught him better though he never did get the airborne quality, the quantum jump from accuracy to setting the idiom vibrating just right, that came naturally to Mark Twain, Tarkington and Lardner.

yet keep it as nourishing as pemmican. His view of the worlds he knew and
handled—professional and amateur sports, Broadway, the conspicuous
wastelands of Long Island, winter resorts—was as melancholic as his own
appearance. Dos Passos recalled "A tall sallow mournful man with a
higharched nose . . . dark hollow eyes, hollow cheeks, helplessly drunk," [101]
for periodic booze fighting was the saddest thing about him. Elmer Davis
considered him "the most bitterly misanthropic of American writers . . .
[he] merely happens to be more mature than most of our current gloom
spreaders." [102] Maybe that maturity was what saved him from his contemporaries' petulant way of blaming their own escapist misanthropy on the
crudities, brutalities and puerilities that they took to be peculiarly American
insults to their emotional integrity.

When he wrote farce, as in the case of the Nebraskan yaphounds afflicted
with the blanny in *The Big Town*, the characters stayed three-dimensional
even though he could count on the reader's eyes blurring with the tears of
hysteria. Effortlessly he slid into such a mastery of the absurd that
intellectuals taken unawares compared him with the new Dada cult in Paris.
Actually Dada was supposed to disintegrate Art, whereas Lardner was
achieving a four-dimensional vertigo that just for a second there felt like
higher integration, as though one had inhaled a cigar for the first time. The
germ of this may have been his surefooted syntactical atrocities. Seldes'
favorite was: ". . . the hotel has all the modern conveniences, but the
barber is also the valet so a man can't look their best at the same time." [103]
It flowered into *Dinner Bridge* and *I Gasperi* (The Upholsterers), the cast of
which includes "Ian Obri, a blotter salesman; Johan Wasper, his wife . . .
Ffena, their daughter, later their wife; Egso, a pencil guster; Tono, a typical
wastebasket," and other brief encounters with the higher expressionism. Some were privately acted out, and I wish I had been there. The
Translator's Note to the cast of *Clemo Uti* ("The Water Lilies") is: "This
show is written as if people were there to see it." [104]

Hats off. The man had it.

Little Blue Books with "birth control" in the title sold well though about
all they said was that contraception was feasible and socially advisable—no
how-to at all. This reticence came of federal laws against sending obscene
matter through the mails in force since the 1870's and vigorously supported
by volunteer watchdogs. Much of the drawing power of "birth control"
was, like the phrase itself, the work of still another frequenter of Mrs.
Dodge's pre-War salon—Margaret Higgins Sanger, daughter of an Irish
stonemason in upper New York State. Mrs. Dodge thought her "a
Madonna type of woman." [105] A decade later she looked to me like a
wispily determined Salvation Army zealot. Both observations were faulty.
There was small piety about Mrs. Sanger's endorsement of irregular
couplings as recommended by her close friends H. G. Wells and Havelock

Ellis. She was mother of three but so far from Madonnaism that she spent most of her steel-spring energies defending her right to teach the theory and practice of less motherhood. It is significant that though her heavy hair was chestnut brown, people usually recalled it as red. They also remarked how fragile she looked, not like the cultural earthquake who would leave a deeper mark on America than any other of Mrs. Dodge's guests—and a mark that badly needed making.

She came legitimately by her taste for discontented ideas. Her father was a cracker-barrel admirer of Henry George, Lucifer of the heretical single tax, and Colonel Bob Ingersoll, whose witty agnosticism made him hero of the Little Blue Books set. As the young wife of a radical-minded architect she came to espouse the fashionable causes—feminism, pacifism, anarchism. But in becoming First Lady of Contraception, she was more directly motivated than is usual when the maverick rebel settles on a specific concern. In time she realized that birth control was a social tool and potential factor in the world's cancerous population problems. Some opposing her saw baby prevention as deplorable aggravation of "race suicide." But the unusually direct basis of her career was experience as a trained nurse concentrating on maternity cases. The more she saw of the emotional and economic as well as physical results of too frequent or unwilling or inadvisable pregnancy, the more strongly she felt that the curse of Eve could do with some lifting.

Her radical bent naturally got into it when she perceived that by and large that curse applied in inverse ratio to income and education. With discreet illegality the doctors of affluent families instructed patients in the methods of contraception then available—chiefly douching, condoms, suppositories. None was too trustworthy, but among them they accounted for the prevalence of one- and two-child families in silk-stocking districts, whereas in slums. . . . The reasons were partly economic, for in families nearest the margin the cost of drugstore supplies was discouraging; partly cultural, for the proletarian wife seldom met opportunity to learn about reliable contraceptives, and too often her husband, to whom intercourse was likely to be a chief gratification, was impatient of precautions or clung to the widespread folk notion that the sole proof of virility is to impregnate women; partly religious, for Roman Catholicism was firm against artificial contraception and America's urban slum-dwellers were mostly Catholic. Immense bitterness resulted. Many poverty- and child-ridden slum women believed that the rich deliberately withheld from the poor the secret, whatever it was, of keeping families small. (Actually, of course, most of the money and much of the moral support in press and courtroom that kept Mrs. Sanger's cause afloat came from millionaires or their wives, few of whom were radical-minded.)

A strong sense of husbands' brutishness, dooming their wives to a new baby each year, led to affinity between feminism and the birth control movement. A decent society, feminists held, would educate men away from feckless randiness while birth control would enable women healthily to enjoy conjugal doings. Once it learned the Fifth Avenue techniques, the Lower East Side would be in a better position to secure husbands' consent to precautions. "No Gods, No Masters," said the masthead of Mrs. Sanger's pre-War magazine launched in that same early 1914 that saw Henry Ford announce the $5-a-day wage. The flavor of the *Woman Rebel* was as hotly feminist as its name. The New York *Call*, America's largest Socialist English-language newspaper, had been printing her series of sex-education articles, *What Every Mother Should Know* and *What Every Girl Should Know*, which eventually circulated very widely, particularly as LBB's. At the time they got the *Call* into trouble for using the specific words "gonorrhea" and "syphilis."

Soon Mrs. Sanger was indicted for alleged obscenities in the *Woman Rebel*. Reacting with wonted vigor, she published for lower-income women a pamphlet, *Family Limitation*. Her husband was arrested for selling a copy. His wife had already sailed from Canada under an assumed name for Europe, leaving the district attorney a letter promising to look him up when she returned. The War had begun, but no mere world cataclysm would keep her from increasing her arsenal by learning Old World contraceptive techniques, particularly those of the Netherlands, where a new system of birth control clinics meant the world's lowest death rates for mothers and town-born babies. There she met and brought home the Dutch secret weapon—the Mensigna pessary, still a good nonbiochemical contraceptive to protect against regardless husbands. Armed with this and buoyed up by a nolle prosequi of the *Woman Rebel* case, she went home and late in 1916 opened the nation's first birth control clinic in the Brownsville section of Brooklyn—then largely Jewish. Some local people, anticipating today's black militants, suspected that the general purpose was genocide against Jews. But it was the Catholic-dominated New York City police who raided the clinic as a public nuisance defying state laws against circulating contraceptive information.

The battle to unshackle contraception would go on for forty years and is not over yet. Mrs. Sanger's doughty sister came near death in a hunger strike while serving a stiff sentence in the workhouse. In and out of jail herself, Mrs. Sanger took every opportunity to make her case whether before a committee of the U.S. Senate or before the ladies' auxiliary of the Ku Klux Klan in Spring Lake, New Jersey. She lacked Miss Addams' stateswomanly presence but was otherwise of the same order of social prowess. The point here is that the devices and new insistence on using them that she brought undermined fear of pregnancy as deterrent to a maid's way with a man at just the time when Freudianism was eroding the allied moral deterrents. That is, Ford, Freud, feminist, flapper and the frustration of spermatazoa—five principal reasons why those post-War women would be different from their mothers—were all gathering speed before Sarajevo was ever a household word.

Another premonitory vagary with a capital *F* was Fundamentalist religion. Its high-water mark—the Scopes trial in 1925—ended in stalemate. Afterward it withdrew into the revival industry of Dixie, the eccentric tabernacles of Oklahoma and the Southwest and the storefront shrines of city slums. But in the following generation radio and then television gave it a new lease on life and the flamboyant ministries of today's Reverend Dr. Billy Graham, Reverend Dr. Oral Roberts and Reverend Dr. Rex Humbard indicate that its claws were only temporarily cut. In its day it was taken to be symptomatic of much of what ailed the nation* and gave native and exotic Americanophobes heavily exploited ammunition.

It began and remains as ingenuously simple as its adherents—Bible-reared Americans who need unblinkingly to believe everything in the King James Version, particularly its accounts of the Creation and the gaudy, vindictive pageantry of the Apocalypse. Its enemies naturally blamed the War for its gains after 1918. Such heaped-up horrors, they said, persuaded the ignorant and literal-minded that the end of the world, just as in Revelations, seven-headed and ten-horned beast and all, must be at hand, and Wartime strains had set people seeking something more nourishing than the apologetic theology of "Modernist" Protestantism. Fundamentalists accepting this told of numerous instances of soldiers whose souls as well as lives were saved when their pocket Bibles stopped bullets, and exploited Wartime emotions by emphasizing the German origin of much of the Higher Criticism—the analytic study of Scripture that cast doubts on the Bible God's cosmogony and led to the heresies of Modernism.

Actually Fundamentalism had been gathering force since 1900 among millions of American churchgoers, chiefly Baptists and Methodists. The Reverend Dwight L. Moody's elaborate revivals of the 1880's had begotten the Moody Bible Institute in Chicago to train hot-gospelers to counteract "the advancing apostacy predicted in the Bible." [106] Entrance required only a common school education or equivalent. By 1919 the institute's ancillary correspondence school of reactionary theology had 10,000 students. In 1907 two pious millionaire brothers, Lyman and Milton Stewart, had founded Moody's chief rival, the Los Angeles Bible Institute. Several dozen smaller schools emulated these Vaticans of Fundamentalism, teaching what an expert liberal theologian described as "a very precise theology . . . [they] insist quite rightly that the Bible means what it says, and hold that if the Bible be, as they believe, the revealed word of God, nothing contrary to it can be true or ought to be taught." [107]

* Actually, as the Reverend Dr. Kirsopp Lake pointed out (*Atlantic Monthly*, June, 1925), much the same thing had developed a generation earlier in the Netherlands, and the schisms that it created among local Protestants had political repercussions graver than anything Fundamentalism accomplished in America.

In 1900 the Niagara Bible Conference, highly heresy-sensitive, set up "Five Points" of essential belief that, in one or another version, became touchstones of the movement. They required literal acceptance of every word in the Bible; of the divinity of Christ; of His Virgin Birth; of His "substitutionary atonement," that is, the success of His suffering and death in lifting the guilt of sin from those believing in Him; and of the certainty of His actual physical return to judge mankind as the Bible predicted. It was implied that this Second Coming was far nearer than sinners expected—and wouldn't they have a nasty shock! That checklist gauged those professing what a favorite Fundamentalist hymn calls "That old-time religion! . . . It was good for Paul and Silas/ And it's good enough for me!" A copy of the Los Angeles Bible Institute's reprint of *Jesus Is Coming*, basic document of Fundamentalist propaganda, was sent to every ordained minister in the United States. A quarter million copies of its twelve-volume encyclopedia, *The Fundamentals*, from which the movement took its name, were distributed. None of its tenets would have troubled Paul or Silas or, barring details of the Atonement, any of the founders of Calvinism or Methodism. Kirsopp Lake, brilliantly liberal and discerning professor of ecclesiastical history at Harvard, called it all "a reaction against the intellectual chaos which has often been allowed to serve as a substitute for liberal theology . . . it is we who have departed from the [early Christian] tradition, not the [Fundamentalist], and anyone who tries to argue with [him] on the basis of authority will be worsted." [107]

Chaos was not too strong a word for the Modernist's position. Once Higher Criticism had shown the two accounts of the Creation in Genesis to be inconsistent, bang went the infallibility of the Bible. Further, geologists showed that neither version allowed for the millions of years needed to lay down the multiple strata of sedimentary rocks. Evolutionists said that the fossils in such rocks ruled out Genesis-style creation of all known creatures in a single day and made it overwhelmingly likely that, far from being made in God's image, man came of a long line of slowly evolving, apelike ancestors. These crosslights robbed the Bible of its holy authority as cosmology, deposing it to the status of either a rich literature or a valuable, if obscure, source of anthropological data.

Many parsons as well as Bible-reared laymen found these views disturbing. Only Unitarians, a small group unable to believe much beyond a generalized Goodness basic to the universe, had no theological hostages to fortune to lose. (Bert Leston Taylor, pre-War columnist of the Chicago *Tribune*, defined a Unitarian as "a Retired Christian.")[108] Catholics firmly ignored the issue. That was wiser than to try, as many Protestants did, to reconcile the new science with the Biblical basis of what they taught their communicants. Their subterfuges were various. Plaintively they suggested that those "days" of Creation were a Divine metaphor for geological eons allowing a Divinely sponsored but naturally slow evolution of species, and that the creation of Eve out of Adam's rib was a Divine symbol of solicitude for man's emotional fulfillment through love. For such strained interpretation, after all, the Bible on the pulpit contained ample precedent in those chapter headings treating the candid eroticisms of the Song of Songs as symbols of the mystical union of Christ and His Church.

Those thus wholesomely eager to help God update His message were "Modernists." Others, often though not always less cultivated, refused to try because they were either more honest, more loyal, more ignorant, more stubborn, more authority-minded or more superstitious. They saw with dismay that Modernist views made nonsense of most of the traditional hymns and the values implied in the childhood instruction received by most of their communicants. Hence this "uprising of orthodox supernatural-ism" [109] as a Fundamentalist paper called it. All over America preachers, chiefly Methodist and Baptist, pounded the pulpit and shouted that they did too believe that God created man out of the dust of the earth instead of letting him evolve from something mighty like an ape; that the fish did swallow Jonah and cast him forth again according to God's plan; that Balaam's ass did speak and the Red Sea part for Moses; that Jesus Christ did rise from the dead just as sure, my friends, as He died on the Cross to take away our sins, hallelujah! and that He will rise again in that great day when the heavens shall roll up like a scroll and Alpha and Omega be as little children, praise God! One really logical Fundamentalist maintained that though he couldn't controvert rocks and fossils and contradictions in Genesis, he didn't need to; God put all that stuff into Holy Writ and the Triassic limestone to test man's loyal eagerness to believe in spite of it all.

Certain eminent people—including professors at august Princeton Theological Seminary aware of the eroding effect of logic and science on Divine authority—stayed on God's side without completely formal adherence to Fundamentalism, like the "fellow travelers" so useful to Communism in the 1930's. A Fundamentalist satirist effectively derided the position of the Modernist who, once the Bible no longer meant what it plainly said, saw the Ten Commandments and the Beatitudes become matters of personal taste:

> Holy Bible, flecked with spots,
> How I love thee, marred by blots;
> Word of God, in thee I find
> Each according to his mind. . . .[109]

Most in the public eye was Bryan lecturing from coast to coast against Modernism on "Tampering with the Mainspring" and "They Have Taken Away My Lord. . . ." Crucial support came from the road-show revivalists of the day following the lead of the Reverend Billy Sunday, raucous king of the profession. Operating chiefly in cities large enough to underwrite his costly shenanigans, he did much to preserve an urban aspect of Fundamentalism. Huge numbers of city folks heard him rail against "[that] old bastard theory of evolution" as "jackass nonsense," [110] "Bunk, junk and poppy-cock." [109]

For though Fundamentalism ran deepest in the bucolic South, it had representation in the regional metropolis. The Reverend William Bell Riley, lecturer-missionary, founder of the World's Christian Fundamentals Association, was pastor of the First Baptist Church of Minneapolis. Boston's large Tremont Temple housed Fundamentalist Reverend Dr. Jasper Massee. A few hundred yards from New York City's sinfully elegant Plaza Hotel was Calvary Baptist Church and the Reverend Dr. John Roach Straton bellowing against evolution, Rum and dirty plays. Two churches on the semismart Upper West Side had Fundamentalist incumbents. Obviously thousands of New Yorkers—many probably immigrants from west of Pittsburgh—liked to hear of the glory of the Millennium and the sinfulness of slandering God's image as a glorified monkey.

Nevertheless, the largest Fundamentalist flock in America was Southern —the 10,000-strong congregation of the Reverend J. Frank Norris' First Baptist Church in Fort Worth, Texas. A magazine reporter called him "the shrewdest, strongest and most romantically adventurous figure in the movement." [109] The cover of his house bulletin showed him playing a Navy searchlight on the Devil; in the mid-1920's he built a 6,000-seat church (since demolished) crowned by a real searchlight visible Hollywood-premiere style for thirty-two miles. Loudspeakers on its walls sent his blistering sermons booming through downtown streets. Billed as "The Texas Cyclone," he made a publicity-rich sideline of revivifying big-city churches with high-pressure revival sermons followed by intensive fund raising and during much of his career combined serving his Fort Worth church with directing the affairs of an equally obscurantist congregation in Detroit.

High-chinned, hard of face and eye, he seemed to me more like the foreman of a wildcatting crew than a minister of the Gospel. One easily believed his boast that he had three bullets in him from a youthful brush with rustlers. In Fort Worth he and his staff were once indicted for arson; they were thought to have burned the church down to force the factious congregation to finance a better one. When a mass meeting threatened to run them out of town after acquittal, Norris and friends barricaded themselves behind a machine gun, legend said. Norris replied it was a lie, all they had were sawed-off shotguns. In 1926 he shot and killed a political enemy who came blustering into his office in the church. The following Sunday he preached on "All things work together for good to them that love the Lord." [111] Acquitted on grounds of self-defense, he went on to exploit radio as the new mass-appeal tool that would keep him a local power among the red-necks until he died in 1952.

He was full of rant about "that hell-born, Bible-destroying, deity-of-Christ-denying, German rationalism . . . evolution" [112] and predictions of a "literal, personal, bodily, visibly, imminent return of our Lord to this earth as king." [109] Fundamentalism preferred those two of the Five Points. Dwelling on the Virgin Birth risked lewdness, and the subtleties at issue in the Godhead and the Atonement were over the head of the average Fundamentalist preacher and in any case would have bewildered his hearers. Emphasis on the Millennium as gratifyingly near at hand put them closer than Modernists to the original Christians, who had been achingly sure that Christ would return any day. It also tempted some Fundamentalists into a harsh, though not illogical, mistrust of democracy and social reform. Autocracy was "God's idea of government. What we need is . . . [a] Kaiser Jesus," said the Reverend Dr. Reuben A. Torrey, head of the Los Angeles Bible Institute. "Man has no inalienable right except to be damned," [109] said a colleague. And if Christ might bring a new heaven and a new earth next year or next week, it was pointless and maybe sacrilegiously presumptuous to beat the drum for slum clearance. Fighting booze, white slavery and gambling was different. Those soul-destroying sins threatened the individual with immediate hellfire if he died before the Second Coming.

The Reverend Dr. Shailer Mathews, president of the Baptist-founded University of Chicago, a leading Modernist, admitted in 1923 that Fundamentalists controlled one in four "evangelical" * churches in the Eastern states, one in two in the Midwest, three out of four in the Far West. The enemy claimed nine out of ten such congregations—probably a high estimate but still formidable even when cut in half, signifying near dominance of the South. Fundamentalist power lost nothing by subsidy from old-time religionists of wealth such as George F. Washburn, real estate magnate of Boston and Florida, who gave lavishly, particularly to the Bryan University presently founded in Dayton, Tennessee, and to the Bible Crusaders of America, a missionary phalanx of Fundamentalism. The Reverend Dr. Albert C. Dieffenbach, Modernist editor of the *Christian Register*, gave another clue to the flavor of Fundamentalism in calling it "religious Kukluxism." [109] Some of its leaders, notably Straton—egocentric, foolish but no manipulative knave—repudiated the Klan. But Norris and his likes welcomed hood, lash and fiery cross. In many contexts Klansmen gave the pro-Bible cause cordial help, and it was no coincidence when Edward Y. Clarke, ejected from the Klan's high command, founded a competing order of the Supreme Kingdom to propagandize Fundamentalist principles.

As his and his Lord's power grew, Norris took the warpath against evangelical colleges that allowed their faculties to teach the theory of

* Meaning those relying for doctrine on the Bible instead of authority; in practice Methodists, Baptists and the numerous offshoots from their many schisms. At the time this took in at least 60 percent of American churchgoers, maybe 80 percent of Americans enrolled in Protestant congregations.

evolution. At Baylor (Baptist) and Southern Methodist Universities he forced the resignation of professors by rousing local Fundamentalists against their poisoning students' minds. He wrote an article about the evolutionism befouling Wake Forest University, mailed a copy to every Protestant preacher in North Carolina and came within a hair of forcing its president to resign. Every such foray, of course, meant that dozens of presidents of freshwater colleges heard the thunder of Norris' terrible swift wings and advised their biology instructors to take in sail—the effect sought by Senator Joseph McCarthy in other contexts thirty years later. When Carl E. Akeley, expert on big game, was to lecture on gorillas at a Southern college, the president begged him not to mention evolution lest the newspapers pick it up.

This was piecemeal, however, and limited to evangelical campuses. In Kentucky the Reverend Dr. J. W. Porter, Baptist head of the Anti-Evolution League of America, turned to the law to succor righteousness. Through the Baptist State Board of Missions he introduced into the legislature in 1921 a bill banning "the teaching of Darwinism, atheism, agnosticism or evolution as it pertains to man in schools wholly or in part sustained by State funds." [109] The press called it "the monkey bill." Bryan came to urge its passage, vowing to "drive Darwinism from our schools." [109] Such resort to law to prevent occasions of unrighteousness had a long, if not honorable, history. New England's and Virginia's early Puritans shared with their Old World preceptors the belief that good men sinned when they did not destroy whatever might lead a brother astray. Hence a godly society must ban brothel, gambling hell, saloon and lascivious book, picture or show. Hence federal or state laws against lotteries, whoring, intoxicants and use of the mails for obscene matter. In the Fundamentalist view, to tolerate Darwin or the Missing Link in high school or college was to expose maturing youth to the means of sin—a risk properly inviting legislation. Yet—the proposed law was clever—it could not be denounced as blanket suppression of scientific ideas. It did nothing to prevent non-tax-supported schools from teaching evolution or agnosticism.* It merely relieved Kentucky's many thousands of Fundamentalist taxpayers from being forced to finance having their children taught things that they considered not only false but poisonous to the soul.

Norris and Sunday joined Bryan, of course, in praising the social morality of this proposal. The Louisville papers denounced it as vociferously as the Bible thumpers extolled it. In the end it was ominous that the lower legislative house of one of the South's least unenlightened states

---

* The point is sound as far as it goes. But it fails to recognize that the line between private and tax-supported schools is less than clean-cut. Most private schools could not survive without exemption from taxation on their property. Suppose the law made that indispensable exemption conditional on their renouncing the teaching of evolution or gained the same end by wiping out such exemptions, as is now widely urged in the case of church properties.

rejected it by one slim vote—cast by a Hard-Shell Baptist from the hills who, though against evolution, thought the proposal a threat to personal freedom. This narrow squeak encouraged Fundamentalists in other states to sponsor such bills. They failed in Iowa, Minnesota and Florida but passed by narrow margins in relatively backward Oklahoma and Texas.

In Tennessee it was thought that legislators voting for the monkey bill had done so to help the governor in a close election in which his signing it would draw Fundamentalist votes. On signing he said nobody expected much effort to enforce it. But it caused newspaper stories, and the American Civil Liberties Union, self-appointed watchdog agency set up to help radicals caught in the Palmer Raids of 1919–20, offered legal help to anybody challenging it in court. Dissolve to Dayton, Tennessee, a county seat of some 3,000 souls in the southeastern corner of the state—TVA country now, sluggishly out of the way in 1923. There frequenters of the local drugstore persuaded themselves that to take up the ACLU's offer would put Dayton profitably on the map. For a test case they recruited John T. Scopes, teacher of general science in the high school and coach of its athletics. A friendly indictment arraigned him for having taught evolution in class. After the consequent trial was over, he confessed that he had done no such thing. The day the class reached that part of the book a special athletic occasion kept him from being there.* The pupils testifying against him in court had to be crammed the night before on what evolution was and what Mr. Scopes would have said about it had he been there to touch on the subject.

The soda-fountain junta did indeed put Dayton on the map—of a grinningly astounded world as well as of America. The prosecution had the eager services of Bryan as chief counsel. The ACLU countered with Darrow, fresh from keeping Nathan Leopold and Richard Loeb, intellectualized thrill killers, from the electric chair; Dudley Field Malone, conspicuous divorce lawyer, Democratic politician of New York City, candid enemy of Prohibition and friend of Women's Rights; and Arthur Garfield Hays, the ACLU's own famous counsel-champion. Three big-city men—an insistent agnostic, an Irishman and a Jew—against Bryan, the string-tied idol of the WASP small towns where Main Street was paved with the Ten Commandments. Among them they embodied the chronic quarrel between the county seat and the godless metropolis that already bulked large in Populism, Prohibition and the Klan. The American Association for the Advancement of Science sent expert witness to defend the evolutionist against the Fundamentalist position. Special correspondents and wire service and newsreel teams came flocking, foremost among them Mencken,

---

* This section is greatly indebted to L. Sprague De Camp's admirable *The Great Monkey Trial* (1968), a book specially needed because *Inherit the Wind*, a conspicuous play and movie about a Scopes-like situation (1955) deplorably diluted and defused the valuable ironies of the actual participants and procedures. Scopes' recent autobiography is also valuable here.

then at his peak. His prolix filings to the Baltimore *Sun* dripped with the contempt for grass-roots America for which his public valued him.

He had small need to exaggerate. Dayton was awash with ignorance and corny opportunism—crackpot prophets, hot dog vendors, souvenir hawkers and two rival trained chimpanzees whose showman-owners presented them as the creatures that the arguments in the sweltering courtroom would refer to. The judge was grotesquely eager to pose for photographs. The jury, who had sought service to secure front row seats, almost mutinied because technical arguments made it necessary to exclude them during the juiciest infighting. The sanest touch came from Alfred W. McCann of New York City, a lay nutritionist and author of *God—or Gorilla*, a disarmingly earnest attack on the paleontologist view of the descent of man, when Bryan asked him to join the prosecution: "I disapprove of the entire proceedings . . . we can't hope to bottle up the tendency of men to think for themselves." [113] The worst taste was shown when the defense lawyers, plus the Reverend Dr. Charles Francis Potter, archfoe of Straton, and Mrs. Potter invited Little Joe, the smaller chimpanzee, to dinner.

Bryan was the focus of the trial. Shiny with sweat and ill-advised zeal, trusting in his forensic renown, he took the stand as expert witness on the infallibility of the Bible. Darrow, gallused and shirt-sleeved to look as cracker-barrelish as Bryan, took him apart like a dollar watch. It was too easy. A few years later Lippmann wrote: ". . . if Mr. Bryan had been as acute as his opponents, he would have conquered them in debate. Given his premise, the logic of his position was unassailable. . . ." [114] What may have seemed to Darrow another fine moment came when the judge, objecting to his insolence, said that he hoped counsel meant no disrespect, and Darrow replied: "This court always has the right to hope." Frank R. Kent of the Baltimore *Sun*, less flashy than Mencken, condemned the whole proceeding as "trivial . . . full of humbuggery and hypocrisy, conducted by publicity-seeking lawyers, sensation-hungry correspondents, a befuddled jury, a popeyed crowd." [115]

In order to get a clear ruling on constitutionality from appellate courts, which an acquittal would prevent, both sides hoped for conviction. They got it—"guilty as charged," $100 fine. The eventual results varied between nil and significance. The judge, failing of reelection, exploited his recent prominence by going lecturing for the anti-evolutionist Supreme Kingdom racket. A few weeks after the trial Bryan died in his sleep. Scopes' appeal to the State Supreme Court was upheld but not on grounds involving the constitutional issue. So it did not get threshed out until forty years later, when the U.S. Supreme Court rejected Arkansas' anti-evolution law.* The

---

* Mississippi's monkey law, last of the species, was repealed on April 14, 1972. But there is a new movement centered in California hoping to force textbook publishers by law to include the Fundamentalist-endorsed Biblical account of Creation in biology texts as an equal-footing alternative to theories of gradual evolution.

hot dog and souvenir boys failed to make as much money as they hoped. But Dayton, though little better off economically for its blatant fame, at least had plenty to talk about for years to come. And Scopes came off fairly well. Some of the scientist witnesses procured him scholarships for graduate study in geology that gave him a new profession. With the screening of *Inherit the Wind* came a preretirement career as Exhibit A lecturer promoting the movie.

Gilbert Murray, one of Britain's symbols of deep-thinking cultivation, called the Scopes case "the most serious setback to civilization in all history." [116] Thus to set it ahead of the barbarian invasions of old Rome—only one possible rival—was overstating. Temporarily the verdict encouraged the obscurantists. Mississippi passed a monkey bill in 1927, Arkansas (by referendum) in 1928. When the legislature of Texas balked in 1926, Governor Miriam "Ma" Ferguson ordered all pages mentioning evolution torn from state-supplied textbooks and procured new expurgated editions. Yet several other monkey bills were withdrawn, and the impulse behind them seemed to have lost its spring. The ablest student of the case, L. Sprague De Camp, though granting that the defense's "grandstand show" was discreditably "raucous, clownish and undignified," nevertheless thought the net effect "A telling blow at the [Fundamentalist] crusade." [115] Six years after the trial Stewart G. Cole, historian of Fundamentalism, described its adherents as "recently . . . content to maintain their faith without attempting to convert liberals." [117] In view of the threat that the Norrises had been representing, there was, in spite of Murray, a victory for civilization—at a deplorable cost. For the Scopes affair, gleefully reported all over the Western world, had made America sound pathologically absurd, crude and vicious.

Yet it was possible intelligibly to describe Fundamentalism as betokening things ailing America. Its anti-intellectualism went back 250 years to Quaker and Pennsylvania Dutch mistrust of learning beyond the three R's—one stupidity that cannot be laid to New England's Puritans. Add the Colonial populace's sulkiness toward Tory Master Broadcloth, who knew more than blacksmiths and backwoodsmen did. In the late 1700's the new parts of the country learned from Baptist and Methodist missionaries that schooling not only was not necessary, but might even clog spiritual skills. A cognate theology drew settlers west of the mountains away from Calvin's elite of arbitrarily saved souls into the Methodists' equalitarian salvation of all spiritually eager for it. This old-time religion that made headlines 100 years later dwelled on the direct link between God and dependent man. That indirectly glorified the spiritual gifts of the individual at the expense of his reason and nudged him toward faith healing as crowning evidence of nearness to God. Its Bible-minded smugness also committed him to the morals that Mother used to make. Yet Fundamentalism had its up-to-date aspects. Though it never fused sympathetic schismatics into an ecumenical Fundamentalist church, it did develop a powerful press of its own and form large associations of Fundamentalist preachers and lay zealots crossing sectarian lines. Those Bible Institutes sending out thousands of glib missionaries employed typewriters and telephones in the same sort of organization that had been created by and for highly secular business enterprises.

Such organizations were a specialty of America's. Many Americans took scale and efficiency as good things in themselves in any field, why not in religion? By 1914 the Mormon empire between the Rockies and the Sierra Nevada shows how ruthless discipline and selective proselytizing could make a flourishing economy out of a religious movement born of mental disturbance. Mormons' flocks and herds, banks and retail profits were making the ghostly wealth of such caretaker foundations as New York City's Trinity Church look meager. Hostility from Gentiles did not vanish overnight. Former Senator Frank J. Cannon, the renegade Mormon leader, was widely and lucratively booked for Chautauqua lectures. Mormon elders contributed to his publicity by denouncing him on street corners on the day of his booking and sometimes invaded the tent demanding to be heard in rebuttal. Once lightning struck the tent while he was speaking. But soon after the War it was plain that the prestige due economic weight and the Saints' renunciation of polygyny—a custom that had made social acceptance difficult—were lifting Mormonism toward respectability in a public relations victory as striking as what Ivy Lee did for the Rockefellers. The great dome of the Mother Church of Christian Science in Boston told another such success story, celebrating the other American, a lady this time, who had woven of her own fantasies a net to accommodate any amount of power and others' dollars. Mormonism and Christian Science as they now stand, though both had some success outside the United States, are among the few things of which it may well be true that they could have happened only in America.

Two cousin examples of the Christian Science version of mind-over-matter flourishing as the War arrived—New Thought and Unity—adapted to religious uses those American innovations mail-order selling and the correspondence school. The parent of New Thought was the same faith-healing cult, child of Phineas P. Quimby of Belfast, Maine, that taught Mary Baker Eddy, mother of Christian Science, that disease is only erroneous belief that the material world exists. While she expounded that and expanded her following, certain restless ministers of the Unitarian, Universalist and Swedenborgian persuasions were independently polishing Quimby's teachings into a rival identification of the Spiritual with the Healthy with the Christ-like Divine so windily that it ended up meaning practically Nothing—except that Mind could make man almost blasphemously Godlike and keep him ailment-free. Soon came emphasis on the spiritual duty to exercise one's solar plexus, a knot of nerves below the wishbone then on the public mind because Bob Fitzsimmons, heavyweight champion of the world, was said to win by battering his opponents in that crucial region.

This "Boston cult" of dilute mysticism officially became New Thought in the 1890's. Presently it purveyed a sort of subpsychiatry in a sanitarium where more or less disturbed persons were rehabilitated—sometimes—by various mixtures of inspirational lectures, hypnotism and electric shock administered through a fancy gold crown on the patient's head; Max Eastman tried it without success on his backaches and general malaise. By 1914 its devotees' New Thought Alliance booked paid-admission lectures by leaders and prospered even more from the written word—works with such titles as *In Tune with the Infinite* and *All's Right with the World.* The author of those was Ralph Waldo Trine; the names of New Thought authors often sound as if cooked up by Sinclair Lewis trying too hard: Frank Channing Haddock, Gaius Glenn Atkins, Orison Swett Marsden. . . . Queen of New Thought literature was Ella Wheeler Wilcox, a Wisconsin poetess then famous for overstuffed verses. Her panegyric of the cult comes as near as anybody ever did to defining it:

> All sin is virtue unevolved,
> Release the angel from the clod—
> Go love thy brother up to God. . . .
> When the great universe was wrought
> To might and majesty from nought,
> The all creative force was—*Thought.*[118]

Mrs. Wilcox's poems on New Thought were obtainable for 10 cents sent to the Elizabeth Towne Company of Holyoke, Massachusetts, official source of its books, pamphlets, spiritual diets and magazine, *Nautilus,* presumably so named from the line "Build thee more stately mansions, oh my soul!" in "The Chambered Nautilus." Mrs. Towne paid young Sinclair Lewis $250 each for serials about how New Thought solved the woes of newlyweds and salesgirls. Its advertisements were as familiar in national magazines as those of mail-order taffeta petticoats, collar buttons and cures for baldness. *Nautilus* by no means neglected the faith healing on which the cult relied. Its readers' testimonial letters cited emotional and spiritual as well as physical wonders. One man following its mail-order therapy not only cured his deafness, which had baffled doctors, but also acquired a wife as a sort of premium with the cure. A girl in Enterprise, Mississippi, was mentally deranged after influenza; the doctors gave her up, but mail-order treatment from New Thought headquarters set her right in three days. The portrayal of Christ as what one wishes Him to have been—social agitator, witch-hunter, Progressive educator—never went farther than in a New Thought pamphlet asserting that He "wore good clothes, ate good food. . . . The comforts and luxuries of some of the best homes in Jerusalem . . . were his . . . and among his friends were many men and women of wealth." [119] By 1920, however, emphasis was shifting to psychological catchwords newly fashionable. Advertisers in *Nautilus* offered courses in "bio-psychology and psycho-analysis" or shouted: "Don't Pay Me a Cent if I Can't Give You a Magnetic Personality—Five Days Free Trial!"

The Unity cult, exactly contemporary with New Thought, originated among laymen, hence has less of the pseudo-pantheistic flavor that had recommended the latter to Boston's well-thought-of Metaphysical Club. The mother of Unity, Mrs. Myrtle Fillmore, was consumptive. Her husband, Charles, crippled from childhood, had been a railroad clerk, an assayer and a mule skinner before getting into the real estate boom in Kansas City in the 1880's. The boom and his gains vanished simultaneously. Financial troubles piled on physical apparently transmuted Myrtle into a more highly conductive organism. Both had dabbled in the self-styled metaphysical movements of the New Thought stripe; Fillmore boasted of having been through forty-odd courses of the sort. From that spiritual compost now sprouted in Myrtle a timely belief that proper application of "fixed divine law" to daily life would thwart "negative or destructive agencies" [120] and solve their problems. It did too. Her lungs healed, his shrunken leg lengthened, and when she took the good word to afflicted acquaintances around Kansas City, they too felt more robust and even began to prosper economically, while the Fillmores found that free-will offerings from those thus benefited were relieving their own pecuniary difficulties. They planned a new movement to be called Unity, "not a sect or a church but a school for investigating and demonstrating the scientific principles taught by Jesus," [121] and lest any misunderstanding arise between them and the collaborating Powers, they drew up and signed a mutual pledge to "dedicate ourselves . . . all we have, and all we expect to have . . . to the Spirit of Truth. . . . It being understood and agreed that the said Spirit of Truth shall render unto us an equivalent for this dedication in peace of mind, health of body, wisdom, understanding, love, life, and an abundant supply of all things necessary without our making any of these things the objects of our existence. . . ." [122]

Rather than compete with existing sects, Unity urged its faithful to carry the new Truth into the churches they attended, just as Fundamentalism founded no churches though hoping to lead existing ones into literal interpretation of Scripture. At least Fundamentalism had a definite body of dogma. The Unity convert asked by his pastor just what he had in mind would have had to reply in terms even vaguer than New Thought's. Spokesman "Papa Charley" taught that though Unity was not primarily a means to healing and prosperity, it should bring both in its wake. Eventually came a theory of reincarnation—he had been early attracted to Theosophy—and the teaching that those perfected in Unity, hence bolstered by hygienically true and beautiful thoughts, will not only never go broke but also never die. In adolescence, however, Unity was little more than polysyllabic babble about faith healing—of fiscal as well as bodily ills—that employed the term "science" for the same purpose of window dressing that had led Mrs. Eddy to it.

And psychogenic ailments being always with us, naturally it worked. Among the testimonials, doubtless all genuine, in Unity's publications consider the man who restored soundness to his decayed teeth by telling each in succession: "I am God's child of perfection and nothing but perfection can be manifest through me";[123] the woman who, caught by the hand in an electric wringer, shut off the power by declaring the truth about God; the man whose constipation was explosively relieved only two hours after he mailed to Unity headquarters a letter asking prayers in his behalf.*

For while elder healing cults relied on the laying on of hands, Unity extended Mrs. Eddy's "absent treatment" into mail- and phone-order healing in Sears, Roebuck style presently imitated by the radio-racketeers of the bootleg Mexican border stations and most recently by the Prayer Tower function of the Reverend Oral Roberts' headquarters-university in Tulsa, Oklahoma. In Unity Village, southeast of Kansas City, Missouri, a striking group of pseudo-Spanish, yellow-walled, tile-roofed buildings like a private World's Fair, lights burn all day and all night in the rooms housing "Silent Unity"—the arm of the cult that opens letters and takes telephone calls from ailing or troubled people seeking help from Unity's prayer experts. Yearly some 700,000 such requests come in response to Unity's printed propaganda and nation-blanketing radio spot broadcasts. No charge; the free-will offerings by which the Spirit of Truth kept that contract with the Fillmores continue ample for staff salaries and the upkeep of the village. Cheap night rates keep the phones ringing, but there are still many letters. Economic motives can be innocently candid: "A few weeks ago I asked that you pray that my son might find a better job. A few days after . . . he . . . received a promotion . . . the financial gain was terrific. . . ."[123]

Unity's printing plant now turns out 70,000,000 pieces a year—magazines, prayer manuals, hortatory leaflets, Sunday School lessons, courses in self-development—to mail to anyone that thirsteth. *Good Business*, its magazine for businessmen, has vanished, but *Wee Wisdom*, bait for small fry, edited until she died by "Mama Myrtle," persists. Both she and Papa Charley have gone to their reward a good while since. The implication that

* On both New Thought and Unity this section is greatly indebted to Charles W. Ferguson's *The New Books of Revelations* (1928), which gives invaluable detail about the movements as of the late 1920's. I found it fascinating to visit Unity headquarters forty-odd years later.

neither had properly achieved perfection in Unity, which would have kept them alive, doesn't seem to bother the 250-odd posthumous employees who keep Unity Village very much of a going concern.

Mail-order methods were not the only way in which the ebullient America of 1914 gave the religious urge a business flavor. New heights of disciplined organization were then attained by the impudent revivalism of the Reverend Billy Sunday, ally of Fundamentalism. Ballyhoo had made him so conspicuous that he tied Carnegie for eighth place in a national magazine poll to choose America's greatest man. Being American-born, unlike Carnegie, he epitomized even better the cliché of strive-and-succeed. He actually was born in a log cabin on a small farm in Iowa; son of a Union private who never saw the child he begot before he marched away and died in camp; scantily schooled in an orphanage for veterans' sons; daring base stealer and sensational outfielder for the Chicago White Stockings (now White Sox). Professional baseball paid little then—he broke in at $60 a month—so he eked out winters by firing locomotives. The fuel being coal and automatic stokers unknown, it must have kept him in shape for next season. Ballplayers then had few of the suburban tastes that press agents now claim for them. Sunday drank his share and ran after women somewhat but was stable enough to double as business manager—presaging his later talent for organizing—went to church now and then and was courting a nice, churchgoing Chicago girl.

One tipsy afternoon he was cajoled into a skid row mission where they sang the old come-to-Jesus hymns he had known in Iowa. Another visit or two, and in the jargon of revivalism, he "publicly accepted Christ as his Saviour." It was his Road to Damascus. He gave up drink, refused to play ball on Sunday, studied public speaking at Methodist-controlled North-western University, threw up a next year's contract for $500 a month, turned roving soul saver for the YMCA, married the Chicago girl. And soon baseball's loss of a fine outfielder became the gain of the Reverend J. Wilbur Chapman, an eminent evangelist working the Midwest, who hired him as advance man at $40 a week.*

Advance man was a term from show business. It meant the traveling harbinger of minstrel show or road company of a Broadway hit who made town well ahead of the troupe, arranged details with the theater, alerted the transfer man to expect such and such baggage and scenery, staked out rooms in hotel or boardinghouse, wangled posters into store windows and got large ones stuck up on billboards and board fences, buttered up the press with drinks and free tickets as well as paid advertising, bribed the law

---

* This section owes much to *Billy Sunday Was His Real Name* (1955), a rich biography by William G. McLoughlin, Jr. The surname Sunday was not assumed to fit a preaching career but was a true family name, once "Sonntag," from a German immigrant ancestor of four generations back.

as indicated . . . and then did it all over again in the next town on the schedule. Evangelism being so much a branch of show business, Sunday's functions were similar along lines worked out decades previously by Moody's field organization.

Methods differed only in scale, whether the soul saver was Moody or B. Fay Mills, his chief rival, or a well-considered second-rater like Chapman in towns like Peoria, Illinois. First, one arranged to be invited for a week or so of revivals by the town's Protestant churches of evangelical tone, each sect sinking its doctrines and local rivalries in a "union revival" that, it was hoped, would elevate local morals by diminishing drinking, whoring, gambling and general lightmindedness and in any case fatten each congregation with some of the prospective converts. In many towns these festivals of redemption became as much annual events as circus day; in some parts of the South they still are. The evangelist's basic cadre consisted of himself; a "songster" to manage the local choirs and coax the audience to sing its hearts loose for God; a woman assistant, usually Mrs. Evangelist, to handle distaff arrangements—and the advance man, usually though not always a preacher himself.

In that role Sunday called on the ministers of the allied churches, shook down their affluent church members for guarantees of advertising costs and the rent of the town's largest hall; if it was too small, he negotiated a site for a tent, probably the same lot that the circus used—and the circuslike look of the tent there was in itself good publicity. With the ministers' advice and consent he fused the several choirs into a more or less harmonious group to mass in white robes on the platform behind Chapman and make a joyful noise unto the Lord under the coaching of the songster. He also formed and briefed publicity committees, plate-passing committees, women's committees, committees of "personal workers"—church members of both sexes assigned to counsel and hold hands and sweat with sinners whom Chapman's exhortations and the soaring, gushing rhythms of the singing had persuaded that they felt salvation coming on. Women's meetings in the morning, odd prayer meetings at private houses, special doings for the children and the businessmen who bulked ever larger among backers of revivals. . . . And unless the next stand was demandingly imminent, Sunday stayed as Chapman's right hand during the actual earlier doings, supervising the special events, keeping an eye on the plate passing on which solvency hung, easing frictions, helping process souls struggling for rebirth in the "inquiry rooms."

For all these accretions the purpose was still the same that underlay the original open-air orgies of hellfire and glory in the Kentucky backwoods almost a hundred years earlier—to assuage itching of the soul, to melt and recast souls into the shape that God preferred. Only vulgar cynicism can doubt the loyalty of Moody, Chapman, Sunday *et al.* to this end. But the minor purposes—to get more warm, cash-offering bodies into the churchgoing habit; to make local big shots feel righteous; to check local vice; and, on the principle of not muzzling the ox that treadeth out the corn, to make a good, if strenuous, living for the boss preacher and his crew—required more and more such ironically secular-flavored organization. The last thing a well-established evangelist of 1914 would have dreamed of doing was to set forth, as Christ recommended, without staff or scrip, taking no thought for the morrow.

In 1895 John Wanamaker prevailed on Chapman to accept a conventional pulpit in Philadelphia, which wiped out Sunday's job. Only momentarily considering return to baseball, he decided to set up as evangelist in his own right. In order to be able to call himself the Reverend Billy Sunday, he cajoled an examining board of Presbyterian divines into ordaining him in spite of his grinningly candid ignorance of any of the theological issues about which they questioned him. He began his new career imitating Chapman's formal rig-out, earnest style and elaborate sermons. Gradually he taught himself to turn into a shrieking mountebank, tearing off coat and collar, dramatizing his athletic past by leapings and skippings and bits of baseball lingo, squawking holy billingsgate and vaudeville-style wisecracks at the Devil and defiant sinners and those doubtful whether Joshua really made the sun stand still. Much of it was semiblasphemous exaggeration of the red-neck-folksy, hog-calling style of a well-known soul saver, Sam Jones, who worked the South and put on a good show. On the county seat circuit Sunday so ripened Jones' methods that in time even big-city reporters conceded that his platform impersonations of various kinds of sinner had big-time professional quality.

Soon he shifted from soul saving as such to rasping, sweat-soaked denunciations of current moral menaces likely to appeal to local parsons and holders of safe-deposit boxes—the Demon Rum, politics-backed vice, the soul poison of Modernism. He used each new trick of evangelistic showmanship as it came in fashion: The church organ accompanying the choir gave place to double pianos and the blare of trumpets and trombones. The songster starting "Shall We Gather at the River?" at the right moment amused the crowd by ordering them to sing the first stanza, whistle the second, hum the third; only women to sing the second chorus, only men the third, now, boys, let's outsing the girls! Fundamentalist preacher factories taught budding evangelists and songsters such aids to holy glee. Homer Rodeheaver, Sunday's music chief, was like Moody's Ira D. Sankey, almost as famous as his principal, writing and publishing his own hot-gospel hymns and developing special gimmicks. He often recruited a local child of five or six to pipe "Jesus Wants Me for a Sunbeam" to massed thousands in the great tabernacle. For a Sunday revival in Washington, D.C., he borrowed the Navy and Marine Bands with the consent of that genially churchly Southerner, Secretary of the Navy Josephus Daniels. In Boston he had chorus girls from Al Jolson's *Robinson Crusoe, Jr.* render hymns at an afternoon session. And much to the annoyance of the liquor trade he featured among his Temperance numbers a darky-dialect number, "The Brewer's Big Horses."

From circus and minstrel and Tom shows Sunday borrowed the preperformance parade. His advance man had him met at the railroad station by brass bands and hymn-singing, handkerchief-waving thousands, who, with police in the van, marched through town ahead of an open touring car displaying God's noisiest press agent all smiles and flailing arms. The town was already knee deep in publicity aimed at filling the huge wooden tabernacle knocked together to hold the nightly 10,000, 12,000, 15,000 expected as the size of the pitches grew. To reduce reverberation, sawdust was thick underfoot. The air was thick with the glare of strings of unshaded electric bulbs and the pungency of resin from the pine planks nailed to joists and plates so lightly that in a fire panic the crowd could burst through to safety. These huge matchboxes were heated by coal stoves; since no disasters occurred, God really must have been on Sunday's side. He employed a full-time architect to see each tabernacle to completion. When it was all over, with the Devil and the brewers presumably licking their wounds, he dismantleu the thing, sold the planks as salvage lumber for the benefit of the guarantors and sifted the sawdust for coins dropped by bemused souls when fumbling for the "free-will offering" that was Sunday's specific reward.

"This is a tabernacle, not a tabernickel!" [124] shouted the Reverend Bob Jones, one of Sunday's ablest emulators, to let sinners know that he wanted an average of 50 cents a head in the collection plates. In Scranton, Pennsylvania, Sunday's love offering came to $21,000; in Pittsburgh $29,000; in Philadelphia in 1915 $100,000—better than baseball at even $500 a month. But travel, publicity and the snowballing payroll must have kept the net low enough to justify asking for advance guarantees. In 1917, when Sunday finally played New York City—the Rockefellers lent him Ivy Lee as publicity consultant, as if Knute Rockne were asked to advise Jim Thorpe on football—the requisite full year of preparation employed seventy-five persons in a twelve-room suite of offices. By then the production staff included not only the architect but also three auxiliary preachers, five other men specialists, seven assorted women for group activity—and "Ma" Sunday, the quondam nice girl from Chicago who kept the books and made the dates. Chautauqua crews encountering the Sundays when Billy filled in summers as a star lecturer found him easy to get on with but described Ma as "tougher than whang leather." [125]

As center of this planetary system of sponsors, jerry-building and ballyhoo, Sunday was incandescent. His hoarse diatribes gave hearers the pleasure of tension-relieving shock. A minister accepting evolution was "a stinking skunk, a hypocrite and a liar"; a society woman playing cards "worse than any blackleg gambler in the slums." [126] He spattered slang all over his audience. David "soaked [Goliath] right between the lamps and he went down for the count." The Bible said that as Christ prayed, "the fashion of his countenance was altered," so: "Ladies, do you want to look pretty? . . . spend less on dope, pazzazza, and cold cream, and get down on your knees and pray!" [126] He could spice the values of a striptease with ascetic horror: "Herodias shoved Salome out into the room to do her little stunt. . . . She didn't have enough clothes on her to flag a handcar. And she spun around on her toe and stuck her foot out at a quarter to twelve. The king . . . said, 'Sis, you're sure a peach. . . . You can have anything you want. . . .'" [127] Sunday dripped and slobbered thus over many issues, but the lessening number and substance of women's garments c. 1914 particularly tempted him to outvulgarize himself:

"Ma and I stopped to look at a ball. . . . I'll be hornswoggled if I didn't see a woman there . . . [wearing] the collar of her gown around her waist," and on into a bit of doggerel he was fond of:

> Little Girl, you look so small,
> Don't you wear no clothes at all?
> Don't you wear no shimmy skirt?
> Don't you wear no petty skirt?
> Don't you wear no underclothes
> But your corset and your hose? [126]

Dean Andrew West of Princeton University adduced that to show why he refused to allow Sunday on campus. As for the close-contact dancing new in that day: ". . . watch your wife folded in [a stranger's] long, voluptuous, sensual embrace, their limbs twining and entwining, her head resting on his breast, they breathe the vitiated air beneath the glittering candelabra, and the spell of the music, and you stand there and tell me there's no harm in it!" [127] He borrowed much material from John B. Gough, strongest Temperance orator of the mid-1800's, and from atheist Bob Ingersoll. But his own style came out clearest in denouncing those who, for one kind of reason or another, deplored his way of fighting God's wars for Him. To secure new communicants, preachers might let him call them "ossified, petrified, dyed-in-the-wool, blown-in-the-bottle, stiff-as-a-poker, cold-as-a-dog's-nose Pharisees." As for the "cocktail-drinking, gambling, indecently dressed, automobile-riding, degenerate, God-forsaken gang you call society," [126] their bankers were among those guaranteeing Sunday's costs. But there was a limit to his rhetorical license. When he called the liquor trade "the most damnable, corrupt institution that ever wriggled out of hell. . . . It will steal milk from the breast of the mother . . . take virtue from your daughter . . . close every church in the land . . ." [128] the Commercial Club of Louisville, capital of bourbon, forced local ministers to withdraw an invitation to come over into Kentucky to help them.

As he became a national plague, the Progressive-to-Socialist element, already strong, also found reason to deplore him. George Creel, firsthand observer of Colorado's sickening war between reactionary management and radical labor, pointed out the suspicious likelihood that Sunday would be invited into a given area to attack booze and sin wherever employers, harassed by militants, needed their men distracted from prevailing wage scales and the class struggle—not only in bloody Colorado but also among the mines and mills of West Virginia, Pennsylvania and New Jersey. Woundingly Creel connected the sponsorship of Sunday by the grimly anti-union management of Philadelphia's Baldwin Locomotive Works with a bit from one of his sermons: ". . . a lot of good-for-nothing lobsters think they are called by God to go up and down the country harping for a limitation of wealth and cussing and damning the rich man for every dollar he has, while they sit round and cuss . . . and never work." He described Sunday's sociology: ". . . the slums of Philadelphia are not the result of low wages, but the direct result of balls, card parties and drinking. Let the worker cut out bridge, and the tango, the cocktail and the highball, and in a flash he will find himself possessed of a large income and a fine house." And its results from Sunday's revival in Philadelphia: "God is now in Pennsylvania. Wages haven't been raised, strikes are still crushed by armed force, the spy system and black list are still in vogue . . . but God is there." [129]

John Reed, covering the Philadelphia revival for the radical *Metropolitan Magazine*, listed among Sunday's backers twelve major industrialists, twelve major bankers, four eminent corporation lawyers and the president of the Union League. The disproportion between Mammon and God in this phase of Sunday made poet-radical Sandburg almost as shrill as his target:

You come along . . . tearing your shirt . . . yelling about Jesus . . .
               Where do you get that stuff?
               What do you know about Jesus? . . .
          You slimy buckshooter . . . belching about hellfire
and hiccupping about this Man who lived a clean life in Galilee. . . .[130]

That the powerful tried to use Sunday to "substitute brotherly love for better wages" [129] was obvious. In my view he understood that and, in order to finance reaching a maximum number of potential converts, let himself be so used. For not even John Reed, whom Lippmann accurately described as incapable of objectivity, certainly the last reporter to let an antilabor hypocrite down easy, doubted Sunday's sincerity: "I do not believe . . . he could put the fire and passion . . . into his words and actions if he were not sincere. . . . As to the social, economic and political relations of the world . . . I think he is just ignorant." [131] Or say that, being a striking case of the self-made man—the folk hero of his day—he could heartily preach the tenets of the archangels of the tradition, such as Carnegie and John

Wanamaker: Booze and running around are bad. Mother and hard work are good. Honesty is the best policy. Unions are the workingman's enemies; immigrants are dangerous. Even in degenerate big cities the brewer's big horses won't run over me. And shouting those undeniable truths got tabernacles built and the greatest possible number of sinners exposed to the possibility of salvation.

The revival industry blossomed in the sunshine of Sunday's example, and the Bible colleges taught his platform tactics. By 1914 the Interdenominational Association of Evangelists, swapping showman's tricks and tips like tramps and medicine-show doctors discussing which towns were easy marks, had some 600 full-time and 100-odd part-time members. Several Grade B soul savers billed themselves as "The Cowboy Evangelist" in imitation of Fred Seibert, who had joined Sunday's staff. Boy Evangelists were also rife.

One of the most raucous was Bob Jones, son of a small-farmer Confederate veteran in southeastern Alabama, who was only thirteen when he began making Populist stump speeches and preaching to neighborhood gatherings. Grown to six feet, lean, so thin-lipped handsome that he looked girlish, he earned his way through a Fundamentalist college by itinerant summer preaching that brought countless free Sunday dinners and love offerings. His string of urban scalps was never as impressive as Sunday's— only Atlanta, Columbus, Ohio, Grand Rapids—but he made New York City a year ahead of Sunday and took a newspaper reporter on a gabby tour of "tango tea emporiums, lobster palaces and cabaret restaurants," commenting, "Drink and dance, dance and drink. That's their merry round to the devil. I had rather have a young daughter of mine drink arsenic than cocktails . . . a cocktail pierces a woman's armor. . . . The dance gives her the thirst, the drink robs her of her senses. . . ." [132] In 1921 he made even St. Petersburg, Florida, already full of old folks presumably too far gone for much vice, sound sinful enough to draw 10,000 an evening to his tabernacle. He dwelled on cardplaying, bootlegging and dancing but also got the city's famous sunshine into the act: "There is too much damnable immodesty among St. Petersburg's women. When the sun is shining they ought to have to walk on the shady side of the street." [133] His blasting and gargling sometimes rivaled Sunday's, as in his indictment of the saloon-keeper:

He builds his house out of human hearts and uses life blood for mortar. The plastering on his walls is made from the lining of human stomachs. In his shop of hell he hardens human brains out of which to make tiles for his bathroom. His window curtains are widow's weeds. . . . The music by which he dances is the wail of

the widow, and the cry of the orphan ground by the hand of the
devil from hell's awful organ. . . .[134]

In the mid-1920's Straton brought to New York City glib little Uldine
Utley, the Girl Evangelist, who worked the silk-stocking district with some
success, though her pitch and personality struck me as watery. Loudspeakers on the outside of Straton's church on Fifty-seventh Street filled the
neighborhood with her yelping voice, which elicited bitter protests from the
American Association for the Advancement of Atheism, whose offices were
in nearby Carnegie Hall. Since the evangelical sects supplying the run of
revival audiences had no strong tradition of she preachers, lady evangelists
were few. The outstanding exception was, however, a beauty in all senses.
In 1917 Aimee Semple McPherson, converted at seventeen to the Holy
Roller kind of Pentecostalism, daughter of a former lady worker in the
Salvation Army, brought her handiness at faith healing, a leaky secondhand
tent and the charm of her tall, redheaded, winsomely vigorous person from
her native Canada to troupe America. By 1918 she could buy a new touring
car, load into it her mother-manager and her pulpit wardrobe and drive
across the continent to storm Los Angeles, which was already the ideal
culture medium for religions of the absurd. She filled the largest hall in
town. That success floated her on a major foray—by Pullman now—into
Denver, St. Louis, Washington, D.C. . . . But her affinity with Los Angeles
tamed the gipsy in her. On New Year's Day, 1923, she consecrated there her
5,000-seat Angelus Temple, Vatican of her "Four-Square Gospel" that soon
dotted the West Coast with eighty-odd branches.
    Crushed seashells mixed into the concrete made the dome of the new
temple glisten in that California sunshine. The blue tinting of the ceiling
gave its double-balconied auditorium the illusion of open sky. A huge
painting of the banks of the Jordan was background for the fancy symbolic
tableaux, always centered on Aimee—who had a good deal more ham than
halo about her as it turned out—and interpreted in sacred song by a choir
of 100. Nightly special streetcars filled the place with transplanted
Midwesterners admiring "Sister" posed in sou'wester and slicker at a ship's
wheel while, against a medley of storm sound effects, the choir urged her to
"Throw out the lifeline! Someone is sinking today!", a standard gospel
number. The middle-aged flock's rallying song:

> Are we downhearted? No! No! No!
> Troubles may come and troubles may go;
> We'll trust in Jesus, come weal or woe.
> Are we downhearted? [All whistle] No! No! No! [135]

"Are you Foursquare?" is still the in-group question asked by the temple devotees. Aimee herself defined her field of fire invidiously but probably accurately: "I bring religious consolation to the great middle class leaving those below to the Salvation Army and those above to themselves." [136]

Her hold on her following was so firm that they stayed loyal even when the press, checking her story of having been kidnapped more thoroughly than she had counted on, learned that actually she was covering up a season of sin with the announcer-manager of her radio station. This crisis merely put her showmanship on its mettle. Public identification of her bedmate inspired her to lead the faithful in a new version:

> Identification may come, identification may go,
> Are we downhearted? No! No! No! [137]

and packed houses of them sang it gleefully. In protest against being indicted for perjury she preached on "Slavery Days" wearing Cindy Lou hoopskirts against a background of a cotton field in which an overseer with a cowhide whip bullied cotton pickers. To express the poignancy of her martyrdom, she staged a special communion service under a huge Crown of Thorns with tableaux beginning with the Crucifixion and proceeding into the agonies of St. Stephen, St. Paul, Nero's victims, Joan of Arc. . . .

Permanent tabernacle headquarters in a large city was the new approach as the elder, traveling-circus tradition—and Billy Sunday's career with it—dwindled. The tradition of the town's yearly religious debauch in tabernacle or tent, though not wholly vanishing, withdrew into the cultural backwaters of the South and Southwest. Aimee was also a pioneer in using radio to make such a fixed center of righteousness available over a wide area. Her KFSG was the third broadcasting station to go on the air in Los Angeles.

The post-Dayton encysting of Fundamentalism left American Protestants more exposed to the self-styled Modernist who considered his church less a means to redeem souls than a community center and seedbed of social-minded good works—anyway good words. Such a religious plant might differ from the nearby schoolhouse only in its vestigial tower and electric sign on the lawn advertising next Wednesday's chicken supper in letters as large as those announcing the Reverend Dr. Mundane's coming sermon on "The Church as Christ's Cooperative." His church as auditorium/shrine was overlaid by Sunday School, gymnasium, kitchen, dining room, meeting rooms for Epworth League or Christian Endeavor, missionary and sewing societies, Boy Scouts, Girl Scouts, staff offices—business-style organization again, this time for largely secular ends. One of its groundbreakers was the Reverend Dr. Edward Beecher, half brother of the lady who wrote *Uncle Tom's Cabin*, whose "home church" in Elmira, New York, in 1873 already had a kitchen with its own china and silver to serve

300, a free library—and a dancing room, a billiard room, a "children's romp room with . . . the complete fittings of a theater." [138]

Catholics had been multiplying sodalities and lay philanthropic guilds to lure the unregenerate, particularly young ones, within the gravitational pull of God. Prospering Fundamentalist churches too laid such snares. Angelus Temple was an extreme example with a Prayer Tower where two-hour relays of men and women kept up unceasing supplication, its sewing circles making layettes for poor mothers, brotherhoods finding jobs for recently freed convicts and a round-the-clock commissary supplying emergency food, clothes or rent money. Very probably Christ would have looked favorably on those latter activities. They made a Fundamentalist Baptist editor uneasy: ". . . the doctrine of social service is very plausible and attractive but it is . . . a dangerous misinterpretation of the teachings of Jesus to assert that civilization and environment are Christianity . . . [that to] surround the individual with a good environment [means] salvation will result. No greater or more insidious heresy ever issued from hell." [139] In the pulpit at least Fundamentalist and Catholic still often preached the perils of sin and the hopes raised by the Crucifixion. The sermons of the Modernist incumbent of one of those sacred settlement houses usually cast him as director of amateur social services, dwelling on "Inasmuch as ye have done it unto one of the least of these my brethren ye have done it also unto me." A noble text but only a minor aspect of Christianity.

Most Modernists owed much to the Christian Socialist movement of the later 1880's—in its American version the Social Gospel. Its leaders dwelled on Christ's uncharitableness toward rich men and money changers and labor's struggles against smothering alliances of employees. Entering his long incumbency at the originally Unitarian, soon nondenominational Community Church in New York City, the Reverend Dr. John Haynes Holmes first preached "a series of sermons on evolution. Then . . . I stated my belief in trade unions, my growing interest in Socialism, and my general conviction that churches . . . must work out . . . the social application of religion." [140] Such ideas were shared with the abortive Church of the Revolution soon founded by the Reverend Bouck White, a Congregationalist turned Unitarian turned Socialist-maverick, for admirers of his who were wont to gather Sunday afternoons in a Greenwich Village studio to sing Socialist songs. Its basis was White's wishful belief that Christ had been a horny-handed proletarian agitator done in by Jewish capitalists and Roman lawmen. It had its own prolixly liberal marriage service, a catechism and a sort of confirmation dedicating children of members to the revolution— White preferred the nonviolent kind—and naturally its office was on Washington Square.

Born in the spring of 1914, it came just in time to plague the Fifth Avenue Baptist Church, pet of the Rockefellers, to which White sent a brotherly invitation to join in investigating the recent Ludlow Massacre—the occasion when forces of alleged law and order protected the Rockefellers' Colorado Fuel and Iron Company by killing strikers and their families wholesale. When the Fifth Avenue's minister paid no heed, White, warning the press beforehand, went to the next Sunday's service. Before he could get out more than a few words, he was arrested by police staked out in the vestry. He got six months for disorderly conduct and, knowing as well as John Brown, a hero of his, the usefulness of martyrdom, was lukewarm about getting his able lawyers to file an appeal. The next spring he made the same gesture with a few followers at Calvary Baptist Church and cleverly inveigled the police into clubbing them. After a second stretch behind bars he boasted to the press that the consequent publicity had brought his church forty-seven new members. He might have made something cogent out of this ideological toy had not the confusions of the imminent War roiled the waters that he launched it in.

When the Social Gospel grew too explicit, support from affluent members of Modernist congregations naturally tended to waver. Even in the swimmingly liberal climate of Holmes' church Henry H. Rogers, a great man in Standard Oil and economic godfather of Mark Twain, came less and less often and finally came no more. But such falling away was not invariable. Local magnates' consciences sometimes nudged them into continuing to finance a nominally Christian divine who pungently and often justifiably denounced them and their greedy ways. In 1914, the trustees of Holmes' church, for instance, still included the president of the New York Cotton Exchange and a first vice-president of the New York Central. In 1917 when Holmes denounced war in general, then that War in particular, then America's entering it, his trustees, all pro-War, supported his right to go on tilting at windmills in their pulpit—a credit to their own delicacy as well as to Holmes' very probably sincere courage.

Much of the religion-flavored pacifism of 1914–21—except that of Quakers, the Pennsylvania Dutch "plain" sects and Jehovah's Witnesses— arose in this Social Gospel/settlement house axis. In some ways the complex was salutary. It reminded the godless that kindness between man and man is good taste and the godly that it is a Christian's moral duty. It did not point out, however, that no socioeconomic system, not even the Cooperative Commonwealth after which queasy-conscienced parsons yearned, guarantees against man's inhumanity to man, still less against the vicissitudes of age and death. It neglected to foster what the old-time religion supplied as anodyne for those ills—a sense of healing contact with and support from the supernal. The Modernist Presbyterian minister intertwining social service and congregation baits while preaching the spiritual beauties of doing one's society good—and eagerly treating such political topics as his moral tastes suggested—was doing little more than inspirational journalism. Faced with this emotional sterility, again "the hungry sheep look up and are not fed," as Milton said when reproaching other parsons for other neglects several centuries ago.

Maybe that was why by 1914 millions of Americans were drawn into the orbit of Christian Science or Unity, and millions more repelled by both Fundamentalism and the Social Gospel were letting religion go hang. They were likelier to do so because the function of church as place where one went to see others, stay in touch with the neighbors, relate to others' lives—interaction, in short—was newly supplemented by the growing number of amusement resorts allowed to open on Sunday and by the movies.

The list of 1914's social solvents in F major should certainly also include "films"—only as yet America preferred "movies" or "moving pictures" to that British-flavored term. Effort to substitute "motion pictures" had small success though it did enable Hashimura Togo, Wallace Irwin's syntax-cracking Japanese Schoolboy, to put his Oriental finger on the essence of the new medium in the fall of 1914—he called them "the emotion pictures." [141]

Gilbert Seldes, adept observer of America's arts and antics, saw 1914 as "turning point . . . of the American moving picture." [142] He had in mind the momentous merger of the Ince and Griffith interests with the Keystone comedy company including Mack Sennett. By then movies had unmistaka-bly added a new dimension to American—and Western—culture. In two decades those quivering shadows of actors and backgrounds had advanced from the peep show for a cent to the vertical white screen for a dollar. Producers were now at home in the values and techniques that remained basic until talkies came in—in many respects until today. This new kind of pantomime entertainment was nearer universal than literature or spoken or sung stage shows, all bound to one or another self-limited language, or than instrumental music, which is so dependent on the hearer's cultural heritage of arbitrary scale and rhythm. Thus the Polynesians unprepared for *La Bohème* or *Macbeth* took to horse opera almost as precipitously as their great-grandfathers had to the white man's Rum.* Hence, movies spread all over the world. But really wide impact came first in America. The contrast persists. Television did little more than move the movie screen into the living room, and so far America's is the most television-bound culture.

The War may intrude here. D. W. Griffith and Anita Loos, both veterans of the pertinent period, thought that to some extent America owed domination of the world screen to the War's smothering the vigorous film industries of France and Italy. In any case, the impression that America

---

* Their one difficulty came of the movie hero's being, in their terms, usually too much of a laggard in love. Island audiences used to jeer the strong silent hero playing the waiting game instead of throwing the heroine down and going to it.

invented the movies is vulnerable. The technical breakthroughs of the mid-1890's were as much the work of Europeans, such as the French brothers Lumière (appropriate name!), as of Thomas A. Edison's boys. The Edison camera and projector were better than rivals on either side of the ocean but did not necessarily imply American dominance. Edison never bothered to patent them outside the United States, so Europe was free to borrow and improve on them as moviemaking hit its stride. Indeed the success with which Edison's patents were administered may have retarded the American movie until enforcement came apart in 1914.

In the first fifty years, however, European movies affected America through technical stimulus rather than as a major part of what the American public saw. Though Europe made the first beginning-middle-and-end movie stories, it was an Edison employee, Edwin S. Porter, who, in a screening of an *Uncle Tom's Cabin* troupe, then in *The Life of an American Fireman* (1902) and *The Great Train Robbery* (1903), turned the American movie from a peepshow into a promise of entertainment in its own right—a new medium shifting scene, character and point of observation around as no previous medium had been tempted to try to do. American moviemen were probably also first to supplement nonverbal action with printed subtitles. Also, whereas early Europeans confined their story films to variety theaters, with relatively affluent patrons, America found a vast secondary market in the penny arcade, which grew into the nickelodeon*—usually a darkened retail store equipped with nondescript chairs and a white sheet on the back wall. That was the institution that planted the movie show at America's grass roots—make that curbstones. Five cents bought quite a nickel's worth of melodrama, garish sentiment and clowning, chosen with shirt-sleeved tastes in mind, not only in the straitened neighborhoods of big cities but in smaller state capitals and important county seats. The chairs were hard and rickety, the atmosphere fetid, the quality of projection poor. But the nickels flooding into the tiny box office fronting the street showed that what was being projected vastly entertained the customers.

Richard Griffith, curator emeritus of the Museum of Modern Art Film Library, has called the founders of this flourishing new industry "a ragtag and bobtail of small-time operators . . . mostly newcomers to these shores . . . some of them hardly knew enough English to read a financial statement." [143] Some came from the margin of show business—rep shows, medicine shows, carnivals; others from small retailing and the fur and

---

* This fusion of the American slang for a five-cent coin with the Greek for "concert hall" was probably first used for a movie show in Pittsburgh in 1905. But the *Dictionary of Americanisms* takes it back to 1888, apparently applied to amusement arcades offering nickel-in-the-slot primitive phonographs with ear tubes—a nickel concert hall. As Edison's mutoscope peep show machines came in, they stood alongside or were synchronized with the phonographs while the nickelodeon name persisted for the whole establishment. Eventually, as in Pittsburgh and then all over the country, the movie ousted the phonograph without the anomalous name's being changed.

garment trades. Edison thought movies an evanescent toy. Even after he became an outstanding movie director, Griffith thought them probably a passing fad. But these Jewish immigrants sensed an opportunity that better prepared Gentiles failed to recognize. Groping into the darkened world of the nickelodeon, pirating Edison's patents and cutting one another's throats for all those nickels, they were the hormone-rich compost whence the new medium grew like Jack's beanstalk. Not that Jewish dominance was as marked as in the garment trade—a sizable minority of those swinging weight in those early days were named Sheehan, Powers, McManus. . . .

As this new way to quick profit spread like a new slang term, social effects soon appeared. Drys were pleased, brewers dismayed, to find the nickel movie competing with the nickel beer for the spare time and spare change of the wage earner. Vachel Lindsay, the only still-considerable poet of America or any other nation to have been a sincere Temperance lecturer, called "the cheap photoplay house . . . the best known rival and eliminator of the slum saloon." [144] Jacob Gould Schurman, president of Cornell University, said his undergraduates were now seeing movies instead of going to town for beer and pool. I know of no such effect on the pubs of London or the zinc-countered wineshops of Paris. Anyway, consequent hard feeling between movie exhibitors and saloonkeepers may go far to explain the strong antisaloon tone of the early American screen. In movieland the bar was either a scabrous dump or a gilded haunt of vice; one drink spelled one kind of ruin for a man and another for a girl. The movie that so impressed Tarkington's Penrod in 1913 "depicted with relentless pathos the drunkard's . . . conversion to beer in the company of loose traveling men; pursuing him through an inexplicable lapse into evening clothes and the society of some remarkably painful ladies, next, striking . . . [his] pleading baby daughter with an abnormally heavy walking stick . . . finally . . . picturesque behavior at the portals of a madhouse." [145]

At sixteen frames a second the standard 1,000-foot reel of film ran fifteen minutes. C. 1908 a full reel might show several short items—a glimpse of a baseball game or a parade, a slapstick routine, a dance routine, a couple spooning on a park bench. For early moviemen, many up from the depths themselves and aware that penury seldom sharpens wits, considered their public too sluggish to tolerate more than a few minutes on a given topic. (Later the carriage trade, movie-minded at last, complained because it was still thought advisable to leave subtitles on the screen so long to accommodate those who could not read at normal speed or were ill acquainted with English.) Yet once a few daring trials showed that audiences were up to 1,000-foot movies, innovators like Griffith ventured on to two-reelers, four-reelers, five-reelers. Part of the stimulus came from the five-reel Italian screening of *Dante's Inferno* brought over in 1911, the first movie "road-showed"—offered as sole attraction in a theater hired expressly for the purpose—in America.

Within two years other long European movies were thus influencing America. Italy sent two versions of *The Last Days of Pompeii*, Lord Lytton's pseudo-religious novel about goings-on in ancient Rome, and topped them with *Quo Vadis?*, nine reels from the equally famous novel by Henryk Sienkiewicz. Stage versions of both books were already popular with American touring troupes unable to afford the chariot-race effect in *Ben Hur*. Filling Broadway's elegant Astor Theater for months at a dollar top, *Quo Vadis?* carried its own orchestra, heightening its message of gorgeous vice and wide-eyed virtue. Twenty prints of it filled large theaters coast to coast, vindicating the acumen of (George M.) Cohan & (Sam H.) Harris, eminent Broadway producers who had backed it when veteran moviemen fought shy of its length. Then here came Italy's *Cabiria* of *twelve* reels, almost three hours, a spectacle brewed up by the strutting poet Gabriele d'Annunzio, and a twelve-reel French version of *Les Misérables*. No, it wasn't Hollywood that invented the supercolossal clambake, only the adjective. Soon Griffith's *The Birth of a Nation* was roadshowing twenty-eight prints, each with two baggage cars of special equipment and fifty persons, including a miniature symphony orchestra, stagehands and publicity staff, ballyhooing and hippodroming this epic of the Ku Klux Klan in the style to which it had rapidly grown accustomed.

The celluloid *Quo Vadis?* carried several warnings. Its usurpation of large theaters built for live actors presaged what the screen would do to the American stage. And time and again in the next fifty years importations from European studios—sometimes movies, sometimes directors or performers—would cross-pollinate American movies to the great benefit of the world's screen public. This modified the idiom that, probably with more respect than it deserved, Edward Wagenknecht called America's "closest approach to folk drama" [146]—the prefeature-length movies of Biograph, Vitagraph and so on. Soon enough the glories of *Quo Vadis?*—its high point was a naked girl riding on a bull in a Roman arena—bore American fruit in the four-hour length and baroque vulgarities of D. W. Griffith's *Intolerance* (1915), megalomaniac sets, shield-and-helmet goriness, seductive pagan girls and episodes of religiosity* as concessions to the churchgoing element. With unwonted taste Griffith soon dropped that sort of thing. It was Cecil B. De Mille *et al.* who made it an international institution as the industry's soaring profits enabled it to finance the hundreds of thousands and then millions of dollars needed for such explosions of visual delicatessen.

The sham-archaeological, pseudo-religious epic was not the only durable

---

* Iris Barry's *D. W. Griffith* (20) says that Griffith disliked implications that movies like *Quo Vadis?* showed him the way to *Intolerance* and maintained that he had never seen it. Maybe he hadn't, but by that time it was not the only item to find such suggestion in. *Cf.* also Robert M. Henderson, *D. W. Griffith: The Years at Biograph* (151).

movie genre born between 1910 and 1914. In three and four reels came crowding the parka-malamute-and-Royal-Mounties story; the jungle story, heroine in breeches and sun helmet, supported by shopworn lions and elephants borrowed from a circus or rented from agencies already supplying the new industry; the sea story of mutiny or piracy, hero in a plumed hat; the Civil War story developing the battle stuff that Griffith would refine in *The Birth of a Nation*. The actor-stuntman in an early novel about Hollywood, *Buck Parvin and the Movies* (1913), says: "I'm a veteran of Bull Run, Lookout Mountain, Shiloh, the Wilderness, Gettysburg. I held Grant's horse at Appomattox . . . I've been in Libby Prison twice . . . I'm a Yank one day and a Johnny Reb the next." [147] Nor was it *The Sheik* that founded the dynasty of venturesome blondes, also sun-helmeted, carried off to the black tents against a background of moth-eaten camels and the Mojave Desert. In 1912 the scenarios rehashed for *Motion Picture Story Magazine*—a cross section of the movie crop—included also the coonskin-pioneer story, the caveman-and-cavegirl-in-fur-tunics story, the lumberjack-Timberrrrr! story, several European-made Bible stories and a version of Lady Godiva. The Answers-to-Questions column insisted that she had not only been hidden among cascades of crepe hair but all the time wore a "living picture suit"—skin-color fleshings. In 1913 here came the South Seas-beachcomber-wriggly-brown-girl in *Tale of Old Tahiti* and *Ballad of the South Seas*. Movies even dealt with social problems—the woes of convicts, the evils of predatory speculation, the contrasts between showy wealth and the results of slumlordship. Griffith did several such.

Those shifting pastiches of stock situations and characters did not replace the Western and the he-done-her-wrong story. But they did provide new, soon well-trodden avenues into which the lengthening "feature" grew. Higher production costs of longer efforts forced admissions up to 10 cents, even a quarter in large cities. The public absorbed that and "went to the movies" in greater numbers. One reason may have been that longer running time allowed closer coherence and situation buildups with emotional pulls stronger than only six or seven minutes of situation establishment and action allowed. More elbowroom enabled the "emotion pictures" better to exploit their birthright of suspense, vicarious fear and sentimentality. Those with the new habit of going to the movies once or twice a week could be fairly sure that whatever the Idle Hour or the Bijou offered would trigger plenty of hormones. Exhibitors began to hold these longer movies over two or three days instead of changing program daily. That let word of mouth get round the neighborhood and fill the house the next night with those who heard that this new three-reeler was Maurice Costello at his best.

As cash intake grew, ambitious exhibitors, beginning in the South and Southwest, began to build handsome new theaters designed primarily for movies, more comfortable and lacking zoolike smells. Presently the industry's press noted with pride that at such new establishments "it is no uncommon thing to see carriages and autos drive up . . . and discharge wealthy passengers in opera cloaks and evening clothes." [148] Very citified, but even in Wellington, Kansas (pop. 5,000-odd), Burford & Glamman's Majestic Theater had a seven-piece orchestra and advertised itself as "Cooled With Ice In Summer." Note that orchestra. The movies were "The Silent Drama" in only their most primitive days. By the time of ten-cent admission few movie houses lacked the tireless piano player hammering out musical clichés to match those visible on the screen—"Pony Boy, Pony Boy" for horsey action, "O Promise Me" for when His lips met Hers. The pianist might be the owner's wife or the local lady piano teacher or a seedy refugee from a honky-tonk required not only to accompany the action on the screen but also to coax the house to sing along with the tinted stereopticon slides showing Sycamores, Mother and the Moon to lend vividness to "On the Banks of the Wabash."

Well before 1914 the newly elegant city movie house, following Californian examples, had the refined grandeur of a church-style pipe organ thundering swooningly in storm or battle sequences and imitating the birdies high in the treble as He and She strolled down by the old millstream. Then management lent class to this or that specially pretentious feature by hiring a string quartet to do a sort of overture and supplement the organ. One way or another it was assumed that movies needed music as interpreter and emotional emphasizer. The thing had another aspect. Screen actresses were sure they were regarded seriously only when the director supplied on-the-set musicians to play the sort of schmaltz that would soften them into "registering" optimum teariness as the hero was hauled off to durance vile for a crime he didn't even know of. Whatever emotional catalysis occurred on the set, the customers of the Family Theater in Lacrosse, Wisconsin, presumably got the benefit six months later. Its organist making the pipes whistle and snore to match was unwittingly showing how "Heard melodies are sweet, but those unheard are sweeter. . . ."

Supplementing sight with sound came into its own in April, 1914, when the Strand Theater, first of the movie palaces, opened on the upper edge of New York City's theatrical district. The particular point of this largest showshop yet built expressly for movies was that the house was as much part of the show as the feature. Its prototype was the Regent Theater in Harlem (then still largely a prosperous semisuburb of German flavor) gussied up for its owner in 1913 by the world's most plush-minded manager—S. L. "Roxy" Rothafel. Son of a cobbler in Stillwater, Minnesota, former sergeant in the U.S. Marines, he got into show business by turning the upper room of his father-in-law's saloon in Forest City, Pennsylvania, into a vaudeville house showing many movies; then he made movies alone pay in a white-elephant theater in Minneapolis. At the Regent his splashy gimmickry—ornate auditorium bathed in tricky light-changes, luxurious seats, ushers in musical comedy uniforms drilled in snappy,

Marine-fashion courtesy, on the stage a large orchestra of competent musicians discoursing semiclassical numbers from among potted palms and gilded columns—had made Harlem feel pampered as well as entertained. Such luxury for two bits naturally became the talk of show business. Now Mitchell and Moe Mark, two former nickelodeon kings of Buffalo, New York, putting their profits into an effort to outdazzle the Great White Way on its own grounds, hired Rothafel away to work with their architect, Thomas W. Lamb, in applying to their projected Strand the same approach, only thicker and shinier still.

That is just what Roxy's Strand did. Its myriad ushers were glittering, solicitous automatons. Its Corinthian-columned auditorium gave every balcony seat a clear view of the screen without distortion and offered at extra cost an area of "loges" (pronounced *low*-juzz) with loungey wicker chairs and ample legroom. At the opening, thick with celebrities, a fifty-piece orchestra played "The Star-Spangled Banner" punctuated with cannon fire, then the *Second Hungarian Rhapsody*. During the travelogue about Naples a genuine, live Italian tenor sang "O Sole Mio" back of the screen, which was made of something called Radium Gold Fiber. A newsreel of the afternoon's ball game in Brooklyn preceded a rendition of the quartet from *Rigoletto*. . . . By the time the nine-reel feature—the first screen version of Rex Beach's *The Spoilers*—came on the audience had already had its money's worth, particularly when one counted in the glories of the plaster-of-paris ambience. One of the refinements even made sense. The feature was not broken into by "One Moment While the Operator Changes Reels," for Lamb had installed multiple projectors, each loaded with a print of the movie, and zeroed in to take over without a break when the film in the first machine ran out. This arrangement, borrowed from the 5,000-seat Gaumont Palace in Paris, was soon standard in American movie houses of any standing.

The Strand so flourished that in 1915 Rothafel was hired away to daub showmanly glitter on a projected competing house down the street, the Rialto. In 1916 he was hired away from the Rialto to do more of the same for the new Rivoli. Lamb and others were drawing plans for even fancier houses in Chicago, Los Angeles, Atlanta. . . . Thus, the lavishly garish movie theater so often thought to reflect the values of the 1920's was already an esthetic menace-in-being before the War. Sir Philip Gibbs, visiting America soon after the War, listed the key institutions of Westchester suburbs he visited—bank, post office, school, church, movie palace. "It is impossible to overrate the influence . . . exercised by that house of assembly," [149] he wrote, averring that fast and deep as movies had spread in Britain, the effect in America was much greater.

The year 1914 also saw Charles Spencer Chaplin, a comic from the rough-and-tumble British variety halls, reach Los Angeles and go to work for one of its lively movie studios. The one-reel slapstick genre that he would glorify was already well in being—pie throwing, subhuman police-men, chases and all—as a staple of neighborhood movie house fare. Chaplin's pantomime had an incisiveness and impudence that were both gamey and engaging—and whatever else describes the inscrutably inde-scribable. Anyway it was soon known throughout moviedom that to book a Chaplin short meant buckets full of extra dimes. In a matter of months he was a special twinkle in the star system that the nickel-and-dime public's eagerness to play favorites had forced on the new industry.

In the old days—ten years earlier, how fast movies grew!—actors went nameless: no identifying credits, no names in the lobby frames. The girl escaping from the villain was either unknown outside her Chelsea boarding-house, or when she was a stage actress of some standing making $10 a day while "at liberty," she preferred not to be identified, for the profession looked down on movies. Griffith's passion for anonymity for everybody but himself kept even Lillian Gish's name unmentioned in the original prints of *Intolerance*. In earlier years, however, the industry's emphasis on company trademarks—Biograph, Essanay and so on—at the expense of the cast had crumbled under public pressure. In particular Mary Pickford, the arch charmer with the corkscrew curls identified with Griffith's work for Biograph, known to moviegoers from subtitles only as "Little Mary," was so taken to the public heart that anything she appeared in meant capacity business—so once she got out from under Griffith's rule, her name was most profitably exploited. Alice Joyce, a meltingly stately beauty playing a great variety of roles, and John Bunny, the fat funnyman who died before the movies meant millions, were other powerful early name draws. It was the exhibitors, receiving the direct impact of such special popularities, who taught producers that it paid to put names on and advertise these revenue-attracting persons.

Thus the star system came to the screen. Never did camel get inside a tent to greater effect. The term "star"—a performer with top billing on posters and program—had long plagued the stage. Certain stage stars, such as the matinee idol-actors who made salesgirls in the second balcony tingle all over and swallow their gum, had had large personal followings. "Lillian Russell" or "Anna Held" on a marquee meant instant ticket sales. But the theater public was a largely urban minority, whereas as movie outlets multiplied, those feeling a personal glow at the thought of Francis X. Bushman or Clara Kimball Young were a majority in tank towns as well as big cities.

Corollary to the movie star was the movie fan, showing better than the theater patron could that the eyes are a wonderful way into the viscera. "Fan" came from baseball, properly so, for the goggle-eyed adoration involved was as fanatic as that of the office boy for Joe Jackson. In 1910 a furor (doubtless aided by press agentry) was created by press reports that Florence Lawrence, once the anonymous "Biograph Girl," now star-billed by the IMP company, had died in a streetcar accident in St. Louis. Excitement swamped the city when she and her leading man got off the train in St. Louis to show her mobs of admirers, assembled through more press agentry, that her death had been greatly exaggerated. In so short a time—four or five years—public thirst for identification with source of emotion had created this mass of millions of movie fans gloating in semidarkness over the object of love or concern or fear, laughing or hating in tune with his or her vicissitudes. Nor was this the old melodramatic stage with flesh-and-blood hams chewing the scenery. What movie fans took so seriously was only a beam of artificial light undergoing a series of calculated obscurations. A pointless point, of course—the movies were vicarious living. As such they beat reading Laura Jean Libbey or gossiping over the back fence and brought irresponsible tears or erotic arousal to many who had never read a book or seen a ten-twent-thirt tearjerker. The everyday public had found the ideal entertainment.

For most of it the relation to the star was—and still is today—intensely personal. Hence the movie fan press, already hatched in 1911 and working toward the complete panoply of portraits of stars, interviews with them, narrative rewrites of their scenarios, pages of answers to inquiries whether it was Wallace Reid who played the younger brother in *Hank of the Yukon*, producers' offers to send pictures of stars to admirers, advertisements of schools in such unlikely places as Boonville, Indiana, eager to teach scenario writing by mail. The only difference between this and the fan press of thirty years later was that fans had to pay 10 cents or a quarter for that picture. Among thirty-three Vitagraph stars thus offered in 1912 were not only Lottie Pickford (Mary's sister), Norma Talmadge and Maurice Costello but also Jean the Vitagraph Dog and Eagle Eye, the studio's otherwise anonymous specialist in the Noble Red Man business. Pathé, the French company active in America, countered with Max Linder (a European pioneer in short comic movies), Pearl White, queen of cliff-hanging serials, and matched Eagle Eye with Red Wing, specialist in winsome Indian maidens. Those pre-War years do not sound so unfamiliar! The slick magazines carried humorous fiction about moviemaking, technicians were perfecting schemes to synchronize screen and audible dialogue and, though they had only four to five reels to work with, producers were squeezing into screen form literature of prestige and great bulk—*Martin Chuzzlewit, The Deerslayer, Vanity Fair*—advertised as painless ways to assimilate the classics. Broadway plays were adapted. . . .

Inadvertently but not at all grudgingly the dime-bearing millions who created the star system afforded their idols showers of gold fit to make Danaë jealous. As stars became the road to riches, producers naturally raided one another's stables of talent. The girl lead's $10 a day of 1907 became $200 a week, $1000 a month, $20,000 a year—and on firm contract too. By 1915 Mary Pickford's primacy was confirmed by her $100,000 a year plus a share in the profits. A few months later Chaplin exacted $10,000 a week, $500,000 a year at a time when federal income tax was still relatively negligible, from the screaming and bleeding film magnates. Doubtless they suffered the more because the publicity that such deals puffed up, lending the glitter of gold to a star's already septic glow, promised to raise even higher the cash value of the actors thus transfigured under the Sign of the Dollar.

Such exorbitant salaries plus costly promotion and the permanent vogue of long features forced another round of raised admission charges. Coin kept flowing unchecked into box offices, and the producers made their own millions to match what the stars shook them down for. It was the fanciest bonanza America had seen since the Spindletop oilfield blew in in 1901. By 1914 17,000-odd movie houses of all sizes were enjoying an average of 10,000,000 patrons a day. Since most of them "went to the movies" once a week, the movie audience was already the bulk of the adult population. The public appetite for shifting shadows required enough film yearly to go around the earth almost three times.

In Southern California Griffith was shooting *The Birth of a Nation*, the movies' tallest landmark since *The Great Train Robbery*. Unmatched as moneymaker, it grossed $18,000,000 on an investment of some $100,000, a datum that has inspired producers of "epics" ever since. It was also as nasty a piece of racism as was ever screened outside of Nazi Germany.* Nevertheless, its intrinsic merits as a movie drew approval from drama critics previously condescending to mere movies and "compelled the acceptance of the film as art," says A. R. Fulton, movie historian.[150] Stage-minded critics might still complain about the broken-up scenes of movie continuity—the very devices that made movies a new art—and denounce as grotesque the close-ups that gave the screen actor a tool his stage predecessor never had. But because increasing movie advertising had been persuading newspapers gingerly to install movie reviewers a new force-in-being came into play. The newspaper stuff was vapid enough to begin with. But something else was occurring in the *New Republic*, weekly organ of the cultivated liberals, where Vachel Lindsay was attempting what he considered serious movie criticism.

Years of devoted moviegoing in Springfield, Illinois, his home town, had him lovingly acquainted with the new medium. He wrote soundly that "Edison is the new Gutenberg." [151] He warned that the travelogue would so familiarize moviegoers with the look of China and India that travel would

---

* Griffith denied that it was antiblack. In his defense Lillian Gish says (*The Movies* . . . , 202) that one of his World War I movies, *The Greatest Thing in Life*, of which no print survives, showed a racist white officer in a shell hole tenderly ministering to a mortally wounded black who has saved his life. Supposing all that true, the emotional impact of *The Birth* is still as antiblack as the rabid novel it was made from, and it must have represented Griffith's own sympathies.

never again have the same utility. He deplored subtitles as clogs on the flow
of pure movieness, deplored the damage that musical clichés did to the
screen's emotional climate, foresaw that eventual sound systems supplying
realistic dialogue would change movie methods. . . . But he was too
Whitmanesque and sentimental to grope toward the esthetic core of the
movie as Griffith and the great Germans of the 1920's would shape it. The
movie, he wrote windily, would "build the American soul broad-based . . .
with dreams the veriest stone-club warrior can understand and lead him in
fancy through every phase of life to the apocalyptic splendors. . . ." [152]
That sounds like a bit from a subtitle in one of Griffith's worst pseudo-
historical aberrations.* His admiration for Mary Pickford was based on her
ability to be at will "a doll, a village belle, or a church angel. . . . Why do
the people love Mary? Because of a certain aspect of her face" [153] that
reminded him of a Botticelli in the Chicago Art Institute. Since he was a
remarkable poet when doing himself justice, it is probably unfair to reprint
his verses to Mae Marsh as star of *A Girl of the Paris Streets*:

> She is madonna in an art
> As wild and young as her sweet eyes;
> A frail dew flower from this hot lamp
> That is today's divine surprise.
>
> Despite raw lights and gloating mob
> She is not seared; a picture still;
> Rare silk the fine director's hand
> May weave for magic if he will. . . .[154]

A subtle version of what's a girl like you doing in a place like this?

Lindsay was the typical fan in dwelling on the star, never mind the
context. For him it was "MAE MARSH / in / *Blur*. . . ." Then as now
movie reviewers paid no heed to the scenarist's names for characters but
wrote only of how the movie had Wallace Reid elope with Bessie Barriscale.
It fitted with Griffith's fancy for making characters semi-abstractions as in
The Mother and the Law peopled by the Boy as unlucky hero, the Dear One
as his wife, the Musketeer of the Slums as the gangster who has the Boy
framed and tries to rape the Dear One. The audience could be counted on
joyfully to identify her as Mae Marsh. Poor Mae, born to trouble as the
sparks fly upward! Only a few months earlier she was just as close to a fate

---

* It is astonishing that one can still find Griffith being described as a "versatile and elastic
genius . . . at home in a variety of realms of thought and feeling—the social, the psychological,
the philosophical, the poetic and the religious . . . more important and more lasting than mere
entertainment." (Seymour Stern, introduction to Lewis Jacobs, *Introduction to the Art of the
Movies*.) Griffith certainly felt himself at home in all those fields, but it was largely an illusion
consequent on his manifest megalomania. To be impolite, he was the Elbert Hubbard of the
screen as well as its greatest natural genius.

worse than death at the hands of a leering black in *The Birth of a Nation.* So she jumped over a cliff and died in the arms of her Confederate officer-fiancé.

Nowadays The Musketeer of the Slums would be shown as scoring. In 1914, however, the movies were well into their first serious try at self-censorship and making no more sense of it than in any later efforts. In 1909, just when longer movies were making less imbecilic content possible, New York City closed all movie houses in town on the grounds that they were immoral influences. The larger producers chose not to fight head on. Instead, they asked social workers connected with the People's Institute (an arm of the Cooper Union foundation for popular education) to police their wares suggesting changes in or rejecting footage unfit for public showing. To forestall other attacks, the producers would make such changes not only locally but coast to coast.

The resulting, candidly named National Board of Censorship was no posse of ignorant bluenoses. On its advisory board were Jacob Riis, the muckrakers' expert on poverty; Felix Adler, founder of the respected Ethical Culture Society; representatives of the Children's Aid Society. A leading spirit was John Collier, later a most imaginative U.S. Commissioner of Indian Affairs. Frederick C. Howe, enlightened U.S. Commissioner of Immigration and husband of Marie Jenny, bitterest man hater among local Women's Righters, headed the Executive Committee. It seems not to have occurred to these well-meaning persons, as it would to their likes today, how precarious the intellectual position of even the most cultivated censor must be. Volunteers from among their conscientious acquaintances sat through gluts of one-reel Westerns, vest-pocket dreams of mother love, spicy glimpses of how girls go wrong and shouted Foul! whenever settlement house values were threatened. Arson, suicide, poisoning were taboo "although in classics like Shakespeare or the Bible they are reluctantly allowed to pass"; generally "no sensationalism or representation of crime, except with the object of conveying a moral lesson." [155] Already the industry had set up that exception to allow it to get away with murder and most other crimes the box office seemed to take kindly to.

On that basis New York City's movie houses were allowed to reopen. The new board showed its diligence and good faith by scrapping or toning down 10 percent of the footage inspected the first year. As producers and the film exchanges that distributed movies gradually learned what the board would and would not stand for, the rate of breakage declined. Its sponsors included only larger sources of movies, however. When the small fly-by-nights supplying some 5 percent of the annual crop stayed troublesome, a subcommittee of the board rode herd on them. Soon in several hundred urban centers local committees were using the board's lists of approved movies to guide law agencies. The board properly advised them to pay heed to local peculiarities in moral or religious emphasis—anything within reason to keep public censorship from taking over. In all this the board's position was rather like that of the New York Stock Exchange relative to local financial markets—extragovernmental but swinging a great deal of weight.

In terms of its day the National Board was fairly tolerant. It passed the skintight caperings of Miss Kellerman's mermaids, even let an inspirational feature, *The Hypocrites*, personify Truth as a stark naked girl. Those glimpses in *Intolerance* of Belshazzar's harem, not exactly naked but juicily suggestive, got by though they were probably as lewd as anything the board ever cut. Maybe because of this slackness, the states of Ohio and Pennsylvania and the cities of Chicago and San Francisco had their own boards of movie censors with arbitrary power to ban before public showing. Chicago went beyond issues of physical decency, barring not only the Kellerman sort of thing but also sequences of a policeman taking a banana from a pushcart and a man kissing another's wife—and *The Merchant of Venice* for its anti-Semitism. By late 1914 such usurpings of the industry's self-policing went so far that liberal Norman Hapgood protested: ". . . when enlightened public morals [*i.e.*, the National Board's] are in harmonious cooperation with enlightened business [*i.e.*, the larger moviemakers] . . . it is a pity to have the harmony broken by local police . . . deficient in training . . . too often within the reach of devious influence." [156] When the antiblackism of *The Birth of a Nation* stirred up riots and a few local legal suppressions, Griffith complained: "Had intelligent opposition to censorship been employed when it first made itself manifest it could easily have been overcome . . . the pigmy . . . has grown to be a giant. A people that would allow the suppression of this form of speech [the movie] would unquestionably submit to the suppression of the printing press." [157]

It was not that simple. The very existence of the National Board—whereas no such institution to watchdog books or plays had even been suggested—argued that the social impact of movies was of a new order. The unprecedented relative size of the audience, the emotional immediacy of the screen and its attendant star system had embedded it in the psyches of millions more deeply than novels or rep shows ever were. The screen's visceral approach to the grave problems of crime, the saloon, child labor, the incitements to racism and religious bigotry in Griffith's best movies constituted wider scope and heavier idea forging than *Uncle Tom's Cabin* or the Hearst press had ever achieved. That was clear even to a prim lady writer telling the juvenile readers of *St. Nicholas* how splendid it was that movies propagandized for good causes like peace and Prohibition, Women's Rights and laws reducing child labor: "Every picture shown is making some impression . . . for good or the reverse, depending on the story told." [158] For the next sixty years America, sidling and limping through the frustrations incident to the Hays Office and the Breen Office and the Hollywood Ten case and so on, would try to learn how the screen can reconcile responsibility with freedom. No solution yet visible.

Other implications surfaced. As the newsreel grew more elaborate, its contrived events, dependence on sports and cheesecake and tolerance of stuffed shirts created much of the stock-in-trade of today's TV news. Anticipating another aspect of television, movie backgrounds and props did much to acquaint isolated or poor people with the dwellings, clothes, artifacts and alleged folkways of those more luckily or more centrally situated. Millions of Americans owed the screen their first sight of a trolley car, a décolleté gown, a bathing beach, a woman smoking a cigarette, an ocean liner, a room full of books, a fixed bathtub. The movies' examples of such things might be absurd or tawdry, but they did convey the general notion. They also heightened social coherence as common awareness of the Keystone Kops, Chaplin, Mary Pickford, the Theda Bara "vamp"—created by Frank Powell for William Fox in 1914—widened the range of images instantly familiar to the bulk of Americans. That range had previously been limited pretty much to the flag, Christmas and the recurrent characters of newspaper comic strips—images that for the first-generation immigrant were culture-bound. The flag symbolized a strange and not necessarily benign government. The idiomatic talk lettered out in balloons in comic strips probably puzzled even many newcomers who knew the alphabet. Most movies, however, were flatly self-explanatory, and moviegoers' habit of reading the subtitles to themselves aloud, however it exasperated the fastidious, sometimes helped the immigrant patron improve his grasp of English—screen English, true, but better than none.

For fresh air after the stuffy gilt-and-glory of Roxy's Rialto and the doctrinaire sensuality of the early Freudian consider the summer camp—a clue to certain pre-War things and ways as wholesome as the stewed prunes it served for breakfast, as innocent as the theories of physical and mental hygiene creating it. It was child of Physical Culture, all Indian clubs, parallel bars and cold water, brought from Germany in the 1830's by political refugees to permeate the loose American educational system—with overtones of the YMCA kind of uplift. The first recognizable camp for boys whose parents wished to buy them a summer of roughing it was opened in the 1880's by Ernest Balch, a businessman of New York City with amateur gymnastics and clean living as hobbies. The first such girls' camp was set up a generation later by Luther H. Gulick, a leader in Physical Culture, colleague of G. Stanley Hall in child study and a founder of the National Board. C. 1900 the camp idea had a most favorable climate—Gifford Pinchot's conservationism calling attention to the hygienic beauties of wild waters and woods; Theodore Roosevelt's trumpetings about the red-blooded outdoors of strenuous riding, swimming and study of wild life; and the insistent cult of "fresh air" that, as breathed among hills and woods, would be prophylactic, morally as well as physically, for the sons of affluence as much as for slum boys.

By 1914 some 50,000 boys of various ages regularly summered in some 600 clusters of sleeping cabins or tents, dining hall and sports grounds concentrated in New England—the usual leader in American education— but also sporadic wherever lakes or forested hills occurred north of the Ohio River. The cost for eight or nine weeks ranged from $200 * to much more, depending on prestige and elaborateness. A popular camp was profitable to its owner, often doubling as director, often with a tireless wife as staff captain-housekeeper; in winter they taught school or worked for a staid religious organization. The industry gave a new kind of summer jobs to tuition-earning college boys skilled enough in swimming, ball games, canoeing, boy wrangling to qualify as "counselors." Many preferred it to waiting on table or stringing utility lines. In those simpler days extra dollars and cool nights plus board and lodging also attracted schoolteachers.

Camp taught all but the most inept to handle themselves in and on water, brought out potential knack in baseball and track and field, maybe tennis, in expensive camps maybe riding, and forced on all prebreakfast calisthen-ics good for both young and weedy and young and plump. The handicraft and woodcraft programs were mildly educational. Part-time tutoring for boys with school shortcomings to make up was usually offered at extra cost. And the timid or spoiled egocentric boy got a jostling among his peers often, though not always, salutary. Harvard's Charles W. Eliot had some reason to say that this institution was "the most important step in education that America has given the world." [159]

For parents who could afford it the result was near the best of both worlds. They were giving Jimmy what everybody said was an optimum healthy summer while sparing themselves the duty of keeping him out of trouble in that long idleness between school years. In a culture where even the very well-to-do and pretentious seldom sent their sons away to school before they reached fourteen or so, this respite was welcome to both parents and offspring. "Only one thing remains," *Life* said in 1917, ". . . to extend summer camps into winter . . . boys . . . come home from camp in the fall . . . track mud all over the house ruin the furniture . . . send them off to some camp in the winter for not more than two or three times what it would

* This book gives dollar costs as little as possible because it is difficult to convert such data into terms meaningful from one decade to another forty years later. Expectations of output per hour and notions of what goods and services are necessary have changed the tenor of real wages drastically. How, for instance, can one relate the dollar cost of that sound mechanism, the Model T Ford, with that of the lowest-priced Ford of today, all glitter and gadgets that the customer feels unable to do without, all adding to manufacturing cost, which in turn is made up of wildly changed costs of labor and raw materials? Take the above about summer camps as meaning that a family sending a child there in 1914 had an income high enough to contemplate an out-and-out luxury.

cost to keep them at home . . . [and] we might begin to feel as if there was, after all, some pleasure in raising children." [160]

Girls' camps, soon almost as numerous as boys', cost about the same for the same regimen, down to rigid partition of the day by strident bugle calls. Though athletic programs were modified—less strenuous hiking, boating and swimming, the softball version of baseball—parents expected to get daughter back almost as husky and brown as her brother. This flapper-to-be who would soon be meeting Yale juniors under the clock at the Biltmore was already far from the delicate lady tradition of her grandmother's day. Her camp uniform—sailor-collared middy blouse, baggy bloomers, dark stockings, rubber-soled tennis shoes—was based on what had kept Mother decent while exercising in the school gym. In that garb girls sang around campfires, toasted marshmallows or popped corn, listened in a sisterly glow to the counselor who went in for wholesome storytelling or alleged Indian lore. The name of the Gulicks' pace-setting girls' camp on Sebago Lake, Maine, was Camp Sebago-Wohelo; Sebago was Indian all right, though Wohelo stood for Work, Health, Love. The mistreated Indians had a fine revenge in the wildly transliterated names of camps in the rugged New England upcountry. One occasionally met Camp Tall Pines or Camp Eagle Rock, but the usual sort of thing—greatly to the benefit of dental surgeons—was and still is Camp Kenjocketee, Camp Kokomoko, Camp Wynegonic. . . . It could hardly have been worse in Wales.

Most of the boys and girls probably liked the illusion of roughing it—under conditions that would have seemed rather luxurious to their *Mayflower*-Knickerbocker ancestors. Nor might it have marred their fun had they been aware that they were being nudged away from their elders' tradition of self-play, of have-your-own-fun apart from institutional initiative and prodding. A camp's organized sports, rigid schedules, standards of achievement in lifesaving and pseudo-Indian beadwork amounted to extending school into a new context, usurping the time and energy that one's grandfather—assuming he didn't have to spend the summer at farm chores—devoted to scrub baseball, shack building, lie swapping, swimming holes, desultory fishing, all loose as ashes and spontaneous as sneezing. What it lacked in skill learning it made up in imagination training. In his prosperous Midwestern social stratum Tarkington's Penrod Schofield, contemporary with the early boys' camp, was the last of this tradition. Even after allowing for the author's ingenuity in getting him into complications, one sees that Penrod needed nobody to organize him in his summer vacation. He would have resented the mere visible presence of an adult while he—alone or with collaborating peers—exploited this rich fund of free time. Yet had the Schofields been in their relatively favored position in Boston, say, instead of a disguised Indianapolis, Penrod would probably have been sent to camp. By the late 1920's the custom was strong in the

Midwest, too. *C.* 1938–39 Penrod's own son would certainly have been thus favored if the Depression had left his father able to afford it.

Or a depleted family purse could have sent him to a religion-affiliated camp partly subsidized by, say, the Episcopalians or the YMCA. For American religion went early into camping in the belief that, the groves being God's first temples, as the poem said, there was indirect connection between holiness and seasonal outdoorsiness—hence all those godly-flavored summer resorts like the Methodists' Ocean Grove on the Jersey Shore or the Quakers' sleek Lake Mohonk in New York's Catskills. An offshoot of this combined with a simpleminded hygiene to effect some genuine benevolence in the Fresh Air movement for slum children begun in 1877 by a former social worker, the Reverend Willard Parsons, incumbent of a Presbyterian pulpit in Sherman, Pennsylvania. He nagged his hearers and some of his former colleagues into taking small children out of the fetid, heat-tortured tenements for a ritual two weeks among green fields and friendly animals and milk fresh from the cow on the farms of conscientiously welcoming country folks. "Fresh air" was an obsession of the day, of course, because hygienists considered open windows and lack of stenches to imply proper oxygen content. The great Dr. L. Emmett Holt, author of the manual of baby care on which my generation was reared, wrote: "Fresh air is required to renew and purify the blood . . . just as necessary for health and growth as proper food." [161] In the camp context it referred particularly to the tuberculosis that still seriously threatened all economic strata but mostly the poorest.

In 1881 the notion was taken up by Whitelaw Reid, publisher of the New York *Tribune*, and affluent friends of his, who raised money and gave their own to send to summer farm homes a yearly average of 8,000 children. It is dubious whether a mere 14 days away from the pollutions and straitened diet of Hell's Kitchen did much good, since 351 days remained. But the children usually had a good time, a thing healthy in itself; so was the stimulus of learning of another world, one smelling and looking so much better. The heartwarming drama of it moved *Life* independently to solicit its prosperous readers for money to set up a regular summer camp, essentially like Camp Tall Pines, for slum children near Ridgefield, Connecticut. (For several seasons $100 or so came to this fund from juvenile shows staged at Westport, Connecticut, by subadolescent Robert E. Sherwood, already theater-minded.) In 1905 the *Tribune* added to its country vacation program a camp in the same area, then went into several more. For the next thirty years *Life*'s promotion of its Fresh Air activity was a miniature national institution. Taken over by the New York *Times* after the *Herald Tribune* died, such schemes still send some 15,000 children for salutary vacations each summer and operate seven camps on special reservations in Dutchess County, New York.

Summer camp, like most other things, sought patriotic pertinence when the War came. To a mother's question: "In this year of stress and sacrifice should I send my daughter to a summer camp?" the editor of a woman's magazine replied: "More this year than ever. Those girls of 12 to 18 . . . will mold a generation . . . help to produce an army of mothers enthusiastic, strong, vigorous, joyous, as well as loyal devoted parents." [162] This try at bricks without straw blandly assumed that to remove an adolescent girl from her family was a good way to help her become a model mother-to-be—a doctrine that, whatever its merits, would have dismayed such a mother of previous generations as the Marmee of *Little Women*. Already, however, the elder belief that a framework of parents and siblings is the best support for the emotional skeleton of the immature individual was fraying at the edges. Third-person society, no blood kin, was offering to take over much of the adjusting-training previously done by the largely hit-or-miss attrition and imitation that made the family a focus alternately repelling and attracting a girl. The leak in it was the extramural school immersing the child in a legally prescribed artificial microcosm five days a week, often forty weeks a year, that might already be trying to handle "the whole child." Summer camp and among Protestants Sunday School and the YMCA and the YWCA were all part of this process. And for year-round piecemeal equivalent of summer camp for the offspring of lowish- to middle-income families the nation had recently acquired Boy Scouts, Camp Fire Girls and Girl Scouts.

For these Britain and Canada supplied the germ, America the early shapes, Britain the eventual form. In the 1880's a pious Glasgow business-man, William Alexander Smith, created a Boys' Brigade to calm his unruly Sunday School pupils with military drill; by 1904 he had 50,000-odd boys in such units. At the same time a Canadian* naturalist-writer-artist, Ernest Thompson Seton, was publishing deservedly popular, self-illustrated stories about North American fauna—wolf, bear, cottontail, etc. His writing was able, his marginal sketches even better, and his attitude only half as foolishly anthropomorphic as that of most "nature writers" of the time. In 1903 he wrote for the *Ladies' Home Journal* a series about boys creating shelter, food and garments in the woods Indian-fashion; then he used this material in an autobiographic fiction, *Two Little Savages*, about an Ontario town boy's joy in woodcraft as remedy for both a weak chest and emotional conflicts with harsh parents. On the success of these writings he founded a boys' society, the Woodcraft Indians, of local "tribes" bringing boys together under adult supervision to do things described in a new Seton handbook, *The Birchbark Roll of the Woodcraft Indians*. Then the *Woman's*

---

* Americans seldom realize how often and variously Canadians settling south of the border have contributed to American life. A list of the first coming to mind: James J. Hill, D. D. Palmer, Raymond Massey, Mary Pickford, Father Charles W. Coughlin, Aimee Semple McPherson, Cyrus M. Eaton, John Kenneth Galbraith, Guy Lombardo, Mack Sennett. . . .

Home Companion took over from *Recreation* magazine a similar boys' movement, the Sons of Daniel Boone, organized by Daniel C. Beard, once a fellow student of Seton's at the Art Students' League, now a magazine illustrator specializing in nature and animals.

With outdoorsiness then much in the public mind, such schemes prospered. Mindful of his parents' English origin, Seton took his Indians to Britain, lecturing about them and founding several tribes. There he met Sir Robert Baden-Powell, one of the few generals to come out of the Boer War with credit. Expert in reconnaissance, he had written a training manual, *Aids to Scouting*, that certain British teachers adopted to set their boys using their brains in the open air. At a review of Smith's Boys' Brigades, Baden-Powell said they drilled well, but it was too stiff and limited. Smith suggested making *Aids to Scouting* the base of a wider movement. The general was considering this when he heard of Seton and met with him to learn more about the Woodcraft Indians.

Doubtless all those opportune happenings mean that some such thing was in the air. Smith/Baden-Powell/Seton gave Britain the Boy Scouts, training boys from all social classes—in England an innovation—in campcraft and citizenship. Since much of what they learned would be handy for soldiers, they had a paramilitary air. Local units were "troops" made up of "patrols"; the disciplined drill included a hand salute; the uniform of neckerchief, khaki shorts and shirt was like that of Baden-Powell's South African Constabulary. The wide-brimmed, four-dinted felt hat was his own personal attribute borrowed from America; in West Africa he was known as "man with a big hat."

His prestige caused Scouting to flourish in Britain. America became infected when a Chicago publisher, W. D. Boyce, losing his way in London, met a clean-cut stripling who saluted him snappily, asked might he be of service, sir, and showed the way to the obscure address sought. Boyce tried to give him a shilling, but the boy said, "A Scout accepts no reward for a courtesy or a good turn" [163] and vanished like a leprechaun guardian angel. Boyce traced the origin of this apparition, visited Baden-Powell and within a year had set up an American counterpart as near like the original as American conditions in 1910 allowed. The uniform retained Baden-Powell's hat and, with realistic regard to poison ivy and mosquitoes, also borrowed from the U.S. Army the doughboy's laced canvas leggings and riding breeches, so the first American Boy Scouts looked like midget members of the garrison of Fort Sheridan.

Seton was Chief Scout the first five years. Beard was equally involved; soon his benevolent, goateed face under the four-dinted hat (now best known as an attribute of Smokey the Bear) was as familiar as Theodore Roosevelt's. And Roosevelt, of course, sponsored Scouting along with a strikingly mixed bag of notables—Admiral George Dewey, hero of Manila Bay; Hamlin Garland, gloomy Son of the Middle Border; G. Stanley Hall, as keen on Scouting as on Freud; David Starr Jordan, idealist-pacifist president of Stanford; Major General Leonard Wood, stiffest of militarists; the Reverend Dr. Charles H. Parkhurst, snorting scourge of red-light districts; Mortimer L. Schiff, powerful Jewish banker; Lincoln Steffens, most subversive of the muckrakers; Judge Ben B. Lindsey, crusader for juvenile courts, who said that if Scouting got proper "moral and financial support . . . the Juvenile Court will soon no longer be needed." [164] Such hopes soon had churches, Catholic as well as Protestant, sponsoring troops; also granges, lodges and (as they came into being) service clubs. Young churchgoing types acquired merit in their communities by volunteering to be Scoutmasters—a term that Baden-Powell borrowed from grim Oliver Cromwell's army—and frantically learned knot tying and lifesaving to stay one jump ahead of their eager charges. By 1916 the Scouts had a federal charter with the President of the United States as ex officio president, and in 1917 a Broadway play showing California's Japanese house servants and farm labor turning overnight into a fifth column army had them foiled by the radio skills of a Boy Scout.

Certain radicals deplored the Scouts' submilitary flavor and verbose patriotism. They did so the more when after the War the veterans' organizations, particularly the American Legion, made a point of sponsoring new troops, drilling them and featuring them in parades. But much of that was perfunctory, and in any case the radicals would have disliked anything tending to keep youth content with society as then constructed. More widely the sight of Scouts conspicuously hiking through the landscape enriched America with jokes about the assiduity with which they helped old ladies across streets without being sure they wanted to go; about rubbing two Scouts together to make a fire; about the formidable list of the Scout's virtue-duties that the Tenderfoot (neophyte) had to gabble through. But a residual affection persisted, and even in most unregenerate circles the pejorative epithet "Boy Scout" was never quite as harsh as "Christer."

Inevitably girls also were thus organized. Emulating the Woodcraft Indians with Seton's blessing, using Sebago-Wohelo as pilot plant, Gulick launched the Camp Fire Girls in 1912. His wife, a devotee of artsy-craftiness, designed for them Indianistic uniforms with beaded headbands—she forbade sticking feathers in them, for Seton said that was for braves only—and "authentic squaw dresses" [165] of fringed and beaded cotton. Actually "squaws" in pre-Columbian eastern North America stripped to the waist in summer, but after all! Whatever their flaws, such Indianana had an important result for real Indians. John Collier was a founding sponsor of the Camp Fire Girls and credited the Gulicks with thus bringing him "for the first time into contact with authentic Indian folklore . . ." [166] through [an Indian] symbolism at once rich and profound" [167]—which made him so valiant a friend of the red man. That was a good thing even if it was rather like learning to value and befriend the ancient Gauls by seeing a performance of *Norma*.

The Camp Fire Girls' equivalent of Tenderfoot was Wood Gatherer; the higher ranks were Fire Maker and Torch Bearer. Their ritual hinted at a high-minded pyromania that might now trouble both psychiatrists and conservationists. More innocent was Mrs. Gulick's naming groups of smaller girls Blue Birds after the symbol of happiness in Maeterlinck's morality play then so admired by the wholesomely cultivated. At the age of eleven a worthy Blue Bird advanced to Wood Gatherer and acquired merit by learning to make ten standard soups; or recognize three different baby wails; or sleep two months with windows open; or organize the girls on her block to beautify the front yards—for Gulick valued domestic arts as well as bird book and canoe paddle. He wanted "girls to be womanly . . . as we desire men to be manly . . . to copy the Boy Scout movement would be utterly and fundamentally evil." [168]

That was probably aimed at the Girl Guides, a modified Scouting then developing in Britain. Within a year Juliette Gordon Low, a firm lady from Savannah, Georgia, married to a Briton and friend of Baden-Powell's, brought the Girl Guides to America as Girl Scouts. She did emphasize womanly virtues as well as superficial imitations of Scouting. Over the years her Girl Scouts took the play away from the Camp Fire Girls. Not for the first time invaders from Britain outlasted and bested the Indians. Maybe one reason was that in addition to laundry skills and rather unsound teachings about nutrition, Girl Scout manuals taught the best way to truss up a burglar.

All three organizations surely helped, as Anne L. New wrote of the Girl Scouts, "to fill the gap left in the education of youth by mechanical progress, urban living and other complications of modern civilization." [169] As fragmented settlement houses for adolescents, they heightened youngsters' new dependence on group activity arranged from the outside at outsiders' instance. That further eroded family and home as sources of ways of doing. Too much could be made of it, but the Scout Oath didn't even tip its hat to the Fifth Commandment.

In such respects Scouting was an arm of what was already called Progressive Education—a thing so much on American minds today that it seems hardly possible that, under one name or another, it has roots going back two centuries. One of its later stated purposes was to train children in the handling and savoring of life on the assumption that urbanization and mechanization were robbing them of full development. Homer Croy, Missouri farm boy turned post-War novelist, said that Scouting merely taught boys "to do what [country boys] had to do every day" and wondered whether the "self-reliance and self-dependence we developed wasn't [*sic*] better for us." [170] Scouting and such were part time, however, and voluntary, whereas systems inclined to Progressive Education usually made attendance compulsory up to, say, age fourteen and sought to fill the pupil's time five days a week. Home was chiefly for sleep and major meals. In Newark, New Jersey, indeed, some elementary schools kept open till 9 P.M. to give pupils a clean, quiet, well-lighted place for homework. In compensation for this weaning of children away from home such schools also often reached out for their parents too with evening classes for adults in handicrafts, languages, civic problems, theatricals. . . .

This amounted, as some educationists half recognized, to applying the settlement house approach to white- as well as blue-collar neighborhoods, even, as newly expanded country schools felt the tide, to rural populations. Tacitly it was assumed that, since Mom and Pop were in no position to shape their offspring right, the school, acting for the community, must and, *sotto voce*, could do a better job than they ever could have anyway. John Dewey said it was "obvious that . . . in every Western country the increase of importance of public schools has been at least coincident with a relaxation of older family ties." [171] John Keats (no, not the poet), speaking for troubled parents, recently felt justified in writing that today's educationists tend to "regard the child's home with undisguised contempt." [172]

When Progressive Education was barely teething, educationists had envisioned the schoolteacher discerning that in the world of city-based technology children had new needs—so sights were raised, classrooms to be freed from the straitjacket of the three R's and supplemented with richening, life-anticipating handicrafts, fine arts, performing arts, sports, hygiene, basic industrial and domestic skills, knowledge of the workings of the approaching world of jobs and government. This called for expanding the schoolhouse beyond mere classrooms into nurse's office as well as principal's; studios for painting, carving, dancing, ceramics; tool-rich carpentry and foundry shops—all once new and remarkable. Visiting a high school in St. Louis new-built on such principles, Julian Street, crack magazine journalist, marveled at its "auditorium like a very simple opera house," its façade "like Hampton Court Palace brought up to date," its greenhouse for botanizing, workshops, library "like that of a club," and, as culminating joy, a scientific ventilating system that kept it from even smelling like a school—it lacked that "rather zoological odor of dirty little boys. . . . Can it be that the school smell is gone forever?" [173]

C. 1914 the prime example of Progressive Education's superschool, with specially heavy overtones of settlement house, was in Gary, Indiana. The town was a left-handed creation of the United States Steel Corporation at the south end of Lake Michigan—a halfheartedly sponsored company town* attached to an enormous new complex of steelmaking installations.

---

* It was often pointed out that U.S. Steel neither sought nor deserved credit for the virtues of Gary's schools. The company's contribution to the community consisted of its name (after

It's employee residents were mostly New Immigrants, its slums not much more livable for being newly jerry-built rather than venerably fetid. Self-consciously new, it had no previous educational mistakes to clear away and was stimulatingly near the educational ferments of Hull House and the University of Chicago, where John Dewey, that most significant American educationist, had been working toward what he hoped the proper place of education in American life could be. Gary was still wet behind the ears when, in 1907, it employed one of Dewey's ablest disciples, William A. Wirt, to install there the Progressive methods with which he had made himself a name in the rural county seat of Bluffton, Indiana, the other side of the state.

Part of it was economic—two-platoon, specialist-taught, rotating classes, shop and exercise periods, that kept the school plant in full use all day. That, he claimed, meant lower overhead cost per pupil as in a factory on double shifts. But economy, however welcome to school boards wearing their fiscal hats, was not where his heart lay. He loved the imaginative range of curriculum and plant that gave Gary's children, mostly from alien-born parents in low-income brackets, a new life of flower and vegetable gardens, wading pools, miniature zoos with animals to care for, experience with musical instruments. . . . Industrial arts were taught not by normal-school teachers with some shop training but by veteran machinists, carpenters, printers. Experienced gardeners, plumbers, painters led the pupils to do most of the upkeep of the school plumbing, corridor walls, floors and so on. Lunches that the girls cooked in the household arts kitchen were sold at cost to teachers and pupils who could afford not to bring their own. What Wirt avowedly sought was "a genuine children's community, where the children's normal interests are centered . . . [making up for] the comparative failure of the public school to care for the city child. . . ." [174] The wide freedom with which pupils browsed among electives, dropping this, nibbling at that, with inadequate follow-up on who was doing what, struck Abraham Flexner and Frank P. Bachman, surveying the system in 1917, as its weakest feature. Yet some regard for the three R's remained. Which elementary sciences a pupil dabbled in was pretty much up to him or her, but English, arithmetic, geography and history were, however relaxedly taught, compulsory.

Wherever possible one kind of learning reinforced another. Thus scorekeeping at athletic games turned into arithmetic practice. In Indianapolis, where some of Dewey's principles were being tried out in a rather gingerly way, a teacher needing a cold frame for botanical plantings enlisted a mathematics group for specifications, a draftsman group for the

---

Judge Elbert H. Gary, head of the company), building several hundred houses for upper-echelon personnel and selling building lots to any able to pay. Big Steel thus avoided the headaches the Pullman Company brought on itself by paternalism in creating Pullman, Illinois. (*Cf.* Bourne, *The Gary Schools*; Flexner and Bachman, *The Gary Schools*.)

plans, a carpentry group for building the thing. Seventh and eighth graders made group visits to the city's water, health, fire and police departments and to factories "to teach them the relation between industry and life" [175]—old stuff now but conspicuously novel then. The boys of a solid black elementary school rehabilitated three rattletrap dwellings—one becoming a clubhouse, the second a shoe repair shop mending the neighborhood's shoes, the third a demonstration center for the girls' cooking, sewing, laundry and so on. Parents were encouraged to come and learn to slough off the slatternliness in which they had been reared.

Gary went well beyond settlement house terms, however, when installing promotion by subject, not by graded class. That is, in today's jargon the pupil learned at his own pace, staying with fellow pupils at the same level in arithmetic or reading no matter how their calendar ages varied—which also is common now, was radical then. With that went further libertarian notions, particularly a great crying out against the Screwed-Down Desk—one of Dewey's favorite symbols. Rigid ranks of fixed little desks and seats to match, standard in schoolrooms sixty years ago, stultifyingly implied learning by rote, compulsory silence, harsh punishments exultantly contrasted with the consequences of freely movable seats and worktables that fostered spontaneous grouping, eager interest and discipline confined to moral suasion. Further elements in the syndrome were the notion of the Whole Child as the school's concern; of Learning by Doing; of tailoring subject matter to the pupil's nascent (now read "relevant") interests; of taking the Child as entity in his own right, not a miniature grown-up as he was taken to be in the old portraits and the elder schooling; of the school's duty to foster cooperative impulses; of its wider duty so to shape children's sympathies and understandings that as adults they will make the world juster, gentler, more civilized—all those were Dewey's ideas bubbling away under certain experimental schools, school systems and teacher-training institutions.

This most remarkable man—a great intellectual and educational catalyst, responsible participant in many movements always decent, though occasionally ill advised—would never have claimed much originality for these ideas. *Schools of Tomorrow* (1915), his collaboration with his eldest daughter reporting on Gary, Indianapolis and several other proving grounds, is rich with passages from Jean-Jacques Rousseau. And Gary did well to plan to name a new school after Johann Heinrich Pestalozzi, Swiss father of the school as child-centered, motherly equivalent of home—a concept central to Dewey's thought—who died in 1827. Ever since Rousseau persuaded the Western mind that Natural Man—and by extension still more the Natural Child—was innately good and potentially clever, every thirty years or so some Continental educationist produced a new-sounding version of Rousseau-*cum*-Pestalozzi, and after a certain lag, American admirers applied it practically. A sort of proto-Progressivism has been around a long time. Edith Wharton regretted that in her childhood (the 1870's) "The sentimental theory that children must not be made to study anything that does not interest them was already in the air . . . it made my parents turn my work into play. . . . I never learned to concentrate except on subjects naturally interesting to me." [176]

The resulting schools were usually private, small, concentrated in the Northeast, much discussed, little imitated, little more significant than the occasional vegetarian restaurants. In the 1880's, however, an innovative Yankee, Colonel Francis W. Parker, who had taught a country school, studied advanced educational methods in Germany and conspicuously improved the schools of Quincy, Massachusetts, was called to Chicago to administer the Cook County Normal School. He made it nucleus of a pedagogical power grid that transmitted the glow and tingle of Progressive Education to most of America's public schools. Dewey called him "father of progressive education." [177]

Parker's basic tenet was innocently Wordsworthian: "The spontaneous tendencies of the child are the records of inborn divinity," and Cook County Normal's practice school was to be a "model home, a complete community and embryonic democracy." [178] Note that this extension of Pestalozzianism was announced well before people began to worry about the gap between child and environment that was later thought to have brought on Progressive Education as antidote. (This book often deals with carts rigged forward of the horse.) Yet Parker's school sounds like a good, if oppressively euphoric, place. As benign father-deity he imbued the pupil/teacher relationship with sympathy. His programs seethed with watercolors, playacting, spontaneous discussion, individual reports on how the spider built its web—and trailblazing emphasis on correlating previously separate fields of learning. Nature study fed into the laboratory and vice versa. Writing, spelling, reading, memorizing fused into what we now call "communications arts." All a good ninety years ago!

From Cook County Normal zealous young teachers fanned out into the public schools of the core area of the Midwest. Until then Rousseau, Pestalozzi and Company had been merely stimulating jostles. Now they broke through the arterial wall into the nutrient-bearing bloodstream of American schooling. (Again, as in poetry, industrial methods, mechanized agriculture, architecture, the Midwest called a tune that the nation would dance to.) Gradually teachers' colleges, springing up all over to supply the demand for formally qualified teachers, felt secondary but definite effects. The classroom teacher's job is so exacting that he—usually she, for by then four in five American teachers were women—can hardly be blamed for inclining toward any promising theory impressively vouched for. Compulsory attendance laws sluicing larger loads of unlikely pupils into the schools had made conventional education—rigid curricula, punitive discipline, neglect of individual needs, in brief the Screwed-Down Desk—look worse than ever. "Had there never been a progressive movement," says Lawrence A. Cremin's masterly *Transformation of the School*, "had there been no social settlements . . . no William James, Stanley Hall, Edmund Thorndike or John Dewey, the mere fact of compulsory attendance would have changed the American school." [179]

Dewey sent his two eldest children to Parker's school. When, under University of Chicago sponsorship, his wife and he set up their famous Laboratory School, it was candidly based on Parker's but, having research more than teacher training in mind, played even more by ear. In ten years the Parker-Dewey two-stage rocket had been pilot plant for most of what workable Progressive Education had come to mean. Sidney Hook calls the second (Dewey) stage "the most important experimental venture in the whole history of American education." [180]

It probably was. One consequence has been unfair to Dewey as cavilers heap on his deservedly eminent name the blame for all that doctrinaire sentimentalists have done in the name of Progressive Education. He never succumbed to the child worship of Pestalozzi and Parker. His common sense mistrusted even so appealing an abstraction as the Rousseau-Blake-Wordsworth image of the Child. Aware of the egocentric handicaps of immature human beings, he set modification of them as one purpose of the ideal school: ". . . childhood's interests . . . are neither to be humored nor repressed," he taught as early as 1897. "To humor the interest is to substitute caprice and whim for genuine interest." [181] Yet he also promised that if "we [teachers] identify ourselves with the real instincts and needs of childhood and ask only after its fullest assertion and growth, the discipline and information and culture of adult life shall come in their due season." [182]

In his devoted hands Parker's clusters of interests became sweeping projects steering pupils into using their muscles, eyes, tongues, brains and cooperative impulses to work out in class the whole process of, say, textile making—taking the wool off the sheep's back through washing, carding (with homemade cards), spinning (with homemade spindles), weaving (on homemade looms). Instead of just reading in a textbook that until the cotton gin came in, the difficulty of deseeding short-staple cotton hampered its usefulness, the pupils were set to removing seed by hand to make them realize how slow it was. Simultaneously the pupils of the Francis Parker School (going on after he died in 1902) studied Greek culture by building a Greek house, making Greek costumes worn daily in class, playing Greek games, fighting the Trojan War with wooden swords and barrelhead shields, and held a "Dionysiac festival . . . with prayers and dances and extempore song. . . ." [183] War and festival must have been fun. But they also illustrate the pitfalls of Learning by Doing. If the lads had really reproduced a Dionysiac festival by getting staggering drunk and tearing off those Greek costumes. . . .

Dewey expanded Parker's Pestalozzian "model home" into "doing systematically . . . what for various reasons can be done in most households only in a comparatively meager and haphazard manner . . . the life of the child becomes the all-controlling aim." [184] He enlarged Parker's "embryonic democracy" to present the child-centered school as "the fundamental method of social progress and reform . . . the teacher . . . engaged, not simply in the training of individuals, but in the formation of the proper social life . . . is the prophet of the True God and usherer in of the true kingdom of God." [185] Hence, Cremin says, the "Progressive" label for this necessarily diverse and confused movement. It was close kin to the contemporary sanguine but bitter, generous but smug mind of the muckraker/Christian Socialist/settlement house worker/Bull Mooser Progressive of, say, 1885–1915. Donald Barr, current headmaster of the Dalton School in New York City, sees "a good deal of simple populism in progressive education." [186] Anyway Progressive Educationists often took it rather for granted that the ends they sought, the minds and hearts they hoped to shape would be antipathetic to U.S. Steel and sympathetic to that never well-defined but then widely shared hope of so many of goodwill, the Cooperative Commonwealth.

In 1904 Dewey became the star of the Department of Philosophy at Columbia. To New York City along with him migrated the capital of Progressive Education, for while with one hand he trained brilliant young philosophers at Columbia, with the other he planted a teeming crop of the new ideas in pedagogy at Columbia's Teachers College. It became to American education what bagpipes are to Scotland, the chief means of what Cremin calls a "conquest of the [American] organized teaching profession." [187] Year after year it sent out better and more impressively trained true believers, not only classroom teachers but influential young EdD's carrying the word into the nation's hundreds of teachers' colleges. By 1917 the pedagogical showcase was no longer in Chicago but on Manhattan Island—Teachers College's Lincoln School, supported by Rockefeller money at the instance of Abraham Flexner, reformer of American medical education. There children of interested parents—by definition a picked group, as had been the faculty kids from the University of Chicago in Dewey's Laboratory School—went from kindergarten to college entrance under picked teachers guided by not only Dewey but also by other rising Progressive Educationists such as William H. Kirkpatrick and Harold Rugg.

Not that Teachers College monopolized the gospel—or anyway its exaggerations. Already famous was Marietta Johnson's go-as-you-please "organic" * school on, of all unlikely spots, the eastern shore of Mobile

* Nothing to do with the pupils' diet—just the lady's way of saying that her methods were nonartificial and spontaneous.

Bay, where pupils were discouraged from learning to read or write until they reached eight or nine years. C. 1912 the materials-centered kindergarten methods of Maria Montessori came from Italy temporarily to quicken the already effervescent reaction from mixing Freud and self-expression into educational theory. Freud's repressed child as traumatized parent of the neurosis-ridden adult was, even when misconceived Village-fashion, valuable to the hyper-Progressive Education mind. Helen Naumburg's Children's School in New York City leaned frankly on psychoanalysis—she had been a patient of Brill's. Among peripheral ventures were the Moraine Park School of Dayton, Ohio, backed by Charles F. Kettering, father of the self-starter, and the experimental play school created by Caroline Pratt, a well-grounded teacher, for the children of low-income families in the Village. Intellectuals eager to foster the life creative moved their offspring in on it. The resulting City & Country School, founded on the belief that at bottom the Child, any child, is a free-style artist whom blockage of self-expression will cripple, became as much a Village institution as the Jefferson Market Courthouse. Pupils of Progressive schools, one of the movement's high priests promised, would develop "a productiveness . . . of those same exquisite values which characterized the pre-Raphaelite art." [188]

Proliferation of such schools, many aborting but while they lived as charming as basement tearooms, led to an advisory Bureau of Educational Experiments that became today's Bank Street College of Education. Presently Helen Parkhurst, who, like Miss Naumburg, studied under Dr. Montessori, brought to New York City her "Dalton Plan" named for the Massachusetts village where she applied it to a high school situation under encouragement from Mrs. W. Murray Crane, Lady Bountiful of the Crane paper fortune. Miss Parkhurst's first innovation came of the realization that many a child learns more faster when teaching younger children things he has just learned himself. She discovered this, she said, when, teaching a country school of forty pupils ranging through all eight elementary grades, she marked out the room into eight different areas in which elders taught youngers in specific subjects.* This evolved into her Laboratory School system in which pupils above the age of eight or so signed up to carry out specific education-fraught projects and worked at them on self-evolved schedules in one or another separate laboratory where all ages pursued a given field of learning. "[The pupils] can wander from one room to another," [189] wrote a wondering early admirer. The only penalty for not completing a self-imposed task was the disapproval not of teacher but of one's fellow pupils, which, it was averred, invariably snapped the laggard to. It seems to have occurred to nobody that this was the very individuality-

---

* She seems not have been aware that this resembled the Lancastrian System, widely adopted in British schools for the lower orders in the early 1800's and tried in America—it soon petered out here. Something like it was attempted in Gary; Flexner and Bachman found the results highly unsatisfactory.

warping, conformism-encouraging group pressure that Progressive Education and its allies presumed to be anathema.

Then in 1919 a young man zealot, Stanwood Cobb, persuaded certain eager women in Washington, D.C., to form a national Progressive Education Association headed by Charles W. Eliot, who had done his bit for the cause a generation earlier by practically abolishing compulsory courses in Harvard College. Its members wrangled a good deal over which could best free the Child from warping forces, but for all that it flourished; its influential journal seethed with ingenuity, energy and the best intentions. As the young products of proudly unbuttoned Progressive schools went on into college, they often acquitted themselves well and were recruited into higher education's faculties. Through them the value demands of Progressive Education permeated the whole American educational process. By the early 1930's new colleges such as Bennington and Sarah Lawrence, then Black Mountain, were deliberately created in the Progressive Education image.*

As the farther reaches of the movement approached self-parody—as usual when a principle is carried too far—they made its leaders uneasy. Dewey warned the association in 1928 that the necessary air-clearing, "negative phase . . . of protest . . . deviation and innovation . . . removal of artificial and numbing restrictions" was finished and "such freedom is not an end in itself." [190] Miss Parkhurst told an early interviewer that she dreaded wide attention for her Dalton Plan lest those failing to grasp its inner essence pervert it. "The child who 'does as he likes' is not a free child," she wrote later, sounding first like Spinoza and then like a Victorian governess. "He is . . . apt to become the slave of bad habits, selfish, . . . unfit for community life" [191]—adjustment to which was, of course, an avowed prime purpose of the Progressive Education movement.

Aldous Huxley saw another hazard. It "stressed the importance of non-verbal activity. . . . History . . . is . . . taught in . . . projects. Stonehenge is reconstructed with the brickbats in the yard . . . the Middle Ages . . . reproduced minus, of course, the dirt, the violence and the theology . . . the essence of that life. Whether children learn more through these mud-pie techniques . . . I do not profess to know." [192] Keats heretically wonders "whether the trip to the factory is really worth while in view of the crumb of knowledge to be carried home." [193] Much depends on which factory, of course, which teacher leads the expedition and which child takes part. One of the most depressing sights in the world is a gaggle

* The self-congratulatory conclusions that Progressive Education drew from its products' doing so well in college relative to those of conventional schooling have a possible catch: Most pupils of the Lincoln School, say, had unusually intelligent and literate parents, the sort likelier to send their progeny to such a school and to be interested in Progressive Education—and likelier to produce unusually educable children who probably would have learned well in maybe not all but certainly most systems.

of schoolchildren being herded through and talked at in an art museum. Yet one never knows when a first look at "La Grande-Jatte" will start an eight-year-old on the way to being a great painter. A knottier problem lies in the description by a staff teacher of the "central core of subject matter" taught at New York City's Little Red Schoolhouse in the late 1930's as "mainly . . . the social sciences . . . history, geography, sociology, economics, government—in fact, Life *on a level with the child's understanding*." [194] (Italics mine.)

Huxley also suspected that Learning by Doing lost much value because "the doing . . . is left unanalyzed . . . nothing to choose between one kind of doing and another. . . . John Dewey himself knew better, but his followers . . . ignore his qualifications of the learning-by-doing doctrine." [192] This shortcoming suggests what may be the movement's most stubborn trouble—dearth of proper subalterns. Visitors to the Laboratory School and other pace-setting experiments were usually struck by the devoted brilliance of the teachers carrying out the innovators' ideas. It probably reflected both the leaders' skill in choosing staff and the natural affinity of such schemes with aspirants likely to handle them well. Once Progressive Education became dogma in teachers' colleges and among younger faculty on campus, however, handpicking of vessels to receive the fire had to cease, and much of it went out for lack of proper tinder.

Or say that even in mild dilution the movement demanded far more of teachers than did the elder keep-quiet-and-study-three-R's routine. The Little Red Schoolhouse proudly proclaimed: "All the ingenuity, all the resources, all the imagination, which the most gifted teacher possesses is called upon to give [pupils] the training, the creative outlets, and the discipline [they require]." [195] It was wildly sanguine—yet implicit in wide application of Progressive Education—to expect any culture to supply enough persons able to become the requisite imaginative, charming, well-adjusted, unflappable, astute, fatigue-proof, liberal-minded teachers, each well enough versed in psychology, anthropology, sociology, the handicrafts and biochemical hygiene to coordinate them into what the movement sought. "There may seem to be a dearth of such teachers," Stanwood Cobb wrote rather sulkily in 1929, "but more . . . would be available were there more opportunity for . . . their abilities." [196] That was sheer gratuitous assumption. One might as well ask the nation for enough ballplayers of major-league quality to field 100,000 teams. So, as Dewey complained in 1952, teachers' colleges turned "the ideas and principles [of Progressive Education] . . . into ready made rules . . . applied to educational problems externally . . . [like] mustard plasters." [197]

Progressive Education did not go unopposed. Teachers used to elder ways and school boards all too sure what voters would say about newfangled notions fought rearguard actions. Widened curricula drew from

humorists things like Abe Martin's "Miss Fawn Lippincutt's little niece is
. . . jes' doin' fine at cookin', dancin' an' sewin' but she's havin' trouble
with th' alphabet." [198] Small private schools proud of pupils' using teachers'
first names and cherishing the Child's creativity drew disproportionate
notice that did disproportionate harm. All things considered, it was a credit
to either the open-mindedness—or the latent guilt feelings—of parents that
the idea of "the child-centered school" gained such currency within a
generation. It took far longer for it to gain solid footing in Britain, and
though so much of it originated on the Continent, it is not yet well
established there.

Somehow millions of American parents/taxpayers were won over to the
Whole Child and Learning by Doing—irresistible phrases. Who cared to
advocate dealing with fragmented children and learning by not doing?
Though promising attempts were made in Gary, at the Lincoln School and
elsewhere, Progressive Education never succeeded in one objective—to fuse
elementary and secondary schools in an unbroken sweep of creative
development. But as the graduates of the new training accumulated on high
school teaching staffs and as the proportion of the population entering high
school rose, the Whole Child—by then the Whole Adolescent, and a
handful he was!—took over in high school too, needing shops, studios,
theaters, gyms, field trips, cafeterias, a welter of special-interest clubs,
solicitous training in how not to fall over one's own feet—and a wealth of
elective courses to choose from. As yet discipline slackened little. A high
school boy seen holding hands with a high school girl within eyeshot of the
school was in deep trouble. But there was no checking the gradual but
resistless flooding in of the notion that anything a preadult wanted to do
should not be forbidden unless there was a devastatingly strong case against
it—Russian roulette, say.

What then seemed to be extreme permissiveness in educational theory
was more widely accepted in America than elsewhere possibly because
America's unusual receptivity to Freud had specially prepared the way. The
popular version of the don't-frustrate-your-child-with-arbitrary-patterns-of-
discipline approach was bound gradually to infiltrate the women's magazines. They held out longest in the pretoddler department. The chief
pediatric manuals of the 1920's, dominated by Dr. L. Emmett Holt's
archaic *The Care and Feeding of Children*, clung to pretty rigid discipline
about feeding, crying, excretion. Following that preeminent lead, *The Baby
Book*, compiled for *Women's World* in 1927 by Dr. Herman N. Bundesen,
Chicago's health commissioner, sponsored by the American Medical
Association and a panel of 100-odd eminent pediatricians and sold by
millions, allowed feeding only at rigidly regular times and forbade paying
heed to persistent crying once safety-pin and fouled-diaper trouble was
ruled out. If the baby were "allowed to cry it out . . . even though the
crying lasts for hours and is repeated for a number of days," the habit

would be broken. "The real trouble is that he has been given his way too much" by being cooed at and cuddled or fed when he sounded off. Bundesen recommended beginning pot training at two or three months, arbitrary measures against thumb-sucking and laid it down as one of Mother's Ten Commandments: "Thou shalt not spoil the baby by humoring him." [199] In the same late 1920's John B. Watson's also influential advice to mothers worked out to about the same thing—rear a baby to the talking age about the way you'd rear a promising puppy.

But the post-toddler, preclassroom situation softened up earlier. Maybe young parents accepted it more readily because to give one's young unusual latitude had long been an American trait. For a century European travelers had reported home that American small fry were holy terrors because nobody controlled them Old World-fashion. This was not one of the peevish libels that visitors borrowed from their predecessors' clichés; the testimony is so consistent from so many witnesses that doubt is impossible. The indiscipline of the younger generation appeared more or less simultaneously with the rise of American women to cultural hegemony, but that may be coincidence. Anyway by the end of the 1930's it had got so far that the Little Red Schoolhouse warned: "Some parents take the teachings of 'progressive parenthood' too literally . . . do not exercise enough restraint over their children, fearing foolishly that they may be unduly blocking some important impulse. This laxity . . . robs the child of the very security he needs in order to grow normally." [200] Chorus of conscientious parents: "You can't win!"

The policy of asking the school to do for progeny what parents could not or anyway did not do well enough gained momentum after 1908 through a new women's organization—the National Congress of Mothers and Parent-Teachers Associations. Its origin was even more gynocratic than its name. It was born as the National Congress of Mothers, created by able and nippy Alice McClellan Birney, who had hoped to be a doctor but as a young widow had a lucrative career in advertising in New York City (c. 1890!) and then remarried to bear and rear a family in Washington, D.C. The idea came to her, she said, with her third child: "Filled as my mind was with the great mystery of birth, the solemn responsibility of parenthood, and the utter helplessness of the little being by my side, I built in imagination a new world, such as . . . might be . . . if each newborn soul might enter life in a happy, uplifting environment." [201] Like-minded ladies at Lake Chautauqua to whom she opened her mind encouraged her. And when she got to the money-raising part she found a good angel-godmother—Mrs. Phoebe Apperson Hearst, wealthy widow of Senator George Hearst of California, fond of good causes in education and mistress of, among several quasi-royal residences, an overpowering Romanesque mansion in Washington. She had only one child but, as in the fable of the lioness, that one was William Randolph Hearst, king of yellow journalism. With that son she could not doubt the nation knew she was a mother.

At Mrs. Birney's call American mothers proved so aware of their world-refining mission that the clubwomen, lady educators and becorseted reformers representing them swamped the organizing meetings of the NCM and brushed aside the frivolous demurrer of a man who rose in that sea of bulbous hats to say, "What the world needs is a little more father." [202] They were addressed by, among others, Anthony Comstock on pornography; but there was more potential in Frank Hamilton Cushing, expert on the Zuñi Indians and mothers in primitive cultures, and in G. Stanley Hall with the classic Progressive Education doctrine that in school curricula the Child's "interests must be utilized, each at its golden period." [203] Mother . . . child . . . school was by then a natural progression. In 1901 the national NCM convention was sending out leaflets telling how to organize Parents' and Teachers' Auxiliaries in local schools. The eventual change of name to National Congress of Parents & Teachers only formalized a *fait accompli.* Nationally PTA's have worked on ancillary matters—juvenile courts, for instance—but as most of us now know, they concentrate on the public schools and have yet to rid themselves of the original postulate that mothers are *the* parents, fathers incidental—a point that biology seems to share.

It was a little graceless thus to ask schools to do for the Child what Grandmother would have considered her responsibility—and then insist on breathing down the schools' necks. The schools had the cleverness to approve, however. They badly needed sympathetic liaison with parent/taxpayers, for Progressive Education assumed that aside from the settlement house function, schools could do most for children when parents accepted purposes and methods. This tact was rewarded when many PTA's rallied behind Progressives when other taxpayers scolded and made schoolboards nervous. In the early 1920's, for instance, PTA's began to do what had probably been inevitable once they submitted to the embraces of G. Stanley Hall—formally support Progressive Education's most ticklish application of *in loco parentis,* classroom instruction in Sex.

Freud cannot be credited here. His hopes for sex education did not stand out among the teachings attracting his early following. Long before he reached Clark University, this innovation in pedagogy was already vigorous. It owed most to discovery of the exact etiology of syphilis and gonorrhea. Common sense had long known them to be infectious and contracted through carnal indulgence. But the new immunology spelled out their cryptic symptoms—infertility, blindness in the newborn, psychosis and so on, and the Problem Drama of Ibsen and Brieux used syphilis as a stage prop to the applause of the conscientiously well informed. At the time effective cures were lacking and prevention was the only reliable strategy,

So seventy years ago health-minded persons in Europe and America went to war against VD's two chief allies—prostitution and ignorance or disregard of the disease risks in promiscuity.

Nice Nelly still flourished, so prostitution was "the social evil," syphilis and gonorrhea "the social diseases." But the seriousness of the war was soon manifest in the Mann Act (1910), in the Rockefellers' sending Abraham Flexner to study prostitution in Europe and in radical-flavored agitation about the lack of economic opportunity for women that allegedly drove so many into whoring. Also in Progressive Education's adding sex education to Teacher's lengthening agenda—after all, without genitalia the Whole Child could hardly be considered whole. In 1904 an eminent dermatologist,* Dr. Prince Albert Morrow of New York City, fresh from a conference in Brussels on VD, published the first pertinent American text, *Social Diseases and Marriage*, and set up what became the American Federation for Sex Hygiene. Its sponsors included the ubiquitous Charles W. Eliot and G. Stanley Hall, plus Maurice A. Bigelow of Teachers College as bridge between the new frankness—for frankness it seemed at the time—and the school. This was no reluctant undertaking of onerous duty that would otherwise be scamped. Progressive Education volunteered with a whoop to tame Aphrodite and Priapus with sweet reason.

The scamping was real, however. Once society asked itself how children were supposed to learn the facts of reproductive life in spite of Nice Nelly, it could only mumble about their observing what went on in farmyards and the traditional role of parents in fielding Junior's or Sister's spontaneous questions. This was weak. Fewer and fewer children were in a position to observe farmyards, nor was what went on there good preparation for a society favoring monogamy. In the experimental Porter School in Adair County, Missouri, Mrs. Marie Turner Harvey, its genius teacher, had to give parents as well as pupils sex education precisely because farmyards and haylofts were so handy. She deplored that "almost morbid feeling of secrecy and shame that surrounds anything pertaining to sex in country districts. . . . If children know no more than what they see and have acquired a strong feeling of secrecy about [it] . . . they are . . . much more apt to succumb to temptations . . . based on curiosity." [204] To help parents handle younger offspring's queries, she imported specialist lecturers for schoolhouse meetings of fathers and mothers reared to stammering reticence; older pupils were also given instruction emphasizing social responsibilities and penalties.

When storks and cabbage leaves still obscured so much, about the best a child could expect was "You'll understand when you're older." In 1910 an

---

* Since the symptoms of syphilis often include skin lesions, it was traditionally in the dermatologist's province. I do not know how Dr. Morrow came by his curious name. It must somehow have been part of the mid-1800's respectful awareness of Queen Victoria's consort that put the name "Prince Albert" on a pipe tobacco and a variety of frock coat.

article by highly respected novelist Margaret Deland written for the *Ladies' Home Journal* on the causal relation between illegitimate conceptions and ignorance of how babies are begotten produced more than 30,000 subscription cancellations from readers indignantly certain that such topics should never be publicly mentioned under any circumstances. Actually, of course, many a not too dull city boy put together an approximation of the biological facts by blending his playmates' snickering hints, his elders' occasional unguardedly crude remarks, sometimes accidental observation, sometimes older girls' ministrations. Bigelow found that most normal boys had thus learned the score by the age of twelve; all but the most carefully shielded girls by the age of fifteen. But sex hygienists deplored such "learning from the gutter." Nor could one count on it; else it would not still be true—even now that the new frankness fills the air—that social workers find many a slum-reared adolescent an experienced fornicator without being aware that's how babies are made. For such reasons Nearing's survey of *The New Education* (1912) included sex instruction as another field in which parents had failed society, so the schools must take over. Confidently he proclaimed: ". . . it is ignorance of sex matters that leads to immorality or disaster." [205]

It sounded good at the time even though Dr. Richard C. Cabot of the Harvard Medical School did grumble that detailed knowledge of the physiology and sociology of reproduction never kept his medical students out of trouble. The experts' poor opinion of parents as tutors in erotica was probably justified. Indeed, *c.* 1923 John B. Watson, America's leader in behaviorist psychology, branded them as "the most dangerous of instructors [in sex]. I have yet to see the parent whom I would like to have instruct a child of mine." [206] But any kind of family life implied such persistent risk of the subject coming up that Watson eventually had to make recommendations for all intending fathers and mothers based on the experience of a few of his acquaintance who were receptive and realistic enough—and if you weren't like that, you had no business having children to begin with. Mrs. X, for instance, encouraged her little boy to be present during her bath. At twenty months he knew the names of his and her sexual equipment; at three years he had Daddy's all blueprinted too and yearned for pubic hair. When Mommy had another baby, he followed the pregnancy with great interest. She grew anxious after his fourth birthday because he ceased to inquire into such matters. Dutifully she broke through this ominous reticence with a motherly chat about broody birds and gravid tigresses. . . . Watson prescribed further briefings around the age of ten from a superhumanly knowledgeable and tactful physician, much reading in biology during adolescence and for college students a forthright course in "the *ars amandi,* for certainly love is an art and not an instinct." [207] He did not say whether the course should carry academic credit. The curious part is that much as he despised the romantic psychology behind Progressive Education, his

Behaviorism brought him out at much the same place, maybe farther along. In any case his widely influential preachments had as much to do as the nascent cult of nudism and misinterpretations of Freud with the number of young parents of the late 1920's who learned and practiced the duty of stripping for Junior.

Watson's was counsel-of-perfection stuff, however. Teacher, gamely accepting her assignment, was understandably inclined to be more gingerly. She avoided part of the issue by supplying Mommy and Daddy with bright little pamphlets on what to say when. Soon a bird meeting a bee hardly knew where to look for blushing. Secondary schools were not to have explicit classes in sex-as-such—as is often done today—but to tuck into courses in biology and home economics disguisedly pertinent data gradually to fuse into fumbly knowledge. Teachers College set up a course in sex education for teachers-to-be not planning to take biology. For explicit sex instruction, Bigelow advised, boys should be segregated from girls and only "very mature women" chosen to teach the boys if no man were available, for "I fear danger for some boys if they are frankly instructed by attractive young women . . . only ten to fifteen years older than their pupils." [208]

In spite of those risks such schemes doubtless had residual healthy effects, particularly toward sex hygiene's original purpose—to check VD and concomitantly promote monogamy as basis for social stability. Much of the patter on that point anticipated the early birth control crusaders' praise of connubial joys as ecstatic sacrament. Elder overtones were borrowed from *The Idylls of the King, Silas Marner, Tess of the D'Urbervilles,* to set the stage for a new attitude toward licit erotics. Maybe knowing of the disasters that struck King Arthur's realm because Guinevere and Launcelot couldn't leave each other alone did keep some hard-pressed girl from succumbing in the hay. More grimly sex education also borrowed the Temperance crusader's trick of securing captive audiences of youth by taking over so-called hygiene or physiology courses in high schools. Detailed descriptions of general paresis were the same sort of tool as the Temperance lecturer's luridly colored lithograph of the alcoholic's hobnailed liver. The drugstore corner loafer's destructive byword that a dose of clap was no worse than a bad cold was constructively rebutted. And though nobody dared recommend the condom as either prophylaxis or contraceptive, the epidemiologist (if not the psychiatrist) welcomed the teaching—which was then necessarily a practical fact—that both syphilis and gonorrhea were likely consequences of pre- and extramarital goings-on.

For another ticklish subject *c.* 1914 the preferred doctrines about masturbation were harsh and obviously weakly grounded; old wives' tales about idiocy and physical debility were only very gradually modified. On such a topic militancy was inevitable, however. Few parents were then ready to have Teacher virtually tell Junior go ahead, why not? as might be done today. But they could stay fuzzy-minded about it because comfortably aware that once school took over this aspect of child rearing, they could neglect it more flagrantly than ever. So in one watery, twitchy form or another, sex education was encouraged to spread not only into public schools but also into YM-YWCA's, Scouting, certain private schools—in *Dodsworth* (1929) a preadolescent girl giggles because "telling us about sex" makes a teacher in her private school "scared and silly" when "all us kids know all about it already." [209] (How that teacher must have envied the nuns in the Catholic girls' high school the other side of town, confident that they would never be told now, Sister, we must work some sex data into your botany class.) The pace was glacier-slow, however, and small steady advances were kept more undercover than was thought necessary after the 1930's.

Good tactics—particularly because in the 1920's the USSR's zeal for sex education gave it an embarrassing pinkness impertinent but awkward. As part of the unchaining, bourgeois-flouting new day Lenin's Communism embarked on a syndrome of emancipating women, reforming whores, loosening relations between the sexes with contraception as corollary—and adopting Progressive Education as the powerful social tool that its Western leaders represented it to be, fostering collectivist attitudes and breaking down the family as dominant social unit. With all that sex education was, of course, cozily at home. Before the new regime got schools properly coordinated, some local experiments went as far as arranging for classes to observe how dogs do it and ornamenting the classroom wall with charts showing incidence of first successful masturbations among normal adolescents by sex and age and the practically unanimous preference of Moscow's university students for extramarital relations instead of marriage. As things cooled down, educational authorities backed away with warnings that sex education could readily "arouse the sexual emotions prematurely and . . . cause tremendous injury" and that "before showing such [materials as those charts] to the pupils . . . one would have to lose all pedagogical sense." [210] But the USSR remained the only nation formally committed to what was still described *c.* 1930 as "Frank sex teaching . . . of all ages . . . lectures, books, pamphlets . . . radio, travelling exhibits and demonstrations. In the school simple lessons in nature study and biology are followed by lectures on the anatomy and physiology of sex organs and on general sex hygiene." [211] It sounds as if those in charge had EdD's from Teachers College. Ella Winter, volunteer propagandist for the USSR and wife of Steffens, admired the sex-oriented captions of high school wall newspapers: "What Role the Pioneer Movement Plays in the Diminution of Masturbation. . . . All Forces to the Venereal Front!" [212]

"Demonstrations" above brings up sex education's built-in trouble as a branch of Progressive Education—what about Learning by Doing? It was thrown back on the didactic, word-bound methods of instructions deplored in all other contexts. Another hitch, maybe related, is that, as Donald Barr has pointed out, classroom treatment of sex, supposing it stays this side of the arousal that Teacher must avoid, omits its primary nature: ". . . the sexual drive . . . has always been particularly difficult to reconcile with civilization. Schools transmit civilization. What, if anything, are they to do about sex? . . . We need to help pupils reach out for . . . emphasis on sexuality, not sex. Sex without a valued sexuality can result at best in a series of nervous explosions, orgasms which are just sneezes of the genitalia." [213]

When studying Mrs. Harvey's rural-Progressive school, Dewey's saga- cious daughter Evelyn was dismayed by the poor quality of local farming. In spite of earnest agricultural missionary work by federal and state governments Adair County in 1914 still planted and harvested with little more knowledge than its grandfathers had commanded and little more foresight than the Scriptural sluggard. The same reproach could have been laid on the whole America of which Missouri's degenerating soils were only part—lack of national husbandry in the widest sense. A growing demand for sweeping reform in this area of concern was firming up in what was already called a "conservation movement."

On the train between Frankfurt and Bad Nauheim that peaceful spring of 1914, Owen Wister, cosmopolite author of *The Virginian*, hence a chief creator of the Western genre, admired a prodigiously tidy and well-man- aged forest. He learned it had shown a profit for its owner, the city of Frankfurt, for seven centuries. He "thought of American forests looted and levelled . . . of ourselves toasting our glorious future while we obliterated the future's resources . . . [of the] hasty American . . . [with] nobody to make him look after [his country] while he rushed about climbing . . . to a higher skyscraper." [214] Crony of conservation-minded Theodore Roosevelt, Wister was a bitter foe of his own country's poor planning and worse housekeeping. The eloquence of his bitterness fitted its occasion. Concern for trees, the earth-cumbering vegetables that had so hampered early America, was long overdue. And it was concern for trees that led America into our present complicated struggle so to reshape the "hasty American" and his environment that he can survive his noxious effects on it.

Even in pre-Revolutionary times a township uneasy about supply might ban the felling of certain kinds of tree or the killing of deer immobilized by deep snow. George Perkins Marsh, learned and original-minded politician diplomat from Vermont, published his *The Earth as Modified by Human Action* in 1864; few heeded its warnings. But concern was not altogether lacking. That same year certain Californians' respect for the venerable redwoods of Mariposa and the majestic Yosemite Valley persuaded the U.S. Congress to set them aside as public parks, and since Uncle Sam had no administrative machinery to look after them, the state of California became their caretaker. Eight years later, at the height of the Gilded Age, when sordid gain was supposed to engross politicians, agitation about the geysers, waterfalls, bears and other wonders of the Upper Yellowstone moved Congress to make the area the first National Park with a caretaker Park Service to match.

Simultaneously a thoughtful journalist-politician, J. Sterling Morton, prodded the relatively treeless state of Nebraska into starting a national Arbor Day movement to encourage towns, schools and such to plant trees with due dendrophile ceremony. This emphasized shade rather than forest planting that was even worse needed; besides, to most Americans the word "arbor" conveyed only an openwork thing for vines to climb on. But at least Arbor Day reversed the pioneer's view of trees as usually nuisances. In 1873 Congress again moved toward conservation by giving special privileges to any settler on the public domain (largely Western) who planted and maintained for ten years forest-style a given number of trees on his 160-acre homestead. The theory was that settlement and the departure of the Indians—who used prairie fires as hunting aids—had lowered the hazard of fire, that the vanishing of the buffalo, browsing enemies of natural reforestation, had made young trees far likelier to live, so that some restoration of the stands of trees that had off and on graced the Great Plains in pre-Indian and -buffalo times was practical. And so it might have been, only the homesteader seldom planted the right kinds. The arrangement became only another way to legal subterfuges under which individual and corporate land grabbers could raid the nation's free acres.

Yet a tingle of promise came in 1891 when Uncle Sam, trying again where individuals had failed, made experimental plantings in Nebraska that eventuated in the great shelterbelt program of forty-odd years later under the New Deal. And that same year private initiative took a momentous step toward intelligent forestry in America, the results of which are still spreading today. Of three men responsible the unlikeliest was George W. Vanderbilt—heir to a great share of the famous fortune, then ornamenting the hills outside Asheville, North Carolina, with a pseudo-ducal estate centered on a huge pseudo-chateau of French Renaissance flavor built in Indiana limestone. Fortunately this did not mean he was altogether a crass plutocrat of the pseudo-chateau sort, instead "a slim, simple and rather shy young man . . . unmarried but without racing stables or chorus girls in his cosmos." [215] To landscape his extensive new toy he had hired the great Frederick Law Olmsted, creator of New York City's Central Park, the Chicago Columbian Exposition of 1893 and dozens of other highly influential projects that made him the father of imaginative land esthetics in the United States. Studying the thousands of Vanderbilt's acres on which the original forest had been annihilated by lumbermen's ruthlessness and then inhibited by the ignorantly destructive farming methods of local hillmen, Olmsted advised calling in a young friend of his—Gifford Pinchot, fresh from learning European-style forestry in France. This context of

Frenchness and Monseigneurial forests, tantara! probably helped. So, probably, did Pinchot's proving to be a tall, lean, charming Yale man from an affluent Pennsylvanian family of standing even though not smothered in millions Vanderbilt-style. So, maybe, did his contention that sound forestry applied to Vanderbilt's land could pay for itself from the start. Anyway Vanderbilt gave him his head at Biltmore, thus doing his country an ecological favor so large that it may well have more than compensated for the shell games with which Commodore Cornelius Vanderbilt made that fortune.

Pinchot gave the credit to his own father, John Pinchot, grandson of an émigré officer of Napoleon's. He, like Wister, admired European forestry, loved the woods of the family estate on the Delaware and had once asked his outdoors-minded elder son, "How would you like to be a forester?" At the French government's forestry school at Nancy the boy learned theory and practice as alien to American ways as cannibalism—the forest as a farm for trees cut when mature, grown again for future cutting in "sustained yield," making a profit on land unfit for other use and acting as water controller, climate gentler and game shelter for its neighborhood. Pinchot took it all in while yet aware that European methods would have to be modified to suit American conditions—a point neglected by the few European foresters previously come to America. But he did not modify his purpose to keep sound forestry economically self-supporting on Biltmore's fouled-up hillsides.

In 1893 a striking display of how it was done drew fertile notice at Chicago's Columbian Exposition. It made Pinchot Mr. U.S. Forestry and, suppose any single person deserved the name, Mr. U.S. Conservation. As leading edge of the U.S. Forest Service he steered President Theodore Roosevelt in expanding the system of National Forests that now keeps a tenth of the country under federal control. Of all TR's bustling achievements his ecological work—creating new National Parks, game refuges and bird sanctuaries and beginning to revive the waterways—have probably been of greatest long-run benefit. It was Pinchot and staff who (borrowing unaware from Marsh and Britain's foresters in India) tagged the trend "conservation." Then, quitting Washington when President Taft's administration proved unsympathetic, Pinchot became Mr. Forestry for Pennsylvania to show what a state could do with trees and intelligence.

In his European-trained view forests were not to be mined like mineral deposits or turned into tree museums, but kept productive by cutting and regrowth—and within reason other uses. Cattle and sheep, for instance, might graze within the new boundaries but only on the Forest Service's terms aimed to safeguard trees and long-term supply of forage. This caused tumult among stockmen used to grazing that ruined the public range regardless of posterity's interests. Further tumult arose among lumbermen hoping to acquire by hook, crook or any combination of the two the rich timberlands still publicly owned. But eventually it appeared that in National Forests intelligent harvesting had a place. Private loggers willing to keep their noses clean and protect young trees and the land as required could buy and market mature trees at a profit. Some loggers, already gnawing into the tremendous forests of Oregon and Washington after plundering those of the Lake states, saw so much light that they dabbled in sustained-yield reforestation themselves. By thus serving as huge demonstration project, National Forests would have been worthwhile had they not also protected watersheds and, as economics took hold, brought in cash revenue in nine figures—20 percent of it going to the counties, usually lean ones, where the system holds land. The service's example of fire prevention begot the never-ending but long since rewarding battle of engineering, organization and public relations to check the national disgrace of forest fires. When young Pinchot returned from France, more timber was burning each year than regrowth replaced.

As the War approached, it was still possible for a lumberman answering a Forest Service questionnaire to reply to "What do you do about reproduction?": "No such thing allowed in my camps." But sooner than might have been expected of so hard-nosed an industry some large companies acquired such realistic habits as employing professional foresters, leaving "seed trees" for windblown propagation of certain species in logged-off areas, refining logging methods and tools to minimize damage to young growth— notions new then but now rather widely practiced. Note that it was necessarily soulless corporations that led in following the Pinchot-created public example. The rugged individual settler or small logger was not likely to see in a fine stand of timber anything but so many car- or schoonerloads of lumber or an encumbrance to a potential plowed field or open pasture. He never dreamed of reforestation partly because most trees take too long to become another crop of usable wood. Being naturally geared to short-run economics, he had no interest in schemes that would show returns only well after he was dead. Large corporations, on the other hand, derive from being soulless the privilege of living far longer than most people. For them, once it was suggested and proved feasible, tree planting in 1914 for harvest in 1970 could be seen to make sense.

New technologies further supported the forester. It was widely accepted that forest around upper courses and headwaters meant deeper, steadier flow of river systems. Particularly west of the Rockies river systems were already indispensable to vast irrigation projects making farms of what had been desert—also to hydroelectric power created by dams. The first came of examples set by Spanish missionaries in California and the amazingly regenerated Mormons of Utah. The second was born in Appleton, Wisconsin, in 1882 and boomed when George Westinghouse invented the transformer system that took turbine-made current long distances by cable, whisking energy from dam site to far-distant factory or city. Once water-spun dynamos were big business, forestry could get a hearing by stressing the relation between forest reserves and rivers. As flush toilets and daily baths took over, cities had to have vastly enlarged reservoirs also dependent on tree cover in their catchment areas—and that too strengthened forest-mindedness.

The effect could be unpretty. The Hetch Hetchy basin near Yosemite, also a potential National Park, was instead devoted to holding water for Northern California and ceased to be a wonder of nature. When the Niagara & Mohawk Power Company made hydroelectric use of West Canada Creek on the southern edge of the Adirondacks, the roaring cascades of Trenton Falls, as famous as Niagara a century ago, were destroyed. Today's public is better aware of these issues. Conservationists doughtily resist the felling of redwoods and overzealous dam building, just as lumber companies publish advertisements patting themselves on the back for sustained-yield forestry. Such a pat is often not ill deserved—only it is most unlikely they would ever have got around on their own to replacing tree mining with tree farming.

Pinchot's personality was part of it all. Light-stepping and slender as he aged, mustached like a Remington trooper, he combined Don Quixote and D'Artagnan and, though he belonged to the best clubs in the East, was no textbook-bound tenderfoot. He could ride, shoot and lose his temper at the right time with any cattleman or miner on whom his rangers kept tabs. A fine example of something new among sons of moneyed families—TR was another—the boy preferring public service to the factory or bank that made the family wealth, working as hard and effectively as if he were young Cornelius Vanderbilt with a fortune to make.

While Pinchot and Roosevelt showed that Knights of the Silver Spoon could be invaluable public servants, 1914 saw the first impact of reforms boding ill for silver spoons such as theirs. The year before Sarajevo a new constitutional amendment erased a long-standing U.S. Supreme Court decision and opened the way for a graduated federal income tax; with it came a graduated inheritance tax. Both were already established in the Old World. At first this two-edged weapon was applied too gingerly to hamper the bloating of existing fortunes and the sprouting of new ones under the forced draft of the War and the renowned boom of the 1920's. Over the decades, however, the effect was to some extent what liberals had sought and reactionaries dreaded. It grew harder for old money to be exuberant and for new Vanderbilts, Rockefellers or Mackays to create personal economic empires.

Slippery lawyers and complaisant tax agencies and legislators have heavily braked this, of course. The classic example—depletion allowances in the extractive industries, particularly oil—is the reason why most of the nation's large personal fortunes today are oil-connected. Less dramatic but heavy modification has come through expense charges, capital gains clauses, stock options, trust funds, tax-exempt securities and good-works foundations. In spite of ingenuity, however, Morgan's huge yachts and the Vanderbilts' hyper-gaudy palaces have had few American successors. One reason may be that it is widely recognized—except west of the Sabine River—that ostentation is poor public relations. Another certainly is that it is now more difficult to lay down the extra-deep layers of pecuniary fat required. Economic empires are less often personal than in William C. Whitney's and Samuel Insull's time. Now they are likely to be bank-mid-wifed, multilayer monsters steered by teams of extravagantly paid managers succeeding one another through an arid gamesmanship not unlike revolutions in Central American countries. Less scope for the various but always showy idiosyncrasies of Goulds and Flaglers.

Henry Ford was one of the few resisting that trend. He sloughed off his first financial backers early. The second set he got rid of in 1919—after making them large fortunes of their own—by his only major resort to bank money. The economic buoyancy of the Model T and the blackjacking merchandising methods with which he distributed it enabled him to get clear of the banks with amazing speed. Early in the 1920's he was permanent personal master of a vertically integrated industrial kingdom of the billion-dollar order—as self-centered as Selkirk on his island, as anachronistic as the McGuffey school readers that he lovingly reprinted. A striking spectacle, but about all it meant was that his crackpot genius was close to unique. In 1913–14 his real significance was not at all anachronistic but as timely as Freud. He was giving the world its classic, most advanced example, never substantially improved on till automation loomed up, of mass production by complexly timed, moving assembly lines—a chief key to the rising production-per-man-hour that was revolutionizing American standards of living. And on January 5, 1914, he smashed previous clichés about wages—both Marx's and those of the National Association of Manufacturers—by proclaiming a basic minimum wage of $5 a day,* more or less double the going rates, in his factory in Detroit.

His reason for this flashily unnecessary step, apparently a suggestion from James Couzens, a close associate, was a vague belief that to pay more to the labor doing the manufacturing would help keep demand for manufactures high. Or say that thus to dramatize the link between rising production and the need to broaden consumer demand recognized the new efficiencies of his Highland Park assembly line. At the time he was groping toward profit sharing and paternalistic uplift. Being disinclined to think things through and temperamentally unable to stick to a subject, he was also muttering about timing annual layoffs to coincide with the harvest

* At least that was what his statements led others to believe. The actual pay scales resulting were confusing but did tend to create a rather undulating flow at the $5 level and did recognize the importance of taking account of the wage earner as consumer.

season, so Ford workers could lend the farmer a hand. But little of that got into the headlines. The glowing notion of a great industrialist of the strive-and-succeed sort showing up conventional employers as myopic penny pinchers made him world-famous overnight, better known to the masses from Poland to Hawaii than any other American in history. Of all his grandstand plays—and as the Peace Ship would show, his knack with them matched P. T. Barnum's—this was the masterpiece.

Whence Couzens got the idea is unknown. Shrewd, tough and tireless, he was very valuable to Ford and, after selling out for millions, made a second career as a far better than average U.S. Senator. He could never have thought of it himself. Some of its ingredients were already in the air in Detroit and elsewhere. In 1910 industrialists opposing rises in rail freight rates told Congress that the railroads wouldn't need rises if they would only cut their costs by applying the revolutionary new "Taylor System." This fixed national attention on a certain Frederick Winslow Taylor, a deftly practical theorist from Philadelphia, who had been doing more than others before or since to show mankind how to get the most out of modern industry. Specifically as to the automobile industry, says Keith Sward's cogent book on Ford, "[Taylor] anticipated all the production methods that were to take Detroit by storm." [216] A disciple of his had applied some of his ideas at General Motors, and in 1909 Taylor himself had brought the gospel to Detroit in a four-hour lecture to the Packard Motor Car Company's top echelon. In 1914 he returned sponsored by the Detroit Board of Commerce to lecture to foremen and shop superintendents from every automobile plant in the area.

After 1910 the Taylor System was more intelligibly called scientific management, in its early phases more familiarly time-and-motion study, and its creator was famous (deservedly) among industrialists and growingly infamous (rather undeservedly) among labor. His specialty was to look at manipulation—tools, materials, shop arrangements—as if neither he nor others had ever seen such a thing before and question down to the bone whether that was the best way to handle, shape or arrange it. He had always been like that. He may have been the first to pitch a baseball overhand. He invented a special-shaped tennis racket that he used to become an early U.S. doubles champion. He designed his own golf clubs and, to get good turf on the putting green on his suburban estate, put as much research and ingenuity into grass, fertilizer and consistency of soils as he ever had into the belting, machine speeds and positioning of lathes to turn steel axles for the Pullman Company. This driving originality of mind meshed with his technological ingenuity to make him the second American—Eli Whitney first, Ford the third—revolutionizing world industry. Nor was he the tunnel-vision expert seeing only that to do something in less time with less energy was good because it could be so done. Taylor believed—and spent much of his later life trying to persuade others—that his work could not only bring out the best in industry as producer for consumers but also reduce the rankling tangle of industry's labor relations.

He was born to cultivated affluence and went on into strive-and-succeed. His parents were well-to-do, dilettantish, comfortable in Germantown, then a choice suburb of Philadelphia. Fred had foreign travel, Exeter, Harvard Law School. His eyes went bad; he entered a pump-manufacturing plant to learn the machinist's trade. In the hard times of the late 1870's he did pick-and-shovel common labor in the Midvale Steel Company. Soon surfacing in a skilled trade, he operated a lathe daytimes and studied engineering at night. Presently foreman of the machine shop, he gained early fame in the industry with a radically original design for the largest steam hammer ever built. Less conspicuously he tinkered with imaginatively changing the layout of the plant's machine tools and adjusting labor time to production needs. By 1893 he was an independent consultant, first into a profession he himself invented and defined portentously on his business card as "Systematizing Shop Management and Manufacturing Costs." [217] In a few years the great Bethlehem Steel Company made him its manufacturing superintendent. Now he had the major industrial plant he needed as testing ground for ideas he was bursting with.

He was admirably equipped. He was a crack machinist. He had had horny-handed experience forcing a shovel into a pile of sand. Having worked alongside both the skilled and the unskilled, as one of the crowd, as foreman over them, he knew from both sides of the coin the vast amount of waste motion, some deliberate, some customary, some just wrongheaded, plus sheer shirking, that went on. In his view the wages of even the typical skilled man were both unconscionably small and seldom fully earned. Everybody he had observed as he strove-and-succeeded—boss, foreman, skilled workman, laborer—took it for granted that the way a man shoveled slag or poured castings or figured piecework rates was more or less up to him and that industrial wage earners would, as they always had, adjust their pace to that of the slow men in the gang to shield them from being fired and the whole gang from threat of being overworked. Everybody but Fred Taylor. He was temperamentally unable to admit that things had to be done clumsily, wastefully, sulkily and, as he saw it, unfairly to all.

Bethlehem let him experiment in corners. With stopwatch and slide rule he studied laborers shifting 98-pound iron pigs from stockpile to railroad car, the simplest of tasks—pick up pig with both hands, carry it up a ramp, put it down, go back and do it again. The gang averaged 12½ tons a day. Analysis gave interesting hints as to the temperament and bodily build best for such work, the best way to pick up a pig, the rhythms of alternate exertion and rest that minimized fatigue. Taylor chose a notably stolid Pennsylvania Dutchman whose stamina was attested by his habit of jogging a mile home after wrestling pig iron all day and persuaded him, by hope of increased pay, to be experimented on. "Now pick up a pig . . . now walk

. . . slower . . . now sit down and rest . . ." said the man with the stopwatch day after day. Gradually Schmidt shifted more and more iron with less fatigue until he was up to 47½ tons a day, feeling better than ever before when the whistle blew *and* taking home $1.85 a day instead of $1.15. Taylor persuaded others in the gang to take the same training, moved those physically unsuited to it to other tasks in the plant—and pig iron was being loaded 300 percent faster at an added cost of only 60 percent more wages paid.

The new light was turned on shoveling—iron ore, coal, ashes, limestone, sand, slag. . . . Customarily each laborer had his own shovel and worked just briskly enough to keep up with tacit standards set by mutual mistrust between foreman and hands. Stopwatch, slide rule, scales and imagination worked it out that to minimize fatigue, 21 pounds was the optimum shovel load, given a certain timing of rest intervals. Since 21 pounds of ashes are bulkier than the same weight of coal, Taylor issued different sizes of shovel for each material handled and trained the shovelers in the most efficient motions. To break up defensive slowdowns and let each man show he was personally earning prospective higher pay, each was assigned an ash heap or carful of ore all his own. Again those not physically up to the new pace were shifted to other jobs. And once the procedures were shaken down, the average shoveler was moving 59 instead of 16 tons a day; pay up from $1.15 to $1.88.

To keep track of individual assignments and results, daily production, tool issue, car positioning and other such details in this new way of running, a plant required many new-hired planners, checkers, stockroom and tool help—soldiers in the new army of scientific management. But even with their wages counted in, the average cost of moving a ton of sand or ore was down 54.5 percent. Applying these principles to manufacturing departments, Taylor found—not at all to his surprise—comparable savings:

> The work of every workman is planned out at least one day in advance . . . written instructions describing in detail the task . . . as well as the means to be used . . . not only what is to be done but how . . . and the exact time allowed for doing it . . . whenever the workman succeeds in doing his task right, and within the time limit . . . he receives an addition of from 30 . . . to 100 per cent of his ordinary wages . . . if [he] fails to do his task, some competent teacher should . . . guide, help and encourage him, and, at the same time, study his possibilities. . . . So that [if it's indicated] he [may] be shifted to another class of work. . . .[218]

It was soon clear that most industrial operations were fair game for these methods. An eminent disciple of Taylor's, Frank B. Gilbreth (also famous in the 1940's as the exuberant and prolific father of *Cheaper by the Dozen*), won his spurs in the new field by spectacularly revising the venerable trade of bricklaying. A ball-bearing factory called Taylor in to improve the efficiency of its women employees inspecting the product for flaws. He used tests not unlike those of modern psychologists to pick out girls of specially quick visual discernment and worked with them to set up new patterns of alternate eyework and relaxation. In the end 35 girls were doing what had previously required 120; accuracy was two-thirds higher, and they were getting double their former pay for an eight- instead of ten-hour day, plus two days off a month for a physiological need that employers had seldom recognized before.

A Philadelphia engineer, Carl Barth, became Taylor's right hand, developing subtle mathematical formulas for this new science and diabolically complicated slide rules to manipulate them. "A plant that [Barth and Taylor] made over was made over from top to bottom," said the New York *Times* at Taylor's death. ". . . from the duties of the boy who carried drinking water to the unskilled laborers to the duties of the President . . . emphasizing the necessity for the humane treatment of labor." [219] By 1911, very comfortably retired on the royalties from his 100-odd patents, Taylor enjoyed himself as unpaid consultant for any management sincerely interested. "At least 50,000 workmen in the United States are now employed under this system," he announced, ". . . receiving from 30 to 100 per cent. higher daily wages . . . while the companies employing them are more prosperous than before . . ." Emphatically he added: "In place of the suspicious watchfulness and the more or less open warfare which characterizes the ordinary types of management there is universal friendly cooperation between the management and the men." [220] For he went on believing that proper use of his methods, always respecting the need to give employees enough time to understand that stopwatch and work sheet would probably mean higher pay, less fatigue and pleasanter working conditions, could leach away the poison spoiling industrial relations. He had seen it happen. The "soldiering" that his conscience hated—the slowdown to protect clumsy habit, the square peg in the round hole or the born dawdler—dwindled away in shops through which the cleansing wind of scientific management blew. Good feeling thus created was, he taught, insurance against strikes as well as the road to profit.

To complaints that the benefits were uneven, that while the boss' costs fell sharply, wages, though higher, did not rise in proportion, he had two replies, the first paternalistic and shaky: Studies led him to believe that though well-earned pay rises up to 60 percent made workers "not only more thrifty but better men . . . they . . . begin to save money, become more sober," rises above 60 percent often proved demoralizing, leading them to "work irregularly, become more or less shiftless and dissipated." [221] The second was good economic statesmanship: Sound management would not pay out all new cost savings in dividends but use much of it to reduce the sales price of the product, undercutting competition and directly or indirectly widening use of the product. That is, lower prices for pig iron led to lower prices for steel in threshing machines, lower prices on ball bearings led to lower prices on bicycles, hence expanded sales of both. Look beyond workmen and employers, Taylor said, "to the great third party—the consumers, who buy the product of the first two and who ultimately pay the wages of the workman and the profits of the employers . . . this great third party should be given its share of the gain." [222] It also followed that scientific management would not only give the workman more dollars, each dollar would buy more—a rise in "real wages" enabling him to want and have more. Time study and work sheets led to this classic doctrine—the standard of living rising in consequence of rising production-per-man-hour resulting from rising efficiency of men and machines.

Doubtless a garbled version of that is what Couzens and Ford had in mind when dazzling the world with $5 a day. I do not know Taylor's opinion of their gesture. This candid man of immense ability and significance died the next year, fortunately before the severe disappointments to which his ideas were doomed could overtake him. One trouble was the self-styled "efficiency experts" who, borrowing a few tricks and phrases, used them to cram poorly masked speedups down the throats of poorly prepared work forces. Their "historic place in management engineering," wrote a disciple of Taylor's in the early 1930's, "is comparable to that of the quack and shyster in medicine and law." [223] They gave Taylorism a bad name among diehard bosses and to an unfortunate extent among labor leaders. Another trouble was that in any but the cleverest hands Taylorism made the workman feel like what it actually doomed him to be—a temporary part of the machine. Detroit's use of time-and-motion study, gouging out of Taylorism the cruder, obvious elements, did produce the split-second nightmare that Chaplin so brilliantly exploited in *Modern Times.*

At best the psychological skills that Taylor taught to his genuine disciples could only distract from the essence of the situation—that (in terms of today) the workman is bartering a quarter to a third of his adult life for a powerboat and a portable TV. Something like that had always been true of shovel labor; only in Taylor's youth the equation was half-your-life = bare livelihood. But when Midvale Steel's machinists accepted Taylor's detailed instructions how to set up, time and handle the turning of axles instead of working out their own, often wrongheaded ways . . . that made them flesh-and-blood forerunners of the little black automation box that now sometimes replaces them in operating lathes.

Taylorism was probably in for cumulative trouble anyway because it was incurably unilateral. The girls in that ball-bearing plant owed vastly improved wages, hours and working conditions not to the employer's sudden good-heartedness, or a strike, or collective bargaining with goodwill lubricating good faith, but to outside experts. Taylorism grasped the necessity of securing the workman's willingness to be retrained on the grounds he would get more and—it was hoped—better dollars. But it seldom sought his help in improving methods—Taylor obviously felt that a common laborer's notions of shovel handling were probably wrong, as indeed they usually proved to be—or dealt with him as anything but a warm body under pressure from grocers and mortgage holders. To read Taylor's *The Principles of Scientific Management*, one would never suspect labor unions existed; casual mention of strikes is the only hint. In 1910, of course, the bulk of labor was still unorganized. But this was poor preparation for the future. Even supposing a Taylorized plant's die casters did belong to an AFL craft union, the programming of their work, the tools they handled, the timing of their tasks, the determination of how much extra pay accrued to them from the consequent cost savings, all that was determined on high and handed down with, at best, great courtesy—never a nod at the union leaders, no awareness of the maxim of today's experienced management: Never appear to originate better wages, hours or working conditions. Always make sure that they look as if wrung from a more or less reluctant boss by the union strategists.

In a funeral tribute to Taylor, Justice Louis D. Brandeis of the U.S. Supreme Court, a staunch liberal with a concern about the labor movement and the less savory aspects of industry, noted:

> Those for whom he labored most, the working people, are not represented at this meeting. It was Taylor's purpose to make the laborer worthy of his hire; to make the hire worthy of the laborer; to make the standard of living and the conditions of working worthy to be called American . . . [he] met . . . widespread opposition from those whom he particularly sought to help . . . due to misunderstanding . . . [it] can be overcome only through securing the affirmative cooperation of the labor organizations. . . . The obstacles are great. Twenty-five years may be required to remove them fully. . . . In no other way can we attain in full measure the increase of productivity upon which our well-being so largely depends.[224]

Twenty-five years later, in 1940, America's production-per-man-hour had most impressively increased and the harsh 1930's had taught management something about arriving at consent of the employees through their own leaders. Taylorism had ramified into techniques of shop betterment, market research, personnel policies that had been only gleams in its father's eye. But thanks to its basic unilateral grain and maybe to lack of imagination among labor leaders, it was too often applied Detroit-style, and sometimes hardly at all. Consider American railroads. Had Taylor been turned loose on that snug harbor for featherbedding, already stagnant in his time, as was suggested in 1910, it might not now be our outstanding economic disgrace. Still, suppose railroad management had invited Taylor in, the brotherhoods would probably have fought him to a standstill.

Since Taylor's fame among industrialists and nervous labor leaders did not entail equal public awareness of what his work meant, the Ford-Couzens gesture had its point. However backhandedly, it served notice on the American economy, already deeply affected by the synergism between industrial mechanization and consumer-aimed advertising, that the breadwinner as consumer was coming into his own. The implied upward surge in the gross national product would have occurred without Ford's dramatizing the possibility, and one cause would have been Taylor's ideas even though skimped or fragmentarily applied. But when Ford chose unilaterally to pay wages higher than the labor market then required, with a rising standard of living as specific aim, he so strikingly called attention to the consumer's future that this in itself probably did much to accelerate it.

The future of Ford's consumer as beneficiary of increased efficiency was brighter anyway through improvement in retailing, notably of food.

Come back sixty years to the corner grocery that sold most of what America ate in 1914. Typically family-owned, it afforded a fair living to Lester Ratcheese, its proprietor; his two sons, one in the meat department, the other doubling as sales assistant and driver of the delivery wagon; one daughter doubling as bookkeeper and backup sales assistant; only in the Saturday rush did Mrs. Ratcheese leave her housework next door and rally around. Enter their typical customer, Mrs. Clyde Pincenez, who lives within walking distance, approaching the counter behind which Mr. Ratcheese stands uttering deferential Good Mornings. The lady fumbles in her bag, eventually finds her grocery list, studies it and says she'd like some prunes, how much are they? . . . Well, two pounds. Mr. Ratcheese walks 15 feet to the case of bulk prunes, scoops out what should be 2 pounds into a paper bag, weighs it, frowns, returns to the case to fetch three more prunes to make the full weight, brings the bag to the counter and places it before her as deferentially as a retrieving dog. And a dime's worth of soda crackers. Mr. Ratcheese walks 10 feet to a rack of large, glass-topped, cubical biscuit boxes, puts crackers in a paper bag and lays it before her. Is the new cabbage in yet? Mr. Pincenez likes coleslaw this hot fall weather. Mr. Ratcheese goes 20 feet to the vegetable bins, fetches a sample head, learns two small ones is what she had in mind. . . .

Through thirteen items and sixteen minutes this unhurried ceremony gradually strews the counter with nourishment. At its other section Mabel Ratcheese is doing the same, with rather less deference, for the maid-of-all-work of Mrs. Pincenez's next-door neighbor, but Mrs. Pincenez is conscientious about doing her own marketing except in bad weather and seldom allows herself what more and more women are doing, telephoning the order so they never see what they're getting till the wagon brings it. "Soon as Jack's back, I'll have this over to you in a jiffy," says Mr. Ratcheese, making out the sales slip to add to Mrs. Pincenez's bill. She is already entering the butcher's department behind its glass partition to ask straw-hatted Russell Ratcheese the relative prices of frying and roasting chickens, complain about the price of soup meat and eventually settle on roast beef for Sunday dinner this time. And some bologna for the washwoman's lunch. It's more than a jiffy before the order is delivered, however, because a salesman for Staples, Hogshead & Company, the Chicago jobber that supplies the Ratcheeses, turns up two days late for the weekly order and Jack must wait on customers while father resists blandishments about a new line of canned fruits.

That counter system survives today only at the extremes—in the "fancy groceries" of the largest cities and most affluent resorts and in marginal neighborhood stores of the slums and remote country hamlets, which charge just about as much for basic items. Credit! Item-by-item assembly! Catch-as-catch-can stock control! Traveling salesman economics! The waste of man-hours and foot-pounds was obviously sinful, and the consequent unnecessary cost to the customer deplorable. Think what Taylor would have said about such a final stage of food distribution had his analytic mind been turned loose on it. When he died, this opportunity had not yet presented itself. The problem was working itself out spontaneously, however, in several disparate reforms that fused into the gigantic self-service, cash-and-carry chain supermarket of today. Its basics are: Make the customer do much that Mr. Ratcheese used to. Buy in quantities large enough to squeeze maximum discounts out of suppliers. Reinforce the consequent savings by keeping profit margins low. Never hesitate to go into wholesaling or processing when it looks tactically advisable. Overblown and sluggish with success as the supermarket now is, perversely as it fouls its economic nest with loss leaders, trading stamps and dubious alliances, it still gives a far better average money's worth (in terms of real wages) of nutritional necessities than any retailer could c. 1900. And most of its building blocks were formed or forming by 1914.

Chains of retail stores under identical insignia and close control of operation are at least as old as the transatlantic cable, say five generations. They arrived Ford-fashion without substantial help from banks for the understandable reason that their vivacious policies and dependence on low-income customers did not inspire confidence in the banking mind. Today's typical old-line chain financed itself by plowing earnings back into expansion. A salient example of the 1860's was the Great Atlantic & Pacific Tea Company, ancestor of that national institution, the A&P in the shopping center. Its chain of several dozen stores identically tricked out in scarlet paint outside and allegedly Oriental gimcrackery inside sold tea and coffee at bargain prices in Northeastern cities. Its merchandising was cluttered up by heavy dependence on premiums, chiefly showy dishes for which housewives exchanged accumulations of coupons; by mail-order "clubs" sending mass orders at cut prices; by company wagons rattling from farmhouse to farmhouse taking and delivering orders. Several rival tea companies used much the same methods, and the germ of modern merchandising being in their bloodstreams too, some of them also turned into national supermarket chains. In the 1880's J. C. Penney and F. W. Woolworth separately applied the chain principle to the five-and-ten (variety) store for the masses to whom nickels and dimes bulked very large; in the South, stirred by the same economic impulse, the term was "racket store." Shoes, drugstores, tobacco retailing developed chain operation, and by and large such application of massed purchasing power to manufacturers and wholesalers meant real savings for the consumer in all those contexts. But the omens are clearest in the story of the A&P.

A century ago its pilot was a Maine Yankee, George Huntington Hartford, whose flamboyant promotional methods went with financial caution in just the right proportions to set the growing chain on its way to billions. In the 1880's he combined convenience for the tea-buying housewife with higher gross per store by expanding stocks-in-trade—first local butter, then spices, then baking powder. At the time he was breaking in two teen-age sons, George L. and John A., whose gradual involvement in company affairs would keep them busy for the next sixty years. George, stodgy, bulky, rumpled, was watchdog of the treasury and even as a youngster began the A&P's policy of making many of its own wares—happening to learn how simple a mixture baking powder is, he persuaded his father to hire a chemist to make the company's own brand in a back room to save middleman's profits. Brother John was contrastingly slight, nippy, boiling with schemes, eccentrically committed to flowing bow ties—rather giving the impression he was being played by Walter Huston. He handled selection of the gaudy crockery in the premium displays, made the decision to go into trading stamps when they came in around 1900—and eventually put into effect an original scheme of his that, in 1912, showed grocery chains the way to glory.

By then steady expansion of items stocked had the A&P, like its rival chains of "tea stores," deep in the general grocery trade. Their credit accounts, high rent on good locations, delivery wagons, fancy decorations keeping up the pseudo-Oriental motif meant overhead as high as the independent competition's, and the cost of the premium gimmick kept the advantage of chain buying, though real, tantalizingly slim. In 1912 cartoonists were all drawing Mr. and Mrs. John Q. Public shivering under a Sword of Damocles labeled "HCofL"; fleeing mammoth spiders labeled "HCofL"; forced by grinning demons to swallow bitter doses from bottles of "HCofL"—that is, High Cost of Living, for over the previous decade food prices had risen nearly 30 percent. Proposing a complete revolution of policy, John told his father and brother that the A&P should recognize this public cost-mindedness by cutting out all fancy work and reducing prices to an even slimmer margin of profit, counting on increased volume from bargain hunters to make the difference. Specifically he wanted the whole chain shifted into "economy stores"—small, drab, in low-rent locations, no premiums, no delivery, no charge accounts, no payroll but a manager-clerk paid partly on sales commissions and a sweeper-outer/can-stacker helper, not even a gilt signboard, just a windowfull of groceries marked with attention-demanding prices.

He failed to convince the others but did wrest from them $3,000 of company money to experiment with. Around the corner from one of the A&P's largest and most profitable units in Jersey City, where company headquarters were, he set up a pattern economy store. In six months his David had put Goliath around the corner out of business. Father George and Brother George moved fast. Showing how seriously they took John's demonstration, they went to the banks for the first time in company history, borrowed $5,000,000 and embarked on a conversion program that within two years gave the A&P 1,000-odd units mostly of the economy type. They were in effect the Model T's of retailing and succeeded for many of the same reasons. They didn't look like much, but their crude efficiency and exploitation of mass economics gave the breadwinning American a fine dollar's worth with a minimum of frills. It was even true that, like Model T's, all A&P economy stores were exactly alike—red paint on the street front, withindoors a standard system of stock shelving so the canned beans were always on the third shelf ten feet to the right.

The cash-and-carry feature was not applied all the way. Until 1940 some larger A&P units under stiff competition from rival chains kept up short-radius delivery here and there. Nor was cash-and-carry in itself original. Customers of crossroads stores and chain dime stores had always carried purchases home. The originality lay in applying it to the most down-to-earth stratum of grocery retailing as another in the array of money savings enabling the A&P to maintain those seductive low prices. In effect it was paying the customer for doing his own home delivery.

As these low prices on standard, nationally advertised comestibles undercut the sales of independent grocers and the jobbers supplying them, complaints piled up on the processors' doorsteps. Could the Campbell Soup Company do something about it? Here they were selling directly to the A&P at discounts so heavy that it could knock a cent or two off the can at retail—which bade fair to put both retailer and middleman out of business. And once the independents were gone and the processor found himself dealing with only a few giant mass-buying chains wielding greater economic leverage than his. . . . Apprehensively certain processors heeded Lester Ratcheese's wails and tried in court and elsewhere to make minimum retail prices stick on their products. In periodic pulling and hauling about fair trade laws this problem still haunts American retailing. The result the first time around was to put the A&P, harking back to Brother George's baking powder, into processing on its own. It would still buy, shelve and sell nationally advertised Brand X laundry soap at the X Company's minimum price if that was the way it had to be, but nothing prevented the A&P from marketing its own brand of laundry soap looking, smelling and washing clothes the same and shelved next to Brand X at a few cents less.

Eventually a quarter of the company's sales came from such "private brands." Long before Women's Liberation imaginary domestic types like Jane Parker and Ann Page were big wheels in the moneymaking machine over which Brother George watched obsessively well. Indeed the processors had done the A&P an inadvertent favor. As packer of sockeye salmon, say, it needed no costly sales force, no national advertising to sell its entire output of x00,000 cases a year to itself as sole customer. So its salmon cannery showed a whopping profit on invested capital even though the product was retailed well below nationally advertised brands. In slightly different terms much the same applied to the produce-buying organization that the A&P created so successfully that it got into a famous antitrust prosecution. "This is the key," says one economist observer, "to much, if not most, of the advantage which the grocery-chains have over the independents." [225]

Yet it was not the A&P that stirred self-service into the chain supermarket brew. That came from California, where a small Los Angeles grocery chain, Alpha Beta Stores, took a hint from the local cult of the cafeteria and made the customer do her own fetch-and-carrying in 1912.* Consequent savings in employee man-hours translated into helpful lower prices. The notion was brought explosively to national attention by Clarence Saunders, a bright wholesale grocery salesman, who opened the first of his revolutionary Piggly Wiggly stores in Memphis, Tennessee, in 1916. He explained the name as having been chosen to make people ask questions. His system combined the cafeteria with the amusement-park crazy house, in which the patron, once within, must go through the whole to get out. The customer entered through a turnstile, was given a large basket and launched on a tour of clearly priced, easily reached, well-selected displays of standard grocery items from which she plucked her needs. Thus encountering things not on her list, often a number of items she hadn't known she needed till she saw them . . . here "impulse buying" took on importance. As her basket gained weight, she set it on a knee-high shelf that ran all around under the displays and pushed it along like the tray on the

---

* Much of the above is from my "Mr. George and Mr. John," *Saturday Evening Post*, December 31, 1939, and my "Behold the Supermarket—It's Colossal!," *Forbes'*, December 15, 1941. It also draws on more recent sources, including Edwin P. Hoyt, *That Wonderful A&P!* (1969).

cafeteria rail. At the exit the cashier whisking up the total on an adding machine—good-bye pencil behind the ear and sprawly digits on a paper bag—might be the only employee encountered throughout.

In four months Saunders had six Piggly Wigglys open in Memphis. Subsequent expansion was in franchise deals with chains paying for the valuably well-known name and installation of the attached self-service layouts and price and purchasing systems. Then he got in over his head exploiting his success in Wall Street jugglings and lost control of his brainchild.* But meanwhile self-service so pleased his client chains that it was adopted pretty well all over food retailing, then over retailing in general. By now it dominates everything but bartending and prescription filling. Then, as the end of the 1920's neared, California rounded out the supermarket by supplying grandiloquent Hollywooden name and huge size—both typical of the land of big trees and colossality.

Saunders' innovations would have pleased Taylor; so would those supermarket carts with a rumble seat for Junior that replaced basket and shelf. The father of scientific management might have solved the only aspect of supermarketing yet to be streamlined—the piecemeal restocking of cans and packages. But he might have been baffled by the problem built into self-service—shoplifting, by now so pervasive an institution that much of the potential money savings from supermarket methods disappears into the pockets of the light-fingered.

Taylor's slide rules rationalized breadwinners' industrial jobs. The Hartfords' and Saunders' rule-of-thumb rationalizations helped Mrs. Breadwinner get the most provender for extra money thus earned. About the same time a third such rationalizing revolution arranged better treatment for the Breadwinners from American doctors. Not public health insurance or better doctor/patient relations—on the American side of the water those were far in the future, even nominally. This was, however, a logical preliminary—a deliberately sought rise in the quality of American medical practice effected by drastic reform of American medical schools. Here gradual does not mean slow. The earthquake came in 1910. Twenty-odd years later—blindingly fast in such a context—the rather bilious *Encyclopedia of Social Sciences* averred that whereas not long since "the standard of medical education in the United States was incredibly low . . . [American] medical schools now rank with those of other countries

---

* In the late 1940's Saunders was back with a "Keydoozle" system of self-service that showed the customer coded display samples from which he ordered by punched numbers, picking up the automatically accumulated order at the cashier's counter. It did not catch on possibly because it did best with prepackaged nonperishables, and much of the stock of the supermarket is meats, perishable green stuff and other things that then sold better when the customer could handle them; this would apply less nowadays when most such stock is prepackaged. The present Piggly Wiggly Corporation of Jacksonville, Florida, uses the name on buying and merchandising franchises for supermarkets in some thirty states.

. . . are probably on the whole better equipped . . . and . . . attract advanced students from abroad." [226] By 1973 Dr. Robert H. Evert of the Harvard Medical School spoke confidently of "the worldwide dominance of American medical education and American biomedical science" [227] consequent on the prime occasion of it all—the famous Flexner Report.

Abraham Flexner was one of the most remarkable of the many west-of-the-Delaware, American-born Jews gaining national importance. As undergraduate at the new Johns Hopkins he took its German-based academic standards much to heart. After college he set up in his native Louisville, Kentucky, a preparatory school for boys so effective that it drew the inquisitive notice of Harvard's President Eliot. His subsequent career in education made him a sizable peak in the American educationist range dominated by Horace Mann and John Dewey. He conducted the crucial survey and report on American medical schools here discussed; had a large hand in the Lincoln School of Teachers College; provided the most cogent analyses of American higher education, no less brilliant because most campuses smiled bleakly and looked away, leaving him an honored but hardly heeded Cassandra; then in the 1930's midwifed the utterly important Institute for Advanced Studies in Princeton, New Jersey. For an added and unique distinction he wrote his reports on it all without abusing sociological or pedagogical jargon, in an idiom so vigorous that—well, who could believe that many pages of something called *Universities: American, English, German* financed by a giant foundation and published by a university press could be such downright vivacious reading?

Sixty-odd years ago his tour of medical schools had to be made without help from planes or automobiles. Steam locomotives, streetcars and horse-drawn vehicles took this tireless, incisive, already middle-aged genius of a fact finder, usually without auxiliary staff, to cover everything from the seminal example of Johns Hopkins, one of America's very few centers of adequate medical teaching in 1909, through the slipshod, lecture-clogged typical big-city medical schools to the abject diploma mills of the Midwest and Pacific coast and the state licensing boards through whose negligence and occasional back-scratching venality poor teaching remained the rule. A striking bit in the consequent Report Number Four of the Carnegie Foundation for the Advancement of Teaching was the high mortality among new MD's seeking posts in the U.S. armed services, whose examinations, though not unreasonable, were far stiffer than those of state boards. In the previous few years the Navy had flunked 46 percent of those confident enough to apply in spite of the notoriously high relative standard. The U.S. Marines flunked 86 percent.

A doctor-short society such as ours now is may blink at Flexner's opinion that in 1909 we had too many doctors—in large cities one for every 400 residents, whereas German cities of such size did nicely with a ratio of 1 to

1,000.* In his view this came of "enormous overproduction of uneducated and ill-trained medical practitioners . . . in absolute disregard of the public welfare . . . [reflecting] the existence of a very large number of [commercial] medical schools, sustained in many cases by advertising through which a mass of unprepared youth is drawn out of industrial occupations in the study of medicine. . . . In [an American] town of two thousand people one will find . . . five to eight physicians where two well trained men could do the work efficiently and make a competent living. When . . . six or eight ill trained physicians undertake to gain a living in a town which can only support two, the whole plane of professional conduct is lowered" [228]—a polite way to say all such jostling rivals had to eke out frustrated, frowsy careers based on obstetrics and the half-ignorant application of dubious medicaments to often misdiagnosed ailments.

What he meant by unprepared youth was simple: Only Johns Hopkins and Harvard Medical Schools required bachelor's degrees for entrance, and both sometimes relaxed that. Even when the requirement was lowered to two years of college, which Flexner deemed the tolerable minimum, only 16 of 155 medical schools in the United States and Canada qualified. The rest, some with nominal university affiliation, some without, enrolled fresh high school graduates, or in the lower reaches of homeopathic and eclectic schools, where formulas were often winked at in the hope of cash customers, any hint that the applicant had at some time attended a high school somewhere was acceptable. Many better-quality schools might scamp work on cadavers and seriously neglect the laboratory subjects—bacteriology, organic chemistry, pathology and so on that newly scientific methods imposed on the profession—in favor of didactic lectures on symptoms, diagnosis and how much of what to prescribe. From these the professors, often local practicing physicians, drew the lecture fees that were such schools' basic reasons for being. Also probably scamped was the bedside or dispensary experience with actual patients that today's hospital-affiliated medical schools find indispensable. So though better students from second-level schools probably could spell psoriasis and impetigo, pronounce them, maybe even recall what to prescribe for them, they were distressingly shaky about recognizing cases of them when they began to practice.

Whereas the professor's purpose too often included revenue, the student's was to store his mind with enough patter about symptoms, drugs and bones to pass examinations for his MD, then for the license to practice that opened for him the world of office hours and fees that he had promised himself when signing up. Since his preceptors were usually veterans of the

* Comparing these with today's ratios is pointless since the proliferation of public medical agencies and the rise of industrial medicine has greatly increased the exposure of the population to doctors.

days before immunology was well developed, since endocrinology was hardly born yet, graduates of any but the best schools were ill grounded in such fields even in book and lecture knowledge, let alone clinical experience. Society could only hope that after entering practice, the better new MD's would sharpen their clinical skills by observing what happened to their patients and by reading medical journals—for which they would have less time as their practices grew. Fortunately medicine often attracts youngsters of brains and goodwill, so, in spite of the crassness and sluggishness of their training, able physicians often came out of this process. No wonder, however, that before the War American boys (and some girls) whom taste or family tradition drew toward medicine preferred to go for professional study, when they could afford it, to Edinburgh, Berlin, Vienna or Paris.

The ideas about medical schools and standards with which such expatriates returned were part of the background of Flexner's report. His assignment had not just come out of the blue. As laboratory and clinic grew in weight, as the old calomel-and-mustard-plaster school dwindled, uneasiness mounted among leaders of American medicine, of whom many were European-trained. For some years the *Journal of the American Medical Association* under editorship of Dr. George H. Simmons had been saying increasingly sharp things and investigating individual flagrant cases. The medical schools of some universities were already raising their admission standards. So when Flexner challenged them to come out from under archaic shadows and convert into counterparts or better of the Johns Hopkins example, the situation was already well off dead center, the stimulating formula was now in print: Not only jack up and enforce admissions requirements but provide "adequate endowment [to eliminate lecture fee commercialism], well equipped laboratories conducted by modern teachers, devoting themselves unreservedly to medical investigation and instruction . . . [a school-attached hospital] in which the training of the physician and the healing of the sick harmoniously combine to the infinite advantage of both." [229] The pain of the huge expense involved was eased by millions from one or another of the good-works foundations to which Flexner's long-standing connections gave him access. Though the War slowed the first burst of reform, its consequences were brilliant by the end of the 1920's.

America thus acquired the educational and clinical tools to shape better doctors. It has yet to solve the problem how to get optimum use of their skills and knowledge. In its own right, however, this burst of medical creativeness was a remarkable bit of cultural emancipation. In one generation American medicine, once as colonialistically dependent as American sculpture,* say, not only cast off Nurse Europe's leading strings

* This should not obscure the sporadic occurrence of important originalities in pre-War American medicine, notably in surgery, anesthesiology and epidemiology.

but in many respects was soon showing the old lady the way—analogously, though probably not significantly so, to America's simultaneous shift, largely because of the War, from being a debtor to a creditor nation.

In medicine the swing was felt even among deviant medico-therapeutic cults. Time was when the westward-setting tide of phrenology, homeopathy, hydropathy, Freudianism and so on was only slightly countered by eastward flow to Europe of such items as galvanic tractors, spiritualism and Christian Science. But the upward trend of responsible American medicine —say it began in 1893, when Johns Hopkins Medical School chose to require four years of college for entrance—was bracketed by the founding of Dr. Andrew Taylor Still's American School of Osteopathy at Kirksville, Missouri, in 1892, and of Daniel David Palmer's College of Chiropractic 100-odd miles away in Davenport, Iowa, in 1898. By the early 1930's America's impressive medical coming of age was impishly travestied by the 12,000 osteopaths and 18,000 chiropractors practicing legally in the United States, and both movements were taking root in Europe. America was rolling its own with a vengeance.

Of the two, osteopathy was elder and, though remarkably crude in its early days, better—at least not quite so bad. Its probably well-meaning founder, Dr. Still, was an eccentric youth in frontier Kansas whose father had been, among other things, a self-styled doctor. Son did some doctoring among local Indians and claimed to have a degree from a course at the Kansas City School of Physicians and Surgeons, which c. 1860 must have been a pretty sketchy institution. After an interval with the militia in the Civil War he developed special interest in alcoholics and drug addicts and the anatomy of his Indian patients who died. The obvious mechanical absurdities of the human body seem to have blended in his mind with the then newish evolutionist's notion that man's ancestors went on all fours. This suggested that the Missing Link's assuming upright posture, for which he was badly engineered, led to many of his descendants' ills. Still's attention centered on the spine, the jointed ridgepole from which the skeleton hangs when on all fours but which must act as combined hat rack and construction boom when one stands upright. And since the spine also contains the core of the nervous system, something out of kilter there might transmit miseries all over the body.

Actually man's upright posture is one source of certain ailments. Some of them do originate in spinal anomalies. Only, as is likely among incautious and ill-grounded theorists, Still carried a good guess too far. From the notion that some things that doctors treat come from maladjustment of the spine he came wishfully to assume that not only some but many . . . then most . . . then about all were thus to a large extent accounted for and that optimum alignment of the spine and associated bones was the royal road to normal health. Hence osteopathy, which, being interpreted from its Greek roots, means "bone treatment." The pathological conditions that it postulates are "osteopathic lesions." The American School of Osteopathy that Still set up in Kirksville, where his shingle was hanging at the time, taught its matriculants to reduce such assumed lesions by using the hands to restore spine and skeleton to harmony. He not only taught in Kirksville but also sent out missionaries of the new good word, including a former vendor of a cure for hemorrhoids and a former lightning rod salesman.

Osteopathy often worked. Most MD's admit that maybe half the patients consulting them suffer from psychogenic ailments. So the laying on of hands, impressively done, whether by a D.O. (Doctor of Osteopathy) in a white coat or a Siberian shaman in a fur leotard, has been sporadically useful therapy for millennia. Further, the crude physiotherapeutic effects of osteopathy from pushing and kneading may often benefit orthopedic ills particularly when the DO is long experienced. Many MD's send those with stubborn creaks in back or limbs to the osteopath around the corner.

Because osteopathy sometimes worked, seven more schools teaching it sprang up, mostly in the Midwest. Though organized MD medicine fought every step of the way, organized osteopathy had and has able lobbyists, and within a generation every state in the Union was licensing DO's after examinations of varying severity. In view of what Flexner found in even medical schools of some repute c. 1910, nobody need be surprised to learn he thought schools of osteopathy ineffably incompetent. The teaching their 1,300 students got for fees averaging $150-odd a year he called "inexpensive and worthless" [230] for the training in diagnosis that even in its own dubious terms osteopathy needed. Curricula were weak in anatomy, weaker still in chemistry, sketchy on pharmacology because osteopathy was tempted to renounce drugs altogether in favor of exclusive "manipulation." The students, seldom with even high school diplomas behind them, were usually "crude boys or disappointed men and women" attracted by advertising reeking of "commercialism . . . [and] hysterical exaggerations alike of the earning and of the curative power of osteopathy." The Los Angeles College of Osteopathy shouted: ". . . many of our graduates are earning as much in a single month as . . . formerly by a full year's work." The Central College of Osteopathy claimed: "The average osteopath has a better practice [i.e., more lucrative] than ninety out of every hundred medical practitioners" [231]—much the same tone as in advertisements of that day offering spare-time selling of patent medicines or celluloid collars.

Obviously osteopathy had nowhere to go but out or up. It went up. Its present condition—9,000-odd DO's in practice, many doing surgery; getting a few grants from the U.S. Public Health Service; operating half a dozen schools giving DO degrees and claiming to do osteopathic research in cancer and psychiatry—seems to promise that, as happened with homeopathy, it will finally upgrade itself into fusion with modern medicine.* So long

* I understand that one reason for the survival of some vestiges of homeopathy in hospitals

as its separate identity persists, however, it will remain to some degree what Dr. Morris Fishbein, high in the American Medical Association, called it fifty years ago: ". . . an attempt to enter medicine by the back door." [232] One likely reason for its rise toward respectability has been its avoidance of the mistake of claiming *all* illness for its panacea's province. It always retreated at the last minute from the urge to denounce "allopathy"—the deviants' name for MD medicine—root and branch. Another may have been the simultaneous rise of chiropractic, the embarrassingly brash by-blow of osteopathy that, in spite of strong family resemblance, made its sire look good by contrast.

We owe chiropractic to Daniel David Palmer, a Canadian-born grocer settled in Iowa who dipped in and out of spiritualism, phrenology, osteopathy, magnetic healing—the same crankish constellation underlying Christian Science, Unity and so on. In the 1880's he was a magnetic healer in Davenport, Iowa. But his great discovery seems to hark back to osteopathy. He cured a local janitor of deafness by pushing back into place an allegedly misaligned vertebra, or so he said. Then he cured a heart case by realigning the vertebrae involving the nerves that in his view regulated the heart, or so he said. From such successes he came to the full-blown theory of chiropractic (= Greek roots for "hand" and "action")—that all diseases are caused by "interference with nerve transmission, due to pressures, strain or tension upon the spinal nerves." [233] (Whatever its virtues, the theory is wildly inconsistent with the cure of deafness that set Palmer on his way, for the hearing nerves go nowhere near the spine.) The causative spinal deviations, cousins of osteopathic lesions, of course, are called subluxations. Since realignment of vertebrae is fundamental, it follows that in any clinical context drugs, surgery and prophylaxis are useless, wasting the patient's money and the doctor's time. For lockjaw, appendicitis, typhoid fever, diabetes, pellagra, gallstones and on through all the infections, surgical emergencies and biochemical anomalies to tinker with the associated subluxation is not just the method of choice, it is *sine qua non.* Indeed, chiropractic's delusions of grandeur went even farther. The legislative bill admitting chiropractors to practice in New Jersey in 1920 defined their science as "the study and application of a universal philosophy of biology, theology, theosophy, health, disease, death. . . ." [234] Osteopathy never went that far. But by going farther of the two chiropractic by no means fared worse. In the ensuing competition for patients and dollars in the early 1930's chiropractic was taking in 50 percent more cash than osteopathy.

Palmer's School of Chiropractic in Davenport began with no admission requirements. Anybody able to pay a few hundred dollars was taught

and medical schools once devoted to that "sectarian" deviant is that important parts of their endowments represent bequests made on condition that homeopathy be advanced and supported thereby.

medical patter from a home-remedy book and how to adjust subluxations, and supposing Palmer was right, they really needed no more to qualify for the previously nonexistent degree of DC. As fees came in, other such schools naturally appeared, mostly in the Midwest—again parallel to osteopathy. But the Kirksville College of Osteopathy, still flourishing, by the way, never had such a crisis as that of 1906 when D. D. Palmer was jailed for practicing medicine without a license, sold his school to his son Bartlett Joshua, in what sounds like a necessitous bargain, and disappeared into outer darkness on release. For fifty years following, the son was, as Ralph Lee Smith says in *At Your Own Risk*,* "the guru [of chiropractic]," describing his Davenport enterprise as "on a business, not a professional basis. We manufacture chiropractors . . . hold no entrance examinations." [235]

At least it maintained classrooms and lectures; whereas correspondence schools were soon offering handsome DC diplomas to hang on the office wall to those able to read the advertisement in the back pages of second-rate magazines—and pay $68.75 in installments if preferred. The advertisements said up to seventy-five patients a day could be handled at $2 each, and "frequently . . . a wealthy patient is so grateful . . . that he . . . insists upon the chiropractor accepting a substantial sum over and above the regular fee." [236] In 1915 George Creel, then a prominent magazine reporter, found that the American University of Chicago, which advertised thus, consisted of one dingy room and the entire staff was a self-styled "dean" and a couple of mail clerks. Down on the South Side was the National School of Chiropractic in a run-down dwelling house equipped with one blackboard and a few examination tables for manipulating volunteers who ventured in for free diagnosis; that made up the bulk of the training course. A diploma awarding the DC came at the end of three months and cost $75, but the school also advertised a correspondence course leading to the degree of Diploma in Chiropractic for only $40. "Some of our very successful graduates have taken this course alone," [237] they said.

As often happens in such cults chiropractic split between the still-lively Davenport school and a rival in Illinois, plus many splinter movements. A recent advertisement of a New York City chiropractic clinic offers: "All latest advanced painless methods: Palmer, Carver, Reflex, Pressure, Spears [name of a large chiropractic hospital in Denver], Gonstead, Zone, Logan-Basic, Traction, Grostic, Merric, Diversified, De Jarnette, Non-Force, Bennet, Concept, Shelton-Nat'l Hygiene, Toftness, Spastic Muscle, Illi (Switzerland), Lorenz (Austria), Locke (Canada), Garten & Oriental Methods. PHONE NOW or just come in." Said the spider.

---

* This admirable piece of firsthand research and reporting published in 1969 is recommended to any inclined to look more favorably on chiropractic than this section suggests.

Osteopaths particularly abounded in California, Flexner noted. His neglect to try to explain why is significant of the reputation California already had in 1910. It is harder to find reasons for the fact that though the cafeteria, child of the barroom free lunch and the fetch-it-from-the-counter-yourself lunchroom, probably originated in Chicago, it flourished so mightily when transplanted to California that the nation took it to be another of those Californian innovations. (An incidental caution—many early cafeterias had luxurious carpeting, Art Nouveau lighting fixtures, linen tablecloths and string quartets rendering pop concert numbers among potted palms; such refinements persisted here and there until the Depression smothered them under white enamel tables, tiled floors and slovenly dish busing.) Take cafeteria and supermarket as typifying a momentous shift in cultural center of gravity well underway before the War—a new tendency for waves of the future, large or small, to wash eastward instead of, as with automobiles and poor whites, westward from the elder states. The movies were the most striking instance, of course, both in their own right and as carrying the screen industry's strange notions of the chief traits of American life. Movies were no crucial factor, however, in the emergence of California as major force. "California" had been a magically glowing word long before Hollywood took the bit in its capped teeth. First gold, then oranges, sunshine . . . and as 1914 ripened the Golden State was more than ever on the public mind because the Panama Canal had opened and California, egocentrically assuming it had been dug primarily for her, was preparing to celebrate it.

Most states would have been content with one great festival. California staged two 500 miles apart. No doubt one reason was the overemphasis that was already a local failing. Another, however, was the actual existence of two Californias so different and dissonant that—as is so often said both sides of the line—they should be separate states with the boundary at the Tehachapis.

The capital of one was San Francisco, vaunting itself on an allegedly cosmopolitan, cultivated and yet raunchy spirit capable of baking sourdough bread every bit as good as any *flûte* in France—a venerable tradition already sixty years old when in 1904, the year after the Canal became an American project, she began to plan her Panama-Pacific Exposition. In 1906 the earthquake-fire gave the scheme a second purpose—to show how gamely the city had rebuilt and gained new momentum. The capital of California II was Los Angeles, which San Francisco found abjectly bourgeois, upstart, crass as befitted a place where the chief industry was selling bungalow sites to retired Iowa farmers and the unique feature not the Golden Gate but oil derricks on the beaches. A promising new port at San Pedro gave Los Angeles as much or more than San Francisco to hope for from the imminent Canal. But the march that had been stolen on her so disheartened her that Los Angeles left it to San Diego, stepchild port of

California II, to insist on the region's right to a front pew at the wedding of the Atlantic and Pacific oceans. Weighing in in 1909, this lightweight sparred so pluckily that San Francisco agreed to live and let live, provided San Diego confined her scope to regional matters and did not seek accreditation as a world's fair entitled to invite foreign nations to build exhibits. Beyond that it was hoped—and it worked too—that two fairs for one fare would attract even more Easterners than San Francisco's gorgeous plans could alone.

Gorgeous they were. The architects fetched westward to create a showcase for American plus international enterprise with Latin-American overtones were the nation's most eminent: Henry Bacon (Lincoln Memorial, then a-building); Carrère & Hastings (New York Public Library); and inevitably McKim, Mead & White, dominant American exponents of the then continuing Beaux Arts tradition of colonnade and cornice. The site chosen opposite Alcatraz Island was an industrial wilderness of gasworks, iron foundry, power plant. What replaced them set no architectural fashions, as had Chicago's Columbian Exposition in 1893, but did most judiciously combine a pseudo-Roman classicism with Baroque buoyancy. The thronging statuary was supervised and in part modeled by Karl Bitter, Austro-American veteran of such work at every important American exhibition since Chicago in 1893, and A. Stirling Calder, able father of the Alexander Calder now best known for his mobiles. The usual glut of allegorical figures—Youth, Autumn and so on—was varied by statues of Cortez, Pizarro *et al.,* politely recognizing that Alta California's past and the site of the new Canal both had a strong Latin-American flavor.

The lighting effects, suitable for what was basically stage scenery, were mere elaborations of those so admired at Buffalo's Pan-American Exhibition of 1901. But they were greatly heightened by the pastel color contrasts, such as neither Vitruvius nor Bernini had known, created from building to building by Jules Guerin, a famous muralist of the day. The focus of the whole, Carrère & Hastings' Tower of Jewels, a loftily elegant Baroque affair hung with tin colored mirrors shimmering in the wind through the Golden Gate, looked, Emily Post said, "like a diamond and turquoise wedding cake," [238] and gave just the combination of gaiety and imposing scale that the occasion needed. ". . . in its time and place it was a thing of magic," R. L. Duffus wrote forty-five years later, recalling how as a young reporter of muckraking bent he had mistrusted the whole show as "a spurious bit of publicity . . . I wish I could tell it now how much I loved it." [239] That rings nearer true than the judgment given at the time by Edwin ("Man with the Hoe") Markham, California's unofficial poet laureate, that the exposition at night was "the greatest revelation of beauty that was ever known on earth." [240] Superlatives were as unconfined as joy. The relatively cautious official history of the show called its Palace of Fine Arts "in many respects the most beautiful building in the world." [241]

Though the Canal did not open formally until July, 1915, it had actually been transiting ships for months. The North Atlantic liners *Finland* and *Kroonland* were scheduled to take exposition-bound passengers through its engineering wonders. As a triumph of American skill—and epidemiology—brilliantly succeeding where the Old World had failed, it was satisfactorily impressive—not least because it was a gigantic work of peace in a world gone to war a few days before the first ship used it. ". . . the building of the Panama Canal by the American Army is perhaps the greatest victory an army ever won," [242] Walter Lippmann wrote late in 1914. Yet on the exposition grounds homage to the Canal as acknowledged occasion for all the doings was strangely scanty. The one large gesture was a five-acre model, like something in an amusement park, that put miniature ships through miniature locks and reaches. The visitor was likelier to be impressed by the Santa Fe Railroad's huge diorama of the Grand Canyon and starkly accurate reproduction of a Southwestern Indian pueblo adjacent to, of course, a Fred Harvey shop stocking Navajo rugs and silver-and-turquoise jewelry. The territory of Hawaii's official exhibit—an aquarium teeming with incredible fishes, a Kanaka quintet doing authentic wonders with versions of local music far superior to Tin Pan Alley's, and dioramas of Waikiki and the view from the Nuuanu Pali—was so attractive that 1916 saw tourist trade to the Islands rise by 50 percent.

The honky-tonk department—called the Zone in vague reference to Panama—necessary to such festivals ever since Chicago's raucous Midway of the previous generation, made the usual announcement that a certain dignity would be maintained. This led to confusion between the dignified and the lugubrious. Authentic movies, lectures and memorabilia from the heroic disaster of Captain Robert Falcon Scott's party frozen to death on their way back from the South Pole in 1913 failed to prosper. An equally jolly miniature enactment of the flood that almost wiped out Dayton, Ohio, the same year did poorly. A mock-up of the very recent sinking of the *Lusitania* roused Germany's consul general in San Francisco to hot protest. The Chinese consul general reacted just as strongly to a concession called Underground Chinatown, stiff with recumbent Chinese, pigtailed hatchet men and almond-eyed daughters of joy (alleged). The Somali Dancers disappointed a public led indirectly to believe that they would stage exhibits of cannibalism; when the management closed them out, they refused to go home and had to be forcibly deported by the U.S. Immigration Service. But Captain Sigsbee, the educated horse, prospered. So did the Jimtown Dance Hall, though its insistence on offering real gambling-for-keeps kept it in hot water, and the Tehuantepec Village presenting life in Old Mexico as conceived by its creator, G. M. "Broncho Billy" Anderson, the movies' first cowboy star.

King Karlo, a Flathead Indian from Oklahoma, whom show people rated the best barker on the grounds, extolled the charms and winning ways of the Mayan Maidens of Anderson's Village. But the barker whom visitors best remembered did the spiel for the Stella concession that gave the nip of prurience that Midways always need. Stella was a barroom nude painted in high detail, side view, reclining. The showman had it in a very deep frame so lighted that only a little credulity was needed to think the lady real. Stare and stare and hold your breath and you'd swear you saw her breathing. The Palace of Fine Arts, as the historian of the exposition noted, had on display free of charge half a dozen nudes just as voluptuous and much better painted. The difference was the barker working up his pitch: "Have . . . you . . . seen . . . Stella? Have you seen *Stell*-ah? Is she alive or is she a pict-you-ah?" In that long-vanished moral climate the possibility of seeing flesh-and-blood beauty naked as a jaybird fetched them in droves at a dime a head, and "Have you seen Stella?" was the watchword of the fair long remembered in tranquillity by her admirers.

Many of the same men also remembered the hulking diesel engine that turned all the wheels in the Palace of Machinery, the display of dinosaur-scale power in caterpillar tractors, then new to the general public, and the Ford display, a miniature assembly plant taking in a miscellany of parts at one end and turning out at the other Ford Model T's driving away under their own power. Most found the airplane stunts even more memorable. That began on opening day when a radio beam activated a key on President Wilson's desk in Washington, D.C., with which he started the huge diesel and signaled Lincoln Beachey to come barrel-rolling his monoplane over the grounds and releasing a flock of doubtless indignant pigeons. Later Beachey showed off the size of the Palace of Machinery—eight and a half acres—by making the world's first indoor plane flight in it. His daily stint was odd stunting, some pioneer skywriting—and then one day the public got an unscheduled thrill when he crashed and was killed. Art Smith, another flying barnstormer recruited as replacement, presently crashed in turn—surviving, true, but hardly making aviation look as if its glorious future were all the public fancy painted.

The show was an economic success. Its profits—and any profit from such a project is unusual—built San Francisco's municipal auditorium. Even in this respect, however, little San Diego's show went big sister one better, not only paying all debt off the first year but going on into a highly profitable second year and leaving the town with a permanent and most commodious civic center of numerous buildings. That was planned from the beginning. Usually such affairs are largely temporary, at best leaving one permanent building to be remembered by, such as Chicago's present Museum of Science and Industry from 1893 and St. Louis' Art Museum from 1904. But all the structures constituting the quadrangle nucleus of San Diego's Panama-California Exposition, personally designed by Bertram Grosvenor Goodhue, the eminent Eastern architect who supervised the whole complex, were built to stay. In 1935 they were focus of another important regional exhibition and to this day continue buzzing with civic activities and cultural uses.

With both taste and showmanship Goodhue disguised the steel and concrete with tile roofs and unabashedly souped-up Spanishness of the kind unpronounceably called Chirrugueresque. Pigeons were installed in the various plazas to tease visitors into feeding them. Teams of vaguely Spanish minstrels singing to guitars strolled about. Such Hispanicistics made San Diego's show more specifically Californian than San Francisco's; on the whole, the thronging visitors preferred it.

Further Californiaisms were the transplanted groves of full-grown orange trees flourishing where, the year before, had been a semidesert mesa top and the language of the advertising: ". . . the air of the Exposition is soft, balmy, healthful and strength-giving . . . the bay and sky, the islands and the sparkling sea . . . enhanced by the colorings of the most exquisite flowers and enhanced by the perfume-laden air—a paradise for the man or woman who has not known the joy of such an atmosphere of peace and rest." From the grounds visitors could see over on Point Loma the pastel-tinted domes of the Aryan Memorial Temple and Raja-Yoga College of the International Theosophical Headquarters ruled by Madam Katherine Tingley; the second year her Spanish Mission-style proselytizing branch was going full blast on the exposition grounds. The Isthmus, the amusement area, sounds mediocre: Neptune's Wonderland, the Palais de Danse, the Japanese Streets of Joy, Cawston's Ostrich Farm. . . . But the California II note is strong in its Nature Man, wearing very little, "the way he believes best," and living on "simple meals of uncooked fruits, vegetables, nuts and oils which had brought him to his present state of healthy vigor." [243]

The reliable balminess of California II's climate was dramatized by a gift from the Spreckels family, sugar refiners and biggest names in San Diego—a mammoth outdoor pipe organ playing tricks with a chime of church bells, drums and cymbals. It accompanied Carrie Jacobs Bond, who had become a local resident, singing for great crowds her "The End of a Perfect Day." The second year the Isthmus acquired a badly battered painting of a naked woman said to represent St. Mary Magdalene, said to be the work of Murillo, said to have been stolen from a Mexican cathedral, said to be worth $50,000. Down from the dismantled San Francisco exhibition came not only the educated horse but also France's rich loan collection of paintings from the Luxembourg. Beauty received further tribute in the homage paid to Miss San Diego—an ancestress of Miss America-to-be—a gorgeous brunette who weighed a slender 135 pounds at five feet nine in her stocking feet and combined looking very Spanish with being, the committee said, "the typical San Diego girl." [244]

The also highly Californian purpose of the whole doings was candidly to promote settlement and land sales in this relatively undeveloped corner, so its most original feature was what the advertising called "moving, throbbing, real life" demonstrations. That is, instead of just showing the latest farm machinery in an Agricultural Hall, here was an impressively extensive model farm with the machines actually out there plowing, cultivating, ditching. For the other school of farmer, here was a model five acres to show what irrigation could do in intensive cultivation—orchards of walnuts and four different fruits with all kinds of garden truck flourishing between the rows of trees and a model farm family inhabiting a model California bungalow with such fancy modern gadgets as an automatic electric pump and a vacuum cleaner. . . . San Francisco had arranged to be terminus of a Lincoln Highway transcontinental motorcade showing the joys of motoring, but that frayed apart when between bad roads and time-wasting publicity capers en route the junket took two months coast to coast. San Diego more cleverly exploited the growing affinity between California and the automobile by giving special medals to motorist visitors coming more than 500 miles; staging special welcome days for touring cars, roadsters, trucks; pitting one make of car against another in climbing contests and tugs-of-war—with results so stimulating that the second year the exhibition had to install history's first large-scale, paid-admission parking lots, a very weighty omen of the future.

Even little sister's renunciation of formal international standing worked out to her advantage over big sister. For the outbreak of the War six months before opening day played havoc with San Francisco's international plans. The management was far too deeply committed to consider canceling, but much of the original carried away in the ensuing high winds. Out went the international yacht race, the round-the-world airplane race. The celebration of "One Hundred Years of Peace Among English-Speaking Peoples"—it was the centennial of the end of the War of 1812—fell apart because the other English-speaking peoples were too busy fighting. Nor could Britain carry out the scheme for an elaborate exhibit midwifed by Herbert Hoover, adopted son of the Golden State already well established in London. Alone among the belligerents France did not withdraw. German participation consisted of San Francisco's German colony, or the militant fraction thereof, staging jeeringly hostile demonstrations in the French exhibit, which consisted principally and unaggressively of those paintings from the Luxembourg.

In the preceding August the nation's cards, ranging as usual from important to insignificant, had lain fairly well. True, unemployment was uncomfortably high and Colorado was a bloody mess between local miners and the Rockefellers' Colorado Fuel and Iron Company. U.S. Representative J. Thomas "Tomtom" Heflin had just succeeded in foisting Mother's Day on the country. But U.S. Representative Richmond P. Hobson's proposed Prohibition amendment to the Constitution, launched with great hullabaloo and considered a substantial threat, had failed to pass the House. The Wilson administration had unlimbered the Clayton Act, a stronger weapon against trusts, and the Federal Reserve System, a device for the more responsible handling of credit. And at some indeterminate time that year two momentous portents, not even identified until later when the statisticians had tidied up, appeared. For the first time the per capita national product of the United States—the sum of goods and services made or performed divided by number of Americans—exceeded that of Britain. And for the first time the shift of Americans from farm to town domiciled more of them in urban than in rural situations.

Both had developed without help from the morbid stimuli of war. But now came the War to erase all possibility of ever knowing what they would have worked out to under more or less normal—anyway peacetime—conditions. For the Europeans' War that became ours too would be a spoiler. The hand could never be played out. Whatever was tried was always trumped by another peremptory ace of spades.

III

1914 and All That

Once we have a war, there is only one thing to do.
It must be won. For defeat brings worse things
than can ever happen in war.

—ERNEST HEMINGWAY, intro-
duction to *Men at War*

ST. *Nicholas* was the magazine for proper young Americans from the age of seven or so well into the teens. It had a department, the St. Nicholas League, to which the ambitious submitted for publication, on topics announced monthly in advance, snapshots they had taken with their Kodaks ("The Great Outdoors"), pictures they had drawn ("What We All Like"), bits of prose ("A Close Call") and verse ("The Eagle"). First publication earned a silver badge, the next a gold badge, the third an Honor Membership. The cultural climate of 1914 was such that though *St. Nicholas* tried to attract boys with jolly pieces about handicrafts and baseball, nine out of ten things that the league published came from hair-ribboned, cotton-stockinged WASP girls named Elizabeth M. Dukes, Edith Anderson, Emily Lucile Weed. . . . One sometimes recognizes with a start E. Vincent Millay, Eudora Welty, Stephen Vincent Benét, Cornelia Otis Skinner, Corey H. Ford, Rachel L. Carson.

In September, 1914, the league carried "An Object of Interest" by Harold Drake, age sixteen, probably drawn from a postcard, showing a three-funneled ocean liner with "VATERLAND" on her starboard bow. No cut-line ever fitted better. When that September issue had been put to bed early in July, the world was at peace. By the time the mailman delivered it the greatest Object of Interest in New York Harbor, endlessly discussed by ferry commuters, was that very *Vaterland*, brand-new pride of the German merchant marine, largest ship afloat, laid up at Hoboken to keep her safe from British cruisers. A few years later, renamed *Leviathan*, she lent her speed and size to ferry tens of thousands of American soldiers Over There.

The day after Belgium was invaded Washington proclaimed official neutrality. It took thirty months completely to shred away. But the process began at once on so large a scale and in such quarters as to perplex later observers trying to attribute it to deliberate manipulation. The very next day Charles W. Eliot, president emeritus of Harvard, America's nearest thing to an elder statesman, bade President Wilson enter "offensive and defensive alliance" [1] with the anti-German powers. William Dean Howells, dean of American letters, whipped off to the *North American Review* an ironic piece on belligerents' prayers for God's help that gave Germany the worst of it—and deservedly, for Wilhelm II's early appeals to heaven were in even worse taste than those of his foes. As soon as *Life* could get into print, its pithy editor, E. S. Martin, observed: "The unanimity of sentiment in this country against Germany is surprising . . . spontaneously . . . the American mind records the impression that the English, French and Russians are fighting . . . in behalf of the liberties of all the world. . . ." [2] On the opposite page a cartoon, "Back to Barbarism," showed Wilhelm II wielding a spiked club and dragging a girl named "Europe" away from a radiant cross marked "Civilization." Simultaneously *Harper's Weekly's* double-truck cartoon by Boardman Robinson, best draftsman among radical cartoonists of the day, had a Godlike judge scolding the German and Austrian emperors in custody of a policeman labeled "Civilization." Three weeks later it ran a new translation of Alphonse Daudet's "The Last French Lesson," which was to French Germanophobia after 1870 what "The Wearing of the Green" was to Irish nationalism a hundred years ago.

Suddenly many young Americans whose studies or travels in Europe the War had interrupted came marching together behind the Stars and Stripes to recruiting offices in France. So did some young Rumanians, Italians (whose nation was nominally a defensive ally of France's enemies), Spaniards, Greeks and so on, manifesting the headiness of mixing adventurousness, Francophilia and dismay over Belgium. Across the Atlantic young Americans went to Canada to enlist. By the end of the War 6,896, including a large number already resident there,* had donned Canadian uniform. The supply of European hotheads in Paris soon dried up. But the seepage of Americans into the meat grinder from which their own government stood aloof hinted strongly at eventual involvement. France absorbed likely ones into the Foreign Legion, whence they could transfer to various arms of the service without risking their American citizenship. Once Britain surmounted legal technical ties, Americans also appeared in khaki-clad units deep in the mud of Flanders—for instance, James Norman Hall, romantic Iowan who wrote so popularly after the War about the South Seas in collaboration with Charles B. Nordhoff, another American enlisting for France. Those two survived. Others, such as Alan Seeger, a young American poet who loved Paris, did not.

Motives for thus meddling in others' quarrels varied with individual temperament. High among effective stimuli was Germany's dunderheadedness. On the steps of Amiens Cathedral Owen Wister asked an American boy what had moved him to leave home to enter the French Army. "When the Lusitania happened," he said. [3] An American joining the Royal Canadian Flying Corps still recalls the pull exerted on affluent youth like himself by the photographs in the *Illustrated London News* of dashing young British officers who had "Died for King and Country." And peril so charged with adrenalin—the "bright eyes of danger" sort of thing—natu-

---

* Official total from Canada's ministry of National Defense, which makes hay of the extravagant claim in Robert E. Sherwood's *Waterloo Bridge* (112) that 25 percent of the Canadian Army in the War were American.

rally drew the brashly restless. Apparently that was confined, however, to pro-Ally or anyway non-pro-German boys. The War found many male, young Americans in Germany, some fond of the *gemütlich* country where they were sightseeing or studying. Until early 1917 any American bent on wearing a *Pickelhaube* could get to Germany through Scandinavia with only minor risk and trouble. Yet though large numbers of the Hohenzollerns' and Hapsburgs' subjects living in America went home for duty as reservists, I know of no American whose thirst for adventure or love of Germany took him into what soon proved to be what it had always said it was—the ablest army in the world. Those close cultural ties between America and Germany so talked up in pre-War years failed to stand the first major strain.

A sort of portrait of the pro-Ally volunteer emerges from the roster of the Lafayette Escadrille, a French pursuit squadron manned by Americans. The first dozen members were transfers from the Foreign Legion or ambulance services. (A couple of hundred like them also flew and many died as members of regular French flying units.) The insigne of the specifically American unit—a war-bonneted Red Indian—might have been a winged silver spoon. Its organizer, Norman Prince, was an affluent, polo-playing Francophile from the North Shore of Massachusetts—his family had a hunting estate in Gascony—who learned to fly to get into the War. Through knowing the right people in Paris he finally overcame official reluctance to create a separate unit of aliens from a single neutral nation. The clinching argument—to have American boys conspicuously flying for France was good propaganda—speaks well for the acumen of the French brass. Middle-aged reservations about Prince's impetuosity dwindle when one learns that it cost him his young life in a landing crash.

Outstanding sponsors of the Escadrille were Theodore Roosevelt, soon pro-Ally, and William K. Vanderbilt, Jr., who paid the sea passages of the few unable to do so themselves and supplemented the pay of those lacking private means to live up to the outfit's standard. (At first only the French commander was commissioned, only a few senior pilots ever were; the rest remained noncoms with officer privileges on nomcom pay.) Death in combat or accident steadily thinned the roster; steadily it filled up again with fresh applicants largely from the Northeast, almost all from east of St. Louis. New Yorkers, the largest single group, included some from Squadron A, the silk-stocking unit of National Guard cavalry. Philadelphia sent two Biddles and a Drexel. An Ivy Leaguer summed it up: ". . . men from all colleges and men who don't know the name of a college . . . half a dozen from Harvard, as many from Yale, some from Dartmouth . . . all-American football stars [but also] a colored boxer. . . ."[4]

What most struck him—in 1916 it was very striking—was "the corporal of our room . . . as black as the ace of spades but a mighty fine fellow . . . the next two bunks are occupied by Princeton men of old Southern families . . . the best of friends with him . . . This black brother has been in the

French Foreign Legion, wounded four times, covered with medals. . . ." [4]
But dilution with footloose adventurers and air-minded boys from Kansas
did not keep the Lafayette Escadrille from having been primarily a
picturesque, brave gesture made by affluent WASPdom, Ivy League
branch. Another letter writer wondered how the boys from "the better
classes" would stack up alongside the soldiers of fortune in combat. No
need to be uneasy—in its first twenty-two months this gilt-edged outfit lost
only six of its own pilots (one to antiaircraft fire) to thirty-two German
planes confirmed. As Finley Peter Dunne's Mr. Dooley said early in the
War: ". . . th' on'y rason there are-re more brave poor men thin rich is
because there are-re more poor." [5]

Adventurousness heightened by hands-across-the-sea led other Ivy
Leaguers into a different path to the bright eyes of danger. Early in the War
Richard Norton, archaeologist of august family and repute, "a Harvard
man of the old nineteenth-century school, snob if you like, but solid granite
underneath," [6] said Dos Passos, created an ambulance service of Americans
to succor French casualties. The purpose was proper for neutrals, the
motive humane. A complementary American Ambulance Service also gave
other college boys a way to alleviate suffering, save lives and prove their
courage under fire. When unable to find ambulance work, they might sign
up with the French munitions transport, gamely aware that an enemy shell
exploding too near their eastward-headed loads of shells for the famous
75mm field guns would send them to glory in a fashion much too emphatic
to be taken personally.

In certain articulate cases the reasons given for such volunteering seem
strangely self-centered. Some had a more or less conscious feeling, as much
cerebral as cerebellar, that, as E. E. Cummings, one of them, told Charles
Norman years later: "World War One [would be] the experience of my
generation." [7] "Although I was an enthusiastic pacifist," Dos Passos
recalled, "I wanted to get into the ambulance service to see what war was
like. . . . The attraction was enormous . . . many other young men of my
generation felt the same way." [8] Ambulance rosters showed other names of
later literary note: John Howard Lawson, Sidney Howard, Robert Hillyer,
Nordhoff (who shifted from ambulances to the Foreign Legion to combat
flying). Malcolm Cowley's munitions-transport section included other lads
who later became poets, novelists, architects. Cummings' and others'
impulse to take the worst thing that had yet happened to Western mankind
as occasion for intellectual-cultural sightseeing led to several cases of later
severe revulsion in print and onstage—and important social and esthetic
results over several decades. This cross between sociological duty and
self-conscious hunger for subjective experience makes this really new, I
think. Did even a few young esthete-intellectuals thus obtrude themselves
into any previous war?

The strong emotional currents natural between a still semicolonial America and a convulsed Europe also tempted staider youths toward War-flavored doings. Indeed something like that must already have been in the air in the New World. In 1913 some hundreds of undergraduates from state universities and freshwater colleges paid their own expenses at quasi-military vacation camps in California and Pennsylvania. In the summer of 1914—still before War began—the number thus playing soldier almost tripled. In 1915 Major General Leonard Wood, physician turned soldier-administrator, Roosevelt's colleague in the renowned Rough Riders and almost Teddy's equal in drawing public attention, fired the imagination of much of the nation with a Citizens' Military Training Camp at Plattsburgh, New York. There fraternity boys, businessmen, lawyers and amateur sportsmen from Eastern big cities mustered in the belief that it was wise as well as showily red-blooded to learn some of the art of war in a world mostly under arms. Junior Roosevelts, Fishes and Milburns, both the mayor and the police commissioner of New York City, eminent lawyers like Dudley Field Malone and George Wharton Pepper, made the roll calls, said Walter Millis, expressing post-War disillusion in 1933, sound like " 'Who's Who' and 'The Social Register' combined . . . very strange, very fascinating and very democratic." [9]

The prestige of Plattsburgh's rookies made the existing National Guard of state-recruited, federal-sponsored part-time soldiers meant to back up the regulars look inane. The next year three more Plattsburghs were humming, financed secretly by Bernard Baruch, Wall Street's most renowned operator. Their physical benefits, as of "health farms" conducted by the numbers, were much talked up. Sent to Plattsburgh for his health, Robert E. Sherwood, future Pulitzer Prize playwright but then the weediest undergraduate at Harvard, gained ten pounds, and the drilling came in handy in 1917, when he enlisted with the Canadians. Hunger for "something closer to contemporary reality" sent Edmund Wilson, just out of Princeton, there: "very boring . . . it completely convinced me that . . . I did not want to be a soldier." [10] Most of the participants, however, seem to have had a powerfully infectious glow of patriotic energy. In 1916 came a Women's National Service School at Silver Spring, Maryland, where clear-eyed young American womanhood in deep-pocketed khaki shirts to the shoe tops and four-dinted campaign hats lived in tents, did "Sk-wads right . . . HARCH!" like their brothers at Plattsburgh, learned wigwag signals and radio and heard lectures on the new and still vague science of nutrition.

Higher on the same stem bloomed a "preparedness movement" led by emphatic viewers-with-alarm: Roosevelt, Wood and Hudson Maxim, chemist creator of smokeless powders and author of *Defenseless America*, a widely read call to arms. Behind fell in William T. Manning, Episcopalian Bishop of New York, the Reverend Dr. S. Parkes Cadman, eminent

Congregationalist (both British-born as it happened), and the Reverend Billy Sunday. Four months after the War began *Harper's Weekly* printed "The Attack on New York," a military fantasy concocted by a disciple of Wood's and endorsed by Henry L. Stimson, recently President William Howard Taft's Secretary of War, as "containing nothing outside the bounds of military probability." [11] The *Metropolitan Magazine*, by no means reactionary, countered with a piece by Richard Harding Davis, America's ranking war correspondent, on the same theme. Its illustrations showed the Germans entrenched in a sand trap on a Long Island golf course and using the Piping Rock Country Club as headquarters—a detail likely to send millionaires' sons flocking to Plattsburgh. For a wider public a highly successful movie, *The Battle Cry of Peace*, showed what spike-helmeted invaders would do not to well-rolled fairways but to defenseless American women and children.

At first the Wilson administration was lukewarm about Preparedness. Wood's tunnel vision of what the nation needed—Dr. Leonard Wood's ideas carried out by General Leonard Wood—probably irked the President, whose bent was, though not exactly pacifist, pacific.* But as those invisible, intangible but inevitable transatlantic induction currents grew strong, Wilson adopted and promoted Preparedness with parades, speeches and fresh millions for expansion of the Army and Navy. In view of the way the War was going, emphasis should have been on light, fast craft for submarine hunting. But Jutland had not yet made it clear that Germany's capital ships would never get loose, and rising frictions with unstable Mexico and growingly powerful Japan were chronic reasons to build up any given kind of war strength. Boy readers of *St. Nicholas* were soon afforded articles on the firepower of the Navy's new battleships, the tactical difference between them and battle cruisers and the latest in destroyers and submarines.

In a paradox that dwindles when examined, Preparedness was popular with many who also liked President Wilson's campaign slogan for 1916: "He kept us out of war!" But for vastly different reasons Preparedness greatly disturbed and gained little ground with three conspicuous groups: the numerous and often articulate pacifists of practically all stripes, including many whose pacifism was part of a generalized collectivist radicalism, the more *Vaterland*-minded German-Americans and the most unreconstructed Irish-Americans.

The latter two had already allied themselves in another context in an agreement between the German-American Alliance and the Ancient Order

* Wilson's comment on a sequel to "The Attack on New York" published early in 1915 to promote vacation training camps for college boys: "I am very much interested in the successful working out of the idea . . . the students will derive not only . . . physical benefit . . . but also . . . practical military instruction . . . useful . . . in case their services should ever be required." (*Harper's Weekly*, January 2, 1915.) A model of benign caution.

of Hibernians to support each other in opposing federal restriction of immigration. The Irish were, however, the simpler case of "hyphenated American," * as simple as their venerable axiom: "England's necessity is Ireland's opportunity." The force created by Preparedness was likely to be employed on the Allied—the hated Sassenach's—side. The corollary pro-Germanism arising among Irish-Americans as soon as the War began was almost pure Anglophobia, for in the past the only German element for which the Irish had much use was lager beer. Now the War made Uhlans and U-boat commanders heroes to those editing Irish-American papers, heading local branches of the Ancient Order of Hibernians, preaching cryptic Irish chauvinism in Irish-Catholic parishes. Add the hundreds of thousands of first- and second-generation Irish whose difficulties in adjusting to the New World, which had deplorable manners in such contexts, kept them dependent on the partisan bitternesses of the Old. Note, to be fair, that Irish-Americans responding strongly to the snarls of Jeremiah O'Leary's *Irish Echo* were only a minority and that, once the nation declared war, many thousands of Irish Catholics loyally volunteered into uniform. But particularly in that day before public opinion polls, to politicians a noisy minority could sound like a majority. So the concentration of Irish-American voters in big-city Congressional districts tended to brake the gravitational pull toward belligerency that the party in power— the Democrats, specially sensitive to the Irish vote—felt more strongly as the War went on into months and years.

Among most of the hyphenated groups in 1914 ethnic ties as such had less to do with side taking. Huge numbers were from the friable Austro-Hungarian Empire that was nominal cause of the War. Chicago's Bohemians and Slovaks, for instance, might hope the Hapsburgs would meet defeat that might mean—as it proved to—national independence for their Old Country cousins, but they weren't as hot about it as Chicago's Irish on the other side. Hungarians, Croats and Slovenes, though also considering the Hapsburgs encumbrances on their homelands, were no more militant. Most of those groups responded well when, after Uncle Sam got into the War, official propagandists set about swinging them into line. Early reluctance among the non-German Central European enclaves was mostly the low-grade pacifism of the peasant culture.

In their view governments, any governments, were primarily harsh enemies of common folks like themselves and war was one of the whips of scorpions with which rapine, taxation and conscription were visited on the

---

* A phrase much used during World War I, notably by newspaper cartoonists and Theodore Roosevelt; the *Universal Oxford Dictionary* traces it back to 1893. The meaning was always clear; the intent long pejorative. By now, however, much of that is past, and this book uses the phrase as a handily concise way of saying "More or less definite group of Americans clinging to ethnic values brought over from the Old Country." Note that in the pre-War decade the German-American Alliance had no distaste for the hyphen.

just and the unjust alike. Jane Addams, founder of Chicago's Hull House settlement and pacifist leader, was reproached by one immigrant in 1917 for having persuaded him to take out the U.S. citizenship that made him liable to the draft. "I went into the citizenship class because you asked me to," he said. "I have to thank you if I am sent over to Europe to fight." [12] No hint of refusal, however, only annoyance because he had been led to hope that this American government was not just as bad medicine as any other for the little man. The trend of this aimlessly anarchistic reflex, being neither pro-German nor pro-Ally, was merely isolationist. Its leverage on votes and national policy was stronger after the War than during it. German efforts to exploit it among recently arrived industrial workers to hamper American production of munitions for the Allies came to nothing, though full-page advertisements warning Hungarians, Poles, Croats and so on that the stuff would be used to kill their kin in the Old Country were lavishly spread over sixty-eight newspapers in sixteen languages.

German-Americans were likely to share this kind of antiwarism. Ever since the influx of the Pennsylvania Dutch (mostly Rhineland Germans) in the early 1700's hatred of conscription and mistrust of rulers had been among emigrant Germans' reasons for uprooting themselves. What differentiated German-Americans of 1914 from Danish-Americans was a snowballing ethnic pride exceeding that of any group except the Irish. Germans coming to America since 1820 had averaged a high proportion of literate-to-cultivated people conscious of ethnic history and the cultural value of Old Country habits and language, which made them a more positively ambitious element than the Irish. The German-language press was out and away the strongest non-English press in the country. *Turnverein, Sängerbund* and German churches, both Lutheran and Catholic, were rife not only in proverbially German-rich Milwaukee, Cincinnati, St. Louis, Chicago but also Indianapolis, Baltimore, New York City's York-ville—wherever Germans' special skills, talent for hard work and cohesive-ness lent them the self-importance that goes with prospering. Their leaders were smugly aware that America's new higher learning in the graduate schools springing up around college campuses was built on German models and that every year more American students of both sexes sought genuine scholarship at the fountainhead in German universities. In the American mind German chemistry, German medicine, German music loomed larger than any rivals, and the superiority thus acknowledged was genuine. German ships were running British ships hard for top prestige on the North Atlantic. German Social Security laws guided the thinking of American reformers. . . .

To such sound reasons for admiring their Old Country cousins many German-Americans added the glory of the German Empire created by victory over France in 1871. That was easier because hope of a unified Germany had been dear to German liberals in the early 1800's. During the four decades since Sedan the growth of the new empire's sense of worldwide mission, pumped up by German publicists, professors, preachers and the German-American press, had seized on susceptible German-Americans' imaginations. After the Spanish-American War set Germany looking hard at waxing American power, Germany made a deliberate effort to widen intercultural bridges between the Fatherland and German-Americans. So high were hopes for New World *Deutschtum* that in certain cities where Germans had special weight they forced classes in German into the public elementary schools—on a voluntary basis, true, but no other ethnic group could thus entrench itself at the cost of all taxpayers. Norwegian-Americans seeking to bolster their peculiar values had to finance their own ethnic schools.

This must not be overstated. Any number of second-generation Germans were as apt at intermarriage and taken-for-granted assimilation as at brewing, piano making and farming. The mushrooming telephone system's directories were full of German names of households hard to distinguish from the Smiths next door or the McIntyres across the street. As the War came on, however, the German-American world must have been the envy of Irish Anglophobes and Czech Sokol leaders for the scale as well as the depth of its ethnic power. Just as the German Army was the most effective because best organized. . . . The National German-American Alliance, formal aspect of *Deutschtum*, founded in 1908, hence predating the pressure of the War, boasted* some 2,500,000 members and support from some 10,000 German-American organizations.

At first whether the United States entered the War was not crucial. Both Central Powers and Allies were assured by their respective experts that fighting would last only a few weeks; hence the force of a militarily unready America could not come to bear in time. Hence also the early lag in the Allies' propaganda pressure on America? (Luckily for them, the Germans provided everything needful by invading Belgium.) Germany's careful readiness, however, seems also to have extended to its public relations in America. Six days after Belgium was attacked there appeared in New York City *The Fatherland*, a new weekly "devoted to Fair-Play for Germany and Austria-Hungary," edited by George Sylvester Viereck, a journalist-poet of some standing in Greenwich Village. His father had been a member of Germany's Reichstag; he himself was New York City-reared and City

* Word used advisedly. In a short-lived Broadway play seeking fairer treatment for German-Americans in the spring of 1915 Justus Miles Forman had his protagonist wealthy German tell a German intelligence officer: "You haf been mistaken about us and it is partly our fault. We are like the parrot, we haf talked too damn much . . . calling ourselves German-Americans, German-Americans, German-Americans . . . you have heard it so often you . . . say to yourself American-Germans! . . . With our German papers and our German clubs and societies we haf held ourselves too much apart." The play was called *The Hyphen*. Its producer, Charles Frohman, was drowned in the *Lusitania* a few weeks after it opened. I make a present of that to any conspiracy-happy writer who has got tired of Lee Harvey Oswald.

College-educated, so his new paper, strongly as it smelled of the German-American Alliance, couched in workmanlike English its instructions to Americans on how to think and feel about the war.*

Viereck's subtle and poetic powers are apparent in his apostrophe to Wilhelm II as "Prince of Peace":

> May thy victorious armies rout
> The savage tribes against them hurled,
> The czar, whose scepter is the knout,
> And France, the wanton of the world.
>
> But thy great task will not be done
> Until thou vanquish utterly
> The Norman brother of the Hun,
> England, the Serpent of the Sea. . . .[13]

His genius for hyperbole is clear in his analysis of "the roots of the war . . . a war between German efficiency and English inefficiency, between German Democracy and the Feudalism of Great Britain and Russia. . . . The German Army is the most democratic institution in the world."[14] His sense of tact let him call President Wilson a "weak-kneed sophist"[15] for dealing too gently with Germany's foes at just the time when his political enemies were screaming at him to get tough with Germany and let him charge that Elbert Hubbard, a culture hero of freshwater esthetes, who drowned in the *Lusitania*, was a "paretic"[15] which sounded bad even to those who didn't know what it meant. He prepared America well to see in the paper that the national president of the German-American Alliance had told cheering thousands at German Day at the San Francisco Pan-Pacific Exposition in 1915: "What Greece was to Rome, that Germany is . . . to [America] . . . only . . . the Greek brought to Rome with his culture disgusting sensual vices while the German with his culture brings to his new home sturdy integrity and a pure and happy family life."[16] The next month Germany's unofficial representative at the exposition told a local meeting of the alliance that "it is better to be a hyphenated American . . . than to be a hypocritical Anglicized schoolmaster . . . in the presidential chair."[17]

Actually—as is often true of *ad hoc* publications, whether *Ramparts* or the *National Review*—*The Fatherland* probably reached few readers who did not already share its views. It nevertheless irked those edging toward sympathy

---

* After the War Viereck (*Spreading Germs of Hate*, 49–54) said that the paper was hastily cooked up and financed by $200 raised by himself and three cronies—a banker, a chemist, an accountant—with a first run of 10,000. Testimony before the U.S. Senate Committee on the Judiciary in 1919 makes it clear that his memory was faulty. Even Viereck's own account rouses suspicion that the German steamship offices in New York City, always close to the German government as Cunard was to the British, had a hand in the amazing rapidity with which *The Fatherland* was launched at the same time that its seagoing namesake was interned.

with the Allies. So did the Germans' frank purchase of the unprofitable New York *Evening Mail*; its new publisher was Edward A. Rumely, a German-educated Hoosier developing tractors for the American farmer. Also irritating was Dr. Bernhard Dernburg, former German colonial minister sent to America ostensibly to represent the German Red Cross but actually to support Viereck and Rumely in print or on the platform wherever he could wheedle a way in. "We Germans love the French and Belgians who were forced into the war," he told an audience in Westchester County.[18] With equal tact Congressman Richard Bartholdt of Missouri warned his colleagues to ban exports of munitions from America to the Allies on penalty of losing the votes of the 25 percent (a gross overestimate) of Americans with close relatives in Germany.

Only aggressively self-conscious German background can explain the lip-licking unction with which Mencken and Dreiser felicitated each other when Germany crushed into northern France and it seemed to be all over with the Allies. ". . . it would be an excellent thing for Europe and the world," Dreiser told the highly receptive Mencken, "if the despicable British aristocracy—the snobbery of British intellectuality were smashed and a German Vice-Roy sat in London." [19] By 1917 Mencken was pulling in the horns of his Nibelungen-style helmet. But well after the United States declared war, Dreiser sought publication for a sarcastic piece on "American Idealism and German Frightfulness" that the *Century* magazine, among others, rejected as clearly giving "aid and comfort to the enemy." [19]

The penalty for such vaporings was that Germany might take them seriously. It startled James W. Gerard, U.S. ambassador to Germany, when the No. 2 man in the German Foreign Affairs Office warned him that if America went to war over submarine warfare, the German and Irish-Americans would rise in revolt. "I thought he was joking," Gerard said, "but he was actually serious." [20] Adolf Hitler may have had such illusions about the German-American Bund. Whom the gods would destroy they first tempt to believe their own nonsense.

Within two months of the outbreak of the War the *Atlantic Monthly*, playing fair, printed articles supporting Germany from Hugo Münsterberg, eminent German psychologist at Harvard, and Kuno Francke, chief of Harvard's new Germanic Museum. These respected men (both already lending their names to the masthead of the *Fatherland*) told the *Atlantic*'s cultivated readers that the basic meaning of the War was that Germany, the world's model of dynamic order, was no longer to be put upon by other and less worthy nations. The next spring the *Lusitania* affair gave Francke misgivings. Münsterberg died before the declaration of war forced pro-Germanism underground.

Meanwhile, these ethnic champions had help from native, non-Teutonic Americans. Hearst's chain of sensational newspapers fervently preached isolationism, which suited the Germans nicely. Hearst's discernible reasons, doubtless cogent in his own eyes, were, as usual, personal. He wanted no preoccupation with Europe to distract America from his pet bugaboo, the Yellow Peril, and the chronic chaos, often tempting America to intervene, in Mexico, where he had large ranching and mining interests. So he financed *Patria*, starring Irene Castle and Milton Sills, a movie waving flags and repeatedly imperiling the heroine, to persuade the public that the real menace was imminent alliance between Mexico and Japan in unspeakable dirty work. But then he would probably have been isolationist anyway. He had long hated Britain, and his papers in Boston, New York City and Chicago depended heavily on the urban masses of Irish- and German-Americans. Much of the money with which Arthur Brisbane, Hearst's chief editorial aide, bought the Washington *Times* came secretly from German-Americans of the alliance. One reason why they backed Brisbane was his zeal for exempting light wines and beer from Prohibition. But add a tacit assumption that a Brisbane-managed paper would sing Hearst's song about perfidious Albion and the iniquities of ammunition makers and the banks financing their sales to the Allies.*

Another volunteer, Senator William J. Stone of Missouri, isolationist chairman of the U.S. Senate's Foreign Relations Committee, may have been mindful that St. Louis was almost as German as Milwaukee; anyway he wrought so unscrupulously that Lippmann described him as "the type of senile and slinking politician . . . which the basic evils of our congressional system throw up." [21] Senator Robert M. La Follette of Wisconsin was a different case. Had Milwaukee not been the largest city in a state with a generally heavy German population, his neo-Populist instincts might well have set him against banker- and Northeast-flavored foreign entanglements anyway. It may also have weighed with him—or his supporters—that feeling from Lake Michigan to the Black Hills was, as it tends to remain, residually isolationist; it is somehow associated with the high proportion of Scandinavians as well as Germans.

That tradition was pungently expressed in the career of Charles A. Lindbergh of Minnesota, handsome son of Swedish immigrant farmers, leader in the neo-Populist Non-Partisan League, already father of a son destined to fame in aviation, isolationism and conservation. Lindbergh, Sr., kept his ideas to himself after war was declared no better than did Dreiser. Such sharing with others is courageous in inverse proportion to the hero's

---

* Besides two English-language papers in New York City, Hearst also owned the German-language *Deutsches Journal*, washing it out early in 1917. Anybody seeking a defense of Hearst here may turn to *The Big Money*, where Dos Passos, deep in revulsion against the War, includes in an otherwise unflattering portrait: "Sometimes Hearst was high enough above the battle to see clear. He threw all his powers as a publisher into an effort to keep the country sane and neutral during the first world war. He opposed loans to the Allies, seconded Bryan in his lonely fight to keep the interest of the United States paramount over the interests of the Morgan banks and the anglophile businessmen of the East; for his pains he was razzed as a pro-German. . . ." (532.)

egocentricity. The U.S. government suppressed his *Your Country at War*, a compilation of his speeches that, though sometimes saying, "Now we are in the war [we] must prosecute it until we have established peace," also accused an "inner circle . . . [of] money sharks" [22] of tricking the United States into war by deliberately exposing Americans to danger from the Germans at sea; the motive was, of course, profits from War industry and War banking. "If you really are for America first," he complained, "solely for the masses primarily, then you are classed as pro-German by the big press . . . supported by the speculators." [22] Such talk is almost as morbid as that of Henry Ford and Populist Ignatius Donnelly, though, so far as I know, the elder Lindbergh never shared those statesmen's anti-Semitism. His paranoid flavor was sharpest when he ascribed support from "big finance speculators" [22] for the American Red Cross to plans to use it after the War for economic control of prostrate Europe. Then as cures for the nation's ills he lamely prescribed public ownership of banks and the rail, telephone and telegraph systems, for he suspected the Money Trust of tampering with press filings and private messages.

In the sultry air of the Cotton Kingdom the War stirred up another Populist, former Congressman (and future Senator) Thomas E. Watson of Georgia. This sincere friend of the underdog had turned Catholic- and black-hater and now allied himself with Hearst and the IWW against the War. The U.S. Post Office's list of periodicals barred from the mails as violating Wartime laws against hampering the War effort duly included his *Jeffersonian* magazine alongside *The Masses*, organ of America's Red radicalism. One reason was Watson's editorial of August 8, 1917, accusing America of entering the War solely to protect J. P. Morgan's loans to the Allies: "*Where Morgan's money went, your boy's blood must go,* ELSE MORGAN WILL LOSE HIS MONEY. That's all there is to it." [23] Neither Lindbergh nor *The Masses* ever said it so concisely, though both tried.

Early in the War Watson had warned his red-neck public that Preparedness was a scheme to transform the nation into a German-style military camp, then that the declaration of war came of "the most ravenous commercialism that ever cursed a nation." [23] After all, many of his readers were grandsons of poor whites for whom Dixie's Civil War had been "a rich man's war and a poor man's fight" as the Confederacy tried to enforce conscription. He urged his following to resist registration and induction and raised $100,000 to challenge the draft law in court. Yet, though the government smothered his paper, he was never threatened with jail, and having several times been prosecuted for obscene libel of the Catholic clergy, he was used to court troubles. After the War his antics as U.S. Senator from Georgia were so grotesque as to imply a periodic paranoid state heavy with delusions of persecution and retrospective falsification—a sad end for a leader who when younger and sounder had done much against Bourbon neglect of the one-gallus man. He and the ideological pacifists made strange bedfellows, but then Watson was used to that. The man who financed his first paper was Colonel W. D. Mann, owner-publisher of *Town Topics*, America's most profitable blackmail sheet.

Emotions farther from paranoia—maybe only civilized alarm—led G. Stanley Hall to warn America that between Germany's military genius and her Nietzsche-inspired ruthlessness there was no stopping her. However regretfully he reached this conclusion, to state it did Germany a favor. One wing of effective war propaganda always shows that the belligerent client is morally right; the other that it is in any case irresistible. Sometimes these theses conform to the facts better than usual, sometimes worse. The technique does not vary.

For all such paid and volunteer help, however, Germany lost its propaganda game in America within weeks of the outbreak of the War, eight months before the *Lusitania* again brought calamitous bad luck, as if a supernal dealer had stacked the cards. The Allies won the first propaganda round partly through their own Blimpishness. For months they barred reporters, including their own, from seeing action, kept them dependent on scant communiqués and behind-the-lines interviews. Not until spring, 1915, were a few specially sifted correspondents, all English, allowed to visit British trenches. In contrast, the Germans, as Harold D. Lasswell noted in his hindsight study of propaganda in the War, "favored the war correspondents of foreign countries before the Allies woke up to their importance." [24] Maybe the reason was mere pride in their impressive military machine. Anyway, they accredited many neutral reporters, including such crack Americans as Richard Harding Davis, Will Irwin, Irvin S. Cobb and John T. McCutcheon, under whose eye-catching by-lines American newspapers and magazines soon carried vivid accounts of how German armies went through a country they mistrusted. Davis' terrifying picture of the field-gray columns penetrating Brussels like a disciplined avalanche had great minatory value for the German cause. But much of the others' copy was about household goods clogging streets where German looters had thrown away less prized items; German soldiers piling straw in dwellings to be burned; a child's doll "flat in the road—a cannon wheel had passed over the head . . ."; [25] German troops using civilians as shields when entering villages. . . .

Such details increased the harm done the German image by the invasion of Belgium and the burning of the University of Louvain. The Allies' added charges of mutilation and rape, coming along in due season, were hardly needed to dismay homebodies who had never seen the ruthlessness often accompanying and sometimes inseparable from war. Besides, immediate severity in occupied places was Germany's predetermined policy, a calculated use of the *Schrecklichkeit* that Allied propaganda thenceforth harped on so effectively. An old man peers at German troops through his opera glass? Cut his throat. A German officer finds his coffee bitter, suspects poison? Shoot the man and wife supplying it. In at least one instance Uhlans burning a Belgian village stood up and shot a twenty-year-old civilian solely because he was a potential soldier.[26] Such instances reported not by Allied propagandists but by American journalists working behind the German lines at Germany's invitation were necessarily impressive. Evidence from both sides suggests that much such harshness came of exasperation with the Belgians for showing fight. German troops had been promised that the Belgian Army was small and sloppy—which it was—and would at most offer only token resistance. When Belgium rejected Germany's request for free passage and dead Germans piled up round the forts of Liège—which imperiled the timetable vital to German strategy—many German officers seem to have felt outraged. So they tended to wink at arson and looting, welcomed rumors of civilian sniping that, in their view, called for mass execution of civilian hostages and often let their men go uncontrollable on the wine and spirits in the village inn or the local magnate's house.* ". . . drunk with looted liquor and destruction" [27] was neutral Gerald Morgan's eyewitness description of the Germans burning Louvain.

"German atrocities" require attention because propaganda embroidery made of the original allegations a fecund folklore for Americans as well as British, French and the minor neutrals in Western Europe. Stimulating to both adrenal and lachrymatory glands, it was essential in bolstering America's will to fight after entering the War. Conversely, sharp revulsion from it after the War gave disillusion disproportionate sting.

The groundwork was laid soon after the first round of alleged horrors. In September, 1914, five American correspondents, including Cobb, McCutcheon and Harry Hansen,† who had been with the Germans in Belgium jointly cabled their editors that in contrast with reports in the neutral press, they had seen no "unprovoked reprisals," "wanton brutality" or drunkenness and had no firsthand evidence of atrocities. As far as this cable went—on analysis not as far as Germany's eager use of it implied—it was significant. In December a colonel in British intelligence told a British

---

* I know of only one case in which looted drink was beneficial: A mixed bag of civilians were under guard in a barn at Sisonne to be shot the next day. A Saxon soldier came on a quantity of wine, used it to fuddle the guards—and a pregnant woman and two children among the prospective victims succeeded in escaping. (Friedel, *Over There*, 320.)

† In 1929 Hansen (New York *World*, February 8) said that some weeks later he filed stories about "the shooting of civilians at Tamines and various German acts of violence . . . I helped provide the Germans with a choice bit of propaganda [but] . . . I never believed in their complete war innocence." Will Irwin, on the same beat, did not sign. Asked why in 1929, he "strongly [implied] that he did not sign because he believed in the reality of the atrocities." (*Cf.* Mock and Larson, *Atrocity Propaganda*, 29 n., and the further note of Irwin's not having been with the other five.) For a sound try at reconciling soldiers' with civilians' evidence on atrocities see Hueffer, "What 'They' Do in Flanders," *Harper's Weekly*, January 30, 1915.

reporter not to put "too much weight in these atrocity stories." [28] The liberal, strongly anti-German editor of *Harper's Weekly*, Norman Hapgood, wrote that though a German general had told him, "We did a lot that was very terrible in Belgium," the public should be warned that "a large proportion of the stories against the Germans are false." [29] The radical-minded *Metropolitan Magazine* said in an editorial in May, 1915, that atrocity stories had been so glibly promulgated by "the press of the Allies and so gullibly swallowed . . . [that] impartial people began to doubt whether . . . Louvain and Dinant had been burned."

With the end of the War queasy memory furthered skepticisms. In Dos Passos' *One Man's Initiation* (1919), an early clue to this soon-to-be-modish attitude, a silly woman tells juicy atrocity yarns to the radical-minded hero en route to France to drive an ambulance; precociously he demurs, "I wonder if it's all true." [30] Cummings' autobiographical "I" in *The Enormous Room* (1922), asked by a French officer, "You are doubtless aware of the atrocities committed by the Boches? . . . You do not believe?" shrugs it off with "Ça se peut." [31] (The pulse of authentic poetry beat in Cummings as soundly as in Vachel Lindsay, Ezra Pound, T. S. Eliot, but a true poet, whether being peevish about war or about the USSR in *Eimi*, is not necessarily a sound observer-diagnostician.) Both set down gossip about Allied soldiers abusing German prisoners and likely enough incidents in which Germans behaved handsomely. Robert Graves' *Goodbye to All That* (1929) laid mutilations shown by Belgian civilians entirely to shellfire, maybe from friendly guns, and set down his fellow officers' views as of 1917:

> Propaganda reports of atrocities were ridiculous . . . while the Germans were in a position to commit atrocities against enemy civilians, Germany . . . never had an enemy on her soil. We no longer believed accounts of unjustifiable German atrocities . . . knowing the Belgians now at first hand . . . we meant rape, tortures and mutilation, not summary shooting of suspected spies, *franc-tireurs,* or disobedient local officials. . . . We did not believe that rape was more common on the German side of the line than on the Allied. . . . It was unnecessary.[32]

That some Allied soldiers abused prisoners and many Germans behaved well is common sense. As the worst tales shocked an ill-prepared public, *Life*'s Martin wrote: ". . . to believe all the . . . German cruelties and reject . . . anti-German cruelties is not intelligent . . . War . . . lets loose hordes of men, the bulk of whom are humane . . . many who are not . . . excites and intensifies the passions and may even brutalize the kindly. . . . It is the war that is terrible, not these poor, dreadful incidents." [33] A little later: "In a great war there will be all kinds of participants and all kinds of behavior, and also innumerable tales that are not true." [34] Soon, however, *Life*, hot anti-German from the beginning, ran a cartoon of an aviator awarded the Iron Cross for killing "a dozen." "A dozen soldiers?" asks his charming mother. "No," says pretty sister, reading the paper, "three were nurses. He dropped a bomb on a hospital." [35] (The cartoonist was Reginald Birch, Briton long resident in America, illustrator of such hands-across-the-sea works as *Little Lord Fauntleroy* and *Master Skylark*.) Then it pictured Wilhelm II decorating German submariners carrying as trophies baby shoes from babies drowned in ships they had sunk. About the same time Madison Grant's *Passing of the Great Race* contributed the theory that Germany's habit of unchivalrous brutality came of the "annihilation of [its] gentle classes" brought about in the 1600's by the Thirty Years' War.

Graves had one point. Fighting only in their own or friendly country, the Allies lacked the battle-drunk temptation to savage enemy persons and property. But that vitiated his hint that Belgian women were so compliant or venal that no randy German ever needed to take one by violence; that even supposing a few Germans guilty of rape, their British counterparts would have done the same in the same circumstances; that no German ever wantonly mutilated a civilian; that the only Belgian civilians shot were identified snipers or saboteurs. . . . Sir Philip Gibbs' *Now It Can Be Told*, attempt of an eminent War correspondent to fill in omissions imposed by censorship and discretion, told of Frenchwomen rubbing thumb and finger together to explain why the Germans had no need "to use violence in love-making. There are many volunteers." [36] But not even this debunking book ruled out rape, and Gibbs' next book still used Germany as an example of how a nation can "lose all sense of reason and play the wild beast." [37] In any case there had been wide distribution of eyewitness testimony taken pretty fresh from Belgian and French civilians about the first few weeks of the German invasion of 1914—source of the rich early crop of atrocity stories.

After 1920 these publications were cried down as either self-deception or deliberate faking. Fifty years later to apply to them reasonable views of evidence—not court-of-law evidence but commonsense reporter's evidence —may suggest that the post-War reaction against them was immaturely facile. These accounts of what A or B saw or went through often include details of a lame vividness that probably spells reliability. Some witnesses generalize hysterically; others obviously apply hearsay to their own cases. But an open mind comes away ghastly sure of mass shootings of civilians up to some hundreds at a time, including women and children obviously guiltless of sniping; unconscionable looting, arson and vandalism; mutilation (though rare) and a certain amount of rape, sometimes of women of an age inconsistent with Graves' sneers. The scale of it was probably not as bad as what John Reed and Robert Dunn, war correspondents who had recently been with the Germans in France and were skeptical about atrocities there, learned about the Hungarian invaders of Serbia in 1914–15. But by Western standards as of 1914, German actions in the first few weeks in Belgium badly needed the whitewash that later writers were so ready with in order to give warmongers a black eye.

Britain's casebook relied on Belgian refugees to England examined by barristers noted for skill in interrogation. It has instances of German officers shot for rape after drumhead court-martial. The chairman of the presiding committee, Viscount Bryce, was the most respected ambassador whom Britain had ever sent to Washington and an honored friend of German culture. That wool was pulled over his eyes to the extent later suggested is hard to believe. The impressiveness of some of the data published by the French came from their including German soldiers' field diaries with reproductions of the scrawled on-the-spot texts. One noted what happened when a local sniper fired (allegedly, and quite possibly he did) on the invaders. "The village was surrounded, our men a yard apart so nobody could get out . . . any who tried were shot down. Then the Uhlans set the fires house by house. . . ." [38] Keep in mind that this was no faction-poisoned, exasperatingly prolonged, guerrilla-embittered war such as blighted Spain in Napoleon's time and Vietnam in ours. It was, instead, the first few days of a formally declared, fully uniformed, highly disciplined invasion of an open, civilized countryside, and fifty years earlier the American Civil War, bloodiest the world had yet seen, had few such incidents. In 1914 *Harper's Weekly* made the same point about the American occupation of Veracruz the preceding April: "There was sniping in Vera Cruz just as there was in Louvain. Louvain was burned by order. In Vera Cruz snipers were captured [by the American military]. Not a house was destroyed. Not a prisoner was shot." [39] And the cultural gap between leathernecks and Mexican guerrillas, hence the likelihood of xenophobic violences, was far wider than that between the German subaltern and the Belgian village official facing the firing squad.*

The Germans' countercompilation of instances of Belgians sniping, mutilating wounded and so on was published in America. Much of it rings true but suffers from scarcity of cases and deriving chiefly from officers. It is difficult not to respect the summing-up of the Bryce Report which, with sound historical sense, admitted that few of its data would have been much out of the way in Louis XIV's or even Wellington's time:

> The ill-treatment . . . rape, plunder . . . widely committed [by
> Germans] . . . [were] more numerous and shocking than would be

---

* Harry Elmer Barnes (*The Genesis of the World War*, 294) said that Bryce, asked after the War about the validity of the Bryce Report, said that in wartime one may expect anything. Barnes took that to mean it was invalid. Yet it may merely have been harking back to some of the general comment about human orneriness in the foreword to the report. Neither *Genesis* nor Barnes' *In Quest of Truth and Justice* (1928) is impressive. The best case against atrocities-as-fact is James Morgan Reed, *Atrocity Propaganda* (1939), which discredits many a deliberate propagandist and sensational reporter but still leaves the Germans smelling bad.

expected in warfare between civilized powers, but they differ rather
in extent than in kind from what happened in previous though not
recent wars . . . in every large army there must be a proportion of
men of criminal instincts whose worse passions are unloosed by the
immunity which the conditions of war afford. Drunkenness . . .
may even turn a soldier who has no criminal habits into a
brute. . . .[40]

The report's data on the widely publicized Belgian babies spitted on
bayonets are explicit, but a nice taste in evidence rejects them as probably
reflecting vindictive hysteria. (The same criteria reject the Germans'
contention that Belgian civilian sniping was officially planned guerrilla war
and official Belgian posters ordering civilians to refrain from rashness were
the activating signals.) The grisly tale of the crucified Canadian officer did
not hold up when Gibbs checked it. The bit about the Germans shipping
their dead home to be rendered into War-scarce soap fats died when it
came out that the *Kadaveren* in the evidence cited were those of horses, not
men. But even such scorners of the Allies' moral position as Veblen and
Francis Neilson, former Member of Parliament and author of *How
Diplomats Make War*, grudgingly conceded that, as Neilson wrote, "The
Belgian people have had almost every kind of atrocity inflicted on them." [41]

Even after those disastrous first few weeks, the German knack of making
oneself look bad had kept the Allies' public relations work in America
pretty much done for them. With exquisite tact German-American agencies' mail circulars asking money for relief supplies for blockaded German
civilians carried the slogan *Deutschland über Alles!* In a far more grisly error
Germany gave the Allies a glowing martyr by shooting Edith Cavell, a
British nurse confessedly guilty of helping Allied prisoners escape from
occupied Belgium; life imprisonment would have fully answered the
authorities' purpose. Germany shipped thousands of Belgians of both sexes
into exile as forced labor, which, in the view of James Morgan Reed, expert
on propaganda in the War, was crucial in keeping America inflamed against
it. (It was those two subjects—the Cavell case and the callous exploitation
of forced enemy labor—that gave George Bellows material for his two great
propaganda paintings; when Joseph Pennell reproached him for handling
the homecoming of worn-out peasants in "Return of the Useless" when he
had not personally witnessed such a scene, Bellows said he never heard that
Leonardo da Vinci had been at the Last Supper.) Germany's treatment of
Belgians in Belgium in effect blackmailed the neutral world into having to
feed them, and every fund raising for Herbert Hoover's Committee for
Belgian Relief—which he managed so well that it set him on the road to the
White House—poignantly reminded Americans of how Belgium had been
overrun and, one kept hearing, fearfully mistreated. Hoover's deputy liaison
with the German military government of Belgium was Vernon Kellogg, a

biologist of Leland Stanford, Jr., University who had done his graduate work in German universities, spoke the language well—and in his tours of inspection had unusual opportunities to see just what had gone on. "We were not haters of Germany when we went to Belgium," he said. ". . . inescapable sights and sounds and knowledge forced on us" [42] emotional causes of hating them. He thought it would be no wonder if, after the War, "the people of the world, when they recognize any human being as German, will shrink aside so that they may not touch him as he passes." [43]

And Germany sank the *Lusitania*, a Pyrrhic victory largely accidental. The submarine doing it had no specific orders about this prima donna of Britain's maritime prestige. Indeed the U-20 was going home to refit when those four great funnels climbed over the horizon in range of her periscope. The torpedo used was next to the last on board. The decision to send it on its momentous way seems to have come of the U-20's identifying officer's assumption that four funnels meant the *Mauretania*,* the huge sister ship known then to be in service as a troopship. But just before the *Lusitania* had sailed from New York City, German interests—Viereck took credit for this second greatest publicity blunder of the War—ran newspaper advertisements warning neutrals off British ships. That made it look as if the Kaiser's sneaky U-boats had been specifically set on the great ship carrying hundreds of neutral passengers. It was worse luck—for German propaganda as well as for the lost passengers—that slack precautions, untrained personnel and rapid foundering led to high loss of life, including many women and children. Elsie Janis, a star of the musical stage, later the entertain-the-boys heroine of the American Expeditionary Force, appearing in London in 1915, wrote widely reprinted verses about the *Lusitania* showing how to use it to rouse anti-German feeling—a lead zealously followed for years:

> Where are You, God? . . .
> I can't believe that You have seen

---

* This point about mistaken identity is the major contribution of *Lusitania*, Colin Simpson's recent book about the old propaganda controversy. Otherwise his book is admirably zealous homework wrongheadedly applied. True, for instance, the *Lusitania* was nominally a Royal Navy auxiliary fitted with gun mounts; but on her last voyage, by Simpson's own account, her deck guns had been removed, and if, as he strongly implies, she had others mounted between decks, there is no evidence that her inexperienced scratch crew included the gun crews needed if they were to be used. True also, she was carrying a few hundred tons of munitions, some clandestinely, and some of her passengers may have been Canadian Army personnel. But the quantity of either was inadequate basis for the *post facto* German claim that she was sunk as an armed auxiliary cruiser carrying military forces and munitions and therefore fair game. Indeed the error about the *Mauretania* makes it clear that the U-20's people were unaware of her identity and knew nothing of the grounds for such a claim. As for Simpson's contention that, for propaganda purposes, the Admiralty tempted the Germans to sink her when she had a large complement of neutral passengers, that is strictly for those who enjoy believing that John Wilkes Booth was part of Edwin A. Stanton's conspiracy to assassinate Abraham Lincoln; and that Lyndon B. Johnson had a hand in the assassination of John F. Kennedy. The seagoing snafu that Simpson embroiders to substantiate this is obviously partly brass hat stupidity as usual, partly fumbling owing to previous inexperience in antisubmarine operations.

> The things that they have done. . . .
> And yet upon this earth of Yours
> There still exists the Hun. . . .
>
> Where are You, God?
>   In whom I put my trust?
> You must be there,
>   And You are great and just.
> Your mighty sea they've turned into a grave,
> A little baby slumbers on each wave. . . .[44]

Then Germany allowed a private designer of what he called satirical medals to circulate abroad one showing the *Lusitania* sinking with guns and airplanes on deck under the words "No contraband" and on the other side passengers boarding her under "Business as usual." The British found one in Holland, saw its value as evidence of Germany's callous barbarity and distributed some 250,000 reproductions where they would do most good.

The Imperial Navy did not need bad luck to make its submariners look inhumane. At one point it announced that U-boats were under orders to sink hospital ships, no matter how well marked, with the purpose of forcing the British to withdraw convoy craft from high-seas duty to protect them. After unrestricted submarine warfare resumed in 1917, a U-boat that had sunk the British freighter *Belgian Prince* and taken her crew on deck, stove in their boats, removed lifebelts from most of them and submerged. Four survived to tell about it. Such nastiness was unusual, cannot possibly have been standard operating procedure; the U-boat skippers probably were on the whole little more ruthless than their British opposite numbers would have been in such ticklish duty up against Q-ships and merchant skippers ordered to ram enemy submarines if possible. But no such palliations apply to the Germans' industrious destructiveness in retreat late in 1918, when the War was obviously ending. Allow some military excuse for blowing up evacuated villages that might shelter the advancing Allies and for felling the tall trees that usually line French highways, to block the roads with their trunks. But there was none for taking the time and trouble to fell fruit trees that had survived three years of neglect and damage. Wister, touring the War zones in the spring of 1919, mourned "the murdered fruit-trees . . . the symetrically amputated orchard, dead, on its knees, so to speak, as if had prayed its destroyers to spare the other orchards' lives. Since this land was not to be the invaders' booty, as much of it as could be killed should die." [45] The number and scope of such fellings showed they were not the whims of sulky individual officers but done on orders down the chain of command. In 1960 Duffus, a liberal and civilized nonhater, wrote thoughtfully: "I am inclined to believe that in 1914, as in 1939, the Germans—bearers of so much light, drinkers of beer, lovers of music, exponents from time to time of an orderly sort of liberty—were under an evil spirit." [46]

Maybe the angels were puzzled when the Columbia University branch of the Collegiate Anti-Militarism League sent President Wilson a telegram advising him to do nothing about the *Lusitania* affair because it had "no legal or moral significance." [47] Yet angels might have been prepared for such ingenuousness—or casuistry—by previous observation of the American pacifist movement that had probably drawn their sympathetic interest in its pre-War phases.

In early 1914 the prestige of pacifism was high, its ramifications subtle, its emotional basis—revulsion from even potential violence as a factor in international situations—most engaging. Its wide acceptance had many well-placed, articulate and, in some cases, acute Americans disillusioned about the War before it began, hence particularly open to post-War disillusion. Like most American reformist movements, old or new, it was a transplanted version of a European-cosmopolitan model. An American "peace movement" with international roots had waxed and waned since William Lloyd Garrison's time. Its post-1900 waxing was associated with the immense renown of Count Tolstoy and the persuasive indictment of war sometimes explicit, more often implicit in *War and Peace* as well as in his didactic writings. At the time his picturesque eccentricities and curious death in 1910, added to world esteem, gave him a position in the public consciousness as if the prestige of Mahatma Gandhi had been piled on that of Dr. Albert Schweitzer. A great many people would have agreed with Judge Lindsey that Tolstoy was "the man with the greatest vision that has found any expression on this planet." [48]

Sympathy for such pacifism came from those with other kinds of prestige. Alfred Nobel founded his Peace Prize with money made from dynamite— as handy for military demolition teams and experimenters with naval ordnance as for civil engineers. With money made partly from steel armor plate Andrew Carnegie lent the American touch and a cruder irony by building at The Hague a Peace Palace, a sort of international sanitarium for the god of war. And the war-deploring gospel of all but anarchists and hot Marxists was *The Great Illusion* (1910) by Norman Angell, an erudite and persuasive Briton much at home in America. He taught that post-1900 economic and social interdependences made large-scale war about as much of a calamity for the victor as for the vanquished; in any case was a game no longer worth the candle. Hence war was far less likely to occur than ever before, supposing governments understood as much. To make sure, he proposed that peace-minded majorities in Britain and Germany particularly—working people, plain people, thinking people, people of goodwill— cooperate across frontiers in *pari passu* political effort to check aggressive policies and freeze armaments. He was aware of but heeded too little men's sporadic abilities to grow not just careless of but passionately blind to their own best interests; thus the failure of Europe's Socialist parties to resist the War spirit of 1914 shattered Angell's hopes. In any case he had overweighted his major premise, only a half-truth to begin with. Though it was impossible to win a large war, it was nevertheless still possible disastrously to lose one—as Russia learned in 1917 and Germany after 1918.

The new War did not take the wind out of pacifists' sails to the extent that might have been expected. The Reverend Francis Green, who had done well in Chautauqua tents with a lecture, "The Key to the Twentieth Century," showing there would never be another war because civilization had got beyond that, merely dropped that line of talk and took up "The Truth About Japan"—the Mikado had personally assured him that there would never be a war between Japan and America. But the kind of thinking that Angell led to—one cannot directly blame so good a mind for its admirers' excesses—was blatant in a letter to *Life* after four months of fighting, suggesting it would have been better had nobody opposed the Germans. Suppose Belgium had done as Germany wished, numbly bowing the invaders on, so the Germans' right wing could walk into Paris on schedule. Suppose France had agreed to pay the huge indemnity that Germany would have imposed, suppose the Entente powers had handed over the colonies and spheres of secondary influence that Germany desired: "The German soldiers . . . would have become ashamed of their job; the Socialists would have come to the top in Germany; German students would have flocked to the Sorbonne. . . ." [49] How ashamed General von Kluck, as grim a soldier as Tilly or Gneisenau, would have been as he led his footsore divisions down the Champs-Élysées!

At the other end of the intellectual spectrum from Angell soon glowed the aniline dyes of gut appeal from Tin Pan Alley:

> . . . in her lonely years
> I heard a mother murmur through her tears:
> CHORUS
> I didn't raise my boy to be a soldier.
> I brought him up to be my pride and joy.
> Who dares to place a musket on his shoulder
> To shoot some other mother's darling boy?
> Let nations arbitrate their future troubles.*
> It's time to lay the sword and gun away.
> There'd be no war today
> If mothers all would say:
> "I didn't raise my boy to be a soldier."†

* This probably reflects the intensive diplomatic campaign, which resulted in numerous fine-sounding treaties, that Bryan, as Secretary of State, had been waging for bilateral agreements between nations sending all future disputes to arbitration.

† "I Didn't Raise My Boy to Be a Soldier," words by Alfred Bryan, music by Al Piantadosi. Copyright © 1915, renewed Copyright © 1943. Leo Feist, Inc., N.Y., N.Y. Used by permission.

The cover shows Mom laying aside her knitting to cuddle her boy, behind them a vision of soldiers and bursting shells. The whiny tune, no great thing, was nevertheless worth stealing; a fellow composer soon had a court verdict of plagiarism against Al Piantadosi, who had set Alfred Bryan's lyric to music. That did not affect its popularity. Alexander Fichtlander, principal of P.S. 165 in Brooklyn, even taught his pupils to sing it in assembly and lined the corridors of the school with supplementary pacifist posters. When a local National Guard unit, then trying to fill its ranks, took a dim view of this, Fichtlander said: "I am doing all in my power to breed in the schools a wholesome horror of war" [50] and told the press he had the explicit backing of his superiors.

The success of "I Didn't Raise My Boy . . ." early in the War showed not only that Tin Pan Alley could be just as mawkish for peace as for war. It also meant that many grass-roots Americans already feared lest their country be somehow sucked into the War and that the good cause of pacifism had some appeal for gossipers over backyard fences as well as for settlement workers. Early in 1915 the B. F. Keith vaudeville theaters, no haunts of the intelligentsia, had great success with a one-act drama, *War Brides*, starring the intensely exotic Alla Nazimova. In a vaguely European village most of the men are called up to fight, and the government urges bachelors thus drafted to marry before leaving to breed fighting men for the future. Nazimova, already pregnant by her drafted husband, denounces such marriages, for only by ceasing to give birth can women prevent future wars. Learning that her husband has been killed, she shoots herself to spare her unborn child the ordeal of life in a war-ridden world. In 1916 she had a far wider success in a movie version, and at the same time Thomas H. Ince's *Civilization*, a pacifist sermon in celluloid, showed further that the screen was a fine vehicle for propaganda of whatever purport, Preparedness, Pacifism or Prohibition.

Pacifism and Preparedness knew each other for natural enemies like cobra and mongoose. To pacifists Wood's Preparedness meant either that Americans were already War-destined or that its parades, halftones of brawny lads in campaign hats and movies about alien hordes despoiling God's country would soon make them so. Underneath it all the radical pacifist smelled a "new demand of American industrialism for armament orders at home, for . . . foreign markets . . . for the discipline of military patriotism . . . against developing social strains . . ." [51] as Millis retrospectively summed it up. These *post hoc* suspicions were ingenuously clear in a manifesto of the Women's Peace Party of New York City printed late in 1916 in the *Survey*, organ of American social workers, calling "the radical peace movement . . . America's best answer to the war," defining its purpose as "to stop the war . . . organize the world for peace at the close of

the war . . . warn democracy (or such democracy as we have in America) *
about the subtle dangers of militarism . . . military training is bad for the
bodies and souls and minds of boys . . . free minds . . . undrilled to
obedience are vital to the life of a democracy. . . . To hold the fort for
liberty over here . . . until . . . every fool can see the folly of war
preparations . . . is a task worthy of the grimmest and gayest fighters
among us." [52]

Women's movements, whether radical or just morally energetic, whether
for peace, votes-for-women, Prohibition, birth control or the suppression of
the corset or of cigarettes, were unfortunately prone to such foot-tapping
tactlessness as calling "fools" those they hoped to convert. In pacifist
women's view Man made and valued War, Woman repudiated its
heart-rending slaughter of the children she bore and the individual men she
loved. As spontaneously as a spider spins thread out of her innards, women
had spun themselves the implicit hope—or conviction that it was true
because it ought to be—that if people, mostly women, only deplored war
heartily and long enough, it would disappear. To that end they held
elaborate women's meetings to promote international goodwill, bypassing
governments, and to nag or wheedle men into settling international disputes
peacefully.

Fortunately for the dignity of a worthy cause the figure who was
Woman-as-Peace-Incarnate-in-America was no peevish radical or veiled
seeress but solidly serene Jane Addams, whom Vachel Lindsay apostro-
phized early in 1915 as "Our Lady of Light, and our best woman and
Queen. . . . Stand now for peace (though anger break your heart). . . ." [53]
She had been standing for peace, indeed outstanding for peace, for a
decade. Her pacifism came of gratifying experience with the hyphenated
groups for whom her Hull House sought to soften the ordeals of the New
World and the industrial big city. She shared her sisters' horror of the
wasteful savagery of war and Angell's view of its senselessness. But for her
the worst of it was "its total prevention of mutual understanding of peoples.
. . . When a South Italian Catholic [she wrote] is forced by the . . .
situation [in a factory] to make friends with an Austrian Jew, representing
another nationality and another religion, both of which cut into all his
established prejudices, he . . . gradually loses them. . . ." [54]

Her grasp on that doctrine—it recalls hopes, some of them realized,
raised by FEPC laws in the late 1950's—brought her hegemony among
women meeting to tell one another that war was intolerable and women
would destroy it. Soon after the War began, she was a founder and first

* This slur on American democracy was no surprise in anything signed, as the manifesto
was, by Crystal Eastman, handsome sister-aide of Max Eastman (editor of the *Masses*) and
eminent militant feminist. She soon married Walter Fuller, a Briton then managing the
American tour of his three sisters' concerts of folk songs, and with his help organized the
American Union Against Militarism. (Eastman, *Living*, 563.)

president of a new Women's Peace Party, then of an Emergency Peace
Convention held in Chicago. In April, 1915, peace-minded women from
both warring and neutral nations invited her to preside over a meeting at
The Hague to form a Women's International League for Peace and
Freedom. This choice doubtless reflected both her prestige and the hopes,
already high on both sides of the water, that the goodwill and international
leverage of the United States would create a post-War world purged of the
most toxic hatreds and equipped with a sort of sprinkler system to damp
wars down before they burst into flame. Britons as dissimilar as G. Lowes
Dickinson, learned lover of ancient Greece, and Winston Churchill, *enfant
terrible* of Parliament, saw such prophylactic world revisions as fitting fruits
of the War almost before it began. Dickinson also plumped for the
self-determination of small peoples that proved so dangerous to the Paris
peace talks and promised America that "A Europe thus rearranged . . .
would be ripe for a permanent League." [55] A few months later Angell,
charting post-War possibilities, saw the United States as anchor of a system
of international boycotts—the luckless "economic sanctions" of the League
of Nations-to-be—to penalize nations refusing arbitration and international
indictment.

The values beneath all this were hinted at in 1916 by Albert Rhys
Williams, social worker turned magazine writer, and soon zealot for the
Bolshevik Revolution. He came out of a look at the War, which he dubbed
"The Great Calamity," as it surely was, believing "that in the New
Internationalism mankind will lay low the military Frankenstein . . . and
realize the triumphant brotherhood of all human souls." [56] Thus isolation-
ist-pacifist-radical Americans strengthened their hope that America could
best work for a better post-War world by remaining loomingly and flexibly
neutral. Such talk also appealed to Americans of goodwill who merely
felt—in a tradition as old as John Adams that could sound almost as
overweening as Germans vaunting their *Kultur*—that America was the
example and hope of the world. Hence twittering acclaim for Wilson's
Fourteen Points set forth in 1917 as scaffolding for the peace that would
come some time. It was to Miss Addams' meeting in Holland that he owed
the earliest expression of several of those points.

Not that Woman monopolized the movement as well as gave it its wishful
tone. As the War went on, Secretary of State Bryan became much less the
prudent pilot of the nation's foreign affairs than adherent of what Millis
called "old-fashioned, evangelistic pacifism." [57] He resigned to return to
lecturing, his preferred career, eloquently crying peace, peace where there
was none and proposing simplistic cures for complex troubles—a habit that
our forebears also had. Soon the booming business that American industry
did with the Allies roused alarm "deeply rooted in . . . great areas remote
from Europe . . . so ignorant as to feel that the sale of armaments to
Europe was indistinguishable from the sale of small-arms to a gang of

homicidal maniacs" [57]—Millis again. John Wanamaker, who shared Bryan's faith in peace and Prohibition by fiat, suggested that America end Europe's agony by buying Belgium from Germany for a few billion dollars. David Starr Jordan, deservedly respected president of Leland Stanford, Jr., University, and Rabbi Stephen Wise, leader of Reform Judaism, severally assured the nation that they personally found the War so abhorrent that it was unthinkable the United States would enter it. Mrs. Wharton, returning from France soon after War came, was baffled by her fellow passengers' prevalent "vague feeling that war was an avoidable thing which one had only to reprobate enough to prevent its recurring." [58]

So far most such pacifism had roots in Benjamin Franklin's dictum—inconsistent with some of his own doings—that there never was a good war or a bad peace. This appealed to the stolid isolationism endemic west and north of Chicago where distance from the War bolstered attitudes inherited from European peasantry, a geography clear in 1917 when the filibuster against a bill to arm American merchant ships was made up of six Republican and five Democratic Senators, one each from Missouri, Wisconsin, Iowa, Nebraska, North Dakota, Minnesota, Arkansas, California, Oregon, Mississippi—and a Senator from New York named James A. O'Gorman.

On the other flank the Addams-Jordan kind of pacifist, gamely risking jobs or careers in a climate growing less cordial to deviancy, were arm in arm with articulate radicals whose insistence that the nation stay neutral meant chronic mistrust of or grim hostility to Western civilization. These often shrill persons ranged from genuine if oversuggestible well-wishers of their fellowman like Amos Pinchot, brother of the great conservationist, through the Eastmans and the interlocking but usually backbiting sects of American Socialism to Emma Goldman, spirit of chronic anarchism. The women frequently linked peace-mindedness with feminism, pursuing both gleams with as much militancy as each temperament supplied. The flavor of the milder strata distills from the organizations joined by John Haynes Holmes: the Moral Resistance League, the League for the Limitation of Armaments, the Anti-Enlistment League . . . all bound to the seductive proposition that the risk of having to fight wars is directly proportionate to persistence in arming—never mind the contrary instances of Sweden and Switzerland.

Among these jumbled bedfellows the most intelligible were the Quakers, whose doctrinaire renunciation of all violence, personal or institutional, gave them a consistent position otherwise possible only to extremist nonresistant anarchists; indeed, Quakerism contains a gently stubborn residue of anarchism. Not only around Philadelphia but also in New York City, the Midwest and Southern California, Quakers had social and economic leverage disproportionate to their small numbers. At the farthest remove from their solipsist boycott of war lay the hatred that threw a bomb into San Francisco's Preparedness Day parade in 1916—which railroaded Tom Mooney and Warren Billings, sulky radicals, into the penitentiary. As trench warfare took over and the Allies' need of American-made supplies grew critical, then as it began to look as if only American military intervention could break the tactical deadlock, growing pacifist outcry against Preparedness and Wall Street had the effect—usually inadvertent, of course—of doing the Central Powers a favor. In the end counterpressures were far stronger. But there was sense in the action of John Spargo, British-born crusader against child labor, who quit the American Socialist Party because of its policies "favoring precisely the things desired by Germany and . . . opposing the things [it] opposed." [59] Indeed, Bertram D. Wolfe described the Greenwich Village radicals, of whom he was then one, as "inclined to sympathize with Germany as the 'underdog,' the late-comer among the colonial and trading nations who had arrived when everything was preëmpted. Not much to choose—but the Entente seemed more 'hypocritical.' " [60] W. J. Ghent, Hoosier-born veteran Socialist, saw it in ethnic terms. The specifically German emotional drag on the American Socialism of which Germans had always been chief props, bolstered by the Germanness of the Jewish culture also strong among them, seemed to him to have tricked his comrades into a false position.

The avowed aim of the Women's International League for Peace and Freedom was to set up permanent mediating bodies to halt the War that, to hear the belligerents tell it, none had wanted and that now bade fair to destroy both sides. This plan was born to Julia Grace Wales, a Canadian teacher of English at the University of Wisconsin given to trances during which she thought she was Joan of Arc. During one such she had seen neutrals mediating in Switzerland. The Wisconsin legislature endorsed the notion. It had already occurred without ghostly auspices to an intense Hungarian mover-and-shaker, Rosika Schwimmer, cosmopolite feminist, friend of social justice and pacifism and well-accepted frequenter of high-minded gatherings. It was not essentially absurd. Responsibly handled, it could hardly hurt mankind's interests and just conceivably might provide helpful lubrication. Only fate and Mrs. Schwimmer turned it into a laughingstock.

In the spring of 1915 the lady came to America with a bag of alleged secret documents that she never let leave her grasp, to lecture and buttonhole in the cause of Continuous Neutral Mediation. The well-meaning were cordial, yet she got nowhere with President Wilson. Hoping to dramatize her cause with sponsorship from eye-catching names, she chose Henry Ford as focus-in-chief and went after him. He had combined his famous $5-a-day with a solicitous, if paternalistic, program of uplift among his employees urged on by his wife and her spiritual guide, the Reverend Dr. S. S. Marquis, dean of Detroit's Episcopal cathedral. That gave Ford enough savor of social conscience to attract such as Mrs. Schwimmer. He had also been making headlines with roundhouse swings at Preparedness and War-mindedness: "Take away the capitalists and you will sweep war from the earth. . . . War is nothing but preparedness." [61] He threatened to remove his and his company's accounts from banks doing business with anybody buying any of the Morgan loan to the Allies. He pledged "half my fortune to shorten the war by one day" and offered a fat prize for a new history of war "in all its horrors." [62] Best of all, he could certainly finance an international peace movement all by himself if he felt like it.

A large *if,* for he was known to be a cross-grained lone wolf. When his staff worked out a slightly refined version of the Model T during his absence on a first trip to Europe before the War, he prowled around it, then silently and savagely tore it to pieces so far as one man could on the spur of the moment with simple tools. When the Lincoln Highway plan came up in 1913 and the automobile industry eagerly supported what would obviously expand their business, Ford alone neither gave a cent nor lent his name. Yet on a Tuesday or Thursday he might also catch at somebody else's striking notion and fervently pursue it; thus he got his $5-a-day, his pacifism, probably his anti-Semitism. Maybe it was Tuesday or Thursday when Mrs. Schwimmer penetrated his screen of understrappers. Her firm ally was Louis P. Lochner, later an able newspaperman, then a young idealist who had worked with Miss Addams and Jordan and taken fire over Continuous Mediation.

Mrs. Ford was to head a women's movement to flood the White House with telegrams. Ford, who took a fancy to Lochner and was in one of his manic phases, entrained for Washington and New York City to badger the world into applying Continuous Mediation to its severe hemorrhages. He too failed with Wilson. But in the heady atmosphere of New York City, rich with interviews and headlines, he got airborne. At a luncheon with eminent pacifists Lochner suggested that a ship be chartered to take august Americans to set up Continuous Mediation on the spot in Europe*— beyond which, as Charles Merz, liberal reporter, later said, there was "no plan of action save a devout wish for peace and a great willingness to do something in a hurry." [63] Exploding with dollars and energy, Ford engaged the *Oscar II* of the neutral Scandinavian Line and sent telegrams inviting many prominent people to make the world-saving cruise.†

His cable asking support from Pope Benedict VII in Rome was not delivered because the Holy Father thus designated had died A.D. 953. Of

---

* He may have got this notion from Mrs. Schwimmer, who had already been talking about a Women's Peace Ship as attention-drawing propaganda stunt.

† Text of the telegrams: "Will you come as my guest aboard the *Oscar II* . . . sailing from New York Dec. 4th for Christiania, Stockholm and Copenhagen? I am cabling leading men and women of the European nations to join us enroute and at some central point to . . . establish an international conference dedicated to negotiations leading to a just settlement of the war." (E. A. Ross, *Seventy Years of It,* 239.)

state governors invited the only one accepting was L. B. Hanna of South Dakota, a staunch Preparedness man. Others invited were President Wilson's daughter Margaret; ex-President Taft; Miss Addams; Bryan; Julius Rosenwald, philanthropic head of Sears, Roebuck & Company; Helen Keller, famous for overcoming blind deafmutism; Ida M. Tarbell, queen of muckraking journalism; the Reverend Jenkin Lloyd Jones, eminent nondenominational minister of Chicago; John Burroughs, the naturalist; Luther Burbank, the rule-of-thumb plant breeder; Edison; John Wanamaker. . . . The press was invited. Ford wanted lots of press copy filed by radio from the high seas and promised "the big Marconi gun" would dominate the Peace Ship's armament, flooding the world with the collective wisdom of the passengers' deliberations. His slogan for the trip was "Get the boys out of the trenches by Christmas!" It was already late November.

Press acceptances were ominously many. Owing partly to the suddenness of the summons—passenger aviation did not exist, so some invitees hardly had time to pack and reach dockside in time to sail—but also partly to some pacifists' failure to share Ford's euphoria, the roster of notables shrank. Miss Addams sent regrets from a hospital bed. Wanamaker was sympathetic but doubted the wisdom of the scheme; when Lochner came to urge him, all he got was the merchant prince's usual gift to visitors, a copy of Eleanor H. Porter's *Pollyanna*, the then best-selling novel of fatuous optimism. Bryan said he could do more for peace by talking at home, but he came to Hoboken on sailing day to give his unctuous blessing. So did Edison, but his deafness increased every time Ford besought him to make the voyage. Mrs. Ford also declined to brave the December Atlantic but, dismayed by the extravagant growth of the seed Mrs. Schwimmer planted, sent along the also dismayed Dean Marquis to cool Ford off and, if possible, abort the scheme. Sinclair Lewis, who had resigned from the Adventurers' Club of *Adventure* magazine to protest its interventionist tone, announced he would sail in the Peace Ship, but apparently he received no invitation.

Mrs. Schwimmer and the black bag sailed, however. So did the Reverend Mr. Jones, his Whitmanesque white hair and beard blowing in the chill wind off the Hudson River. So did B. W. Huebsch, avant-garde publisher; S. S. McClure, quondam king of muckraking publishers but now representing the German-tainted New York *Evening Mail*, which he had joined unaware of the taint; Inez Milholland, loveliest of Women's Righters, whom Ford would soon denounce as a vampire; Mrs. Mary Fels, zealous crusader for the single tax hobby of her soap-manufacturer husband; May Wright Sewall, another eminent feminist; Judge Lindsey of juvenile court fame; and certain Grade B cranks sponsored by Mrs. Schwimmer.

On sailing day the Hoboken waterfront had a high old time. The author of "I Didn't Raise My Boy to Be a Soldier" tried and failed to get on board, but the ship's band played his song. Another band supplied by Hoboken's heavily German population struck up *"Deutschland, Deutschland über Alles"* while the pro-Allied tried to drown it out with *"La Marseillaise."* The Reverend Mr. Jones was marrying Berton Braley, taking the trip for *Collier's* magazine, to his girlfriend so she could go along. Dr. Charles Giffen Pease, head of the Anti-Smoking League of America, to whom some joker had sent a telegram of invitation, possibly to satirize Ford's anti-cigarette-ism, was being thrown off the ship. Another joker of a symbolic turn of mind released a crate of white pigeons at what seemed a suitable moment in the hullabaloo. Still another, mindful of the high proportion of "nuts" on board, gave Ford two gray squirrels in a cage.

Soon after sailing, the captain had to marry Braley and lady all over again because somebody pointed out that the ceremony had taken place in New Jersey, where Jones' license to marry was invalid. Within a few days the passengers fell to bickering about who said what about whom behind whose back, then over the position that the party should take on the Preparedness issue. The reporters duly filed stories about this lack of harmony. Most of them gave in to the temptation to satirize, and radio, Ford's favorite toy, took their irreverences all over the world. The circus at Hoboken had already badly flawed whatever chance the Peace Ship had of being taken seriously. Bert Leston Taylor, conductor of the Chicago *Tribune*'s "Line o' Type or Two" column, had lampooned it in a version of "The Ballad of the Snark" with Ford cast as the Bellman. Bud Fisher, creator of the *Mutt and Jeff* comic strip, added slapstick to the confusion by booking Mutt and Jeff as passengers. "Noah's Ark" was the kindest comparison that most papers could think of, so the press corps of the *Oscar II* had no reason to feel discretion was called for. Elmer Davis for the New York *Times* and William C. Bullitt, later first U.S. ambassador to the Soviet Union, for the Philadelphia *Public Ledger* kept themselves more or less responsibly in hand, but on the whole the effect was that of a severe hazing. (A young member of the Peace Ship staff eventually had a little revenge on some of the most raucous reporters by booking them into a grimly strict Temperance-and-vegetarian hotel in The Hague.)

The ship's captain asked Ford's leave to censor flagrant fictions turned in at the radio shack. Ford refused. It was about the only intelligible thing he did after sailing. Having launched this adult Children's Crusade, he now went into one of his fits of lone-wolfishness and snubbed it, using a heavy cold as pretext for never leaving his private suite-and-deckspace. For the only interview he granted—to a British reporter-stowaway—he was rewarded by a dispatch about how Lochner had shackled him to a bedpost to keep him under control.

Norway's government and local pacifists warmly welcomed the peace pilgrims to wintry Oslo. Ford, though still snuffly, seemed at first to relish being lionized as symbol of American originality in international affairs as well as in industry. But Marquis had made good use of his time. Within a few days Ford let himself be whisked away home without a word to his protégés. He paid their expenses as they milled about, eventually mustering in Stockholm an unofficial commission drawn from half a dozen neutral nations to juggle ideas of mediatory tenor. It floundered through to early 1917, when Ford withdrew the subsidy. About all its members had accomplished was to hearten exile pacifists in Switzerland and to endorse certain post-War possibilities already fashionable, such as an international organization to impose peace and self-determination of small peoples. Negatively, of course, it had brought discredit on whatever life Continuous Mediation might have had, and made serious peace seeking sound like a cause for crackpots only. Returning via London, McClure, gruff and ungracious, told the British press, "All talk of peace efforts is now sheer idiocy. Ford's peace expedition was a sheer phantom. I only went for the fun of the thing." [64]

Ford showed no sense of guilt for what Lochner called his "sensational defection." [65] When an aide mentioned that the affair had cost half a million dollars, Ford said, "Well, we got a million dollars worth of advertising out of it." [66] He did tell the press that he no longer blamed bankers and munitions makers for the War; really the blame lay on the peoples of Europe for putting the wrong men in office. Beyond that he was not the man to admit he had perpetrated the worst—at least the most destructive—of the Ford Jokes. Instead, he was soon again nursemaiding the universe, publishing huge anti-Preparedness advertisements so harsh— particularly those attacking Hudson Maxim, the Navy League and *The Battle Cry of Peace*—that the producer of the movie sued for libel. In an interview with John Reed, Ford promised that his new light, cheap farm tractors would sell so well that meeting the demand would leave no factory labor available for munitions plants. Anyway, he said, "the workingman . . . is going to refuse to obey orders when his rulers tell him to go to war." [67] As for the Peace Ship, he'd do it again, only this time embarking not thinkers but the whole population of Dearborn, Michigan. And rather than participate personally in an American war effort, he'd stand up and be shot.

During the flurry over the Peace Ship, Bryan, teaching his famous shirt-sleeved Bible class in Royal Palm Park in Miami, Florida, could felicitate himself on having avoided taint from the derisory scheme and yet kept Ford's goodwill. One of the sights of Miami that winter was Bryan's Ford, a token of esteem from the maker, with silver-plated—some said sterling—radiator shell, tie rods and lamps and, on the curbside door panel, a great silver plaque engraved with fulsome praise of the pacifist spellbinder whom Ford delighted to honor.

Throughout 1916 Ford and Bryan stayed anti-War along with Viereck,

Senator O'Gorman, Miss Addams, Upton Sinclair and the IWW, which had sent a delegation to cheer the Peace Ship off. The Wobblies were clear, if not subtle, about their collectivist-radical hatred of war that often seemed to mask a general hatred of Western society. William D. "Big Bill" Haywood's summary as of 1916 fashionably blended cynicism and simplicity: "The industrial magnates of the United States realize that a victorious Germany would be a strong contender for the markets of the world . . . [even after the *Lusitania*] the Middle West and the western part of the country were decidedly against the nation becoming involved. So it was necessary for . . . Wall Street to start a preparedness campaign." [68] At an anti-Preparedness meeting in San Francisco two days before the bombing that jailed Mooney, an IWW speaker advised Europe's soldiers to solve everything by shooting their officers and going home.

In mid-March, 1917, the February Revolution struck Russia.* This might have helped to bring milder radicals—though not such pure haters as the IWW's leaders—around to the Allies' side. Czarist absolutism had been making that cause look queer as self-proclaimed champion of freedom and democracy. Now a Czar-free, wide-suffrage, even Socialist-flavored Russia under Kerensky's Provisional Government could be far more appealing, and it was still conceivable that his nation could be kept in the War, a newly liberal force-in-being to keep reactionary Germany from concentrating all of the Central Powers' weight on the Allies. That could have been acceptable to many readers of the *Masses* had it not threatened them with coming up on the same side as J. P. Morgan, General Wood and Bishop Manning. As it was, though they were as starry-eyed about events in Petrograd as Adam and Eve at their first sunrise in Eden, they could not bring themselves to relinquish the joy of denouncing and despising anything those gentlemen approved of. America's most stalwart Reds withheld their imprimatur from the February Revolution and went right on maintaining that support of the Allies was a venal crime.

When President Wilson severed diplomatic relations with Germany on February 1, 1917—a step virtually committing him to war—radical pacifists automatically protested solely in terms of capitalism usurping national powers to protect the munitions deals of Bethlehem Steel *et al.* Just as automatically several months later they besought all right thinkers to sign petitions of protest when Washington installed conscription early in the War instead of increasing strains by delaying the inevitable—a mistake made in the Civil War. This innocent consistency in the teeth of changing circumstances was rewarded late in the year when, just as the Germans hoped when shipping Lenin into Petrograd, the October Revolution put the anti-War Bolsheviki in the saddle. American Reds seized on this as

* The apparent anomaly in months comes of Russia's having used the unreformed calendar that left a discrepancy of thirteen days relative to the Western world's reckoning. For the same reason the October (Bolshevik) Revolution of the same year got into the wrong month.

vindicating the soundness of their instincts. Long before they had the
opportunity to devour John Reed's *Ten Days That Shook the World*, they
were already welcoming Lenin's *coup de main* as the *real* Revolution,
demolishing the bourgeois-mindedness with which the Kerensky regime
was tainted and curing Russia of the War, that disease of capitalist
imperialism. Now the struggle between Allies and Central Powers could
show its true nature—imperialist rogues had fallen out, and honest workers
and peasants were coming by their rights.

The Allies, vainly hoping to salvage some military nuisance value from
Russia, occupied Archangel and Vladivostok and otherwise supported the
several counter-Revolutionary armies of varying degrees of unsavoriness
that arose under czarist officers. Obviously this was militarist capitalism
trying to rob the newly freed of their victory. Through the Red-tinted
glasses much worn in Greenwich Village and Carmel and Western
bunkhouses the October Revolution was finishing the job by protecting the
Russian masses from being used as imperialism's catspaw. "In Soviet
Russia," Dos Passos recalled much later, "they were finding the righteous
cause their fathers sought in following Wilson and Roosevelt and Bryan. To
them the soviets were spontaneous selfgoverning assemblies like New
England town meetings . . . massacres conducted in the name of the
proletariat were shrugged off as temporary phenomena in the war against
. . . enemies financed by capitalist governments, or as capitalist fabrica-
tions." [69] Henceforth the Bolsheviki—and, when it came formally into
being, the American Communist Party (né American Workers Party)—were
a mass object of hero worship among Americans of a certain emotional
bent. With many it remains today as pervasive and durable a commitment as a Southerner's reflex about Robert E. Lee, "Dixie" and Reconstruction.

The purest pacifism, horror of war undiluted by extraneous hatreds,
appeared in Jeannette Rankin of Montana, first woman to sit in the U.S.
House of Representatives. In the first roll call on the declaration of war on
Germany she abstained; the second time around she said, "I want to stand
by my country but I cannot vote for war." [70] That is still poignant though it
was true then as now that nobody feeling like that should take the
Representative's oath to uphold a Constitution including the warmaking
power. Others unable to change their views when war became official had
varying fortunes. Some eloquently pacifist parsons, such as Jenkin Lloyd
Jones and John Haynes Holmes, suffered only abuse privately and in print,
and there was nothing inexplicit about Holmes' statements: "If war is right,
then Christianity is wrong, false, a lie. . . . Other clergymen may pray to
God for victory—I will not. . . . No man is wise enough, no nation
important enough, no human interest is precious enough to justify the
wholesale destruction and murder which constitute war." [71] In view of his

experience Holmes concluded that "to be an absolutist in the moral life is to secure an understanding and protection not otherwise or elsewhere possible. . . . the [conscientious objector] of the extreme type, true to himself and to the Word, was little questioned and still less condemned." [72] But this theory failed the Reverend Irving St. John Tucker, convicted after the Armistice of violating the Espionage Act with pacifist-Red talk likely to obstruct the War effort; the Reverend Herbert S. Bigelow of Newport, Kentucky, who, though not opposing the War, was horsewhipped for praying from his pulpit for the souls of the Hohenzollerns; and the Reverend Clarence H. Waldron of Windsor, Vermont, who got fifteen years for distributing his pacifist pamphlet stating, just as Holmes had advised, "Under no circumstances can I undertake any service that has for its purpose the prosecution of war!" [73]

The campus also saw inconsistency. J. McKeen Cattell of Teachers College, editor of its influential *School and Society*, doughty battler for academic freedom, was dismissed for calling conscription for overseas duty unconstitutional. Columbia dismissed Henry Wadsworth Longfellow Dana, grandson of the poet and amateur Marxist, for encouraging students to oppose the draft law while it was still under debate. Others on whom the edge of the mortarboard was used as guillotine were Emily Balch, sociologist-feminist dismissed from Wellesley, and Scott Nearing, sociologist-Red gadfly, whose pre-War quarrel with the University of Pennsylvania over ideas repugnant to its administration had already been a *cause célèbre*. The most grotesque gesture was that of David Starr Jordan's Cornell classmates asking rescission of his degree as penalty for his pacifism.

Cornell did not oblige. Nor did President A. Lawrence Lowell of Harvard, a stout friend of academic freedom, act against members of his faculty whose anti-War clamor was brought to his notice by his distinguished professor of history Albert Bushnell Hart. In protest about Cattell and Dana, Charles A. Beard resigned from Columbia, saying, "I have, from the beginning, believed that a victory for the Imperial German government would plunge all of us into the black night of military barbarisms. . . . But thousands of my countrymen do not share this view," and recommended "Arguments addressed to their reason and understanding" [74] instead of punitive action to convert them. Dewey did not resign but denounced Columbia as "nothing but a badly run factory." [75] Cattell and he had been principal founders of the new American Association of University Professors just before the War. In today's contexts its Committee on Academic Freedom and Tenure would be expected to rally to the defense of such cases. But in 1917 this eventually formidable arm of embattled professordom endorsed dismissal for several kinds of faculty opposition to War and the draft. At the time most cultivated Americans probably agreed with *Life*: "LIFE ordinarily has much sympathy with dissenters . . . is loath to see peals silenced from a lot of fine belfries because there are bats in them. But

. . . citizens . . . prosecuting the war now have the floor. If the citizens opposed to it will hold their peace for a spell, their opportunity for declamation will come after the close of hostilities." [76]

Beard took Spargo's position, accepting the War as opportunity "to put an end to the Prussian oligarchy. . . . Every advocate of peace at any price . . . is now playing into the hands of Prussian militarism." [77] Dewey, writing on the aggressive cultural narcissism of German philosophy, commented on the elegant chauvinism of General Friedrich von Bernhardi: "Outside of Germany . . . it would be hard to find [a cavalry general whose] appeal for military preparedness would be reinforced by allusions to the Critique of Pure Reason." [78] A year earlier Josiah Royce, a philosopher of the same order, had come out hot for the Allies, calling Germany "the wilful and deliberate enemy of the human race" [79] and recruiting into a Citizens' League for America and the Allies eminent colleagues of his at Harvard—the mathematician Leo Wiener, the philosophers Ralph Barton Perry and William Ernest Hocking.

As the bandwagon rolled, the Reverend Dr. Washington Gladden, apostle of Christian Socialism, and the Carnegie Endowment for International Peace climbed aboard. Even before war was declared, Henry Ford went to Washington to put his industrial empire at Uncle Sam's disposal. Upton Sinclair, garrulous foe of war as well as capitalism, alcohol and meat, lent belligerent America the dubious advantage of his support on the grounds that victory over the Kaiser was necessary to the progress of Socialism. John Sloan resigned from the *Masses* on the sounder grounds that its comments on the War made it a mere propaganda organ. George Bellows, whose early years in the Village had him vibrating between Marx and the anarchists, abandoned both camps and went into painting official propaganda posters. But the most striking result of the emotional impact of the War was that the declaration silenced Bryan-as-pacifist. Though he could not bring himself to abandon lecturing—his livelihood as well as his joy—his only contribution to public affairs throughout the War was a very proper telegram to President Wilson to the effect that now War had come, it had to be carried on vigorously and finished right.

It was not true that, as *Mutt and Jeff* hinted, Ford's dry-mindedness closed the bar of the *Oscar II*. As the storm winds did blow, the Friendly Sons of St. Vitus, a scratch fellowship of reporters and the more worldly pilgrims, drank plenty and sang to match. Their favorite number was:

> It's a long way to Copenhagen,
> It's a long way to sail.
> It's a long way to Copenhagen
> But we'll get there, never fail. . . ." [80]

It appears they still had the ship's destination wrong. But all certainly knew accurately and *ad nauseam* the original of this lyric. "It's a Long Way to Tipperary" was a great hit of the day—except in German-American beer gardens. Just another popular song in pre-War England, it was taken up by the British infantry for route marching and, though it did not mention war, became the international symbol of the Allied fighting man. Labeled "The Song They Sing as They March Along" over a gaudy picture of a kilted Highlander piper, it stood on the music racks of American pianos along with other favorites of Tommy Atkins, the generic British private: "Sister Susie Sewing Shirts for Soldiers," "Pack Up Your Troubles in Your Old Kit Bag." . . . For Americans vicariously patriotic for their cousins in the trenches of Flanders, it was a singing war long before it was declared on their side of the water.

Soon best-selling books also immersed Americans in the British version of the War. There was Ian Hay's *The First Hundred Thousand* (1916), deftly humorous semifiction about a battalion of Scots volunteers from mustering in to the bloody smother of the Battle of Loos; its amusingness did not rule out a few effective bits about atrocities. Its author detached in major's uniform to exploit the popularity of his book had a fine propaganda lecture tour of the States. Far grimmer was *Rhymes of a Red-Cross Man* by Robert Service, a Canadian road-company Kipling still remembered for "The Shooting of Dan McGrew," a souvenir of his days in the Klondike. Driving ambulances on the Western Front, he saw and metrically celebrated several aspects of the bloody stalemate—some appalling but giving a strong residual impression of British bulldoggedness. Weightiest among writings likely to affect Washington's policies was H. G. Wells' lively and many-angled *Mr. Britling Sees It Through*, from the Socialist-minded Briton whose novels did so much to turn cultivated Americans toward hope of social decency. He refused to make his German character a monster, denounced the bunglings of professional soldiers, yet attributed the worst atrocities to the error of entrusting war to conscripts: "Most of the barbarities were done . . . by an excited civilian kind of man . . . [who] thought every Belgian had a gun behind the hedge. . . . Half the Germans and a lot of the French ought never to have been brought within ten miles of a battle field." [81] But the sinister bent of the Kaiser's regime was also there full scale, and the gist of the whole, the more impressive for its scruples, was that civilization's only hope of post-War health was generally to rely on a Socialist God, specifically to trust in Britain-in-arms.

Hay's and other firsthand accounts of the trenches soon taught Americans a pungent new jargon from French as well as British usage: "fag" = a cigarette, not a homosexual; "dud" = a shell failing to explode; "Blighty" = England as yearned for by Tommy Atkins; "barrage" = a prolonged curtain of shellfire; "camouflage"—some of which words we still use, not always accurately. In the late 1960's, for instance, TV men used "barrage" for any artillery fire exceeding a single salvo. By mid-1915 American newspaper readers also knew that "poilu" meant the tough, bearded French opposite number of Tommy Atkins and that France's soul resided in a slim figure in fancy armor named, as Mark Sullivan noted, "Jona Vark." [82] Tin Pan Alley wrote songs about her. General and women's magazines ran copious coverage, pro-Ally in indirect effect, of the Western Front and the emotionally entangling work of American volunteers of both sexes in hospitals and refugee relief. For the *Saturday Evening Post* Wister wrote able articles marshaling copious evidence from "the utterances of Prussians, the Kaiser and his generals, professors, editors and Nietzsche" for the finding that "Germany is [mentally] a hospital case. . . . [of] the mania of grandeur complicated by the mania of persecution . . ." [83] *—the chief stigmata of classic paranoia. And American editors were soon reprinting the drippily horrendous anti-German cartoons in which Louis Raemaekers of the Amsterdam *Telegraaf* showed how a nominal neutral could make the blood simultaneously boil and chill.

Here was the American press voluntarily cooperating with British and other propagandists. Encouragement from Washington had no part of it. Soon after the Armistice F. Scott Fitzgerald told his numerous readers that once America declared war, the administration gave the word and the press "began to whoop hysterically." [84] Here is a warning example of how unreliable post-War cynicism was. Long since the relative unattractiveness of the Central Powers' cause and manners had reinforced the feeling of many influential WASP's that blood was thicker than water. Awareness of growing economic commitment existed, but to see it as major is naïve. Well before credits for the Allies were negotiated, sentimental individuals and organizations were doing a better job than deliberation could have to erode the nation's first impulse to shy away from Europe's bloodbath. Hence the Lafayette Escadrille; hence Lasswell's bilious summary of the importance of "persons as channels of influence . . . business man to business man . . . journalist to journalist. . . . When a lance was broken in public for the British cause, it was done by an American and not by a foreigner. There were no obnoxiously evident Britishers as there were Dernburgs in America. It was the social lobby, the personal conversation . . . which forged the strongest chain between America and Britain." [85]

Once rising bellicosity became belligerency, however, America created an

---

* During World War II Dr. Richard M. Brickner, an American neurologist-psychiatrist, arrived at a similar notion with modifications derived from anthropological crosslights: *Is Germany Incurable?* (1943). Apropos, early in World War I Francke, Germany's most impressive apologist in America, wrote in *Harper's Weekly* (November 28, 1914) that "megalomania" was identifiable in Nietzsche, Wagner and Wilhelm II, whom he considered the significant exponents of German attitudes; megalomania, he explained, was inseparable from genius, and its permeation of German life had had fine results in the integrated solidarity of the German state and people.

immense, deliberate internal propaganda to supply the other half of complete commitment. Its nucleus was a Committee on Public Information to coordinate news and useful data about the War. To manage it, President Wilson chose George Creel, a rugged, somewhat radical-minded trans-Mississippi newspaper editor and magazine journalist, who had been associated with his Presidential campaign. Between natural ebullience and intuitive grasp of this unprecedented situation, Creel improvised a multiplex, ever-expanding idea machine that flooded all channels to the public mind, heart and glands and probably had more than any other factor to do with developing the modern public relations industry.

The United States had never before known such a project. During the Civil War neither side had had much notion of organized public relations, nor was much more done in the Spanish-American War. Before 1915 national propaganda work of such scope was also unknown in Europe. This was an unusual kind of war, however, throwing off unusual by-products, one of which was deliberately massive, if often ill-coordinated, apparatus to blacken the enemy, create sympathy among neutrals and buck up the home front as well as the troops. The special demands of conscription played a part here. Peacetime conscription, all able-bodied youth under arms for some years in rotation, long established in all the belligerent powers except Britain, had never been popular. The conscript mobilization of 1914 not only took Fritz, Ivan, Jacques or Guglielmo away from home but, since this was shooting in earnest, meant a grim chance of his never returning. That put an even worse face on the system. It called for all possible intramural propaganda about fatherland loving and aggressor hating. Add that all belligerent peoples had been assured that no modern war could last more than a few months. The ensuing years of slaughter led to deepening dismay and resentment of the deprivations of Wartime. Only massive appeal to the back of the national neck could keep disillusion from clogging the national will to fight.

Germany, always thorough, seems to have done an excellent job of the requisite propaganda on all domestic levels. Paradoxically Britain did well because, hoping to make volunteer enlistment do, it pulled out all stops before turning to conscription, which was against all precedent since medieval times. America's experience with the badly framed and worse handled draft in the Civil War had left sour memories still lively in 1917. This time a better-drawn "Selective Service Act"—the title itself was able public relations—passed within six weeks. Its machinery had already been set up and registration forms were already on the press when Congress acted. To persuade Americans to put up with the draft was in itself challenge enough to stir Creel into not only playing all the tunes that European precedent suggested but also to find new ones to blend into a landmark in American life. In the 1930's his methods were reactivated to get the Blue Eagle of the National Recovery Act soaring. In the 1940's they were again unlimbered to help Uncle Sam fight two great wars at once. In the 1920's its immediate example lent crushing momentum to the rising profession of managing public relations for large institutions—industrial, financial, benevolent, religious—on national and world scale. Two of Creel's chief aides, Edward L. Bernays, Vienna-born press agent for concert artists, and Carl Byoir, promoter of the Montessori Method in America, became giants in the equivocal business of showing great corporations— and good causes, sometimes bad ones—how to set that best foot forward.

Another by-product of Creel's virtuosity was to add to the post-War intellectual's anxieties the belief—just near enough true to make it toxic—that given enough money and cleverness, anything could be put over on America any time. Just after the War the hero of Dos Passos' *One Man's Initiation* says, "What terrifies me is their power to enslave our minds . . . the gradual unbaring of teeth, gradual lulling to sleep of people's humanity and sense by the phrases, the phrases. . . . America . . . is ruled by the press. Who shall ever know what dark forces bought and bought until we should be ready to go blind and gagged to war? . . . We are slaves of bought intellect, willing slaves. . . ." [86] The War thus adduced was a poor case in point. Germany probably spent more than the Allies on pre-1917 propaganda in America, and all it got for it was the landing of 2,000,000 American soldiers in France. Eastman was nearer actuality when writing in 1927: "Publicity is a fearful thing . . . whimsical . . . not calculating . . . no controlling it. Its method is to spring up, and the whence and wherefore no man knows . . . until afterward. . . ." [87] Yet in 1920 *Life* had to say, apropos of the undertakers' efforts to persuade bereaved families to have their war dead brought home, that "the art of starting movements is getting to be too well understood. It will have to be regulated. . . ." [88] That will be the day.

Most of the nation's eminent historians, some still notable—Carl L. Becker of Cornell, Wallace Notestein of Yale, Frederick J. Turner of Harvard, Carlton J. H. Hayes of Columbia—put themselves at the disposal of the Creel Committee or ancillary groups. The printed word, whether in learned pamphlets or newspaper releases—Creel's men are said to have invented the PR handout in its modern form—was only one of many media exploited. The Liberty Bond campaigns were multimedia convulsions using schoolroom blackboards, door-to-door solicitation (often downright bully-ing of ethnic minorities), posters, "Four Minute Men" speakers bobbing up wherever two or three were gathered together, movie stars such as Douglas Fairbanks, Chaplin, Miss Pickford, making in-person speeches—very likely this begat that later national menace, the stage or movie star shilling for political candidates. John Philip Sousa, whose "The Stars and Stripes Forever" already rivaled "The Star-Spangled Banner" in popularity, cobbled up a "Liberty Bond March." Many needed no official prompting to make propaganda. Quite spontaneously George M. Cohan, mindful of his fame as Yankee Doodle Dandy, wrote "Over There!"—as successful as it was deliberate. The song industry was prodded up, but in any case its sharp sense of timing—the same that came up with "I Didn't Raise My Boy . . ." soon after the War began—would have led it heavily to exploit War feeling. Of the results that fill seven stout volumes in the New York Public Library maybe the gooiest to reach great success was "Just a Baby's Prayer at Twilight." There was also "Hello, Central, Give Me No Man's Land" and "If He Can Fight Like He Can Love." Among the best were Howard Johnson's and Percy Weinreich's "Where Do We Go from Here?" * and Irving Berlin's opinions of Army hours and punctual buglers: "Oh, How I Hate to Get Up in the Morning." Those two held their own with "Mademoiselle from Armentières" even in the mud and stench of the Western Front. Wartime sheet music often carried a plea from Hoover's United States Food Administration: "Save Wheat/Do Your Bit/Help Win The War/Eat More Vegetables, fish, poultry and save beef, mutton and pork for our fighters!"

Creel was a genius and his staff large and able, but even so propaganda had failures. Efforts to dub the American rank-and-file "Sammies" to match Britain's "Tommies" got nowhere though Edward Streeter used the term in his humorous best seller, *Dere Mable*, about an egocentric rookie's troubles. Actually no equivalent of World War II's GI appeared. "Doughboy" was hampered by its referring properly only to the infantry. The handsome, austere figure of General John J. Pershing and his nickname, Black Jack, were striking, but the home folks never gave him the warm hero worship that their grandfathers gave Lee, Jackson, Sherman, even Grant. It was a different war. The shoulders of the heroes who did develop bore no stars: Major Charles W. Whittlesey of Massachusetts, commander of the savagely beleaguered Lost Battalion, and Sergeant Alvin C. York of Tennessee, once a conscientious objector, whose hillman's marksmanship and gumption enabled his patrol to bag 132 German prisoners at one haul. Since the incidents bringing them fame occurred in the Argonne within a few months of the Armistice, their propaganda value came too late.

For each misfire, however, Creel scored ten bull's-eyes. James Montgomery Flagg's poster of Uncle Sam pointing bonily at young men: "I want YOU for U.S. Army" was as potent as its British prototype employing Lord Kitchener. Howard Chandler Christy's poster goddess sold Liberty Bonds like debutantes' kisses at charity fairs. The movies, as opportunistic as Tin Pan Alley, weighed in with a celluloid panegyric of Jona Vark starring Geraldine Farrar, the only opera star of her day pretty and slim enough to risk the silent screen, and *To Hell with the Kaiser*, *Wolves of Kultur*. Dos Passos' queasy summary conveys them: ". . . soldiers in spiked helmets

---

* Like "Tipperary," this song, though so closely associated with the AEF, had little to do with the War as originally written; the singer is represented as a New York City taxi driver addressing peacetime fares.

marching into Belgian cities . . . bayoneting the civilians . . . setting fire
to the buildings . . . spitting babies on their long swords. . . . Then . . .
flags blowing very hard. . . . The Yanks were coming . . . fast, fast across
the screen. . . ." [89] The cycle peaked with *The Kaiser, the Beast of Berlin*
colossally ballyhooed and offering a free seat to anybody willing to admit
being pro-German. The British hired Griffith to bring the Gish sisters to
France to make *Hearts of the World*, just as sticky as the title.

The cultural range of Creel's efforts ran from Edith Wharton's ladylike
but cogent magazine pieces about visiting the Western Front to the
slaverings of Billy Sunday briefing Divinity on behalf of the U.S. House of
Representatives: "Thou knowest, oh Lord, that no nation so infamous, vile,
greedy, sensuous, bloodthirsty ever disgraced the pages of history. . . . Oh
Lord, smite the hungry, wolfish Hun whose fangs drip with blood, and we
will forever raise our voices in Thy praise. . . ." [90] The juvenile department
bubbled with Creel's insistence on leaving no stone unturned. In Cleveland
the Reverend Dr. William H. Hubbell extracted from the Sunday school
pupils of his Presbyterian church a dime each to help build a warship for
Uncle Sam. In any town's P.S. No. 9, 10 or 11 both sexes were taught to
knit soldiers' scarves and at assembly all sang "Tipperary" and "There's a
Long, Long Trail." Boy Scouts sold toward half a billion dollars' worth of
Liberty Bonds and War Savings Stamps. *St. Nicholas* explained that though
"government could easily dispose of this issue [of bonds] to relatively few
persons . . . it prefers to scatter [them] as widely as possible because the
patriotism and determination of a country at war are largely judged . . . by
the number of citizens willing to lend. . . . Germany is watching this bond
sale." [91]

Every other story in *St. Nicholas* was about a heroic little French girl
helping a soldier or a sturdy American boy smelling out a submarine
hideaway. The pages that once told how-to-build-a-tree-house now bristled
with machine guns and tanks. The letters of Lieutenant Colonel Frank E.
Evans, USMC, to his small son, jauntily illustrated by the colonel's own
pen, took *St. Nicholas*' readers right into Belleau Wood: ". . . a pretty
wood . . . when we left there, five weeks later, it was a famous battle-field
full of dead Heinies and Fritzies . . . lots of little wooden crosses where we
buried the brave Marines who were killed in those pretty woods . . . and
don't you hope that [they] died a little happier thinking, just for a teeny
second, of the green fields and red poppies before the angels took them to
heaven? I think they must have been French angels, for the brave Marines
died for France, and soldiers always go straight to heaven when they died in
battle." [92] A huge new department, "For Country and For Liberty," beat
the drum for bandage rolling, canteen serving, vegetable growing. To judge
from my early-teen memories of these goings-on the extra quotas of goods
and services thus produced cannot have been large, nor can the grimy
atrocities committed on good yarn by child knitters have been worth the

trouble. But the pains taken thus to indoctrinate even people ten years below military age when not even the blackest pessimist thought the War could last so long show how ardent was the heat worked up between the Germans and Creel & Company.

Recruitment of the Women's Land Army, more popularly the Farmerettes, followed British example to fill gaps in the agricultural labor force left by the War's drain on manpower for the armed forces and munitions plants. In the Civil War farm wives and daughters driving the reaper had presaged that sort of thing but not on such a scale. Thousands of robust young schoolteachers, college girls kept fit by compulsory exercise, hearty business girls who could get supplementary leaves of absence readily spent summer vacation strenuously tending crops. Mustered into small gangs like the traditional migrant farm labor, chaperoned by elder volunteers from among clubwomen and school supervisors, they earned their $2 a day and keep in harvest field, orchard and truck patch. That was the more notable because America had renounced the European acceptance of women doing fieldwork. According to surviving memories, the girls also enjoyed it in a wholesome, all-sisterly-together sort of way. It alleviated the sweat and creaky backs of the daylight hours when mandolin and banjo rang out and they all started singing "The Long, Long Trail."

Women filled other War-created gaps as messenger boys, mail carriers, elevator operators, streetcar conductors; New York City enlisted six for regular police duty. Management was forced to hire women for light production jobs in munitions plants, whereas previously they had worked only in food, textiles and garments. The U.S. Navy enlisted them as yeomen—the neologism "yeowomen" was too much of a proofreader's nightmare—because it had no precedent for hiring civilian clerks. So did the Marines—here was the weaker sex sworn into the armed forces. Several hundred telephone girls, all trained to handle French too, actually went overseas with the U.S. Army Signal Corps. None of it was on the scale that made WAVES, WACS and Rosie the Riveter conspicuous in World War II. But these women's activity greatly eroded archaic notions about relative weaknesses and the need of rigidly separate subcultures for the sexes—particularly important at a time when legislatures were under culminating pressures for the Nineteenth (Woman's Suffrage) Amendment.

Creel's committee directly touched every American civilian old enough to walk and talk. So did the Food Administration—FOOD WILL WIN THE WAR!—set up to keep the Allied as well as the American armed forces adequately nourished while so many productive hands were in uniform, yet without stinting civilians of essential nutrients. Its chief was Herbert Hoover as if by acclamation because his handling of relief for German-occupied Belgium had been so able—and this was his second firm step toward the White House. Less in public consciousness but of immense importance was the third great improvisation (again, of course, with European precedents)—the War Industries Board steered by another gifted figure in the right job, Bernard M. Baruch.

A Jew, a Wall Streeter and self-styled speculator, a lone wolf in that usually clubby calling, by definition he was an unlikely choice for the job defined by Mark Sullivan as making "the whole United States a single factory dominated by one management with the relation of the departments . . . worked out as smoothly as in Henry Ford's factory." [93] But he was highly respected among moneymen and just as high in President Wilson's confidence. In order to be the shrewdest stock gambler of his day, he had taken pains to learn an ungodly amount about raw materials, markets, transportation, engineering and the all-too-human nature of the American businessman. Choosing as a connoisseur, he put the best managers to work for Uncle Sam—not necessarily all famous big shots, many being "the real doers" in next-to-top or next-to-next slots, "keen, dynamic, forceful, purposeful, transilient vice-presidents and managers and superintendents" [94] as an admiring colleague saw them. Those presumed to have ample private resources were flattered by being made "dollar-a-year man" because the value of their services was incalculable and it was illegal to pay them nothing. After the War many a $1 check from the U.S. Treasury hung uncashed and framed over the desk in a huge office in Chicago or San Francisco.

Partly through Baruch's shrewd allocations, partly through individual suggestions from management eager both to help and to stay in business, "The carpet manufacturer [who] could not make shells . . . could make blankets and duck. . . . The maker of refrigerators could turn to hospital tables. . . . The corset maker . . . could easily master belts for the Medical corps . . . pipe-organ factories . . . were very good at making mosquito nettings." [94] Yet the coordinating machine was not even in tentative motion until early 1918; the whole project not in full sweep until late summer, so the accomplishments were spotty. Fuel, textiles, ships and rifles came out the far end in adequate quantity. But the much bragged-up fleets of planes and parks of artillery were still largely on paper. At the Armistice Americans fighting in France were still using French-made guns and French-make planes. Not that the lag was altogether discreditable. Much of it came of a decision temporarily to concentrate on sending the materials of planes, guns and shells for manufacture in existing French factories. The building of indicated American munitions plants was on second priority as hedge in case of a much-prolonged war and possible collapse of France.

Thus America learned in 1917 what Britain and France had learned in 1914, that a twentieth-century power entering a major war would have done well to imitate pre-War Germany in preplanning an industrial mobilization in step with military mobilization. Gestures in that direction had been made in President Wilson's first term but had never got near practicality. Maybe the eventual achievement was the more impressive for its handicaps. In the end, thanks to Baruch and his gung ho cadres, the United States had "a more far-reaching and compelling control of industry than . . . any other of the warring countries . . . accomplished . . . with a mere handful of executives and a few hundred clerical helpers—not as many persons on the official roll . . . as a single bureau of the British wool control . . . successful, cooperative, democratic self-control of industry for national purposes." [95]

Indeed these zealots committed to competition as the breath of enterprise grew fascinated by this new game that subordinated competition to planning and efficient production routing—a vision more sweeping than that of any trust magnate scrounging and bullying thus to coordinate a mere single industry. Well after the structure was dismantled, Grosvenor B. Clarkson, its historian, had another thought: "When one reflects that [Baruch's crew] for months on end thought and toiled for the public welfare, without thought of pay or substantial reward, he is prompted to speculate on what might be accomplished by the collectively powerful but feebly acting machinery of the State if such men were to administer its affairs." [94] An interesting point even though there is reason to wonder whether some of the War Industries Board's keymen were quite so disinterested in all their doings.

For ironically the board had given the collectivist, particularly recently Socialized Russia, a brilliant demonstration of how, make the occasion pressing enough, the state could manage a whole economy as a single enterprise—a thing never actually done before except in the meager and simple economy of pre-Columbian Peru. How much attention the Bolsheviki paid is problematical. But the lesson was not lost on America. In the 1930's, when President Franklin D. Roosevelt sought to check the Depression by harnessing industry, his National Recovery Administration followed Baruch's example. Its chief, General Hugh S. Johnson, had been one of the ablest of the War's miracle organizers, first under General Enoch H. Crowder in shaping the draft machinery, then under Baruch. And George N. Peek, first head of the New Deal's complementary Agricultural Adjustment Administration, was, naturally, another graduate of Baruch's College of Howtodoit. When World War II loomed up, the nation had only to dust off the old models of Creel's committee and Baruch's board and say to a new generation: "Do it pretty much this way."

The zeal behind America's War may have come partly of the exhilaration felt, rather cryptically, by a nation at last become the New World member of the club summoned to redress the balance of the Old. Presumably a right to a major hand in the New Order was to follow. It reminded one of the self-conscious expansionism—the hankering of a new nation after colonies and cruisers as status tokens—that produced the New Navy of the 1890's and the Spanish-American War. The likeness grew when Theodore Roosevelt, the same who had stepped out of line to alert Commodore George Dewey in 1898, banged his drum for Preparedness and for joining the Allies. "Made in USA" on the great tractors towing big guns through French mud in 1916 caused Arthur Guy Empey (American volunteer in the Canadian Army) to flush with pride in his country's international weight. Or so his book said; anyway he felt no flush of shame at what Eastman and Hearst were calling American capitalism's ghoulish meddling in an imperialist war.

The emotions, such as prideful zeal, that war rouses behind the lines are clumsily visceral to begin with. When deliberately heightened, they lead to cooperation, comradeship, the helping hand, and also fire up persons given to meddling, posturing, panic or hate—whoever it was who threw that bomb in the San Francisco Preparedness parade and the mob that flogged the Newport parson. President Wilson foresaw that kind of thing. The night before he asked Congress to declare war he told Frank Cobb, editor of the New York *World*, that Americans, once at war, would "forget there was ever such a thing as tolerance . . . ruthless brutality will enter into the very fibre of our national life, infecting Congress, the courts, the policeman, the man in the street." [96]

The man in the street lived up to that in antics ranging from minor absurdity to lynching. He sought to rename sauerkraut "Liberty cabbage" and, not so amusingly, sometimes forced Liberty Bonds on farmers of German extraction. He was tempted to act thus by advertisements in which Creel's committee not only asked citizens to button the lip: "The Hun . . . asks no better service than to have you spread his lies of disaster to our soldiers . . . [about] scandals in the Red Cross, casualties, neglect and wholesale executions in our camps . . ." but also to report to the Department of Justice anybody spreading "pessimistic stories . . . cries for peace . . . or [belittling] our efforts to win the war." When the Authors League expelled Viereck, it took a tender mind to feel much chagrin; one wonders why it took fifteen months after the declaration of war. Less can be said, however, for the citizens so noisily aggrieved by the high proportion of *Deutschtum* in normal American musical life. Pittsburgh's women forced cancellation of a concert by Fritz Kreisler, then the ranking violinist, because, as a former reserve officer in the Austrian Army, he might send some of his earnings to finance Franz Josef's creaky war. In East Orange, New Jersey, the mayor barred Kreisler. Providence, Rhode Island, was outraged when Miss Farrar gave them an all-German program as soloist with the visiting Boston Symphony Orchestra. The Chicago Federation of Musicians ousted all German members who had not bothered to become citizens and denounced German-born and -reared Frederick A. Stock, conductor of the Chicago Symphony, who, though he had been with the orchestra thirteen years, had let his first papers lapse. Only by lying low and renewing first papers did he get reinstated early in 1919.

It was worse for Karl Muck, equally German conductor of the Boston Symphony, when Providence included him in the row about Miss Farrar because he refused to open concerts with "The Star-Spangled Banner." In vain he explained that patriotic airs did not fit the repertory of an august orchestra; neither he nor his enemies brought up the ambiguous example of the *1812 Overture*. Major Henry Lee Higginson, redoubtable cavalry veteran of the Civil War and chief subsidizer of what they were calling "the Bocheton Symphony," [97] got nowhere threatening that if Muck were forced out, he would disband the orchestra and sell sacred Symphony Hall. Even though Muck gave in and played the bone of contention in his programs, he ended in a federal detention camp in Georgia on charges of fraudulently claiming Swiss citizenship. After the War he went back to Germany to resume there the distinguished career that he had interrupted to bring Major Higginson a talent worthy of Boston.*

In other areas the snarling was even nastier. When the Reverend Dr. Lyman Abbott, parson turned publicist-editor, urged the U.S. Senate to expel La Follette for stubborn opposition to national policies, one could at least say that was the Senate's privilege under the Constitution (if one read it thus) and in any case Abbott was pushing eighty-five and maybe his judgment was slipping. But when the Reverend Dr. Henry van Dyke recommended shooting Morris Hillquit, Socialist-pacifist candidate for the mayoralty of New York City, the proposer was barely in his sixties and widely considered still responsible. Yellow paint was smeared over the dwelling of Henrik Shipstead of the Minnesota legislature (later U.S. Senator) and a leader of the isolationist Non-Partisan League. (After the War he found it politically valuable to have been thus made conspicuous as isolationist-pacifist.) That was part of ugly frictions in the northern wheat belt between the league, which Creel believed to be politically motivated, and overheated patriots who often went as far as tar-and-feathering and runnings-out-of-town. Elsewhere amateur spy hunts led to scores of cases of mobbing ranging from being forced to kiss the flag to two lynchings. Most of the victims were unpopular or defiantly outspoken men of German background. The second lynching was that of Robert P. Prager, German-born Socialist, in Collinsville, Illinois, a tough coal-mining town. The mayor and police made fumbling efforts to protect him, but he was hauled through the streets, forced to kiss the flag, hanged by a rope hauled on by teen-age boys, let down to be screamed at before he strangled, then hanged

* At the time Walter Damrosch, another eminent conductor of German background working in America, thought Muck's behavior tactlessly rigid. All he had to do, Damrosch, said, was to let an assistant conduct "The Star-Spangled Banner" and explain that "as a loyal citizen of Germany," he could hardly be expected to do so himself. (New York *Times*, November 3, 1917).

again—permanently. Eleven mob leaders were tried for this noisome contribution to the War effort and acquitted by what probably was indeed a jury of their peers.

The tone of all that could be matched by the mobs, harried law officers, hot-eyed officials and zealous editors in the American Revolution, and too many still alive in 1917 could recall how Copperheads had been dealt with during the Civil War. In view of such national precedents it is a matter of wonder that a sense of proportion persisted as well as it did. Consider that whereas Britain thought it necessary to intern every one of the 45,000 German nationals resident there in 1914, the United States interned only 6,300 of 500,000 resident here in 1917. Berlin, New Hampshire, voted against changing its name, whereas Berlin, Ontario, renamed itself Kitchener. In spite of the rank Germanness of their origin, lager beer and hot dogs stayed in favor. But it was undeniable and undeniably unhealthy that the means of mass stimulus were far more effective under Wilson than they had been under Lincoln. The difference may have been more than one of scale. As Creel & Company exploited press, parade, pulpit, mass meeting, school, bank, grocery store, screen, stage, their methods broke a sort of sound barrier in social indoctrination. The chips fell where they might, and some were very sharp underfoot.

Forced-draft patriotism often got the CO (conscientious objector, not commanding officer) handled more roughly in the press and on street corners than among the military in charge of him. Laurence Stallings, a maimed veteran who hated war and brass as heartily as any, considered Sergeant York's case "commentary on the spirit of civilian officers who handled Doughboy draftees . . . [his] new major, who might easily have sent York to prison . . . worked so manfully not to" [98] that the nation acquired a very decent hero and the Germans a formidable foe. In mid-1918 perplexing CO cases were looked into by an itinerant commission dominated by Dean Harlan F. Stone of the Columbia University Law School (later Chief Justice of the United States) and Federal Judge Julian W. Mack, acknowledged to have been one of the great jurists of his time. The commission's tone is deducible from a case cited in Norman Thomas's post-War pamphlet that, even while deploring the draft and its results, gave the commission good marks, faulting it only for appearing on the scene so late. Carl Haessel, a Rhodes scholar and radical recalcitrant, testified that though he had three times refused noncombatant service, his treatment had been "courteous and forbearing" and that Judge Mack had gone out of his way to get him described as "good and sincere"; [99] under the circumstances, Haessel said, he would not complain about the penalties he incurred. But that admirable picture was badly flawed in other cases by sporadic barbarities: beatings, "the water cure," cells unheated in winter. . . .

The law let off combat service anybody already professing a religion of established antiwar principles. This took care of Quakers and the several kinds of Mennonite and smaller sects sharing their religion-based pacifism. Many Quaker boys did not claim this civil privilege. I knew a Midwestern Quaker meeting (of the kind deeply tainted with un-Quakerish trimmings) that hung up the usual service flag with some dozens of stars on it signifying members gone to war. Its salaried minister wore the YMCA's pseudo-military uniform to preach his farewell sermon—a sight that would certainly have brought on George Fox's epilepsy. Soon exemption was also allowed to nonreligious pacifists willing to turn to for the nation if only in factory or farming. Many served well in hazardous medical work or reconstruction overseas—a decent solution for all. But harshness often befell the "absolutist" CO bound by principle, religious or merely ethical, to renounce anything to do with war even indirectly and the anarchist or Red collectivist so bitter against capitalism and all its alleged works that he worked actively to obstruct the War effort, often the draft, and urged others to join him. The first impulse was strong in Joseph F. Rutherford, head of the International Bible Students' Association (known as the Russellites after their founder, now usually called Jehovah's Witnesses), as he advised a drafted disciple to refuse duty: ". . . present institutions are unrighteous . . . if you feel you cannot conscientiously have anything to do with the present war you will refuse. . . . You will probably be confined in prison or shot. . . . If confined in prison it may be the Lord's way of giving you an opportunity to witness to His truth. . . . if you are shot . . . that will be a quick method of entering His glorious presence." [100] Judge Rutherford (he had been a minor judge in his preprophetic days) and seven of his adherents drew twenty years each.

The Wartime laws against acts likely to aid or support the enemy were sweeping, and in view of inflamed public opinion, one wonders why they were not invoked more often and more severely. In a population of more than 100,000,000 only 1,532 were arrested for disloyal talk; only 10 for actual sabotage. In Massachusetts, where the U.S. district attorney was George W. Anderson, a most open-minded and level-headed lawyer, later a distinguished federal judge, nobody was prosecuted under the catchall Espionage Act throughout the War. In the expert opinion of Zechariah Chafee, Jr., of the Harvard Law School, the nation's chief exponent of the law of civil rights, few judges handling Espionage Act cases were "guilty of prejudicial conduct," though too often they failed to distinguish clearly for the jury "between expression of opinion with intent to obstruct and expression in accordance with the First Amendment regardless of possible obstruction." [101] A notable exception to that last was Federal Judge Albert B. Anderson of Indianapolis, considered pretty tough, giving the jury in a sedition case a long tirade about the evils of Socialism, then saying, "Free speech means the right to say foolish things as well as the right to say sensible things," [102] and directing them to acquit. Doubtless it will remain hard for bench and jury box to balance nicely between that unimpeachable principle and the post-Armistice opinion of famously liberal Justice Holmes upholding the constitutionality of the Espionage Act: "When a nation is at war, many things that might be said in time of peace are such a hindrance to its effort that their utterance will not be endured as long as men fight . . . no court could regard them as protected by constitutional rights." [103]

Conspicuous radicals denouncing capitalism's War were tried openly with no hint of Star Chamber. Among those sent to penitentiaries were Eugene V. Debs, the most appealing leader whom American Socialism ever had; Rose Pastor Stokes, Russian-Jewish firebrand (conviction set aside early in 1920 on appeal); Victor Berger, Austrian-born Congressman-editor-organizer of the German-flavored Socialism so rife in Milwaukee (conviction set aside early in 1921 on appeal). Even under the emotional stresses of Wartime, Scott Nearing was acquitted, though the allegedly seditious book that got him arrested was banned. After two mistrials with hung juries, charges against Max Eastman and John Reed were dropped partly on the grounds that the War was already over, partly that both had—rather quaintly—denied any purpose to reflect on the U.S. Army by making such statements as "Sending troops to Russia was an adventure of brigands." [104] Under Presidents Harding and Coolidge the next three years saw all Espionage Act prisoners set free on one or another kind of executive clemency.

Mildly though the act was applied to Socialists, it was, however, used to throw the book at the IWW, which had ostentatiously chosen not to follow most labor unions in renouncing strikes for the duration. The Wobblies' militancy threatened production of copper and other critical metals and of lumber from the Douglas fir country on the West Coast. Late in 1917 federal marshals took over their leaders' persons and files. In a five-month trial sternly handled by Judge Kenesaw Mountain Landis most of them were sentenced to stiff terms. This so crippled the IWW that it never again carried weight in American affairs. A strange little melodrama ensued. Free on bail pending appeal, not only did Haywood and nine of his colleagues skip their bail—which ruined several of their loyal bondsmen—but Haywood also smuggled himself out of the country to a new career as exotic revolutionary hero in Bolshevik Russia. He died in fumbling exile in Moscow in 1928. His body was cremated and the ashes buried, as he wished, half under the Kremlin wall, half in Chicago near the graves of the anarchists' Haymarket martyrs. The rank and file of the IWW are said never to have forgiven him for defecting, for it was at his urging that some of his colleagues gave themselves up for trial to begin with. Had he stuck it out and died in federal prison or as a fugitive from the law, Bill Haywood would have been as fertile a martyr as the Haymarket men.

The U.S. Supreme Court has recently come nearer to clarifying the legal position of the philosophical absolutist pacifist. But, as Joyce Cary once wrote, "governments simply do not know how to deal with martyrs." [105] Particularly society has yet to resolve the issue of the citizen of a sovereign state who, like the consistent Quaker, enjoys its economic fruits and civil protections while refusing attendant responsibilities that may entail or support formal fighting. Beyond those subtleties of conscience, some 160,000 youths out of 10,000,000 subject to draft were thought successfully to have evaded it by either failing to register or hiding out. Few of them would probably have been good military material anyway.

The War expanded transatlantic cultural—a wildly broad use of the word—interchange. The means of warfare were heavily Americanized well before America entered. The suicidal standoff of trench warfare was based on machine guns and barbed wire. Wire entanglements were first used in the American Civil War. The barbs that made them more effective were invented by Americans seeking better fencing for livestock. Machine guns were largely creations of B. B. Hotchkiss, Hiram Maxim, I. N. Lewis and J. M. Browning, Americans all. The submarine that almost starved Britain out and brought Uncle Sam in was sired by American inventors—Robert Fulton and Simon Lake—and perfected by J. P. Holland, an Irish revolutionary teaching in a parochial school in New Jersey. The caterpillar tread of the tanks with which Britain almost broke through trench warfare was worked out by Alvin Orlando Lombard of Maine for the steam tractors that snaked big logs down icy woods tracks, then adapted to the swampy delta of the San Joaquin River in California by Benjamin Holt, "McCormick of the Pacific Coast." Airplane and field telephone were American-born. Indeed the only technological items not of American genesis that made that War different and on the whole worse than earlier ones were use of poison gas, internal-combustion motor, radio, self-propelled submarine torpedo and rigid dirigible balloon—and the last proved to be of small military significance.

Items coming the other way to Americans emulous of European belligerents included the British officer's toothbrush mustache; the "trench buckle" from his "trench coat" adapted to civilian caps and jackets; the wristwatch once considered for women only, now associated with combat officers. Once in the War, the U.S. Army borrowed European styles in military garb, mostly for the worse. In soldiering too one culture borrowing from another usually chooses the worse things. The wide-brimmed, four-dinted campaign hat, symbol of the professional and glumly competent "Old Army" that kept sun out of the eyes and rain off the face, gave way to the useless "overseas cap" version of the Scots glengarry. Its only virtue lay in being a relief from the "tin hat" shrapnel helmet worn in combat. The Old Army's laced canvas leggings were replaced by the spiral puttees that Britain took over from the sepoys of the Indian Army. It took weeks to learn to wind them securely; meanwhile, the new soldier, already despairing of ever learning so many new things so quickly, was always getting chewed out because ten feet of loose puttee were trailing behind him.

There was a different kind of borrowing in America's acquisition of what might be called the Whatpriceglory complex that bulked so large after the War. *What Price Glory?* (1924) was a well-staged rough tribute from Maxwell Anderson and Laurence Stallings to the professional fighters in a U.S. Marines outfit in and just behind the lines in France. But it also contained an off-key episode that deeply impressed little groups of serious people and supplied the piece's title—a nonprofessional officer suffering from battle fatigue bursts out: "What price glory now? Why in God's name can't we all go home? . . . I won't stand for it! . . . you can shoot me, but I won't stand for it!" Battle fatigue, fulminating or chronic, often showed itself in young Europeans in that filthily prolonged stalemate—the world's first experience of reciprocal siege warfare 600 miles long. But the reverberations in post-War American ears of the Whatpriceglory phrase from American sources obscured the exotic origins of much of the Lost Generation's Post-War Disillusion. For the curious fact was that a great deal of it *preceded* actual experience of the War itself. The record shows a heavily literary, wistfully or bitterly cynical, pacific view of war well established before Sarajevo in Britain and in radical intellectual circles on the Continent and naturally radiating into America.

Pre-War Britain had a clear example in Robert Graves, who, in his last year at a famous public school, was "a strong anti-militarist" quitting its cadet corps in revulsion against "implicit obedience to orders" [106] and alarm at a display of barbed wire and machine guns at a summer training camp. The case of Belgium moved him to suppress his pacifism and enlist. Under the strains of the War, however, he became one of the first to publish verses on its miseries, dangers and horrors. Those are, of course, proper materials for art, as Callot, Goya and Arnold Zweig have shown. But Graves' printed reactions carried a peevish self-reference, a demand to know what the universe meant by putting him, *him,* through such ghastly things. The same could be said of his poet peers as hero spokesmen for the disillusioned, Wilfred Owen and Siegfried Sassoon. ". . . the soldiers in [Sassoon's] poetry," Rebecca West wrote in 1925, a woman saying what few men had said, "are the kind of people who in a railroad train would have to travel with their backs to the engine. Peace can have but few corners padded softly enough for such sensitives." [107]

The soldier-poets who, though well aware of the ugliness of war, did not take it as a dirty trick played on them personally, were well received at the time but went abruptly out of fashion after peace came. Rupert Brooke had dwelt lyrically on his prospective soldier's grave "in some corner of a foreign land/That is forever England." Alan Seeger, who enlisted in the Foreign Legion because "I could not go on enjoying the pleasant things [in

Paris] . . . for the defense of which my [French] friends were shedding their blood," [108] gamely regretted his probable "rendezvous with death / On some scarred slope of battered hill. . . ." Brooke died unblooded of something enteric and Mediterranean; Seeger of machine-gun slugs in the Battle of the Somme. Had they survived, maybe piled-up attrition might have embittered them too into Sassoon's gloating fantasy of leading his men "to clear those Junkers out of Parliament" while the rest of the regiment bayoneted the "Yellow Pressmen" who had made War propaganda. But Seeger's last letter home, after he had seen plenty of combat, showed no emotional waverings.

Here is the reaction of poetic James Norman Hall to the disastrous, frustrating butchery of the Battle of Loos in 1915: ". . . we could not get away from the sight of the mangled bodies of our friends. . . . One thinks of the human body as . . . a beautiful and sacred thing. The sight of it dismembered or disemboweled, trampled in the bottom of a trench, smeared with blood and filth is . . . hardly endurable . . . whichever way we looked, there were the dead." So far not unlike the tone of *All Quiet on the Western Front*—only Hall's feeling in 1916 led him to not self-pity but respect for the grit and resilience of the British rank and file he served with, not men of fighting tradition, white-collar city types, "drapers' assistants, clerks . . . [but] less than a dozen natural-born cowards. . . . It gave one a new and remarkable faith in his fellows." [109] The War's best-known verses, "In Flanders Fields," came from Lieutenant Colonel John McCrae, Canadian medic and veteran of the Boer War, who, commanding dressing stations at such slaughters as Second Ypres, saw all there was to see of what so shattered some of his juniors, yet his by no means detached conclusion was that this fetid, slimy, grisly, screaming hell was a job that responsible persons had better see through to a finish: ". . . If ye break faith with us who die,/We shall not sleep, though poppies blow/In Flanders fields." Apropos he was killed in line of duty.

As 1915 became 1916 . . . 1917 . . . 1918 . . . the time factor steadily heightened the tension between strain and personality, of course. An articulate young British officer described it to Gibbs:

> . . . the length of the war . . . does one down. At first . . . the excitement . . . horrible as it was, kept one going. . . . At first we all searched the papers for some hope that the end was near. We don't do that now. We know that whenever the war ends . . . this little crowd will be mostly wiped out. And why are we going to die? . . . "In defense of liberty." We are slaves under shellfire. And as for the Empire—I don't give a curse for it. . . . [The Germans] are in the same bloody mess. They hate it just as much. We're all under a spell together, which some devils have put on us.[110]

Among Americans, however, the time factor could apply chiefly to those entering foreign combat service at the beginning and serving straight along. None such were among the writers who led Post-War Disillusion in the United States. Hemingway, for instance, was an ambulance driver who did not get overseas until the spring of 1918 and saw only three weeks at the front before a trench-mortar shell ended his contact with action. The debacle of Caporetto so ably described in *A Farewell to Arms* had occurred the previous fall while he was still in Chicago.*

In his novel *1919* Dos Passos has two Harvard boys planning ambulance service in France tipsily telling each other "how it was the fate of Beauty and Youth and Love and Friendship to be mashed out by an early death, while the old fat pompous fools would make merry over their carcases." [111] That was written after the author had seen war. But he had put the same feeling into his diary years before when he was only on his way to war: ". . . all young men are frightfully decent. If we only governed the world instead of the swagbellied old fogies. . . . Oh, what a god damned mess they've made . . . the bankers and brokers and meatpackers and businessmen!" [112] Such cases encourage the surmise that Post-War Disillusion contained a derivative element. The epigraph of Sassoon's second volume of verse was a bit about the War's brutalizing all ranks and nations from Henri Barbusse's *Le Feu* (in English *Under Fire*). This prototype War novel from a middle-aged hot anticapitalist Frenchman of talent boiled with hatred of war as France waged it—and in 1916 the book won the Prix Goncourt. It was to the embittered radical mind of the day what *Main Street* would be to the antihinterland mind of the 1920's. In *1919* a radical newspaperman recommends it to a nice Chicago girl crossing to France for Red Cross work. In *A Farewell to Arms* the elegant old Italian nobleman recommends it to the disgruntled hero. Hemingway's preface to *Men at War* (1942) called *Le Feu* "the only good war book to come out of the last war . . . the first one . . . to show us . . . you could protest . . . the gigantic useless slaughter." [113] It dealt not with the ordeals of officers, as did Tolstoy and British malcontents of the 1920's, but with the miseries and exasperations of the French *poilu*. It smelled of blood, carrion and bewilderment as would no other War fiction until Arnold Zweig got into his great tetralogy (*e.g., Education Before Verdun*) in the late 1920's.

---

* This does not at all imply that for all its brevity Hemingway's war record was not good. Badly mauled by mortar fragments, he nevertheless fetched a wounded man on his back to a dressing station and was most deservedly decorated for it. His subsequent record as observer of combat in France and Spain was admirable. Actually little relation can be traced between the extent and kind of a person's involvement in the War and his literarily expressed feelings about it. Maxwell Anderson was never in uniform; Stallings lost a leg in combat. Dos Passos, Hemingway, Cummings were in ambulance service, but Cummings never saw action. William Faulkner and Fitzgerald got into uniform but never saw combat. In the Canadian Black Watch Sherwood saw plenty. . . . I have no wish to make anything of these data. One can learn a lot about the ugliness of war in a short time.

How *Le Feu* managed to reach so many readers in the Allied world is strange. Andreas Latzko's *Men in War*, the Central Powers' equivalent, shriller than Barbusse's but of the same tenor, got into print in America—Dreiser gave it a cordial review—in 1918 but was almost immediately suppressed. Even so, it seems to have got around. Acquaintance with such exotic items on the mental bookshelves of Americans who felt Post-War Disillusion gives one the feeling of reading their significant works before they were written. Latzko's Austrian captain's gorge rises against the prebattle speech he must make to his men in 1914: "Twenty-five years ago . . . 'oath to the flag' . . . had seemed . . . the sum and substance of all things. . . . But now . . . he had grown deaf to the fanfaronade of such words." [114] A soldier dying on the shell-tortured ground over which he must lead his unit fills him with "impotent rage against a world that had inflicted such a thing on him." [115] Ten years later Hemingway's Lieutenant Henry is "always embarrassed by the words, sacred, glorious, and sacrifice . . . [in the War] I had seen nothing sacred, and the things that were glorious had no glory and the sacrifices were like the stockyards at Chicago if nothing was done with the meat except to bury it." [116] Maybe as America entered the War, the Old World was not only drawing the New into its whirlpool but also supplying the young American literary leading edge with ready-made reactions to it. The analogy is, of course, to the White Queen, who screamed with pain the day before she injured her finger.

Youth often plays Wise Guy, seldom gracefully. Dos Passos even countenanced the theory that the chief purpose of sending the AEF to Europe was to have it on the spot to suppress the Revolution that was bound to follow the War. It was more ominous when he showed the college boy ambulance driver of *1919* so metamorphosed by experience at the front that he says it will take a "huge wave of hope like a revolution to make me feel any self-respect again." [117] This led into the smug We-vs.-Theyism that Mary McCarthy sensed in the body of Hemingway's works; that has kinships with Fascist emotions; that already permeated Sassoon's verse; that persuaded Cummings and his garrulous crony that the pitiable, trouble-prone misfits among whom the French locked them up were "the finest people in the world" [118]—a cliché already as overworked as the prostitute with the heart of gold. It seemed to these two young narcissist-misanthropes that in thus isolating them from the values and pressures of organized society, the world had paid them a high compliment. Note too that for the college boy of *1919* the coming revolution was valuable primarily because it would make *him* feel better. The innocence of his self-reference is exquisitely true.

Such misanthropy and nihilism are not to be confused with soldiers' gripes, which often, not always, come of actual grievances. In that War a favorite irritant of the enlisted man's was the YMCA and its shiny-putteed, prim "secretaries" managing the recreation huts, leading songfests, selling

chocolate and—grudgingly—cigarettes to fighting men resentfully aware
that the Salvation Army's refreshment teams gave coffee and doughnuts
free. Even the farcically numb hero of *Dere Mable* complained that in Y
huts, "as soon as you get ritin [a letter] a bald headed fello jumps up and
says 'now fellos well all sing.' . . . They got one in every Y.M.C.A." [119] *Life*
called the Y-men "priggish and incompetent . . . lazy louts whose main
concern was to shut down at six o'clock or . . . goody-goodies." [120] The
decision to employ the Y as canteen and recreation agency had reflected
encouraging experience with the organization in that job in Britain, where it
originated, and on a small scale along the Mexican border in 1916. On the
large scale it was found too late that the stiff Protestantism of its personnel
put off the hundreds of thousands of Catholics in uniform and that the
secretaries tended to be meechy little Bible belters insistent on "prayer
meetings camouflaged as movie-shows . . . antediluvian tracts . . . resistance to Sunday baseball . . . reading rooms inundated with proselytizing
church magazines," [121] as Alexander Woollcott sketched the trouble soon
afterward. What ailed the Y was epitomized in the secretary who told
Wister with thin-lipped pride how "I used to come out between vaudeville
acts and speak to our boys about social purity and kindred topics of a
serious nature." [122]

Mark the distinction between the buck private cursing the Y's red
triangle insigne and the hyper-Pharisaism of the *Three Soldiers-1919*
attitude—not thanking God because they were not as other men but
reproaching Him for not making other men more like the Cultivated Wise
Guy. The latter was using the world's agony to scratch his personal
emotional needs. Sherwood, who had seen plenty of fighting in Flanders
and shared Dos Passos' hatred of war and armies, nevertheless took *Three
Soldiers* to task because the author let "his hatred . . . blur his vision . . .
coat his tongue . . . he has poisoned what might otherwise have been a
remarkable novel . . . almost photographic . . . yet . . . a false document . . . he loses all sense of proportion . . . splatter[s] black paint all over
his canvas . . . every officer is an inhuman tyrant, every non-com an
illegitimate, every chaplain a smug, sleek hypocrite, every Y.M.C.A. worker
a sissy, and every private a surly anarchist. This conception is no more
authentic than one which represents the army as a galaxy of Galahads." [123]

What Sherwood asked for came along a few years later in Leonard
Nason's *Chevrons* (1926). The author, a combat noncom who had been in
the thick of it from Château-Thierry to the Argonne, used the confused
foulnesses and interludes of War as background for a highly creditable
mass portrait of good and contemptibly bad officers; brave, patiently
enduring and cowardly rank and file; sadistic head nurses, venal orderlies
and doctors too overworked to be humane—all set down with no
whimpering, just a sturdy sense of very well, that's what the human race
would be like under such brutal strains. But it was the *Three Soldiers* sort of

thing that became stock-in-trade for five decades of novelists reacting to this and following wars.

Their prototypes seem to have been the "Sorbonne detachment" of literate young Americans staying in the Army while Uncle Sam supported them at French institutions of higher learning, an expansion of the American colony in Montparnasse that would greatly influence the arts in America for the next twenty years. In that spring of 1919 the prevailing clime among them was of "savage joy and bitter hatred . . . the world was a lousy pesthouse of idiocy and corruption, but it was spring." [112] The marked talents of many of the creatively ambitious youngsters in that frame of mind were widely accepted by a Western public overstrung by the War to the point where exasperation and slackness were pleasures. People were understandably weary, and the brighter the wearier, of George Creel and "Over There!" But those emotional luxuries came high in damage to cultural cohesion—the ambient medium that buoys up a society, without which it is wracked by heavy, potentially backbreaking strains like a ship lacking the support of water. From decade to decade the jargon differed, but as favorable conditions recurred, the same phenomenon surfaced, always leaving a fertile residue like the leaven of sourdough bread to start fermentation in the next batch of susceptible, narcissistic individuals. Cummings' *The Enormous Room* + Nathanael West's *Miss Lonelyhearts* = Joseph Heller's *Catch-22*.

The culture medium for the leaven was specially nutritious because of discontent caused when Angell's major premise proved up: The Allies could not win this war, nor had they done so. They came out nominal victors but with a third of the economy of Europe in ruins and the rest twisted all out of shape; most of their best young men dead and some of the survivors emotional cripples; the proclaimed high ends of their fighting— "to make the world safe for democracy . . . to give self-determination to small peoples . . . the war to end war"—looking foolish in view of what wrangling, secret treaties and international shell games had brought about at Versailles in 1919. Friction between President Wilson and the U.S. Senate forced the League of Nations, the peace ark on which civilized hopes had been set since 1914, to sail under jury rig and with a strong tendency to ride down by the head. Disillusion, disappointment, revulsion and just plain emotional weariness smothered the question of what would the world have been like a year after Germany had dictated another peace at Versailles. Suppose that push for Paris in 1918 had succeeded, as it almost did. Suppose American supplies and soldiers had not got past the submarines in such unexpected quantities. . . .

Dr. C. J. Hexamer, president of the National German-American Alliance, had given some of the answer in October, 1914:

Germany was willing to spare France if England would remain neutral. . . . But . . . Now Germany, strong in the possession of

eastern Belgium, holding France to good behavior by an enormous
indemnity, making peace on terms that suit Austria and herself,
fastening Italy to her leadership by bonds stronger than any paper
promises, will dominate Europe . . . her coming navy, built for her
by the war contributions of France, Belgium and England, will
leave no room for fear of England.[124]

Even more ominous is his failure to mention German dominance of the
resources of European Russia that would have followed such a victory, that
Germany was avidly clutching for after Russia disintegrated early in 1917.
About the same time Lippmann was envisioning "a German-Russian-
Japanese coalition against the Atlantic world" as a threat to "If not
civilization, at least our civilization" [125] and a compelling reason for the
United States to give the Allies whatever support circumstances demanded
to bring them victory.

While the Versailles Treaty was still brewing, Wister was touring the
battlefields with an awed dismay worthy of Barbusse. He had happened to
visit Berry-au-Bac in 1914 just before the War broke. What had happened
to the lovely countryside in less than five years daunted him:

> I could no more have recognized this spot than you could
> recognize a dead man who had been lying out in the open for a
> year. . . . The dead! . . . It was written all over the face of the
> region . . . not alone through the sight of a great cemetery . . . to
> our right, to look at the mere earth was enough. [It] had died in
> torments. I can evoke the vision of its twisted corpse today. White
> [this is chalk country], dislocated, crumbled, distorted . . . This
> ancient doorway between the Ardennes and the Ile de France was
> a shrivelled, gaping mouth. The pastures, once so calm, were flung
> up into shapes white and wild, like a herd of screaming ghosts
> petrified into silence suddenly as they crouched and gesticu-
> lated. . . .[126]

Recently I took occasion to visit some parts of France where the fighting
of World War I was especially heavy. North of the Marne, along the
Somme—lovely little rivers heavy with death—the face of the country is
healed, in some places healed again from a second round of damage as
World War II came through. Only here and there an anomalous twist in the
lie of a green field or the slope of a knoll hints at a shell crater not yet quite
filled or a deep dugout collapsed as its props decayed. The replacement
roadside trees are tall and massive-trunked. But the cemeteries for those
who were not taken home are still there, achingly well maintained by
French workmen under American supervision at American expense. The

Stars and Stripes on the tall pole in the center remind one that since President de Gaulle ejected the U.S. armed forces, these are the only American troops remaining on French soil.

The grave markers are elegantly shaped white marble crosses—or Stars of David in appropriate ratio. (French and British markers are of concrete; those for the African Moslems who died for *la France métropolitaine* duly turban-shaped.) The long, eye-compelling perspectives of white crosses on green turf tend to exaggerate the relative numbers of Americans dying to show Lafayette and the Kaiser that the Yanks were not only coming, but had arrived. The 6,000-odd denizens of the typical cemetery at Fère-en-Tardenois north of the Marne need thirty-six acres for their last rest. That works out to a vast expanse of personnel in extended order far more accurately aligned than live soldiery, however well drilled, ever achieved on parade.

Crosses for the unidentified bear the same words as those on the grave of the Unknown Soldier at Arlington. The names of the missing are on the walls of the presiding monuments. Officers, noncoms and privates lie higgledy-piggledy in an equalitarianism that no army ever yet knew. Another sort of equality puts Private James Goelet du Bois Tiffany of New York in the same context as Duffey, Callarino, Jones, Mortensen, Bernstein, Danaschke. . . . Several aspects of America come to mind as one works down the row whispering names: Oscar August Vollrath of the U.S. Marines, obviously no adherent of the German-American Alliance, got a posthumous Croix de Guerre; nearby are men named Graf, Eicheldorfer, Steinbach. Those whose crosses carry "Joe" or "Willie" are not Bill Mauldin's GI's from World War II but come from Alabama, Texas, Georgia where nicknames often crowd out originals. Joe Stinson, private in a Louisiana labor battalion, was certainly a black doing for his country the only service that the War Department's then sharp segregation policy would permit. Private Moroni Kleinman (Second Marines) must have been a Mormon boy dying for the country that Brigham Young hated. Perley Raymond Hamilton was still in the French ambulance service when his number came up. The few women were nurses.

Soon after the War came the problem whether to bring the dead home or leave them in the ground they died to protect. *Life* said that the first would be a "great mistake in sentiment and an injustice to the dead." [127] A third of the families agreed. Today's visitor feels that it was surely right to bury the leathernecks and doughboys killed in Belleau Wood in the shadows of the new trees sprung up to replace those that shellfire shattered. "It is time to speak of these," wrote Stephen Vincent Benét years ago but years after they died

> Who took the long, strange journey overseas.
> They were men of my age and country, they were young men

At Belleau, at the seaports, by the Aisne.
They went where their passion took them and are not.
They do not answer mockery or praise. . . .
It is hard to think back, to find them, to see their eyes
And none born since shall see those, and the books are lies,
Being either praise or blame. . . .[128]

IV

Symptoms of the Morning After

. . . it is vastly easier to begin a great war than to
end one.

"The Watch Tower," *St. Nicholas,*
February, 1916

TO be fair: Those attributing a certain aspect or trait of 1919 to the War were not always wrong. For instance, Wartime shortage of paper was the real reason why the dimensions of popular sheet music shrank and, since nobody cared, remained smaller. The War-occasioned trick of making ships of concrete vanished, but that of building ships of prefabricated subassemblies lasted. From War-born experiment came the quick-frozen fish industry. The trend begun by measures to save leather had men as well as women in low shoes early in the 1920's.

Some such consequences were important as well as innocuous. To supply nitrates for explosives and fertilizers, Uncle Sam built on the Tennessee River the Muscle Shoals hydroelectric plant that, after fifteen years as political football and white elephant, became nucleus of the New Deal's showpiece, the Tennessee Valley Authority. For grimly obvious reasons the War brought great advances in plastic surgery. The need for rehabilitation behind the lines set American Quakers helping their British brethren early in 1917. The resulting American Friends Service Committee not only enlisted conscientious objectors for such work but persisted after the War as the Quakers' salve for man-made misery whether in Syria or West Virginian coalfields, whether caused by war or by civil meanness. In more worldly context War wages and full employment heightened the standard of living, most notably in clothes and amusements. That stimulated the economy of the 1920's and maybe lent extra edge to the discontents that labor organizers found handy. But beyond such things the extensive sequelae were usually deplorable. What else was to be expected of the greatest social calamity the world had ever known?

The capitalization of the Armistice to mean that the end of this unique War was uniquely hopeful set the stage for feeling that the subsequent disappointments were uniquely frustrating. The sourness fouling the national breath after November 11, 1918, represented several ferments. Some of it was retrospective yearning after a former world shattered but still tantalizingly near in time. Many people's viscera, lacking experience with international cataclysms, sluggish after the tingles of Wartime, yearned after what had been familiar on July 4, 1914. Add high awareness of the Bolsheviki, and of the shipyard workers' silk shirts that irritated stay-at-home civilians as well as low-paid doughboys, and the dismay of millions of buyers of Liberty Bonds, unaccustomed to the ups and downs of securities, on finding that those pieces of paper which, the Minute Men had promised, would always be as good as gold, take Uncle Sam's word for it, sank after the Armistice toward 90 cents on the dollar . . .

Then the international primacy into which events had hustled George Washington's standoffish confederacy had on the whole been unsought. The intramural response was flurried retreat into the irrational and parochial. The economic facts were imperative. German-owned enterprises in America had been confiscated. The great holdings of the Allies, particularly Britain, had been sold to foot the bill for Allied purchase of American supplies, and the new owners of those railroads, breweries, mines, ranches and so on were mostly Americans. A former debtor nation with a colonial-flavored economy now held vast obligations in War loans made to the Allies and in any case exerted further huge leverage on the world by its sheer existence. Defying these omens, Americans resisted the temptation to exploit and rejoice in hegemony not so much on anti-imperialistic principle as out of diffidence tinged with xenophobia. "By analogy to what happened in past eras," Mark Sullivan wrote fifteen years later, "we should have become the most important mercantile nation . . . the great lender, put the dollar in the place of the pound in international trade, built the largest navy . . . accepted the role that fate thrust toward us. But America did not care for the power, or did not know how to use it; she did not take the responsibility." [1] So the Senate rejected a League of Nations (child of Europe's as much as of America's wishfulness) and the American Legion of American veterans set "100% Americanism" among the goals in the preamble to its constitution.

The returned servicemen made many dents—a strange one at news-stands, for instance. *Home Front*, a well-edited magazine employing some of the former staff of the AEF's well-handled newspaper *The Stars and Stripes*, died after a few issues. But soon procurable was a different sort of publication for veterans, a two-bit, pocket-sized affair published in a suburb of Minneapolis, *Captain Billy's Whizbang*—nickname of a German projectile of evil memory. Self-defined as "an explosion of pedigreed bunk," it was "Edited by a Spanish-American and World War Veteran. . . . Dedicated to the Fighting Forces of the United States and Canada." The owner was Wilford H. Fawcett, a chunky Minnesotan who had enlisted young in the Old Army, got wounded in the Philippines, come home to newspapering, been a captain in the AEF and in 1924 acquired supplementary fame as captain of the U.S. Olympic trapshooting team.

The original aim of his paper was to amuse hospitalized veterans with as juicy examples of their sort of humor as the mails allowed in 1919. Leering old vaudeville gags; bowdlerized versions of stag party songs; diffuse comments from Captain Billy on mothers (favorable) and Prohibition (unfavorable)—for at least a large minority of veterans the formula must have been well calculated. They floated it until, after a couple of years, it forgot about hospital wards and was pushing toward a circulation of half a million among the pimply-minded. References to old times in France, never plentiful even at first, tended to vanish. In the mid-1920's came a section of jokes of the "I Phelta Thi" sort culled from campus magazines of undergraduate humor, and another of full-page photographs of voluptuously underclad pretty girls procured from the Hollywood and Broadway amusement industries. The humor, stressing the privy and double entendre about a goose making a broad jump, leaned toward burlesque rather than vaudeville. Before it died in 1935, the *Whizbang* was largely snickery cartoons and captions that the artists could sell nowhere else. But its profitable early years had enabled Captain Billy, a good businessman who also dabbled in banking, to launch other shrewdly aimed magazines, among them the ancestor of today's *True* and the first of the confession books. Hence the special-interest magazines and paperback imprints of today's Fawcett Publications, Inc.

Maybe also on the credit side was the *Whizbang*'s share in eroding the Nice Nelly standards of what could be published and circulated that the 1920's inherited from preceding decades. Even so the balance remains on the whole negative. The same could be said of those major results of the War, the veterans' organizations already making themselves heard as Johnny came marching home. Such things follow wars elsewhere too—the British Legion, the Germans' Stahlhelm. . . . Presciently in 1913 splinter groups of veterans of the Spanish-American War had fused into the Veterans of Foreign Wars in time to compete in 1918 with the newborn American Legion for the nostalgic loyalties of former members of the AEF.* In the previous generation the Grand Army of the Republic, blue-coated, brass-buttoned, black-slouch-hatted, each year stepping a little less briskly to fife and drum in its annual "encampment," had kept it worth political candidates' while to go on waving the bloody shirt thirty years after Appomattox; the United Confederate Veterans were their counterparts in Dixie. The GAR, however, though born in 1866, had been sluggishly small, not reaching peak membership of 400,000-odd pension-hungry voters until the 1880's, whereas the American Legion, also theoretically welcoming all who had worn the uniform, no matter where or how briefly, was huge from the beginning.

It had the advantage of the wider and keener, War-born publicity techniques that similarly boomed the once-puny Ku Klux Klan in 1919–20. One may also suspect among the boys in khaki a pervasive disgruntlement

* The American Legion's name, which Alexander Woollcott, a delegate to its founding caucus, called "too silk stocking," came from the organization to promote the Plattsburgh idea set up in 1915 by Leonard Wood and Theodore Roosevelt. Theodore Roosevelt, Jr., an officer in the formidable First Division, was high among the new Legion's organizers. (Raymond Moley, *The American Legion*, 58.)

of a sort that fewer boys in blue felt. Grant's and Sherman's men, having won clean-cut victory, saved the Union and freed the slaves, were entitled to a sense of accomplishment, however futile some of it looked later. Most of Pershing's men who saw fighting disliked what they saw of the foreign parts they were saving. A great many never got overseas. Sudden peace and a dawdly discharge after all that drill and moving about were, however welcome, anticlimactic. And on getting home and doffing the old olive drab, they became aware that far from having made the world safe for democracy as advertised, they had, a growing number of the home folk thought, only made it safe for swindler politicians enjoying overseas seats of power.

Many from formerly Wet areas resented the Prohibition imposed during their absence. Few condoned the way industrial labor, including hundreds of thousands of draft-exempt aliens and physically disqualified natives, had lived high on War-inflated wages while better men were doing squads right at $1 a day. They particularly resented the way the physically fit, including new heavyweight champion Jack Dempsey, had taken jobs in shipyards that entailed exemption from the draft. Worse, the new-hatched Bolsheviks were, by all accounts, stirring up foreign-born Reds to undermine Mother, the flag and the girl next door. Soon came an impression that veterans banded together under no-nonsense leaders were the best safeguard against subversives. . . . On the cordial side the Legion and the VFW offered nostalgic maintenance of the lie-swapping, foulmouthed comradeship that had made Company C or Battery D tolerable, even something to look back to, in spite of mud, KP and short-arm inspection. On the material side veterans' organizations promised to make Uncle Sam show the nation's saviors due gratitude—which soon meant not only good care of ailing and disabled veterans but also pressure for bonuses and looser disability criteria.

Without those latter functions the Legion and the VFW alike might have simmered down into mere rivals of the Elks and the volunteer fire company as ways for a man to get away evenings. The Legion's annual conventions, soon so drunken and rowdy that cities half dreaded to compete for the free spending that they promised, became part of American folklore with their fantastically costumed bands and drill teams and the cuttings up of the Forty-and-Eight crews—the Legion's privileged jesters whose name commemorated the stencil on the French boxcars in which troops were shipped around: "40 HOMMES/8 CHEVAUX." For street showmanship the Legion beat the Shriners (pseudo-Oriental, high jinks affiliate of Masonry) and the New Orleans Mardi Gras. But serious, if often misguided, purposes remained the core of the Legion with evident effects on the nature of its rosters. By no means all former servicemen bothered to join even during ardent membership drives—the total was never higher than a third of those who had been inducted—so a tough automatic self-selection doubtless occurred. By and large the typical Legionnaire tended to be more aggressive, suspicious-minded or aggrieved by what he found in civilian life than the veteran failing to sign up. And the leaders whom such members chose for local, state and national officers were likely to reflect such emotional habits or even inculcate them as conducive to local and national action.

Antidotary efforts to organize veterans of radical bent aborted. Soldiers' and Sailors' Councils imitating the Russian revolutionary pattern to the extent of barring officers and favoring recognition of the Bolshevik government soon petered out. Only in chronically disgruntled Minnesota and the Dakotas did the World War Veterans, Inc., allies of the populist-radical Non-Partisan League, take root for even a few years. One may wish more might have come of the example of New York City's Willard Straight Post of the Legion itself, named for the eminent, liberal-minded banker who died in uniform in France in 1918. It hoped to show that veterans of goodwill and cultivation could at least dilute the reactionaryism toward which the Legion was leaning. Its roster was stiff with young and middle-aging names already eminent or soon to be so,* well able to get a hearing when time and again their post publicly opposed dubious Legion policies on such issues as the veterans' bonus, institutionalization of veterans' orphans, ironclad preference for veterans in civil service jobs. The New York State Legion, goaded to action by a ruling from the national level, revoked the Willard Straighters' charter. Their membership included several with excellent access to the best legal talent of the day and the suit they brought forced the Legion, after losing an appeal, to rescind the revocation. But they remained only an encysted thorn in the Legion's organism.

Deplorably soon members of the Legion or the VFW were often in the van when IWW or Marxist meetings were broken up. Lodi, California, Desdemona, Texas, Astoria, Oregon, Santa Barbara, California, Cincinnati, Ohio, Wilkes-Barre, Pennsylvania, saw Legionnaires, sometimes acting as a unit, sometimes as cooperating individuals, run suspected Reds out of town or horsewhip editors printing the wrong sort of talk or vandalize the headquarters of radical political groups. Such capers were not overtly stated official policy, and they seemed to occur oftenest in the more mob-minded parts of the country. But occasional disclaimers from on high could not modify the commonsense impression of radical groups that veterans' organizations often had a hand in such doings. That was why the IWW of

---

* Such as Adolf Berle, eventually ablest analyst of the overgrown corporation and a power in the early New Deal; Sidney Howard, soon to be Broadway's most intelligent liberal playwright; W. W. Norton, solidest of highbrow publishers; Charles Merz, ornament of the editorial board of the New York *World*, then of the New York *Times*; Carlton J. H. Hayes, a highly eminent historian; Walter Lippmann . . . and Francis Rivers, a black judge who was a pillar of the National Association for the Advancement of Colored People.

Centralia, Washington, hid members with rifles in and near their red-draped new meeting hall on Armistice Day, 1920. The local parade, dominated by the Legion, came down that street, and when a hitch in the timing brought a Legion unit to a halt in front of the hall, the riflemen, thinking attack imminent, opened fire. Three Legionnaires were killed outright. Before it was over, a mob had taken one of the IWW riflemen from jail and castrated and hanged him from a bridge.

The ensuing trial—of the surviving IWW riflemen, for nobody expected any action against the mob—brought heavy sentences for second-degree murder. The Legion's leaders praised the Centralia post for having cooperated with law and order but made no effort to deny that Legionnaires were in the mob. The net effect of the IWW's gorgeous stupidity was to stiffen the Legion's already vicious militancy. As the kindred odors of Fundamentalism, Prohibition and the Klan were showing or would soon show, the prospects of reaction in post-War America were already bright enough. The last thing needed was such coast-to-coast sodalities of edgy young men egging one another on to repressive doings in the name of a 100 percent Americanism that men even brighter than their leaders could never have defined. Yet that was the organized veterans' chief contribution as their country tried to shake off the toxicities left by aborted war.

Legionnaires and VFW's needed intelligible aims the less because their chosen antagonists were often obligingly flagrant. The occasion was, of course, Russia's October Revolution in which Lenin's Bolsheviki ousted the moderate radicals of the first (February) one. Its connotations, noxiously embittering life in America as well as the Old World, were the greatest and saddest consequence of the War. For without such strains on the friable Russian society, the long-overdue explosion there might not have been as shattering and might not have developed such hopes of infecting other polities.

The disintegration created within Russia by its second convulsion would have seemed to promise victory to Germany before America would make its weight felt. Outside Mitteleuropa, however, that contingency was so repugnant that most ignored it. Particularly seekers of "peace without victory" assumed at worst stalemate, at best defeat for Germany, and then diverged in directions appropriate to the two kinds of temperament involved.

Those drawn toward the pole of goodwill—the settlement house/Mr. Britling/fatherhood-of-God-brotherhood-of-man sort—planned a world more promisingly organized because butchery in the trenches and the miseries of War-sparked revolution had forced mankind to renounce the habits of Kilkenny cats. The implicit compliment to the human race was undeserved, but that was clearer twenty years later. Others flowed more or less peevishly toward the pole of righteous violence, of *ruat caelum* social justice—the IWW/Thorstein Veblen/*le bourgeois à la lanterne* sort of thing sometimes in a Pickwickian but often in a literal sense. They relished the prospect of chaos, however bloody and arbitrary, a romantic shattering to bits that, as Omar suggested in another context, led to reshaping "nearer to the heart's desire"—the heart in this case being that of the radical zealot, whether orthodox Marxist, syndicalist, anarchist, sentimental collectivist or plain nihilist. Not only the agonies of Russia but the tumults presently arising from defeat in Germany and victory in Italy struck all such—under such conditions they had good reason to hope—as good growing weather for the Revolution.

A year before the Armistice the October triumph of the Bolsheviki convinced American radicals of several stripes that the great day was come. ". . . the air was freshening," Dos Passos recalled in *The Big Money*. "In Russia the great storm of revolt had broken, seemed to be sweeping west . . . in the east the warsodden multitudes began to see again." [2] Germany would explode first, the Marxist press vehemently predicted; then Italy; nor would Britain and the United States be far behind as their toiling masses felt the breath of the Russian hurricane stirring their hair. Lenin himself wrote for the American Marxist press—readers of which naturally included agents of the U.S. Department of Justice—that in America the workingmen were coming out into the streets for the decisive struggle and that 1920 would assuredly see the triumph of the International Socialist Republic promised in the Bolshevik version of the Red anthem, "The Internationale."

Also among the powerfully affluent many suspected grimly alarming substance in these confident projections. Philip Gibbs, who saw much of American coupon clippers in 1919, reported home that he was hearing a great deal about an impending "social revolution in the United States on Bolshevik lines . . . Fifth Avenue swept by machine-gun fire . . . Pittsburgh, Detroit, and Cleveland in the hands of revolutionary committees of workmen after wild scenes of pillage and mob passion . . . the rich daughters of millionaires stripped of their furs and their pearls. . . ." [3] Gibbs thought the odds against such melodrama but, hardheaded reporter though he was, found the possibility not absurd in view of the inflammatory contrasts between the overheated ease of American plutocracy and the dead-end squalor of American slums, once the leaven of the Russian example got working. As early as March, 1919, *Harper's Bazaar*, handbook of these millionaires' daughters, warned: "There is a plague abroad in the land . . . bolshevism . . . the cure is a thorough inoculation with Americanism. . . . If you haven't found your place in this greatest of all reconstruction work, write to . . . [a lady editor]. . . ." [4] And Griffith, then planning *Orphans of the Storm*, nominally about the French Revolution, said he hoped to make its account of "the maddened mob under blood lusting rulers" into "great anti-Bolshevik propaganda." [5] It all heightened tensions and set stubborn doctrinaires on collision courses. In later years hindsight discerned a Red Scare deliberately cooked up to justify the harsh antiradical gestures of tunnel-vision reactionaries. In creating this cliché, hindsight was wrong, as it sometimes is. The scare was there before the crackdown. Then, no doubt, the crackdown somewhat heightened the scare.

Ardent fans of the October Revolution did their best to warn capitalists what they planned for them while forming the two wings of devout Marxism—the Communist* Party and the Communist Labor Party—that Lenin lashed into fusion as the eventual American Communist Party. "Commie," however, was at first no part of the popular idiom. "Bolshevik" or "Bolshie" or "Bolo" identified the Leninist menace. Such terms were necessarily blurry, for many anarchists and amateur Marxists had not yet perceived that the new god of the Kremlin was a jealous god who would have no other leaders' notions before him. Since technical distinctions among Bolsheviki, anarchists and the anarchosyndicalist IWW were unclear to parlor radicals, Americans had some general excuse for mixing up the shifting groups of foes of things-as-they-are.

"Just now," the Chicago *Evening Post* said late in 1919, "in popular parlance a Bolshevik is anybody from a dynamiter to the man who wears a straw hat in September. In more enlightened circles [it] includes paternalism, socialism, syndicalism, and anarchism." [6] The soberly conservative *Review of Reviews* spoke of "the Anarchistic movement . . . whether called Anarchist, Communist or Bolshevist." [7] Anarchism was much on the American mind because of a well-spaced series of episodes—the Haymarket bombing in Chicago (all too probably an anarchist gesture bringing about grievous miscarriage of justice in the penalties applied); the attempt of Alexander Berkman, eminent anarchist, to kill Henry C. Frick, a steel magnate; the connection with anarchists of the psychotic Leon Czolgosz who killed President McKinley (which led to a federal law, inconvenient for anarchists after the War, barring all stripes of anarchist aliens from the United States); the killing of Italy's King Humbert by Italian anarchists who had worked out their plans in America. Hence the man in the street made the anarchist the archstereotype of rabid revolutionary—a wildly bearded, slavering demon with a foreign accent. *Life* got most of it into rhymed clichés of high density:

> A cubic yard of whiskers rank,
> A bomb in each big fist,
> And murder in the ebon heart—
> You have a Bolshevist! [8]

* "Communism" as distinctive label for the Kremlin's variety of Marxist Socialism seems to have been first used not in Zürich or Moscow but at a convention of the faithful in Chicago late in 1919.

Actually the bomb as notice-rousing—and soul-relieving—"propaganda by the deed" was largely the specialty of one faction of anarchism and met little favor among Bolsheviki, who thought anarchism stupid or frivolous. The element of foreignness in the stereotype was statistically sound, however. True, certain prominent American devotees of Bolshevism were 100-proof WASP's: John Reed, Albert Rhys Williams, the Eastmans, William Bross Lloyd, Nearing, Haywood (alias Mr. IWW) and some of his lieutenants. But on the Coast the Wobblies' ranks included many Scandinavians, and the industrial populations of New Jersey and Pennsylvania, where they scored propaganda coups, were mostly immigrants from Eastern Europe with, regardless of religion, a low proportion of applicants for citizenship. A chief ingredient of the Communist Party would be the hot-Marxist Federation of Russian Workers, with several thousand members in 100-odd branches called People's Houses.

Into this volatile mixture of dreads, hatreds, adrenal throbbings and post-War strikes persons unknown threw bombs late in the spring of 1919. Twenty-nine, disguised in department store wrapping, were mailed to eminent men, starting with J. P. Morgan. All but one were defused in time; two women were hurt. Five weeks later a smaller series of planted bombs drew headlines. The most successful blew in the front of the dwelling of A. Mitchell Palmer, a Quaker politician-lawyer who managed the confiscated German assets during the War and was now U.S. Attorney General. Whoever planted that one could not be identified, for the bits of him found across the street on the steps of the dwelling of Franklin D. Roosevelt, then Assistant Secretary of the Navy, were too small. An anarchist leaflet found among them made it likely that this was a gesture with the anarchists' black, not the Marxists' red flag. Palmer was not an ideal target. He had been cold to a still War-nervous Congress' hopes to extend into peacetime the curbs that the Espionage Act imposed on dissent. Only a few months later, however, the Palmer Raids were to become indelible history, the moral of which varied with the observer. Did they show how a nation should handle subversion? Or how America on the war path can flout constitutional rights? Or how, when extremists get striking minatory attitudes for one another and trading threats, civilization usually suffers?

The end of the War had erased federal antisedition acts, but some states were planning, and a few passing, measures of that sort that would do great moral damage. Assuming—correctly too—that most of America's resident anarchists and militant Marxists were unnaturalized aliens, Palmer secured help from the Department of Labor, which handles aliens, and got from Congress funds for a new General Intelligence Branch of the Department of Justice to round up aliens "advocating the use of force or violence against property, the government, or its officials" for Labor to deport. Trial runs bagged a few, including Berkman, out on parole after serving fourteen years for his attack on Frick, and undaunted Emma Goldman, recently released from a jail term for obstructing the draft. Then, late in 1919, as radicals gathered to celebrate the anniversary of the October Revolution, Palmer's men, led by young J. Edgar Hoover, burst in on their dances and speechifyings and arrested hundreds of members of the Russian Workers in New York City, Chicago, Boston . . . New Haven, Connecticut, Jackson, Michigan. . . . Innocents and U.S. citizens caught in the net were winnowed out fairly soon. Within four weeks a U.S. transport, the *Buford*, called "the Soviet ark" in the press, took back to Russia via Finland 184 alien Russian Workers, 51 alien anarchists and 14 nonpoliticals otherwise answering the law's definition of an undesirable alien. There was little protest from a still War-jangled public mindful of bombs and Red spokesmen's bluster—except from the Reverend Billy Sunday, who complained that it would have cost less to shoot the *Buford*'s passengers, a notion elaborated by Leonard Wood, saying "S.O.S., ship or shoot . . . place them all on a ship of stone with sails of lead and . . . their first stopping place should be Hell." [9]

In most cases the shipping was legal. Some of the shippees were "happy to get a free trip to the workers' fatherland." [10] But too often the method was too summary for the requirement of the Fifth Amendment that no "person" (not just "citizen") be "deprived of liberty or property without due process of law." Constitutional guarantees suffered worse the day after the first Palmer Raids, when New York's Lusk Committee sent local peace officers to break up Communist meetings and screen those present for liability under state law against criminal anarchy. Several key Communists thus caught were convicted and imprisoned until pardoned in the early 1920's. In both affairs lawyers' protests were ignored. On New Year's Day, 1920, Illinois tried the edge of its new antisedition law in a premature swoop on Communists in Chicago that again resulted in some convictions. The next day Hoover's men made a far wider series of violence-marred raids, picking up 6,000-odd presumed members of Bolshevik-oriented organizations. U.S. citizens, aliens able convincingly to deny Communist membership and certain IWW's among them were soon freed, but a number were duly deported as Communist aliens.

In such state proceedings though "many sentences were handed out . . . few [were] served," says Theodore Draper, able analyst of Communism. "Nevertheless, at the time, the fact that the bark of the inquisitors was worse than their bite could not be known." [10] By early 1920, however, higher-ups in Washington were growingly uneasy, and the rising buzz among lawyers was hard to ignore, particularly after Charles Evans Hughes, recent Republican Presidential candidate and former member of the U.S. Supreme Court, spoke up sharply in a widely publicized speech. As public zeal abated, many hot-Communist aliens were turned loose after more or less confinement and harsh treatment—ready-made martyrs back on their chosen ground. *Life,* though hotly anti-Bolshevik, surmised that

"Mr. Palmer's net [has] gathered in too large a proportion of comparatively, or wholly, innocent people. . . . Order without Liberty is no slogan at all for the people of these States. . . . So inquisitors and deporters are now moving unobtrusively toward the back benches, and it is time they did." [11] At his first Cabinet meeting after his disabling stroke, President Wilson, hearing Palmer extolling the good effects of deporting irksome aliens, roused from his apathy to say, "Don't let the country see Red." * [12] His daughter, Mrs. Francis B. Sayre, had been one of those going to Deer Island in Boston Harbor to alleviate the hardships of aliens awaiting deportation there in freezing weather with no heat.

This Red Scare, as it was subsequently known, whatever its origin, was petering out, readily nudged off front pages by the Presidential campaigns of the summer of 1920. In September it was momentarily revived by the Wall Street Explosion at lunch hour at the curb outside the office of J. P. Morgan & Company, which killed thirty persons but neither Morgan nor any other symbol of capitalism. The never-identified perpetrator used so much dynamite that the shabby wagon and decrepit horse that some noticed drawn up before the Morgan corner just before the world came apart were blown into smithereens; all that was left to show they ever existed was two hooves and some fragments of axle and hubs. But not even that caused reverberations enough to keep Bolshevik hunting fashionable.

Those compiling the score of what Zechariah Chaffee, Jr., stalwart liberal professor at the Harvard Law School, called "the greatest executive restriction of personal liberty in the history of this country" [13] had some noteworthy items. Mass arrests and conviction obtained during the War smashed the IWW beyond repair. A few stubborn souls like Joe in the hit play *They Knew What They Wanted* kept going through Wobbly motions, but the crackle was gone. For a while the new-hatched Communist Party too looked hopelessly shattered as its faithful went to jail or to their spiritual or actual Russian homeland. Yet as Benjamin Gitlow saw it after he quit the party in the late 1930's, the Palmer Raids—about which he remained indignant—did Lenin's cause great favors. They separated "the wheat from the chaff," he said, by reducing membership to 16,000 bitter-enders eager for "the rigors of Communist life [underground], its regimentation and strict discipline." Nor were most of the 60,000-odd thus disaffiliated lost to the cause. Already used to its moral climate, they "remained staunch communist sympathizers . . . generous supporters . . . a dependable layer between the . . . membership and . . . fellow travelers† who, in 1920, numbered over 600,000." [14]

---

* Interesting problem: Had Wilson been fit, would Palmer and Hoover have been allowed to go so far? Wilson had been out of touch, dependent for information on tiptoeing intimates, since before the Palmer Raids began. True, he had sought and used the wide powers of the Espionage Act in Wartime. But he was also known to mistrust America's talent for overdoing.

† In this context the term may be an anachronism, but when Gitlow was writing (in the 1940's) it had been widely used for fifteen years.

If Gitlow saw irony in this backhanded result of the Red Scare, he did not say so. More ironic was the founding, in January, 1920 of the American Civil Liberties Union as result of the Palmer Raids. Every action, says physics, has a reaction equal in force and opposite in direction, and the moral and emotional energy of the young ACLU grew in proportion to government's zeal in overhewing to the line. Thus a number of salutary hobbles in which the law must now work are referable to the synergism of the reactionary and the collectivist radical created by the War—which was the occasion of both Russia's Revolution and America's temporarily destructive intolerance.

For that matter the linear ancestors of the ACLU were products of the strains of Wartime. First an Anti-Preparedness Committee of 1915—articulate pacifists, some of religious flavor, some collectivist, some only self-committed: John Haynes Holmes, Lochner, the Eastmans, Rabbi Wise, Oswald Garrison Villard, a couple of eminent Quakers. . . . In a few months this became the American Union Against Militarism, enlisting Amos Pinchot, suggestible lawyer brother of the great conservationist. In the crisis of 1917 over resumption of submarine warfare the AUAM recruited Roger Baldwin, a doughty social worker of pacifist and tenuously anarchist leanings, who created for it a Civil Liberties Committee to aid those in trouble with the draft law. Help came from able lawyers, some of whom were no pacifists but preferred good law to bad. Then Norman Thomas, ardent Socialist though still a Presbyterian minister, tried to tie the AUAM to the People's Council for Democracy and Peace—a presage of the Communist front organizations of the 1930's. From resulting schisms emerged an independent, narrowly labor- and peace-minded National Civil Liberties Bureau headed by Baldwin. He became Mr. Civil Liberties, and it became the ACLU.

His view of liberty was limited. He sometimes sounded as though he thought it chiefly a social means to moral ends, necessary to man's sustained collective well-being, like vitamins, whereas the 200-proof libertarian feels that liberty is a primary good in itself like a healthy *joie de vivre* and its hygienic virtues, real as they may be, are secondary. Baldwin's view is understandable, however, in a social worker who had toyed with the IWW and was drawn toward anarchism. In view of his leanings and the ACLU's family tree, the wonder is that it and he did not become fronts for militant Marxism. Danger of that, ever present in the organization, was not always strongly enough resisted. The consequent heavy list to port made maintaining more than a demi-virginity difficult. In these twisty matters, however, even demi-virginity is, as in the well-known case of Rosie Gore, "some record for this vicinity." Through the 1940's at least the ACLU maintained a nominal token level of nonpartisan loyalty to the Bill of

Rights. It occasionally defended rank reactionaries as well as radicals and watched sharply for infringement on the separation of church and state. In so doing it has brought about much clarifying restriction on government as well as on aggressive individuals and private groups—which makes it still more ironic that in a manner of speaking Palmer was its great-grandfather.

A different, grimmer irony came to the archsymbol of what Palmer was assailing—John Reed. His generation at Harvard included more young brilliance marked for nonacademic fame than the place has turned out since: Lippmann, Gilbert Seldes, T. S. Eliot, Conrad Aiken, Seeger, Broun, H. V. Kaltenborn, Willard Huntington Wright, Van Wyck Brooks, Gluyas Williams, Kenneth Macgowan, Lee Simonson, Robert Edmond Jones, Edward Sheldon, Robert Benchley. . . . Dos Passos, Cummings, Sherwood were right behind them. Of this amazing group (strangely few of them New Englanders) Reed was in some ways the Hemingway—burly and handsome, rather a womanizer. Forty-five years later Miss Ferber recalled him as "the blue-eyed babe of the [Greenwich Village] crowd . . . laughing, talking, eager, young." [15] His writing showed a natural wrist, a prancing narcissism so candid as to seem innocent, a high skill with pungent detail. His magazine pieces about Pancho Villa, then on the War in the Balkans and on the Eastern Front showed that, for all his relish for radicalism, he was at bottom (this too is Hemingwayish) the paragraph-hunting journalist-tourist. His first sight of Villa's raucous, ragged rebels caused him to write not how fiercely they were sweeping away injustice but "What pageant material!" [16] But Steffens, at the behest of Reed's Progressive father, had cultivated the boy's radical bent, and the pageant Reed wrote for the IWW in 1913 made him a culture hero overnight in the Village, Provincetown and Carmel. Lippmann, a college contemporary, had some reservations:

> [Reed] assumed that all capitalists were fat, bald and unctuous . . . all newspapers were corrupt . . . made an effort to believe that the working class is not composed of miners, plumbers, and workingmen generally, but is a fine statuesque giant who stands on a high hill facing the sun. . . . He talked with intelligent tolerance about dynamite . . . has no detachment and is proud of it, I think . . . not a professional writer or reporter . . . a person who enjoys himself. . . .[17]

America's entrance into the War outraged him. He knew as well as his avowedly Marxist cronies that it was nothing but profit madness triumphant and that the February Revolution was a bourgeois fraud. In the *Masses* he predicted that "the real thing" would soon be along to create "a new human society upon earth." [18] A bad kidney kept him out of trouble with the draft. He married a Red-lining, militantly feminist, attractive newspaperwoman, Louise Bryant. She went to cover the New Russia for a news syndicate.* Reed went for the *Masses* on money raised by Eugen Boissevain, affluent businessman and husband of Inez Milholland, handsome Joan of Arc of votes-for-women. Reed's consequent book, *Ten Days That Shook the World*, based on personal experience in the October Revolution, lacked the crackle of his coverage of Mexico and the War and must have been superficial since he had too little time to learn Russian adequately. (One recalls Phyllis McGinley's travesty of Red-minded British poets of the 1930's: "For though I understand Spain I do not understand Spanish." [19]) Bertrand Wolfe, a veteran Communist who eventually apostasized, said *Ten Days* showed Reed to be "an innocent who did not know whether he was attending a wedding or a funeral." [20] But its pungent partisanship and Reed's infectious hero worship of Lenin—he had been the same about Villa . . . for a while—got him canonized as a Bolshevist saint. To a moderate Socialist deploring such slanted reporting he replied: "You are correct when you call information about Russia Bolshevik propaganda, for the great majority . . . who learn the truth about Russia become convinced Bolsheviki." [21] Inclusion of *Ten Days* among Communist Scriptures was well advised. Granville Hicks wrote in 1935, when he was still firmly Communist: ". . . it would not be easy to compute the number . . . whose interest in Communism dates from the reading of *Ten Days That Shook the World*." [21]

Returning home, Reed, an able speaker, exploited his *Mayflower*-ed ancestry to show that WASP's too could go Bolshevik and defy muzzles as well as any. In spite of several indictments, he worked dauntlessly for his cause while out on bail. Maybe he was stiffened by the persecution feelings that led him to think it sinister when the Harvard Club of New York City posted him for an unpaid bill. Eventually he smuggled himself out of the country on money raised by Boissevain again and became one of several Americans working for the Bolsheviks' propaganda mill in Russia. In 1920 he died of typhus in Moscow and was buried in the Kremlin wall as a party hero.

Maybe it was just in time. One story had him dismayed by the vulgarities of a top-echelon junket to Baku in a lavishly stocked special train traversing famine-gaunt country. The party leaders had already snubbed him for trying to buck the steamroller at a party congress. It seems likely that his last days were almost as sick with disillusion as with typhus;† neither

* Before a U.S. Senate Committee on German and Bolshevik Propaganda in early 1919 Louise Bryant expressed one reason why American feminists often looked kindly on the Bolsheviki: "I have never been in a country where women were as free as they are in Russia . . . not treated as females but as human beings . . . a very healthy country for a suffragist." Feminist Bessie Beatty, social worker turned newspaperwoman, had much the same reaction after a stay in the Soviet Union at the same period.

† Draper (*Roots of American Communism*, 284–93) sums up available data in a gingerly fashion; the issue is fogged by several witnesses' confusions: "Was Reed a 'disillusioned'

ailment is benign. He could have blamed this personal wrench at least partly on the War that set off the Revolution that failed him and then cynically ignored his revulsion—the associations of American Red-minded writers of the early 1930's were called John Reed Clubs. But such things · happen to his sort. In *26 Jayne Street*, Mary Austin's novel about the Village of her and John Reed's day, a feminist describes a former lover* who has just been giving a firsthand account of the Bolshevik triumph: He never loved me, she says, nor do he and most of his beglamored hearers "love economic justice. . . . They love the effect of ideals of freedom and justice on themselves." [22]

America created her share of radical saints for the Communists' use. The Sacco-Vanzetti case was a mystery deeper and more poignant than that of John Reed's probable disillusion.

Had Palmer's arrogant raids not put the wind up both local police and alien radicals in early 1920, Nicola Sacco and Bartolomeo Vanzetti might never have been arrested on a suburban trolley car in southeastern Massachusetts and found to be carrying firearms. Their lame explanations of why and how they had those particular weapons made them as widely known as Captain Alfred Dreyfus and as dear to radicals as John Brown to Abolitionists. In prison, between emotional crises, they, like Brown, came to see that their being executed would further the good cause—in their case that of the anarchist's law-free, hate-free, exploitation-free good time coming. Each was probably stabler than Old Ossawotomie. But it is good to know that supposing they had to die in the electric chair, they died persuaded that their fate had meaning. Indeed it had. A recent student of the case, no partisan of theirs, calls their ordeal "the only significant intellectual occurrence in the United States between the first World War and the depression" [23]—an exaggeration almost sound.

The mass of books about them makes summary unwise. Yet an attempt must be made because Sacco and Vanzetti are now mere names of a golden shimmer like Dr. Schweitzer's. They were Italians come to America as grown men seeking a better livelihood. Both had the reflex mistrust of authority and money power that went with the sentimental but tough anarchism endemic among low-income Italians of their day. Both were active among Italian anarchists around Boston. Neither knew more than enough English to manage wage jobs. Sacco was a machine tender in shoe factories, Vanzetti an odd-job drifter, just then peddling fish to the Italians

---

Communist? . . . the burden of proof [is] on those who claim a definite break. But if disillusion is understood intellectually and emotionally rather than organizationally, Reed was probably as disillusioned as it was possible to be and still remain in the movement." The recent *So Short a Time*, Barbara Gelb (1973), is pretty positive that Reed was disillusioned and gives supplementary evidence.

* Justin Kaplan's recent *Lincoln Steffens* (p. 208) identifies this character with Steffens; the psychological point does not, however, depend on whom she had in mind.

of Plymouth, Massachusetts. Neither had applied for citizenship, so neither was subject to the draft. Yet both went to Mexico to avoid the registration required, for their principles forbade any such cooperation with belligerency. Hard times for refugees in Mexico sent them back to the States—and apotheosis.

Late in December, 1919, a group of gunmen bungled an attempt on a payroll in Bridgewater, Massachusetts, and managed to escape. In mid-April, 1920, a similar group struck in South Braintree, Massachusetts, killing a mill paymaster and his bodyguard and getting away with a payroll. One night in May local police following down a possible connection between local anarchist aliens and the robbery picked up two previously unnoticed Italians sitting together in an interurban car. On the mustached one (Vanzetti) were found shotgun shells and a loaded revolver later identified as that taken from the dead payroll guard; on the smooth-shaven one (Sacco) a Colt automatic and a mixed lot of obsolete and rare ammunition for it, the caliber and brands of which coincided with those of spent shells found at the site of the Braintree job. Police ballistics men later called the bullets from the dead guard's body "consistent with" having been fired from Sacco's pistol.

Several witnesses identified Vanzetti as the Bridgewater gang's shotgun man. He was convicted of armed robbery in a trial presided over by Judge Webster Thayer, who also presided over the trial of the subsequent (South Braintree) affair. Several identifications, contested and blurred by the defense, put Sacco and Vanzetti both in the Braintree holdup party, but it was chiefly the firearms that convicted them. Their best explanation for going armed was that being liable for deportation as alien anarchists made them apprehensive. For Sacco that was specially weak because he had just arranged to reemigrate to Italy—his alibi hung on his steps to that end—and deportation would merely give him a free passage. Then he said he had come on the Colt when packing to leave and stuck it in his waistband and forgotten he was carrying it—unlikely in view of its weight and bulk. Vanzetti said he carried a revolver because his fish route obliged him to carry substantial sums on his person, but his several stories of how he came by a weapon exactly corresponding with the dead guard's were damagingly confused.

Harsh, tiny Judge Thayer, who had asked for the assignment to try them, despised aliens and radicals—a frame of mind not alleviated by the Red Scare—and bragged foolishly outside the courtroom about what he would do to those "arnychists," as he called them. In court he was correct enough for the record, indeed sustained more objections from the defense than from the prosecution. But it was charged that he so marred the atmosphere with unrecorded snorts and scowls that there was reason to feel he had unduly influenced the jury. Stifling summer weather did not help, nor did the chief defense counsel, Fred Moore, brought in by Carlo Tresca, prince of Italo-American anarchists, and Elizabeth Gurley Flynn, a mainstay of the Communist Party, because of his past successes in defending Wobblies out West. Loud, swaggersome in a cowboy hat, Moore outraged the prim judge by shedding not only his jacket but his shoes when the thermometer approached 90° F. Maybe Thayer would have behaved badly without goading. Anyway certain radical-minded Bostonians and some of the press had a strong impression that he had warped the jury's collective mind and that Moore had gravely damaged the defendants' interests.

A third impression, deepening among such persons with the years, was that the two had been convicted not because they were proved guilty beyond reasonable doubt but because as anarchists and aliens they were ethnic and ideological victims of a corrupt, hidebound society. Presently, since many able minds are not immune to fashion, it became a vociferous certainty that they were harmless idealists guiltless of crime, railroaded by an ambitious prosecutor, Red-hating police, a radical-baiting judge and a biased bourgeois jury. Thus they joined the Haymarket martyrs (some possible guilty as accessories), Dreyfus (railroaded), and Tom Mooney (probably so) as symbols of the savagery of capitalism. Some held that the issue of their guilt was secondary to another: "Had their trial been fair? Why not try them again?" Most of those interested, however, took it as read that it had been grossly unfair, since no fair one could possibly have convicted these innocents fed to the bourgeois Minotaur.

Much of that sentiment was of Moore's hatching, the rest that of the International Labor Defense, American arm of Communism's International Red Aid. During appeals and other delays Moore created what he probably had planned when taking the case—a great public relations drama to rally liberal-to-radical opinion not so much behind his clients as against the society arraigning them. At first publicity had been extensive only in the local press. The Defense Committee that paid counsel and monitored proceedings consisted mostly of sympathetic Italians. After the verdict, however, Moore and allies made wide and effective appeals to the radical-chic and Villager type of mind vulnerable to the anarchist/Communist version of what had gone on. To Gardner Jackson, ardent member of the later Sacco-Vanzetti Defense Committee, the devotion of such supporters seemed, in retrospect in 1930, to come of "a sense of purely personal frustration. In their radical activities for the first time in their lives they attain a feeling of self-realization and self-importance. . . ." [24]

Francis Russell, ranking student of the case,* reared a partisan of Sacco and Vanzetti, recalls his "Aunt Amy . . . [Boston] social worker . . .

---

* His *Tragedy in Dedham* (revised edition 1970) is, with its new lights on the ballistics and new post-execution data, a principal reason why it is very difficult nowadays to stick to the classic position that the pair were very probably guiltless and in any case unfairly tried. Anybody who wants to be encouraged to stick to that, however, can turn to Herbert B. Ehrmann, *The Case That Will Not Die* (1969).

convinced of the two men's innocence . . . the way one had to feel if one was a social worker." [25] To admit the possibility that one or both might have had a hand in crime would have flawed the elemental picture of a brutal society savaging the innocent. Writers and artists exposed to this verbal cartoon fell in line. For the next several decades literature was rich with Sacco and Vanzetti. Dos Passos tucked them into novels wherever it would make America look bad. Miss Millay wrote Eliotish verse about them. Maxwell Anderson's plays about the case made sweepingly tender or harsh assumptions about them and their persecutors respectively. Ben Shahn drew and painted them and their story at tireless length. Inevitably came the feeling that because they were guiltless, hounded and enjoyed the flowers that lady partisans sent to their cells, they were saints. Toward the end Phil Stong, interviewing Vanzetti for a newspaper syndicate, obtained a brave statement of his attitude toward being a significant martyr that, widely reprinted, completed his elevation to radical archangel.* Thirteen years later in his play, *The Male Animal*, James Thurber used reactions to this statement as touchstone for distinguishing between reactionaries and decent people on a Midwestern university campus. Twenty-two years later in his novel *The Big Wheel*, John Brooks used attitudes toward Sacco and Vanzetti the same way in the context of New York City in the 1930's.

Late in 1924 Moore's relations with Sacco soured, and he quit the case. Miss Flynn went to William G. Thompson, a well-placed, able Boston lawyer whom the case had disquieted. Reluctant to monkey with this buzzsaw, he asked a sizable fee in advance. Miss Flynn borrowed the bulk of it from the radical-committed Garland Fund under guarantee from the Amalgamated Clothing Workers and the International Ladies' Garment Workers. Thompson consented. Never did lawyer earn a fee better. For the next three years he struggled to extract his clients from the tangle of bad law and misrepresentation that controversy had woven around them. As staid clients shied away, he half ruined his practice, of course. It was a great help early in 1927, when Ellery Sedgwick, editor of Boston's *Atlantic Monthly*, printed a strong attack on the prosecution's case by Felix Frankfurter, professor in the Harvard Law School, already almost as conspicuous a figure as he would be later in the New Deal and on the U.S. Supreme Court. It was less than no help, however, to the personal interests of the accused that the Communists had pretty much taken over, neglecting their standing feud with anarchists in order to borrow Sacco and Vanzetti as sticks to beat the capitalist dog with. Wherever Communism had a party or a front, there were demonstrations and fund raisings for this hapless pair.

---

* Felix (*Protest*, 178) disagrees with the usual opinion that Vanzetti's prison studies of English made him a remarkable, if not always, correct writer of it and implies that Stong, who became an able popular novelist, prettied up the famous statement. This is probably unjustified. Other bits from Vanzetti not open to suspicion of tampering show a sound feel for this tongue that was not his own and a fine boldness of idiom.

Of hundreds of thousands thus raised only a few thousand dollars ever reached the Defense Committee, but neither the givers nor most of the agitators knew that, and the propaganda effect against capitalism and the America that symbolized it was immense.

The archaic law of Massachusetts left the basic responsibility for ordering a new trial to the judge of the original one. That enabled Thayer, indubitably a nasty little man, to play dog in the manger. That was the mildest thing that liberal rallies now called him, making sure he would never relent. Final recourse lay with the governor of Massachusetts, a self-made rich man of some conscience, Alvan T. Fuller. He studied the case intensively and chose a board of leading citizens to go back over the ground and, if they found it advisable, recommend a new trial. The chairman was A. Lawrence Lowell, president of Harvard, expert on the British Constitution, conspicuous defender of academic freedom; with him President Samuel Stratton of MIT and Judge Robert Grant, eminent probate lawyer, Sunday writer of novels of liberal tenor and a founding father of the Authors League of America.

Fuller probably expected them to recommend the new trial that would get him, Massachusetts, the United States and the private-enterprise tradition all off the hook. After exhaustive hearings Lowell's panel did not so recommend. Frantic appeals to members of the U.S. Supreme Court for this or that stay were rejected; liberal Justice Holmes said no twice. The uproar before U.S. embassies and the picketing demonstrations in American cities played up by radio and newsreel as well as the press—the whole new battery of on-the-spotness—gave the passion of Sacco and Vanzetti publicity a million times greater than that for the death of Socrates, the Crucifixion or the burning of Joan of Arc all put together. One still hears the faithful recall where they were that hot midnight of August 22, 1927, and who said what to whom—like people recalling Pearl Harbor.

As for the pair's standing with the Recording Angel: Moore came privately to believe both guilty, the purpose of the crime to raise money for their cause; the amateurish methods of both crimes lend weight to this. Tresca, who knew both men personally, said Sacco was guilty, Vanzetti not. The case against Vanzetti was clearly weaker. He may have been merely unlucky—the damning revolver may have been misidentified or he was not aware of its past use. The case against Sacco grew very strong fourteen years ago, when new ballistic techniques applied to the trial exhibits left no practical doubt that the bullet that killed the guard was fired from the pistol found on Sacco when he was arrested. In view of that, the elaborate confessions from jailbirds that fouled up the latter phases of the case stand up little better than Vanzetti's accounts of how he came by the revolver.

Certainty must wait for Judgment Day. Two weighty results remain now. Adding this case to the indigenous self-contempt in *Main Street*, the antics of dollar-happy Americans abroad, the social inanity of Prohibition, the organized nastiness of the Klan, the innocent ignorance of the Scopes episode completed the overseas intellectual's impression that America was a howling wilderness socially backward, culturally sterile, economically irresponsible and morally brutalized and hypocritical. The last was further strengthened when Europeans ill versed in the U.S. Constitution were asked to believe—obviously a capitalist subterfuge—that protests to the White House were useless because neither President nor Congress had any power over what a state did about murder. Anatole France, Bertrand Russell and Knut Hamsun had been Americanophobe enough already. This world-shocking cause won them a far more sympathetic hearing on the subject with the uncommitted. However distorted, or true, the above account of America, the point is that down to today international emotions to which Sacco and Vanzetti contributed heavily still warp relations between America and overseas, still create important feedback into the American mind through the influence of non-Americans whom many Americans respect. Not a bad inadvertent revenge for those whom Vanzetti's eloquent testament called "a good shoemaker and a poor fish-peddler."

Directly too the growth of their legend while they were in jail crucially sensitized many Americans, mostly young, to radicalizing notions. James Joll, authority on anarchy, calls this a *"cause célèbre* in which a whole generation of American liberals came of age,"[26] rather like what *Ten Days* did for those seven or eight years older. In my time—that of those too young to have got into the War—the post-War ferments fizzing in post-War writings were already laying ideological-emotional groundwork. But for many the radio bulletin on that steaming summer night—the switch thrown on Sacco first, Vanzetti next—acted like light fixing the potential blacks and whites of a photographic negative. "They" had gone ahead and done it in spite of all. Thenceforth the world that put up with "them" would never feel quite the same. Once again the blood of the martyrs was the seed of the church.

Federal Prohibition—Eighteenth Amendment plus Volstead Act—poses nice distinctions between War-caused things and others. Its deplorable results are hardly disputable, but its origins may need resketching.* The returned soldiers' complaint that it was "put over" on the nation while they were overseas and unable to protest is untenable. As Herbert Asbury, expert on uncouth Americana, pointed out, the whole House of Representatives and a third of the Senate that passed the Eighteenth Amendment were elected in 1916 before there was an AEF. Passage late in 1917 came of the formidable power long exerted by Dry organizations, notably the Anti-Saloon League with the Women's Christian Temperance Union running its

---

* This section is mostly condensation from my *Life and Times of the Late Demon Rum*, wherein readers may find further references and discussion.

interference. Ruthlessly the Drys exploited a flaw built into two-party representative government—the ability of a disciplined minority of voters to swing close elections. In a legislative district where the ASL's local leaders pledged, say, 5 percent of the voters to vote Republican or Democratic solely according to the candidates' stands for or against Rum, promises to support Dry measures often brought the margin of victory— were, in any case, good insurance against defeat. Such leverage on the U.S. Congress was stronger after 1914, when election of U.S. Senators by popular vote began.

Even in 1913 the Drys had enough Senators as well as Representatives chained to their chariot wheels to pass, over President Taft's veto, the Webb-Kenyon Act, a federal ban on delivery of liquor in Dry states by express companies whose exemption from state laws had long annoyed the Drys. That victory was probably what led the ASL to plump for national constitutional Prohibition, whereas its previous announced goal had been only annihilation of that social ulcer, the saloon. There were other presages of success: Four weeks before Sarajevo Secretary of the Navy Daniels ordered alcoholic drinks out of officers' messes—fair enough since the regulation tot of rum for the hands at six bells had long since vanished. But the consequent flood of derision in the press called attention to the power of the Drys just when that suited the ASL's new strategy. So did the uproar when Secretary of State Bryan made a point of not serving wine, nothing stronger than water or unfermented grape juice, at his first luncheon for the diplomatic corps in Washington.

Bryan and Daniels represented the small town, Methodist/Baptist, Midwestern/Southern, lips-that-touch-liquor-shall-never-touch-mine sort of Dryness fundamental to the WCTU and the ASL, sworn foes of the vice-polluted, Catholic-, immigrant- and millionaire-ridden big city in a quarrel that explained much of the emotional drive of Prohibition. This powerful church-supper element had recently been joined by important industrialists and urban merchants. Some were former country boys retaining Sunday School notions of drink. All were aware that the saloon at the factory gate or down the street from store or roundhouse meant Monday absenteeism, on-the-job accidents and often a local nest of union organizing in that small meeting hall over the barroom. John Wanamaker, J. L. Hudson (his store was the Wanamaker's of Michigan), H. J. Heinz of the "57" varieties, S. S. Kresge, great name in dime stores, followed Carnegie and the Rockefellers in giving large sums and lending prestige to the Dry cause.

Famous guardians of public health had opened another front. Dr. Harvey W. Wiley, father of the U.S. Food and Drug Administration; Dr. Charles H. Mayo, of the nation's best-known diagnostic center; and the American Medical Association denounced Rum as a menace best suppressed. Equally impressive support came from what seems to have been a misguided group of settlement house/goodwill figures—Jordan, Upton Sinclair, eminent Women's Righters. . . . This combination of faith in Prohibition with causes that many still find worthy—pacifism, alleviation of social injustices—went back to the early days of the antislavery movement and had not yet been spoiled by the abject failure of national Prohibition. Also auspiciously for the Drys the white-collar man with a merely normal liking for booze and little taste for uplift was almost neutral. ". . . the great mass of drinkers," *Life* said, "are apathetic. They dislike the prohibitionists . . . but . . . Most of them think rum-selling and saloon-keeping are detrimental and even disreputable. . . . The brewers and distillers have too earnestly [competed] in establishing saloons . . . inviting the attention of buyers with as much energy and strategy as though they were selling soap. . . . The liquor trade has spoilt the liquor business by making it a public nuisance." [27]

Yet for all these omens and the ASL's skill in pressure-bloc blackmail and luck in getting the Rockefellers, Upton Sinclair and the *Ladies' Home Journal* on the same side for once, the Drys might never have won without the War as pretext.* They hitched their cause to the War effort as cleverly as did Tin Pan Alley. They dwelled on the dangers of the saloon to soldier boys away from home for the first time; on the crime of wasting room in drays and railroad cars to move kegs of beer and cases of rye from manufacturer to victim; on the inability of topers to pull their weight in field or factory; on the cereals and fuel taken from the nation's supplies to make soul-destroying booze. But the best of it was that the brewers, who made the most popular drink and controlled most big-city saloons, could be identified with the foe's Germanness.

Though Britons had been buying heavily into American brewing, the brand or corporate names and managers of four out of five breweries were still candidly German: Ruppert, Feigenspan, Pabst, Lieber, Schmidt. . . . Lager beer, long the American choice, had been an import from Germany in the 1830–40's and *Braumeister* came along to show America how. As saloonkeepers and bartenders German-Americans were second only to Irish-Americans, particularly in the Midwest where every sizable Wet town had at least one saloon known as the Dutchman's. The beer gardens that shocked the Methodists of those parts by purveying music, dancing and seidels of suds on Sunday were as German, of course, as the goose step. As the War went on, it leaked out that German brewers' money went to the *Fatherland* and those portentous purchases of the New York *Evening Mail* and the Washington *Times*. Well before the United States declared war, common sense was aware that the National German-American Alliance

---

* This agrees with Andrew Sinclair (*Prohibition*, 20): The War was "a murderous stroke of luck" for the Drys. Asbury (*The Great Illusion*, 136–37), was not so sure: "At most the war may have hastened ratification by a few years. It is extremely doubtful that anything could have stopped it . . . the American people wanted prohibition and were bound to try it."

and the United States Brewers' Association were as close as the Sinn Fein and the Ancient Order of Hibernians—and had far more money. To abolish alcoholic drinks would not only reduce hazards associated with saloons—DT's, accidents on the job, brutalized wives, squandered pay, whoring, gambling—but also dry up profits financing God only knew what treasons. Much of that was unfair to brewers whose noses were clean, but it made good Dry propaganda all the same.

By 1916 so many Americans lived in jurisdictions at least nominally Dry that Anheuser-Busch launched a product it had been foresightedly nursing for years—Bevo, a beerlike soft drink of .005 percent alcohol legal in Dry country and, thanks to use of yeasts from making real beer, with a cozily reminiscent taste. It sold so well—5,000,000 cases a year—that the company built the world's largest bottling plant to supply the new market. Then side effects from Prohibition smothered it. When the plants were not making real beer, they lacked the yeasts essential to Bevo's happily illusory flavor. The company tried again with "Anheuser" and then "Budweiser" brands of the near beer that other brewers were producing, made by removing alcohol from real beer down to legal level. The flavor was, however, too often like what was left in the glass from the night before. All that saved near beer—and it lasted well into the 1920's—was the custom among barkeeps and home drinkers of spiking it with enough illegal alcohol to reproduce the *status quo ante* in biochemical effect, if not in flavor.

In the fires of the War the ASL shaped two irons for striking. It revived the constitutional amendment proposed and defeated in 1914, got it passed and sent to the states for ratification. Wavering Senators were shown the provision that it would lapse if not ratified in seven years—too short a time, the Drys whispered, to get the necessary thirty-six states into line, so Senator X could placate his Dry constituents by voting Yea without threatening John Barleycorn. The ASL also sponsored a "War Prohibition" act to save grain and so on by banning manufacture of alcoholic drinks until after post-War demobilization—Canada already had taken similar steps—and forbade sales of beverage alcohol after June 30, 1919. The Drys' skill at bullying and confusing got this passed *ten days after the Armistice ended the fighting that was its occasion.* Sixty-nine days later Senators who had trusted the seven-year safeguard woke up to find that the ASL had dragooned state legislators into ratifying the amendment in little more than a year. In final roll call 85 percent of state senators had voted for the Dry cause; 78 percent of members of lower houses.

By such deftness with pea, thimble and blackjack it came to pass that on January 18, 1920, from Eastport to San Diego and Seattle to Key West, "the manufacture, sale or transportation of intoxicating liquors . . . for beverage purposes" became a federal offense. The Volstead Act, the necessary enforcing statute passed over President Wilson's veto, defined "intoxicating liquors" as any over near beer's .005 percent of alcohol—less

than that in sauerkraut, it was peevishly pointed out. Thus formally ended
the battle begun eight decades earlier when the innocent old Temperance
movement turned to law for help in clothing erring neighbors on with
righteousness.

The day after the Volstead Act went into alleged effect the Drys' prayers,
hymns and smug rhapsodizings sounded like those that their grandparents
had afforded the Emancipation Proclamation. Most of them really did feel
that they had lifted from mankind a major cause of misery and self-destruc-
tion. In Washington the ASL's chiefs and their Congressional vassals met to
hear an exultant sermon from Bryan and assurance from Daniels that the
great amendment would "last as long as the preamble [to the Constitution].
. . . No man living will ever see a Congress that will lessen the enforcement
of that law! The saloon is as dead as slavery!" Elsewhere the nation's
gaudiest Bible thumpers, Sunday and Norris, staged elaborate funerals for
giant effigies of John Barleycorn. So did a few New York City cabarets. But
among the ungodly rites of passage were halfhearted. Previous high jinks
mourning the advent of Wartime Prohibition had taken the edge off. And
for many of normally convivial habits it appears to have been a sort of relief
that the shoving, backbiting, moral and scientific faking of which both sides
had been guilty over the years could now simmer down. The responsible
public was not unwilling to see the saloon disappear from the street corner
and the soak given a better chance to rescue himself. Some of the
professionally emancipated, Floyd Dell, for instance, welcomed Prohibition
and the promised death of the saloon in hopes it meant "Men and women
would . . . spend more of their play-time together, with benefits to
American civilization. . . . My prediction came true, though I had no
notion of the speakeasy as a coeducational institution. I very naively
believed that Prohibition would work." [28] Lardner, anything but an uplifter,
had nevertheless, says his recent biographer, drunk "enough to develop an
obsessive sense of guilt . . . and . . . believed that the manufacture of
alcohol should be entirely prohibited; for medicinal or industrial uses a
substitute could be found." [29]

In view of the experience of the previous eighty years it was curious how
little heed was paid to the core of the problem—enforcement. The Drys had
so persistently preached that nationwide Prohibition was a sure road to
drought, once stocks were exhausted, that many seem to have halfway
believed it. Yet nothing was less likely. Since Massachusetts' Fifteen Gallon
Law in 1838, severe restrictions on liquor in whatever form, often that of
flat statewide Prohibition, had always broken down under the attrition of
stubborn violations. "Blind pig," "hooch," "home brew" were part of the
language long before the ASL won its game. A sequence in *Intolerance*
(1914) shows two shirt-sleeved ruffians tending a table-size still with the
subtitle "Instead of mild wines and beer—each man his own distiller." Too
many well-worked-out techniques for evading Prohibition were waiting in

the wings when the curtain rose on the Drys' cold sober heaven on earth. But they had no misgivings. Sweepingly their great spokesman, Bryan, predicted: "Now . . . the man who peddles liquor, like the man who sells habit-forming drugs, is an outlaw. . . . The sanction given to prohibition by law . . . reduces its [enemies] to those whose fondness for drink, or for the profits obtained by its illicit sale, is sufficient to overcome conscientious scruples . . . this number will constantly decrease as the virtue of the country asserts itself." [30] Indeed, having cleaned up their own country, the Drys were already laying groundwork for an international Prohibition movement to make an arid heaven on earth of the rest of the world. Trials of sweeping restrictions on drink in Scandinavia and Canada encouraged them. No isolationism here!

In that same 1920 when the Volstead Act was launched came onstage an even less savory phenomenon—the Ku Klux Klan—for which the War was at least partly responsible in its major post-War phase.

This national ulcer was sired by William J. Simmons, a seedy Southern pseudo-colonel who had read a book about the white-capped night riders who bullied black freedmen during Reconstruction. This inspired him to organize something like that. He saw a vision, right there on the wall of his room, of the old Klansmen riding in their white robes and swore on his knees some time to found a fraternal society as a memorial to the Ku Klux Klan. In his precarious past he had been a recruiter-on-commission for the Woodmen of the World, one of the many "lodges" combining minimal life insurance with secret rituals and good fellowship. For his neo-Klan he took from the cornily ugly old movement its rank racism and the white robes and rigmarole that he borrowed to attract those with a few dollars and a half-baked anxiety about "Protestantism . . . the Christian religion . . . [and] the eternal maintenance of white supremacy." [31]

The probable reason why he chose 1915 to launch his scheme belongs to movie history. Early that year began road-show bookings of *The Birth of a Nation*, which stirred up the adrenalin almost as strongly about the glories of the old Klan as about bestially uppity blacks. Very, very likely Simmons was one of the millions entranced by Griffith's masterpiece, and it revived his vague ambition to reap glory and concomitant profit from a Klan of his own. Walter F. White, then a shrewd investigator for the National Association for the Advancement of Colored People, believed that *The Birth* "did more than anything else to make successful the revival of the Ku Klux Klan." [32]

So with heaven knows what windy blandishments Simmons recruited thirty-four neophytes—"splendid citizens . . . of Georgia," [33] in his description—on Stone Mountain (awesome geological freak near Atlanta now carved into portraits of Confederate heroes) to form a "Patriotic, secret, social, benevolent order . . . Knights of the Ku Klux Klan." In the words of its papers of incorporation, its motto was "Non silba sed anther." Simmons' explanation of this gibberish sheds light on how his mind worked: "Many wise men have puzzled over that motto. I made it up myself . . . part Latin and part Saxon. . . . I was reliably informed that 'silba' is an old Saxon word meaning self and 'anther' means other." [34] The organizational titles as well as the hooded disguises of sleazy white cotton came from the half-whimsical, half-minatory old Klan: Meeting place = Klavern; meeting = Konklave; minor leader = Kleagle; chaplain = Kludd. . . . In higher echelons euphony vanished: state leader = Grand Dragon; regional leader = Grand Goblin; Simmons himself was Imperial Wizard.

During the War, for all his dreary experience in persuading crossroads storekeepers and livery-stable owners to become Woodmen, his Klan languished. Its charter forbade members to derive profit from it. By 1920 the Imperial Wizard, who had obviously hoped for a good living from initiation fees and sales of regalia at a whacking markup, was observing that clause dismally well. Membership was barely 5,000. The Imperial Palace where the Wizard wove his spells and kept sloppy records was one room in a dingy office building in Atlanta.

Rescue so brisk that it resembled kidnapping was at hand. Among Simmons' recruits was the son-in-law of a certain Elizabeth Tyler, beefy, able veteran of Wartime fund-raising campaigns for the YWCA, Red Cross and so on. One Edgar Young Clarke, also a renowned local fund raiser, was, though married, her occasional bedfellow. He had once been a newspaper reporter and, more to the point, a recruiter for the Woodmen. Mrs. Tyler and he pooled their War-whetted skills in a partnership, the Southern Publicity Association, one of many such enterprises sprouting in the climate created by Creel's example. Seeking paydirt, they thought of this white supremacy lodge that son-in-law belonged to. Simmons was eager for help. Tyler and Clarke took over and changed his Klan, says a recent student of it, "from a somewhat easy-going southern fraternity of patriotic whites into a violently aggressive national organization of native-born, white Protestants." [35]

In the ensuing membership drive Mrs. Tyler was Clarke's right hand and also led a ladies' auxiliary, the Kemalia. Their SPA took the profits on robes and 80 percent of each $10 initiation fee, the rest going in minor commissions. At the peak the pair were making at least $40,000 a month. Simmons got the use of a fine house in Atlanta called Klankrest and an ample cash allowance to keep up his dignity as Imperial Wizard—a title largely honorary by then, for as Imperial Kleagle = executive officer, Clarke ran the show. Gnawed at by frustration, Simmons crumbled into blasphemous delusions of grandeur. After Clarke's successor took from him even the Wizard's title, his rantings drew on the Scriptural glibness of his early career as a Methodist revivalist: "I am the door of Klankraft; no man may enter therein but by ME. . . . I am the way, the truth and the life in the kingdom of Klankraft. . . . Come unto ME all you who yearn and labor after Klankraft. . . ." [36]

The Klan's sudden success in the lower South in 1921, contrasting with Simmons' early fizzles, may reflect the SPA's superior promotional methods. With white supremacy and anti-Catholicism (the meaning of pro-Protestantism in this context) as bait, its techniques might have done well even in normal times. Before the War Georgia's notorious Thomas E. Watson, foulmouthed foe of "the interests" turned reactionary, had shown the way by preaching hate against blacks, Catholics, Jews and Socialists. Georgia had few of any but the first category, but Watson's slavering exploitation of all four drew him a following with which he dominated his state's politics. Watson probably had no hand in launching the Klan, says C. Vann Woodward, his biographer, now the shrewdest historian of the South. "Yet if any mortal man can be credited (as no one man may rightly be) with releasing the . . . human malice and ignorance and prejudice [that] the Klan merely mobilized, that man was Thomas E. Watson." [37] In other Deep South states the same wool-hat boys and red-necks responded to the Klan's Watson-style appeals. But—enter the War again—the boys were probably in an unusually accessible and inflamed mood because the South's black soldiers were coming home disinclined to resume the cringe and shuffle going with "Yassuh, boss." As labor troops they had seen little or no combat. But at least they had had better food and shelter than most of them had ever known and learned that over there whites felt no need to Jimcrow blacks. The northward migration of black labor during the War already irked Southerners as their heritage of docile, ego-building black help dwindled with every train leaving for Chicago. Now they suspected uppityness overt or lurking in these black veterans who had been allowed to lose the habit of knowing their place.

Clear and present danger to white supremacy—and to meet it, here were secretive strangers or whispering neighbors from down the road offering in exchange for a few dollars (but enough to show the proposition meant business) a place in a brotherhood sworn to keep the "nigger" where he belonged like in that movie.* Maybe the prospective recruit had seen

---

* Some observers in the 1920's saw War-roused feelings as even more deeply involved than this. Thus the sociologist John Moffett Recklin (*The Ku Klux Klan*, 121–23): "The Klan owes its marvellous growth to the disturbed post-war conditions. The war, with its hymns of hate, its stories of poison gas and human carnage, its secret spyings upon fellow Americans, its accounts of Belgian atrocities, its imprisonment of radicals, its fearful tales of Bolshevist designs upon American institutions . . . opened up the fountains of the great deep of national feeling . . . we had cultivated a taste for the cruel, the brutal, the intolerant, and the un-Christian that demanded gratification. . . . The Klan offered just what the war-torn, distraught emotions of the nation demanded." The writer's heart was obviously in the right place but. . . . Difficulty One: In that case the Klan would have flourished all over the nation, because the whole nation had been subjected to the influences listed, whereas actually the Klan made important headway only in the South, the lower Midwest and to some extent the

newspaper pictures of a mystic circle of Kluxers, all white of robe as well as skin and soul, burning a fiery cross at night against an eerie background that showed no sign of being only the mule pasture of one of the members. It must often have turned out that the neophyte already knew some of the boys who had previously joined. Them Kluxers had blood-chilling oaths and passwords and grips like in any ginuwine lodge, and it wasn't only niggers they got after neither—it was moonshiners that sold to niggers and trashy women that put out for black as well as white, and even suppose they did draw the line at dark meat, a good whipping never done that kind no harm. And Kluxers sticks together. Some Sheriff's deputies belongs, and they don't make no fuss when an uppity nigger gets burned out. Neither did the Baptist and Methodist ministers whose bitterness against loose women, liquor and blacks and, when they remembered, the Pope and the Jews made them Klansmen. A Kludd blessing a fiery cross and praying the Lord to save white supremacy got the same emotional charge as the disgruntled white trash mill hand out of disguise and flickering flames and the deep satisfaction of righteous hate.

Duffus' masterly reports on the Klan as of 1923 described its Southerner converts as "the short-witted, the bored, the vindictive, the bigoted, the ambitious." [38] Nobody knows how many such Clarke and Mrs. Tyler recruited. The millions that stories in the Northern press so freely tossed around were probably exaggerated—and excellent promotion for the Klan. Simmons told a Congressional committee that his cause owed a great deal to such Yankee scare stories picked up by the Southern papers and to the Congressional investigation that they set off. "Congress made us," [39] he said simply. Actual numbers were soon formidable enough, however, to implement borrowing the Anti-Saloon League's tactics of using minority blocs to sway political primaries in the Deep South. Hushpuppy County might contain only 500 Klansmen, but an aspirant to county office suspected of hostility to the Invisible Empire might lose to a more tactful rival by 400-odd votes—and the Klan would have made the difference. It was acknowledged to have elected its own governor of Georgia, secured majorities in the legislatures of Texas and Oklahoma, grown weighty in all the cotton states plus Florida. Many more or less well-placed people attracted by its flag-waving, glib piety and loftily defined notions of white supremacy also joined. It so effectively encouraged buying, selling and backscratching among members—presumably to the loss of their Jewish and Catholic competitors—that local merchants often came in. Bootleggers did so as insurance against the whippings and runnings-out-of-town that the ostensibly Dry Klan often visited on their likes. Responsible opposition varied with the cultural level of the community. It was usually silent. One

---

West Coast. Difficulty Two: No emotion-rousing war had preceded the successes scored in the 1880's in the Midwest by the American Protective Association, which had a very Klannish smell and similar objectives.

articulate focus of it was Hearst's Atlanta *Georgian*—credit the man for siding with civilization in this area. His New York *American* also rivaled the New York *World* in exposing the Klan's viciousness, which reminds one that much of the paper's readership was big-city Catholic.

How much bullying and flogging was policy from above, how much the natural result of preaching hate to men already deep in racism, bigotry and courthouse politics is not clear. Nor is the reason why the relative appeals of its various stimuli shifted as the Klan gathered speed. In its first boom the already outrageous incidence of black lynching rose, but it was soon eclipsed by the harryings of WASP's of both sexes whose conduct or ideas displeased Klansmen. This hints at a generalized paranoid pattern with religio-ascetic and sadistic as well as xenophobic overtones, most sensitive to the race context but spreading into others familiar elsewhere. In corroboration the Invisible Empire, once as basically Southern as hominy grits, presently overflowed into non-Southern regions where Dry sentiment, Fundamentalist doctrine, anti-Semitism, anti-Catholicism and reactionary anti-Redism were already lively.

As expansion accelerated, Clarke and Mrs. Tyler were swept off the quarterdeck by scandal—they had once been caught in an establishment that neither of such pillars of morality should even have known about. She died in 1924. Clarke drifted away to leeward dismasted by federal indictments for misuse of the mails and then misuse of females; his conviction under the Mann Act brought a $5,000 fine. (His next avatar was as founder of the Supreme Kingdom, a hot anti-evolutionist society consequent on the Scopes trial; its local cells were "castles," its officers dukes, earls and such.) This disaster at the top did not, however, ruin the Klan. Many Kleagles, Grand Goblins, Exalted Cyclops and other such wordy bugbears resigned under clouds or in revulsion, but the latent vigor of hate kept it a fast-growing concern. When the dust settled, Simmons had been kicked even farther upstairs into a cushiony limbo as Emperor of the Invisible Empire. The new active chief, shogun to his Mikado, was Imperial Wizard Hiram Wesley Evans, a Texas dentist; the Klan had taken powerful hold in the oil and cotton country.

Stocky, blue-eyed, at home in the right phobias, deliberately behaving like what he professed to be, "the most average man in America," Evans described his expanding empire's aims with impudent candor. He admitted "the mistakes it has committed" in a magazine interview in 1925 but went on to show he was talking tactics, not principles. ". . . actual social equality between whites and any other race is not practiced to any important extent anywhere on earth," he said. "The Klan will not argue about it. It merely rejects it, as almost all Americans do. Neither will we argue about . . . white supremacy. . . . American stock . . . has proved its value and should not be mongrelized. . . . [The] Klan is intolerant . . . of the people who are trying to destroy our traditional

Americanism . . . aliens who are constantly trying to change our civilization into something that will suit themselves better . . . liberalism . . . is
seriously in danger from the Klan movement. At least we hope so. . . ." [40]

Outside Dixie this version of the Klan did best between Appalachia and
the Great Basin; not badly in California and Oregon; sluggishly in the
Northeast, though Pennsylvania and Maine had severe spasms of the
disease. Its chief raids across the Ohio and up from Texas meant not
deliberate strategy but the gravitational pull of kindred attitudes. Up to at
least latitude 40°N, say Pittsburgh-Indianapolis-Springfield-St. Joseph, the
Midwest had a dilute but discernible Southernness because most of the
adult inhabitants' grandfathers had come from Virginia, Tennessee and
Kentucky—states kind to Klannish emotions. The grotesque anti-Catholic
American Protective Association of the 1880's had been strong among
WASP farmers raising corn in Indiana and Illinois and the merchants and
bankers they dealt with. A juicy anti-Semitism was part of the panacea
cocktail that Populist leaders in those parts offered in the same period.
Wartime pay scales had drawn northward not only blacks but also into the
same overcrowded and jangled cities hundreds of thousands of Southern
poor whites. Their stay-behind cousins who had struggled a precious notch
upward, Snopes-fashion, were the core of Southern Kluxing. Doubtless
Chicago, Indianapolis and Detroit could have worked up their own black
and alien haters, but these newcomers from the hookworm belt were eager
teachers by example.

On the Coast the Klan had Chicanos and Japanese to fear on Tuesdays
and Thursdays and despise as aliens seven days a week. In Maine the target
was French-Canadians, probably the most standoffish and dependent on
the parish priests of all Catholic immigrants, who had swarmed into New
England's textile mills from over the border. In 1924 the *American Journal
of Sociology* printed an interview with an Ohio farmer, leader of the Klan in
Harding's own county, showing how, when it had to, Klannish hatred did
not need blacks to point to. Catholics dominated 80 percent of the nation's
newspapers, he said. Jews made the movies, all worthless and immoral,
gobbled up the money with their crossroads stores, and were also selling
into white slavery 60,000 to 75,000 young girls a year; they hired men to go
out in automobiles and pick them up on country roads.

Blundering here, floundering there, weakened by the intramural squab-
bles usual among cliques of chronic haters, the Klan's recruiters nevertheless got value out of their cards. In Kansas, in one of their few efforts to line
up labor, they signed up striking railroaders by playing up the black
strikebreakers whom management brought in. Oregon credited the Klan
with the passage of laws suppressing Catholic parochial schools by
requiring all children to go to public school—a great victory until the U.S.
Supreme Court rejected this perversion of Jefferson's hopes. Billy Sunday
openly endorsed the Klan's "aggressive evangelism and . . . staunch

Prohibitionism." [41] Less openly so did Bryan, opposing an anti-Klan resolution in the Democratic national convention of 1924 on the weasly grounds that "we can exterminate Kluxism better by recognizing their honesty and teaching them they are wrong." [42] W. R. Pattangall, attorney general of Maine, denounced the Klan at that convention and the next year at the polls took a beating that the Klan and he agreed was their doing. He had not, he told a reporter, thought the Invisible Empire could raise a hundred converts in so un-Southern a state, but their propaganda took unexpected hold in rural parts mistrusting the town-dwelling Catholic Irish and French-Canadians. Thousands, Pattangall said, "had no idea they were being abused until the Klan told them so";[43] also that President Lincoln had been killed by order of the Pope, the Knights of Columbus had poisoned Harding and in the War nine out of ten deserters had acted under the church's instructions.

In its best days the Klan could bully politicians on state and county levels in downstate Illinois and nearly took over Kansas soul and body. Indiana became, in Duffus' words, "a sheeted Tammany." [44] In Colorado, led by a physician whom the Denver County Medical Society refused to admit, backed by three local parsons (one Methodist, one Presbyterian, one Disciples of Christ), it filled every major state office from the governor's down and secured a majority in the lower house of the legislature. The degree of its violences varied; always despicable, they might be mere intimidation—veiled threats to recalcitrant Jews or Catholics or local politicians failing to bow to the Invisible Empire's notions. In Denver hoodlums drove through the Jewish neighborhood on the Sabbath bawling obscenities, a restaurant advertised that it served fish every day but Friday; but nobody was actually assaulted. Sometimes as in Perth Amboy, New Jersey, the Klansmen's militancy so roused local resentment that it was they who got mobbed for a change. But within Dixie's sphere of influence, methods closely followed the local traditions of playing really rough.

Semi-Southern, semi-Western Oklahoma, for instance, was the more rugged in the 1920's because on top of its usual problems with a neglected major population of Indians, it was oil-drunk and bootlegger-ridden. This atmosphere encouraged the Klan to corollary "whipping parties" at which the instrument of choice was a leather strap three inches wide, slit into three thongs, that took off the skin like a gradual blowtorch. When the yearly incidence of such functions, to which guests were invited as if to a ball game, reached over 2,000, Governor J. C. Walton put Tulsa County, including the state capital, under martial law. The Klan burned 260 simultaneous fiery crosses ostensibly as protest against failure to enforce Prohibition and in honor of the recently deceased Harding. For persisting in defying the Klan, Walton was presently impeached and removed from office. In Louisiana and Texas, white as well as black victims were drowned in swamps or burned under what local people had every reason to believe were Klan auspices. (That there was any uncertainty shows the frequency with which such things happened impromptu down there.) In Texas the Klan took over large cities as well as dusty county seats. A local magnate described Fort Worth as in "almost a complete state of anarchy . . . officers of the law seem to be either afraid of those fellows or are members of the infamous outfit themselves." [44] And, to leave Dixie, Indianapolis was the Klanniest large city north of the Ohio River.

All that in five years! The new cadres of Cyclops, Goblins and Kleagles had reason for delusions of grandeur. But by 1925 weather was blowing up. On the hyposympathetic Eastern seaboard appeared a National Vigilance Association to watchdog the Klan and press for laws banning masks on the street and to compel publication of the memberships of secret orders; some states passed such laws. Commendably the American Legion, though given to harsh patriotism, denounced the Klan. So, less surprisingly, did the American Federation of Labor. Then came the misstep of D. C. Stephenson, the overweening Texan who had become Grand Dragon of Indiana. "I am the law in Indiana" was his brag, backed up by a special terrorist force based on revival of the pioneer- and vigilante-flavored Horsethief Detective Associations. His downfall began when Evans deposed him in an intramural struggle. But he knew where so many bodies were buried that his political leverage remained strong. The disaster of 1925 was his own doing. He kidnapped a local girl and raped and so brutalized her that she took poison and died partly of that, partly of injuries he had inflicted.

He got twenty-five years to life,* but the stench necessarily clung to the arrogant Invisible Empire of which he had been so tall a pillar. "His removal," Elmer Davis wrote, ". . . set up two discordant factions among the sheeted paladins . . . doubtless the pro-rape and anti-rape factions . . . perhaps the Klan's enthusiasm for female purity proceeds ultimately from a jealous cherishing of the droit du seigneur." [45] Only slightly less noisome stenches arose in 1928 when a struggle for power within the Klan in Pennsylvania reached federal court and washed in public such very dirty linen, including responsibility for riots, a nasty kidnapping and the lurid

---

* In 1950 Governor Henry F. Schricker of Indiana, for reasons best known to himself, followed the recommendation of the State Clemency Commission that, for reasons best known to its members, Stephenson be paroled. To protests from certain Hoosiers—including the late Elmer Davis and Rex Stout—the governor replied with the old nonsense about how Stephenson's former colleagues in the Klan had framed him. (There is no inherent improbability in the notion that the Klan might have framed somebody. But I have in my files letters from friends who were reporters in Indianapolis at the time, knew the girl as a neighbor down the street and repudiate any such possibility. A privately published book, *So They Framed Stephenson*, by Robert A. Butler (1940), was, until the cranks began to speculate about the assassination of John F. Kennedy, the most grotesque bit of absurdity extant.) Stephenson rewarded the governor's slackness, humaneness or whatever it was by running out on his parole as soon as he was freed. Arrested in St. Louis for molesting a girl, he was returned to the Indiana penitentiary. Presently paroled again, he married and was said to have settled down—only to disappear once more. At present writing his whereabouts are unknown.

details of lynchings in Texas under Evans' particular leadership, that the judge threw the case out, denying both plaintiffs and defendants. "They come with filthy hands," he said, "and can get no assistance here." [46]

For those and subtler reasons the Klan was slipping. William Allen White, whose Emporia *Gazette* had consistently fought the Klan in Kansas, had reason thus to hail a promised visit of the Imperial Wizard: "He will find what was once a thriving and profitable hate factory . . . busted . . . the cock-eyed he-dragon wails for its first-born, and the nightshirts of a once salubrious pageantry sag into the spring breezes and bag at the wobbly knees." [47] Evans' conciliatory gesture of ordering masks left off failed to help. By 1929 national enrollment was down to 200,000 from a putative peak of some millions in 1924, the year when the Klan was the grand divisive issue in the Democrats' national convention. In Florida sporadic activity persisted into the 1930's. The race crises of the late 1950's saw notable savageries from petty revived Klans. But that particular version of America's sinister side probably has little more future than classic anarchism. In 1922 Duffus pointed out that such hate movements appear among us every thirty years or so and seldom last a decade—such as the Know Nothings, the APA and (it might now be added) Senator Joseph R. McCarthy's creepy confusions of Red Judas goats with woolly-headed pink sheep and occasionally innocent white lambs.

Thank the Lord, however, that the Klan's fangs were drawn before the Depression. Think how it might have exploited the fears and hatreds of the worst times the nation ever knew, particularly had it had dynamic leadership. Evans was a good PR man but lacked fire. In his time, too, the radio was not yet the vehicle of national emotion so well exploited by Huey P. Long and Father Charles E. Coughlin. Suppose Long, riding high on radio waves, had had the Klan's continent-straddling secret cult of white-robed haters to back him in the punch-drunk 1930's. Huey was no Klansman, but his Louisiana was rotten with Kluxery, and he had consistently failed to face the issues that it represented. . . .

For a massive, still-growing hangover from the War consider the black enclaves of Chicago, Cleveland, Pittsburgh. . . .

In 1914 such non-Southern industrial centers already had distinct black districts housing descendants of local pre-Civil War blacks and slowly growing as immediate descendants of slaves trickled up from Dixie. The latter were likely to be those least able to stomach Mr. Charley's notion of the "niggra's" place and how to keep him there. Their migration had recently been lubricated by a decision of the U.S. Supreme Court in 1910 curbing the "debt peonage" that tied the rural Southern black to the soil. Many were enticed northward as strikebreakers recruited by labor agents offering free rail tickets and high pay on arrival. If the boss won the strike, they might get permanent sweep-out work easier and better paid than

cotton chopping. If the boss lost and they liked the Northern version of Jim
Crow better, they got other jobs and settled down. Further, an entomologi-
cal event was disquieting Southern field labor. The boll weevil, ruinous to
cotton, had come into Texas from Mexico, swept into Louisiana and
Arkansas and jumped the Mississippi to gnaw at the rest of Mr. Charley's
shaky Cotton Kingdom. It looked bleak for him and worse for the hired
hands or sharecroppers, black or white, who worked his land and for the
many blacks who had taken Booker T. Washington's advice and bought
and painfully paid for small holdings of their own. Now with little or no
crop to pick. . . . Eventually it proved that the boll weevil had done Dixie a
favor by forcing it to diversify land use into tree and cattle farming. But at
the time one saw only threats of bankruptcy and very hard times for the
Cotton Kingdom's field hands.

This dislocation sent many blacks into the South's growing industrial
cities—Atlanta or steel-boomed Birmingham, whose black colony inspired
Octavus Roy Cohen's stories about Florian Slappey and the Sons and
Daughters of I Will Arise in the *Saturday Evening Post*. Other blacks found
the boll weevil a hint to get away altogether from Mr. Charley. By
thousands they migrated into the existing "nigger heavens" of the North
such as Indianapolis' Indiana Avenue and Detroit's "Saint Antwine"
neighborhood. Presently War-created opportunities drew hundreds of
thousands after them. War cut off normal trade with the Europe that
bought most of the cotton of the states not yet crippled by the boll weevil. It
took away from the North's labor force thousands of aliens going home to
fight for their belligerent fatherlands. It dried up the annual fresh supply of
strong-backed and easily exploited immigrants on whom American industry had come to count. And conversely, as Allied demand for American-
made munitions grew, it heightened Northern need for the unskilled, docile
labor no longer coming from Sicily and the Balkans.

So in slatternly Southern county seats where few blacks saw much cash
after the advance on the crop was paid off, labor agents swung down from
the accommodation trains of the Louisville & Nashville or the Illinois
Central once more to sing that siren song of free tickets to Chicago or
Detroit and $3 or $4 a day when you got there. The same song also sent
poor whites northward in separate cars, for cotton's troubles, forcing many
small white Southern farmers off the land, inclined them too to go
proletarian on Northern industrial payrolls. But poor as Tobacco Road's
prospects were, viciously as it hated the plantation landlord and the
crossroads storekeeper, its reasons for leaving were rather less cogent than
the black's, and the consequences of its migration, though still marked,
were less far-reaching. Indeed at the time the poor whites were helping the
blacks to decide to leave. Competition between poor whites and blacks for
what cottonfield work remained led to exasperation and a boom in
lynching, and black leaders in the North noted that "Every time a lynching

takes place . . . down south . . . colored people from that community will arrive in Chicago inside of two weeks." [48] To such push from behind add the pull of enticing letters from those up North to those back home: ". . . colored men are making good," a black in Chicago wrote to his former pastor in Alabama in June, 1917. "Pay is never less than $3 a day for ten hours. . . . They do not hurry or drive you. . . . Nothing here but money and it is not hard to get. Oh, I have children in school every day with the white children." [49] It was the same kind of letters that had traditionally stirred white immigrants to come join their folks who had found the industrial slums of America preferable to the rural slums of Calabria and Transylvania.

Northern black papers with substantial circulation in Dixie carried labor agencies' advertising and editorial offers of advice and help in coming North to better things. The *Journal of Negro History* once published a selection of Southern blacks' responses to these stimuli well before the draft began further to constrict the nation's manpower. The sample is necessarily confined to those able to write a comprehensible letter to the Chicago *Defender* or the New York *Age*; the proportion of town wage earners among them, often at least semiskilled, is also unduly high. The data are nevertheless eloquent. The inquiries come almost entirely from the Deep South, though the Northern black press was widely read in Virginia and Kentucky. Reasons for contemplating migration are predominantly economic. From Gonzales, Texas, in May, 1917: ". . . if a man from the south come north, such as common laborer, stationery [*sic*] engineer, gasoline engineer, fireman, or janitor . . . is there a likelihood of . . . lucrative employment?" From Mobile, Alabama, in April, 1917: "This is my native home but it is not fit to live in just as the Chicago Defender says it says the truth and my husband only get $1.50 a day and pay $7.50 a month for house rent and can hardly feed me and his self and the children. . . . I want to get out of this dog hold [*sic*]. . . . I want to get to Chicago and my husband crazy to get there because he know he can get more to raise his children. . . . He get there a while and then he can send for me." From Houston, Texas, in April, 1917: "[I want] to leave the South and Go any Place where a man will Be any thing except A Ker. . . . I am 30 years old and have Good Experence [*sic*] in Freight Handler . . . would like Chicago or Philadelphia. But I dont Care so long as I Go where a man is a man. . . ." [50]

On arrival this northward flow behaved in the American big city as had the westward flow of Europeans. Blacks too clumped together for the mutual support of their own ways of doing, speaking and cooking. First crowding into dwellings already holding too many of their own kind, then overflowing into adjacent buildings, then adjacent streets, they created expanding enclaves of high homogeneity. "You can hardly get a place to live here," said another black's letter home. "I have rented me a place for boarders. . . . I have fifteen sleepers." [51] The same process had created those half self-established, half pressure-shaped Little Italys and the Jewish city on New York City's Lower East Side. As usual it meant fat profits for slum landlords and real estate brokers exploiting the dismay of the new enclaves' neighbors—whether named Schmidt or Kelly—who found the houses in the next block becoming noisome slums with half a dozen newcomers to a room. For the folkways and sanitary procedures of peasant Galicia or black-peon Alabama—or, for that matter, Tobacco Road—did not suit big-city needs and annoyed Germans and Irish approaching the lace-curtain stage of upward mobility.

The Southern blacks took over what had been petty bourgeois neighborhoods in Chicago and also the long, southward-stretching avenues of the elaborate dwellings of the affluent. They said the first black-foot-in-the-door sale of a Grand Boulevard mansion was made by a lady brothelkeeper who, having bought the place for professional uses, wanted revenge for the neighbors' complaining about her. Other things being equal, the frictions need have been little worse than those between Irish and French-Canadians in New England. But things were not equal. These enclave makers had dark skins with ominous old connotations. Their color kept reminding the incumbent previous residents that they not only talked queer, ate strange things and competed with local breadwinners for jobs but were also "niggers" associated in pervasive American folklore with jungle ancestry, body odor, puerile crime and the alleged Biblical infliction of blackness on Canaan. Add identification with strikebreaking. . . .

Such strains had once combined with those from mishandled conscription to set off the bloodiest race riot* in American history—the so-called draft riots of July, 1863, in New York City. A generation later the Chinese who did California's menial tasks and pick swinging had the same trouble on a smaller scale. Surely the curse of varying skin color has proved worse than the curse of Babel! C. 1916 matters were probably all the nastier for the presence in the same Northern cities of those numerous Southern poor whites talking racism to their benchmates at just the wrong time. Nor did it help that the field hand blacks prevalent in this weevil-and-War migration were less presentable than many of their established Northern cousins. As hack drivers, livery-stable hands, waiters, house and yard servants—sometimes skilled workers or owners of small catering or livery businesses—Northern blacks often had a certain standing, however equivocal, as solid, clean, tidy and often fiercely self-respecting persons, provided, that is, they were skilled in the wider but subtly severe Northern version of the color line. Now here were swarms of the products of the South's black peonage stultified by contempt and neglect, many, we can now suspect, mentally

---

* C. 1920 this term usually meant an outbreak of violence among whites against blacks. The blacks often violently defended themselves, but the onus was typically on whites. The term is used only in that sense here.

stunted by malnutrition—flap-footed, dull-eyed, slack-jawed, dilatory, inarticulate, ragged or, after the first few paydays, cheaply garish, fecklessly violent among their peers, inevitably reminding whites of the razor-toting, chicken-stealing, thick-witted caricatures of the comic strips and the movie screen. (Many of the parallel poor whites were just as poorly housebroken, but white skins kept their visibility lower.) Thanks to the War, the black was putting his worst foot foremost.

Even before America entered the War, the influx of blacks was stimulating the vicious propensities of blue-collar whites. By 1917, well before the first draft lottery was drawn, bullying of blacks and labor leaders' warnings about their being potential strikebreakers had grown common in East St. Louis, a drab industrial excrescence in race- and violence-minded southern Illinois. Early in July a race riot burst into burnings and killings. Local police and then militia hardly bothered to try to cope. Small boys were seen emptying revolvers after fleeing blacks. Young girls brandishing clubs led mobs of men. It seemed a grim omen, but once the dead were buried and the ashes cold, the nation saw no more major race violence until 1919. Then July heat accentuated accumulating racial strains—this time from post-War letdown, maybe heightened by the demobilization of many hard-nosed young haters unable to find jobs—and set off horrible riots, in which whites again were the aggressors, in twenty-six cities.

In Washington, D.C., discharged soldiers and sailors, many still in uniform, led the rioters. With some justice the black papers blamed the playing up in the local paper of blacks' molestations of white women. In Omaha, Nebraska, the mayor defied a mob's effort to seize a black for lynching and was lynched himself, strung up twice and twice cut down just in time; the rioters then burned the courthouse, pride of the town. Chicago's episode is straight out of yesterday's headlines: Black boy swims beyond the unmarked, mutually observed customary line between whites' and blacks' exclusive segments of a Southside beach on Lake Michigan. White boys stone him; he falls off a diving raft and drowns. Black spectators demand that white policeman present arrest the stone throwers. He refuses. As the victim's body is carried away, whites and blacks stone one another, and for three days the margins of the city's Black Belt are a guerrilla battleground of stonings, arson and gunfire leaving twenty-three blacks and fourteen whites dead. Lippmann called it "infinitely more disgraceful than that Mexican banditry or Red terror about which we are all virtuously indignant." [52]

By then Chicago's Black Belt was a city-within-a-city of 125,000 blacks. Its black-owned and -operated enterprises included five banks, three retail cooperatives, seven drugstores, a life insurance company, a building and loan association, many real estate brokers adept at blockbusting and the largest single Protestant congregation in America, Olivet Baptist Church,

8,500 strong; also noisome craps and poker parlors and flourishing sales of dream books for the numbers game that dismayed the black bank cashiers, lawyers, physicians and so on who lived in and tidily maintained large houses taken over from prosperous whites. They also deplored the pawnshops and storefront churches of shouting religious splinter sects that, in the prospering blacks' view, reflected moral and spiritual as well as economic poverty among their racial comrades.

In hopes of sounder interracial public relations they sought to refine these raw field hands who, having always thrown refuse outdoors in Dixie, did the same in Chicago. "I will arrange my toilet indoors and not on the front porch . . . refrain from loud talking . . . on street cars . . . do my best to prevent defacement of property, either by children or adults," [52] ran a leaflet from the Urban League, a national organization set up by blacks in 1910 to ease Northering immigrants into their new lives with minimum friction. But the heavy strains of dislocation dragged many down. In two blocks on Dearborn Street in the heart of Chicago's raffish Black Belt in 1919, a black reporter found almost all the boy children truant from school while "most of [their parents] were away from home so much they were out of touch with the children." [53] Of eighty-three households willing to be questioned, forty-three were broken by "death, desertion, divorce, drink, promiscuity or degeneracy." [54] Twenty-eight fathers, twenty mothers were heavy drinkers. Forty mothers worked all day. Sanitary habits were as poor as the available facilities. Add drug problems, and it would sound very like today. The fragile family relationships that slavery imposed on blacks, still part of their ways-of-doing two generations later, were poor preparation for stability in the big city.

As the post-War sag in employment began to disappear late in 1919, the northward flow of blacks resumed, heedless of the previous race riots. The South had no sag in "lynching, disenfranchisement, inferior schools, confinement to menial and lower-paid employment" [55]—Walter White's list of reasons why blacks left Dixie—so by 1922, the U.S. Department of Agriculture noted, 13 percent of Georgia's field hands had moved North. The *World's Work*, monthly Bible of current affairs for Americans of reasonable standards of information, rather woundingly approved of this migration:

> If these Negroes stay north . . . [and] work regularly in industry, the country will greatly gain . . . the earning power of the Negroes must be larger and their production greater than in the South where many of them work but intermittently and with no great results. . . . The Negro . . . is a burden . . . carried easiest where it is widely spread . . . where there are few Negroes race questions are not so serious. . . . To those in the South who believe that cheap labor is a blessing the movement will be viewed as a

calamity, but cheap labor is not there or anywhere else a real benefit.[56]

Many Southern whites probably shared this wrongheadedness about the black's low potential. Nonetheless, counterrecruiters were sent North to distribute leaflets saying come on home, calves are fattening down here where winters aren't so cold. Few blacks heeded. The yeasty and often new-hatched Northern black press—Chicago alone now had six weekly black papers led by the *Defender*, which ranked with the Pittsburgh *Courier* in national readership—rejoiced because Mr. Charley was hurting and laid it on heavier than ever. "Look around at your cabin," said one salvo zeroed in on vulnerable targets, "look at the dirt floor and the windows without glass! Then ask your folks already up north about the bathrooms with hot and cold water . . . the steam heat and the glistening hardwood floors which down home you see only when you polish them. . . . What chance has the average [black] to get these things down home? And if he does get them how can he be sure but that some night some poor cracker will get his gang together and come around and drive him out? . . . step on a train and ride for a day and a night to freedom. . . . Your nickel is worth as much as the other fellow's nickel in the [Northern] streetcars and you sit wherever you can find a seat. . . . You tip your hat to no man unless you desire to do so. . . ."[57]

Some black preachers organized mass migrations of their congregations to the Northern fleshpots. Many Southern urban blacks writing for encouraging advice mentioned groups ranging in size from a few families to scores and hundreds eager to come North. No wonder it was risky for a Southern black to be caught with a Northern black newspaper. The process thus promoted has continued.

Some of that migration may well have been part of the general shift of country folks into cities. But among blacks the War did give it a very special push. Indeed, supposing the Kaiser to have been as responsible for the War as propaganda said, he did as much as Abraham Lincoln to alter the American black's economic circumstances, on the average much for the better. Beyond that, unfortunately, the rule that lasting side effects of the War were usually deleterious still holds, for they did little to improve interracial relations. That was the sadder because on the whole blacks performed creditably or better in War industry and in uniform. The black soldier particularly had reason to hope that when demobilized in a world made safe for democracy, he would be some steps above his previous second-class citizenship. His mistake was soon clear. In 1919 the South lynched ten returned black soldiers, some still in uniform. Two were burned alive.

Indeed even during the War morbid tangles, all primarily the fault of whites, plagued black soldiers. Harlem's own black National Guard regiment, become the 369th U.S. Infantry, was sent to train at a camp near Spartanburg, South Carolina. At a local hotel newsstand Sergeant Noble Sissle—great early missionary of jazz and concertmaster of the 369th's remarkable band—was beaten for not taking off his hat. A black company officer was thrown off a streetcar. Their white colonel, William Hayward, a Manhattanite blueblood, had great trouble keeping his white officers, of the same social stratum, from leading the outfit to teach the town a retaliatory lesson. Fortunately somebody in the War Department had the sense to order the 369th north to Camp Mills, Long Island, and when Southern units there made trouble, shipped it prematurely overseas, the first National Guard unit to land in France. Brigaded with the French, it spent more time in the front line than any other regiment in the AEF, had more casualties and more individuals decorated than most and was the first outfit to pass through New York City's Victory Arch returning home.

A regiment of black regulars, the 24th U.S. Infantry, showed less restraint when the devil's brew of white viciousness boiled over in Houston, Texas, in the summer of 1917. The detonating incident sounds dismally familiar: There had been so much trouble between local police and the MP's of the 24th that its officers had disarmed them. Local patrolmen known for bullying blacks swoop down on respectable black household. Private of the 24th who happens to be there objects. Patrolmen beat up unarmed private. MP corporal, very popular in the regiment, intervenes. Patrolmen beat up and kill unarmed MP. Some hundreds of his comrades defy their white officers and besiege the jail. In the ensuing gunfire fifteen whites are killed, including a little girl struck by a bullet going through a wall. Houston kept its collective head better than might have been expected. No citywide mob rose up. Military law could take its course, and though Wartime exigencies could be pleaded, it proved severely grisly. After two mass courts-martial and much proper agitation for clemency, the score was: 8 acquitted; 100-odd imprisoned for life; 13 hanged. Few newspapers, Northern or Southern, joined the Buffalo *Express* in urging the War Department to begin "playing fair with its black troops" [58] by ceasing to station them in Dixie. A generation later in World War II the War Department had not yet learned that lesson.

Nobody in 1917 even considered integration of black volunteers or draftees with their white counterparts. The U.S. Army had seen nothing like that since the Continentals of the Revolution. As for the U.S. Navy, it persisted in enlisting blacks only as messmen and would no more have contemplated commissioning a black than it would have hoisted its ensigns upside down.

In France the best black combat units' fine records did not spare them the stupidity of white staff officers in spite of the alleged "lifelong respect and affection" [59] that long service with the black 10th Cavalry was said to have given General John J. Pershing, commander of the AEF. Mess table talk attributed to them inability to fight well after dark. As in one of Berton Braley's *Buddy Ballads*:

> Send 'em over in the daylight when the Boches they can see
> And they'll rush 'em with the butt or bayonet;
> But at night, or in the gray light, when the dawn is strugglin' free
> You can't trust the crazy dinges on a bet! . . .[60]

The famous 369th's officers were mostly white on the long-standing theory that black officers could not keep blacks steady under fire. But the company officers of the 367th—another black National Guard regiment with a record of the same order—were all black, which certainly did not mar its fighting capacity; its homecoming parade up Fifth Avenue in a snowstorm culminated in depositing its colors in the Union League Club, the Civil War-founded headquarters of stuffy WASP affluence that, in memory of the old days of Honest Abe and Emancipation, had given the regiment those colors in the first place. Even more significantly the 370th, a black National Guard outfit from Illinois, had all black officers from the colonel down and fought so well that it could show sixteen Distinguished Service Crosses, seventy-five Croix de Guerre and more battlefield citations than any other regiment in the AEF. The AEF's top brass rewarded this demonstration of what must have been able leadership as well as courage by gradually replacing its black officers with whites, beginning with the colonel, just before the Armistice. The men objected stormily: "That Blue Eyes ain't our colonel! Duncan [second-in-command] is our colonel!" [61] But discipline held, they did not mutiny and the Armistice blunted the issue.

Others of the new black combat units did not live up to the examples set by these National Guardsmen. Note that the laggards lacked the good luck of being brigaded with the French. French brass, aware that their army's West African black troops were as tough as their battle habits were grisly, thought well of black fighting men. Black labor troops brought to France, largely from the South, for stevedoring and construction behind the lines moved dirt and cargo with a powerful efficiency that awed Allied onlookers. That, in the typical American general's view, was what "niggers" were for, not, for God's sake, to be trained in arms and even given command. Since the example of the 370th was so bright that most eyes closed against it, nobody ever determined how the several hundred black officers commissioned in the War would have handled combat, for few had their chance. Most remained company officers in supply regiments.

So it need surprise nobody that the black veterans' peacetime status in the American Legion proved to be second-class in most Northern contexts and nonexistent in many Southern ones. Indeed Jim Crow was among the first Legionnaires to join. In June, 1919, Major J. E. Spingarn, in civil life an eminent academic critic and pillar of the NAACP, telegraphed Lieutenant Colonel Theodore Roosevelt, Jr., a pillar of the newborn Legion, to protest, as a prospective delegate to the organizing convention, that for it to exclude blacks, as the press was predicting, would be unthinkable. His and others' agitations accomplished little against the weight of hundreds of thousands of Southerners and some millions of more or less melanophobic Northerners among the prospective members. This association of returned heroes let the issue roll to the outfield in an ignoble compromise that left the lifting or imposing of the color line to the several state-level headquarters.

It followed that black veterans seeking to join Legion posts forming in South Carolina, Mississippi and so on learned that these were for whites exclusively. In some, bylaws limited membership to "Caucasians"; in others, the restriction was no less rigid for being informal. Outside Dixie, local reluctance to admit blacks led to state-level charters for what were meant to be—and were, though the charter never said so—Jim Crow posts. This followed the War Department's policy of segregated units, so it had a certain sad logic. Many black veterans put up with it, particularly after the NAACP advised it as a way to keep a black voice in the Legion's affairs. Posts admitting blacks along with whites were all in the North and very few.

Several Southern state headquarters soon refused charters even to posts accepting Jim Crow status. At the first national convention late in 1919 this was fiercely attacked by the dozen black delegates, mostly from the Midwest, and by Spingarn and Hamilton Fish, Jr., former Harvard football star, Bull Moose Progressive, later a reactionary Congressman, who was proud of the blacks he had commanded in France and eager to raise hell for them. But even though Ham Fish was in many ways the ideal Legionnaire leader, Southern finagling and the lily-white leanings of most of the delegates once more smothered the issue.

Common economic and cultural origins made the North's black enclaves much alike west of the Alleghenies. On the Northeastern seaboard some had special traits. As center of federal white-collar jobs for blacks and site of Howard University, one of their outstanding centers of higher learning, Washington, D.C., had a stable and staid black community little affected by the northering flood of former field hands; after all, there was no manpower-hungry industry to attract them. And Harlem, the blacks' new capital city on the far end of Manhattan, had a distinctive texture with different origins. For one thing, blacks migrating into New York City after 1910 were dominantly from towns and cities, hence better prepared for the pressures and hopes of city life than their rural cousins streaming into the Midwest.

C. 1900 Brooklyn had a colony of prosperous, literate black families whose forebears had fled Manhattan after the riots of 1863. The focus of Manhattan's larger black population was "San Juan Hill"—the Fifties and

Sixties well west of Broadway, its center of night life under the Elevated on Fifty-Third Street. A shift northward was imminent, however. The district of Harlem had been overbuilt with apartment houses and single brownstone row dwellings intended for middle-income whites but renting sluggishly because rapid transit serving most of them was inadequate. Black real estate men saw an opportunity for the swelling black population and helped Harlem landlords fill this vacuum with self-respecting black tenants. They hoped to avoid enclave forming; one of their manifestos denied the assumption that "Negroes must be confined to certain localities . . . that it is not practical to put colored and white tenants together. . . . Race prejudice is a luxury. A respectable, law-abiding Negro will be able to rent wherever his means will permit." [62] That failed to allow for whites' setting such frantic store by prejudice that they would pay its heavy cost in economic loss and social stultification.

As blacks grew conspicuous in Harlem, local whites organized resistance. But psychological as well as economic slippage was against them, and rising panic opened the way for blacks to buy as well as rent. By the late 1920's they owned $50,000,000 worth of Harlem real estate, including the whole street of elegant private houses designed by McKim, Mead & White that, as pride of Harlem, the insurance-company owner had tried to hold onto. Unhappily, inevitably, as all strata of San Juan Hill flowed into the newer, cleaner, roomier quarters that Harlem's whites sulkily relinquished, they tended to grow dirty and horribly crowded to match the persistently low earning power of the average city black that had made San Juan Hill slummish.

It was piecemeal defeat for the civilized hopes in which black Harlem originated. The net result, for good or ill, was a new, racially homogeneous city, a true cultural capital for an ethnic group such as America had not previously seen except in San Francisco's Chinatown and, rather less sharply demarcated, the Eastern European Jews' Lower East Side on Manhattan. On the face of it Chicago's Black Belt could have rivaled Harlem. But only in its press did Midwestern blackdom lead. One reason probably was the grip that New York City had on national attention. There grew most of the country's songs, theatrical productions, movies (as of 1914), best sellers, styles, lurid domestic scandals, financial manipulations; there were the headquarters of the newspaper wire services and most national magazines; there most transatlantic liners docked. So thither gravitated the growingly numerous ambitious black writers, songsmiths, entertainers and confidence men for the same reasons that drew their white counterparts.

To the above-mentioned specially urban background of most blacks settling in Harlem add a unique element—a strong leaven of West Indian immigrants, some from Spanish- and French-flavored islands but mostly from British-influenced Jamaica, Barbados, Trinidad, the Leewards, the

Virgins, Bermuda. . . . They were fleeing the stagnating poverty of what had once been the slave-devouring sugar factory of King Cane. New York City got the bulk of them because the ships they came in usually docked there, also because New York was as much a magic word in Basseterre or Kingston as in Atlanta or Porgy's Charleston.

The slave forebears of these West Indians came from the same West African lands as did American blacks. Why the two groups turned out so different is puzzling. For surmise: The sugar islands usually had first pick of slavers' cargoes, leaving only a minority of middling to lower qualities to trickle directly or indirectly farther along to the secondary slave markets of the Carolinas and Virginia.* Thus the original West Africans sold in the mainland colonies, ancestors of the United States' native blacks, may have averaged less vigorous or otherwise less likely. Whether the genetic differentials were strong enough to show up in the traits of West Indian and American blacks today is uncertain. Anyway, differences have long been discernible. The West Indian's speech—listen to a genuine calypso singer— lacks his Dixie cousin's drawl, is chirpily flat with odd stresses that tempt some to hear Irish in it. As black observers have described him, he laughs and jokes less, moves less relaxedly. His facial trim is often tauter, and if he is light-colored, he has probably had more education. James Weldon Johnson, brilliant elder statesmen of American blacks, considered West Indians "characteristically sober-minded [with] something of a genius for business." [63] It may be significant that some 80 percent of them came not from the stagnant rural parts of their native islands but from the port capitals. In Harlem their bent for small retailing got them called black Jews. The epithet "monkey-chasers" reflected popular notions of the semitropics whence they came:

> When a monkey-chaser dies
> Don't need no undertaker,
> Just throw him in the Harlem River,
> He'll float back to Jamaica. . . .[64]

Both names hint that they and American blacks felt some of the same frictions familiar between white Americans and Britons. Harlem grumbled about the West Indians' habit of "waving the Union Jack," dwelling on how much better they did things in Bridgetown—which they had left presumably because America sounded more attractive.

Any native usually dislikes any immigrant competing for jobs. In Boston and Chicago Italians from the Abruzzi and Italians from Basilicata develop frictions cognate to these. But much of the above may also be ascribed to

---

* This comes of the navigational necessities and time factors of the slavers' voyages to New World markets; *cf.* my *The Americans* (121).

West Indians' imported notions of caste and race. American racial nonsense is two-ply in theory and largely so in practice. White = upper crust; "black" (or "Negro" in the usage of twenty years ago) = anybody with a discernible or reputed black genetic heritage—that is, from blue-eyed, fair-haired, fair-skinned Walter F. White, who chose not to pass but to remain classed as black, through the coffee-with-cream girl dancer at the Cotton Club to the blue-black Gullah of the Sea Islands. In the British West Indies, however, absentee ownership of plantations plus economic devolution after the slaves were freed in the 1830's created a three-ply situation. A sparse handful of dominant whites exerted primary leverage on the colonial government headed by whites sent out from Britain. Minor administrative and clerical posts, many of the professional berths and the skilled trades were filled by "colored" hybrids of many shades of brown—a color caste corresponding to middle and lower-middle classes. It floated on the dark brown to black masses assigned to the strong-back toil of canefield, fruit plantation, fishing boat and dock.

Contact between lily-whites and colored, though never quite even-footed, was rather easy; indeed many a lily-white was tacitly aware that indiscreet search would probably find him a quadroon great-grandmother. But the colored group fought shy of their genetic cousins among the black proletariat of the ports and the black peasantry of the upcountry. "There is no fixed color line in the sense that a black may not rise to middle class status," says E. David Cronon in *Black Moses*, "but . . . color looms large in island thinking." [65] Other things being equal, opportunity and prestige went by relative lightness of skin, and the black resented the mulatto's contempt about as poignantly as the mulatto despised him.*

West Indians landing in New York City naturally brought along these fixed presumptions, just as Sicilians brought ashore the attitudes that buoy up the Mafia. Hybrid color as social advantage was known to American blacks. Skins averaged significantly lighter among the wives and daughters of black lawyers and doctors who, in Washington, Philadelphia and so on, ornamented debutante balls very like those of affluent whites. Preparations for undarkening the skin were heavily advertised in the black press. It meant one thing when Negroid dolls for little girls became available and sold well late in the War; it meant another that light-brown ones sold best. Out of this hankering after white physical traits Madam C. J. Walker, a black lady from Indianapolis, made a fortune with a pomade (applied with hot combs) that modified the kinkiness of most blacks' hair. Her chain of beauty shops, its anchor a Georgian mansion on Harlem's West 136th Street, reached into the black enclaves of the Midwest and South. Her upriver estate was grand, her daughter an arbitress of Harlem society.

* From much the same causes much the same things developed in the French West Indies. In Haiti, French owned until Napoleon's time, the topmost stratum of whites has now pretty much disappeared, leaving a light-colored *élite* despising *les noirs*.

Thoughtful blacks mistrusted this rejection of the way God made them. Light-colored W. E. B. Du Bois, militant leader of black intellectuals, said in 1922 that it was "the worst possible taste for a Negro ever to refer to differences in color." [66] To do so was disloyal to one's race as well as impolite to one's fellows in a segregation based on racism imposed by white arrogance and stupidity. Yet Du Bois' magazine, the *Crisis*, gave Madam Walker a most respectful obituary as a great example of black abilities and, since her methods required meticulous cleanliness, a crucial missionary of personal hygiene.

So the black West Indian often made trouble when he stormily assumed that light-skinned Harlemites despised him as they would have in Spanish Town. The light-skinned West Indian offended when he treated his black Harlem neighbor toploftically. Yet once these newcomers got adjusted, their wider experience with responsibility, better schooling and probably in some cases their better-integrated personalities lent them disproportionate weight. West Indians (or their children) conspicuous among us have been Bert Williams, Claude McKay, Stokely Carmichael, Shirley Chisholm, Caspar Holstein (the numbers king of Harlem in the 1920's), Sidney Poitier, Harry Belafonte, Bayard Rustin, Malcolm X. . . . The first black deep enough in Democratic politics to be chosen a Presidential elector was a West Indian. So was the first to be a Democratic district leader in New York City. Today's American black owes much, and most of it good, to the West Indian's example of well-managed energies and the crosslights that he cast on the race problem.

The crosslight causing the longest eventual shadow blazed up during the eight active years in America of West Indian Marcus Garvey, founder of the Universal Negro Improvement Association and African Communities League. He was very black. His very black father, a village mason of frustrated ambitions, proudly claimed descent from the Maroons—the runaway slave outlaws who held their own against the white government of Jamaica in the 1700's. The thickset country boy rose young to an unusual success as foreman of a Kingston printshop. When labor troubles barred him from his trade, he went odd-jobbing in Central America, then to Britain with the gnawing purpose of studying the background of blacks' difficulties. In London he read *Up from Slavery*, inspirational autobiography of Booker T. Washington, founder of the famous Tuskegee Institute in Alabama. In 1914 many whites and many blacks too still saw Washington's ideas as the pillar of fire that would lead the American black into as much of a Promised Land as he could reasonably expect. Suppose that as farmer or craftsman, teacher, doctor or lawyer for his own kind he pulled himself up by the bootstraps to self-respecting quasi autonomy apart from whites but interpenetrating and parallel with the white economy—then whites would discern his merit and accord him equality to match.

Only white America did not deserve this trust in its fairmindedness. North as well as South any postponement of the quest for *de facto* equality was taken as resignation to segregation and race prejudice. As frustration grew more painful, Du Bois and the NAACP rejected Washington's theory as poor strategy and probably Uncle Tommish. They reasserted the black's right to an immediate fair share of his American homeland and in a program called the Niagara Movement went militant against segregation and defamation. Respect for Washington led Garvey to toy with his theory, but its sweet-temperedness was alien to his nature. Soon he spiced it with a harsh xenophobia diametrically opposite to the Niagara Movement. His Universal Negro Improvement Association would lead blacks, particularly *black*-blacks, into their own separate society free of the false values and genetic corruption with which whites and mulattoes mongrelized the glorious black race—"emphasizing a color line within the colored world," [67] said Walter White. The UNIA would campaign in the West Indies, Central America, the United States, wherever white brutality had settled blacks. But its focus was West Africa as the blacks' homeland. Mass return of black-blacks thither was always high among Garvey's aims. And a minor curiosity of the ensuing ethnic misery was that nobody pointed out he was so zealously recommending a part of the world he had never laid eyes on nor ever did.*

"Back to Africa" was not new. The feebly independent black Republic of Liberia in West Africa, conspicuous in Garvey's plans, was a relic of the Colonization Movement of the early 1830's—a showy but futile effort to settle free and freed American blacks in their "homeland" that Theodore Draper called "mainly a white man's fantasy for Negroes." [68] Maybe for that reason it left cold the bulk of those it was meant to help, or maybe the motive of the august white Americans sponsoring it was too transparently an unflattering hope to abate the nuisance of free blacks. A very close minor parallel to Garveyism had just recently flickered out. In 1913 Alfred C. "King" Sam, a black from Oklahoma, set up an Africa-for-the-Africans movement selling $25 shares entitling the holder to a free trip to Africa and free land when he got there. The means of transport was a ship bought with $200,000 of the money thus raised. She took the first contingent of shareholders from Texas to Liberia in 1914. They were flounderingly stranded there, and Sam had the good sense never to return to America to face the consequences. But it is a great tribute to Garvey's magnetism that within six or seven years of this notorious and wishful swindle he could work up high enthusiasm for just such another scheme.

The analogy between Zionism and these movements is often noted. In

---

* Truman H. Talley's more than fair piece on Garvey in the *World's Work*, December, 1920, January, 1921, says that Garvey's travels after his stay in London included North Africa. I know of no substantiation of this, nor would some acquaintance with North Africa qualify him to recommend West Africa, as different as India is from Kamchatka.

another aspect what Garveyism did was to exploit in America the West
Indian's kind of color-mindedness. Of seventy-five leading Garveyites
thirty-seven came from the West Indies. The UNIA's first headquarters was
in Garvey's native Jamaica. In 1916 he brought it and himself to the
thousands of West Indian blacks in Harlem. He and it fumbled at first. But
Harlem's black leaders gave the tense little newcomer some countenance
and at just the right time the post-War ferments of 1919 provided hormones
for explosive growth of the UNIA, as they also did for the Klan. Many
black newcomers from the West Indies as well as from Dixie were dismayed
by the crowded realities of the North's "nigger heavens"; angered by
post-War race riots; irked by black soldiers' failure to find the democracy
they were said to have fought for. Naturally many warmed to "Back to
Africa!" and the projected Black Star Line of ships to take them there and
the Negro Factories Corporation's black enterprises to underpin the
scheme. For a while several hundred thousand members of the UNIA in
black enclaves coast to coast paid thirty-five cents a month each; the sick
and burial benefits included were like those of the black benevolent
societies imitating those of whites. Many also took money from their
meager earnings to buy $5-a-share stock in the economic programs, among
which the Black Star Line drew most attention.

The UNIA's colors were red for slave blood, green for the allegedly
boundless fertility of Africa, black for her children's skins. The logotype of
its paper, the *Negro World*, featured an Egyptian head, for the glories of the
Pharaohs often kept Africanophiles from seeing how far it was in miles and
culture from the Nile Delta to the Grain Coast. It dwelled on past black
slave risings, the little-known empires of the Niger Valley and refused
advertising for hair straightener and skin bleach. The UNIA's nerve center,
basement of a half-finished Harlem church on West 128th Street, called
Liberty Hall, held some 6,000 people. There Garvey expounded the blacks'
future in Africa and created his lieutenants Duke of Uganda or Duke of the
Niger or member of the Sublime Order of the Nile. For the many parades,
stiff with marching bands, the Garvey Militia wore sober dark-blue
uniforms with red stripes down the trouser seams. The Black Star nursing
corps, 200 strong, among whom few had had any training in nursing, were
in long-skirted aseptic white. Gorgeousness was reserved for Garvey in a
full pseudo-military explosion of cocked hat with red, green and black
plumes, epaulets of heavy gold, pounds of gold lace and medals, Sam
Browne belt, fancy sword—as innocently gaudy as any white hardware
dealer got up for the national convention in Omaha as Grand Imperial
Hetman of the Thrice Cantilevered Order of the Arcane Forest. Garvey
lacked the figure for it, but the same was true of Mussolini and was no
handicap to him either.

For the UNIA convention of 1920, which drew 25,000 members, Garvey
wore academic cap and gown of purple, green and gold; what degree from

what university he had in mind was not clear. The convention insisted that the press capitalize "Negro"—a point largely won by the late 1940's—expanded the Sublime Order of the Nile, bestowed the title "Fellowman of the Negro Race" on each paid-up member and created Garvey Provisional President of the African Republic back to back with his existing title of Lord High Potentate of the UNIA. He vowed that once he had the world's blacks organized, they would stop at nothing:

> If the Negro does not show in the next century that he is the equal of the white in capacity, in fighting power, the white man will . . . [push him] to an extinction as complete as that of the American Indian. . . . It is the purpose of this movement first to prove the hollowness of the white man's claim to racial superiority by developing within our race capacity for industry, civilization [vestiges of Booker T. Washington's teachings], for war, then . . . complete independence of Africa from the white man's rule.[69]

Garvey's leucophobia was not only a good focus for emotions that blacks readily felt, it had the minor advantage of immunizing him against the blandishments of Communists hoping to use him to the party's advantage. Marx, Lenin, Robert Minor, all Reds were white, by definition immutable enemies not to be trusted. But Garvey was willing to try to exploit whites' open hostility to widen the gulf between the races that suited his purpose well. As soon as the Klan became a national scandal, Garvey conferred half openly with Clarke, its opportunistic chief, seeking alliance and money for the ailing Black Star Line. "I never built any street cars or railroads," he told his new hooded friends apropos of Jim Crow. "The white man built them for his convenience. And if I don't want to ride where he's willing to let me ride, then I'd better walk." [70] Responsible black leaders and most of the black press, already troubled lest the UNIA's black racism play into the hands of white racism, were aghast. Du Bois called Garvey and Clarke "indeed birds of a feather, believing in titles, flummery and mumbo-jumbo and handling much gullible money." [71] Scornfully he told white readers of the *Century* magazine that though the UNIA claimed enrollment of some 4,500,000,* 80,000, mostly Harlem West Indians, was more like it. And the epithets that others, such as A. Philip Randolph, hero leader of the Pullman porters' union, applied to Garvey got almost as contemptuous as those applied to Mr. Charley.

The UNIA's spiritual arm, the African Orthodox Church, was headed by the Reverend George Alexander McGuire, a black Church of England clergyman from the West Indies radicalized by Jim Crowing in Arkansas

---

* At the time black population was almost 11,000,000, so in effect the UNIA claimed that it included every American black adult.

and thwarted hopes occasionally to occupy white pulpits. He created a new ritual based on the Book of Common Prayer but diverging to teach that Christ, His mother and the angels were black or at least dark enough to be Jim Crowed. Most black leaders repudiated this too, but its appeal was deep. McGuire told of an old black woman who gave one of his clergy $5 for having preached a black Christ; she said she had never been able to believe that any white man would die on the Cross for her. That has the same emotional truth as white Roark Bradford's bitter parable "Nigger Deemus": Christ's Disciples are peevish with hunger; He "passes a miracle" creating "fried chicken and ham and cake and beans . . ."; the white disciples fall to, but the black disciple, Nigger Deemus, is fobbed off with only "a little bitty lump er cold cawn bread." [72] When sentimentalizing Bradford to make *The Green Pastures*, Marc Connelly omitted that.

On balance African Orthodoxy was probably an asset to Garvey. It was his economics that ruined him. There was potential sense in the Tuskegee-inspired projects that he set up in Harlem as black services for blacks—a laundry, a restaurant, cooperative shops, milliners, tailors, dressmakers. . . . But hope of Liberia as port of entry and economic bridge to Mother Africa foundered on a reef against which Garvey had been amply warned. Liberia was a tight colonial-style oligarchy of American-descended blacks exploiting native black tribesmen in ways often close to quasi slavery. Even had the ruling clique been willing to share power for the sake of black prestige—as distinctly it was not—hostility from Washington, D.C., and the reluctance of European nations to see black nationalism infect West Africa would have been fatal handicaps. And the Black Star Line proved a smothering Old Man of the Sea. In each deal for a vessel, whether rusty tramp, wind-broken yacht or rickety old excursion steamer, the UNIA let itself be pitifully swindled; each effort to use them was a failure damaging to prestige; each search for adequate cadres of black officers futile. Some $800,000 that loyal blacks could ill spare went down with the Black Star.

By 1924 anti-Garvey pressures from blacks and the UNIA's flagrant stock-selling capers got Garvey and three of his staff indicted for using the mails to defraud. Garvey insisted on being his own lawyer. Notably fair-minded Judge Mack* went out of his way to keep this egoistic gesture from damaging the defendants' cause. But the jury convicted, and Mack gave Garvey the maximum five years. A comeuppance was overdue. During the trial Garvey showed clear symptoms of an eroding grasp of reality. He railed at the prosecution as instigated by mulatto enemies of the black champion of black-blacks and openly threatened them with sorcery, the black obeah of which his West Indians were specially conscious. His ostentatious costumes and rantings about black African empires past and to

---

* Fax (*Garvey*, 198) makes much of the suggestion that Mack was Jewish and the severity of the sentence reflected his resentment of Garvey's frequent outbursts of anti-Semitism in court. To anybody with an acquaintance with Judge Mack this is obviously nonsense.

come had long manifested his delusions of grandeur; toward the end he promised to return after death in "whirlwind or storm." [73]

His three years in the penitentiary were not likely to restore an emotional stability he had never enjoyed. Pardoned in 1927, he was deported as an alien convicted of felony and returned to Jamaica to build up the local arm of the UNIA into what its Harlem pattern had been. Newspapers were founded, new uniforms designed, new mass meetings exhorted into frenzy in the very island where he had first learned the folk duty of black-blacks to hate. But this West Indies phase of the movement gradually dwindled in step with the American one. Garvey died of pneumonia in London. He was buried in Kingston, Jamaica, as honored father of the new cult of pride in blackness of which white hating is the obverse. The honor was well deserved.

In Garvey's time many American whites and some blacks thought him a figure of fun. Randolph's *Messenger* called him the "Supreme Negro Jamaican Jackass." [74] But James Weldon Johnson saw the potential future in his rousing "a latent pride of the Negro in his blackness." [75] And Du Bois mistrusted this rather too successful tempting of blacks to think white hating a necessary element of black self-respect, "[opposing] white suprem-acy . . . by a crude and equally brutal black supremacy . . . [had he been] canny, shrewd, patient, dogged . . . [he] might have brought a world war of races a generation nearer . . . deprived civilization of that previous generation of respite where we have yet time to sit and consider if differences of human color must necessarily mean blows and blood." [71] Such a Garvey would not have been quite so dynamic a demagogue, hence his cult might have lacked optimum momentum. But the apodoses of that comment are well worth a second look today.

A study of demagogues in Garvey's black America would include William Hale "Big Bill the Builder" Thompson, mayor of Chicago for twelve of the sixteen years (1915-23; 1927-31) after the first impact of the War. He was white, born rich, crude. When Chicago's blacks needed him most—during the race riot of 1919—he failed them, using police too gingerly and refusing Governor Frank O. Lowden's offer of the National Guard. Yet throughout Thompson's raucous career he was the Black Belt's hero.

His inherited minor fortune came of Chicago real estate amassed by his Yankee father. Many of his age peers in the Gold Coast stratum of Chicago went east to Yale or Harvard. Young Bill went west to learn beef ranching largely on his own as hired cowhand. This led his father to buy him a ranch in Nebraska. He did well with it and earned the right to exploit this picturesque past as Cowboy Bill. In a wide-brim Stetson he made his maiden office-seeking speeches *c.* 1900 in Chicago's Second Ward—adja-cent but distinct layers of silk-stocking mansion dwellers; blacks forming the nucleus of the Black Belt-to-be; the pimps, whores and bouncers of a lively red-light district. Hat and name were not the only traits he shared with Hearst, whose Chicago papers gave Thompson his only newspaper support in the 1920's. Hearst too was tall, ranch-minded, Anglophobe, isolationist, power-greedy, had prolonged fits of political ambition, never thought twice about braying away about anything coming into his head consonant with his emotional vices, was born to affluence and ably increased his patrimony. As for differences: Big Bill was an ardent, crack amateur athlete in water polo, indoor baseball and the Chicago Athletic Club's football eleven—until jowliness and paunchiness coated his rangy frame with tallow. And while there was something sinister about Hearst, Thompson's coarseness and blatancy had a sort of rancid innocence.

Though nothing really explains him, the War had much to do with his saliency. Chicago politicians saw small reason to pay much heed to blacks until the War brought so many black potential voters to town. And by the time they constituted a major force they were already Alderman Thompson's personal following—a powerful springboard for the ambition that set him running for mayor in 1915. When the growing Black Belt of 1913 had celebrated the fiftieth anniversary of Emancipation, Thompson, introduced by an eminent black clergyman, had been chief speaker and roared like the guns of Mobile Bay about his father's Civil War service as Admiral Farragut's aide. When Chicago's blacks denounced *The Birth of a Nation* in 1914 and local liberals withheld help on libertarian grounds, Thompson got the permit to show it rescinded. As mayor he so diligently opened the city's payroll to blacks—redressing a long-standing unfairness—that Chicago called City Hall "Uncle Thomp's Cabin." Twelve years and several elections later another black clergyman was still laying it on thick: "God made William Hale Thompson and forgot the mold . . . let there be righteousness . . . come to earth. Call it William Hale Thompson." [76] The worth of such loyalty is not altogether obscured by the intimacy between this incarnate righteousness and the black chiefs of the Black Belt rackets—craps, policy, brothels . . . and by then also with the Capone mob.

One clue to this lasting affinity may be at least a semisincerity in Big Bill's solicitude for blacks. His early crony George F. Harding, another young Gold Coaster, had refrained from sloughing off his South Side real estate as the black tide rose, instead increased his holdings there and tried to be a good landlord to decent black tenants. Neither that nor his securing city jobs for blacks hurt Harding when he needed black politicians' help in political jugglings. But goodwill does seem to have been involved, and maybe it rubbed off on Thompson playing the same game at Harding's elbow. If so, it was about the only civilized thing about Big Bill. In mitigation of Garvey's exploitation of blacks' sense of their plight, one can say he was a sick man, all the sicker for the way whites abused those of his complexion. Thompson's capers had no roots in reaction to racial discrimination. He threw his weight about in politics because he liked the spotlight that came with power. Nothing scratched his puerile itches as gratifyingly as making a sympathetic crowd rise to his nonsensical bellowings.

The other anchor of his career, the other bloc of votes counted on through thick and thin, was the Germans, Chicago's largest ethnic group. This too brings in the War. Soon after it began, they gave him lasting fealty because he thundered against pro-Allied propaganda and those suspected of hoping to involve the United States in the morbid struggle. Such cards took the winning tricks in his campaign for the mayoralty in 1915. What he could do about foreign policy as mayor of Chicago he did not explain, but then he counted on his admirers to feel instead of think or even read anything not in large type. Late in 1914 the Chicago *Tribune*, no friend of his, though isolationist, ran under big headlines pro-German articles by one Robert Thompson, a former U.S. consul in and admirer of Germany: THOMPSON DENOUNCES BRITISH ATROCITY PROPAGANDA . . . THOMPSON SAYS BRITISH DIPLOMAT STARTED THE WAR. . . .[77] Big Bill's boys distributed thousands of reprints with those headlines in the German wards to persuade the unwary that *Alderman* Thompson used the city's largest newspaper to defend the Fatherland against perfidious Albion's calumny.* German clubs clamored for him as speaker, the German-American Alliance made him an honorary member. . . .

As protégé of a small local boss, William Lorimer, later U.S. Senator, Big Bill was Republican—and American blacks were still emotionally tied to the party of Lincoln. So were the Germans, though less consistently. Chicago's important Irish population, first- and second-generation, was traditionally Democratic. But Big Bill's diatribes against Britain as fomentor of war—again hardly pertinent to the office he sought, but again that didn't matter—doubtless attracted many Irish votes into the 390,000 that elected him. Not that he owed his Anglophobia to the War. His earliest campaign speech fifteen years earlier had drifted away from lashing the crooks in City Hall into denouncing a certain British journalist who had described fair Chicago's whoring, gambling, dirt, noise and so on as exceeding those of other American cities; every Britisher he had ever met, Thompson assured the voters of the Second Ward, had been "seedy and untrustworthy." [78] But the War exacerbated everything, including his well-timed aversion to the Allied cause because it was Britain's.

When an Allied commission (Lord Bryce, Marshal Joseph Joffre, France's most renowned general, and René Viviani, its finance minister) was to visit Chicago, Big Bill refused to issue an official invitation to what

* I owe this and much more in this section to Lloyd Wendt and Herman Kogan, *Big Bill of Chicago* (1953); also much to John Bright, *Hizzoner Big Bill Thompson* (1930) and Elmer Davis, "Portrait of an Elected Person" in *Show Window* (1927), a lovely piece of witty political analysis.

he was going out of his way to remind the nation was the sixth largest German city in the world. Ten years later articulate Chicago Germans, when asked how they could conceivably vote to restore to City Hall a slob like Thompson, told Elmer Davis, "Damn him, we know he's no good; but he made life livable for us in 1918, and he gets our votes." [79] The City Council invited the Joffre party on its own. Thompson came down off his high horse long enough to greet them, then climbed back on again. His personal political house organ, the *Republican*, went back to shouting that it was a "moneybags' war" and American participation was "unnecessary, unwise, unwarranted, and contrary to the self-interest of this country and its people." [80] For the duration Thompson blew hot and cold and then somewhat colder with a nice, though not exactly delicate, feeling for what the city would bear, and an obvious belief that if Congressman Lindbergh, John Haynes Holmes and Senator La Follette were still at large, the mayor of Chicago had little to fear. When Lochner sought a permit for his pacifist People's Council to meet in Chicago, Thompson granted it and fended off Lowden's threat to break it up with the National Guard. But after Rotary expelled Big Bill and the Veterans of Foreign Wars, yelling, "Hang Kaiser Bill!," burned him in effigy on the lakefront, he rescinded his order barring City Hall to Liberty Bond sellers and eventually bought a $5,000 bond himself. That effect was largely lost next year, however, when, while the outcome of the War was still chancy, he ran for the Republican nomination for the U.S. Senate with the slogan "America First!"—which he kept intermittently alive until doctrinaire isolationists picked it up in the late 1930's—blaming the Democrats' ineptitude for the nation's being at war at all and promising an end to foreign entanglements as soon as it was over.*

Though at last he was seeking an office with leverage on foreign policy, a landslide of hostile Republicans downstate lost him the nomination. Never mind, Germans, blacks and Irish plus the city's many pacifist-minded Scandinavians carried Chicago for him by 18,000 votes. This was an amazing result in a nation that was at war and—according to the revisionist history fashionable for two generations—had been doped and duped by flagrant propaganda, bullied by patriotic snoopers and brutalized by a War-intoxicated government. That such a thing occurred undermines that conventional lurid picture of War-drunken America *c.* 1918.

So far Big Bill's tactics had made enough ward-politics sense to pass for

---

* A curiosity of the literature of post-World War I revisionism is Harry Elmer Barnes' introduction to a 1930 book about Thompson: ". . . the standing puzzle why the uninformed Thompson came closer to the bull's eye of the war than the learned and statesmanlike. . . . [He] was the only conspicuous American . . . outside of Senator La Follette, to have sized up the matter in a manner consistent with the facts . . . since . . . established by scholars and publicists in all civilized lands." (Bright, *Hizzoner* . . . , xxii). Actually many conspicuous and cultivated Americans had taken the line of a "moneybags' war," and the moral to that probably is that, given the same basic temperament, PhD's and football stars are the same down among the viscera.

rational. Now he took off into rhetorical fantasy, concentrating on the Anglophobia he had begun with. Thenceforward, no matter who his opponent, no matter what the issues in a given primary or election, he always ran against King George, whom, in his best-known pronouncement, he vowed to punch in the snoot if His Imperial Majesty ever had the effrontery to visit Chicago. When it was plain that Harding was winning the election in 1920, Thompson said to an aide, "Let's have the Star-Spangled Banner now . . . we will not have to sing God Save the King." [81] Running again for mayor in 1927, he revived "America First!" to spark such obiter dicta as: ". . . who says 'America Second!' speaks the tongue of Benedict Arnold and Aaron Burr," and "I'm pretty old and fat but I'll guarantee to lick any Britisher of my weight . . . why don't they send over someone to lick Jack Dempsey? . . . All this argument for the world court is a lot of propaganda for the King of England. They tell me we ought to trust England . . . well, the King got control of all the rubber and raised the price enough to pay all their debts to us." [82] Running yet again for mayor in 1931, he left off his occasional flirtations with the Drys (the usual politician's cynicism, for he was an earnest drinker) and shouted, "Who benefited from Prohibition? Did you ever hear of an Italian or German or Scandinavian rum fleet? Who owns the rum fleets that are peddling hundreds of millions of dollars worth of poison booze off the American coast? The British. . . . Tell the King to go to hell!" * [83]

He got in his best licks on King George, however, when he tried to eliminate pro-British (or anti-American, synonymous in his mind) "propaganda" from books in the Chicago Public Library and the histories recommended to Chicago's schoolteachers. For Thompson King George was to blame for any efforts at commonsense objectivity about the origins of the Revolution. Much of that sort of half-witted reaction to the "debunking" historians and biographers of the day was then going on among veterans' organizations and women's clubs. The fumbling crony whom Big Bill chose to purge the library promised public book burnings; none was burned, but the threat made headlines for days. Even showier fireworks soared up over Lake Michigan when suspect texts for teachers were made part of the grounds for dismissing as insubordinate William McAndrew, an eminent educator whom the previous Democratic administration had made superintendent of Chicago's public schools. His insubordination consisted chiefly of having rescued the school system from its

---

* This may be Big Bill's high-water mark, for none of it made any sense at all. Britain, like other liquor-exporting nations, would have been better off had Prohibition not imposed clumsy clogs on dealings with the American market; indeed the Drys blamed propaganda against Prohibition on British money. Most of what the largely British-owned rum fleet sold was not poison but genuine. By 1931 Rum Row was a vastly diminished factor in the nation's liquor supply. And for a final effrontery, at the time he said this Thompson was hand in glove with Italian-dominated mobs who really were among the forces making the biggest profits from Prohibition.

previous plight as grab bag for patronage and graft, and it is still strange to read that because his housecleaning reduced the leverage of the teachers' union, its leaders were as hot as any boodler in Thompson's gang against their stiffly independent superintendent. Ousted by a subservient board, reinstated by court order but disdaining to return, McAndrew often told in public lectures how, when Thompson was asked whether he had George III or George V in mind, he said, "My God, are there two of them?" [84] Thompson, who liked to be called Big Bill the Builder because certain items in Daniel Burnham's Chicago Plan were carried out while he was mayor, dusted his beefy hands and began to hitch his star to the great Chicago Century of Progress Exposition of 1933.

In 1931 a bustling Bohemian-American Democrat, Anton J. Cermak (who died of an assassin's bullet aimed at Franklin D. Roosevelt), defeated Thompson for the mayoralty—maybe a token that the Depression was creating a new ball game. The Chicago *Tribune* saw no reason to be gentlemanly about it: "For Chicago, Thompson has meant filth, corruption, obscenity, idiocy and bankruptcy. He has given the city an international reputation for moronic buffoonery, barbaric crime, triumphant hoodlumism, unchecked graft and a dejected citizenry. . . . He is not only out but he is dishonored . . . goes from the city the most discredited man who ever held place in it." [85] The *Tribune* spoke too soon. Though the ailing Thompson's campaign for governor in 1936 was a disaster, events in Europe were setting the stage for a postscript triumph before he ran down like a grease-clogged watch. As Spain, Japan and Hitler's Germany made World War II look all too imminent, Thompson came down with a severe case of *déjà vu*. In 1937 he set up the William Hale Thompson Association to Keep America Out of Foreign Wars, and the ballot of an Illinois election actually carried the question. "Shall the people of Illinois approve the William Hale Thompson public policy . . . that all members of the Congress . . . from . . . Illinois shall vote 'No' on all legislation for the drafting of American boys to fight on foreign soil?" The press made it clear that no such gesture had binding force. By then, one would have thought, Big Bill's name on a proposal to wipe out cancer would have defeated it. Illinois voted for this windy futility 1,700,000 to 960,000.

When Thompson died in 1944, the Chicago *Daily News*, kinder than the *Tribune* in 1931, called him "the most amazingly unbelievable man." [86] In his prime, however, the international press had eagerly found this florid monster believable—significant of America as well as characteristic. The latter word is dubious; the former holds good. He was significant of a major flaw in democracy as practiced in America. Universal suffrage electorates often vote as if elections were popularity contests.

Out of the three-ply synergism of blacks, Chicago and the War, largely responsible for Thompson, also came the musical pandemic that named the

Jazz Age. New York City audiences sobbed when, in Samson Raphaelson's *The Jazz Singer*, George Jessel, playing the cantor's son, strayed into show business and "defended jazz as a sort of incantation . . . from the very soul of the American people." [87] It was a false provenance. Jazz, like the spirituals that had already delighted the Western world, came out of the *black* segment of America. So did ragtime, harbinger of jazz in showing what syncopation could do. In due time white musicians got the hang of ragtime, then jazz. On exposure to it the young white world danced to it with a passion that struck their elders as nearly pathological. But its core, and the ancillary blues, remained black. For parallel take ice hockey, long dominated by Canadian players no matter how zealously Americans played and supported it.

"Jazz" (sometimes "jass" *c.* 1910) is said to be somehow West African referring to copulation; he jazzed her, she got jazzed. . . . For complicated reasons West African influence was stronger in New Orleans than elsewhere in black America. Any given treatise on jazz guesses at African contributions to this musical idiom evolved for funerals and festivals by blacks using mostly white men's instruments: syncopation, percussion-mindedness, neglect of conventional harmony and, boldest of all from the white point of view, improvisation. Sometimes as solo against the rhythm of the other four or five instruments, sometimes in intertwisting but never actually harmonizing simultaneous improvisations, jazz was free, informal musical utterance. Hence, as Winthrop Sargeant's admirable study says, "Large scale jazz can never be hot jazz. Three or four men can collaborate in a collective improvisation without getting in each other's way . . . for fifteen or twenty it becomes impossible." [88]

No more performer's thralldom to composers. Jazzmen might take off from some street tune known to them all, but the chief point of what ensued was their subjective reactions to it and their fellows' reactions, never the same from each, probably never twice the same from a given player. These were no music school variations-on-a-theme but wild and yet inner-disciplined arabesques of tone and timing flaunting high and far, then wrung out and flaunted again. Soon whites tried ploddingly to set down on striped paper dry notations of these virtuoso ecstasies. But whether a given jazzman could read them made no difference at all. He needed only jazz in the back of his neck and the skill to blow, thump, pick or bow life into an instrument: clarinet, trombone, cornet, guitar or banjo (the only one of black invention), maybe violin, double bass (or tuba), drums with assorted hardware—a limited and in today's terms unfamiliar armament. The piano, ragtime's tool of choice, infiltrated jazz only gradually, maybe because most early jazz was played either in street marching or from a wagon bed too crowded for anything so bulky. Sixty years ago the jazz bull fiddle was bowed; the first to pluck and thump it, one hears, was Bill Johnson, who broke his bow one night in Shreveport, Louisiana, and learned this new technique by impromptu efforts to keep on getting some noise out of the ungainly thing.

The saxophone, valued for generations in military bands, seems not to have moved in on jazz until the early years of the War. Once in, it became the symbol of the Jazz Age, visual as well as sonorific: ". . . a player standing up with [a saxophone] to his lips could by dipping and swinging . . . sudden starts and rigidities and tremors . . . swoops and swerves, give to the instrument an effect of sentience . . . the union of music to ear and motion to the eye . . . comedy, surprise, dismay, satisfaction . . . As for the sounds . . . [the saxophone] could be onomatopoetic as no other instrument could . . . the yowl of a cat, the moo of a cow . . . the whinny of a horse . . . a lunatic asylum in which were segregated victims given especially to maniacal laughter . . . a yawn, a grunt, a belch. A skilful [sic] player with an acrobatic tongue slapping against the reed, his fingers fluttering over the score of keys, could achieve titillating arpeggios, glissandos . . . he could toot and he could tootle . . . blare and blast . . . bleat and blat . . ." [89] to quote Mark Sullivan's tribute. All manifesting the impulsively fluid qualities that made it the ideal instrument for improvisation.

Small groups of black jazzmen groping northward on river steamboats set up bridgeheads in the black worlds of Memphis and St. Louis. By 1905 the drift reached New York City. A black song-dance-and-instrument ensemble billed as the Memphis Students (actually mostly musicians playing for dances on West Fifty-third Street) did well at Proctor's Twenty-third Street Theater, then at Hammerstein's Victoria, with what seems to have been jazz-flavored or anyway hyper-ragtime material. Their subsequent prosperous year in Europe may have been the Old World's first taste of such music. In 1911 Bill Johnson found in California enough jazz-skilled blacks to form his Original Creole (connoting New Orleans) Ragtime Band—ragtime being the current craze and the line between it and jazz vague at the margins—that took the message pretty much all over the country. In the first year of the War stray black jazz groups tried their luck in Chicago, in the Black Belt at first, of course, but soon this rich, wayward innovation created by blacks for blacks followed through the breach made by ragtime into whites' self-conscious favor as a rowdy, dynamic musical miracle.

One important bridge was a white group emulating black jazzmen, up from New Orleans the first year of the War—the Original Dixieland Jazz Band. Their success soon got them booked into Reisenweber's famous dine-and-dance place in New York City. But their greater influence came of their being "waxed" by Chicago's lively recording industry in the first jazz discs to attain major national sales, which spread jazz to every American hamlet containing a phonograph. Particularly their "Tiger Rag" introduced millions to the new style. Purists now call that and its sister recordings dilute and vapid, not representative. To know the great early style, it appears, one goes to the later recordings made by New Orleans-trained *and* black King Oliver's Creole Jazz Band in Chicago after the War. At the time, however, for the nation as a whole, as well as for Reisenweber's paunchy patrons and their gussied-up women, here was enough jazz flavor to be novel and memorably stimulating. Subauthentic though they may have been, the Original Dixielanders were to ragtime what a joyride in a Stutz Bearcat was to a fast spin behind a trotting horse.

Now the War got into the act. The brothels of Storyville, New Orleans' remarkable red-light district, had been hiring local jazz combos as regular entertainment-*apéritif.* The consequent boom in the jazz trade in its cradle city squared and cubed it. In 1918 the U.S. Navy tired of Storyville's ravages among sailors ashore and closed the whole district as a war measure. Doubtless the girls and madams found less gaudily organized livelihoods one way or another. The members of the black house combos were in straits, however, and many of them migrated to Chicago, already known as a city where jazz fared well. During the next decade this concentration bubbled up into the "wild, winds-of-Chicago [school of jazz] full of breaks and surprising dynamics" [90]—as raucous as the wide-open joints that employed it, as famous as the big-shot hoodlums who patronized them.

Beyond this localized episode the War also introduced at least a protojazz to a wide transatlantic audience through the memorable band of the famous black 369th Regiment. Secretly subsidized by William B. Leeds, the tinplate king, it had as concertmaster Sergeant Noble Sissle (soon immortal with Eubie Blake for, among other things, the groundbreaking black Broadway revue *Shuffle Along*) and as bandmaster Lieutenant James Reese Europe, once a Memphis Student, then musical director for the Vernon Castles and founder-chief of the Clef Club for Manhattan's black musicians. Soon after landing in France the 369th's band held concerts in Brest and Nantes and was so warmly received that headquarters, clever for once, sent them touring twenty-five French cities, ragging and jazzing whatever came to mind—Sousa marches as well as distinctive jazz numbers. Thence it was only a step to the post-War concerts in London's concert halls—the white tie kind—of black Will Manson Cook's Southern Syncopaters jazzing Brahms and Dvorak. For once the Old World's groping for significance among American-oriented cultural data had something valid in its grasp.

Presumably nobody danced in the aisles at Cook's concerts. But in those days there wasn't much just sitting and listening to jazz as spectator sport. Only occasionally did young folks relax their holds, stop dancing and cluster before the bandstand undistractedly to absorb the clarinetist's auditory and sometimes corporeal antics. Generally jazz and dancing were taken as two sides of one coin. Hence the hurricane of denunciation of this new music, whether authentic or Tin Pan Alley imitation, such as pulpit and printed page would not work up again until rock-and-roll came in. The allegedly morals-corroding effects of jazz got much of the blame for the enormities (or so they then seemed) of the thigh-blending, cheek-to-cheeking fashion in which fox-trot and toddle were danced.

Chronologically this was unfair. The new close dancing had begun before the War as ragtime inspired the bunny hug, turkey trot and so on. By 1914, well before jazz was prominent, Dr. Brill recommended such public intimacies as breaking down "puritan prudery and Anglo-Saxon hypocrisy" [91] so effectively that it had greatly helped a dozen of his psychiatric patients. Maybe he had something there. If so, jazz probably helped even more neurotics because its more rhapsodic, orgiastic nature did lend special savor to the erotic overtones of the dance floor at proms and roadhouses. Ragtime, said Anne Shaw Faulkner, music chairman of the General Federation of Women's Club's, merely "quickens the pulse . . . does not destroy," whereas jazz was "originally the accompaniment of the voodoo dancer stimulating the half-crazed barbarian to the vilest deeds . . . its demoralizing effect upon the brain has been demonstrated by many scientists." [92] The federation's convention of 1923 voted a national crusade to "annihilate" jazz with the motto "Make Good Popular Music and Popular Music Good." [93] The Reverend Dr. van Dyke, then at his height as author-scholar-diplomat-divine, called jazz "a sensual teasing of the strings of physical passion . . . unmitigated cacophony . . . wilful [sic] ugliness and deliberate vulgarity." [92] In Cincinnati a judge enjoined construction of a movie palace next to the Salvation Army's lying-in hospital on the grounds that it would subject newborn babies to "the implantation of jazz emotions" [93] by the bands that the theater would book. The superintendent of schools in Kansas City, Missouri, warned that jazz as social menace would bring on itself prohibitory laws, just as booze had. And in Los Angeles a lady chiropractor so enterprising that she was later indicted for grand theft advertised that jazz caused cancer, which she could cure with appropriately soothing music of other stripes.

To the esthetic outrage among conventional musicians and dance teachers—some of it, not all, born of the realization that nobody needed a teacher to learn to dance like that—was added dismay over what jazz made human bodies do. It was "a signboard on the road travelled by Greece and Rome," [94] wrote John R. MacMahon; touring the Midwest for the *Ladies' Home Journal* in 1921, he described the intoxication it produced in the nation's dancing daughters as leading to worse behavior than alcohol could; sometimes they hadn't touched a drop and yet just look! The owner of a fancy Chicago dance hall said that such dancers should "have a marriage license before stepping on the ballroom floor," [94] and even that would not palliate such public doings. The dance floor version of the Charleston, a frenetic demonstration that the human knee joint could apparently flex two ways at once, made the dancing couple look like one of those multilimbed Hindu idols. But the queen of jazz-inspired antics was the shimmy, a specialty of the bosomy sex since its impressiveness depended even more on mammary than on pygean vibrations. A staid investigator seeing it for the first time in a nightclub said, "If it had occurred in a hospital, the patient would have been covered with six blankets and given ten grains of quinine." [95] Granted that the War had a large hand in endowing America with jazz, here was literally the shaking up that had been so widely and impressively predicted.

Indirectness in repercussions from the War did not necessarily mean puniness—for instance, the gigantism of the modern American highway system is an indisputable War baby. Until 1916 the hopefully christened Good Roads Movement had absurdly lean results, as intercity motorists knew dismally well. The nation's 200,000-odd motor trucks, mostly light delivery jobs, a good many electric-powered, hence of very short cruising range, were more or less pavement-bound in cities and towns. Until 1915, when the rubber industry first supplied a pneumatic tire strong enough for both the high pressures of the day and the weight of a truck, all were further handicapped by speed-inhibiting, frame-shattering solid tires. Already, however, the U.S. Army had the motor truck out into open country with the four-wheel drive invented by Otto Zachow, a Wisconsin blacksmith seeking better performance of his own car in country mud. Trucks incorporating this improvement replaced mule-drawn wagons in Pershing's pursuit of Villa in Mexico in 1916 and performed well. At the same time the Allies were turning to conventional-drive trucks to move men as well as supplies to the front over what shellfire had left of the good French highways. U.S.-made trucks built large and rugged for such work stood out in the logistics that stopped the Germans at Verdun. The AEF procured from American assembly lines thousands more such vehicles to handle its chow, ammo and personnel in the home camps and overseas.

At the Armistice the War Department owned 140,000-odd trucks and trailers, mostly heavy duty stuff, 20 percent still this side of the water. Those already overseas were sold for a song to the Allied governments to use in post-War cleanup. In America a good example of chicken-and-eggery came to pass. Obviously surplus trucks should be sold for civilian use. But without good highways outside town civilians had little use for them. So, supposing such highways were to be provided as existing federal legislation contemplated, what would come in handier than the heavy-duty trucks in question to handle the requisite materials? Indeed lack of just such equipment was what had been holding up plans of the new U.S. Bureau of Roads to subsidize state highway building, so farmers could get their produce to railroad sidings. In a rare example of commonsense cooperation among government agencies the War Department sold some 27,000 trucks to the states, and state engineers adapted them to all aspects of highway making. They not only hauled gravel, concrete and pick swingers but "Ambulances became portable offices . . . tank trucks became sprinklers . . . supply trucks were fitted with dump bodies and . . . hoisting devices . . . [or were] fitted with blades which transformed them into scrapers." [96] Thus was born the bulldozer—grandnephew of the ox-powered snowplow, nephew of the railroads' steam-powered ditto, crossed with the Maine logger's caterpillar tread—that so impressed American power on the world of World War II and has brutalized our landscape ever since.

Engineers already knew how to use concrete and asphalt-bound macadam to heighten highway resistance to wheels and weather. But so far they had been largely confined to towns and cities, and such cumbrous or primitive paving media as wooden blocks, cobbles and brick were still considered rivals. In 1916 the highway from East Aurora, New York, to Buffalo consisted of well-laid brick and, fantastic as it sounds, a beginning had been made on brick surfacing fifteen feet wide from Buffalo to Detroit. Now with War-surplus trucks fetching modern methods and materials, most notably concrete, America had a new major industry—highway construction—and new headaches to match. Fifty years of Topsy-like growth have made the highway builder an ubiquitous menace very difficult to live with because he is so deep in politics and rackets. C. 1921, however, there was only jubilation as ribbons of gritty, grayish concrete unrolled from city to city and the darker secondary network of blacktop gave the small town easy access to "the slab" in most weathers.

Soon came another momentous War baby—the over-the-road truck, child of an emergency improvisation from Roy D. Chapin, chief of the Hudson Motor Car Company and Wartime head of the Highway Transport Committee of the Council for National Defense. The AEF's thousands of trucks came largely from Midwestern factories. For shipment to France they would normally have moved to Eastern seaboard ports on railroad flatcars. Wartime congestion made that unpromising. Chapin sent them to tidewater under their own power and by clever routing and heroic road repair got them through. Further to relieve the railroads, he loaded each with overseas-bound war matériel—showing the nation that given sturdy trucks and worthy highways, the internal-combustion motor could move important quotas of freight over impressive distances. Nobody had tried it before. Doubtless the over-the-road truck would eventually have made its way in any case. But the acceleration consequent on Chapin's policy is a classic example of how the War brought things to precocious maturity.

Ever larger and faster trucks ominously resembling small, self-propelled boxcars began swarming out of Detroit. The railroads and their parasitic express companies (already hard hit by the intrusion of the federal parcel post system in 1913) felt this competition first in short hauls. Trucks could shift goods without delay or rehandling from factory to retail outlet, say, thirty miles away. Soon eighty miles. . . . They carried much less per-man-hour than rails could. But orders were delivered so much faster that the middleman or retailer could often so reduce inventory and warehouse space that the extra cost for driver's wages was more than made up. Only four years after the Armistice the *Scientific American* was deploring the immediate prospect of "absolute chaos in highway transportation. The rapid rate of increase in the number of motor cars and trucks . . . has brought about a congestion of traffic that calls for . . . regulation" and endorsed proposed "motor-truck trunk-line highways . . . wide enough to accommodate several lines of automotive vehicles . . . beltlines around heavy-traffic centers. . . ." [97]

Such railroadlike ideas betokened the economic arthritis to which trucks and highways doomed the rails. The highway that the trucker used was built and maintained at public cost, whereas the railroad had to pay for every yard of ballast tamped, every tie replaced, every switch inspected along its thousands of miles whether much or little freight went through. Taxes on fuel and over-the-road haulers have never yet evened that up. Then the concrete highway further damaged the rails by creating the intercity motor bus—at first a sort of stretched-out sedan but gradually improving in size, upholstery, weight and springing. In the 1920's automobiles and roads were still such that rail day coach was preferable on trips well over 100 miles. Pullman sleeper and parlor car were not really threatened until the airplane joined the attack in the 1930's. But for shorter ranges the bus was bad news for the iron horse long before the Fageol Brothers developed the modern type of engine-underneath, driver-in-a-gold-fish-bowl Twin Coach in 1929. By 1926 it was worthwhile to build special bus terminals in large cities. Down went the interurban supertrolley cars fanning out from urban centers in 60/70/80-mile radii on rails laid only a generation previously. In Indianapolis, an outstanding center of such smooth, silent transportation, the interurban terminal, once pride of the town, was made into a bus station.

The economics of it had odd twists. Most railroads had long considered passenger carrying a nuisance because, thanks partly to featherbedding that wasted many man-hours, it usually lost money. Yet federal and state authorities were disinclined to let the rails drop the function for which they had originally been built, often with public financing or at least encouragement. (The old subsidy debts had long since been settled; it could be maintained that the public had profited from even the least savory deals, but the old moral obligation to the traveling public hung on.) So the plodding old iron horse, forbidden to abandon passenger trains where to do so would have been advantageous, was now bullied by buses charging less than day coach rates and offering a fairly comfortable ride with more frequent, more conveniently placed stops.

V

Self-Moved Revolution

An auto is a helpful thing;
I love the way the motor hums,
I love each cushion and each spring,
The way it goes, the way it comes;
It saves me many a dreary mile,
It brings me quickly to the smile
Of those at home, and every day
It adds unto my time for play. . . .
It bears me into country new
That otherwise I'd never view. . . .
It has its faults, but still I sing:
The auto is a helpful thing.

—EDGAR A. GUEST, "The Auto," *Collected Verse*

THIS book resorts to statistics only when they are unavoidable. Here is such an occasion. In 1920, when Warren G. Harding was elected President, America was chugging along in 9,000,000-odd private automobiles, taxis, motorcycles, buses and trucks—a motorized vehicle for every eleven residents. In 1929, when Wall Street crashed, it purred along in three times as many, one for every four and a half residents, enough to take the whole nation riding at once. The application of internal combustion to the highway cannot account for everything that happened to America in that decade, dear as such integrating diagnoses are to proposers of a Gasoline Age or an Atomic Era. The motor vehicle did dominate many crucial contexts, however, and it is hard, though not impossible, to find contexts with which it had nothing at all to do.

California II was a two-ply example of direct effects. It is hardly necessary to dwell on how its elaborate adoption of the automobile led to an imbecilic diffusion of settlement and destruction of public mass transportation. In that respect Los Angeles County was merely showing the rest of the nation the way it would be going. But south of the Tehachapis this process was greatly and particularly gaudied up by being intimately bound up with California II's culminating oil boom—itself a function of the frantic proliferation of the automobile in the early 1920's. The great oil strikes of Signal Hill, Huntington Beach and Santa Fe springs all occurred in areas already platted out by real estate promoters and disposed of in small parcels to a multiplicity of owners. Previous oil madness in this area, or in Kansas, Texas, Arkansas, Louisiana, all more or less patterned on the original lunacies in Pennsylvania in Civil War times, had been striking enough—gushers, tent cities, overnight fortunes, dry holes, brothels, swindles, just as in the movies. But the results of the discovery of unanticipated wealth in the subsoil of subdivision plots bought because retired Iowa farmers liked the climate were almost as confusedly grotesque as those in Oklahoma that added to the folklore of Coal Oil Johnny, Spindletop and the Rockefellers' power the image of the filthy-rich Indian trying to ride in two Pierce-Arrows at once. By the time the flimflam salesmen had got through with the consequent gusher of suckers oil wells had replaced gold bricks in the American mind as traditional bait for the gullible. They had not yet begun their career as tax shelters.

At more or less the same time on the other side of the continent the automobile was almost as directly adding a third item to the catalogue—the underwater building lot in Florida. Here analogies to California II are necessarily close. Even at their gabbiest and palmiest Florida's promoters obviously owed a great deal to Californian examples. In both contexts too sunshine and oranges were sirenlike accessories before the fact. But the etiology was rather different, and in the end Florida's fever ran higher and probably did more than California II's to help set up the nation for the Great Crash of 1929.

Pre-Boom Florida was a creature of railroads. Henry M. Flagler of Standard Oil and the Florida East Coast Railway and Henry B. Plant of the Southern Express Company and the Atlantic Coast Line had raised it from the status of poor-relation Southern state to that of winter playground-sanitarium for the prosperous-to-wealthy. Their rails needed Northbound freight—citrus fruits and winter vegetables for the growingly nutrition-minded upper brackets. But the basic reason for their huge investments and the enterprises that towed in their wakes was intangible—the romantic heliotropism that developed in the mid-1800's and eventually created Palm Beach and Tampa/St. Petersburg.

Britons, Scandinavians, Germans, Russians—and in due course Americans following a fashion—came to identify the good life negatively with absence of winter cold, positively with generous sunshine and, if possible, palm trees for poetic grace and assurance that the thermometer would stay high. As usual in the birth of resorts the invalids came first, necessarily prosperous ones, largely upper-respiratory cases. The prosperous and healthy relatives who came to cherish them found themselves sea bathing in winter and less given to head colds. Hence Flagler's and Plant's elaborate hotels and the long trains of Pullmans snaking south through the mountains from Chicago, south through the Piedmont from New York City, and on the same tracks high-revenue freight for winter resorters—furniture, lumber and hardware for their hotels and cottages; booze, meat and fancy groceries for their tables; straw hats, bathing suits, golf clubs and tennis rackets, white shoes and voile and dotted Swiss frocks for their affluent persons. Much the same was happening in California II; only it was farther from the nation's centers of population, so more of its climate fanciers tended to be retired folks come to stay instead of Florida's habitually seasonal visitors.

Until after the War the cost of rail travel discouraged the subprosperous from using Florida as antidote to winter. That changed when, after the Armistice, the motor industry converted its facilities from War supplies to turning out sturdy little cheap and middle-priced automobiles—Ford leading but Maxwell, Hupp *et al.* not far behind. A retired couple from Springfield, Ohio, strapping luggage to the rear end and running boards, living on canned and packaged grocery stuff, camping nights in a tent or paying a farmer $1 for the spare room, could make an adventure of driving south before snow made the mountains hazardous and reached Bradenton or Sarasota at the cost of gasoline plus maybe $2 a day—anyway far less than rail even in an uncomfortable and unadventurous daycoach. And when they got there, the Gulf was full of fish and sunshine, the boardinghouse porch full of Midwesterners talking their language. And palm trees one after another all the way down the street and in the park too like the postcards showed. And the car right there for trips to Tampa to see the quaint Cuban quarter and Plant's astonishingly jigsawed Tampa Bay Hotel with onion-shaped cupolas, and to St. Petersburg already full of the elderly retired clustering folksily on the famous green benches, telling newcomers how the St. Petersburg *Times* gave the paper away free on days when the sun didn't shine at all—the whole complex on which Lardner built that fine study of the American mind and tongue "The Golden Honeymoon."

By the winter of 1919–20 the central Gulf Coast was so thick with elderly gypsies on rubber-tired wheels that they had organized a Tin Can Tourist Association claiming 200,000 members. In token of their chief sustenance a tin can was wired to the radiator as insigne. Rattling along in old clothes for the road, they looked dusty, wide-eyed and impecunious. The campsites that sprang up to accommodate them along the way were litter-strewn, frowsy eyesores. At first the entrepreneurs of Florida, already delighted with the elderly arriving by rail, looked askance at the Tin Canners, and admittedly they were not the affluent crowd on whom Palm Beach counted, not even the slightly less elegant fat cats for whom Plant built his Hotel Belleair at Clearwater. Indeed one of the Tin Canners' names for St. Petersburg was "The Poor Man's Palm Beach." But it was soon learned that the shabby Tin Canner's pocket might contain a plump roll of bills and that his savings account back home was readily tapped for a down payment on a Florida lot as Mother and he discovered they liked it down there well enough to come back winter after winter. Sarasota foresightedly catered to Tin Canners with a municipal tourist campsite at $10 a season, latrines and floodlights free. Soon St. Petersburg's Tent City rivaled it, and at both, though shuffleboard was not yet come ashore, horseshoe pitching was rampant.

As better tires, cars and roads gradually made driving to Florida less of an ordeal, the East Coast country south of Palm Beach experienced special side effects from the automobile-born money of the extravagantly extroverted Carl G. Fisher, Miami Beach's Peter the Great. He began as a bicycle racer, then took up free ballooning; but in those times Indiana was a lively rival of Michigan in automobile making, and gasoline was soon this Indianapolis boy's favorite perfume. He raced and sold automobiles. He was a founder of the Indianapolis Speedway, home of the great 500, and promoter of the Lincoln Highway, the coast-to-coast dream that never really came to pass but occasioned ballyhoo tempting many into motoring to California. He was high in the Prest-O-Lite Company, which gave automobiles their first effective headlights; they burned acetylene gas from a tank on the running board. And just before electric lights for cars came in, he sold out and used much of $6,000,000 thus acquired on Miami Beach.

Mainland Miami was then in an early but promising stage of railroad-created sun resort. *C.* 1900 it had been a mosquito-tortured trading post for the Seminole Indians of the Everglades; the sluggish few locals pronounced its name "My-ammah." Flagler favored it with a huge wooden hotel, and the affluent began arriving by rail—Gifford Pinchot, W. K. Vanderbilt, Senator Philander C. Knox of Pennsylvania. . . . Certain plutocrats, such as railroader Arthur Curtiss James and farm-implement heir James Deering, built elaborate winter mansions on Biscayne Bay; the one Fisher bought was the creation of a patent-medicine millionaire.

All this on the mainland. Across three miles of warm, shallow bay lay a barrier key just high enough to curb the Atlantic Ocean. Now smothered under the steel, concrete and plaster gimcrackery of hotels and tourist traps, Miami Beach was then mere sand to eastward and smelly, impenetrable mangrove swamp to westward. Development was limited to two beachside casinos, meaning bathhouses, one with an open-air saltwater pool presaging today's Miami Beach's reluctance to use surf as a way to get wet. A pile-and-platform bridge meant to link town and beach ran out of money, so patrons of the casinos used a ferry service. Barring a few coco palms guyed with wire to keep them from blowing away, the sun-battered, attenuated sandbar was pretty much the way God made and then neglected it.

Fisher liked boats—powerboats smelling oily and making baritone noises—and dredged himself out a bayside basin for them. New land made from this spoil suggested a scheme worthy of the showiness of his Prest-O-Lite millions. Flagler had created Palm Beach on a barrier key. Fisher would do the same here more elaborately—finish the frustrated bridge, wipe out the mangroves, dredge up the bay bottom, pile it where the mangroves had been and sell chunks of the resulting terra firma as sites for hotels and winter mansions. In a sister scheme for his Lincoln Highway he also projected a Dixie Highway southward from Chicago via Indianapolis and Chattanooga to Florida and personally led a Pathfinders' Tour of doughty motorists to inaugurate it late in 1915. Its Florida end was primitive and plagued by toll gates set up by the owners of the ancient Spanish land grants that it crossed. But it met Fisher's purpose—to draw gasoline-powered new people and money into his Florida—and was gradually improved. The name still clings to stretches of the now obsolescent waterside highways between Jacksonville and the Keys.

The War delayed profit from Fisher's huge investment in dredging, clearing, planting, paving, building as he turned a salt-air desert into a fat-cat suburb. But use of Miami Beach as training strip for military fliers—internal-combustion motors again—drew notice to the place. And 1919 came at last, enabling checkbooks to open under the Florida sun, as fresh millionaires—Harvey Firestone, great in rubber, Julius Fleischmann, the yeast king—bought and built near Fisher's new palace on his sandbar. The Armistice also freed newspaper space for Fisher's kind of publicity, which flooded the nation with photographs of Carl and Rosie, his two elephants that pulled stumps and stacked timber in the intervals between entertaining children visiting the beach with parents who might buy. VIP's playing the beach's new golf course were assigned Rosie as caddy—photographers again welcome. The scale of the project set other owners of beach tracts trying to make something of them, and now Fisher's dream was hurrying toward coming true. Elaborate winter villas lined the oceanside, smaller but by no means squalid bungalows filled the bayside. Streams of automobiles and buses clogged the bridge that had once ended in a watery nowhere.

The great villas are now replaced by high-rise hotels, mass vulgarity succeeding individual vulgarity. But Fisher's mark remains deep in southern Florida. He showed it not only what gasoline and ballyhoo could do but also how to help God finish what He had begun in Florida. For, having filled in those mangrove swamps with dredged-up bay bottom, Fisher went a step farther and dredged up more and more to make artificial islands—presto! more land to sell! Both coasts followed this lead most successfully. In 1923 Charles G. Rodes of Fort Lauderdale, a sort of junior Miami benefiting greatly from the Dixie Highway, went Fisher one better by dredging canals through a promisingly located morass and piling the spoil on either hand to make "finger islands" giving each building lot access to a road at one end and waterside on the other. In Tampa Bay D. P. Davis, hot-dog king of Jacksonville, created the Davis Islands and promoted them by free jazz concerts by Isham Jones' famous band. Conservationists now deplore the effect on marine life and the water table of thus disturbing the bottom and infiltrating land with salt water. But it still goes on in developments like Port Charlotte where water frontage for a boat greatly appeals to potential buyers.

Inevitably the waterways between Fisher's new islands got them advertised as the Venetian Islands. Among them for the benefit of photographers, and even the use of the owners, floated prop gondolas built on a model that Fisher's wife, Jane, brought home from the real Venice. Venetianism already infested the mainland south of Miami at Coral Gables, where imported gondolas plied the dredged canals that wound among choice building lots. The municipal swimming pool filling the quarry whence came much of the limestone of which Coral Gables is built was graced by an insistently Venetianish pavilion.

Born as Miami Beach was gathering speed, Coral Gables remains its less raffish foil. Its developer, George Merrick, actually put some of the millions

flooding in from eager purchasers into community amenities—that free-
form quarry pool; a Miracle Mile shopping avenue; a principal gateway
block, once housing the promotional staff, a cross between a triumphal arch
and a Castilian fortress that remains impressive even after one hears
the names of the architectural firm designing it: DeGarmo, Paist & Fink.
The Coral Gables Elementary School could be a church in the
Canaries. The City Hall is generalized Baroque of some elegance. The Coral
Gables-Biltmore is straight Central Park West of the mid-1920's. For
though Merrick's restrictive covenants were as stiff about design and
quality of construction as about race, he grew eclectic about architectural
styles. At first he allowed anything roughly Mediterranean to match the
names of the streets that his surveyors laid out among the orange groves:
Amalfi, Perugia, Caligula, Roderigo, Esteban, Minorca, Corniche—only
Avenue Gondoliere kept up the Venetian franchise. But as his scheme
became airborne, he added clusters of ready-built dwellings—one allegedly
in Dutch style, another South African, another confusingly called "French
Village (City Style)" all built before air conditioning and about as well
suited to the climate as so many igloos.

Such refinement never meant, however, that Coral Gables eschewed
tub-thumping. Merrick is believed to have spent at least $3,000,000 a year
on promotion—free concerts by Paul Whiteman's jazz band, beauty
contests of mermaids in oh-so-briefly skirted bathing suits and below-the-
knee silk stockings, and for barker-in-chief William Jennings Bryan
hollering at the public about the beauties of Coral Gables' present and
future from a platform raft in the middle of the pool; his remuneration
included choice lots as well as ample cash. A gorgeously printed and
swooningly illustrated panegyric of Coral Gables written (for a consideration) by Rex Beach, a very popular novelist, was sent free to all inquirers.
Lyrical advertisements blanketed the press in season: "Will you take the
Priceless Gift of Life? BRONZED, ERECT old men. . . . Round and
brown children. Handsome full-figured youngsters . . . evidences of the
extraordinary vitality and super health that comes [sic] from living under
the tropical skies of Coral Gables . . . the only American tropics will add
years to your life. . . ."

These "only American tropics" were actually 200 miles north of the
Tropic of Cancer. But in spite of fuzzy geography, the basic economics over
the years have borne out pitchmen's patter about how "the value of home
and business sites has increased amazingly every year." [1] Anybody who
bought in Coral Gables in the early 1920's and kept up his payments
through thick and thin came out with a very sound investment. It was
elsewhere and often that the buyer's experience lived up to the line put in
Groucho Marx's mouth as he turns auctioneer in *The Coconuts*, show
business' tribute to the Great Florida Boom: "Now folks, everybody this

way for the grand swindle! Buy a lot, you can have any kind of house you want, you can get stucco—Oh boy, can you get stucco!"

The plethora of stucco that Florida applied both to gas stations and to Vizcaya, Deering's transcendently costly palace that grew for twenty years like a gilded tumor, came of an ardent Spanish-mindedness among builders and promoters who found winter visitors highly susceptible to it. It went back to Flagler's first railroad-fed hotel deluxe, the Ponce de Leon at St. Augustine, its curlicued iron grilles and tile-paved patios betokening Florida's two centuries of Spanish rule—which was taken to mean picturesque romantics instead of the frowsy stagnation that it had actually amounted to. In 1901 the red tiles and Giraldesque towers of the Pan-American Exposition at Buffalo, New York, reinforced the epidemic that eventuated in so many allegedly Spanish post offices, schools, suburban dwellings and—as the movies boomed—picture palaces. In 1915 the hyperbolic and dramatically consistent Spanishness of San Diego's exhibition reinforced public acceptance. But for all these warnings in encaustic tile and crenellated stucco, much of the blame for the confusion of the 1920's between the Floridian and the Iberian peninsulas belongs to the association begun late in the War between Paris Singer and Addison Mizner—respectively the Maecenas and the Sir Christopher Wren of Palm Beach.

California-born Mizner was a tall, plump apprentice of an eminent San Francisco architect, Willis Peck. His addiction to Spanish idioms should probably be blamed, however, on his boyhood impressions of Guatemala, where his father was U.S. minister. Though he knew none too much about architecture as engineering and economics, he was a great stage designer— like many of Baroque's great architects—had the instincts of fashionable portrait painters of expensive women and manifested both qualities in a manner Iberian enough to have embarrassed El Cid. He was Miniver Cheevy-Gil Blas reveling in access to millionaires' checkbooks and private contempt for the millionaires—a dilute version of the view of the world taken by his brother and occasional associate, Wilson Mizner, outstanding wit and Broadway-based confidence man.

It was an odd side effect of the War that subjected Palm Beach to Addison. His patron-to-be, Paris Singer, European-born heir to some $15,000,000 from his father's sewing-machine fortune, was a sleek, suave cosmopolite, handsome, vigorous and openhanded enough to have been one of Isadora Duncan's most cordially remembered lovers. During the War he put some of his money into a hospital for wounded in France, another in England. Then he planned to build one in Palm Beach, of which millionaires' enclave he was a valued ornament. The War made building materials scarce, but Singer's purpose secured him priorities, and Mizner let himself go on the kind of neo-Hispanic palace suggested by the place, his tastes and his patron's resources. So when the War stopped before America had critical numbers of wounded, it left Singer with a prospectively useless hospital of a lofty-halled splendor that no such institution had known since Queen Anne's Greenwich. The story is that a belated sense of the appropriate determined him to convert it into a high-chinned private club of which he would be ruling spirit. As the Everglades Club it flourishes today, a principal pillar of what Palm Beach hopes to go on being.

My guess—the evidence lies in the huge area of the site and the kind of building Mizner put on it—is that Singer had a clubhouse in mind all along. If the War lasted, it would be useful for convalescents. If it stopped soon, he would have secured scarce materials for a head start on an institution that made him social arbiter of the new, post-Flagler Palm Beach. The second paid off. From his sumptuous private apartment in the clubhouse he sifted the membership according to his personal likes and, to keep iron control, canceled all privileges each season for reapplication and review. His portrait—elegantly fitted jacket and flannels, not-too-clipped gray mustache, spine still as straight as when Isadora took him to bed as her Lohengrin—hangs over the chief fireplace in the club to show what *primus inter pares* meant in Palm Beach in the great days.

Until then Palm Beach's showplace was Whitehall, Flagler's gift to a young new wife—a tall columned Beaux Arts affair that, except for not being quite so gaudy, is a Grade A Newport cottage. The advent of the Everglades Club's rich tile roofs, spasms of wrought iron, Moorishistic colonnaded windows and gaunt Iberianesque furniture shook millionaires —or oftener their wives—previously happy in suites at the Royal Poinciana or elaborate Queen Anne private cottages the size of the average high school. One after another money-dripping names—Cosden, Biddle, Stotesbury, Wanamaker, Vanderbilt—besought Mizner to outdo all others with an even more expensively Spanish set for *Don Juan* plus a roof and extravagant plumbing. He was, says Alva Johnston's pungent book about the Mizners, "adept at egging on feuding social leaders to fight it out with Mizner architecture . . . tremendous blows with new Moorish patios . . . savage counter-blasts in the shape of neo-Byzantine loggias, baroque staircases and colonnaded orangeries." [2] The former suave quiet of Palm Beach was ruined dawn to dark by the rumble of trucks taking materials and men to the sites of Mizner's works in progress.

The consequences were wonderingly described in the late 1920's in Joseph Hergesheimer's *Tropical Winter*: ". . . a long drawing-room with a cement floor and a ceiling of exposed beams . . . lemon-colored walls . . . hung with ecclesiastical silks and pictures, in the primitive manner, of saints . . . literally packed with furniture . . . in the ecclesiastical manner, with sharp carved wooden arms and rawhide seats, tall narrow chairs . . .

upholstered in tarnished silver and gold . . . a bookcase on a far wall was practically empty." The master's bed was "Spanish, with no footboard; the headboard, however, was ornamented with a painting, in crude and violent colors, of St. Stephen, stuck . . . full of arrows. The bed was raised on a high platform [which] John Clegg could not learn to remember . . . every night in Palm Beach he severely stubbed and hurt his toes. Clara insisted it was colorful, tropical; Spanish . . ." [3] and the lack of heating plant, the inadequacy of the pseudo-medieval fireplace and the openness of plan made southern Florida's not infrequent chilly spells shivering misery for even Mizner's clients warmed by the thought of how much their goose pimples cost apiece.

A contractor objecting, "This is going to cost a lot of money," when Mizner told him to tear down and revise part of a new-building palace was told: "Listen, these people can't stand the sight of anything that doesn't cost a lot of money." [4] These successive creations had names like El Sarmiento, Sin Cuidado, Lago-Mar, Villa Tranquilla. The Stotesburys' El Mirasol (now demolished) had an entrance hall lined with richly carved choir stalls. One end of Dr. Preston Pope Satterthwaite's dining room was a semicircular Gothic chapel. The swimming pool of the Phippses' Casa Bendita was a flooded cloister. With such implicit sacrilege went the omnipresent pipe organ as elaborate as anything that ever whimpered in a movie palace. The triangular-seated Old Spanish chairs that Mizner doted on and, no matter how their behinds ached, his clients sat on to dine might be genuine antiques from an Aragonese monastery or reproductions made to order and stabbed with an ice pick to simulate wormholes. In either case Mizner Industries, which supplied not only furniture but also ironwork, tiles, latticed balconies and so on, made a nice profit. Add generous kickbacks from contractors to be taken for granted in anything that Wilson Mizner touched. . . .

Toward the mid-1920's Addison went beyond covering Palm Beach with what Stephen Birmingham calls "Walt Disney Castilian." [5] (That is not unfair, yet much of Mizner's work is not as bad as it is easily made to sound; is there such a thing as good bad taste?) Succumbing to megalomania, an ailment then rife in Florida, he persuaded T. Coleman Du Pont to finance his Boca Raton, a super-Palm Beach planned to rise a few miles southward. His backer's name, like his own, was an asset. Du Pont's several previous careers, all strikingly successful, had been in coal, streetcar lines, New York City hotels and then in the great explosives-and-chemicals trust built around his family's holdings. The canals, lagoons and gondolas—electric-powered, if you please—of this synthetic paradise were to outdo anything ever attempted at a world's fair. Its cloisters—"a sort of warmingup exercise and administration building" [6]—got built in grandiloquent elegance and are still the nucleus of a hotel-club for the affluent. But the collapse of Florida's real estate spree came before the Mizners could lay the foundations of what they planned to be Boca Raton's other dominant building—a giant cathedral in memory of their mother.

Florida's Gulf Coast refused to remain given over to Mom and Pop Tincanner. Plant's Belleair Hotel with its own golf courses and rail spur had long served notice of higher things, and in due time Venetianism struck. The West Coast Venice, successfully taking the name away from Rodes' subdivision on the East Coast, was a home-and-small-farm-plus-hotels development below Sarasota into which the Brotherhood of Locomotive Engineers, caught up in the Florida frenzy, sank some $14,000,000 of its war-chest funds. When the Boom collapsed, the union had to bail frantically to keep afloat through assessments levied on the annoyed members. The glamor of the Bride of the Adriatic was even more lavishly invoked when John Ringling, chief of the clan owning the Greatest Show on Earth, moved its winter quarters to Sarasota, pondered the potentiality of the area and decided to do there what Fisher had done at Miami. Prince of an industry gaudier than Fisher's enterprises, he bought the largest local hotel, staging circus acts for the guests in the lofty lobby, and dredged the mangrove-smothered islands of Sarasota Bay into solid respectability— hence today's St. Armand's Key, Longboat Key and so on crowded with expensive shops and winter villas reached by, of course, the Ringling Causeway. For more cultivated interests he created the Ringling Art Museum and filled it with vast numbers of European canvases, mostly religious, so lamentable they are worth going far out of one's way to see; the only worse such collection is at Bob Jones University in Greenville, South Carolina. And next door is the violently Venetian palace that he built for winter residence—an even stranger phenomenon than Isabella Stewart Gardner's famous Fenway Court in Boston.

Its official name, Ca' d'Zan, is said to mean "House of John" in Venetian dialect. It should have been Ca' d'Mable, for it reflected the passion for things Venetian, exceeding that of John Ruskin, that overcame Mrs. Mable Ringling, the showman's wife, during her first visit to Europe. Its Pompeiian red and butter-yellow exterior accented with turquoise blue, ogival windows, arcades and openwork central tower would make a fine "In Old Venice" concession at a world's fair. Beyond that a certain eclecticism arises. The roof tiles are genuine Spanish antiques from a demolished slum quarter of Barcelona. The emphatically German bar was fetched from the Winter Palace Restaurant in St. Louis that Ringling much frequented. The pipe organ—essential in a house obviously bent on reaching Palm Beachy heights—cost $50,000. In the great days Mrs. Ringling was wont to board her specially built imported gondola at the foot of the waterside terrace stairs and glide to her private islet a few hundred yards away. When the hurricane of 1926 broke up the gondola, it symbolized what the more or less simultaneous collapse of the Great Florida Boom did to the Ringling fortune, which was about as overextended as the war chest of the Locomotive Engineers. The Ritz-Carlton Hotel planned for one of Ringling's islands was never finished.

Davis and hot dogs, Ringling and the circus—was there affinity between promotions on the West Coast and the world of unrestrained ballyhoo? As if to clinch the point, the amphibious area below Fort Myers was presently singled out for glory by Barron Collier, lord of Coney Island's internationally famous Luna Park and wealthy impresario of streetcar-card advertising. His plans to bring the modern world to the western Everglades so stirred local politicians that they carved him off a separate Collier County to play with. The Atlantic Coast Line built him a branch through the swamps to his baronial capital-to-be, Everglades. But motoring being already so vital to his prospective customer-purchasers, he also sought to show the accessibility of Collier County by recruiting an expedition of Model T Fords to cross the Everglades to Miami along existing routes. It took three weeks to cover those 80-odd miles. Without Seminole guides the party would probably have succumbed to starvation, mosquitoes or fear of snakes. Miami was first aware they had survived not when they chugged triumphantly into town but when two of their number trudged in on foot to announce that as soon as the final mud-to-the-hubcaps problem was surmounted, those Fords would be along. In a way, however, their arrival did prove Collier's point, and the eventual result was the Tamiami Trail part of U.S. 41—one of the few remaining relics of his scheme, which went down in the Crash like its elders and, in some respects, betters.

In both its Flagler and its Mizner phases Palm Beach was set apart from other Florida resorts by the sheer arrogance of its WASP-minded plutocracy. Jewish wealth got nowhere there. Its gambling house, managed by Colonel E. N. Bradley as stuffily as Singer handled the Everglades Club, had no smell of backing from vulgar organized crime, whereas the roulette wheels of Miami and Tampa, said Kenneth L. Roberts, covering Florida for the *Saturday Evening Post* the winter of 1925–26, were operated by "the ripest assortment of thugs, con artists and gunmen . . . ever concentrated in any state of the Union." [7] Palm Beach alone had the refinement of "Afromobiles"—double wheelchairs propelled by blacks. Yet it was not exempt from the stridency of the Great Florida Boom that began after the inauguration of Warren G. Harding and got its *coup de grâce* from the hurricane of 1926. Up and down the coast for 50 miles junior Boca Ratons and Venices lent themselves to wild jugglings, and Du Pont was by no means the only visiting plutocrat to get into the game. Previously the captain of industry or second-generation coupon clipper in his Mizner-built Casa Dinero was limited to playing distant stock and commodity markets at the end of telegraph wires. Now he could get action on the doorstep with profits almost automatic as Northern sucker money flooded southward to buy into the land boom. And for every such magnate 10,000 Mom-and-Pops were trying their luck along with—sure sign of a boom about to get out of hand—local stenographers, sweeper outers, taxi drivers.

Both southbound Pullman passengers on the railroad and southbound motorists on the newly widened and hard surfaced Dixie Highway saw the same elaborate, lath-and-plaster archways or pylons marking the entrances of new subdivisions—a form of advertising that Florida carried to heights never since attained elsewhere. Beyond them stretched scrubby thickets interspersed with attenuated pines or spiky with palmetto scrub. But in their roadside shadows shack offices spewed salesmen with maps and price lists offering Lot X-109 at $50 a front foot, 10 percent for an option, 100 percent profit in a few weeks—Lot X-110 there changed hands three times in the last month at 75 percent higher each time. Promotion methods were the same as those with which Zephaniah Scadder swindled Dickens' Martin Chuzzlewit into buying into the new city of Eden, Illinois, c. 1840. The East Coast Development Company's new-platted resort of Indrio was "America's most beautiful home town," see the utterly real-looking pictures of "The proposed hotel with an 18-hole golf course . . . salt water bathing casino . . . numerous plazas which will add to the beauty of Indrio . . ." [1] (Twenty-five years later the U.S. Census gave Indrio a population of thirty souls.) There was a great deal of buying long distance, sight-unseen sparked by such advertising in those halcyon days when "Florida was a fabled land of progress . . . God was in His heaven and Cal Coolidge in the White House" [8]—which is Elmer Davis looking back at it from 1932.

Fort Lauderdale, a military post in the Seminole War, then a trading post for alligator hides and egret feathers, attracted almost as many developers as Miami. Its promoters bore down as hard—and as successfully—as any: "Here we reach the very apex of scenic climax. Here . . . Mother Nature . . . broke her mold and threw away her palette and easel and stands forever pointing with unerring finger to the city divided by the New River as the Masterpiece of Her Skilled Creation." [9] A hundred miles farther south Key Largo City paid Ben Hecht, pride of Chicago's gamy journalism, $2,500 a week to write rhapsodical promotion copy. Renouncing the relative dignity of Bryan and Beach as pitchmen for Coral Gables, promoters hired famous press agents from show business (Harry Reichenbach for Boca Raton) and sports (Steve Hanagan for Miami Beach). It was not Ringling but a developer in the Miami area whose circus calliope toured the streets blasting out "There'll Be a Hot Time in the Old Town Tonight" to advertise Amphibious Acres. A free lunch went with the free bus trip to the development to hear the free band concert and then the auctioneer's spiel. Special free buses brought prospective purchasers to Hollywood-by-the-Sea (between Miami and Fort Lauderdale) from Chicago and New York City. Promoters paid lavishly to lure famous professionals down to the new golf courses with which developments and municipalities competed for publicity. Steam shovels created their hazards from the deadly flat Florida terrain. Beyond jazz and golf Miami booked concerts in the largest local Methodist church by Amelita Galli-Curci, most vivacious of the operatic prima donnas of the day, and Ignace Jan Paderewski, notoriously long-haired Polish politician-classic pianist, who was always good for headlines.

Little of this was original. California II's developers had practiced such blandishments for twenty years and, for that matter, had a synthetic Venice before Florida's. What made the Great Florida Boom unique—still part of American folklore like the Chicago Fire and the Johnstown Flood—was the effervescence of its credit system. The sales prospects being mostly persons of slender means dazzled by tales of money doubled in a week, first payments and installments were wildly modified. In Miami in 1922 $20 cash and $10 a month, no interest the first year, sufficed for a $400 lot; for a $1,250 lot, say, $100 cash, $25 a month for ten months, for the next seven years only interest on the balance. Rapid resale spun prices ever higher until toward the climax in 1925 most transactions involved only binders, small-deposit options often changing hands five or six times a day at a premium each time. The binder boys* in white linen knickerbockers and straw hats, talking fast and dealing faster, dominated downtown Miami as the one-piece-suit bathing girl dominated Miami Beach's publicity.

While it lasted, dreams of dazzling profit often came true. That lot at Third and North Andrews that the Fort Lauderdale Methodist Church bought for $1,000 in 1915 really did sell for $80,000 ten years later. Nor was it incredible that a Miami man turned the proceeds from selling two bottles of gin into $75,000 in eight months. Professional con men like Wilson Mizner, Alva Johnston said, were bewildered by this unique "shell-and-pea game in which the swindlers and the suckers were both making money." [10] Vaudeville comics belabored gags about chumps buying Florida lots by mail order and finding on inspection that they were underwater. Large signs standing in six feet of water showed where Sun City's Casino, Roman Plunge and Dancing Pavilion were to be. Very funny, but Florida's prowess with scoop and dredge did make many underwater sites investments potentially as attractive as many above tidemark. When D. P. Davis, creator of those fancy islands in Tampa Bay, announced plans to make more such on the East Coast, he got some $15,000,000 worth of applications to buy within a few hours. Speculation swirled so high that for the first time people swarmed into Florida during spring and summer. Hotels that had always closed on April 1 stayed open and full in the stifling dog days—before air conditioning, remember. Railroads expecting a summer

---

* This seems to have been pronounced with a short *i* as in "hinder," apparently because many of these sharp operators were imperfectly acquainted with English.

lull found themselves adding extra sections to passenger trains. Stuart Chase has calculated that at the height of it all Florida had more staked-out house lots for sale than there were families in the United States.

Plausibility was wearing thin, of course. Northern bankers were moaning because so much money needed for sober investment was draining into sterile maelstroms like Boca Raton. Some plungers grew nervous in 1925, when a temporary downward slump in stocks reminded them that whatever goes up. . . . They had no effect. What broke the Boom was no single crack in a crazy structure but a piling up of tensions along an economic San Andreas fault until slippage was inevitable. Then Du Pont acquired fame as "Daddy of the Bust" by announcing he was getting out of Boca Raton—he had had his fill of Mizners. That stifled sales of lots in nearby developments. In other areas second-payment defaults were spreading. Builders committed to put dwellings and hotels on Boom-priced land were smothering under an embargo on building stuff imposed by railroads when delivery by sea to Miami—then the only deep-sea port between Jacksonville and Key West—stopped because a ship capsized in the only channel. The Bureau of Internal Revenue contributed by a ruling (soon rescinded, but Humpty Dumpty had fallen) that income tax was due on the more breathless turnovers. By early 1926 things were so ominous that *Variety*, no-nonsense paper of show business which had covered the Boom as both sociological slapstick and source of bookings for entertainers, headlined FLORIDA SLIPPING.

Indeed it was. The next few months of crash, shakeout, whatever one called it, wiped out most of the taxi drivers and Mom-and-Pops, most of the binder boys and minor promoters and smashed or crippled even the great ones leading the dance. Fisher, D. P. Davis, the Mizners, Ringling, even Merrick of relatively stable Coral Gables went broke or the next thing to it. Then, late in 1926, floundering efforts to salvage the pieces blew away in the first severe hurricane to visit Florida since it had joined the Follies.

Nobody knew just how hard it had blown, for the government wind gauges carried away when unreasonably asked to record velocity above 120 mph. Newcomers to Florida had no experience with hurricanes, so their buildings included no precautions. Around and in between Miami and Fort Lauderdale some 5,000 dwellings were destroyed, another 9,000 heavily damaged; 25,000 persons were shelterless. The mayor of Miami, fearing for the imminent tourist season of 1926–27, tried to play down the extent of the damage but succeeded only in heading off badly needed emergency help. The big blow cannot be accused of killing the Boom, for it was already dead, says Charlton W. Tebeau's admirable recent history of Florida, but it "certainly buried it in devastating fashion." [11] Among the first things to blow away were, of course, those symbolically flimsy gateways to Amphibious Acres. Winter visitors trickled back in some numbers in the season of 1927–28 but "few spent and none invested," [12] recalls a Fort Lauderdale old-timer. Then to make sure the Northerner's subliminal response to "hurricane" would be "Florida," another struck in late 1928, forcing Lake Okeechobee over its low margins and drowning more than 2,000 people, many of them Bahamian blacks imported in contract labor gangs. As unidentifiable skeletons kept turning up in the swamp grass later, some put the toll over 3,000.

Hindsight sees this sunkissed boom-and-bust as harbinger of the economic earthquake of 1929–30. The notion has merit, though the national phenomenon was so much more complex that close connection is hard to establish. Florida's debauch did absorb billions in cash assets that might have helped when Wall Street had fits a few years later. A patient destined to anemia does well to avoid hemorrhages. But had Florida's troubles been nationally symptomatic, California II's real estate, fermenting with much the same organisms, would have come a similar cropper at the same time—which did not happen.

What Florida and California II had in common was climate plus the WASP American's folk belief that gambling in land was a good way to riches and in any case to a self-admiring sense of shrewd abilities. In 1850 among our forebears named Smith and Jones the smart land speculator, even on a small scale, ranked with the clever horsetrader as a man to take seriously. Land was profitable and honorable to acquire, true, but not necessarily to be clung to, European peasant-fashion. Americans tended to sell out at a premium, take up new land farther west and do it again. And as towns grew into cities, many Smiths and Joneses were well aware how within their own lifetimes the farm Uncle Lester sold for $200 an acre became a bustling suburb in which business lots went at $200 a front foot. Florida's and California II's cookie-cutter lots enabled those of small resources to play this game. That was how Felix Isman, a prominent real estate broker of Philadelphia, explained the great Florida Boom to readers of the *Saturday Evening Post* just before the bubble burst.

What Florida and California II did not have in common—this may be why Florida went bust first—was the same degree of impact from the automobile. For both states it was primarily the snowballing motor industry with its corollary rubber, oil, steel and so on that pumped into the economy the spare money that rained on the subdivision salesman. In both, these subdivision lots would not have been salable had their potential owners not had automobiles or access to them. But the Florida boundary lay only 1,200 miles or less from three-quarters of the population of America, in 1925 already a reasonable motoring distance, whereas it was double that or more to Los Angeles and under worse driving conditions. Hence Florida got a far higher proportion of the kind of winter tourist/potential sucker on whom the Boom fattened. Visitors to Miami and Tampa in the early 1920's were amazed at the wide variety of state names on license plates. Early in the fall of 1925 the typical highway funneling into Florida was so heavily traveled

that Roberts likened it to "an articulated serpent 1500 miles in length." [13]
For the first time more people entered the state by automobile than by rail
and sea combined. Sun-mindedness was similarly affecting Europe's
Riviera, where since the War property values had risen three- and fourfold.
But fiftyfold in Florida—necessarily the peculiar result of the automobile,
which most Europeans lacked. Gasoline-on-wheels was what enabled
America to turn Flagler Street into a madhouse with Standing Room Only.

Even before America's herd of horse and mules actually diminished, the
turn-in on the new car was replacing the horse trade as an important folk
game. In a battle of wits between the veteran of a thousand deals and the
skittish customer the amateur came out winner seldom—but, as manufacturers' pressures on dealers fluctuated, often enough to tickle up those
fancying themselves as hagglers. As for other sports created or fostered by
the automobile, the principle that anything that moves can be raced
operated from the beginning. The Vanderbilt Cup meet annually befouling
the air of Long Island and getting into primitive newsreels was only the
gaudiest American imitation of European road racing. Closed-track racers
were soon roaring around and around the dirt tracks of fairgrounds—hair-
raising nurseries for natives hoping to replace the European drivers who,
like European cars, dominated our first speedways. The now venerable
bricks of the Indianapolis Speedway were laid two years before the War.
The famous 500 soon lost whatever excuse it had as proving ground for
motors and tires. But its basic attraction—the implicit possibility of seeing
drivers die violently at high speed—persisted, so annoying Lardner that he
printed right on the sports page of the Chicago *Tribune*:

> O, to be a race fan,
> And near the speedway stand
> And see somebody drive himself
> Into the Promised Land.[14]

Grandstands and sun-soaked infields counted on drawing sweaty, shirt-
sleeved rowdies from all income groups not only itching to witness sudden
death but by then secondarily addicted to the whine of tortured motors and
the stench of castor-oil lubricants. The next year they had more shrines to
worship in. The wooden-surfaced Chicago Speedway opened in 1915; on
the ocean side of Long Island so did the Sheepshead Bay Speedway with
seating for 130,000 cash customers. The big race was called the Astor Cup.

Using automobiles, hunters and fishermen could go farther afield faster;
hence heavier pressures on populations of fish and game. As road speeds
heightened, groundhogs, cottontails and pheasants suffered out of season as
well as in; skunks, 'possums and raccoons took heavy casualties at night.
Between exhaust fumes and widening of thoroughfares to accommodate

thronging motor traffic, the great trees that were the finest features of Main Street were doomed. Farmwives had to learn that poultry could no longer stray safely. Without low-priced automobiles to take players to their fun, golf might never have pervaded middle-income as well as millionairish strata, for though streetcars served office, church and school fairly well, only the scarce public golf courses were located with much regard to where the trolley line ended.

As for sport afforded by Amaryllis in the shade, the internal-combustion motor really did deserve much of the blame for the Flamingness of Youth. The extent to which American lads and lasses were free of chaperonage had long startled the British and flabbergasted Continental Europeans. The sanctioned buggy ride reputedly—and often actually—led to unsanctioned behavior. But what buggy riders needed optimum weather and surroundings for was no trick at all in even the meager dimensions of the back seat of a Maxwell or Reo. Not that, as previously surmised, motorized "spooning," soon "necking" and then "petting" went "all the way" anywhere near as often as now. But to judge from such internal evidence as that in F. Scott Fitzgerald's early fictions, the effect of the automobile was vastly loosening well before America entered the War. The Reverend Wilbur F. Crafts, national superintendent of the International Reform Bureau (soon to father Hollywood's Hays Office), had reason to demand that Henry Ford "frame legislation that will stop the use of the motor car for immoral purposes" [15] —a thing probably beyond even Henry's high ingenuity. Joe College's car, a Stutz roadster if pop was rich, likelier a secondhand jalopy lettered with slang clichés, was the anchor of his erotic destiny.

Trouble for the streak-of-varnish passenger train loomed up when, soon after the War, advertisements boasted that Buick had equaled the scheduled time of the Southern Pacific's Shasta Limited between San Francisco and Portland, Oregon. The ramifications were many: a grotesque speeding up of funeral processions as well as the death of old industries like buggywhip making. The automobile had a chief part in the enormous growth of advertising after 1919 not only in its own right but also for tires, gasoline, auto horns, tire chains, lubricants, storage batteries. . . . In 1922 some 22 percent of full-page insertions in the *Saturday Evening Post*, pacesetter of printed salesmanship, already represented automobiles or products directly connected, hopelessly outdistancing the former staples of general magazine space—drugstore stuff, health cereals, home appliances, haberdashery. By 1927 the ratio was 40 percent, two of every five full pages. The West Coast attributed the post-War feebleness of the IWW not only to shattering prosecutions in 1918–20 but also to the motorization of migrant labor as the booming market for new cars made secondhand ones available at low cost. Fruit picker-harvest hand-bindle stiffs, largely single men, hopping freights from one seasonal job to another and holing up in urban skid rows in off season, were giving way to harried heads of families

chugging from vineyard to orchard in decrepit Model T's. Pay scales had
risen little, so wives and children also turned to on any fieldwork that could
use them. This not only robbed such families of the domestic integration
that goes with fixed abode, but also broke up the comradeliness of shack,
bunk- and flophouse on which Wobbly organizers counted. The hopeless-
ness of these proto-Okies was unmistakable. No solution has yet appeared.
But how hard it would have been for a Slovene peasant to understand that
any family owning an automobile, however ramshackle, could be called
poverty-stricken!

At the same time the automobile in the shape of the schoolbus was
speeding up creation of the consolidated schools that brought under one
large roof pupils from the one-room schools of several contiguous districts.
Two or three miles afoot being the maximum expected of any pupil in even
those rugged days, consolidation necessitated wheeled transportation. For
some decades sporadic use of school wagons—horse-drawn affairs with
storm curtains and a pupil driver, horses borrowed from farmer-parents in
rotation—had struggled with this problem. The trouble was that a good
part of the school year weather and primitive roads combined to frustrate
wheels and horses. Experiments with motor trucks fitted with bus bodies
showed that in passable weather they could spread the consolidated
school's pupil radius to fifteen miles or so and in the worst weather were
little worse off than horse-drawn vehicles. This extra capacity increased
demand for improved roads . . . and in due time the sealed-surface
highway, creating the intercity type of bus, came along to make sure that
Dick and Jane Farmer would thenceforth be spared the daily, runny-nosed,
overshoe-cumbered, wet-mittened, dawdly struggle on foot that had so
handicapped rural schooling in most of America too much of the year.

The consequent large consolidated school drawing children for ten miles
around was all tapestry brick and big windows, had heating better than the
one-room school's wood stove; had graveled play yards for recess, often a
gymnasium, certainly flush toilets instead of the slatternly twin privies;
offered the stimulating presence of kids from other parts of the county,
yearly change of teacher from grade to grade, maybe departmental classes
in some subjects. It cost less per capita thus to concentrate pupils than to
pay the teacher of the one-room school. The relative reliability of a motor
bus combined with better roads did much to solve the problems of tardiness
and absence that had always plagued previous arrangements. No wonder
educationists thought this consequence of internal combustion was pure
gain. The only people dubious were the drivers of the buses, usually adults
on part time who had to keep order among forty ebullient children while
also keeping both hands on the wheel and one eye on the road. In the
emergency of World War II it proved that by and large women could
handle the discipline better and the bus as well as men. Here was a new job
for country women of a sort that Haynes, Duryea and Ford can hardly

have thought of when so zealously adapting the horseless carriage to American needs and conditions.

Sealed-surface highways lifted not only the curse of mud but also that of dust, despair of the fair-weather motorist. No more dustcoats and voluminous veils muffling up the ladies; away with stuffy goggles that made drivers look like frogs. The rush of air at 20 mph could now be so pleasant that the family motor drive on Sunday afternoon temporarily became as firm an institution as Sunday dinner's roast chicken. The Model T and the secondhand market soon extended this privilege well below middle income. Inevitably, as more and more automobiles took part, traffic congestion leached the pleasure out of that Sunday afternoon drive. There was no more open road to enjoy, and "Sunday driver" came into the language to blame the other cars for the accidents and tie-ups that plagued everybody. The automobile still got plenty of Sunday use but no longer in a drive for its own sake, rather to and from golf course, beach or ball game.

Before congestion stifled it, however, the gasoline-scented pleasure drive begat the modern superhighway—strange as that sounds. When the automobile was largely an expensive toy-convenience, several Eastern cities ornamented themselves with "parkways"—special, genteelly landscaped avenues for see-and-be-seen promenades of the carriage trade in horseless as well as horse-drawn carriages. Some such parkways survive intact—Philadelphia's Roosevelt Boulevard, New York City's Grand Concourse as straightaways, Boston's Fenway for sinuous variations. . . . The usual plan was of dual one-way roadways each with at least two traffic lanes, medians planted with trees, shrubs and seasonal flowers, more planting on outer margins to mask sidewalks, dwellings and delivery wagons. Cross streets were carried under the parkway or dead-ended into flanking service roads, so that refined vehicles could roll through rich, pampered greenery as if in a private estate undisturbed by everyday traffic. The service roads enabled authority to bar commercial traffic and keep private access driveways from fouling up the flow. Add those underpasses and multiple traffic lanes. . . .

An early attempt at pollution control was the next step. New York City's neglected little Bronx River had become intolerably foul. It was decided to clean up its banks and protect it with a motor parkway reservation. The consequent Bronx River Parkway completed well up into Westchester County after War-occasioned delays, delighted the affluent suburbanites of Scarsdale and White Plains with its manicured new scenery, absence of trucks, over- and underpasses to tame intersections and blissfully unimpeded transit from their pseudo-Tudor and -Georgian mansions into town. This example led Westchester County to ornament its suburban lower reaches with a whole system of interlocking parkways of notable elegance. Gracious curves offered successive vistas of prettily tamed meadows and groves. Directional signs were of undressed wood with rustically twiggy lettering. Rough stone made overpasses picturesque and lent a Cotswoldy air to the service stations quaintly pumping gas and fixing flats at proper intervals. Even when the leaves were off in winter, cleverly planned lines of sight kept the sense of isolation strong. In summer only an occasional glimpse of the kitchen end of a suburbanite's house far to left or right reminded the motorist that life is not all chlorophyll. The Westchester parkways even operated their own police force to impose decorous speed limits. The curves were engineered for a then-reasonable limit of 40 mph on the principle presently laid down by Robert Moses, creator of the Long Island parkways: "My idea of futility is to build a beautiful parkway for speed demons who can't tell a flowering shrub from a bale of hay." [16]

For a while Westchesterites not only used the picnic and golf facilities that went with their parkways, but also took leisurely drives along them in spring when the dogwoods made a great show and in fall when oaks and maples were ablaze. A few still do. In time, however, such parkways became mere traffic sluices clogged twice daily as commuting tides set cityward and suburbward. A critical error had been made at the start. They fed into major routes into New York City and New England. The very kinds of motorist whom Moses deplored, intent on getting from Murray Hill to Bridgeport in a hurry, plus traveling salesmen, learned that the parkways' miles without traffic signals, intersections and cars backing out of hot dog joints were far preferable to the miseries of the old Boston Post Road, alias U.S. 1. Such use gratifyingly increased the toll revenues that financed the parkways but also swamped the original genteel purposes.

When Connecticut built its Merritt Parkway to connect with the Westchester system in the 1930's, it retained the term along with the tradition of landscaping, non-eyesore architecture, limited access and ban on commercial traffic. But the Merritt's curves were engineered for a then-realistic 50 mph, and its avowed purpose was not so much recreational as to take the load off U.S. 1 by siphoning off private automobiles unwilling to compete with its thundering herds of long-haul trucks. After World War II Westchester had to fall in line and spend millions setting up dividers, reducing curves, elaborating interchanges—in general engineering the abandonment of the original notion. Ironically the name "parkway" still clings, however, to high-speed, limited-access, sometimes toll-charging superhighways distinguished from freeways only by barring trucks. Maybe somebody in Westchester can derive gratification from the county's having inadvertently helped to create the gaunt, hell-snorting efficiencies of the Los Angeles Freeways and the New York State Thruway.

Drivers were soon delighted with parkways for affording mile after mile without a traffic light. The phrase dates itself. Electricity and remote control did not take over from live policemen and hand-operated GO/STOP semaphores until the mid-1920's. The delay is puzzling. Why was the traffic-directing policeman not an institution long before automobiles took over? By most evidence horse-drawn hacks, buses, drays, grocers' wagons and bicycles often combined with clanging trolley cars to create monumental traffic jams on Market Street, Broadway and Wabash Avenue. After all, a great many such vehicles were all trying to use the same space at the same time, and a cab horse and attached vehicle took up at least as much room as the average automobile of 1920. Nobody had yet thought of definite traffic lanes. The custom of driving to the right was trusted to prevent absolute chaos, and often failed. Yet the police seem to have confined themselves largely to helping timid ladies across.

Anyway the accumulation of automobiles just before the War forced city police to stand in intersections and compel discipline. Thus was born another side effect of the automobile, the most commanding figure of our day—the traffic cop. Burly and resourceful, risky to talk back to, magically governing thousands of tons of hurtling steel and hundreds of mutually antagonistic wills with mere flips of his massive hands, that is the symbol of authority that comes readiest to American minds now that parents and teachers are deposed.

Somewhere, probably by 1914, a member of this new profession devised what educationists call a visual aid to supplement gestures and whistle—circular placards lettered GO and STOP in green and red respectively, a color code borrowed from railroad usage. Then such placards were mounted on a thing like a standing lamp with a handle to twist it to show GO and STOP. Spreading all over the country, this so embedded red and green in the national consciousness that practice moved on to imitate railroad block signals by dropping the letters, using only red and green lights. Presently New York City built the equivalent of a railroad control tower at the intersection of Fifth Avenue and Forty-second Street. Designed with an effort at elegance to suit its location, it looked like a Parisian *pissoir* high on four skinny legs. Godlike therein sat policemen juggling remote-control traffic lights to match traffic flow as observed for a mile or so in all four directions. It was as widely talked about, favorably and unfavorably, as Mencken and Nathan's new *American Mercury*, but torn down in a few years because it seriously impeded the very traffic it was meant to expedite. Meanwhile, its conspicuousness at the nation's most noted intersection had dramatized the docility with which American drivers would take discipline from mere inanimate incandescent bulbs behind red and green glass.

Acceptance was not at once universal. Though its traffic jams reached Manhattan-like proportions, Miami, Florida, did not install traffic lights until 1925, and then most gingerly. But eventually all over America, where Main Street crossed Center Street, where the factory entrance debouched on the highway, then where arterial highways intersected out in the country, various arrangements of clockwork-timed red and green lights overhead, on the corner, presently varied by yellow wait-for-the-change lights and blinking red stop-and-go lights, were dictating—click! br-r-r-r-rm!—what motorists and pedestrians could do. Hence a new cliché for the book-writing European—the strange spectacle of the American driver stationary at a prairie crossroads, no police car or any other kind visible for miles in any direction, waiting good as gold for the guts of an automatic gadget to turn its light from red to green. That, avers the amazed alien, could never happen *chez nous autres*—one of the very few contexts in which Europe compliments America on being law-abiding. It mystifies Frenchmen and Italians almost as much as what seems to them our softheaded willingness to hold relatively still for income tax. They never mention the esthetic aspect of traffic lights, the achingly clear colors of which, seen against a clear sky halfway through a winter dusk, are among the few lovely consequences of the automobile.

The substitution of soulless, if beautiful, red and green for blue-coated men did not, however, abolish the archetype. Precalculated patterns of light change to match traffic needs cannot allow for special occasions and the unexpected. On holidays, during rush hours, fires and so on, society still sends the traffic cop to mediate between traffic lights and the unruly facts of the situation.

The flounderings of early traffic control showed how ill prepared the nation was for the post-War flood of automobiles. Perspective is needed: Congestion was nothing like what it is now. New York City, for instance, allowed parking on up-and-downtown avenues midtown late in the 1920's, and though curb space was scarce after 9 A.M., one could usually find it in the next side street. But public protests against what was already considered intolerable were loud. "A motor car is a handy thing," *Life* said in 1922, "but when the cars begin to crowd the people out of New York it is time to do something," [17] and proposed a complete ban on on-the-street parking, even on private automobiles in Manhattan's streets—measures that, though now ten times worse needed, the city has not yet had the courage to try fifty years later. The same editorial rejected as preposterous, however, other measures now widely in effect, such as banishing trolley cars* and hollowing out parking garages under parks and squares as in Boston and San Francisco. Those in charge have only begun to see that making things handier for automobiles in cities merely attracts more of them and makes congestion worse than ever.

Minor but irksome sequelae appeared as car production in Michigan and

* They took trolleys off the street because the rigidity of their paths on rails hampered growing motor traffic. Buses pulling into and away from curbs to pick up and discharge were the substitute and believed to be more flexible. So they were, but the confusion caused by their persistent lane changing to reach the curb is so marked that in many cities buses are now being confined to buses-only lanes in the middle street—in effect a return to the old system that got the trolleys suppressed—and the trolleys were much less polluting.

Indiana hit its post-War stride. People complained in vain about roadside lunch litter lining the routes to Florida and California and through the best Sunday-driving country. The hitchhiker's thumb was soon an institution, and its owner already had a poor reputation with the law and less softhearted motorists as he learned to take advantage of public good nature. The menace of the roadside slum was yet only faintly discernible, though tourist camps were multiplying. So were roadside stands selling hot dogs or barbecue sandwiches, and the gas pump was moving from in front of the general store or the mechanic's garage (probably a converted blacksmith's shop) to its own establishment across the road, already called a filling station. So were the twenty-four sheet advertising billboards along the major highways, and here too complaints, though heartfelt, were largely in vain.

And compared to public comment on the state of the roads, they were whispers. The country was large, cars newly numerous, demands on the hapless old roads unreasonably sudden. Money and energy were going into highway improvement, but today's Brobdingnagian earth-moving equipment did not yet exist, and to the motorist using tire chains and fence rails to get out of mudholes, progress seemed slow. The summer of 1923, four years after road builders got their post-War start, was, according to the Statler Hotels' advertisements, the first season when highways up into Michigan from Chicago and Detroit could be recommended to tourists seeking enjoyment. James Montgomery Flagg, a ranking illustrator of the 1920's, driving from New York City to California, found the National Road main streets of Ohio towns as full of chuckholes as if "they had been shattered by an earthquake"; Columbia, Missouri, was "an asphalted oasis in a sea of mud." [18] Throughout Nevada the largely hypothetical Lincoln Highway lacked even markers to show where it would run if it did. In identifiable stretches the ruts were so deep that the drain plugs of crankcases had worn grooves between them. California already had ably engineered and usually navigably dry highways that pleased Flagg greatly but eventually meant, of course, that the state was doomed to suffer severely from infestation with cars. Driving coast to coast was still deemed venturesome enough for corny motorists to fly those lettered felt pennants boasting more clearly than mud-covered license plates that this car breezing through Phoenix had come all the way from New Britain, Connecticut.

Yet there were shoals of them. Over such daunting highways 180,000 automobiles reached California from eastward that year. Duffus saw "so large a proportion of our population [being] able to break loose and go on these long and not wholly inexpensive journeyings" as "a sign of surplus wealth widely distributed." [19] For the extent of road improvement was not an infallible index of automobile use. In 1920 seven of the eight states in which the ratio of automobiles to residents was highest were not in the better organized, affluent and better road-surfaced Northeastern quadrant but in the trans-Mississippi farming and ranching country where roads were worst and distances longest; in California, of course, but also in Iowa, Minnesota, Kansas, Nebraska, South Dakota, Montana, Wyoming, where in spring the mud was a bottomless cross between fresh mortar and chewing gum. The Model T, renowned for doughtiness though it deservedly was, had no monopoly on the privilege of bucking these rugged conditions. Six years after Henry Ford had introduced his masterpiece, Hupp, Oakland, Regal, Page-Detroit—ah, the long-extinct brands!—were still outselling him in towns of population under 5,000 as token that they too could conquer roads that would make angels weep.

The farmer was the logical best patron of the American automobile c. 1920 because country folks got the most out of the contraption at the least social cost. People talked about how the telephone, the interurban trolley, rural free delivery (by then covering most of the farm population) and parcel post (inaugurated in 1913) had broken down the stultifying isolation of the farm family. All true as far as it went but soon less impressive because the automobile was revving up in the wings to effect ten times as much. The telephone alerted the doctor quickly, but it was his Maxwell runabout that fetched him 10 miles at speed no horse could match. RFD brought the daily paper, but it was the Model T that took the family to town to see the movies advertised in it. With RFD and parcel post one no longer had to hitch up and drive to a distant express office for one's order from a mail-order catalogue. But such buying was rather a pig-in-a-poke matter, whereas the automobile offered frequent trips to the stores of sizable towns where selection was wider, price comparison clearer, color, size and style more easily gauged. The sociologist in the anecdote asked the farm wife why her household had an automobile but as yet no bathtub; she replied: "You can't go to town in a bathtub." To cope with this new situation the giants of the mail-order industry, Sears, Roebuck and Montgomery Ward, had reluctantly to set up the vast chains of retail outlets that now do most of their business.

Along with the minor conveniences of his touring car, the town dweller also got noise, air pollution, parking problems, higher chance of getting killed in the street and heightened anxiety about his children's morals. The automobile-using farmer's air stayed pure, he parked in the old buggy shed, alien cars did not go by often enough to build up strain in his nervous system or to imperil any but the dogs, cats and poultry and his daughter's behavior in consequence of new, motorized opportunities was at least no worse than the city girl's.* Soon radio and rural electrification would take the farmer even nearer equal command of the new privileges of his day. But

---

* There was a bright lining in that according to an ingenious enthusiast of 1916 compiling the good things about the automobile. By relieving young farm folks of the confined radius of horse-and-buggy spooning, it reduced the menace of local inbreeding in rural gene pools. (James Reed Doolittle, ed., *The Romance of the Automobile Industry*, 1916.)

they too were supplements like the telephone. The vibration and speed of the family car had already shaken and blown most of the hayseed out of the hair in addition to what automobile-encouraged good roads had done for his marketing tactics and the education of his kids.

In America's curious economy—recall Duffus' point about the motorists swarming toward California—the noisy, smelly luxury that Europe invented for the rich became the vehicle transforming millions of farmers and ranchers into Main Street bourgeoisie. Something like that also came to pass in Canada and Australia too, even to some extent in Europe. But in the 1920's it was another of the things that could happen only in America. Henry Ford was near sense when telling an interviewer in 1924, "There are no places 'remote' in this country. The automobile has corrected that." But, being himself, he had to go on into fatuity: "When the automobile becomes as common in Europe and Asia as it is in the United States the nations will understand each other. Rulers won't be able to make war . . . the people won't let them." [20] Morris Markey had a steadier view when on a journalistic prowl of the country in 1932: ". . . farm life in the Middle West has lost the . . . basic element of rusticity. . . . They are no longer rustics at all, those who farm the prairies, but people located at an inconvenient distance from town." [21] For good or ill.

The automobile's role in the thirteen years of national disgrace under Prohibition was peculiar, possibly crucial, anyway needs careful statement and description.

The innate flaws in what President Hoover rashly called "a great social and economic experiment, noble in motive and far-reaching in purpose," [22] might soon have ruined it anyway. In horse-and-buggy times repeated breakdowns of local and state Prohibition had shown how in any accessible community alcoholics, tipplers, barkeeps, grafting politicians, venal police, unscrupulous doctors, bootleggers, moonshiners, home brewers and rum-runners—all characters well known before the Volstead Act in suitable contexts—could keep the Demon Rum snortingly defying the law. In that pre-automobile past, lawbreakers used hooves, wheels and their own feet to frustrate the law's hooves, wheels and feet in so many jurisdictions that it took great naïveté or great wishfulness to assume that federal forces could do any better. Nevertheless, a major reason why Prohibition unraveled so fast that it hardly ever really began was the new use of gasoline transport—a technological advance giving unsporting advantages to un-righteousness. Powerful automobiles of large cubage and springs heavy enough to take 150 to 200 gallons of alcohol in gallon cans; light, fast trucks; overmotored launches—all tactical godsends for smugglers just when Prohibition gave them a golden opportunity.

The law also employed automobiles and motor launches. But it was usually undermanned, lackadaisical or corrupt and always starved for money, so its motorized tools were obsolete and slow, whereas the unsavory characters running booze over the border or down from the hills usually had the fastest wheels available. Little illegal tipple reached the consumer's bloodstream without making at least part of the trip by motorized means. In the urban moonshining that soon sprang up in industrial suburbs and obscure city warehouses, a truck took the corn or cane sugar to the still; another purporting to deliver for a dairy or a bakery took the still's alcohol to the cutting plant; a fast automobile took the resulting bottles of so-called whiskey to the bootlegger, who took them to the customer in any automobile that looked innocent enough.

Most such whiskey was mere alcohol diluted with tap water, colored with caramel, flavored with prune juice—or, if scotch were intended, creosote. It went down better as memory of what real stuff tasted like dimmed. Long before Prohibition the lower barkeeps had employed these arts. Other bootleggers exploited genuine whiskey smuggled in from Canada or Rum Row. One bottle usually begat two or three as the cutting plant added alcohol, water and supplementary flavoring—the same process that makes today's blended whiskey—a rather better tipple that costs more. The labels, unlike the contents, might improve on the originals. The color printing on a fifth of genuine Gordon's gin that I acquired in 1929 from a friend's father's cellar was cruder than that on the counterfeit Gordon's label on bottles from my bootlegger.

In the Northeast genuine-as-labeled liquor came from Rum Row— booze-stocked ships hove to off large cities as near shore as the Coast Guard's harassment allowed. They rigged special chutes overside for rough-weather loading of the stripped-down shore launches that took fifty to seventy cases a trip. This seagoing liquor bazaar had a marked technological edge on the Coast Guard. Not in its ships—they were mostly obsolete auxiliary schooners or elderly tramp steamers, usually British in registry, hence safe from seizure while they stayed outside the territorial limit applying at the time. But the shore launches painted lead color, Navy-style, dousing lights for the night work they preferred, armored forward against machine-gun fire, had the most modern of hairy-chested gasoline motors driving them at 30 to 35 knots, which made the law's underengined small craft look foolish.

Locating the ships at night was easy. To attract the attention of shore buyers, they lighted up regatta-fashion until, the Coast Guard said, the eastern horizon looked like Coney Island. A smallish schooner could safely load 5,000 cases of scotch at Bermuda or Canadian rye at St. Pierre-Miquelon, the French fishing-colony islands off Nova Scotia. The going price of known brands tax free out of bond, $10 or so a case, left enough profit for distiller and jobber. The Rum Row shipowner got $40 or so a case from his tough-bargaining customers in the shore launches. Throughout all dealings the deckhands stayed heavily armed, for informal piracy always hung over the legal limbo of Rum Row. Piecemeal deals took long to empty a ship, but in six months at most she was back at Bermuda with $200,000 in cash; deduct $50,000 for expenses, including high wages for a crew sitting out there so long in view of the lights of Manhattan reflected over Long Island . . . easily 100 percent profit after the owners had bribed the British or French officials to wink at fraudulent clearance papers. (Bermuda and the Bahamas had precedence for such enterprise; during the American Civil War both had prospered from blockade-running.) Soon operations were vertically organized. The Canadian-American Lillian mob had its own shore boats as well as mother ships that stayed 30 miles off the Jersey coast—the new "steaming distance" limit created by international treaties in 1924 to help Uncle Sam cope—and under radio control landed some 40,000 cases a month.

Rum Row's wares were not invariably genuine. Some cargoes consisted of Cuban alcohol cut and flavored at sea into whiskey, gin or whatever, bottled with labels fetched out from shore. But most of what was landed was unimpeachable, and some of it might reach Park Avenue uncut at high prices to match. Likelier, plutocrats paid high and got cut stuff anyway. Their chances were better during their winters in Florida. For fast, small craft Cuba and the Bahamas were only a few hours from Palm Beach, so Rum Row's middlemanning was not needed. By 1922 virgin scotch and Bacardi rum were available in southern Florida at $50 a case retail. Such prices reflected not only the nearness of sources but also the sluggishness of the Coast Guard below Jacksonville and the opposition of local resorts to enforcement that might send thirsty winter visitors to less law-abiding places. A chief of police aware that he'd be fired if he let anybody molest bootleggers was easily bribed. In the economics of Prohibition, keep in mind that since the whole supply was illegal, it paid none of the heavy state and federal taxes that normally make up most of the cost of legal liquor. The kind of pure straight alcohol that goes into licit gin and vodka cost 35 cents a gallon to distil in the 1920's. So what Prohibition did was to turn the nation's power to tax over to the underworld and corrupt public servants. Bahamian rumrunners could have paid their crews well, bought faster, larger boats each year and still given Florida good scotch at $25 a case. Obviously their profits were huge.

In absolute terms the amount of waterborne contraband liquor was not negligible. In 1923 a Coast Guard officer recorded the tonnage of the ships on Long Island's Rum Row and, by observing how high they rode when leaving station, made rough estimates of how much they had sold—an average of 2,000 cases a day, say 8,670,000 bottles, largely fifths. A much smaller amount came directly into New York City and other ports in proportion from the crews of foreign ships. (My shady landlord on Eighth Street did such business with stewards of the French Line.) Say a bottle each for every resident of Manhattan, Brooklyn and the Bronx, babies included. But in view of the Big Town's habits that was only a fraction of what was drunk, and for the nation at large a mere drop in the shot glass, as the Coast Guardsman admitted. In his opinion the bulk of Gotham's exotic supply came by motor across the Canadian border and through the intervening several hundred miles.

That was also true of the northern half of the nation. By the hundreds of roads and trails of all degrees of passability into New England and the Northeastern states, by the broad or often handily narrow waters separating the nations between the Adirondacks and Duluth, booze flooded, trickled or seeped in. College boys in upcountry New England got kicks and supplements to their allowances by amateur forays over the border. ". . . you cannot keep liquor from dripping through a dotted line," [23] said Roy A. Haynes after resigning as chief of the U.S. agency to enforce Prohibition. The volume depended on nearby demand modified by the diligence—or lack of it—shown locally by the U.S. Customs, the under-manned Prohibition Agency and the overworked Coast Guard, always ill coordinated and all proving from time to time to be corruptible. Even when the Canadians regularly informed U.S. authorities of consignments of liquor clearing their customshouses, boats carrying 800 to 1,000 cases a trip plied the Niagara River between Ontario and New York State with suggestive impunity.

If comparisons are possible in a field so wide and obscure, maybe the leakiest stretch was that between Lake Huron and Lake Erie. At Windsor, Ontario, warehouses bulging with liquor lay in full view of the booming, hard-drinking capital of the automobile kingdom of southeastern Michigan. After dark the wakes of rum-running launches were seldom absent from the Detroit River. Some stuff came in by rowboat above Lake St. Clair; I know because on moonlight nights, when visibility was too high for their purposes, the rumrunners let us kids borrow their skiff. At the other extreme the Miller mob of Detroit had three powerboats with a capacity of 400 cases each; they shipped from Detroit by truck and rail to Chicago and even New York City. (Rail shipments were best disguised as carloads of lumber.) A U.S. Prohibition Service investigator wrote in 1929: ". . . conditions on the Detroit River . . . for several years were notorious . . . very difficult to understand why this situation should have been allowed to continue." [24] Any frequenter of the Detroit waterfront could have explained—flagrant bribery and intensive corruption.

More Canadian liquor came out of Puget Sound ports ostensibly consigned to Mexico but diverted into California. The Gulf Coast and the U.S.-Mexican border were leaky on smaller scales. From Mexico direct came mescal and tequila as well as alleged whiskey produced by several distilleries that foresighted gringos had dismantled and shipped south of the border for reassembly. Foreign governments seldom tried to help Uncle Sam square the moral circle. The British and French saw no reason to damage national industries of which America had long been a prime customer. Canada did little to curtail exports to bootleggers that meant higher profit for distillers and handsome revenues from the $7-a-gallon tax on spirits. Theoretically the tax was refunded when the exporter showed a certificate that a legitimate buyer abroad had accepted delivery; but that requirement was seldom met, and Ottawa kept the money. The Dominion's income from that source rose from $18,000,000 in 1914 to almost $50,000,000 in 1928. The Canadian-born Distillers Corporation-Seagrams, Ltd., today's international giant of hard liquor, got its first vigorous growth from slaking America's self-imposed thirst with whiskey sold cash on the barrelhead. ". . . we knew where it went, but . . . I never went to the other side of the border to count the empty Seagrams bottles," [25] Samuel Bronfman, founder of the company, once explained; he died worth some $40,000,000.

On the eve of Prohibition America's per capita consumption of beer was rising, that of spirits falling—which doctors and some sociologists had welcomed. Either drinking habits were improving or the brewers, sponsors of most saloons, were promoting beer more effectively. With Prohibition that trend reversed. It was already known from state efforts at Prohibition that because bulky, low-priced beer was relatively hard to smuggle, bootleggers preferred to handle compact, high-priced hard stuff. The shift was modified, however, by Uncle Sam's laxness about near beer made by extracting alcohol, which meant that numerous breweries were awash with real beer awaiting emasculation. Bribery and undermanned enforcement lubricated clandestine diversion of vast quantities and saved many a brewery from bankruptcy. The nineteen breweries brewing away during Prohibition in Milwaukee alone could have supplied all the near beer the nation could possibly absorb. Producing "wort"—the cooked-up cereal broth that fermentation turns into beer—kept others solvent. Run hot into five-gallon cans, it was legal to sell, and the brewery selling was not responsible if the buyer used it in an "alley brewery" supplying local speakeasies from some dismal abandoned warehouse. Or a brewery confining itself to near beer might prosper in a community where barkeeps mixed into each glass enough bootleg alcohol to restore—or double or triple—the kick. Such spiked near beer was more popular than hard stuff among certain strata of young folks in Detroit in 1925. Sometimes, if rumor was correct—and to judge from the hangover resulting, it was—such "needling" was done with ether, giving a greater kick per cc than alcohol.

The venerable art of household brewing, long since wiped out by federal tax regulations, revived at once. What cereals to ferment how long at what temperatures became a national obsession. A college professor assured a lady reporting for the *Pictorial Review* on the early phase of Prohibition that the taste was hardly noticeable if the stuff was kept very cold. Those too easily put off could use malt syrup, a sort of concentrated, canned wort, just

add water, yeast, and wait. . . . Hardware stores sold foolproof bottle
cappers at $2.50 each, and American folklore soon included bits about Pa's
home brew exploding in the cellar at three A.M. Politicians beholden to
California's grape growers put into the Volstead Act a provision that the
head of a household could make up to 200 gallons of wine a year for family
use. Ethnic groups from wine-growing cultures, notably Italians, Hungarians and Greeks, swarmed through that gap to buy so many grapes that
California's vineyards expanded in six years from 97,000 to 681,000 acres.
"God make dees contry for growin' da grape," exulted the Italian
vineyardist of *They Knew What They Wanted* (1926). "Ees not for pro'ibish
God make dees country. Before pro'ibish I sell my grape for ten, maybe
twelve dollar da ton. Now . . . sometimes one hundred dollar da ton.
Pro'ibish is make me verra rich." [26] The mounting output of both California
and New York State vineyards was sold in bricks of compressed grapes to
be crumbled and stirred into water etc. etc. and in bottles and kegs of grape
juice tagged with warnings how *not* to handle it in a carefully detailed way
lest it turn into illegal wine.

By no means all the results were drunk at home as the law required.
Much found its way to German and particularly Italian speakeasy
restaurants in large cities. Some of the white wines were marginally potable,
but the "red ink" in any given place called Tony's was usually dreadful.
Many Americans for whom that was their first experience with Bacchus
have never since been able really to relish red wine, however glorious.
Morris Markey described the quality of wine in his favorite Manhattan
speakeasy, a very pleasantly decent place, as "based, quite honestly, upon
the axiom that an American doesn't know a good wine. . . ." [27] At least
such wines were genuine.* Nightclub champagne analyzed after seizure
usually proved to be cider carbonated and spiked with alcohol. Its brazen
cost led most whoopee makers to bring their own alleged gin to the Silver
Slipper and pay high for setups of ice and ginger ale, which killed the taste
better than Coca-Cola. On the label of the ginger ale thus sold in a
dancing-and-gambling deadfall across the river from St. Louis (it was called
the Mounds Country Club though it had neither golf course nor tennis
courts) it said: "Reminding you of the eighteenth amendment and the
Volstead Act, the contents of this bottle is sold to you on the understanding
that it will not be used or mixed with any alcoholic liquor." [28]

Such Pickwickian warnings were rife in the moral climate of Prohibition.
Europe exported to America legal because de-alcoholized gins and ver-
mouths analogous to near beer. "REAL VERMOUTH," said Mouquin's
advertisements. "Just 5 ounces of pure alcohol [have been] removed from
each bottle for use in this country." British-made, nonalcoholic Holloway's

---

* A useful by-product of Italian bootleg wine making was *grappa*, Italy's equivalent of
France's *marc*, distilled from lees. In my time it was the least hangoverish and cheapest spirits
available in Manhattan.

gin cost $2 a bottle on mail order. Homemade "bathtub gin" was, of course the staple of the middle-income drinker of the 1920's, mixed with the standard ginger ale or Angostura bitters or with orange juice in an Orange Blossom cocktail, degenerate cousin of the Bronx. We made it not in bathtub lots but a few quarts at a time with alcohol bought by the gallon; two parts alky, three parts water, a scant teaspoon of juniper drops from the drugstore—some bootleggers supplied it with the alcohol—and a table-spoon of glycerine to smooth it. They said age improved it, but the experiment was never tried, and anyway it tasted little worse fresh than what the bootlegger sold in fancy-labeled bottles at higher price—to be exact, 3.3 cents per ounce as against 2 cents. Now that standard gins—rather more palatable, true—retail at toward 15 cents an ounce, those sound like and were bargains even allowing for the vastly lower purchasing power of the dollar. Again set much of the differential down to the exemption of illicit liquor from excise taxes.

Something—discretion? probably not—kept efforts at home-distilling few. Only now and again did chemistry students rig laboratory glass into elementary stills and run off alky to supply the fraternity house. Where all the purchased alcohol came from is not clear. One said and hoped it was diverted "hospital alcohol," pure, hence safe. Gossip, the press and both Wets and Drys (viewing with alarm from opposite bases) dwelt on the risk of blindness or death from hooch made of "denatured" alcohol—industrial alcohol dosed with this or that to make it unfit to drink. The risk was not nil. Early in the 1920's Hartford, Connecticut, Boston and New York City each saw a dozen or two deaths over Christmas from that cause. Commander Evangeline Booth of the Salvation Army crudely advised the Wickersham Commission of 1930 that such alcohol could raise the nation's level of sobriety by killing off the incorrigible drunkards: ". . . 50 per cent of the old soaks kill themselves and 50 per cent quit." [29] Dr. Herman N. Bundesen, coroner of Cook County, Illinois, and commissioner of health in Chicago off and on, told an interviewer that bootlegger-gangsters were "Distillers and Distributors of Death, Unlimited." [30] But then Dr. Bundesen had a keen eye for headlines. Had risks of the order implied been real, they would have shown up in vital statistics—as they did not. What did show up in the U.S. Census and data from the Metropolitan Life Insurance Company was that under Prohibition, meant to lift the curse of overindul-gence, the incidence of deaths from alcoholism—not from poison liquor—crept up from an encouraging .014/1000 population when Prohibition began to the .4/1000 rate that had prevailed in 1911.

Alcohol was denatured in two ways, both legal. One, intended for industry, automobiles (for antifreeze) and chafing dishes and camp stoves, was dangerously laced with toxic and chemical cousins of grain alcohol. Theoretically judicious "cooking" (redistilling) removed these hazards, but the process was so unsure that bootleggers usually procured and cooked only the second sort, intended for use in perfumes, hair tonics and lacquers, so readily reclaimed that even the Drys admitted that more than 5,000,000 gallons a year of it were annually diverted into beverage use. Bay rum containing some 60 percent of it was widely sold for drinking in Knoxville, Tennessee. ". . . the users do not get staggering drunk," the police chief said, "but they do get crazy and their eyes bulge out." [31] A 10-cent bottle from the dime store usually sufficed, but some needed double that for the optimum effect. In Denver, Colorado, lilac hair tonics of the same alcohol rivaled bay rum among underprivileged topers. In Detroit analysis of a bootlegger's stock found that his bottles labeled "Pebble Ford" and "Kentucky Tavern" actually contained diluted and flavored "Parisienne Solution for Perspiring Feet, 90 Per Cent Alcohol." * The one thing to be said for such tipple was it couldn't be as bad for you as the Canned Heat or Sterno, chiefly wood alcohol, that Commander Booth's miserable old soaks drank under the delusion that straining it through a sock made it safe. But Prohibition could not be blamed for that. For years derelicts had drunk such "smoke," heedless of warnings.

The bulk of what bathtub gin makers used was probably virgin grain alcohol from the sizable illicit stills that organized hoodlums set up in or near cities. Lace curtains masked the windows of the bungalow at the corner of Twelfth and Jefferson that they bought from a retired couple moving to California and gutted to make room for mash vats and a three-spout copper still turning out 200 gallons of alky a day. The neighbors often noticed high-powered automobiles entering and leaving the backyard garage by the alley, but for what doubtless seemed weekly good reasons the local police paid no heed. Or the mob might force a nearby farmer to choose between a strong-arm going-over and high rental for the old barn beyond the woodlot. They also made still tending an equivalent of the cottage industry of the 1700's, paying slum families, again usually Italian, $10 to $15 a day to turn their sordid tenement flats into alky factories. Uncle Sam's men, handicapped as they were, knocked over 172,537 stills in 1925, and yet, as the chief of the Prohibition Bureau admitted, for every one thus shut down nine others went on operating unscathed.

A still master who knew his job, and he usually did, kept the quality high. Federal agents confiscating alcohol that analyzed up to standard often gave it to hospitals for laboratory use, so the hospital alcohol that internes supplied their friends might be bootleg in origin after all. Actually bathtub gin made from sound alcohol was healthier drinking than genuine bonded whiskey dependent on minor impurities for its rich flavor. In any industry so ill regulated as moonshining, however, quality was unreliable. In Pittsburgh in 1926, for instance, when a new group in City Hall forced on

---

* The best joke that came out of Prohibition told of the man who, suspicious of a new brand his bootlegger supplied, sent a sample to a chemical laboratory for analysis and received the finding: "Dear sir, your horse has diabetes."

local speakeasies alcohol from a new ring that was "right" politically, patrons buying gin for home use noted with concern that after a few days the new brand developed a sinister green surface scum.

Moonshining's chief transport consisted of battered but souped-up eight-cylinder touring cars in which poured down from the hills growing streams of the traditional corn liquor of Appalachia that many Southerners preferred to revenue-stamped stuff even before Prohibition. Now its gasolinish flavor had symbolic point. New Jersey's applejack from the Ramapos and the Pine Barrens attained national renown. Prohibition agents already vexed by Rum Row had knottier amphibious problems when moonshiners set up stills in swampy places inaccessible save through water up to here—in the Great Dismal between Virginia and North Carolina, source of a famous cypress water whiskey; in the Mississippi Delta and westward; farther north where the Mississippi's numerous cutoffs and islands opposite Tennessee gave the unsavory characters of Arkansas good hiding for stills; still farther north where the same river topography lay close to the triple cities of Moline, Rock Island and Davenport.

Trickles of illegality from drugstores were not new to the federals. In state or municipal previous efforts at Prohibition, the doctor had often flagrantly abused his privilege to prescribe spirits or wine. Obliging or venal physicians wrote sheaves of prescriptions; opportunistic pharmacists encouraged them. Drugstore back rooms became bars for well-known customers; forged prescriptions were rife. To judge by withdrawals from bond of pints of Old Glory on prescription in the early years of Prohibition, a large minority of Americans suffered from whatever ailment 100-proof whiskey is good for. Presently, however, enforcement had its sole success in this field; within a few years withdrawals sank to a reasonably low plateau and vigilance kept them there. The druggist's revenge on Volstead lay elsewhere, in selling quantities of sticky wine tonics—native sherry containing some 20 percent of alcohol plus just enough medication, usually quinine, to qualify as medicine legally salable over the counter. I met this in some fastidious households that would never have patronized a bootlegger. The Virginia Dare brand, 22 percent alcohol, ostensibly recommended for pernicious anemia, was popular among the bedraggled Indians of Arizona and Colorado, who probably got little harm from it except the misery of a wine hangover and a slight ringing in the ears from too frequent ingestion of quinine.

The U.S. Congress' ambivalence toward Prohibition contributed to its failure to get off the ground. While Senators and Representatives shrank from vexing strategic minorities of Dry voters by modifying the Volstead Act as the Wets wished, they were just as reluctant to stir up the taxpayer, already smarting from the intrusive novelty of income tax, by giving enforcement agencies enough money really to test whether Prohibition could work. Leading Drys seemed to feel that since Prohibition was now (a) the law of the land and (b) righteous, it was up to the man in the street to make it stick. Let him stay on the wagon himself, ostracize those who drank and put pressure on local and state authorities to finance underpinning subfederal enforcement. When Wets pointed jeeringly to the striking nullifications of the Volstead Act described above, Drys as well as federal agents accused the states and municipalities of lying down on the job. Give Uncle Sam adequate help from right-thinking state legislatures, district attorneys, local judges and police chiefs, they said, and the Dry millennium would dawn after all.

The reproach made some sense. Failure of Rhode Island and Connecticut to ratify the Eighteenth Amendment had been ominous to begin with. In 1923 New York State repealed its Prohibition law supplementing the Volstead Act. In 1929 Wisconsin did the same by popular referendum more than 3 to 2 for repeal. Particularly in cities—for, other things being equal, the larger the town, the wetter the sentiment—nonfeasance was likely even without corruption. Or where arrests were frequent, the penalties were fines so light that, as one federal investigator justly complained, they amounted only to a local license system. In such climates Inspector This and Alderman That not only neglected to cooperate with the federals, but often sabotaged agents' efforts to do their duty.

State-level attempts to improve enforcement by stiffening laws came to little. The most stringent such legislation was Indiana's "smell law" passed in 1924 under pressure from the Klan, which had virtually taken over the state government and was making a show of Dry energy. Most state Dry laws duplicated the Volstead Act, but this one went beyond anything ever introduced in Congress. To sell, possess or give away liquor risked a mandatory sentence of thirty days to six months (for a first offense); so did the display of a cocktail shaker in a drugstore window; to transport even a spoonful of liquor in an automobile risked jail for from one to two years. Proof of the possession of empty bottles once containing intoxicating liquor was admissible evidence; the smell of the bottle was often sufficient. ". . . a bottle found on your premises, though a passer-by may have thrown it over the fence, is yours unless you can prove to the contrary," Elmer Davis wrote. Yet two years later, though country districts where there never was much drinking anyway were fairly dry, "humidity is as high in Indianapolis as anywhere in the country except for New York and the East Coast of Florida." [32] Granted, Davis was no teetotaler, but here is an investigator for the Prohibition Service in Indiana late in 1929: "Conditions in most important cities very bad. . . . Lax and corrupt public officials great handicap . . . prevalence of drinking among minor boys and the . . . middle or better class of adults." [33]

To judge from other such agents' findings for the Wickersham Commission, most of the other states were much the same. Local variations might occur, as in Columbia, Missouri, where Flagg found that the drink a local newspaperman offered him consisted, to his astonishment, of an orangeade at a drugstore fountain. But even in Kansas, which had a long tradition of Dry-mindedness, a severe state Prohibition law and no large cities, federal agents reported in Kansas City many "joints . . . ostensibly selling soft drinks, etc., but . . . trafficking in liquor." [34] In Leavenworth: ". . . strong evidences of collusion between the police and the liquor interests," and the chief of police and several cronies were under prosecution under the Volstead Act. In coal-mining Cherokee County many unemployed miners were prospering as moonshiner-bootleggers making "fine . . . whiskey . . . carefully blended . . . the best known brands sell from $8 to $12 a gallon . . . pure-grain alcohol made here . . . compares well with the best . . . legitimate alcohol." Wichita had ". . . several large liquor and racketeering groups . . . conditions so bad that the police . . . commenced a general clean-up [but] . . . the county attorney and sheriff are too friendly with the lawless element . . ." [34] Lawrence, site of the state university, was fairly dry, but Topeka, the capital, was well supplied. Kansas' annual deaths from alcoholism, far below the national level before the War, rose more than 300 percent in the seven years 1922–29.

Persons disliking hole-and-corner drinking had a cumbrous but popular recourse in visiting the rum-soaked open bars of Cuba and the doggeries of the scurfy Mexican towns opposite Brownsville, Laredo, El Paso and so on. (Canada's several Provincial efforts at either Prohibition or abolition of the saloon kept it from a major part in Americans' exotic carousing.) Passenger shipping out of New York City and New Orleans did well from the rush to Havana. So did vaudeville jokesmiths and such Tin Pan Alley numbers as "I'll See You in C-U-B-A." As booze-hoisting Yankees discovered that Havana had gambling casinos and brothels as well as bars, American relations with the Pearl of the Antilles suffered. From what Cubans saw of us, and we saw of Cuba, neither culture could possibly respect the other. Think what it must have been like when, in 1920, Delta Kappa Upsilon, a high-ranking college fraternity, held its national old grads' convention in Havana.

But Cuba was at best a sometime thing. Most people unable to be comfortable without a rail under the right foot patronized the speakeasy that, in all versions between wide open and darkly cryptic, plagued Dryness from the moment the Volstead Act went into effect. The word itself was used as far back as 1889 in allegedly Dry Kansas. There was the "club" kind, dues 50 cents an evening for all comers or with a key to the front door given each steady customer; or the cocktail in the teacup in the tearoom; the peephole with the suspicious eye so readily mollified by "Joe sent me"; the false-front business. An undertaking parlor in Detroit never saw corpses but used its hearses to bring in liquor for the ostensible mourners; in a downtown lawyer's office the receptionist politely told inquirers that Mr.

Caveat didn't take such cases as they had in mind, while welcoming people already known into the back room where the bar was. In New York City the International Hair Net Manufacturers' Association displayed a sample hairnet in a frame on the wall plus one rolltop desk and a safe containing a few shot glasses and several bottles of disastrous whiskey. . . .

Such concealment-minded speakeasies usually gave the patron an identification card to spare parley at the door. Worldly people accumulated such cards as their sons did short snorters in World War II. As enforcement slackened and more towns turned wide open, this peephole-and-card routine existed largely to give drinkers the flattering illusion of being insiders. For in the latter 1920's, as Westbrook Pegler, then a brilliantly astringent reporter very much at home in such places has recorded, Uncle Sam pretty well gave up raiding "except in jerky spasms." [35] I knew one nice little French speak where apparently the only entrance requirement was to wish the eye in the peephole "Bonjour." The doors of another a block from Jefferson Market Courthouse stood open all summer breathing beer in the neighborhood's face, bar and drinkers clearly visible to passersby. In Kansas City, Missouri, a restaurant with waitresses openly fetching cocktails and beer operated across the street from police headquarters. In most large towns one of the formerly grand General Grant mansions, usually taken over by chiropractors or masseurs as downtown decayed, became a lavishly curtained speakeasy-restaurant serving affluent locals recognizable cocktails and thick steaks. The same racket took over the chicken-dinner roadhouse on the Branchville Pike. The local German beer hall too exercised folding green reason on the local police. Its policy of substituting near beer for needled after the third round made the carouser wonder why the stuff suddenly tasted better at the time and why next morning he didn't feel worse. At any local hotel a word to the bell captain brought to the room in half an hour a bottle of something reasonably potable but unreasonably priced.

The go-between and the interval were the same as those required to procure a girl, and the prototype of the speakeasy masked behind a business office was the urban candy- or cigar-store fronting for bookmaking. Those affinities meant the more because in a given city the higher-ups in the rum-running-moonshining-bootlegging ring had probably cut their racketeering teeth on pre-Prohibition pimping, gambling and narcotics supply. They already knew how to fix cops and shake down and muscle in on crap joints, brothels and cabarets. They had only to apply those familiar skills to this fourth field opened to them by the Drys' ill-founded optimism. The speakeasy might well still occupy the old premises of the pre-Prohibition saloon headquarters for dope, whoring and gambling, paying graft to the same precinct captain and protection to the same police lieutenant. When the late 1930's showed a tendency to romanticize bootleggers and speakeasy thugs as folk heroes, Pegler scotched nostalgia with the chilly truth that "most of them were criminals by nature or too lazy to work for a fair living . . . [and had] a gift for treachery, robbery and murder." [36]

Prohibition's repercussions were important in proportion to the Drys' failure to foresee them. Proto-Flaming Youth had already been tilting the bottle in a car parked near the country club or down by the old millstream, but doubtless the tingle of conscious lawbreaking further encouraged such behavior, as viewers-with-alarm insisted. Under Prohibition young people could get at liquor more easily anyway because once it was illegal, laws against selling it to minors no longer protected them. Before 1920 the respectable saloon and the established package dealer had had good reason to observe restrictions. Then Prohibition crippled the hotel industry just when, as automobiles began to change travelers' habits, it needed all its strength. For the bar was the little gold mine that kept prices in the dining room reasonable and the books out of the red even when room sales were slack. The guests still drank, but now it was the bellboys and the local hoodlums who profited, not the stockholders of the new fifteen-story Hotel Zenith. And there were international effects as articulate Old Worldlings— and the Cheevyites, of course—took Prohibition as an hypocrisy peculiarly American and uncivilized, forgetting that Finland and a couple of Canadian provinces had also fretted themselves into trying outright Prohibition—and *mutatis mutandis,* were doing no better with it.

The worst damage, however, came of giving the already-tenacious American underworld the resources to become a major force in the economy. Drys and Wets agreed that by the mid-1920's the booze racket in all ramifications employed some 500,000 people. At $40 a week—higher than average city worker's wages at the time, but extra pay went with risks—call the payroll some $1,000,000,000 a year. Add the cost of corruption and millions paid to exotic suppliers, and the industry had to gross some $1,400,000,000 to break even. Since it was fantastically profitable, else the city mobs would not have been in it, assume another quarter billion for profit—total $1,650,000,000. But that is a moderate computation. On another basis: The chief of the Prohibition Agency told Congress in 1925 that enough alcohol to make 150,000,000 quarts of booze was annually diverted. At an average cost to consumer of $2 a quart, say $300,000,000. Add double that revenue from the product of gang-sponsored and hillbilly stills = $900,000,000. Add half that again for beer at bar prices and $150,000,000 for imported spirits = $1,800,000,000 total well toward the $2,000,000,000 accepted in Andrew Sinclair's recent well-researched book *Prohibition.* That is considerably more than the nation spent in 1930 on highway building, maintenance and highway bond interest.

And those were dollars of the 1920's, when the gross national product was not far above $100,000,000,000. That is, from drink alone the mobs took in toward 2 percent of the GNP. Since they usually kept their holds on drugs, prostitution and gambling, put their total economic leverage at at least 4 percent. With resources thus strengthened they could now expand their existing protection rackets—the blackmailing of small businesses—and invest behind dummy fronts in racing plants, the booming highway-construction industry, show business, inconspicuous banks. Such ostensibly legitimate enterprises were useful as camouflage for illegal doings, and anyway something had to be done with all the accumulating loot. It couldn't all be spent on gold-plated women, racehorses, diamonds the size of buckshot, silk suits, foot-long cigars, bulletproof Cadillacs, mansions on islands in Biscayne Bay and $10,000 caskets when something sudden happened to a close associate.

Demand for fancy caskets was high because the several mobs working a given area seldom succeeded in permanently observing spheres of influence. No matter how harmonious agreements sounded, how firmly terms were stated, they fell apart under chiseling as quickly as those of garment manufacturers and railroad presidents. Sooner or later the X gang warned certain speakeasy operators that they owed it to their safety to switch to X-sponsored beer. If the veteran chief of the Y gang, in whose territory those speakeasies lay, protested, he got told he was all mouth and no muscle—and the paid thugs of both mobs began to rack up killings to vary the routine torture, mayhem and bodyguard duty of their workaday lives. In four years of the early 1920's Chicago, become national symbol of wide-open Wetness and gang war to match, saw 215 known gangster killings, an average of 1 a week, most of them making headlines for a fascinated public. When the victim was eminent, his funeral was smothered in huge flower arrangements, mourners with bulges under the armpits and headquarters detectives trying to guess what it meant about future gunplay that a certain hoodlum known as Big Gus was present and another named Packy had chosen to stay away. For gangster funerals were like the lineup of top USSR brass on Lenin's tomb at May Day parades in Moscow—vehicles of economic and diplomatic information important to outsiders. When the latest big shot dying with his handmade alligator shoes on did not have as many flowers as had appeared at last year's outstanding obsequies, it meant not only that the deceased had been slipping but—here was the rub for his henchmen—that his mob was losing clout.

For the general public these grisly, petal-scented occasions made the front page by prescriptive right like the World Series. The first such celebrated the taking off of Big Jim Colosimo, a ranking Chicago purveyor of vice expanded into bootlegging, by Frankie Yale, a hoodlum from Brooklyn sent to do the job by Johnny Torrio, Colosimo's chief rival. The list of honorary pallbearers—a member of Congress, a member of the Illinois legislature, an assistant state's attorney, three local judges and nine aldermen—made the victim's bribe and blackmail power blatantly plain. Four years later the ante was sharply raised by the funeral of Dion O'Banion, king of one of Chicago's three chief mobs, shot dead in his flowershop headquarters. (It really did sell flowers to the public as well as for mob funerals.) His silver and bronze casket was sent from the maker's factory to Chicago in a special express car. Silver angels holding golden candlesticks stood at its corners as the chieftain "lay in state"—the press as well as his courtiers used that phrase—in an undertaking parlor crammed with sightseers as well as hoodlums. The nearby sidewalks were so thronged that mounted police had to clear the way to the hearse for the casket. In the cemetery 5,000 people were waiting to see the interment.

Then the underworld of Brooklyn outdid O'Banion flower-, casket- and hullabaloo-wise in laying to rest Frankie Yale (born Uale) who had become a power in his own right and got killed in turn. But there was no challenging Chicago as gangland par excellence. It might be the hemisphere's greatest railroad center, mother of modern architecture and modern American poetry, "hog butcher for the world." The gangs of New York City, Philadelphia, Detroit, New Orleans, San Francisco might also float on booze and violence and stink to heaven. But thanks to local genius for turbulence and overdoing, the stench of Chicago-as-gangdom, soon concentrated in the squat figure of Al Capone, another importation from Brooklyn, drowned out even the smells of Mayor Thompson and the stockyard district. Particularly the extravagance in column inches—yards, furlongs, miles—of Chicago's press coverage of the most picturesque local industry, with the national and then the world press panting behind, brought this about. The gangster's world became a folk background for commercialized fantasy, and Chicago was to this idiom what Tombstone and Deadwood were to the Western—generically the place where they said "take him for a ride" and "muscle in," where a violin case implied a tommy gun, where George Raft absorbed lead with a pan deader than Buster Keaton's and Edward G. Robinson gave his celebrated imitation of a sadistic gargoyle. In the process, the leading mobsters became heroes (in the classic sense anyway), a mere glimpse of whom in person was a cherished memory.

Now and again an adult Chicagoan objected that such emphasis on one connotation of "Chicago" might give the place a bad name. But the gangster motif was good for daily and Sunday circulation, and by the mid-1920's damage was irreparable. Capone was on the topmost rung of notoriety, his name as recognizable as Babe Ruth's, well before the Valentine's Day Massacre gave Chicago its most renowned gang killing. All over the world, wherever news services and movies reached, those three syllables approximating the Indians' name for "place where wild onions grow" meant killing and corruption—all understood to be inseparable from Chicago = America.

That was grave external damage by stereotype. Internal damage came as Chicago did more than any other place to tempt the nation to believe that bootlegging and the ancillary vices and bloodshed were monopolized by

Italians of the first and second generations. In 1929 the Chicago *Tribune*'s expert on mobs wrote that 85 percent of the chiefs of bootlegging were Italian- or Sicilian-born and another 10 percent were Jewish. Actually of the names mentioned in his windy but reliable account of gangsterism in the 1920's only 41 percent are Italian, whereas 16 percent are certainly Jewish and 32 percent unmistakably Irish. But remember Nathan Glazer's tantalizing remark about "the . . . degree of truth that most stereotypes have, that is, a good deal." [37] Such a head count—it included an appalling number of corpses—does give the group named Lombardo, Nerone, Calabrese and so on a high plurality, and one gets a strong impression that as the years passed, the relative incidence of Irish dwindled, maybe by attrition, and the incoming recruits working toward power were largely Italian. Though WASP America needed no lessons in lawbreaking from the Unione Siciliana, one cannot ignore the affinity between the known ways of the underworld of the *mezzogiorno* and those of the Yales and Torrios. America's first stereotype of the Italian in the New World was the underfed organ grinder. Then came the Black Hand oozing sinister violence. Now it was confirmed on the grand scale. Italy had succeeded Ireland as the accepted mother of organized criminals and crime.

And what symbolized the gaudy Italian gangster? The big black automobile, flagship as well as workhorse of what Prohibition had wrought.

The automobile industry shared the depression that dated nominally from the Wall Street crash late in 1929. So did the steel, rubber and other industries supplying Detroit. But the Depression was not even-handed about blighting enterprises connected with the automobile. Its effect on the bootleg liquor trade, for instance, is inscrutable because the mobs understandably neglected to publish figures, and anyway Repeal cut the ground from under them a few years into the Depression. For surmise, the booze rackets may not have been hurt in proportion to the hardening of hard times. Those hit first and worst—farmers and the lowest-paid wageworkers—were those who had patronized bootleggers least, so relatively little business was to lose there, and the woes of those in higher brackets may have led many to keep up with their drinking. As for that by-blow of Detroit's now called the motel industry, it was gloriously independent of Depression. Every year from its birth sixty-odd years ago it grew and took in more money. In the 1930's, while the nation was tearing its peace of mind and economic traditions apart to assuage its pangs of fear and hunger, this Jack's Beanstalk actually created thousands of new jobs, many for unskilled women doing its housework.

Its founders were obscure opportunists in California and soon Florida, renting campsites to Sinclair Lewis' gypsying Sagebrush Tourists, "Paste-board suitcases lashed to the running-board, frying pans and canvas water-bottles dangling." [38] The numbers of them lacking tents soon suggested to campsite owners the building of marginally weatherproof shacks to rent for 75 cents or so a night. The site probably already offered a latrine, maybe a miniature commissary with sandwiches, basic groceries, pop, tobacco, motorists' sundries. Even after the shacks were known as tourist cabins, they were built just sturdily enough to hold together if it didn't blow too hard. A campsite owner in Arkansas building a few told his wife he'd use them for chicken houses if motorists didn't rent them. Lewis described even the relatively advanced examples in the early 1930's as "apparently constructed by the carpentry class of a kindergarten. The only reason why no resolute burglar had not picked up a couple . . . was . . . they would have been of use for nothing but kindling." [39]

Early specimens in California II were furnished with a dangling electric bulb, a table and benches of rough boards; no bed, for the customers expected to sleep on the floor in their own bedrolls. Even so these houses-that-Jerry-built beat tents and could be run up for some $75 each. The owner of one such layout told a footloose patron from Minnesota that he had rented every cabin every night since they were built. The Minnesotan figured $365 a year gross; investment $75 plus so much for cost of site and taxes . . . within eighteen months he was using materials salvaged from a decayed fairground to build the first tourist cabins in Tallahassee, Florida. Eventually this fast thinker, Herbert Chandler, was an outstanding figure in the motel business in the Southeast.*

For a while it looked as if tourist cabins would get only the least affluent trade because of the "tourist home," the square, verandaed dwelling on Center Street in the county seat that gave motorists what the sordid local hotel failed to—decent comfort in the clean spare room with its double brass bed presided over by a large brown print of Burne-Jones' "Sir Galahad," use of the family bathroom with its smell of Ivory soap—$1 a head, 50 cents extra for a hearty breakfast. By the late 1930's Duncan Hines, compiler of motorists' guides, was recommending several hundred such places in his now-forgotten *Lodging for the Night.* Some still persist and, now that motel prices are so high, often offer good relative value. But privacy is seldom adequate, and they isolate one from one's car. A forgotten map or handbag means sneaking downstairs and maybe waking a landlady who seldom looks as if she takes disturbance kindly. Once motorists above the flivver-campsite stratum proved amenable to $2 a night, cabin owners installed beds—of the cheap flat spring type, true, but with sheets on them—then, as price acceptance nudged upward again, wash stands, toilets. . . . Thenceforth, as motorists multiplied like fruit flies, the future was the tourist cabin's.

Its location on the fringe of town in a shady grove was often pleasant and

---

* These details and more in this section I owe to the files of the *Motel/Motor Inn Journal,* formerly the *Tourist Court Journal.*

usually quieter, and the car stood handy at the door. Additional cabins deployed around three sides of a rectangle with the owner's office-dwelling at the corner near the highway. Upgrading roofed over the intervals between cabins to make carports—and behold the tourist court! or (California's term) the motor court, of the type soon to be immortalized by Clark Gable and Claudette Colbert in 1934 in *It Happened One Night*. Shrubbery and garden furniture made the center space look inviting. For the last 20 miles possible patrons had been wooed by roadside advertising signs promising quiet and comfort at bargain rates and straining for names at once enticing and memorable: Blue Bird Tourist Court, Moon-Winx Court, Autopia Motor Court, The Doll Houses, Dreamland Cottage Court, DanDee Cabins cropped up in the Southwest and Florida, which set the style of the industry. But onomastic enterprise was not confined below latitude 36°N. The Kimball Kottage Kamp, for example, flourished in Kimball, Nebraska, with a name obviously created by George F. Babbitt. In 1939 a local couple bought it, added four cottages with private showers and heated garages, put in 200 Chinese elms—a species noted for ability to survive Great Plains weather—and renamed it elegantly The Elms.

By then America had some 20,000 tourist courts. Almost half offered "cafés" ranging from open-wall sandwich counters to minor restaurants with tablecloths and liquor licenses. In winter resort areas where much of it began, there had been small need for heating; at least sun-seeking customers were told so. But as tourist courts spread northward and year-round use of cars grew, small potbelly stoves came in. Too few of the customers could handle them, so bottled gas heaters came in. Too many customers asphyxiated themselves, so central heating took over. Since that was impractical for isolated cabins, new-built tourist courts began to eliminate the carports in favor of contiguous units with party walls—also a cheaper way to build. But the innocent flimsiness of uninsulated clapboard would never do for party walls lest the snoring or quarreling or too vigorously enjoyed harmony in No. 7 keep No. 8 indignantly awake. Sound insulation through sturdier construction, often poured concrete or concrete block, cost far more but also saved fuel and proved cooler in hot seasons—and lent itself well to the pseudo-Spanish design that, originating in the Southwest, afflicted the highways of the nation for the next twenty years.

The term "motel" came out of California, probably earlier* than the first surviving use of it that I can trace—in San Luis Obispo on Route 101, where the name Motel Inn cropped up in 1925 and still persists on a cheerful complex of California Spanish cottages, each with its own heating,

---

* Doris Elizabeth King, professor of urban history at North Carolina State University, outstanding authority on the history of American public accommodations, believes that the well-publicized use of "motel" in the name of this San Luis Obispo operation was largely responsible for its adoption elsewhere.

bathroom, telephone and garage. Nobody trademarked "motel," so any-body could and some did use it right along. But it did not supersede "tourist court" and "motor court" until after World War II. Some ascribed the tourist court's sudden spurt of widened amenities to the choosier kind of patrons driving to Chicago's Century of Progress Exposition in 1933. Anyway, the late 1930's filled out the essentials that the motoring public came to look for: a single-story range of separate-ingress units each with full plumbing; often some sort of restaurant; and the office at the entrance with two standard features—a rigid policy of pay-in-advance and a VACANCY/NO VACANCY sign. This new American institution, as original as the mint julep, deserved its Depression-defying success. It saved the motorist the traffic and directions problem in finding hotel or tourist home in a skein of strange streets. No extra charge for garage, no problem with street parking. No tipping. And Mrs. Motorist did not have to march through the hotel lobby with no opportunity to tidy up after a day's travel that left skirt wrinkled and hair every which way.

Hints of wider organization superseding the Mom-and-Pop operators going back to shack-and-latrine days appeared in small chains, such as the Alamo Plaza Courts, whose Hispanicistic installations were spreading out from their native Texas, and in the Quality Courts Association, offering guaranteed standards and furnishings and free-to-the-patron advance reservations among members. Most motorists had yet to bother about reservations, however, so court operators often went into attention-calling more elaborate than mere roadside patter: "21 miles to/KIT CARSON MOTOR COURT/Showers—Flush Toilets—Own Cafe." The Tower Motor Court outside Omaha, Nebraska, housed its office in an eighty-foot tower of vaguely "modernistic" design visible to potential patrons for many miles across the flat prairie. Nelson's Dream Village near Lebanon, Missouri, relied after dark on a $2,000 fountain with twelve different spray patterns succeeding one another in changing colored lights. Bain's Motor Court, near Santa Barbara, California, recommended itself with a roadside tableau in highly colored plaster of picturesque pioneers and their covered wagon. Or there was ethnic picturesqueness, as in the Walt Disneyish Danish Village on U.S. 1 in Maine. The effect on roadside scenery was quite disastrous well before Pearl Harbor.

Tourist court owners were realistic enough to provide cooking facilities—California called them "efficiencies"—in vacation areas where stays of several days were usual. Elsewhere they were soon fighting a long, slowly losing battle against patrons' Tin Cannish insistence on at least preparing juice-and-instant-coffee breakfasts, not infrequently using electric rings to prepare hot suppers out of cans. Even where the court had no restaurant thus to lose business, the management took a dim view of the consequent fire hazards, grease on carpets and garbage-choked toilets. But attrition won a tacit victory, and this taboo has gone the way of the notice forbidding ingestion of alcoholic beverages that was familiar forty years ago. Such struggles, sometimes tacit, sometimes overt, are expected in any kind of innkeeping. Widespread light-fingeredness soon taught court owners above the most primitive level to install no lamps or pictures small enough to be readily smuggled away. But in coping with misbehavior in general, management was up against the tourist court patron's having advantages over the hotel guest. His car was right at his private door and his lodging typically "on the outside fringes of town where police jurisdiction stops and county officers seem unable to exert much authority," [40] as J. Edgar Hoover of the Federal Bureau of Investigation pointed out in 1940. Hence the space for license-plate number on the registration card—not that it ever seems to be checked against the actual plate—and the pay-in-advance rule that hotels of any reputation applied thirty years ago only to check-ins lacking baggage.

Further, the relative isolation of most tourist courts combined with the great cruising radius of the automobile inevitably to attract the custom of Mr. and Mrs. John Smith. Their perfectly good dollars tempted less finicky court owners into a "hot pillow trade" comfortably beyond the reach of City Hall. A survey of courts near a large weekend university campus in the late 1930's showed they had housed more than 2,000 couples, far beyond rated legitimate occupancy. To discourage such custom, straitlaced Mr. and Mrs. Momandpop who had always run a nice place, sometimes put up signs: MORALLY CLEAN or OUT OF COUNTY LICENSES ONLY. Yet thus to hint the place had been having trouble might drive legitimate patronage elsewhere. And in any case it was awkward to show a newly registered couple to their unit and stall around till it was plain they had no luggage with a jangly scene ensuing when one told them to be on their way. . . .

Thanks to jerry-building, the second decade of tourist courts saw many instances of structures and respectability coming apart together. A sharp operator with his own ideas could readily buy the Momandpops out of their elderly court that needed costly repairs but would serve his purposes for the few years before it fell down. In his hands it tended to become a haven for call girls as well as noncommercial assignations; or he might build a dine-and-dance joint on the lot with the waitresses doubling in brass. The advantages of being beyond effective police scrutiny might make it further worth his while to see nothing and ask no questions of secretive characters with curiously fitting jackets. Old-line court owners were outraged when radio serials and comic books began to quarter their tough customers—kidnappers, smugglers, blackmailers, international spies—in tourist courts as a matter of course. Their protests to publishers and program directors lost weight, however, when J. Edgar Hoover told millions of readers of the *American* magazine in 1940: "A majority of the 35,000 tourist camps . . . threaten the peace and welfare of the communities upon which [they] have fastened themselves." He admitted that many courts were decent enough but insisted that the rotten apples dominated as "not only hideouts and meeting places but actual bases of operations for which gangs . . . prey upon the surrounding territory." [41]

It was unfortunate that just when tourist courts were upgrading to become places where owners of LaSalles or even Packards might put up, this odor as of the crib house flavored with Cicero, Illinois, should arise. The general accuracy of Hoover's description was borne out a generation later, however, when James D. Saul, veteran editor of *Hospitality*, a public accommodations trade magazine, wrote reminiscently that though "The shock treatment almost killed the patient [*i.e.*, the tourist court industry] . . . Every motel owner [of later times] should be grateful to Hoover." [42] The ensuing cleanup enabled the upcoming motel phase of the industry to develop as straight as was ever expected of hotels, which, after all, have always ranged from the Ritz to the Railroad Avenue House. No great compliment, granted, but marked and persistent improvement did occur. One thing that helped it to persist was the new creation or expansion of county and township police to supplement state troopers in keeping an eye on elderly courts decaying so temptingly just outside city limits.

The problem of Mr. and Mrs. Smith has never been solved, however. It was thoughtful of the automobile, already so propitious to amateur fornication, also to create the faraway roadside lodging. The beneficiaries were probably not so much the young overcome by their own inexperienced hormones as those some years older beginning to lack the extreme limberness required in the back seat. By now, of course, the assumption that accommodations should not be rented to unmarried couples is moribund. But the tourist court/motel was as much a creature of the notorious 1920's as the Charleston. And one is tempted to adduce the marked affinity between it and the Smiths as another example of how Sex somehow imbued most aspects of that decade.

VI

Other Sides of Paradise

O remember not the sins and offences of my
youth!

—Book of Common Prayer

FREUD and Flaming Youth. Bathtub gin. Ubiquitous cigarettes. Scopes trial, Sacco and Vanzetti, pineapple bombs, Big Bill the Builder. War babies, or pre-War sleepers or automobile babies, those items subtend much of what is usually meant by the Roaring Twenties or the Jazz Age. Such labels need gingerly handling. They often develop lives of their own and squeeze this or that all out of shape to make it fit their one-dimensional formulas.

To say "the Roaring Twenties" tempts those born too late for direct experience of that renowned decade into a swirl of clichés: a girl with bobbed hair, a fuzzy permanent and a Cupid's bow mouth dancing the Charleston on a table; raccoon coats and hip flasks; Wall Street spinning like a toddle top; mounted police riding down demonstrators; Hoover's high collars, Coolidge in a ten-gallon hat; two cars in every garage, one a Stutz, the other a Packard; a shining castle built upon the sand. . . . That is the nostalgia-monger's montage. It's all pertinent, only the scope is too narrow for the diverse realities. Yes, the 1920's were like that, only they were so much more, not so much more so.

Such a montage recalls the sequences of symbolic images that a specialist named Slavko Vorkapich used to do for pretentious movies in the early 1930's or those flashy-detail interludes in Dos Passos' *USA*. Both are appropriate because to a large extent the cliché 1920's—as opposed to the actual ones—were created by the printed word and show business, two media swollen since 1910 into respectively the movies and million-circulation periodicals. At the same time a sister set of clichés evolved in Britain—see Noel Coward's early works. The success of both may have meant the same thing as that of the Klan—exploitation in peacetime of new, War-born methods of high-pressure mass stimulus.

The words that thus buoyed up the Roaring Twenties were printed in Sunday supplements and scare-headlined pieces in general and women's magazines about whither-Youth that mistakenly laid the blame on War-jaded morals and lack of corsets in 1919—"that spring which inaugurated the Age of Jazz" [1] in the brash gospel according to F. Scott Fitzgerald. It looked as if a clever publicity firm had been retained to prod the nation into rising alarm while simultaneously giving it plenty of cause. The first gusher to blow in was, of course, Fitzgerald himself. In spite of its anomalous pre-War setting *This Side of Paradise* encouraged Youth to anoint itself with self-pity and its elders dutifully to shake their heads downstage right, and the success of his short stories in *Flappers and Philosophers* displayed the acumen of editors printing them to cash in on Youth's waxing self-esteem. Within two years came the titles supplying the labels that stuck: from Fitzgerald [*Tales of the*] *Jazz Age*; from Samuel Hopkins Adams, an able muckraking magazine reporter, the pseudonymous *Flaming Youth*.

Dorothy Speare's *Dancing in the Dark*, a third winner, duly emphasized the spell of the fox-trot. In most such novels the big ballroom scene was as necessary as the grunt-by-grunt fornication scene today. Even Adams, though pushing fifty, managed the swing of it: "The girls danced by him with their eyes drooping, their cheeks inflamed, a little line of passion across their foreheads . . . each couple a separate entity alone with the surge of the music and what it covertly implied, the allegro furioso of tumultuous untamable blood . . . her lips were lightly parted . . . a little pulse beat in her neck. . . ." [2] In 1925 a rival best seller by an instructor at Brown University, Percy Marks, showed that he had been marking campus folkways as well as themes:

> "He's mine!" cried a pretty, black-eyed girl with a cloud of bobbed hair and flaming cheeks. Her slender shoulders were bare; her round white arms waved in excited, graceful gestures; her corn-colored frock was a gauzy mist . . . she floated into his arms, her slender body close to his. When the music ceased . . . she led him to a dark corner. . . . "You're sweet, honey," she said softly . . . her small, glowing face up to his. "Kiss me," she commanded. [3]

A Frenchman reading that then would have assumed the scene was in a brothel. Marks' title for this novel was *The Plastic Age*. "Plastic" then carried the dictionary sense of "readily assuming a new shape; impressionable; pliable." Today industrial chemistry has it meaning artificial, false, cheap when applied to a culture or a person. In those senses, come to think of it, it fits the cliché-twenties pretty well.

Not all Jazz Age fiction was that bad. Stephen Vincent Benét's *The Beginning of Wisdom*, though as solemn as the rest, had a sure, rhapsodical beat unmatched in Fitzgerald's work on cognate themes. But the canonization of Fitzgerald is now so taken for granted that it may be hard to realize that few then felt a sharp qualitative difference between him and his rivals in exploiting the feedback from his earliest successes. The impression that he was a major writer came later; indeed Malcolm Cowley recently felt it necessary to apologize for not having treated Fitzgerald in a piece summarizing significant new American writing *c.* 1921. The author of *All the Sad Young Men* seemed not at all out of place in *College Humor*, a principal textbook from which Joe College and Betty Co-ed learned what to wear, say and feel—otherwise a monthly founded on cubbish jokes and cartoons from campus humorous publications that attained major circulation with sincere articles and Fitzgeraldish stories about young rebellion. The idiom was born in the Ivy League, but *College Humor* and the Jazz Age best sellers took it to the Coast and into the state universities where pre-War capers on Fraternity Row had already prepared the way.

Textbook illustration came from John Held, Jr., a cartoonist of Fitzgerald's generation. He began in the Wartime *Judge* and *Life* with burlesqued woodcuts (actually linoleum blocks) of pseudo-Victorian feel. His later trick was drawing people like cylindrical wooden characters from an old-time Noah's Ark under expressive tensions. It made his head- and tailpieces for movie reviews in *Life* delightful puppet show summaries of Hollywood's chief personae. But what lent him marked significance was the popularity that came when he applied it to Youth, making him the Du Maurier of the Jazz Age. He had never gone to college, which may account for the sardonic incredulity beneath his handling of the under- and overdressed grotesqueries that he drew. His college boys were peanut-headed, grimacing nonentities. But in spite of the patent contempt with which he drew her, the John Held, Jr., girl, dancing swooningly or frenetically, swigging gin, necking, wielding a long cigarette holder, wearing unbuckled galoshes, hoydenishly leggy about getting into cars and sitting on stairs, translated into a memorable vernacular the long-legged, sleekly coiffed, upstage ideal of the fashion drawings in *Harper's Bazaar c.* 1922. Soon she was not only Betty Co-ed the prom trotter but also stenographer, waitress, mill hand. Fitzgerald went on after the sustaining steed of the 1920's collapsed under him; he came to a dismaying end. Held gave up his Jazz Babies apparently without a backward glance and spent the rest of a long, quiet life as an able watercolorist and art instructor.

The Flaming Youth girl—and Flaming Youth was primarily for girls as a lunatic aspect of the Revolt of Woman—spread so rapidly in lower economic strata because the movies took her there. This flashy genre suited Hollywood almost as well as the Western and the Biblical clambake. Jazz Age fictions begat scores of movies with titles ringing changes on Jazz, Youth, Girls, Free, Dancing, Sex, Campus, Daughters. Thigh-high in the leg, tightly swathed in bosom and behind, Madge Bellamy, Colleen Moore, Betty Compson, Joan Crawford, Clara Bow danced on that table, champagne glass in hand—doing for Flaming Youth what *The Wild One* did forty years later for motorcycling sadists. In 1927 a new item enriched the vocabulary—"It," meaning a generalized sex appeal. *It* was the title and theme of a hard-breathing novel by Elinor Glyn that, in spite of her deserved reputation for titillating the Wednesday matinee set, Hollywood bought solely for the title and her name; the consequent movie threw away the gardenia-skinned heroine and concentrated on Clara Bow masterfully ballyhooed as "The It Girl," an incarnation of girlish gaiety on the loose.* Miss Bow was not gaunt enough for the new standards, but then neither were her rivals on the screen nor yet the choruses of the Broadway musical shows. Show business had the economic good sense to keep a sense of proportion about that fashionable emaciation. The living lady skeleton of great charm and worldly wisdom, with any amount of leg to stand on but no behind to sit on, was confined largely to drawing-room comedy where the tired businessman's dollar did not count for so much.

As expert on Greenwich Village Caroline Ware suggested a close connection between the studio party of 1914 and the generic Wild Party of the cliché 1920's. ". . . what Greenwich Village had liked yesterday was evidently what the suburbs would like tomorrow," [4] wrote Floyd Dell. Actually, however, the sources of the wild party complex that Hollywood so exploited and promulgated were the campus and the country club. As Fitzgerald's young cutups of 1914 married and settled down in Commuter Heights, they often kept up their sprawly social habits—witness *The Beautiful and Damned* and *The Great Gatsby*. It was just as daring to shoot coeducational craps on the new living-room rug as on the country-club floor in "The Jelly Bean." Those uneasy about the finer points of boxcars and Ada-from-Decatur gambled with the toddle top, an octagonal instrument of chance requiring only the ability to read "PUT," "TAKE" and Arabic numerals up to ten. And, as with the bicycle and the automobile, what sports pleased the relatively affluent one year, those of average income went in for a few years later.

The affinity between Flaming Youth and the Village lay rather in shared belief that Youth was peculiarly significant. Women's magazines deplored "a spirit of revolt against all stable and proven things, which has afflicted the youth of the nation." [5] An eminent Methodist lady preacher from Britain said that on both sides of the water Youth "challenges everything, accepts nothing on authority, and is inclined to . . . a brilliantly analytical intellect rather than a constructive one. . . . If the older generation had been right on any important point, why has it got the world into its present state of misery and fear? . . . is the question with which the younger generation . . . meets the appeal of the elder to authority." [6] ". . . after the War," Mark Sullivan said, "an emphasis . . . probably never . . . equalled . . . was placed on the young simply because they were young . . . Pathetically, in many cases, the parent . . . subscribed to the superiority which youth claimed for itself." [7] How familiar that sounds! Elmer Davis,

* This smothering of the printed text was a pity too. Not every novel can boast passages like this: "He had never loved, his mind was too analytical . . . but from his fifteenth year when the saloonkeeper's wife at the corner of his street grovelled before his six feet of magnificent stripling strength, to his fortieth birthday, females of all types and classes had manifested ardent passion for him." (10.)

sixteen years younger but of already wide experience, saw it rather differently at the time: "A good deal of the solemnity of recent literature [c. 1927], like a good deal of the embittered zealotry of recent political radicalism, is obviously the work of earnest young people who are unaware that they are not the first earnest young people in history . . . that the universe is unsatisfactory . . . [is] not exactly a novel discovery, but it is news to most of the earnest young people . . . they feel that something ought to be done, or at least said, about it . . . whoever fails to realize the urgent and immediate duty to take everything seriously is not merely a light-minded and negligible person, but a traitor to society." He ascribed the solemnity with which the 1920's took Youth—and vice versa—to "a reading public which is ninety per cent illiterate, in the sense that it knows nothing of what has been thought, and done, in the past." [8]

That could come from a commentator of 1970. Fits of the *déjà vu* feeling are common when one explores what was done—and said—after 1914. Women's magazines were all in a sweat about what one of them described as parents' bewilderment over "the brutality of their children . . . cruel selfishness that will brook no interference with their modern pleasures and excitements." [9] About obscenity defended on esthetic grounds; about growing use of alcohol among the young; about the effect on children's behavior of incessant violence on the movie screen; about the sinister effect of Progressive Education. . . .

The august principle that "there is no new thing under the sun" is not, however, infallible. It was unlikely that the Jazz Age version of Youth would develop a religious aspect. It is more unlikely that the English-speaking world will soon see a close parallel to the Buchmanism that then harassed certain young Americans and can be regarded as one facet of the Jazz Age. For it was on the campus that the Reverend Dr. Frank N. D. Buchman waylaid his prospective victims, and it was usually Sex that persuaded them into his parlor.

This plump, duly ordained Lutheran parson learned about youngsters as head of the YMCA at Pennsylvania State College, where, he boasted, he brought the campus bootlegger to righteousness and so cleaned up the students' lives that the local gonorrhea quack was starved into leaving town. In the War years he toured the East under the auspices of the Hartford Theological Seminary, supporting the morale of missionaries. In 1921 he visited Britain and at the instance of two Anglican bishops of his acquaintance called on their sons at Cambridge University. This let the wolf (or the shepherd, depending on point of view) in among the lambs. For there Buchman found "a very distressing state of things," [10] an admirer's phrase that, being interpreted, meant not heresy nor agnosticism but rampant lewdness. At Cambridge, then at Oxford for lengthening intervals, he became a self-delegated spiritual therapist saving undergraduates' souls by verbal shock therapy. The lad professing theological doubts was heard out in silence, then bluntly told that what kept him from God was not intellectual misgiving but "Sin! You are a—" masturbator, fornicator or bugger, according to Buchman's skilled reading of cryptic symptoms at which he seems to have been as adept as Judge Lindsey. Nine in ten times, his henchmen vowed, such diagnoses from this master of what he called "soul surgery" were correct. They often led to confession, repentance, reform and entry into Buchman's quasi-mystical fellowship combining backhanded sex appeal with a sort of dilute Quietism that may have rubbed off on him from his boyhood schooling in a seminary of the Schwenk-felders, a splinter sect among the Pennsylvania Dutch. His following, at first called the First Century Christian Fellowship, presently became the Oxford Group, much to the annoyance of many Oxonians; in the late 1930's it became Moral Rearmament, an international cult that an unfriendly expert in Buchmania has described as "a Salvation Army for the middle classes." [11]

Buchman's core phalanx of true believers from Oxbridge rejoiced mightily in one another's righteousness. "We never meet but what we have a good time," said an early member, extolling the "laughter of men who really know there is a way out . . . doing their best to make it known to others." [12] Soon they opened a new way to the marrow of the soul—likely prospects were invited to holy "house parties" usually held in elegant country houses belonging to the families of one or another of the faithful. There, after clean, manly talk and God's fresh air, neophytes were caused to rise on their hind legs before the whole party to confess, usually with retching protestations of self-loathing, their assorted foulnesses—the euphe-mism for masturbation was "the common or garden variety of sin." [13] It was a blend of the "experience meeting" of the hot-gospel tent with anticipa-tions of Alcoholics Anonymous and the Esalenistic encounter session of today. After self-purging, the ransomed soul was drilled in Buchman's "morning watch" or "Quiet Time"—rising an hour before breakfast to put the soul in such order that "God can say 'Hello!' " [14] as one devotee put it, and then give His commands for the day. (In one Buchmanite camp the hired cook, soon as zealous as any, got the day's menus from God at Quiet Time.) The comfortable weekend quarters and throbbing overheatedness of the house party system were soon the chief means of bringing others to swept and garnished fellowship, as crucial to Buchmanism as the pit and bull's blood were to Mithraism. There was always a risk that confessions would be tepid: "One has evaded customs on a small sum; another handed in a paper on a book he had not read through. . . ." * [15] But skilled

---

* For a satirizing British touch: ". . . yesterday in the Strand . . . a [Buchmanite] stood in the middle of the road and said that he wanted to confess to all the great big world that in August . . . about 4:15 p.m., he had lied to his great aunt about the number of lumps of sugar in his warm milk." (*The Best of Beachcomber* [J. B. Morton], 34.)

prodding usually uncovered rich pockets of carnality. Nor was a neophyte drawing on detail borrowed from his dreams likely to be challenged.

Soon Buchman fetched groups of his human trophies to America to regenerate Ivy League campuses. Their wholesomeness and upper-class charm often got these young Britons cordially received by Anglophile deans of colleges and owners of suitable country houses. In 1926 Buchman told me how readily they obtained passage and eating money. When he or a disciple needed sinews of war, he had only to make how much and what for clear to God at Quiet Time, and within twenty-four hours the mail was sure to contain an adequate check sent spontaneously by some admirer. To any expressing wonder at this he said, "Ah, but isn't God a millionaire?" [16] His hidden powers were considerable. There was the Cambridge undergraduate who had never met him, thought of consulting him, began to write him a letter instead—and into his room burst Buchman panting out that he had been on another errand but right there in the street something told him this young sinner needed him and there he was, the soul surgeon, scalpel at the ready.

The supernatural may help to account for the cultural miracle of his otherwise baffling acceptance by many Britons in circles unlikely to tolerate overtly Babbittish Americans. Harold Begbie, his British Boswell, drew him as depressingly "stoutish, clean-shaven, spectacled, with that mien of scrupulous freshness . . . of the hygienic American." [17] Less charitably I described him in print as "pudgy and mild . . . mouth . . . small and weak . . . eyes small and watery . . . hair thin . . . meaty red ears." [18] To me the strangest thing about him was that a man of such batrachian flabbiness so easily ingratiated himself with the well-off and well-placed. Yet support from fat bank accounts was the key to his story. As he talked to me about his supporters, he took his desk copy of the *New York Social Register* and caressed it as though it were a familiar spirit. His right hand in Manhattan was the rector of Calvary Episcopal Church, the Gramercy Park parish, the Reverend Dr. Samuel M. Shoemaker, whose snobbishness as an undergraduate at Princeton was what Edmund Wilson chiefly recalled about him. Some of Buchman's best house parties took place at the Connecticut estate of Mrs. Theodate Pope Riddle, wealthy founder of Avon Old Farm School where the boys wore black ties to dinner every evening. Edison's widow was generous. So were Detroit automobile people. Cultivated disciples wrote admiring pieces about Buchman in the *Outlook* and the *Atlantic Monthly*. The typical house party of the first phase included "college men from Princeton, Yale, Williams and Harvard, girls from Vassar and Smith, debutantes from Baltimore and Boston. . . ." [19]

A Princetonian disciple described and credited to Buchman a momentous change in "the Universities of America . . . a new seriousness among undergraduates . . . visible movement toward a spiritual life. . . ." [20] President John Grier Hibben of Princeton, observing the same thing but taking it differently, ruined Buchman's faith in ivied walls as good social climbing by barring him from campus on what would seem to have been obvious grounds—once somebody came out with it—that he was a morbidly deleterious influence. Unmentioned but maybe involved was Buchman's growing tendency to include girls in house parties. So far as I ever learned, Sex was little discussed in mixed groups, nor were there complaints about scant chaperonage. But fifty years ago the notion of nice girls from good schools rising in a damp-palmed Buchmanite *agape* to discuss even the rest of the seven deadly sins was distasteful to many.

After Hibben's action Buchman's star tended temporarily to wane. Campus religious officers took a second look behind his often-impressive auspices. Gradually he withdrew in good order, keeping his entrée to the check-writing element by holding house parties for affluent recent alumni of the Ivy League who, though getting old enough to know better, were widely regarded as still youthfully flaming, if not more so. Eventually this senior branch of Buchmanism became Moral Rearmament. The point here is that on Ste.-Beuve's and Freud's principle that "There is nothing so much like a bump as a hollow," campus Buchmanites may have been the heads of which Flaming Youth was tails. Without guilty memory of what the Jazz Age believed to be sophisticated behavior during Prom Week, Buchman's cadres would have had much less to work on. Misguided but real revulsion from the new freedom of behavior must often have left youngsters wide open to their blandishments. Indeed one can readily imagine Fitzgerald, or anyway some of his protagonists, breathing hard during a Buchmanite house party.

Joe College and Betty Co-ed, on whom so many in addition to Buchman lavished headshaking, were certainly depressing phenomena—and no less because they were part of a long-developing dropsy afflicting Alma Mater as the post-War era took shape. In 1920 Americans undergoing "higher education"—the nation's potential lawyers, parsons, doctors, scholars, bankers, upper managers, women's club presidents—numbered roughly 600,000, .57 percent of the population. The tissues kept bloating, and that tripled to 1.5 percent by 1940. This merely maintained an upward curve that had begun to rise well back in the 1800's, so the War had little to do with it. From the point of view of a nation needing more and better-prepared teachers, better-trained doctors, more sound scholars—there already were, God knows, plenty of lawyers, parsons and managers—the ratio was still too low. But from that of the college as an enrichening, mind-honing agency, even 600,000 was a stultifying error—at a guess 500,000 excess.

Marked differences certainly existed *c.* 1925 among Harvard College, William & Mary College, City College of New York, Reed College, Whittier College, Wabash College, Hamilton College, Wellesley College, Goucher College and the undergraduate fractions of the universities of

Notre Dame, Georgia, California and Minnesota. But popular usage lumped all as College, and at least two statements hold good of all: They gave baccalaureate degrees, and of none could it be said that a majority of its matriculants had any business in the shade of Alma Mater's elms. That does not apply to institutions like the Massachusetts Institute of Technology or California Institute of Technology, as profession-oriented as West Point and often much more exacting mentally. It does apply to campuses clogged by too many students whose reasons for matriculating had little to do with the intellectual and cultural reasons for Alma Mater's exemption from taxation. The ratios of misfits fluctuated from—at another guess—40 percent at City College to, say, 95 percent at any given prairie Old Siwash. At least a young professor of physics at the University of Wisconsin told Morris Markey in 1930 that though "Most [undergraduates there] can learn the answers out of books . . . ninety per cent of them could not be educated in any college on earth . . . do not possess the eagerness and the flexibility of mind, the downright gray matter to get hold of knowledge." [21]

The reasons behind that were hinted at in the mid-1920's by an impressive witness, John B. Watson. PhD in psychology from the University of Chicago, head of Johns Hopkins' psychological laboratory before he soared to fame as Mr. Behaviorism, he was certainly a jewel in the crown of his Alma Mater, Furman University, Greenville, South Carolina. Yet for him College was not primarily a locus for the mind, rather "a place to grow up in . . . for breaking nest habits [his term for parent-oriented conditioning] . . . learning how to make oneself friendly . . . to keep one's clothes pressed . . . to be polite . . . to use leisure . . ." and at the end of the list, "a place where the student can learn respect for thinking and possibly even learn how to think." [22] Amusedly he confessed that his four years each of Latin and Greek and much history had left him unable twenty years later to make out a page of Latin or name ten Presidents of the United States.

The latter boast may have been exaggerated. His view of College was nevertheless clear. His listed purposes sound as though he were discussing places concerned not with brains but with what, given a change of sexes, were the ends of his day's "finishing schools"—the expensive establishments to which parents with new money sent their mid-teen daughters to learn among the daughters of parents with old money how to eat fruit with knife and fork and acquire the accent now widely associated with Katharine Hepburn. "In the public mind," wrote Walter P. Metzger, recent historian of academic freedom, "the American university was not clearly defined as a center of independent thought, and agent of intellectual progress . . . [rather] perhaps primarily, a school of preparation for minors, a substitute parent for the young." [23] In Watson's world, large and still vigorous, College was the Limbo to which the well-to-do consigned Youth not yet required to earn its own living in hopes it would there find out what it wanted to do and slough off its cruder attributes. A certain affluence and awareness of manners were implied, so a generalized prestige gathered around having "gone to College." Strong among many who had not done so themselves, it was stronger still among those who, having been through Alma Mater's mill, had reason to know how poor her grist was. The average alumnus felt obliged to give his progeny the same four-year privilege if they had to be crammed or chiseled into it. His wife felt the same. She too was likely to be an alumna of dear old Limbo and met him there under the elms or on the sorority house porch.

Mothers with daughters were well aware that a coeducational campus, as at large state universities, was an admirable matrimonial agency. For boys lacking strong commitment to medicine or science the outstanding advantage was socioeconomic. Fathers with their heads screwed on the right way relied on the undergraduate years to equip Junior with well-placed, lifelong cronies with whom to swap back scratchings in careers in business and law. Personnel managers had not yet made a College degree an ironclad requirement for jobs-with-futures, but it was already an asset for the young job seeker in proportion to the prestige of the campus awarding it. In any case Pop was confident that, as Watson, already deep in the great J. Walter Thompson advertising agency, had advised, Limbo U would comb out of Junior's hair any hayseed left from Zenith High School.

Such hitching of Alma Mater to Mr. Worldly Wiseman's wagon was not unique to America. New-money boys had long infiltrated Britain's upper strata through the "public school" (= posh, private, loaded with prestige) and thence either into Oxbridge or directly to apprenticeships in business or certain professions. The chief asset of the young Briton of assured upper-class status has proverbially been peer-level, nickname acquaintance with his school's Old Boys high in this or that government department or industrial complex. The major difference lay in academic standards. In 1925 the average product of Harrow, say, left school at the age of eighteen much better stored with the ingredients and tools of knowledge and cultivation than the average member of the class that Yale graduated that year though, being twenty-one or so, young Eli had had several years' more schooling. He would have compared still less favorably with the average product (also eighteen more or less) of Continental secondary schools such as Germany's *Gymnasium* and France's *lycée,* entrance to which had more to do with examinations and less—though by no means nothing—with economic status and social ambition. By the same token neither the American public high school nor the private prep school emulating British models was much better than a halfway term between elementary and secondary.*

* Abraham Flexner spelled this out late in the 1920's: "[American] secondary education includes the present high school and a large part of college; we are dealing with two divisions

Lack of academic quality under the elms disturbed neither Junior nor his parents. Except when Prexy's welcoming address on Homecoming Day went maundering on about building character by imbuing youth with the best that the past had thought and done etc., etc., they were comfortably, tacitly content that College should be primarily a social club open eight months a year. Learning, sometimes solid, anyway offering contact with the ingredients of cultivated tastes and habits, was usually there for young persons eccentrically so inclined. But for any not so inclined, yet having passable IQ's, which might include the bulk of the student body, required lectures and sporadic nips of study kept them on the rolls of any place with Limbo U's easygoing traditions. Since none of the subject matter interested Junior much, he and his myriads of counterparts created a play world of their own to fill the vacuum—and lo! soon the vacuum fillers were the College's chief reason for existence.

This aspect of most campuses centered on fraternities—small undergraduate clubs identified by odd combinations of letters from the Greek alphabet, vying for local prestige and seldom including a majority of students—for where was the good of exclusiveness if many weren't excluded? A sister complex of sororities deployed the cognate feminine zest for dirty work at the social crossroads; Vincent Sheean, one of the 1920's outstanding foreign correspondents, recalled that at the fraternity-ridden University of Chicago in 1919 "The men did not seem to have the same high degree of social cruelty as the women." [24] With tooth-gritting scorn Veblen, who had seen fraternities at their peak at Cornell, the University of Chicago and the University of California, called them "competitive organizations for the elaboration of the puerile irregularities of adolescence" comprising a "decorative contingent who take more kindly to sports, invidious intrigue and social amenities than to scholarly pursuits." [25]

Quaker, Catholic and the better for-girls-only colleges managed to avoid this numbing disease and at the top of the Ivy League the system had local variations. Pretty much everywhere else fraternities set the climate in which Joe College and Betty Co-ed flourished. The cryptic Greek letters over the door of the fraternity house—often an imposing mansion built by nostalgic brother alumni—implied none of the values of Plato's *Symposium*—indeed quite the reverse. The fraternity system institutionalized and was obsessed by the chronic, itchy heterosexuality that Limbo U owed to its admitting co-eds. The biochemical hungers appropriate to their age group also affected the girls in the sorority houses on the next street en masse and tête-à-tête though not often—as previously noted—"all the way." The fraternity pin was the token of the tenuous campus engagement. Fraternity

---

(secondary education and university education), not with three (high school, college and graduate school) a fact that is made clear by the sudden decrease of students at the end of the second college year." (*Universities*, 214.) For an estimate to the same purpose as of 1912 *cf.* J. McKeen Cattell, *University Control*, 50.

dances were the staple of formal social life. In the annual "rushing" competition for eligible freshmen co-eds Alpha Omega could count on doing well because of its reputation for fielding the choicest girls, hence optimum boy-meeting opportunities for its "pledges." At all-male colleges —scores of such still existed—annual festivals such as Dartmouth's Winter Carnival or the Big Game of the football season, to which fraternity brothers fetched their best girls from all over, were a sort of Olympics for the cloche-hatted cream of Smith, Wellesley and Vassar, Mills, Sweet Briar. . . .

Fraternities' only contacts with learning were their leaders' perfunctory efforts to make the brothers study enough not to flunk out. Occasionally not too unpersonable studious types were pledged to leaven the lump and show to the dean as Exhibit A. Far more important were the fraternities' political alliances and jugglings of the extracurricular activities that supplemented girls as vacuum fillers. A Martian might have seen them as travesty of Progressive Education's school-as-microcosm. Sheean remarked the "Rare and wonderful freshmen [who] went out for everything at once" [24]—that is, for the newspaper, or the monthly funny magazine (business or editorial side), a sport manager-apprenticeship, the glee club, the dramatic club and, as sophomore year came on, a candidacy for student government as well as class office. One could even acquire minor merit from fresh-faced committee work in the campus YMCA or equivalent—the foothold that enabled Buchman to infect the Ivy League—or student-manned settlement work in the local town. In all such bustlings about, the aspirant drew support from his fraternity eager to display "big men on campus" to next year's rushee-freshmen. Sheean thought it might have done "no harm . . . [had] it not been supplemented by a social life of singular ferocity . . . intricate, overwhelming snobbery." [24] But this deliberate busyness necessarily perverted and vitiated those aspects of Alma Mater rightly taken seriously by the submerged minority of students with sound reason to be there. As Bourne said after attending Columbia College, the bewildered old girl "rather let [undergraduates] run away with the college." [26]

Soon other extraneous interests—the catch-as-catch-can professions as distinct from the learned ones, such as law and medicine—were similarly running away with the university. Caution is required in using the term. Its corners were badly eroded by self-styled freshwater universities consisting of 300 students of both sexes whose parents mostly adhered to the evangelical sect that founded them in 1879; ten faculty clumsily teaching what in Europe would have been a secondary-school curriculum; and on the third floor of Old Main a museum containing seven moth-eaten stuffed mammals and a dusty case of Indian arrowheads. Properly, a college seeking university status had to build in the academic air space above undergraduate work several well-qualified graduate schools—typically law, medicine, liberal arts. Here the example of Johns Hopkins, solidly following

German models, was salutary. The best such graduate schools required applicants to have degrees from well-considered colleges. But more usual was an overlapping that allowed the undergraduate to devote most of his latter two years to premedical or prelegal courses that gave him a leg up on the graduate study leading into his chosen profession. Since College curricula were pretty watery to begin with, this usurping of available undergraduate time may not have done great damage. But it did cause confusions between what can and cannot be taught, what vocations are amenable to academic work, and led to masquerading of efforts at vocational training in academic peacock feathers.

Thus, for instance, arose the Graduate School of Education founded on a tenuous science of pedagogy and professing to teach how to teach. Borrowing the apparatus of lectures, examinations and degrees earned by dissertations, these schools imposed themselves on the new teachers' colleges and through them on the secondary schools. The Graduate School of Business Administration developed in two stages—first the example of the University of Pennsylvania's Wharton School of Finance created by multimillionaire Joseph Wharton; then in the early 1920's a huge bequest from multimillionaire George F. Baker expanded Harvard's version (founded in 1908) into what became the pattern for many such schools coast to coast. Abraham Flexner's acerbic study of *Universities** lumped such Business Schools—not to be confused with the business schools that taught stenography, elementary accounting and so on to those seeking white-collar jobs—with Schools of Education, Journalism and Hotel Management as offering to teach what can't be taught. By now some demurrer is possible. Business School faculties often do research into business-as-subculture and certain economic matters that conventional Departments of Economics may neglect. In such institutions businessmen-to-be can learn from lectures, textbooks and case studies much about the terminology and techniques of today's complicated corporations. Nevertheless, the chief reasons for attending a well-thought-of Business School are that it leads to knowing people who are or will be in the right places and that in any case a degree from it is a great help in job seeking and career making.

University-affiliated Schools of Journalism made a fine target for Flexner. Well before the War, special, usually small courses in what is now unashamedly called "creative writing" had sprung up, particularly in the Ivy League, to encourage undergraduates who hoped to be writers to do, under criticism from the instructor and their peers, what they would do anyway were they to be writers. There was no great harm in them except in the misguided precedent of giving academic credit for the work. In 1908 the

* Originally worked out as lectures given at Oxford in 1928, this is the best integrated and liveliest comment on higher education. Most of it is as pertinent today as it was forty years ago.

University of Missouri went one fateful step farther by setting up an explictly named School of Journalism giving multicourse credits.* But the notion did not catch fire until Joseph Pulitzer's bequest created Columbia's version imbued with the prestige of the Pulitzer Prizes. At Columbia or anywhere, Flexner said, such a school "does nothing for undergraduates that is worth their time or money" and unnecessarily fouls up the campus:

> Can the intellectuals really be trained cheek by jowl with students who may veer off into flimsy undergraduate courses in business or journalism? . . . Utter idlers do no more harm than empty benches; but the mixture of students of history or Greek with green reporters or immature bond salesmen is intolerable. . . . Does anyone really suppose that Yale and Princeton, having no schools of business, will for that reason in future be less conspicuous in business and banking than Harvard and Columbia, which have? Or that Harvard, having no school of journalism, will in coming years furnish fewer editors, reviewers, and reporters, than Columbia has? . . . These questions answer themselves.[27]

In spite of the implied sound principle that the only School of Journalism worth attending is a city room, the thing has spread as far as the School of Business. Other such studding sails on the academic ship are university Schools of Social Work, Town Planning, Domestic Science, Library Science, Hotel Management; all train specialists whom society needs, but why universities should be asked to train them is never clear. The practical reason is the supporting community's belief that College owes its supporters any "service"—in this case vocational training—that they think needed. On most larger campuses this produced an amazing proliferation of undergraduate subject matter. One extreme was Vassar's courses in "euthenics"—a coordination of psychology, sociology and so on meant to prepare prospective sweet girl graduates to be expert mothers according to the latest child-study lights. Other extremes were attained in the land grant colleges, soon calling themselves universities, that states set up under the Morrill Act (1862) to foster engineering and scientific agriculture. By the 1920's Morrill

* The School of Journalism founded in General Robert E. Lee's time at Washington and Lee was intended to broaden the background of newspapermen already working in the profession—more like the purpose of the Nieman Fellowships at Harvard—and in any case did not last long. Among the earliest and best of the College writing courses were Charles T. Copeland's at Harvard and first there, then at Yale, George P. Baker's "47 Workshop" for undergraduates hoping to be playwrights. There is small reason to believe, however, that promising students would not have done just about as well in literature and the theater had they never taken these courses. A valuable notion of the feeling of Baker's course can be derived from Book II, Section XVI of Thomas Wolfe's *Of Time and the River*. In my time I knew many undergraduates in Copeland's course but did not take it myself. Fortunately for me "Copey" overlooked that and befriended me with a generosity as notable as it was superficially crabby.

University had been chivied into offering not only undergraduate work in veterinary medicine, swine husbandry and highway design but also ice-cream making, folk dancing, Scoutmastering and filling station operation, all earning credit for a BI—Bachelor of Inanities. Clarence Cook Little, president of the University of Michigan, deplored the trend as resulting in "a uniformly low level of higher education" and an "excess of wasteful, non-essential elements in the . . . institution." [28]

In 1931 Harvard's President Lowell thought that though some students at his august Graduate School of Arts and Sciences were "of high intellectual distinction," most of them "had better not be there." [29] Yet graduate schools, as often happens with institutions of particular purpose, have had unexpected uses. Staying in one, never mind in what field, kept many boys from being drafted to fight in Vietnam—a distasteful job left to their less literate age peers from the boondocks and the ethnic enclaves. And generally graduate schools allow a society uncertain what to do with milling thousands of young folks uncertain what to do with themselves the option of storage in Limbo U a few years more.

The fraternity crowd usually got what they sought, to an extent justifying Pop's money. Students working their way through often got shortchanged. Many boys and some girls paid some or all of their campus expenses by part-time work. Families could not give enough help, available scholarships did not cover enough, and yet—obviously—they were bent on gaining the assumed, sometimes real benefits of College. This specially American custom supplemented a long-standing tradition that, without losing caste, ambitious youth could earn part of the academic year's cost by waiting table at summer resorts. President Little thought the lack of discrimination against such students admirably democratic and worthy of emulation in Europe. So it was—only objective admiration of it tended to mask its strenuous and debilitating realities. Up before dawn to refuel coal furnaces or prepare to serve breakfast in a College dining hall; lectures and quizzes till late afternoon, after which one tutored affluent classmates or minded children or walked dogs or washed cars or pumped gas or tended store or checked out books at the College library. . . . Even the most gilded campuses took this chronic economic emergency for granted and formally or informally maintained employment offices handling off-campus as well as campus jobs. Enterprising students did not always insist on legality. I knew of no such cases as one hears of now of College girls earning their way as call girls. But during Prohibition a major campus probably had several student bootleggers.*

The high unit value of gin probably left the boys some leisure. . . . A few

* At the Treasury Department in Washington, D.C., I was once shown what was said to be the most efficient small still ever designed—creation of a student at a technological college who had earned his way almost through to his degree with it before the revenuers caught up with him.

ironbound heroes managed arduous way-earning and extracurricular life too. Paul Gallico, soon one of the best sportswriters of the 1930's, worked his way through Columbia as stevedore, librarian and gym instructor and also captained the varsity crew. Most of the others had the worst of several academic worlds. Small time for dating and no money; small time (or energy) for better than rote study; inadequate stimulus from lectures or discussions watered down to suit the numb majority. At the end these self-made experts in dollar stretching could call themselves College men and, if ambition dictated several more years of grueling economic scramble, try for the good law or medical schools, for their scholastic records were often superior. A more or less happy ending. Only if the fraternity boys had not fouled up the campus, the way earner would have got a better money's worth. In 1928 Elmer Davis, who burst from the tiny chrysalis of Franklin College (Franklin, Indiana) to a Rhodes Scholarship, said "The logical solution . . . would be the division of our colleges into two groups—those that really tried to educate and those that gave their students the joys of football and extracurricular activities, with a little carefully diluted instruction thrown in." [30]

The strangest way-earners were the football mercenaries whose presence on campus made it unmistakable that somebody up there wanted Alma Mater to look absurd. The athletic kind of vacuum filling also had overtones ironically associated with Progressive Education. The extravagant hypertrophy of "intercollegiate athletics" was innocent in origin. Romantic educationists had soundly held that the emotional and mental interests of the Whole Child entailed regard to his physical well-being. *Mens sana in corpore sano* was incised on the Teachers College headquarters building and duly applied to the Whole Undergraduate, even by colleges imperfectly in sympathy with Progressive Education. Freshmen might be required regularly to work up a sweat. Ability to swim fifty yards was made a condition of receiving one's degree in Romance languages. Beginning in the Ivy League, new Departments of Physical Education were gradually fitted out with swimming pools, tennis courts, sometimes boathouses and golf courses and—the crucial mistake—playing fields for such team sports as baseball, lacrosse, American Rugby football.

Most of it was health-making, but unhappily the virus of gladiatorial rivalry struck early as Harvard and Yale raced crews against each other and then the young gentlemen of Princeton challenged those of Rutgers at football. Rivalries soon sprang up in baseball, basketball and so on, but it was American Rugby, soon bearing small resemblance to its British parent but much to mass felonious assault,* that gave the virus an explosive

* H. C. Witwer, who had managed prizefighters before turning sportswriter, said, "As to the physical and moral courage inculcated by the prize ring, I have seen punishment assimilated in

culture medium. The annual Yale-Harvard football game became a matter of national concern, and emulation of the prestige-rich Crimson and Blue infected the Midwest's and then California's newborn campuses. By 1915 *St. Nicholas'* pieces for teen-agers on "National Stars of the Gridiron" celebrated ends from Penn State, Tennessee, North Carolina, Missouri . . . tackles from Tulane, Texas, Nebraska, Akron . . . as well as from the original centers of the game. The annual All-America ideal football squad chosen by Walter Camp, Yale's pope of football, was compiled in three segments and guarded like a military secret lest thieves publish it prematurely. The Department of Phys Ed tended to become merely the shrine of the football coach who was nominally its employee. At first the undergraduates and their pretty girls at the Big Game, the red-faced alumni and their furry wives, the spastic cheerleaders, the surflike roar of the gibberish-rich college yells, the conscientious oompahs of the college band parading between halves and leading the moist-eyed crowd through "Alma Mater, Yours Forever," made up a more or less private party, a tribal rite with the usual virtues and drawbacks. But it was a good show garnishing the other show of twenty-two large youths butting heads on a chilly Saturday afternoon, and as the general public came flocking to see it, the extra money that they represented had morbid effects on what might have remained innocent nonsense.

False Step One was the thought that money from admissions to football games could be augmented to pay for the college's whole athletic program, and so it proved. Two was the building of huge stadia to seat more spectators—hence higher gate receipts, hence expanded Phys Ed facilities, hence higher operating expenses. (The immediate architectural precedents were the grandstands of racetracks and ball parks, both with ominous overtones of professionalism and commercialism.) The 80,000-odd seating capacity of the Yale Bowl (1914) would have more than sufficed for every member of the university and all living alumni. Three was raising admissions because the bonds financing the stadium had to be paid off. Four was the lesson that the general public was likelier to pay such prices when Limbo U's football players looked like probable winners. Five was the lesson that the annual campaign to extract money from the alumni for operating costs and endowment succeeded best in years when the Limbo Warriors trampled down all opponents, worst when the year's story was two won, five lost. Since the normal student body could not be counted on to field enough redoubtable football talent, "recruiting" was necessary. Enter the quasi-professional student athlete subsidized to put on the kind of show that public and alumni demanded. To make the most of such hired talent, Limbo brought in a nationally famous coach at a salary higher than that of

---

an inter-collegiate football game that would make the average prize fighter jump out of the ring." ("Kill the Big Bum," in Holmes, ed., *More Than a Game.*)

any professor on the faculty, sometimes higher than the president's. He brought with him as transfer students eager to be loyal Limbo Warriors a pair of tackles, a quarterback and a center. A minor college hoping to become major had only to persuade wealthy alumni to procure such a coach and retainers, and within five years it had doubled its enrollment and was gloriously in debt for a stadium.

The sequence varied from campus to campus, of course; some links might be rudimentary. The best Tech schools never let intercollegiate football gain foothold, though admitting competition in less fulminant sports like lacrosse and crew. In 1907, when College football was under fire not only for whoring after "tramp athletes" but also for its physical dangers, an Ivy League-created Committee on the Regulation of Athletic Sports headed by Harvard's Dean Le Baron Russell Briggs tried hard to curb overemphasis on football. Actually, however, it proved grotesquely anticipatory of the Hays Office as dollars, alumni, press and public frustrated its efforts. Twenty-odd years later, after another flurry of anti-overemphasis had petered out, Gallico had every reason to write that "seduced by that nice, crisp, shiny football money, Alma Mammy has become something of a tramp." [31] The most striking demonstration of it was the mileage run up by the football team of the University of Notre Dame, who practically never played a "home game" in South Bend, Indiana, preferring the dividends in prestige and dollars that went with displaying their formidable powers several hundred miles away each weekend.

Intraconference treaties limiting players to three seasons and forbidding flagrant transfers discouraged the tramp athlete as such. But his successors just went underground. In the 1920's the key players of most outstanding football teams were in college primarily to play a game in consideration of advantages not connected with learning—a way of life bringing with it the hero worship of young folk and alumni, the smiles of pretty girls and no doubt the warrior's delight in victory over worthy opponents. Economics was usually present if only implicitly. The fast and powerful left end was a former high school star choosing to attend Limbo U because alumni in his hometown spoke persuasively of the best fraternity, free use of a Jordan roadster and a choice of good jobs after College. The plunging fullback from the wrong side of the tracks would normally have gone from vocational high school to shoveling slag in a steel mill, but other Limbo alumni offered to pay his board bills and supply pocket money while the Phys Ed Department took care of his tuition with what was candidly called an athletic scholarship. Or it hired him to sweep out the field house once a week at wages equaling tuition.

To keep him scholastically eligible to play, they signed him up for the simplest courses, and his instructors knew better than to flunk him so long as he could recall how to sign his name on an examination bluebook, whereas I know of no instance of a coach keeping a boy on the football squad because, though his tackling was never satisfactory, he'd make Phi Beta Kappa if kept in college by that athletic scholarship. Prowess on the football field did secure some worthy boys college degrees that otherwise would have cost them far more in part-time drudgery for wages. Nor is there a real dichotomy between football and brains. College football can point to Rutgers' Paul Robeson, great actor, remarkable singer, impressive black leader; Harvard's Barry Wood, remarkable medical researcher; the University of Colorado's Byron F. White, U.S. Supreme Court justice. . . . On a lower and wider level College football created a new profession. The more astute among capable players could usually make an excellent to fair post-College living coaching, if not at Limbo, at some freshwater college or large high school. With that in view many campuses set up courses in general athletic coaching leading to degrees of various sorts. Normal schools often did the same.

None of it pertinent to Alma Mater's values, of course. The most constructive thing done by intercollegiate football was to open opportunities for ethnic minorities. As alumni and coaches sifted the nation for gridiron talent, they soon dipped into the huge reservoir of muscle and sharp reflexes in New as well as Old immigrant groups. Sportswriters noted with glee that the roster of Notre Dame's Fighting Irish looked like the telephone directory of Warsaw. In 1924 *Life* impishly chose its own All-America first and second teams drawn from Harvard, Dartmouth, Columbia as well as less Ivyish campuses: Rokusek, Goldstein, Michaleske, Schmettisch, Levy, Kowslowsky, Mianini, Koppisch, Molinetti, Dagrossa, Jawish, Zarakov, Cohen, Ropscha . . . a strong contrast with baseball, where box scores still showed few Italian, Slavic or Jewish names fifty years ago.

In those days pressures on colleges to let football swamp their public images were the stronger because professional football, to the dismay of its promoters, had yet to attract major attention, whereas professional baseball had long since drained away whatever general interest College baseball had roused. *C.* 1929 a solemn chronicler of American sport called pro football "a sorry counterfeit of the great spectacle of the campus. Its players perform not like heroes but like hired men." [32] Apparently he was unaware of the high proportion of hired men engaged in most College football games. Their essential commercialism was exposed for the hundredth time in the 1930's, when the powers in charge deliberately reduced the size and weight of the ball to facilitate forward passing and "make the game more of a crowd-pleaser," charged Alexander Weyand, former West Point football captain whom Grantland Rice called the foremost living authority on the game, after which "under pressure from the alumni, the press and the general public . . . proselytizing and subsidization of players increased." [33] Friends of both campus and sport like John R. Tunis, the nation's first writer to apply cultivated criteria to athletics, had been hoping they were seeing "the gradual fall and decline of the football Colossus" [34] as its acceptance in the Ivy League diminished. But that was far too optimistic for the country west of Pittsburgh where nowadays too many important football campuses are virtual farm clubs for the professional teams rampant on TV. And many large high schools are more or less farm clubs for the campuses.

That happened as the vacuum-filling process backed down into the high schools. As their pupil populations rose, filling them with teen-agers with little academic urge to be there, seldom interested in more than the diploma that would be handy when job seeking, emulation of big brother and sister at Limbo U was inevitable. More and more high schools acquired the professional coach not at all disguised as supervisor of manual training or Phys Ed; spring football practice undercutting the lower-keyed track and baseball squads; band, cheerleaders—and in the stands alumni of Limbo who had heard that this Raphael Semmes High had a right tackle worth attention. Some high schools even sprouted Greek letter fraternities that could survive the principals' well-advised hostility. High school prom, high school paper, high school class elections and student government trained College-bound pupils in how to fill vacuums and gave the rest a dilute taste of the snobbishness and shadow boxing they would have enjoyed *chez* Alma Mater had their futures been richer.

The alumnus' College had as rival on Alma Mater's campus the professor's Academe—scholars' shorthand for the totality of persons and institutions "primarily concerned with the advancement of knowledge, any institution of higher learning where knowledge is pursued and not merely purveyed" [35]—a definition by Robert MacIver, a discerning expert in the field of academic freedom. Some thought the two so intrinsically incompatible that undergraduate study should be completely separated from universities. Most scholars, however, allowed a real, if not primary, obligation to expose twenty-year-old youth to Academe's values partly to foster a layman's appreciation of the higher values of civilization among the general public, partly to attract likely recruits to learning. Whatever cultivated tastes and habits of objective thought rubbed off on undergraduates were obviously all to the good all around. So College meshing marginally into the academic faculty had status. The trouble was that as enrollments rose and curricula changed, scholar-teachers were less and less left to their own styles behind the screen of undergraduate doings. And money, crass dollars, also came shouldering in.

Since privately endowed campuses were more and more dependent on shaking down alumni to fund income and finance expansion, Limbo U's president was well advised not only to field winning football teams but also to keep his faculty from vexing its loyal sons and daughters. At State U, operating primarily on public moneys, caution was just as needful, for zealous alumni were relied on to keep pressure on the state budget passers; indeed a sizable minority of the legislators were probably alumni. Most faculty members, mindful of their salaries, which, low as they now sound, averaged in middle brackets *c.* 1910, lay low and stayed in Prexy's good graces. Their predecessors had done the same in the old days when religious deviancy was the chief source of trouble, when undergraduates were on "a restricted diet of classical languages, Protestant metaphysics, rhetoric, logic, and mathematics, natural and moral philosophy, and a smattering of physical science." [36] Over the years, however, religious conformity had ceased to be an issue except on candidly sectarian campuses. College was rapidly secularizing, and those divisively acrimonious disciplines so strangely called the *social* sciences were well entrenched and expanding.

In the new day Professor Headwind's writings and lectures about his research and insights into protective tariffs or strike injunctions might well disquiet the alumnus millionaire momentarily expected to pay for a new dormitory—or the owner of the big paper at the state capital—or the majority leader of the State Senate—or all of them roaring together. Or he might tactlessly make an off-campus speech endorsing some political maverick repugnant to many people bulking large in Limbo U's affairs. In other cases professor-experts' attacks on Populist sacred cows, such as free silver, got them into hot water on Populist-controlled campuses in the corn belt. In either context there was probably an interview with a Prexy urging discretion, and if Headwind did it again, he was likely to be told not to bother coming back next year. Hence uneasiness among not only historians, economists, sociologists, anthropologists and psychologists temperamentally likely to speak out of turn but also among their colleagues in the liberal arts and exact sciences seeing no reason why to be a professor should strip one of a citizen's right to sound off. Some also felt a generalized tenderness about the scholar's professional duty to hew to the line, damn the torpedoes, full enlightenment ahead!

Their problem was particularly American, for their Academe was organized on lines peculiar to America. The typical Continental university had grown up as a state-financed clump of teaching scholars who collectively ran the place about as they pleased and, though by no means exempt from generalized pressures from government and community, enjoyed high job security. Britain's Oxford and Cambridge were autonomous federations of semi-independent neighbor colleges managing their own affairs individually and the university's collectively and, since endowments covered most of their costs, free of any but fairly subtle social pressure. In both systems it was professors who, one way or another, determined what fields of learning should be explored and recruited new faculty on what was virtually a lifetime basis. Think of a private club in which, though the bylaws provide for expelling members, behavior must be outrageous indeed before anybody even suggests such a step—and in any case the whole thing is up to the member peers.

In sharp contrast the American professor could be dismissed pretty much at will, and the executioners were not his fellow professors but Alma Mater's administrator, the president, who had hired him in the first place, probably but not necessarily after consultation with some of his future colleagues. And the president himself was the precariously situated creature of the self-perpetuating locus of American academic power—the board of trustees. This hydra-headed body, basically in charge of finance, personnel, content of programs and so on, contained no faculty, seldom any scholars, consisted typically of locally eminent lawyers, businessmen, maybe a parson, maybe a physician, most of them alumni. In any case their subconscious understanding of Academe was on the average little better than that of the fraternity-minded alumnus, and in money matters they preferred impressive new bricks-and-mortar to increases in general endow- ment to finance research fellowships and laboratory assistants. The president they chose was probably a PhD, often a dean or professor from some campus of the same standing as Limbo U, but hired primarily to act as fund raiser, public relations front and supervisor of policies laid down by the board.

State universities' boards, usually appointees of the governor's, ran to politicians or anyway local chronic public figures, few of whom improved the body's sense of Academe's values. An extreme but hardly unfair illustration occurred in 1950, when the trustee of the University of Illinois moving successfully that the board vote "no confidence" in opposition to the incumbent president on an issue of academic freedom was Harold "Red" Grange, greatest running back of his day, who had not even graduated from the university and whose fragmentary scholastic record while there was no better than expected. In either state or private situations, if Prexy failed to fire Headwind the second time around, the board probably ordered him to do so, and Headwind would begin trying to find a new post on a campus willing to risk a faculty member presumably prone to insult fat-cat alumni. That he often did find a new berth means that even fifty years ago a fair number of presidents and boards made some sense. On the whole, however, "a professor at odds with his employer," as Walter P. Metzger, a shrewd student of these issues has said, "[had] the academic duty to be silent or the academic freedom to resign." [37]

"Academic freedom" was the slogan under which Headwind's more uneasy colleagues rode and still ride to his rescue. Its Martin Luther was a thorny, eminent psychologist, J. McKeen Cattell of Columbia, most recalled now as a prime shaper of intelligence testing, then conspicuous as a founder of the American Psychological Association and soon one of the first heads to fall when the strains of War struck the campus. As Academe's uncommon scold he deplored alumni as "no longer scholars or even professional men . . . any university club could get along better without its library than without its bar," and boasted that he had "incited one of my children to call her doll Mr. President [because] he would lie in any position in which he was placed" [38]—and Daddy did not mean President Taft; he meant Nicholas Murray Butler, president of Columbia University. Since 1900, trustees or presidents had dismissed dozens of minor and some major faculty members for behavior that would have gone scatheless abroad. E. A. Ross was driven from Leland Stanford, Jr., University at least partly because he annoyed California's large employers by decrying the importation of cheap Chinese labor. Scott Nearing was dismissed from the University of Pennsylvania for saying too much about child labor in local industries. . . . Cattell and others rallying behind him worked up demands that the professor be accorded what the general and the federal judge already had—permanent tenure of office, provided they refrained from grossly offensive immoralities and kept their colleagues satisfied of their persisting competence in their fields.

In consequence of such feeling in 1913 eighteen professors at Johns Hopkins, symbol of American scholastic integrity, invited the cream of their colleagues at nine other eminent universities to form a professional guild of academic scholars. Support for what began at Columbia and Hopkins built up promisingly in New England, the Midwest and on the Coast, and two years later was born the American Association of University Professors with John Dewey as first president and among its ruling councils such figures as Roscoe Pound of Harvard Law School, A. A. Michelson of the University of Chicago, Wilbur L. Cross of Yale. . . . Its stated objectives were sweeping: to improve the quality of the new graduate schools and the PhD's they created; to rationalize the hit-or-miss system of faculty promotion, lending itself to all the abuses of patronage without the usual pecuniary rewards; maybe even to police the members for nonfeasance. But all that got smothered in sudden activity consequent on a new wave of nasty dismissals in 1915, giving the organization an immediate baptism of fire on the job security front. Then the confusions of War intervened. When picking up the threads after the Armistice, the AAUP confined itself largely to what it had had its earliest experience with: working toward recognition and clarification of academic freedom.

In 1919, at just the right time, President Lowell of Harvard gave a clean example of enlightened policy. Believing that "suppression of free statements of opinion by professors is worse than anything they could possibly say," [39] this conservative-minded Boston Brahmin refused to countenance the ousting from Harvard's faculty of Harold Laski, alien-born, Jewish, radical, self-appointed gadfly, for speaking in support of Boston's police strike at the very time when Lowell was urging undergraduates to volunteer for emergency police duty. Indeed Lowell told his board that if they forced

Laski to resign, he too would resign the same day. After that other presidents of more or less civilized instincts found it easier to meet the AAUP's views. By 1922 their organization, the Association of American Colleges, had got far toward a concordat with the AAUP. Still able to translate *suaviter in modo,* the AAUP cooled off hotheads urging professors' strikes in defense of harassed comrades and confined itself to following down the most fertile complaints. Where Prexy and the board or the chairman of the Esperanto Department were clearly far out of line, their campus was formally blacklisted—in effect posted: ACADEMIC CLIMATE UNFIT FOR SELF-RESPECTING SCHOLARS. Members were not forbidden to go on teaching there or to accept appointments to its faculty. But the word was out, unequivocal, responsible—and not rescinded till the place mended its intellectual manners.

Applied only sporadically to never-the-same-twice situations, handled with a blend of objectivity and zeal most creditable to the AAUP's leadership, the device was subtly successful. By 1939, twenty years after that anomalous collaboration of Lowell and Laski, trustees were tamed to the point where AAUP and AAC could mutually endorse a nonbinding but impressively recommended Magna Carta of the relations between Limbo U and John Doe Highwind, PhD. If Limbo U wanted to keep him beyond seven years, he was to have tenure—permanent appointment terminable only by resignation, retirement, dire financial straits in the Limbo treasury amply proved or moral or professional shortcomings admitted by a kangaroo court of his academic peers. Until the seven-year mark he was to get a year's notice of dismissal. He was entitled to teach students anything that in his scholarly judgment deserved attention, *provided* he stayed within his special field. Outside the classroom he could say anything about anything, *provided* he kept it in mind that "the public may judge his profession and his institution by his utterances. Hence he should at all times be accurate . . . exercise appropriate restraint . . . show respect for the opinions of others . . . make every effort to indicate that he is not an institutional spokesman." [40]

The accord thus summarized necessarily left what Metzger calls "margins of vagueness." [41] Unreconstructed trustees willing to risk the AAUP's quarantine flag can still drive a truck through its spirit. The last thirty years have seen many skirmishes and rule-of-thumb adjustments. But the same is true of the Wagner Act's requiring "collective bargaining in good faith" of employer and labor union. Both were crucial improvements in projected attitudes toward matters that, when guidelines were lacking and bad tempers the chief tools, unnecessarily depleted the nation's moral resources. George E. Pake, former professor of physics at Stanford, former vice-chancellor of Washington University, St. Louis, recently wrote that now "the faculty holds de facto power in the university." [42] No such thing could conceivably have been said about any sizable segment of Academe fifty years ago. For culminating touch Fred M. Hechinger, education expert of the New York *Times*, pointed out in 1971 that "World War II saw no major violations of [AAUP principles] and the protective screen of tenure did much to prevent a political holocaust of firings during the Joseph McCarthy era." [43] The spadework for all that was done in the post-Armistice decade. No, the 1920's were by no means all flash and crash.

Indeed the shoe is now so far on the other foot that some professors as well as administrators wonder whether tenure is not "numbingly encouraging a certain slothfulness among faculty." [44] It also troubles certain professorial consciences that the AAUP has not disciplined heedless members driving trucks through the proviso conditions on which the accord of 1939 bases Professor Highwind's freedoms. And as the College attitude has encroached ever farther on Academe, a process never slackening to this day, dilution of the caliber of the faculty has made the AAUP's privileges seem—to put it tactlessly—disproportionate to the average faculty member's intelligence and integrity. Maybe it was always so. The niceness of conscience and fear of deluding oneself that the accord demands are qualities almost as rare in Academe as anywhere else. Judge, physician and parson have difficult enough tightropes to walk, but Professor Highwind's may be—and probably should be—the most exacting of all.

Concentration on the flash and then the crash of the 1920's is understandable. It was the prevalent flashiness, for instance, that kept baseball the national game in an era vaunting itself on discarding the traditional. That is, it remained so by virtue of letting itself be deliberately altered in directions in which significance seekers may find the true Jazz Age flavor of extravagance. For after the Armistice baseball fell away from the battle of wits and deftness—the choked bat, hit-and-run, pitcher- and infield-dominated game of Tyrus Raymond "Ty" Cobb and John J. "Muggsy" McGraw and became the *force majeure* long-ball game.

The change had already been working up. In 1910, because sharp pitching had forced batting averages to new lows, they put into the regulation ball a cork and rubber core giving the batter more speed and distance if he did manage to connect. But the resulting mild, if definite, rise in number of hits did not satisfy many carpers, like the writer of a piece in *Harper's Weekly* in 1916 who called baseball "The Dullest Sport in the World" and demanded that the pitcher's box be moved farther back to "give the batsman—and the onlookers—a fair chance." [45] So, once the War was over and newspaper readers' minds were back on double plays, Providence and the club owners combined to make the game as splashy as a Ziegfeld production number and as inflationary in effect on the sport as Wall Street's fever was on the economy. The owners' contribution was the rabbit ball. Providence supplied George Herman "Babe" Ruth.

Organized baseball has never yet admitted that there ever was a rabbit ball. But an executive in an official ball-making company once vouchsafed that "his factory had enlivened the official ball from time to time," [46] a likelier story than the owners'—that tighter winding of a more resilient wool became technically available at just the right time. The right time means the rise of Babe Ruth into apotheosis as symbol of baseball prowess. He broke into the majors as a large and devastatingly formidable left-handed pitcher. He was also such a genius at hitting the long ball that the Red Sox put him in the outfield to get the use of his bat every day—and there too he proved outstanding in spite of his short legs and soon top-heavy build. In the first post-War season the rate at which he turned in home runs caused a tumult of enthusiasm among the fans and the sportswriters who stoked their emotions—a ground swell obviously good for the gate receipts. So some as yet unidentified baseball statesman suggested capitalizing on the new passion for home runs by arranging for others than Ruth also to hit them. Enter the rabbit ball. Lardner explained: ". . . the master minds that controls baseball says to themselfs that if it is home runs the public wants to see, why leave us give them home runs so they fixed up a ball which if you don't miss it entirely it will clear the fence. . . ." [47] The new ball unobtrusively making up the 1920 supply looked the same, weighed the same, behaved the same for the pitcher. But at its core seemed to be something far more resilient than anything known earlier. "Rabbit juice," [48] said Grantland Rice; "kangaroo fuzz," [49] suggested Westbrook Pegler.

Other innovations further helped the batter. The new ball parks had shallower outfields; the old ones sprouted new stands or fences to shorten the distance a home run had to carry. At Yankee Stadium, "The House That Ruth Built," it was only 296 feet from home plate into the right-field stand. Pitchers were elaborately forbidden to scuff and distort the ball, as had been their wont, or anoint it with wax, saliva, tobacco juice, slippery elm or whatever they had been using to reduce air friction on one area so the pitch seemed to break several ways at once as it whirred up to the plate. Still it was primarily the hyperlively ball that was the key to the tactical revolution sweeping over baseball and rejoicing younger fans who wanted things more circus-style than the billiard-player reflexes and crapshooter's percentages of Cobb and Willie Keeler. The new ideal, Ruth, swung from the heels, primarily for distance. Indeed his myriad admirers even loved to see him twist himself off his feet when he missed the ball. His keen eye and the rabbit ball worked together to give him fifty-four home runs in 1920, and baseball was never the same again. For his emulators, hungry for the long ball and the higher pay it commanded, also so eagerly exploited the new ball and the new handcuffs on pitchers that some of them came near his soaring totals of home runs. None were what Pegler called gold standard home runs but "inflated home runs" worth only a third or so as much. "But the customers . . . expressed a wish for more . . . even though they realized they would not be genuine." * [50] Lardner blamed the rabbit ball for his complete loss of interest in baseball after 1920. But the bravado of the booming bats took the post-War nation's fancy, and few heeded such croakings.

The Ruth-occasioned mob scene at the turnstiles was the more welcome because 1920 also brought the Black Sox scandal, which, at some other juncture, might have seriously threatened baseball as national game. Nasty episodes linking ballplayers and gamblers had occasionally surfaced, or threatened to, since the 1870's. But this was the big one and came at a time when the press buildup of big-leaguers as wholesome heroes several times life size was at its height. Every few years when another of the principals dies, the details are again exhumed. The Chicago White Sox of 1919 are often described as the finest baseball club in history up to then, with the Philadelphia Athletics of the end of the 1920's as peers or maybe better. They were 5 to 1 to take the World Series, first since the War, from the Cincinnati Reds, able but not in their class. The fans' interest was so intense that the Series was played best five out of nine instead of the usual four out of seven. Arnold Rothstein, a major Eastern gambler who was said to bet on anything but the weather, which he couldn't fix, arranged to bribe the Sox's two best pitchers, their star outfielder and several others to throw the Series. Smells were noticed the evening before the first game when for no discernible reason the odds on Chicago dropped sharply. After the Sox lost the second as well as the first game a quartet of sportswriters, led by Lardner, who supplied the lyrics, sang:

> I'm forever throwing ball games,
> Pretty ball games in the air.
> I come from Chi, I hardly try,
> Just go to bat and fade and die. . . .[51]

The manager and the owner of the Sox were also suspicious. But it took a year for the mess to reach a grand jury and occasion huge headlines—a cultural calamity for Americans, an economic threat to club owners.

Locking the stable door lest more horses stray, the owners set up a National Association of Professional Baseball Leagues with dictatorial powers over players. Its Rhadamanthus was Judge Landis, who looked like a hillbilly Moses just down from Sinai and had recently been conspicuous

---

* This does not imply that Ruth's homers were typically what came to be called Chinese home runs. He could have hit an astonishing number of homers with a broomstick for bat and a California prune for ball. For he was almost a universal baseball genius, and had he had reason to try, would probably have been in the Cobb and Keeler class as place hitter, though he obviously could never have run the bases like Cobb. The long ball was his trademark, however, and his employers' and his gold mine, so he kept right on with it. See discussion of this point in Red Smith's piece on Ruth in the *New York Times Magazine*, September 16, 1973.

for giving leaders of the IWW severe sentences. Though the eight Black Sox were acquitted in a trial vitiated by the disappearance from grand jury records of their confessions and waivers of immunity, Landis barred them from professional baseball forever. So far as is known the industry has been pretty clean ever since. A smelly little flurry came in 1924, two more in 1926–27. One involved Cobb and Tristram "Tris" Speaker, an outfielder-batter of almost equal renown. But hush-hush work and lack of motive enough to account for the allegations smothered them. It was cleverly arranged for Detroit schoolboys to take petitions of support for Cobb through Detroit office buildings. . . . By then anyway the glory of the home run orgy had public confidence most profitably restored.* It went unshaken through the Depression; indeed its greatest moment came in 1932, when Ruth, in a World Series with the Chicago Cubs, two strikes on him, informed the pitcher and the jeering Chicago rooters by gestures that he would blast the next pitch into the center field stands—and did just that.†

That stayed in the cash customers' consciousness as vividly as Jack Dempsey's knocking huge Luis Firpo out of the ring at a million-dollar fight in 1923—a Ruthian application of power, adrenal as well as skillful. The parallel between these two was so strong that Gallico called both, whom he knew fairly well and felt friendly about, "half-brutes" [52] risen from hobo jungles and orphan juvenile delinquency respectively to fame, affluence and some adjustment to toothbrushes and speed limits. Add that, though both were twenty-two when the War came, Dempsey took a shipyard job that exempted him from the draft and Ruth went on pitching for the Red Sox throughout—many ballplayers enlisted, but many did not, and the War had only five months to go when a work-or-fight order finally cracked down on sports figures.

Both Ruth and Dempsey had their great days still to come. Popular reaction to their lack of fighting records was inconsistent. Nobody commented much on Ruth's case, and when he died in 1948, Grantland Rice published a eulogy with a very curious fourth line, probably not ironical:

> Game called by darkness—let the curtain fall,
> No more remembered thunder sweep the field,
> No more the ancient echoes hear the call
> To one who wore so well the sword and shield. . . .[53]

* Some, Grantland Rice included (*The Tumult* . . . , 105–6), saw causal relation between the rabbit ball and the emergency brought on by the Black Sox affair: ". . . the public wanted to see the ball smashed out of the park—where there couldn't be any question of inside baseball—and the game's leaders moved to help" by juicing up the ball. Actually, however, Ruth had already set off the boom in home runs before the Black Sox were exposed.

† Whether Ruth's gestures at the time really meant that has sometimes been authoritatively questioned. ". . . either it did or did not happen," Red Smith recently wrote (*New York Times Magazine*, September 6, 1973). ". . . I was there but I have never been dead sure of what I saw. . . . When the papers reported that [Ruth] had called his shot, he did not deny it."

But Dempsey had several years of public obloquy. After he came to fame by battering hulking Jess Willard into bloody helplessness in 1919, reference to the new champion as a fighter often elicited sneers about the kind of fighting he had done the previous years. He was actually tried—and acquitted—for draft dodging in 1920, and in the first of the million-dollar fights, Dempsey against overmatched Georges Carpentier, the promoter's publicity cast him as scowling villain against a genuine French war hero—which Carpentier really was.

Maybe it meant something about revulsion against any and all War-related values that five years later, when Dempsey lost twice to handsome Gene Tunney, who had volunteered into the U.S. Marines in 1917, the alleged draft dodger was rather a popular favorite over the War veteran. But by then such issues were all smudged up by the tidal waves of free newspaper publicity with which sportswriters were earning paychecks based on rising circulation. Nothing they did in the 1920's was as noisome as their pre-War campaign to find a White Hope to save civilization by taking the heavyweight title away from black Jack Johnson. More significant of the changing values for which the period was reproached, sometimes deservedly, were the growing numbers of women—not blowzy camp followers of the prizefighters but the shiny, décolletée women of heavy spenders in dinner jackets—in the conspicuously expensive seats at big fights.

To football, baseball and prizefights as occasions for sitting and watching others be strenuous the 1920's added ice hockey, basketball and tennis. The first two were North American. Ice hockey, Canadian-born, infiltrated the States through New England and Michigan. Basketball was invented in Springfield, Massachusetts (under the auspices of the same Gulick who founded the Camp Fire Girls), by a YMCA physical director, James Naismith, to give the boys in the gym something more competitive than Indian clubs. Since it used a smaller playing area and was independent of weather, this bouncy, swirling, upward-seeking blend of soccer and hockey made a better spectator sport than either.

The YMCA's took it all over the country. A version for girls with an extra player and special rules developed. Professional teams began to exploit it. The AEF took it to Europe, where it struck roots as baseball did not. By then College athletic directors, particularly in the Midwest, were booming intercollegiate basketball. Student admissions to knockdown bleachers in the gym more than paid for the coach and the simple equipment. Much of that was infection upward from the high schools, among which the game was feverishly organized before most colleges were strongly affected. Here was something really worth doing in that shiny-floored gymnasium intended to foster physical fitness for all pupils in Decaturville's new high school. Many country high schools lacked enough pupil population to field football elevens. But once standard rules fixed the basketball team at five, an enrollment of say eight or nine senior and a dozen or so junior boys often supplied enough athletic potential. And the nippier or huskier among them were likely to be good basketball timber because on the gable end of every barn for miles around protruded a hoop at which Junior was looping a basketball whenever he was not eating, doing chores or in class.

Teams from small high schools often held their own or better with those from large city schools with hundreds of boys to choose from. In 1920 a Midwestern high school basketball tournament at the University of Chicago, including also teams from the Deep South, was won by Wingate, Indiana, a very small school indeed, defeating Crawfordsville, Indiana, a county seat with a very brisk small sectarian college; a few weeks earlier, Crawfordsville had won a Tri-State championship at Cincinnati with Wingate as runner-up; the two towns were only 12 miles apart. Simultaneously the high school of Franklin, Indiana, another county seat with a small sectarian college, was developing a "Wonder Five" who may well have been the best nonprofessional basketball team that ever trotted out on a court.

The five boys making the nucleus of this demonstration that, for some inscrutable reason, Indiana was then basketball incarnate had all been in the same Sunday school class taught by the high school basketball coach. As high school sophomores they not only won the state title but went into its finals with a win/lose record of 29/1. They won it again in 1921 and 1922; 89/8 was their three-season record against the sharpest opponents in the nation. Moving on into Franklin College, coach and all, as freshmen they went undefeated against a tough schedule of Indiana college teams. As their renown grew, they occasionally scheduled one or another big Midwestern university—by then basketball was important in the Big Ten—and in the next three seasons knocked off, once or several times, Wisconsin, Notre Dame, Purdue, Michigan State; no team from outside Indiana ever beat them. They had become a ten-legged, ten-armed, five-headed but single-minded organism never in a hurry, passing the ball without looking to see if the other fellow was there—he'd be there because he always was. You don't need to look at your left foot to know it's there. They specialized in the Garrison finish, eliciting from a sportswriter on the Indianapolis *News*:

> You can beat them in the first half,
> You can always have the ball;
> But when the game is over
> They ain't been beat at all.[54]

Theirs was not the high-scoring game by beanpole freaks familiar today. The Wonder Five were average-sized or not much larger, and their average scores per season ran between 33 and 39 points. But otherwise the word "average" is shudderingly inappropriate for the virtuosity of their passing game and the uncanniness of their eye for the basket. In my memory they were more impressive than Notre Dame's Four Horsemen football team of a few years later. That, as those familiar with the 1920's will recognize, is the optimum compliment.

As basketball hypertrophied in the Midwest, no sooner was football shelved for the year than it took over to keep high schools' and colleges' mental and emotional energy diverted from proper concerns until the end of the season in March: spring football practice coming up. All too often local leaders, usually alumni of the high school, made its basketball team a civic concern, buying its uniforms, paying the fares to away games; one service club gave the boys a banquet at season's end, another gave the coach, a recent member of Limbo U's basketball squad, a silver trophy. . . . A visiting team committing almost as many personal fouls as the home team might be mobbed by local fans as it left the dressing room for the bus. The school gym had been built for intramural basketball for both sexes—and for girls' cheesecloth dancing, boys' wrestling, indoor track and indoor baseball, ancestor of softball, first played with a broomstick and a boxing glove, enthusiastically taken up by recruits in training camps during the War. Now the trapezes and flying rings gathered dust as the basketball squad took over every afternoon for practice and the place smelled permanently, like a frowsy boxers' hangout, of liniment and ancient sweat. And four months of the year bleachers took up half the available room.

The spectator sports motif can be overdone, however. The pre-War notion that strenuous games were smart soon spread non-teamplay sports into lower-income strata. Municipal golf courses, tennis courts and swimming pools were crowded with devotees doing things once pretty much confined to expensive country clubs; only polo remained inaccessible. When Gertrude Ederle, daughter of a German immigrant, swam the English Channel, the nation was as joyful as when Robert Tyre Jones, Jr., son of well-intrenched WASP's in Georgia, won the American and British Opens and the American and British amateur golf tournaments in one year. Such athletes were almost as well known as Ruth and Dempsey. Skiing in winter, dude ranches in summer—the boys' camp adapted to adults—encouraged individual participations. But wherever possible box offices appeared. The tennis stadium at Forest Hills, suburb of New York City, was nominally adjunct of an amateur tennis club but actually the springboard for coast-to-coast barnstorming tournaments run by country clubs. Each date played eroded the amateur standing of the touring big-name players and aggrandized the shifting cast's chief attraction, William T. Tilden II, who played the best tennis the world had seen till then as if choreographed by Noel Coward. The press said he was primarily a showman. So he was; and what is a showman without audiences? The typical Californian kid who went seriously into tennis—and tennis was as important as oranges out there—had Tilden in mind and did it not so much

for love of the game as for a vision of himself at the center court at Forest
Hills, set and match point, aware of thousands holding their breaths . . .
pow! a cannonball service that aces the defending champ. . . .

Sex as public spectator sport did not arrive till the late 1960's, but the
1920's talked as if it were already there. Reviewing the movie of Elinor
Glyn's once-shocking *Three Weeks* in 1924, Sherwood said: "What we once
considered daringly offcolor in distant 1909 is positively bromidic today.
Sex is . . . old stuff. A healthy sign if you ask me." [55]

Maybe so; but supposing the therapy sound, the dosage was very watery.
The assumption that the new latitude had gone so far it had lost zest was
merely wishful. Even among the liberated, four-letter words were little used
in mixed company and the shock threshold was unbelievably far below that
of the 1970's. A Broadway play would no longer get in hot water because
the hero carried the heroine upstairs for what the Mann Act considered
"immoral purposes." A sociological study of the ethics of capitalism would
no longer be put under lock and key in the public libraries of Cleveland and
Toledo, Ohio, because of its title—*Sin and Society.* But three years after
Sherwood's review, a Broadway play about Lesbianism, *The Captive,* was
heavily harassed—maybe the more so because the treatment was not ribald
but soulfully sticky. Through the decade, notably in Boston, serious novels
taking the new freedom at its word were prosecuted for words or ideas that
would be commonplace now.

The symbol of such bluenosery was a name still remembered—Anthony
Comstock, author and enforcement agent of the federal statute barring
obscenity from the U.S. mails; also head of New York State's Society for
the Suppression of Vice, the subsidizers of which included J. P. Morgan and
John D. Rockefeller, Jr. Dell's account of censorship begins: "In 1915 the
infamous Anthony Comstock died and went to hell." [56] He could be silly
about nakedness, as in the widely publicized episode in 1913 of the nude
painting "September Morn," but mostly he concentrated on hard-core
printed smut. Even his hostile biographers, Heywood Broun and Margaret
Leech, applying common sense to the standards of their day, allowed that
"his actual inteference with books, plays and paintings of sincere intent was
slight." [57] Gustavus Myers, enemy of social repression, said that though
Comstock sometimes overdid things, "on the whole, his vigilance did much
in keeping down commercialized obscenity." [58] The *de facto* ban on
Rabelais, the *Decameron* and so on was as much the work of local antivice
zeal, the police of large cities and the U.S. Customs as of Comstock. And
the book bannings of the Jazz Age were the doing not of Comstock but of
his successor and former lieutenant, John S. Sumner, a gray man but not
fanatic-ascetic enough to deny himself good cigars and (after Repeal, of
course) an occasional cocktail.

Soon after taking Comstock's place, Sumner received from the Western

Society for the Suppression of Vice (*hab.* Cincinnati) word that it had forced Dreiser's *The Genius* out of local bookstores and reported it to the U.S. Post Office as obscene and blasphemous. Simultaneously a Manhattanite sent Sumner what he considered dirty pages torn from a copy of it in the New York Public Library. The book had been out for months. Most reviews found it distasteful; the Chicago *Tribune*'s headline was: MR. DREISER CHOOSES A TOM CAT FOR HERO. Sales had been sluggish. But thus alerted, Sumner browbeat the publisher, the John Lane Company, into withdrawing it. A storm of protest came from not only friends of the book but also many who thought it and its author dismally inept. Probably it should have been suppressed to shield rising writers from its atrocious style—see, for example, the first pages of Book III, Chapter I. But its alleged immorality was what kept it withdrawn until, in 1923, the avant-garde Horace Liveright reissued it. No heavens fell. In 1917 Sumner made another row over *Susan Lenox: Her Fall and Rise*, David Graham Phillips' story of a bastard village girl whom society pushes into whoring, and who then pushes herself into glory on the stage. It had already been serialized in *Hearst's International*, but Sumner cited 100-odd pages as obscene and forced the publisher to substitute a toned-down version. Since its erotic content was milder and better handled than that of *The Genius*, maybe the ironic inversion of the title was Sumner's trouble.

Then he went to France as a YMCA secretary, and the dust settled. In January, 1920, he was home again and brought proceedings against *Jurgen*, chief of James Branch Cabell's fantasies set in a whimsical medieval France, and the *Little Review* for installments of James Joyce's *Ulysses*, then new. Since, after 1915, better writers were acquiring daring, his duty reading was of higher quality than Comstock's. In 1920 an American judge was as likely as Leopold Bloom to think Gertie McDowell's coquetries of obscene intent. The *Little Review* was fined $200 and migrated to Paris, leaving *Ulysses* captive in the U.S. Customs' list of items to be seized on sight.

The eclipse of *Jurgen* was short, however, and, as usually occurs, the banning probably made it sell better when reissued. The unusual aspect of the case was that here Sumner challenged the anti-Philistines to rally behind not a work of earnest solemnity garnished with carnalities (like *Lady Chatterley's Lover*) but a text full of lewd fantasies relieved by odd blasphemies, neither of which flavors was at all masked by a literate, if finicky, style more admired then than it is now* by those dipping into it.

---

* Sinclair Lewis, for instance, called *Jurgen* "sheer magic and beauty." (Schorer, *Sinclair Lewis*, 261–62.) Edmund Wilson, upon rereading Cabell, found him unexpectedly "a comic poet of . . . almost unexampled splendor . . . [creating] a world of swift and witty colloquies, of vivid and enchanting colors." ("The James Branch Cabell Case Reopened," *New Yorker*, April 21, 1956.) In my view that is overstated; but some of the passages I got into again rereading *Jurgen*, usually clean ones, such as the hero's impressions of the ocean and his grandmother's visit to heaven, are delightful just as they were fifty years ago. There is also rewarding reading in some of the literary-moral speculations of *Beyond Life*.

Explicit references to genitalia were couched in dead languages. But it bubbled with candid double entendres, usually phallic, as if W. S. Gilbert and the Gustave Flaubert of *Salammbô* had together written a burlesque show. Upton Sinclair persisted in believing it "the most depraved and depraving book ever published in America" and wondered how many college boys its influence had caused to "suffer atrocious torments from gonorrheal infection, or spend their later years in wheel-chairs as a result of syphilitic infections." [59] That is just the usual Sinclairity of thought, but *Jurgen* did rudely pose the question, answered among us only recently and maybe not permanently, what to do with fresh-baked, deliberate pornography of tenable claims to artistic importance? It was a bad day for logic when the moral-legal system that insisted on cleaning up *The Three Musketeers* let *Jurgen* wriggle back into the water.

Sumner professed not to fret when such slips occurred or the headline BANNED IN BOSTON boomed a book. In his view even abortive prosecution, an expensive nuisance, kept publishers aware that he and his likes were active and tended to keep unwholesome items off spring lists. Maybe it worked. It could have accounted for the cleaning up of Victor Margueritte's *La Garçonne*, published as *The Bachelor Girl* in 1923 in America but lacking the passage in which the gentleman tickles a lady's pudendum at the opera and the one in which the heroine is ministered unto *a tergo* as she bends over her flowers. A bilingual female reviewer protested that this version was "to the original . . . as water is to wine." [60] Direct leverage came up when Richard L. Simon of the newborn Simon & Schuster, uneasy about the sweaty candor of Joseph Moncure March's *The Wild Party* (Saturday night among minor show folks), showed it to Sumner and was warned that anybody publishing it would go to jail. Simon backed away. Only after two years of being admired in manuscript by the right people (and it does have vigorous virtues) did it come out in a limited, unadvertised edition from Covici-Friede. If this sly venture came to Sumner's notice, he ignored it. He also ignored *The High Place*, an item in Cabell's Poictesme series full of the lace-wristed homosexuality of the 1700's. It was not Sumner's New York City but Boston that, through a Catholic prosecutor, a Catholic judge and a Catholic jury, fined the publisher of Dreiser's *An American Tragedy*, at least partly because it hinted that birth control had advantages.

Such lapses were probably partly happenstance, partly owing to Sumner's being human—in spite of talk to the contrary—hence neither omniscient nor superhumanly diligent. Nothing about it all was as simple as the youthful charge of John Peale Bishop and Edmund Wilson that in America "the humanities had little chance against the Anti-Vice Society" [61] or W. A. Swanberg's calling Sumner's assault on *The Genius* an attack on "any mature expression of American art." [62] (This identification of maturity with erotic materials will plague us for another generation.) The decade that published *The Great Gatsby*, *Dodsworth*, *The Stammering Century*, *The Sun*

Also Rises, John Brown's Body, The Road to Xanadu and Ring Lardner's later stories and staged *The Emperor Jones, Beggar on Horseback, Porgy, They Knew What They Wanted* and *Street Scene* managed to do well by the humanities with never a peep out of Sumner.

By now it looks as if much of what then seemed to be sporadic bluenosery came not so much from Philistinism as from conflicting half opinions and eroding principles jumbled in the public mind—hence stupid use of laws aimed at *Only a Boy* to smother texts on birth control. A grotesque case in point was that of Vera, Countess Cathcart, a thirtyish South African with good legs and large brown eyes. When arriving in New York City in 1926, she had not been a countess for some time, but keeping the title made newspaper attention easier to get. The War killed her first husband, a captain in the Guards. In 1919 she married the Earl Cathcart, much her elder, becoming a countess right enough, but in 1921 he divorced her for adultery (the only grounds then valid in England) with a younger, married peer, the Earl of Craven. Post-War Mayfair saw many such episodes. She might well have been soon forgotten at home and unknown in America had she not written a play entitled *Ashes* and come here to interest Broadway in it. Its heroine, a charming South African, married to an elderly peer, elopes with a younger one who proves to be a caddish womanizer, then is reconciled to her noble husband. To discourage any notion that the script might be autobiographical, she planned to play the heroine's role herself.

The circumstances of her arrival bred headlines. Her former lover, Craven, and his countess were also in America. And when Vera filled out her landing papers, she answered the query on marital status: "Divorced." This forced the U.S. Immigration Service to determine whether her divorce entailed the "moral turpitude" that, the law said, barred aliens guilty of it. Like the often awkward Mann Act, this was aimed primarily at commercialized vice. But it sometimes winged a visitor who had been guilty party in a British divorce. As a potential deportee Vera was sent to Ellis Island pursued by reporters asking how a countess felt about such treatment. She told them at length, going on into her plans for her play, her impulsive past and the fog that had kept her from seeing the Statue of Liberty. A fine liberty, she said, that treated as criminal in her what thousands of American divorcées had done, that admitted Craven while barring her when even in the law's own terms, he was equally tainted. Her impeccable logic was almost as striking as her green coat trimmed with red fox fur and her large green hat—*The Green Hat*, Michael Arlen's shiny novel about British high life, a roaring best seller, had just become a Broadway hit graced by Katharine Cornell.

Cables hummed with well-taken strictures on Yankee hypocrisy and prudery. The American Woman's Party, vestige of the pre-War suffrage movement, and the American Civil Liberties Union sent the lady able

lawyers. Some of the consequences were frustrating. The Immigration
authorities so interested themselves in Craven that he and wife, firing
indignant remarks in all directions, took refuge in Canada. Vera's counsel
from the ACLU, Hays again, obtained her a writ of habeas corpus on the
grounds that the law required that the given turpitudinous act be held a
crime by the law of the tainted alien's own country—which, he proved,
adultery was not in South Africa. Immigration officials, obviously relieved,
assured the press that the administrative effect of the decision would be to
temper future use of the turpitude clause with discretion, in effect annulling
it for amateurs. Vera purred to the reporters about how Hays had been "so
human, so handsome, so intelligent," the federal prosecutor "marvellously
just," the judge "really very nice." [63] Throughout the hearings she had been
careful to wear that green hat.

Soon her feeling for publicity made her one of the guests at a famous
party given by Earl Carroll—earls of one sort or another were in her
stars—raided by the police because its entertainment included a show girl
bathing on stage stark naked in alleged champagne. Vera told the press she
had seen nothing heinous. In gratitude or maybe poor judgment Carroll
agreed to produce *Ashes of Love*, as her play was now called. Another
victory—only its tryout in Washington, D.C., with Vera as the winsome,
wayward heroine, was so bleakly received that Carroll sold her back the
producing rights. She brought it into Broadway; it lasted a week. Home she
went, saying that compared to Broadway's and Washington's reviewers, the
Immigration men had been kind. Presumably she rejoined the fiancé who
had loyally cabled the U.S. Department of Labor a protest against "any
reflection on her character." [64]

Net results: The Cravens' stay in the States was spoiled. So were Vera's
hopes of success on the stage. But the British press had had almost as good
a time as it would the following year when Big Bill Thompson squared off
with King George. Broadway had been shown that, contrary to common
belief, it was not true that any script with adultery in it would pay.
And—this was valuable—the Immigration Service had public leave to, for
God's sake, exercise common sense in future.

At the time a movement for a reform called Trial Marriage was trying to
apply something much nearer common sense to that long-standing problem
of who sleeps with whom. Its focus was Judge Lindsey, whom we last saw
boarding the Peace Ship. In 1924 he had been much in the public eye as the
only conspicuous candidate for office in Colorado not to lose to the Klan's
slate. His margin of victory was so narrow and the Klan hated him so—he
had explained their attacks on Denver's Catholics and Jews thus: "They
had paid ten dollars each to hate somebody and they were determined to
get their money's worth" [65]—that they got his election invalidated in the
courts. But that episode was incidental for the little judge. As ebullient

leader in creating juvenile courts to insulate delinquent minors from their
elders and unbetters, he was already nationally known, indeed had tied
Billy Sunday for eighth place in that *American* magazine poll to name the
most eminent living American. A high proportion of those coming before
his Juvenile and Family Court in Denver were, of course, pregnant
unmarried girls; the boys involved; other girls "gone wrong" but as yet not
pregnant; their ignorant and often shotgun-minded parents; the scandal-
ized teachers of the schools they attended or had ceased to attend; married
couples broken down by having to cope with too many children too soon;
children scarred and warped by such parents. . . . Enthusiastically—Lindsey was a cocksure enthusiast—he concluded that "Marriage, as we now
have it, is plain hell for most persons who get into it," [66] and proposed
drastic revision to fit the institution better to human hormones and the
climate of 1920.

Most of his scheme drew on two books that reformers of his day were full
of: Havelock Ellis' *Studies in the Psychology of Sex* and Lippmann's first
major work, *A Preface to Morals*. There he found support for his own
suspicions that unsanctioned sexual congress was not necessarily bad and
the sanctioned kind not necessarily good and that the new birth control
movement made possible a newly healthy rationalizing of attitudes toward
the issue. Mrs. Sanger's gospel thus underlay his recommendation that by
exploiting the recent "perfecting of simple and adequate contraceptive
methods . . . society . . . develop two frankly recognized kinds of marriage which already exist without such recognition . . . one for cohabitation
and the other for the rearing of children." [67] He cited many cases known to
him as confidant of Denver's young folks in which He and She, thanks to
birth control, had shown the way to such new institutions by shacking up
together in "a rapidly spreading conviction that Love without Marriage
may be a moral and chaste thing, harmful neither to Society nor to the two
persons concerned." He named this new thing "Trial Marriage"—"informal
agreement on the .part of a man and woman to live together until they
change their minds—usually with the intention of not changing them . . .
many . . . 'Trial Marriages' ripen into legal marriage especially when
pregnancy results." [68] He likened it to an old Scottish custom, "handfast-
ing," that gave informally betrothed couples bed privileges for a prenuptial
year and a day with the privilege until then of breaking up at any time.

This codification of what Greenwich Village had been practicing and
preaching for years naturally made Lindsey the hero of young rebels and, as
a recent biographer says, "the leading American spokesman for the sexual
revolution." [69] The merit of his doctrine was that it practically recognized
what birth control and urbanization were already doing to the Apostle
Paul's notions of the proper thing. But Lindsey was too restless to leave it at
that. He had to go on: "I don't think Paul would have liked our little
flappers, but I think Jesus would have smiled upon them as he did on all

children." [70] He denounced abortion—a specter familiar in his courtroom—not for its physical risks when illicit but because of an Easter-card morality wildly inconsistent with his policy of arranging secret lyings-in and subsequent adoptions: "I am for children . . . because I am for Society. I insist on the right of the child to be born, and that there be no 'illegitimate children.' . . . for the unmarried mother, as a sacred channel of life, the same reverence and respect as for the married mother." [71]

Blame some of that on the race suicide bugaboo of his day; maybe it also reflected his Catholic rearing. He strayed farther still, asserting that malnutrition led to precocious menarche—the exact opposite is far likelier—hence to delinquency in the early teens. He scolded teachers for not warning girls that constipation—an ailment common among adolescents in his courtroom, he said—could sterilize them as inflammation of the enteric tract spread to the ovaries, a curious contribution to medicine. His estimates, based on interviews in his chambers, he said, of the proportion of Denver's high school boys and girls fornicating were either absurdly exaggerated or Denver in the early 1920's was astonishingly different from the Indianapolis in which I went to high school those same years. He professed to be able to diagnose promiscuity in girls of eleven or twelve years solely from "the look of the mouth." [72] His groundbreaking *The Revolt of Modern Youth* (1925) was rich in alleged case histories, usually of girls from Denver's upper strata whom his advice saved from life disaster, suggesting that this experienced judge either had no ear for liars or was a drawer of pretty long bows. Nor did his yarns sound solider for the book's being run as a serial in *Physical Culture*, flagship magazine of the publishing empire of corny-sexy, crank-minded, paranoid muscleman, Bernarr Macfadden—his other publications were confessions magazines and the New York *Evening Graphic*, wildest tabloid newspaper of the day.

Nevertheless, it was translated into six languages and caused so much stir that lecture audiences all over the country clamored to hear Lindsey, already a veteran of the platform, vociferously defend its validity. Gradually he learned that the emphasis on casually tenuous relations in the book was undermining its acceptability. His next book rather drew in its horns, changing the proposal to "Companionate Marriage"—a phrase borrowed from Melvin M. Knight, a sociologist who had been applying the same sort of reason more cautiously—defined as: "legal marriage, with legalized Birth Control, and . . . the right to divorce by mutual consent for childless couples, usually without payment of alimony." [73] For all practical purposes, he pointed out, the affluent getting collusive Paris and Reno divorces already had pretty much such facilities available; this merely extended it to lower-income brackets.

He tried very hard to convince himself as well as others that this addition of legality adequately emphasized intent of permanent relationships and put the indicated psychological brake on youth's impulsive fickleness. But the public that made the second book a best seller and gave him notoriety parallel to that of Alfred C. Kinsey in our own time brushed aside such obscuring subtleties. Billy Sunday called Companionate Marriage "barnyard marriage," [74] and the world agreed. What it could not agree on was whether society should take a leaf out of the barnyard's book. As the hullabaloo increased, Hollywood planned a movie entitled *Companionate Marriage* (Lindsey to make personal appearances at its openings in key cities), and Bishop Manning preached a sermon in New York City's Episcopal Cathedral of St. John the Divine calling the book "one of the most filthy, insidious, and cleverly written pieces of propaganda ever published in behalf of lewdness, promiscuity, adultery, and unrestrained sexual gratification." [75] Lindsey, who had made a point of attending, rose among the congregation and shouted so loudly for opportunity to rebut the bishop that he was forcibly removed.

Promising as it looked for a while, Companionate Marriage died on the vine—patently because it was needed less and less as years passed. It had served its purpose in dramatizing for the community, particularly for the rising generation, the sociological fact that now birth control was so good a bet, living in alleged sin to see whether marriage would probably work out well was morally practical. That is, they ignored the veneer of legalism and stuck to the original Trial Marriage formula. The 1970's have every reason to feel grateful to the noisy little man, so given to making sense for the wrong reasons, who skipped about the platform in a debate with Rabbi Wise in Carnegie Hall so stridently shouting, "I deny that sex is sin!" [76]

Show business' exploitations of new attitudes toward Sex included Hollywood's lubricious palterings, the Village's doctrinaire pawings and the near nakedness of the *Follies/Vanities/Scandals* sort of thing. Those last and the nightclub shows that aped them had Parisian prototypes and, being basically prurient, were at best esthetically negligible. But the great beauty and intemperate display of their show and chorus girls combined with press agentry to keep Broadway almost abreast of Hollywood as pretty-girl country.

In "the legit" the quasi-incest of *Desire Under the Elms* and the homosexuality of *The Captive* and *The Green Bay Tree* marked the outer limits of subject matter that was not, of course, consummated onstage as it might be today. Certain crude farces leering at middle-aged women and venal young men led the chief magistrate of New York City, confused by the cross tides of public shock and the Big Town's wise-guy permissiveness, to create a standing jury of eminent citizens to review scripts and condemn the smelliest before production—a National Board of Review for Broadway. It was smothered by magistrates' disinclination to take its imprimatur seriously. The emancipation of the American Thespis proceeded as treatment of extramarital pregnancy ranged from the old man's rueful acceptance in *They Knew What They Wanted* to the off-again-on-again plot of *Little Accident* (1928) in which Dell, Villager though he was, mildly ridiculed the emancipated view of moonlit fornication. All very confusing for the police, and the profession, and for that matter intelligent spectators like Elmer Davis: ". . . current opinion permits a freedom of expression on sexual matters that would have been unthinkable ten years ago; but for a few enthusiasts—most of whom know as little about art as the average reformer does about purity . . . show business . . . had all the traffic would bear but they insisted on reaching out for more. And when the explosion came, some of the friends of art . . . wasted their ammunition by standing out for free expression as a matter of principle." [77] One sees now that though at the time it looked like a waste of ammunition, Davis was wrong. Sweeping victory for anything-goes eventually came of keeping on firing for forty-odd years. What would Davis have said about *Oh! Calcutta!?*

Juggling of forbidden fruit on the stage was further confused by a poor relation branch of show business called burlesque that by 1920 had rounded out the special smell of a peculiarly American use of the word. It came into English as French version of an Italian term for travesty of well-known plays. In the mid-1800's it meant a tough French, British and to some extent American tradition of extravaganza with music, knockabout clowns, plump girls with bare shoulders and legs in tights and boots spoofing a standard stage play, *La Dame aux Caméllias* or *The Lady of Lyons*. Gilbert and Sullivan's *HMS Pinafore* and *Ruddigore* were in that idiom albeit far more decorous and parodying types of plot rather than specific items. A near cousin was Britain's Christmas "pantomime" mixing vestiges of the *commedia dell'arte* with extravagant burlesque of one or another fairy tale. In the 1870's the American branch had a transfusion of sex appeal when troupes of juicy British girls in hip-high tights and feathered hats stormed Broadway with *The Black Crook, Ixion, The White Fawn*—spectacle burlesques cousin to Parisian *opéra-bouffe*. Yet for all this exotic background "burlesque" in post-1900 America was a new entertainment almost as distinctive as baseball. Its special audience used its own pronunciation: "burleycue" sometimes corrected by the phonetic spelling "burlesk."

By then it meant a theatrical subculture housed in decaying theaters in New York City, Boston, Chicago, Philadelphia, charging low admission to droopy road shows based nominally on travesty of current plays but relying ever more on the dirty joke and the well-filled pair of tights.* Straight eroticism was provided by featured cooch dancers emulating the Near Eastern dancers who had been the jewels of the Midway of the Chicago

---

* Weber and Fields are often said to have kept burlesque at a high level in their shows at their own Music Hall on Broadway in the pre-War decade. But, as Irving Zeidman says in *The American Burlesque Show* (45–46), though they had come up from burlesque, they carefully called their shows taken off from current hits "travesties": "Actually neither they nor their audiences considered these performances 'burlesque shows.' "

Columbian Exposition of 1893. Several "wheels" of such houses booked weekly program changes through a central office, a sort of foulmouthed Chautauqua. They supplied towns of under 100,000 population only when they had a high proportion of miners or industrial workers. James Barton, harking back to that part of his career, said that such towns' heavily mustached audiences of newly arrived Central Europeans "didn't know what it was all about . . . [didn't] understand a damn word we were saying . . . just came to see the legs . . . though most of them got the meaning of a smutty scene." [78] In larger cities, too, effort at travesty in these bedraggled shows lost whatever point it had once had. Comics could abandon the rags of story line and go into skits adapted from vaudeville and minstrel shows; the chorus girls, with skirts up to there, sometimes a few stepping out of line for specialty dances, drew with no regard whatever to plot.

Men had always dominated the audiences. Now women hardly came at all and—cause? effect?—"burlesque" meant girls as far undressed and lines as blue as the local police would tolerate. In 1909 Sime Silverman, founder of show business' great paper, *Variety*, who long nursed hopes that this part of the industry would cease to be foul and frowsy, wrote: "Were there no women in burlesque, how many men would attend? The answer is the basic principle of the burlesque business." [79] Nothing of the elder ingredients remained but the infrequent production numbers parading the girls onstage while at one side of the proscenium a shopworn soprano or a tenor, who doubled as straight man, sang a June-moon-spoon ballad.

The comics borrowed from other traditions and dirtied up the baggy-trousered, absurdly shod, shave-needing, tiny-hatted hobo. The red-nosed Mick. The blue-whiskered Hebe (= Jew). The elegantly (as burlesque conceived elegance) dressed straight man, bastard son of the interlocutor of the minstrel show. The club-twirling, thick-witted policeman. Maybe a black-face secondary comic as butt for gags and whacks. The silk-and-fur-piece soubrette high-hatted the comic at first but was soon cut down to size. Here came the farmer's daughter in a blond wig and a gingham dress committed to flipping up behind. . . . The routines based on "Schultz, the butcher, with the longest salami in town"; or the feceslike stench of Limburger cheese; or the weak bladder of a comic got up as a child; or a nightgown-clad girl grappling with a shrimp of a lover loudly addressed as Gas-tawn because it was all supposed to be French, the mustached and goateed husband bursting in just as Gas-tawn dives under the bed to find two others already there; or the judge behind a police station desk cracking the accused's lawyer over the knuckles with his gavel and darting, gown flying, after the prisoner's ogling wife. . . .

It all relied heavily on what passed for double entendre on the Bowery or South State Street. Straight man meets haughty soubrette got up to kill. They chat toploftically. Enter tramp comic, greets straight man as old friend, eyes soubrette. Straight man says, "Now when I introduce you to the

lady, go right up and grasp her digits." After shy demur the comic grabs at
her salient bosom and gets knocked kicking. Then she stands back-to with
her behind revolving, and the comic, picking himself up, calls, "Hey, lady,
your engine's running." The Cleopatra legend often appeared in burlesque
for the sake of reference to Cleopatra's asp. Other traditional routines
seemed to be tired, vestigial fragments of nobody knew what persisting long
after losing significance. In one the men of the company swaggered around
the stage in a sort of lunatic Paul Jones stopping every few feet to shake
hands and sing out "Hello Bill!" In another just as cryptic the key line was
"We'll stick to the union!" In a third I recall two comics working
themselves into a lather singing over and over to a tune strangely like "At
the Cross, at the Cross" this succinct lyric:

> At the battle of the Nile
> We was fightin' all the while!

and then they just prowled pantingly offstage apparently exhausted. A
popular motif was skid row's scorn of the dapper straight man and cringing
contempt for policemen. A jaunty tramp meets a blue-coated cop, goes all
obsequious, admires his uniform, his shiny badge, his brass buttons, asks
how does one get to wear such finery? "Oh," says the cop, "I'm a public
servant." "OK," says the tramp, "fetch me a glass of water," and gets
clubbed senseless, but he has had his moment and the house is delighted.
Most burlesque theaters were in the neighborhood of skid row.

In these stock routines the house, knowing what came next, could savor
the given performer's slight variations and subtleties of voice and timing.
Most burlesque comics, as Irving Zeidman truly says in his solid account of
the industry, "resembled the lower rank in any trade . . . just good enough
to be in it . . . not quite good enough for anything better [but] many . . .
recall with the charity of nostalgia occasional hilarious episodes of
enjoyable slapstick or engaging hokum." [80] At their best some could be
marvelously good. Out of prestriptease burlesque came such ornaments of
Broadway as Bobby Clark of the tigerish smile and lightning cane play and
Tom Howard of the peevish voice and starveling slouch and W. C. Fields,
Fannie Brice, Leon Errol. . . . But Sliding Billy Watson and Bozo Snyder,
who did wonders with such material as the above, never got out of
burlesque. The women principals, leading the girls' dancing (so called) and
taking parts in skits, were designated soubrettes—a distant link with the
saucy confidante-servants of Molière and Beaumarchais. They averaged
much prettier than the girls in the line. Fancy troupes carried their own
choruses and even scenery. Drabber ones used dingy house scenery and a
bedraggled local stock chorus. By the mid-1920's the fraying house
wardrobe consisted of brief décolleté rompers or, as daring grew, midriff-

baring brassiere and shorts. Whether fleshings masked legs and midriff depended on the local police and management's willingness to pay.

It became fashionable to profess to be amused by the candid gold teeth and shopworn air of these choruses. Benchley, for instance, just for the hell of it, reviewed a Union Square burlesque show in 1921:

> ". . . each individual [girl] doing something original, instead of confining her movements to a common action. The . . . second from the end, with red hair, introduced an extraordinary shoulder and upper torso agitation . . . her neighbor on the left (whom I am quite sure I recognized as a former algebra teacher) made motions with her hands . . . as if playing the piano. . . . On the other side . . . somebody's mother was executing a carefree prance. . . ."[81]

This minor cult formed on several levels. In the dreary routines of Boston's Old Howard or New York City's National Winter Garden the cultivated Floyd Dell saw "the promise of the dionysiac god to them that toiled and bore harsh burdens." The comic's "hilarious cheapening of the values of normal life" made the underdog-patron "a rebellious child delightedly come into a dream world where all burdens are lifted." [82] This Olympianly patronizing tone was curious coming from radicals chary of the dignity of the toiling masses. Concentrating on the performers, Cummings rejoiced in the ugliness of the Old Howard's girls and "the anatomically unique chorus" of the National Winter Garden, and, falling into estheticism, averred that a certain bit of business used by the star comic there moved him as deeply as anything Cézanne ever painted. He identified Flaubert's *mot juste* in "I'll hit yer so hard yer shirt'll roll up yer back like a windowshade!" and likened the vitality of it all to "the sculpture of Gaston Lachaise, the painting of John Marin and the music of Igor Stravinsky." [83] Dos Passos was at least not quite so far-fetched in saying burlesque as he knew it was "in direct line from Aristophanes, and Terence and Plautus." [84]

When the police closed the National Winter Garden, Cummings turned, on Dos Passos' recommendation, to the Irving Place Theater and the striptease that had been creeping into the industry along with such other nods to Aphrodite Pandemos as runways bringing the girls close to the patrons—a device lifted from the Broadway of 1914. Until then the typical female headliner had usually depended on the erotic violence of her cooch—at its height a demonstration of how a girl could "consummate a marriage all by herself," as *Variety* once described it. Cummings wrote in 1936 that at the Irving Place, "Humor, filth, slapstick and satire were all present but primarily to enhance the Eternal Feminine." [85] At this point burlesque as a distinct bit of Americana was complete.*

---

* Zeidman (*The American Burlesque Show*, 118) says that a certain amount of gradual undressing was in soubrettes' routines in the proto-burlesque lady minstrel and Amazon shows

Brighter strippers—those able to memorize cues and a few lines—played the soubrette parts in skits. But that was secondary to Hinda Wassau or Margie Hart prancing and gliding in a pink spotlight while removing, encore by encore, cape, long gloves, evening gown split over a split gauze petticoat, petticoat, sequined brassiere over a net brassiere, sequined loincloth over a cache-sexe, net brassiere, and—when the cry of "Take it off!" was very loud and the police very lax—finally the cache-sexe and a lightning exit. The music of the basic pit orchestra that went with it had only one virtue—a strong, not to say rancid, rhythm. This new art required new principles of costume structure; fortunately the zipper was soon invented. A typical bill—the show had no title anymore; the marquee just said "BURLESK—Ann Corio—BURLESK"—now fielded three or four strippers, one headlined, and maybe a specialist cooch dancer for change of pace. The basic conservatism of show business was all that kept managers hiring comics and chorus. The straight man and the comics tried hard with ever dirtier gags and broader leerings about homosexuality, but the strip-addicted customers would hardly have noticed had they dried up and blown away.

Stripping reached its moral and intellectual height in the mid-1930's, when Gypsy Rose Lee's version of it graced a benefit for Loyalist Spain and Mencken coined for her the label "ecdysiast" from the Greek for a snake shedding its skin. In 1937, when New York City closed all burlesque houses, several eminent people from the cultivated world testified in protest at consequent hearings. Cleon Throckmorton, prominent stage designer, defended burlesque as "the poor man's theater"; Brooks Atkinson, drama critic of the New York *Times*, said that since censorship was intolerable, the only thing to do about burlesque was to improve the human race; Reginald Marsh, for whose paintings burlesque had long been a favorite topic, protested that it was an integral "part of American life." [86]

But the jig was up for the industry that had once made fat profits and built its own theaters in New York City and Chicago. Stripping fled to minor nightclubs, then, as one of those dreadful but lucrative American innovations, flooded London's Soho. Then Federico Fellini used an amateur strip as a dismayingly sophomoric symbol of the gaminess of modern life in *La Dolce Vita*. Some of the comics cleaned up their old

---

of the late 1880's. He identifies Anna Toebe as a burlesque principal "combining her meaningful shake routine with the equivalent of a modern strip" soon after 1900. After the Olympic Theater in Paris closed in 1970, it was claimed that striptease was invented there in 1895 in a skit, "The Bride Goes to Bed" (Paris *Herald Tribune*, April 11–12, 1970). This was probably the routine (maid gradually undresses girl in a bedroom, elderly bridegroom arrives rubbing hands just as the chemise comes off leaving her in naked-looking fleshings) that Sam T. Jack, American burlesque producer, bought in Paris *c.* 1900 and used in a burlesque, *Orange Blossoms*, in New York City till the police stepped in. (Sobel, *Burley-cue*, 56.) The late William A. Brady once told me that a kind of striptease was common in San Francisco honkytonks earlier than that. Whether or not it was primarily an American invention, America probably did give it its by now conventional form as a standard entertainment device down to bare skin.

routines for summer employment in the Borscht Circuit resort hotels of New York State's Catskills region; a few, most notably Phil Silvers, struggled into recognition on Broadway. This fission completed a degeneration that had begun when the first net brassiere was flung into the wings. However Cummings relished ecdysiasts, what marrow burlesque had went out of it when it let voyeurism submerge the comics. Vestiges may survive, but time has dispersed the faithful audience who knew that after the comic's left hand fondles the soubrette's far hip and she says, "Take that hand away!" he will flourish his right hand and say, "Honey, this is the little devil to look out for!"

Burlesque was America's most raffish public recognition that women are made differently from men and some more attractively so than others. Rather more respectable though just as imbecile was the big-time beauty contest developing simultaneously with the striptease. Its roots were in Hollywood. Mack Sennett's and others' slapstick movies were garnished with prankish pretty girls in fancy bathing suits (often set off by elaborate hats) never meant for water but showing deep décolletage fore and aft and much stockinged leg—even sometimes legs bare from just below the knee to mid-thigh. From their ranks rose several women stars. Gloria Swanson, Mabel Normand had once been "bathing beauties," soon all one word.

They were good incidental advertising for the Californian beaches that they were shown frequenting. As America began to hum after Harding was elected, Atlantic City, the Eastern beach resort, borrowed the bathing-beauty motif. Each of the nation's big cities was persuaded to choose its loveliest girl as "Miss Chicago," "Miss Seattle" or whatever and send her to Atlantic City to compete for the title of "Miss America" by appearing on a stage in a bathing suit as scanty as could be tolerated. This was not quite original. In the sixth century B.C. the Greek island of Lesbos included such a competition among local girls in its annual festival of Hera, queen of Olympus. What prize or privileges went to the winner is not known. In 1921 the first Miss America—fair-haired, blue-eyed Margaret Gorman of Washington, D.C.—got only the kind of loving cup that goes with the municipal golf championship of Peoria, Illinois, and the gratifying knowledge that she was the most attractive girl in America—or anyway the most attractive one willing to be paraded about like an entry in a dog show.

The criteria were simple: face, smile, hair, legs, arms, as much of the torso as could be judged through a cluttery tunic. It wouldn't have mattered if she had never learned to talk. (As the nephew of the man who ran the Miss America contests of the late 1930's explained, it wasn't that he felt the "girls were without talent; he just believed that things would be better if they kept it to themselves." [87]) As yet newsreel cameramen, with no sound track on their minds, could concentrate on the kinds of shots in beach garb or got up like the Statue of Liberty that the sponsors had in mind. It was superb press agentry. Just when the nation was so happily paltering with Sex, the image of Miss America added to the former connotations of Atlantic City—such as the Boardwalk, saltwater taffy, the Steel Pier, Broadway tryouts, sea air for the affluent—the prurient cliché of eagerly exposed girlishness. It epitomized the new technique for creating publicity from the void—cobble up an artificial occasion (Mother's Day) or sport (marathon dancing)* or hobby (flagpole sitting) or conflict (the Scopes trial) and make sure the papers know about it.

Upgrading soon began. The next year the master of the revels was King Neptune emerging from the surf crowned and bearded in the person of Hudson Maxim, who was a chronic cutup as well as inventor of smokeless powder; the next day Miss America led a baby parade on the Boardwalk. The third year the number of entries rose to fifty-seven and the trophy hypertrophied into a golden mermaid seated among golden shells said to be worth $5,000. In any case the winner could count on some $50,000 from fees for personal appearances, vaudeville bookings, endorsements. . . . In 1924 ordeal by evening gown supplemented ordeal by bathing suit, modifying the Minskyish effect as bathing suits shrank; indeed the police once threatened to arrest a contestant for wearing on the beach the same outfit she had used on the judges the previous day. The next year local judges were replaced by some of the nation's best known magazine artists—Howard Chandler Christy, Norman Rockwell among names still recognizable, adding up to still another publicity release.

One of the few national entries to get a break in Hollywood was Georgia Hale, whom Chaplin cast opposite him in *The Gold Rush*; she proved too excruciatingly vapid for even a Chaplin lead. The only early entry to reach real prominence was Rosebud Blondell, Miss Dallas of 1926, who failed to win the national title but changed her first name to Joan and became an amusingly pretty minor screen star. In 1927 the growingly elaborate doings drew such widespread and somewhat raffishly toned notice that Atlantic City's more conservative hotel men decided it was giving the resort a bad name and refused to back it any longer. With one or two minor twitches the idea stayed latent until the latter 1930's, when it had a revival premised on a new dignity and college scholarships under the management of a highly capable lady, Lenora Slaughter, who had learned promotion propagandizing the amenities and beauties of staid St. Petersburg, Florida. Even without Miss America's lead, however, minor beauty contests went on meanwhile. In time, as other nations took it up, it became another thing that America gave Western man, such as syphilis (probably), cocktails, jazz, airplanes, rescue in two great wars, and the works of Upton Sinclair.

---

* Horace McCoy's *They Shoot Horses, Don't They?* and the movie they made of it gave the impression that marathon dancing was Depression-created and based on economic desperation. Actually it began in the booming early 1920's.

Women's Liberation now tells us that beauty contests insult womanhood. Maybe that was why the rest of the world unchivalrously copied them while eschewing most other aspects of American attitudes toward women—always a puzzle outside the United States. Nor were Americans themselves notable for understanding them.

Immediately after the Armistice the stock of Gynocracy Preferred did look as promising as the soft-drink industry. Women had come out of the War with great and, on the whole, deserved credit. They had besides an impressive list of achievements with pre-War roots. More than any other single factor their enterprise exerted in righteous directions had created such strong national reagents as settlement houses, food and drug laws, both timely and untimely pacifisms, PTA's, Prohibition . . . all brought to birth without the advantage of the federal ballot. In 1920 ratification of the Nineteenth Amendment in time for the Presidential election added 9,500,000 women to the 17,500,000 whom state action had already given the vote. All set for the bright new day that feminism had been promising—the cleanup of dirty politics; the diversion of resources from weapons and pork barrels into constructive uses; the creation of effective international agencies for peace! Such prospects were good reason for the American Woman to reiterate her claims to higher morality and finer grain that she had first filed well before the Civil War. On the pedestal of the grouped statues of Lucretia Mott, Elizabeth Cady Stanton and Susan B. Anthony, installed by victorious suffragettes in the basement of the U.S. Capitol, was inscribed: "The three great destiny characters of the world whose spiritual import and historical significance transcend that of all others of any country or age." [88] In 1919 Mary Austin, novelist, feminist and observer of Greenwich Village before she moved to the southwest coast of Bohemia in New Mexico, apparently felt no self-consciousness about using the phrase "the spiritual superiority of women" [89] as something to be taken for granted like their equipment with thicker subcutaneous fat.

Not all favoring votes for women had been so sanguine. Judge Lindsey, though stalwart for feminist kinds of good causes, nevertheless believed from experience on the hustings as well as on the bench that "Women . . . are just the same as men in politics, subject to the same strength and weakness" [90] and said he was tired of talk about women's bringing a better world to birth. Herbert Croly, editor of the liberal *Nation*, said votes for women would "change nothing very radically," could come to no more than a token, though valuable as such, of vast social changes already well toward consummation.[91] Neither man can have been surprised when it proved throughout the 1920's that far fewer women than men bothered to vote, that 95 percent of those who did voted the same as their husbands, that big-city bosses urging their precinct henchmen to get the boys' wives and daughters registered and voted found their majorities gratifyingly higher. It was dismally prophetic of how empty feminist promises had been that the election of 1920, the first with women fully qualified, made the catspaw of the Ohio Gang President and killed all hope of any role for the United States in the League of Nations. Six years later Abe Martin, sage of the Indianapolis *News*, doubtless thinking of Teapot Dome, the Scopes trial and Al Capone, wrote the epitaph "Wouldn't th' way things are goin' these days make a fine argymint in favor of woman suffrage if we didn't already have it?" [92]

As symbol of the New Woman's liberated frankness and freedom the short skirt was stressed in the early 1920's, indeed out of proportion to the degree of shortness. Dropped waistlines hugging what was left of the behind after slimming—the other salient trait of the Jazz Age—appeared in extreme form soon after the Armistice. But the decade was half over before cables about "appallingly short" [93] skirts at the Paris openings warned that just-a-touch-below-the-knee would now be *de rigueur*. That height, never altered until 1929 pulled skirts down again, caused almost as much hullabaloo as miniskirts did in the late 1960's. Actually this high-water mark, moderate though it looks now, had two counterfeminist consequences. Though international in acceptance—indeed British and French girls wore them shorter than ours did—it enhanced the American girl's renown for the most attractive legs in the world, thus perpetuating values that feminism frowned on. And by corollary it committed her, bent on making the most of her best feature, to the relative luxury of silk stockings, for which even typists earning 50 cents an hour had to pay some $2 a pair. Those long silken legs became, as Hollywood knew so well, the decade's chief vehicle of feminine hedonism, of self-conscious feminine attraction for the other sex, and as such quite as distasteful to sober feminists as any beauty contest.

Woman's freedom seeking was also hampered by what was once called her crowning glory. In the Gibson Girl's day only affluent women used the professional hairdresser much, and even they relied chiefly on personal maids for such expert fussing. Most women washed their long tresses themselves at regular intervals, gave them so many strokes with a brush and braided them just before bed, shook them out in the morning and with a comb, a mouthful of hairpins and long-practiced ingenuity arranged them for the day in whatever combination of partings, puffs, coils, braids and whatnot was the current mode. The bother of long hair explains the eagerness with which, aside from issues of fashion and ideology, women took to bobbed hair once the barrier was breached. Girls able to keep themselves persuaded that the shingle cut, close to the head and sleeked down with pomatum à la Colleen Moore, became them—as it often did—were in luck. But this triumph of convenience and sense was never more than marginal. For decades little American girls had been reared to share their mothers' belief that wavy hair was God's finest gift to womankind, not least so because the white American gene pool being what it is, not one woman in ten had it naturally. Hence the familiar smell of singed hair from the curling iron or the wiggly variety of it that produced the marcel wave and Mom's long hours with curlpapers or kid curlers to give little Francine those sausage curls. And now, pretty much in step with the great post-War epidemic of influenza, the French were infiltrating the international woman's world with what they originally called *l'ondolation indéfrisable*, hastily Englished as "permanent wave."

In its early phase this cosmetic miracle was dangerous, clumsy and unreliable. ". . . never before did I realize the force of the statement, *Il faut souffrir pour être belle*," wrote an early subject, telling how they twisted, tweaked and "encased my poor tresses, attaching the cylindrical results to an infernal machine, under which I sat for three hours, looking like the Empress of China and feeling like Absalom." [94] Indeed, the machine being electrical, the process bore an unnerving resemblance to an electrocution in a movie about mad scientists. But between heat and strange chemicals it did alter the cross section of the hair shaft to make it longitudinally wavy, thus correcting God's flagrant playing of favorites. "Permanent" meant what it said, only new-growth hair had not been through the process, so it all had to be done over again every four to six months. Few doubted it was worth it, for not only did it make long hair easier to "do up," but permanent-waved hair also produced, when bobbed, a mass of short curls with a delightful flapper-on-the-loose effect. The "cloud of bobbed hair" of that "Kiss me!" girl in *The Plastic Age* and the football-shaped coiffure of many of Held's co-eds both meant that they had had permanents, wouldn't be without them.

As hairstyles ceased to be so much like stage fright wigs, however, the blow fell. It became clear that to keep such hair elegantly tamed as well as wavy, a weekly "wave and set" was necessary. That is, in order to free herself from hairbrush and hairpins, the American woman had sold her soul to the newly opened beauty shop around the corner. In a remarkably few years here was a once miniature industry grossing well up into nine figures and developing at least the beginnings of the trimmings familiar today— permanents for small daughter too; primitive do-it-yourself kits taking longer than professional jobs and too often reflecting one's imperfect skill; the same hours once spent brushing long hair now devoted to daubing and poking at short hair to keep it in respectable shape until the regular weekly date at Josette's Shoppe de Beauté. The permanent wave machine took all the emancipation out of bobbed hair.

Machines were deplorably unpredictable. Promises that technological innovation would free Woman from Man-forged shackles had been emphatic ever since the new-fledged electricity industry had shown electric stoves and washing machines at the Chicago Columbian Exposition in 1893. But fifteen years later Upton Sinclair still thought of electrical dishwashers as a boon of tomorrow when predicting they would annihilate the "filthy and deadening and brutalizing" chore that doomed women to "anemia, nervousness, ugliness and ill-temper . . . prostitution, suicide and insanity . . . drunken husbands and desperate children." [95] (Did Grandma really find so many social calamities in her dishpan?) Another twelve years and Carol Kennicott of *Main Street* still used the future tense telling her husband: "We women . . . are going to wash [the dishes] by machinery and come out and play with you men in the offices and clubs and politics you've cleverly kept for yourselves!" [96] Meanwhile, Western Electric's advertising showed a charming young wife on the telephone: "Yes, drive right over right away—I'll be ready. My housework? . . . Oh, that's all done. . . . I just let electricity do my work nowadays. I have an electric dish washer and an electric clothes washer, and iron with my new electric iron. . . ." But well into the 1920's, though electric laundry and dishwashing equipment was widely used in commercial contexts, it lagged in domestic use, possibly because the household versions of the big stuff were expensive and clumsy. And in any case the bulk of farm households, most of which had to wait for the New Deal to bring electrification, could not use such contraptions.

In town, true enough, as the 1920's stretched on, vacuum cleaner, electric iron, electric toaster and percolator became common and were gradually supplemented, beginning in the most prosperous houses, by electric mixer and electric refrigerator—all improvements but not necessarily saving much time. It took almost as long to iron Dr. Kennicott's shirt with an electric as with a stove-heated iron. It was less messy to get ice cubes from the new Frigidaire than to chip at a block of ice in the wooden refrigerator, but the saving in time was small. Blenders, storage freezers, automatic ovens (and electric toothbrushes and razors as pretexts for selling more small motors) were still to come.

Even when, as with vacuum cleaners, time saving was substantial, other new living tools nibbled at the accrued advantage—the automobile, for instance. Because group doings for children proliferated in and out of school—part of society's new role collectively *in loco parentis*—Mom found herself driving Child A to and from ballet class this afternoon, Child B to a Boy Scout occasion the next, Child C to a swimming meet the next. As the supermarket sprang up five miles away in one direction and the beauty shop three miles the other direction, a suburban wife could spend twice as much time behind the wheel in a week as her farmwife grandmother needed for the weekly cleaning with mop, scrubbing brush, dustrag and carpet sweeper. And women whose children had grown up or who had none, hence sometimes had free afternoons, were likelier to spend them at the movies or playing cards with the girls than in the thrillingly creative things that Carol Kennicott dreamed of. This was the first large group to show social prophets that more leisure arrived at through technological advance did not necessarily lead to more cultivated or less empty lives.

There never had been much reason to expect better. *C.* 1920 what now seems like an amazing number of wives already had much leisure because they had servants—at least one maid of all work. At the very time Mrs. Dr. Kennicott was promising her sex freedom via dishwashers, her dishwashing was being done by a Swedish girl who was also a better floor scrubber than any machine yet devised. So another reason for the slow spread of some domestic gadgets was that the lady of the house seldom did much of what the door-to-door salesman promised to relieve her of. Only as the 1920's neared their close could gadgetry approach the importance that advertising talked up. That was when the restrictions on immigration successively imposed between 1920 and 1927 began really to be reflected in dwindling annual supply of fresh Swedish, German and Irish girls for American kitchens and indigenous black replacements up from the South were for cultural reasons harder to train, for traditional reasons regarded with less favor. Since 1620 at least, American housewives had, like most others, been complaining about the servant problem. Now very gradually, as erosion of the domestic servant market let them gently downhill all through the 1930's, they came really to have something to complain about.

Nor did it mean much in any but very crass terms that women of the 1920's owned more of the nation's negotiable wealth—real estate, securities, pawnable personal property—than men. This only looked like a triumph of the recently enfranchised sex. The bulk of such holdings was no product of Woman's bow and spear outsmarting or outmanaging Man in the marts of trade or the arena of a profession. Wall Street took it as a striking novelty when in the feverish bull market of 1927–29 certain brokers opened special boardrooms for women who, for the first time, were trading on their own. Woman-held property was merely nominal, result of the legal precaution of putting one's assets in one's wife's name, or represented resources accumulated by the dead—fathers, husbands or other relatives—left to her because she could never make her own way. And because she could not be trusted to manage such assets, though her name was on the deeds and stock certificates, it was trustee or family lawyer or banker uncle or life insurance company that handled them.

The American Woman's Party, militant wing of Women's Rights, fretted awhile as the 1920's grew apathetic about its pet issues, then went into a spore stage like a yeast cell in an unfavorable situation. But it retained a skeleton organization under veteran leaders and a national headquarters in Washington, D.C., proof against infiltration by the enemy through the precautions of the financial angel of its building—Mrs. O. H. P. Belmont, as rich as a lady marrying first a Vanderbilt and then a Belmont was likely to be, and as fanatic a feminist as Alice Paul, her coadjutor in the party. Bitter about the way men had taken over the American Red Cross, which had been founded by a woman, Clara Barton, Mrs. Belmont had the papers financing the headquarters building so drawn that title would automatically revert to her estate "the moment any man is given official position, employment or salary" within its doors.[97]

So far as I know nobody ever took the risk of asking Mrs. Belmont what she thought of beauty pageants, burlesque shows or jazz babies. A pity too, for all three were part of Woman's bursting from the cocoon—rather literally—and deserved places in her wider scheme. The movies, making no such error, by no means confined their recognition to newsreels of Atlantic City's tribal rites and Jazz Age doings. The screen's version of the voyeurism of burlesque began with the juicily exposed houris of *Intolerance* and the underclad posturings of Theda Bara in *The Vampire*.

Dracula and Bela Lugosi eventually restored the meaning of "vampire," but meanwhile, the contraction "vamp" was doubly confusing because on sheet music "vamp till ready" meant to keep chords going till the singer took a deep breath and gave. Now Miss Bara and her imitators made it a noun = an exotic, predatory seductress, and a verb = slitheringly to bring out the worst in a man. (The "baby vamp" was a bobbed-haired, hey-hey junior model.) In 1919 what more the future held was as fully revealed as the National Board of Review would stand for by Cecil B. De Mille in *Male and Female* based—remotely—on Sir James M. Barrie's *The Admirable Crichton*. The mildly sardonic original strands on a desert island a yachting party including a young British aristocratess and the family butler, whom the emergency brings out as a man to tie to. That led De Mille and his scenarist, Jeanie MacPherson, to whom some attribute his reliance on orgies and bathtubs, into an elaborately plushed-up fantasy episode changing the butler into one of those I-was-a-king-in-Babylon types wallowingly adored by Gloria Swanson as a Virgin Slave wearing very little.

The great success of *Male and Female* fatally fixed the movie industry's already lively belief that if nobody cared where the chips fell—and why should anybody?—Sex could be folded into almost any literary property from *Peter Rabbit* (a natural!) to *Walden*. The usual means were: (1) relative nakedness—the modern heroine down to minimum underwear or waving her legs in a bathtub, or the ancient-world enchantress garbed above the pelvis in nothing but a lofty headdress and a few square inches of brocade or shiny metal; or (2) close-ups of protracted kissing. Betty Blythe's versions of the raw-as-a-scallop toast of Nineveh or Tyre were particularly notable, and from her overexposure in *The Queen of Sheba* came the Jazz Age's "sheba" for the generic Dancing Daughter whose male counterpart was the "sheik"—pronounced *sheek*. A cut above Held's vacuous Joe College, he also was movie-born. His sire was banjo-eyed Rudolph Valentino, whose first fame in *The Four Horsemen of the Apocalypse* became airborne when he snatched Agnes Ayres off into the desert on a stallion shod with fire in *The Sheik*, adapted from a best-selling confection mixing sand and sugar.

Yet this hegemony of Sex over the screen must not be exaggerated. It was not the quasi-monopoly of fifty years later, nor was it ever so explicit—the difference between Carmel Myers in a wispy "teddybear" and Ann-Margret in the buff; between marathon kissing and downright copulation. Throughout the decade Hollywood, while leaning on the sexiest girls money could procure, also left ample room for great comics—Chaplin, Buster Keaton, Harold Lloyd—niceboy heroes like Charles Ray, wholesome he-men like Thomas Meighan and Richard Dix, tea-gowned perfect ladies like Katharine Macdonald. The staple movies—the Western, the cloak-and-sworder, the mother-love tearjerker, the pseudo-historical "epic," the bucolic boy and girl down by the old millstream—were only overshadowed, not undermined, by the pseudo-ancient world clambake spectacle and the impassioned tale of affluent beauty following heart instead of head and su-huffering for it. But the leading edge was unmistakable. In the public mind and in the press that strove to follow it, Valentino, Clara Bow and soon Greta Garbo dominated the screen that only a few years earlier had been the kingdom of decorous Mary Pickford and William S. Hart.

In 1925 De Mille outdid himself loading a movie with Sex in *King of Kings*—nominally a screen biography of Christ. Heavy lacing with texts from the Gospels gave it subtitles averaging higher in literary quality than those of any other movie ever made. But instead of opening in the stable in Bethlehem or at Christ's baptism, it begins not with Him at all but in an *Intolerance*-style palace wherein Jacqueline Logan as "the beautiful courtesan, Mary of Magdala, laughing at God and man," sultrily cuddles a pet leopard and lolls about wearing so little that she rouses the passions of all the rich old goats in Jerusalem. She is pining for a lapsed lover, name of Judas, who, she now hears, has gone gypsying with a troupe of beggars led by a carpenter. "Ha!" she says in a really memorable subtitle not out of the King James Version. "Harness my zebras, gift of the King of Nubia!" As promptly as if from a firehouse next door in trot four zebras wearing headdresses like the boots on lamb chops and drawing a ladylike light chariot into which she leaps and swirls off to find Judas, meet Christ—His first appearance—and symbolize her renunciation of sin by donning a long black veil. Half a reel later almost as much footage goes to the Woman Taken in Adultery wearing only a precariously draped bath towel and a startled but impudent facial expression changing so little after Christ saves her as to rouse doubt about her obeying that advice to go and sin no more.

Jews objected to De Mille's showing Judas getting his thirty pieces of silver from a Fagan-like Caiaphas. But few Christians or Jews had the wit to object to this vulgar sandwich of flesh and spirit, a trick as old as early Griffith. De Mille *et al.* took it to glory. Thenceforth sexing up one or another Bible story would be the best, because unassailable, way to circumvent the Hays Office and its successor agencies.

What was the Hays Office? The fine flower of Hollywood. What was Hollywood? A legend, though not a myth.

Greenwich Village and Main Street were not the only folk abstractions in America's gazetteer. The westward shift that made Los Angeles County the Pittsburgh of movie foundries was complete by 1920—a haste made possible by the jerry-built nature of the industry. Just as rapidly, the popular mind came to identify moviemaking with the half-empty suburb of Los Angeles where it centered. Hollywood, that lamely presumptuous name for an area too thirsty ever to support woods, let alone holly, was soon an instantly recognized symbol like Wall Street, Palm Beach, Broadway, the Barbary Coast.*

It owed all that to fan magazines and the daily press, of course, spurred on by press agents and the Los Angeles Chamber of Commerce, for whom the advent of the movie studios was a godsend like that of the navel orange. To the enticements of sunshine and citrus groves was now added the joy of knowing one breathed the same as yet unsmoggy air as Clara Kimball Young and Francis X. Bushman. As Hashimura Togo said: "In Los Angeles [in 1920] . . . everybody lives in a scenario and Goldwyn is taught in public schools." [98] The already-strong influx of the retired elderly followed by quacks treating soul and body was reinforced by a third migration of screen-struck youth self-selected for egocentricity and, often with reason, good looks. Among them the studios recruited extras for mob, street and war scenes, balls and so on, and once each blue moon, just often enough to keep the legend glowing, little Vernella Glockner from Gopher Prairie really made it to stardom as Gloria Golconda.

Years of that process strikingly raised the local level of pulchritude. It was not only that most of the gas pumps and dime-store and lunchroom counters of Los Angeles were manned by young people of banal good looks taking any job available while they waited for the break they knew was bound to come. Seldom was work for more than 2,000 extras offered among 10,000-odd applicants—but few ever went home again. Instead, as hopes dwindled, they settled down in minor economic niches and often married other frustrated aspirants. So thanks probably more to the genes governing skeletal structure than to the climate, their offspring, the pupils of Hollywood High School, averaged far handsomer—if still banal—than those of any other American institution of lower learning. Eventually, in a kind of autarchy, the studios could recruit starlets from homegrown raw material eagerly plentiful on local beaches.

* In fact, by 1922 the name so connoted fame that the developer of a tract of palmetto scrub north of Miami, Florida, called it Hollywood-by-the-Sea and its hotel, overlooking the Everglades from an elevation of ten feet above sea level, the Hollywood Hills Hotel.

Within a decade of its implantation this Jack's Beanstalk of a subculture was well toward maturity and most memorably celebrated in a novel of 1921. Harry Leon Wilson's *Merton of the Movies* was and is to Hollywood what *Moby Dick* is to whaling. A deft Broadway play and several movies were made of it, but adaptations could not retain its great secondary virtues. Many skilled writers with experience of Hollywood—Fitzgerald, Nathanael West, Budd Schulberg, dozens of them—have since tried to distil the essence of the place in his particular time. But for forty years *Merton* has read like a map of the eternal pre-TV verities at the corner of Hollywood and Vine.

There in Merton's Paradise Attained grow the anomalous eucalyptus trees, always in the backgrounds of the elder screen's Fifth Avenue and Dixie mansions. The plot synopses that its moviemakers inflict on one another, the protean changes in situations and story lines as they near the rapids of actual production epitomize what went on in Hollywood from well before the Armistice till long after sound came in. The experienced extra girl sketches for Merton the new Muriel Mercer movie, *The Blight of Broadway*: "Mercer gets into this tenement house down on the east side, and she's a careless society butterfly . . . and this little friend of mine does an Italian girl with a baby and this old man . . . he's a rich swell and prominent in Wall Street and belongs to all the clubs but he's the father of this girl's child, only Mercer doesn't know that yet . . . and he follows her down to the tenements where she's relieving the poor—just in a plain black dress—and she finds out he's the real father. . . ." [99]

The press agentry, tied to the intense personalness of the relation between star and public, epitomizes what made fan magazines profitable between the wars, when they had not yet got into bed with their subjects. About Beulah Baxter, object of Merton's special worship: "In her kitchen, apron clad, she stirred something. In her lofty music room she was seated at her piano. In her charming library she was shown 'Among Her Books.' . . . 'I have my leisure moments from the grinding stress,'" she tells the interviewer. "'Then I turn to my books—I'm wild about history. . . .'" But when Merton asks the magazines' correspondence editors whether she is married, they let him down. "Perhaps," answers one. "Not now," says another. "Twice," says a third. Even when he reached Hollywood and asks the lady at the studio who hires the extras, she says, "Now let me think. . . . I forget. I suppose so. She often is." [100] Obviously the marital customs prevailing in Hollywood were already well formed. Other familiar overtones vibrate in the omniscient heroine's warning to Merton when he is working for Buckeye Comedies. Those so cordial pretty girls who do the minor roles, she says, "work like dogs and do the best they can when they ain't got jobs. . . . If it hadn't been for me this bunch would have taught you a lot of things . . . long before this you'd probably have been hopping up your reindeer and driving all over in a Chinese sleigh. . . ." [101]

Magazine readers following Merton's story knew that meant dope. Press and gossip had them well prepared to believe that life in the film colony was, as Wilson Mizner said, like "floating down a sewer in a glass-bottomed boat." [102] Mizner knew the place from inside. So did Anita Loos, precocious, cute-as-a-bug's-ear queen of the well-wrought scenario and the nifty subtitle, who, having seen Hollywood bud and blossom, testified that "To place in the limelight a great number of people who ordinarily would be chambermaids and chauffeurs [and] give them instant wealth, is bound to produce lively and diverting results." [103] The public, whether movie fans or chronic bluenoses, tended to identify the scandalous with the diverting, and in Merton's year Hollywood was having a momentous run of dirt, apparently confirming the rumors that local home life resembled that of Sodom and Gomorrah.

The studio-lot murder of movie director William Desmond Taylor involved Mabel Normand, queen of rough-and-tumble comediennes, and Mary Miles Minter, an ethereal ingenue of high box-office value. A strong smell of the drug habit hung over the never-solved crime. Drugs soon sent Miss Normand to a miserable end. They also destroyed Wallace Reid, pattern of sleeked-up masculine charm. Pushers working the Vernon Country Club, a resort popular among movie people, had had "an easy time converting these simple young drunks into dope addicts," [104] Miss Loos recalled forty years later. Merton's briefing on the pitfalls of Hollywood ended: ". . . a comedy lot . . . [is] the toughest place this side of the bad one. . . . You can do anything if you wipe up the blood." [101] Maybe the author thought of that with a shiver when, soon after the book was published, Roscoe "Fatty" Arbuckle, an ornament of comedy lots only one rung below Chaplin, gave the decade its most noisome erotic scandal.

Ironically it was not in Hollywood but in San Francisco, where the grinning fat man often went to cut loose, that he threw the drunken party during which the insides of a guest, a minor movie actress, were fatally mutilated. The situation was such that the blood could not be wiped up, and the details reaching the public led to a national plague of labored, very dirty jokes. Tried for manslaughter, Arbuckle got three hung juries and a quashed indictment. But his career was ended. All over the country his movies were hissed. Some Hollywooders insisted that to protect themselves, his friends had thrown him to the wolves; others that the victim was a nice girl and he a monster. That was intramural. The significant result was that the straitlaced element of the public took this scandal as last straw. The screen's lip-licking hudgings into Sex combined with gossip about orgies and drugs had made the bluenosed nervous—and now this hiccuping horror fouling the jolliest figure in the movies' pantheon. Reducing the charge from murder to manslaughter, the judge, one of those afflicted with obiter diction, said: "We are not trying Roscoe Arbuckle alone . . . we are trying our present day morals . . . matters of comment and apprehension to every true lover of our American institutions." [105]

It was disproportionate to demand sweeping reform of moviemaking because an ex-plumber's helper had become a monster under the strain of an income of $250,000 a year. But that was the risk in the screen's practice of keeping the customers' relations with its shadow puppets as personal as ballyhoo manipulating imbecility could manage. The ensuing roar for cleanup and censorship was thunderous. The industry took cover and, while plotting major strategy, sought to cool things off with a flurry of efforts to obscure, blunt, deny, pooh-pooh. Magazine articles depicted Hollywood as nobody there but just us hardworking technicians ploddingly giving the public what it wants, where though "late hours, and undesirable habits may not interfere with the career of a society butterfly . . . they are an insuperable obstacle to the girl who wants to make good in pictures." After that bit—it could have been straight out of *Merton*—the author, a well-known Hollywood executive, advised any girl headed that way to "take your mother or aunt with you, and *live with her*." [106] Will Rogers, already a popular screen star, and Rupert Hughes, a movie-minded novelist with a vast following, made reassuring speeches to women's and service clubs. Chaplin contributed little by protesting that Hollywood really was not full of "hop joints, wild women and all that sort of thing. I wish it were." [107] Studio payrolls were salted with spies ferreting out poor moral risks—hopheads, drunks, satyrs and so on—and performers' contracts began to include the famous "morality clause," entitling the studio to cancel whenever the party of the other part did anything tending to "forfeit the respect of the public." [108] It was such clauses in writers' contracts that set the stage for the strange political drama of the Hollywood Ten after World War II.

No such gestures promised or performed much. But sweeping remedy was at hand not from within the flustered industry but from a Presbyterian parson pushing seventy, the Reverend Dr. Wilbur F. Crafts, specialist in promoting Sunday Schools, Temperance, Purity (meaning continence) and chief of a moral clearinghouse, the International Reform Bureau. His shrillness about Sodomwood's vices secured him an invitation to California to visit the lots and discuss with the makers how to keep the screen clean while yet exploiting the unruly emotions necessary to box-office success. The old gentleman got a long way toward *comprendre tout, c'est pardonner tout*. The more he heard and saw, the less he deplored. He no longer wished censorship widened but instead advised that the product be cleaned up *before* shooting. Self-policed, industry-wide standards of morality and good taste imposed by the front offices on producers, writers and directors could keep the movies acceptably clean, prevent costly revisions of stuff already in the can and shield the innocence of the family trade, the lifeblood of the

neighborhood movie house, against overspiced corruption. In effect Hollywood was to plead guilty and promise to stop hustling on condition of
suspended sentence and release on its own recognizance.

For the means to carry out Crafts' notion the industry recalled the speed
with which Judge Landis had revived confidence in baseball after the Black
Sox affair. In theory the National Board of Review and the scattering state
censorships should have kept the industry's baser urges under control. But
the sheer numbers of movies shot and the large investments involved had
outrun any system founded on surgery once *Silken Sinners* or *The Loves of
Jezebel* was finished. In terms not of today but of 1921 Hollywood had been
getting away with prurient outrages. The *post facto* censorship for which the
straitlaced clamored would, it was assumed, mean not only costly scrapping
of footage but also serious box-office losses if the public were deprived of
the occasionally lively fare to which it was accustomed. Take it for granted
that neither the would-be censors nor the embattled industry had freedom
of creation much at heart.

So into polysyllabic being came a sister of baseball's emergency
prosthesis—the Motion Picture Producers and Distributors of America
comprising and financed by the bulk of moviemaking companies to codify
and enforce a new movie morality. To keep it impressive enough to fend off
public censorship required a counterpart of Judge Landis. Crafts, the
logical candidate, had died soon after having his great idea. The choice fell
on a middle-aged Hoosier politician, Will H. Hays. Spindly, jug-eared, he
was physically no Landis,* but his career as a leading Republican
Congressman, national chairman of his party in the winning campaign of
1920, Postmaster General in the Harding Cabinet, gave him a ripe talent as
a surefooted front man. He knew everybody and had pipelines in many
places. For the next two decades his card sense secreted the insulation—
part grease, part effrontery, part inertia, part casuistry—between Hollywood and its detractors. Landis being "czar" of baseball, Hays was
headlined as czar of the movies and except in the most formal contexts the
organization he led was known in the trade as the Hays Office. Nor was his
effectiveness marred—indeed it may actually have enhanced his reputation
for knowing where bodies were buried—when he proved to be involved
with some of the securities with which bribery was effected in the Teapot
Dome scandal.

Thus the Black Sox and Arbuckle helped to perfect for the new public
relations industry a weapon of high value since widely applied—the trick of
creating *ad hoc* front organizations with fervent and, if possible, convincing
promises of reform to blunt public outcry against a given segment of the
economy. At the time the Hays Office was created nobody raised the

* I saved Hays' life, I believe, at a movie premiere in New York City in 1929. His limousine
disgorged him into a shrieking crowd breaking a police barrier, and he was going down like a
midget in a stampede of cattle. It would have been a dreadful way to die.

question whether for all major studios to agree to eschew obviously profitable dirt was illegal "combination in restraint of trade." Here again a silent consensus distinguished movies from books, plays and paintings as so pervasive and influential that they amounted to a quasi-public utility. That might be bad law but sound sociological observation and handy for industries eventually needing the technique.

The Hays Office's first overt act—an effort to rescue Arbuckle, which was only fair since he had more or less founded it—failed. To test potential public acceptance, two of his unreleased features starring him opposite Mabel Normand were booked into the Park Music Hall on New York City's Columbus Circle—operated by one of the many Minsky brothers who were the backbone of burlesque. One trouble was that Miss Normand too was still much in the public memory as smirched by the Taylor murder. But Arbuckle got the bulk of the smotheringly hostile outcry against the showing. One member of Hays' advisory committee on public relations resigned, and the whole committee, either inadequately warned or putting on an act, publicly told him that to show Arbuckle would be "extremely detrimental to American youth." [109] Many civic organizations agreed, and the clergy were predictably severe. "You cannot purify a polecat," said the Reverend Dr. Straton, ". . . denature a rattlesnake . . . reform a smallpox epidemic . . . even an ex-member of a Presidential cabinet cannot cure organic diseases of screen corruption by treating them with soothing syrup." [110] Hays dropped the matter and began to feel his way into other ways of earning his pay.

After that first discombobulation things went well. The Hays Office's minor practical services included reorganizing the hiring of extra actors to achieve greater efficiency and decency, a long-needed reform. To discourage the whores who had been giving Hollywood an extra bad name by telling the arresting police they were movie actresses—as doubtless some of them had at least tried to be—it hired social workers to interview new extras registered with the new Central Casting Office. Most to the point, however, was the famous Hays Code to regulate the content of movies—that is, to stall off potential censorship while leaving plenty of room to exploit Sex and violence.

The code's spelled-out do's and don't's make curious reading now. Some obviously reflected sensitivity to sin and truckling to aggressive viewers-with-alarm. For the clergy, so nervous about the screen: "Ministers of religion . . . should not be used as comic characters or villains." For the export market, growingly important as costs of production rose, and for second-run houses in ethnic neighborhoods: "The history, institutions, prominent people and citizenry of other nations shall be represented fairly." *"Illegal drug traffic* must never be presented" took care of that ticklish topic. "The use of liquor . . . when not required by the plot or for proper characterization, will not be shown"—clearly a sop to the militant Drys. To ward off complaints that the screen actively suggested crime, the code forbade "sympathy with the crime or against law and justice" and the acting out of murder, safecracking, arson, smuggling and so on in such detail as to tempt amateurs to try their hands. For the many well-corseted clubwomen of the 1920's who still thought movies vulgar: "The treatment of low, disgusting, unpleasant though not necessarily evil subjects, should be subject always to the dictates of good taste and regard for the sensibilities of the audience." Then, having calked those leaks in Hollywood's armor, the code forged a chastity belt for its most vulnerable area. Here are bright sparks from the anvil:

"Adultery . . . must not be specifically treated or justified, or presented attractively. *Scenes of passion* . . . should be so treated that [they] do not stimulate the lower or baser element [apparently it didn't matter if the best people were carnally roused]. . . . *Seduction or rape* . . . are [*sic*] never the proper subject for comedy. *Sex perversion* or any inference of it. . . . *White slavery.* (. . . *Miscegenation* . . . [all] forbidden. *Sex hygiene* and venereal diseases are not subjects for motion pictures. . . . *Children's sex organs* are never to be exposed [the need for any such caution about adults obviously never occurred to the codifiers]. *Complete nudity* is never permitted . . . or any lecherous or licentious notice thereof by other characters. . . . Obscenity in word, gesture, reference, song, joke, or by suggestion . . . forbidden. . . ." These provisions carried far beyond America's intramural taboos. In calling it "a solemn thought that the decisions we make at our desks here . . . may affect the lives of every man and woman and child throughout the world," [111] De Mille was right.

Within a year the *World's Work* magazine congratulated Hollywood and its code on its benefits as in, for example, *The Covered Wagon.* The original script had Kit Carson, famous Western scout, downing a few in a saloon. This distorted history, the Hays Office said, and anyway, Boy Scouts revered Carson, so the scene was dropped, yet, the magazine pointed out, the movie was a great success. Not that results were always so clean cut. *The Green Hat*, Arlen's rhinestone of a novel about elegant adultery, became doubly attractive movie material after Broadway welcomed the stage version. The Hays Office shrank from countenancing it, however. Only after some years of thought did they let it be screened, starring Greta Garbo, on condition that the title be changed to the considerably more suggestive *A Woman of Affairs.*

Minor pledges were fairly well kept. Catholic as well as Protestant clergy were treated respectfully. Opium, morphine, cocaine were ignored. No movie got funny about rape or seduction. Flaming Youth parties, nightclub sequences like that in *The Blight of Broadway* and the old Western barroom business required much drinking, but it was certainly proper characterization and girls indulging were usually shown as either no better than they should be or rueing the day; one of *Our Dancing Daughters* died in a drunken fall. The Irish were solicitously admired; the Germans were spared the rough handling of the War years; Jews as such were usually played by Gentiles and appeared only in Biblical clambakes. Chinese, Japanese and Mexicans continued to furnish stereotyped villains, but that screen tradition was so taken for granted that it is unlikely the drafters of that clause about nationalities had them at all in mind. In major areas the Hays Office was, however, relaxedly accommodating. "Good taste" meant nothing, of course, and even if it had, few Hollywood producers were to be trusted with it. The last hundred feet of the crime movie gunned down the gangster protagonist to show that Crime Does Not Pay, but the preceding 7,900 feet had shown him rolling in money, up to there in fancy girls and using fists, firearms and blackmail to secure those blessings.

As for the bowdlerizing, only the bans on white slavery, miscegenation, sex hygiene and stark nakedness were well observed. In *City Lights*, for instance, released soon after the third promulgation of the code, Chaplin is a street cleaner exasperated by horse droppings, aghast when a herd of mules comes along, devastated by the sight of a circus elephant coming his way. In the boxers' dressing-room sequence his winsome efforts to ingratiate himself with his prospective opponent so strongly imply homosexuality that the opponent refuses to strip within his range of vision, and most of Chaplin's movies of the 1920's included one of his you-chase-me flavored travesties of ballet.* In 1923 Blanche Sweet starred in a movie version of O'Neill's play about Anna Christie, the whore. Adultery was certainly "explicitly treated [and to a great extent] justified" in the person of Lillian Gish in *The Scarlet Letter*, and time and time again in that of Greta Garbo. Dozens of other exceptions sifted through the code's self-denying ordinances. Between the diaphanously garbed orgies from the ancient world—the kind where He props himself on his elbow while She leans over laughing and drops grapes into his mouth—and His and Her attenuated kisses on the tigerskin in the boudoir, "scenes of passion" so persisted that some state censors set stopwatch limits to the duration of osculation.

The purpose was soon clear—merely to set up a "screen of righteous pronouncment [behind which] producers could do . . . approximately what they liked," as an article of mine summed up experience of the code forty years ago. "The screen heroine grew happily or tragically scarlet . . . she seemed bent on justifying all the hard things the reformers had said about her in the days of her comparative innocence. . . . So long as the Hays office would . . . exude enough bland reassurances, muffling querulous complaints in verbose rebuttal, deploring unsympathetic attacks, advocating special pictures for children, it looked as if only an occasional amplification of the code would keep the reformers at arm's length for all

---

* No doubt it was this quirk of Chaplin's that led W. C. Fields, who was usually willing to admit the capabilities of the best among his rival funny men, to call him a "goddamned ballet dancer." (Carlotta Monti, *W. C. Fields & Me*, 74.)

eternity" [112]—a case of that really rare thing, deliberate, persistent hypocrisy à la Tartuffe, lacking any screen of self-deception.

Analogy between Hollywood and baseball in their public relations goes farther than the resemblance between Judge Landis' and Will Hays' functions. Both industries relied on millions and millions of dollars worth of free publicity though in one way baseball's position was weaker—very little of the press space devoted to it was in effect subsidized by paid advertising in any form. But newspaper publishers, aware of what kept circulation up, could no more squeeze down coverage of baseball than they could drop comic strips. Indeed the few papers that had no comics covered baseball most generously of any sport. Movie advertising, whether in daily or Sunday papers, paid for much of the space taken up by reviews, routine trade releases and more or less canned publicity features and pictures. The downright gravy came in the Hollywood gossip columns and straight news space—the movie press agent's dream—devoted to such breathtaking events as Miss Swanson's marriage to the Marquis de la Falaise de la Coudraye. It was hoped, probably justifiably, that the cost to the publisher of such freeloading returned after many days in permanently rising circulation. In spite of the occasional stenches as in the Arbuckle case, most such breaks were favorable as the papers exploited Hollywood and the movies as locus of the larger-than-life vicarious experience that the screen meant to so many.

The classic collaboration among press agents, editors and a mass public was ostensibly built on a corpse, but the beneficiaries were avidly alive—Paramount Pictures and Pola Negri, the Polish actress then rivaling Miss Swanson as public temptress. Paramount was in two minds about the upcoming release in 1926 of *Son of the Sheik*, sequel to the movie that had clinched the deification of Valentino. Public jeering at his image was thought to be eroding his popularity and in any case the movie was so absurdly tempestuous as to rouse suspicions of travesty. At this point Valentino died of a septic appendix. Paramount seized the opportunity to salvage the movie—arranged for him to lie in state at New York City's best-known undertaking parlor and used shills to create riotous crowds mobbing the place, causing police reserves to be called out. . . . After two days of headlines the public, though now barred from the arcanum, were allowed to mass on sidewalks to watch the great stars drive up—just as at a searchlight-garnished premiere, only in daylight—to pay their last respects while the newsreel cameras ground.

The undertaker's press agent secured an honor guard of blackshirt Fascisti showing the esteem in which his native land held the dead hero. When liberals inevitably protested, large front-page pictures resulted. Miss Negri hurried to the scene, called a press conference and, swathed in black, confessed that she and Valentino had been engaged and she was devastated. The next day, again becomingly swathed, she came to the undertaker's escorted by her press agent and fainted by the open casket. During the next few days she fainted and otherwise manifested grief several times more within camera range. When the body was moved to a church for a requiem mass, the streets were clogged with spectators along the route. The mourners included Douglas Fairbanks and Mary Pickford—the screen's royal couple—Madge Bellamy, Richard Dix and so on; the pallbearers were the heads of various Hollywood studios. Nor did burial end it. Some weeks later Valentino's divorced second wife, Natasha Rambova, a conspicuous actress, landed from Europe telling the press that through spiritualistic means she had been in touch with him on the Other Side. He was already playing bits in movies in the spirit world, hoping soon to work up to stardom as had Wallace Reid and Sarah Bernhardt among recent recruits for the ectoplasmic screen.

Thanks to such successful milking of publicity from death, *Son of the Sheik* proved highly profitable. Valentino's share paid his debts and left half a million over.* The bulk of those swarming outside the undertaker's were women. So were the bulk of the crowds in San Francisco who, as Arbuckle left the courtroom, shook hands with him, screeching, "Good for you, Fatty! . . . Hit 'em with a pie, Fatty!" [113]

Unless Hollywood was sore mistaken, the screen had become the particular culture toy of American women as a mass. They were the star makers, the readers of fan magazines, the early standers-in-line who made the difference between profits and bruising losses. One simple reason was that many had more spare time than their menfolk, whose afternoons were usually committed to factory or office. The neighborhood movie theater injected into every day of the week, even in small towns, the matinee habit that had once filled city theaters with middle-aged women on Wednesday afternoons, and the box-office prowess of Reid, Valentino *et al.* showed that the matinee idol was part of it. Yet these better halves' leisure could not alone account for it all. When their husbands could somehow manage afternoon time off, they went not to the movies but to a ball game. (Night ball games did not yet exist.) The other ingredient seems to have been a new kind of matinee idolizing, women enthralled by the shadows of other women. They doted on John Gilbert, true, and Conway Tearle *et al.,* but on the whole it was Norma Shearer or Corinne Griffith whom they flocked to see. This must mean a group narcissism, plus a preening interest in the screen goddess' fine feathers, plus a hankering after the soulful and often sinful carryings-on of Aileen Pringle as the royal Great Unknown of *Three Weeks.* That is, the screen had become a confessions magazine in a marabou-feather negligee.

* This account owes much to M. M. Marberry, "The Overloved One," *American Heritage,* August, 1965.

What was good on balance for Hollywood was the cross-fertilization from Europe of which Miss Negri and Miss Garbo were the least significant part. It began in 1921 with importation of striking movies from Germany. After 1914 the French and Italian moviemakers who had been rivals for America to reckon with—and sometimes learn from—were almost stifled by the dislocations of the War, leaving America a virtual monopoly of the world's screens. Germany, however, cut off from importations, seems to have given strong encouragement to domestic moviemaking for propaganda and morale purposes—a forcing frame for a body of experience and imagination that, as soon as post-War relaxation allowed, proved invaluably brilliant.

The pretalkies screen, remember, knew no language barrier, so German subtitles translated into English, French or whatever were seldom worse than the originals, and the sheer merit of the best of the new German movies took them all over. Since Germany's foreign exchange shortages led to severe limitations in importation of alien movies, Hollywood complained bitterly about this unilateral challenge to its position in the world market. Sherwood, whose new department of movie reviews in *Life* was healthier for the screen than ten Hays Offices, said that actually overproduction and the post-War financial crisis caused the stagnation in Hollywood of which actors and producers were complaining—not the few German movies causing so much talk because "they have proved that it is possible for a work of art to possess elements of popularity." [114] The New York *Times* said editorially that "German films lately shown here are better than anything that ever came out of Los Angeles . . . the real German menace in the field is . . . superior intelligence." [115] The New York *Globe* said that a suggested tariff wall against foreign movies would be as silly as one on Wells' novels or John Galsworthy's plays.

Germany's early *The Cabinet of Dr. Caligari* with sets and backgrounds drawing freely on stage design and easel painting of kinds then thought radical, anticipated European *surréaliste* movies of the 1930's but had little immediate effect because it gave the average moviegoer the squeams. What made Hollywood a believer was three less unconventional movies directed by Ernst Lubitsch, a screen craftsman of the same order as D. W. Griffith and Chaplin—*Passion* (about Madame du Barry), *Deception* (about Anne Boleyn) and *Gipsy Blood* (a sizzling version of *Carmen*). Their box-office draw was as vigorous as their impetuous cutting and acting. In tacit admission that here were higher moviemaking skills than most American work showed, Hollywood fetched Lubitsch over to embark on an American career lasting some twenty fertile years. Shallow people eventually grew peevish about so much talk of "the Lubitsch touch," but for all that it was the surest the screen of his day had ever known.* As other German

---

* Hollywood's respect for things of German flavor had begun a little earlier with the renown as director of Erich von Stroheim, an Austrian rising to screen fame during the War as

directors' movies arrived to carve their titles on American consciousness
and sometimes on American box offices, Hollywood summoned them
too—F. W. Murnau of *The Last Laugh*, E. A. Dupont of *Caligari* and
Variety, Fritz Lang of *Siegfried* and *Metropolis*. . . .

As further sympathetic magic Hollywood also imported the performers
conspicuous in these movies—Pola Negri of *Passion* and *Gipsy Blood*,
paunchy Emil Jannings of *The Last Laugh* and *Variety*. . . . Until then
Hollywood had had few Continental performers; Alla Nazimova was one
of the exceptions. Valentino, like von Stroheim, though alien-born, was
largely of local development. But now Miss Negri's success as sultry spitfire
set off a woman hunt that packed the place with beautiful European screen
actresses, some talented. Prestige now required a major studio to have on
the payroll not only a famous German director but at least one putative ball
of fire from somewhere in the triangle Innsbruck-Bucharest-Stockholm. The
most memorable of these exotic long shots was, of course, Garbo, who, as
early Swedish movies showed her, had been merely rangy and amiable-
looking. Some others of the sisterhood cast discernible shadows, but it was
the directors whose virtuosity—Dupont's emotion-shaping camera angles,
Lubitsch's often witty, sometimes heart-stopping masterpieces of continuity—showed Hollywood how to take up where Griffith had left off in
camera handling and use of the contiguity and succession that, David
Hume said, were all that man can know of how the universe works.

Hence richer texture in the work of America's native directors, for
instance, *The Big Parade*, King Vidor's war movie. Any time, in any idiom,
Vidor would have been a fine movieman. But much of the footage in this
production of 1925 would never have been so juicy had not Lubitsch and
Lang shown the way. The other result was silly, if predictable—a fresh field
for Cheevyism as these German works persuaded the cultivated that only
movies from outside Hollywood were to be taken seriously. This Philistinism in reverse fattened on the well-deserved applause for Robert J.
Flaherty's early "documentaries," *Nanook of the North* (life among Eskimos) and *Moana of the South Seas* (life among Samoans), neither in any
sense a Hollywood product, and presently on the intellectualized adulation
accorded important Soviet Russian (*e.g., The Cruiser Potemkin*) and French
(*e.g., The Passion of Joan of Arc*) movies showing that important overseas
moviemaking was going on outside Germany. Only Chaplin's successive
feature-length movies were spared this proscription.

He and they were also striking and, depending on point of view,
gratifying or depressing examples of sympathetic criticism marring a talent.
The post-War spread of serious theorizing about movies brought a cult of
Chaplin. Overpraise of his best was hardly possible. But this was an esthetic

---

specialist in playing frozenly sadistic Prussian officers; as "The Man You Love to Hate" he
was as well known as the Keystone Kops.

hero worship making every foot of his every movie matter for analysis of a sort that soon caused Gilbert Seldes, who had been one of the foremost shouting that Chaplin was superb, to complain about "intellectuals who so reduced Chaplin to angles that the angles no longer made them laugh . . . followed the score so closely they haven't heard the music." [116] It went beyond the solemn mind's usual lumbering effort to explain the inexplicable, after which it explains aspects of the subject that can be analyzed but don't matter much. This cult proclaimed that Chaplin's funniness was based on a pathos that vastly heightened its significance and that the Little Tramp image that came to dominate his work betokened frustrated Man gallantly confronting the Universe—or words, many words, to that effect. Even Benchley was guilty of such talk.

Yet the Chaplin character in earlier phases—when his work was at its blindingly wonderful best—was generally, as Theodore Huff has said, "unsympathetic, unengaging . . . a sharper, a heel, an annoying blunderer, an obnoxious drunk . . . cruel sometimes. . . ." [117] The first fallings-away cropped up in certain two-reelers from the mid-period—say *The Vagabond*, in which the Little Tramp loves and cherishes a rustic wild rose beauty and is instrumental in restoring her to her long-lost parents only to lose her to the elegant artist whose painting of her cues the way to the great "My cheeild!" recognition scene. Even this exercise in cotton candy opens with a barroom sequence in which the Little Tramp, deftly cynical, collects the spare change the drinkers think they are giving to hard-up street musicians with whom he is not connected. Sometimes I hope that the tearjerking sporadic in much mid-period Chaplin was meant as travesty. If so, it misfired all over its creator. His first full-length feature, *The Kid* (1921) showed how fully he agreed that the Little Tramp was at his best when mawkish. Things were stickier still in *The Gold Rush* as the Klondike dance hall girl neglects to come to the dinner that he so wistfully prepares etc. etc. From then on, though some of the old glory gleamed in each new Chaplin, the inevitable appearance of an ovinely luscious girl always presaged soggy work at the crossroads.

In time the creator of the Little Tramp and the waiter in *The Rink* who makes out the customer's check from the stains on his necktie was telling Beverly Nichols, brash young British journalist, that he achieved "unity of mood and rhythm" in directing his movies by keeping "a certain melody, [say] the Scherzo of the Kreutzer Sonata" [118] running in his head during shooting. Maybe Chaplin could have evolved such palaver without prompting. But the critics tempting him to inflate himself, whether principals or accessories, had done what they could to betray a genius as if they had persuaded W. C. Fields to found a home for stray dogs and foundlings. The great Chaplin in *City Lights* is the one who swoops out of his friend's Rolls to beat a derelict to a discarded cigar butt, not the one recognized by the once blind but now all too clearly seeing flower girl. By

1928 Oliver Claxton, reviewing *The Circus* in the *New Yorker* felt obligated
to say: "Somehow the feeling has got around that a smile-through-the-tears
is happier than a guffaw. Mr. Chaplin rose to his present position by
guffaws and not on streaming tear-ducts . . . most of the other comics . . .
are working below par. Perhaps the reason [is] the fairly recent outbursts of
genius-hailing and the resulting suspicion in the humorists' minds that they
really should be doing Hamlet." [119]

Besides rivaling the ballroom as seedbed of erotic freedoms the movie
theater of the 1920's widened the search for the good life in more prosaic
ways. It countered the usual summer slump at the box office by cooling the
house more and more effectively, then, as competition brought the
thermostats down, down, far too much so. The immediate consequence was
stiff necks and colds in the head. Later improvements in equipment and
common sense in using it were, however, fine promotion for the embryonic
air-conditioning industry that would so drastically alter architecture and
the nation's summer folkways. Meanwhile the marquee promised 20°
COOLER INSIDE in letters so huge as to imply that the feature might be a
minor attraction. But few promising movies were released in summer, and
in any case, something like that was already risked in the grandiosity of the
movie palaces that showed the first runs and set the industry's tone.
Rothafel had shown the trade how a really splashy theater could in itself
draw customers, maybe making the difference between whether a given
couple went to see *Love in Flames* at the gorgeous new Mosque or to see
Flames of Love at the staidly elegant Lincoln. On the consequent principle
that the more visual junk was piled on and in the showcase, the better
business would be, movie-house architecture began to resemble Hollywood's sets for the Queen of Sheba or Nebuchadnezzar or Genghis Khan.
Rothafel's *nunc dimittis* was his Roxy Theater, "The Cathedral of the
Motion Picture," in New York City. Its circular lobby rug was, one
understood, the largest ever woven in one piece and nightly after the last
show experts removed the pounds of chewing gum that had been tramped
into it. Gigantic columns, slathers of festoons, galleries, niches, urns, grated
windows, archways, statues indoors and out showed what architects,
decorators and the Plateresque school of pseudo-Hispanicism could be
goaded into. Particularly since the stagiest of concealed lighting kept
playing colored tricks on what one thought one saw the first time, it was as
if Addison Mizner had acquired brother Wilson's opium habit.
Yet Plateresque was, after all, merely high-strung Renaissance. The Near
and Far East had already been summoned to adorn movie showcases, as in
Sid Grauman's Egyptian Theater in Los Angeles. And soon after the Roxy
opened, Grauman gave the Coast's Chinese colonies cause to believe that
the Yellow Peril had new meaning. It would be rash to say that nobody ever
outdid Grauman's Chinese Theater, however. The Fox Theater in Atlanta,

Georgia, fudged up the whole auditorium into the courtyard of a tremendous Moorish castle with its own artificial sky-ceiling studded with electric stars twinkling at random. Balaban and Katz's Oriental Theater was advertised as "bringing to Chicago the jewelled splendor of the Far East . . . soft silks, subtle lights, regal velvets . . . romance agleam with modern theater-magic." [120] Being interpreted, that meant plaster-of-paris arabesques, peacock tails, lotus buds and vine-and-monkey designs, and the ladies' lounge ornamented with silver elephants' heads against crimson flock wallpaper. The men's lounge of the competing Chicago Theater let gentlemen look through a pseudo-Romanesque cloister into a trompe-l'oeil landscape of the Italian countryside obviously done by an admirer of Böcklin. Persia mingled with Spain (or so the publicity said) for a special synergistic kick in the welter of tortured gilt plaster in the Missouri Theater in St. Joseph, Missouri—outstanding for what Benchley called "the golden kidney school of theater decoration." [121]

The basement lounges and upstairs galleries of these people's pleasure domes were usually hung with too well-lighted genuine oil paintings done between 1850 and 1890 and bought from delighted dealers by the wives of the presidents of the theater chains at, according to the press agent, an average of $x,000 each. The statuary was of the same period in Carrara marble, and the one thing to be said for the paintings is that they were better than these busts of imaginary emperors and half lengths of demure girls holding doves. They probably never corrupted public taste much; nobody looked at them, or at "The Romany Girl" and "The Odalisque" done after the manner of Bouguereau by somebody named Martin Kavel. Nor, for all its massed grislinesses, did movie palace décor probably do much harm. These extravagances were too turbulently exotic to induce anything but inconsequential awe. They were also ephemeral. The Roxy went long ago; the New York Paramount has become office space, the Brooklyn Paramount a college gymnasium. So far committees supposed to preserve and defend significant buildings from the past have done little about these so valuably unedifying edifices. Pittsburgh and St. Louis may have the best solution—turn the gaudy old girls into concert halls for local orchestras.

Fortunately what may be the finest example of the movie palace school of architecture—Hearst's San Simeon "castle" in California—is in no danger whatever of being torn down because it has become a state-maintained museum and popular tourist attraction. Actually, of course, it is no movie palace as such but a money-no-object expression of the willful self-esteem of one man, lord of hundreds of millions of dollars' worth of publications, movie enterprises, mines, ranches, urban property, blending the packrat with the dog in the manger. Yet in the castle-building latter half of his life Hearst was very close to the movie subculture as producer and also part of its social life, and only two distinctions can be made between the esthetic standards of Grauman's Chinese Theater or the Roxy and those of San Simeon: Score one for the theaters, they did keep at least a sort of consistency of ebullience in mind, whereas San Simeon is inconceivably eclectic. Then for San Simeon; almost everything in it, structures and movables, is genuine of its kind, whereas movie palaces were—for economic reasons that Hearst would never conceivably have applied to himself—frequently guilty of Coney Island plaster carving and mock-ups in general.

San Simeon began to ornament the Pacific coast about halfway between Hollywood and Telegraph Hill after the death of Hearst's widowed mother in 1919 gave him unlimited control of the family resources. His favorite spot on the Hearst ranch stretching for fifty miles along the coast was a grove of oaks on a hilltop with an immense view of the Pacific, where family picnics and camping parties took place. There he began to build what eventually combined palace with museum with zoo. To embellish it, he caused to be bought, largely in Europe, masses of antique furniture and splashy works of art—as pre-War plutocrats had done for their Beaux-Artsy supermansions on Fifth Avenue, up the Hudson and in Newport. But Hearst so lacked even a vestigial sense of proportion that he made Vanderbilts look modest. As the project whetted his already-sharp taste for prestige-heavy gimcracks, he bought on and on after the successively built elements of his hilltop pleasure dome were furnished to bursting. The world's most extravagantly compulsive sucker for pictures, carvings, mosaics, tapestries, banners, armor, dower chests, sideboards, rare books, plate and ceramics, he probably spent $1,000,000 a year for thirty years.

Nothing was too costly or too large. At first he only gutted monasteries for refectory beams or palaces for fireplaces; then he bought complete castles, manor houses and abbeys taken apart and sent to America with each stone and rafter numbered for reassembly. When Henry Ford did that to a Cotswold cottage to which he took a fancy, at least it rose again in what had been a Michigan cornfield. With Hearst reassembly was unlikely. As these anatomized structures and other items gained number and bulk, he stored them in warehouses built on the beach of the shore village below his soi-disant castle that, fast and high as it grew, could never house such mountains of expensive, authentic junk. More warehouses were leased in Eastern ports for more and more stuff that its new owner never laid eyes on. At his death most of it had never been uncrated.

The castle began as a cluster of vaguely Spanish Renaissance villas— Hearst had the true Californian tastes for Hispanicistics—successively devoted to guests. By 1925 a second phase blossomed toploftically into a nuclear Casa Grande of 100-odd rooms. Its lofty twin towers between which a Madonna presides over a late medieval carved portal gives this secular edifice the air of a California mission church built by a megalomanic padre; withindoors the glut of religious artifacts maintains the tone. There is no consistency, however. High over the Madonna at the entrance juts out a massive gable of carved teak from Tibet, one is told, stuck up there like a 50-foot bracket fungus because it struck His Nibs' fancy. His architect, Julia Morgan, said to have been first lady architect graduated from the École des Beaux Arts in Paris, never checked his exuberance. La Casa Grande's lofty reception hall is so jammed with legal loot, including a full set of stalls from a medieval Italian monastery, that it looks nothing like its 84-foot length. The only slightly less imposing dining hall has an elaborately carved ceiling from another monastery and is hung with Sienese knights' banners. The library, all Gothic groins and pre-Christian vases, is almost as large as the dining hall. When Dreiser was there in 1930 to see Hearst about Mooney, he noticed that the cumbersome logs for the great fireplaces were hauled into the great rooms by donkeys.

The outdoor swimming pool neglected the Middle Ages for a classic pedimented temple and voluptuously harmonious statuary. The indoor pool is lined with blue and gold tesserae in Byzantine designs occasioned by Hearst's liking for the mosaics of Ravenna. The floor of the entrance hall is a mosaic from Pompeii in near-mint condition. Roman sarcophagi and granite Egyptian gods clutter the grounds, the lawns and shrubs of which grow in tons on tons of topsoil hauled up to this originally gaunt site—at great expense. The only detail not implying great expense is the oaks from the original grove carefully preserved here and there. Hearst called it all "the ranch," and it did remain a huge cattle-raising operation apart from the central acromegaly. The cowhands probably thought this spread of his did have some of the damnedest livestock. Downslope lay a private zoo inside 10 miles of eight-foot wire fence. It included several kinds of great apes, leopards, cheetahs and so on in roomy display pits *ad majorem Wilhelmi gloriam.* In the open freely ranged yaks, aoudads, musk oxen, camels, giraffes, zebras. . . .

Long before rising taxes made it advisable, many of Britain's august peers opened the glories of their great country places to well-behaved sightseers. Lord San Simeon felt no such obligation. All the public saw of what his money could do came through coin-in-a-slot telescopes on the shore aimed at the spiky whiteness miles away on what his toadies reverently called "La Cuesta Encantada"—Enchanted Hill. A closer view was afforded only to servants and guests. Still, that took in a good many. Hearst's guests were reckoned up by ever-changing dozens—not only moneymen, industrialists and politicians asked for tactical reasons but also ornaments of the Hollywood film colony and writers and executives from the upper levels of his publishing empire. To a Hearst man an invitation to "the ranch" meant he was well on his way up.

He had probably been warned about aridity. He got only a single cocktail drunk quickly before dinner. To bring one's own flask for private nightcaps risked its being found by a servant and bang! walking papers. Gossip, probably accurate, attributed this to precaution against the at least part-time drinking problem of Marion Davies, the movie star who was hostess at "the ranch." Yet in many ways this was Liberty Hall. Guests wore what they pleased any time, even for dinner, and had the run of swimming pools, riding horses, tennis courts and mile-long belt of espaliered pergola just as if they had been paying $100 a day at a travel agent's dream of a resort. Since a ranch meant roughing it, the dinner table displayed paper napkins, ketchup in bottles, pickles in jars. Yet one's quarters in La Casa del Monte, or maybe La Casa del Mar, depending on the kind of view, were wildly luxurious in auction-room, satin-bedspread sort of way. A. Edward Newton, famous rare-book dealer as unctuous as a stage bishop, visited the place as it neared its zenith: ". . . one is loath to leave so pleasant a spot, and has the feeling he might stay forever without inconveniencing anyone." [122]

He could have done so without inconveniencing his host, for only exceptional guests saw much of Hearst except at a dinner table seating forty a side. Daytimes His Nibs usually secluded himself in his apartment on top of La Casa Grande, running his affairs by remote control. But just before dinner the rabble of invitees gulping that cocktail in the great hall saw a wall panel open, and there in an elevator, majestically descended from above, a veritable *deus ex machina*, was the tall, paunchy, cold-eyed cause of it all. He moved around the room with a word or so to one or another, then led the way to dinner. After dining he led into a minitheater where each evening he screened a movie—usually new, preferably one of his own productions. Then good night and reascent to insolent isolation—travesty, maybe unintentional, of the life of a king in a grandiloquent setting presided over by a permanent mistress.

When he died in 1951, La Casa Grande was still growing. Half-built elements now stand open to the sky. Busloads of tourists coming up the steep grade of the Enchanted Hill occasionally see zebras, for when the zoo was distributed to towns wanting the animals, some zebras escaped the roundup and now flourish as well adapted to California as the Australian eucalyptus trees that shade them. Visitors may well have heard of Miss Davies, may be aware of *Citizen Kane*; fewer are acquainted with the sordid brilliance with which Aldous Huxley created variations on the San Simeon theme in *After Many a Summer Dies the Swan*.

In their day movie palaces had marked effect, much of it probably unhappy, on American musical habits. Their gargantuan pipe organs bristling with special-effects gadgets had the volume to blast all 3,800 customers eighteen inches straight up from their sybaritic seats. The organist's command-post console, like a cross between Ben Hur's chariot and the control board of a 747, was rigged to rise magically from a corner of the proscenium with a spotlight on the organist poised to "slowly extend his white hands. Silence and then boom!" Aldous Huxley recalled, ". . . the enormous snoring of thirty-two foot contratrombones and bombardes . . . the 'Londonderry Air' on the *vox humana,* 'A Little Gray Home in the West' on the *vox angelica,* and perhaps (what bliss!) 'The End of a Perfect Day' on the *vox treacliana,* the *vox bedroomica,* the *vox unmentionabilis.*" [123] The Roxy had three organists playing at three consoles on the world's largest organ at the same time. Such instruments backed up the house orchestra at need and, in theaters not pretentious enough to keep live musicians in gangs, accompanied the picture to "match in time and shading all the laughter and tears and eternal thrills of the age-old human drama," as the Estey Organ Company's advertisements promised.

The selections thus used as running cliché comment on the action on the screen were less elementary than the pre-War pianist's battery of "Poor Butterfly," "The Skater's Waltz" and "The Light Cavalry Overture." But what merits "To a Wild Rose," "Anitra's Dance" and "The Song of India" possess got diluted and sicklied o'er when thus stirred into the icing on the movie cake. For an arranger objecting to crippling Wagner's Valkyrie music for the score accompanying *The Birth of a Nation,* Griffith cleared up the issue for all time, explaining, "This music wasn't *primarily music* . . . it was music for motion pictures." [124] Montague Glass suggested a Society for the Prevention of Cruelty to Symphonies "[on which] vivisection is being widely practiced . . . for movies." [125] The Largo from Dvorak's *New World Symphony*, he complained, inevitably ushered in lovers' partings and fatal illnesses. The opening of Schubert's C Minor Symphony presaged menacing storms or shoot-outs in gambling houses. The third movement of Tchaikowsky's *Pathétique* usually led into a serious riot. . . .

Some, Sherwood included, believed that sort of thing developed "appreciation of good music in people who previously never thought of Wagner except as the greatest shortstop in baseball." [126] Likelier it did public grasp of music several disservices. It watered down and debased the integrity of works thus cannibalized, turning their themes into clichés deprived of adequate development. For those innocent of standard good music, it took the edge off any future encounter with Dvorak adequately presented, as it half spoils one's first view of a genuine late-medieval half-timber house to have been reared in an Evanston, Illinois, infested with imitations thereof. And it made superb music merely ancillary to the screen, a perversion from which, even when the screen was at its infrequent best, both artistic media suffered. Suppose that at a show of paintings new to you the gallery was pervaded by a sound system voice continually muttering extracts from *Paradise Lost,* Fitzgerald's *Rubáiyát* and *The Waste Land.* Eventually the advent of the sound track enabled Hollywood to stop torturing its betters and move ahead—or anyway away—into hiring music men to cobble up background music *ad hoc* that, however derivative, at least spares the originals.

Movie palaces with large conventional orchestras as well as "Mighty Wurlitzer" organs played the game lavishly, with white-tied orchestral overtures grandly independent of the feature picture, quartets, soloists and pretentious dancing turns between the cinematic items of the bill. Thus New York City's Capitol Theater, Rothafel's concern in 1921, showed *The Voice in the Dark* within a bill beginning with a medley overture from the Capitol Grand Orchestra; then a travelogue of Venice cueing in the Barcarolle from *The Tales of Hoffman*; then the weekly newsreel; then the Salzedo Harp Ensemble rendering "The Song of the Volga Boatmen" (how I wish I'd heard what harps made of that!); then the feature; then the Capitol Ballet and the Capitol Mixed Quartette in a production number of "Selections from 'The Blue Paradise' "; then a Mack Sennett short. . . . In Brooklyn that week the frame for Constance Talmadge in *The Love Game* at the Mark Strand used Dvorak's pianist daughter playing Grieg, a program of favorites from opera and the organist pealing out a Chopin étude.

That sort of thing dominated key-city movie houses coast to coast. Survivals of it persist at the Radio City Music Hall. It did employ hundreds of live professional musicians, scores of sopranos, dozens of rush-across-the-stage-in-cheesecloth dancers, even a certain Dorothy Hecker who, between newsreel and feature, recited Ella Wheeler Wilcox's poems with orchestral interpretation. It was soap-and-water clean for the family trade, often more so than the movie. And given a competent musician on that podium when the elevator majestically eased the orchestra into view, the music purveyed often had quality enough to raise public taste as the sanguine hoped. For many a youngster who would never have attended a concert of the Cleveland Symphony Orchestra paid to see Richard Barthelmess or Lila Lee and thus had to sit through a symphonic overture, it might be the first taste of what no-nonsense music could be.

The most grandiose houses soon had their own permanent ballet ensembles and high-kicking chorus lines, ancestresses of the Rockettes, shifting costumes and themes week after week. Few, however, could stand such production costs. To supply other movie palaces with weekly customer bait came a new theatrical form, the tab (for tabloid) show—a touring package of girls, tenors, costumes and sometimes special props providing forty minutes of glitter three times a day over a circuit of affiliated houses. Chicago this week, St. Louis next, Kansas City, Denver. . . . In very large cities, vaudeville turns—tap dancers, ballad garglers, even one-act plays starring stage names—were booked into movie houses as whipped cream on top. The billing accorded a famous jazz band would practically smother the feature. The Midwest, borrowing from nightclubs, developed a tradition of a permanent master of ceremonies keeping the stage vibrant with his vaunted charm while he patronizingly introduced successive specialties and production numbers. Women and girls came to bask in the glow of Chicago's bushy-haired Paul Ash without caring what was screened between his stints onstage. Managers had stopped bothering with consistency of tone between the movie and the rest of it.* At the Roxy in 1928, for instance, the four-hour Easter show was a welter of seasonal choral and orchestral numbers and ballet bits on all conceivable Easter motifs—and the feature picture was *Why Sailors Go Wrong*.

That harked back to the old, particularly European view of movies as just another attraction on a variety bill. Only in second- and third-run houses did the American exhibitor now ask the average Hollywood movie to draw unassisted. Only the far above average item, usually representing millions of dollars and ballyhooed to match, was "road-showed" in legitimate theaters all by itself, no newsreel, no animated cartoon. And even so self-confident a road show as Griffith's supertearjerker *Way Down East* made much of specially organized pit orchestras oozing a special musical score. For again and again experience had shown that new and brilliant art form though it was, the movie as a mere silent rustle of action on a screen could not, like book, play or concerto, go it alone. Maybe this came of its giving a disconcerting, subliminal impression that one had suddenly gone too deaf to hear anything but the whir of the projector. The nickelodeon's dependence on the pianist probably meant this lack was felt, at least unconsciously, very early.

Further the prompt development of subtitles to set up situations and supply essential dialogue probably meant that movies had an equivalent need of at least a few well-placed words. As movie criticism spread, theory-bound prophets taught that in the interests of pure cinema, titles should not be used at all—look at the long subtitle-free sequences in some comedy shorts. Serious work was sometimes self-consciously filmed in pantomime alone. *The Last Laugh* came nearest to validity; Hollywood's try was Charles Ray in *The Ole Swimmin' Hole*. But the best such only emphasized the dependency. Unassisted pantomime, wonderful as it is in, say, Chaplin's clock-wrecking bit in *The Pawnbroker*, is unavoidably imbecilic when asked to go beyond simple black/white anecdote. Subtitles were always to some extent poisonous, breaking up continuity—and the typical silent movie ran them two a minute on the average. And most of them were incredibly mawkish—at one high point in *Intolerance* when the Huguenot heroine is in the direst straits: "Brown Eyes—ah me! ah me!" But if the screen was to deal in anything more exacting than the ordeal of Little Miss Muffet, subtitles had to be.

* The presumption that such consistency is necessary is modern and probably factitious. Throughout the 1700's and up to the mid-1800's no great actor felt anything out of the way in having his *Hamlet* sandwiched between a one-act light opera and a one-act farce about drunken servants or girls disguised in knee breeches.

A third supplementary tool—vivid, near-normal color—was well in view by 1922. Actually, though Technicolor was in good shape toward the end of the decade, it was little used, maybe because the triumph of the sound track distracted the industry from it. Anyway the extra negative cost of sound had to be digested before color could be allowed to add a second financial burden. And previous experiments of Griffith *et al.* with tinting the film to match the action, reddish for violence, greenish for jealousy, had deservedly withered on the vine and given any use of color a bad name. Yet the strongest thing against it may have been that it contributed relatively little. Even before the Germans' hyperimaginative camera work came in, Hollywood's cameramen, struggling to meet the elaborate demands of De Mille, Griffith *et al.*, could get out of black-and-white 90 percent of what color could promise, and the public's eyes, long used to family snapshots and fine screen halftones, as well as to movies, could derive high satisfaction from it. The crude fact was that it didn't matter enough that Clara Bow's hair was red. Legs and dimples were what did It. None of that meant, however, that the screen was not far better off with music to buoy up the action and with audible words offering still another coordinated avenue to mind and emotions. The sound track rolling with the film came along just in time. Movies then could proceed beyond recycling all the old clichés that were all that dumb show, subtitles and orchestra could handle.

The stage was source of many of the screen's landmark vehicles—*Salome, The Vampire, The Merry Widow, Male and Female* and so on and on—and many of its crucial people—Chaplin, Fairbanks, Hart, Dustin Farnum, Mary Pickford, the Gish sisters, Griffith, De Mille and again so on. So the gravitational pull of Hollywood's waxing bulk necessarily warped it. Some of it was healthy, though painful. Competition from movies gradually smothered that marginal but large part of the playacting industry, the hall, tent and boat troupes doing mostly melodramas and by-gosh comedy for corn-fed audiences. The values of what the Little Gem movin pitcher the*ay*ter showed were as reassuringly simple as those of *The Old Homestead*, their heroes and heroines were better-looking than the *jeunes premiers* of the usual rep show, and the genuine desert into which the movie lovers rode was far superior to the stock scenery of the Decatursville Opera House. Yet this attrition was hard on the troupers for whom *East Lynne* tonight, *Ten Nights* tomorrow were a livelihood. Some, by no means most, found a new one in minor movie roles. But undeniably this disappearance of the typically crudest performers did raise the average level of acting on the American stage.

Eventually, however, it was bad for American acting as a whole, for to some extent these numerous more or less professional troupes were seedbeds of talent, as minor baseball leagues were to the majors. Another such seedbed shrank as movies took over marginal theaters in middle-sized cities and outlying houses in large ones, leaving less showshop room for third, fourth, fifth road companies touring with recent Broadway successes. Some blamed part of this shrinkage of "the road" on the high costs and fouled-up transportation resulting from the War. Anyway, for sample, at the turn of the century Texas had offered six weeks' worth of one-night stands; by 1926 only three houses in the state booked one-nighters. Hence fewer young aspirants getting on-the-job training in minor companies. Along with that narrowing came practical extinction of original productions outside New York City, in effect making Broadway completely congruent with the commercial American theater; formerly Boston, Philadelphia, Chicago, San Francisco had had their own ferments of managerial enterprise and local authorship. Among opportunities for beginners to learn the trade only local stock companies still floated well. In Rochester, Boston, Indianapolis, Denver and dozens of other cities they staged "each week one new play, as a rule a former Broadway success," and depended on "a regular clientele, which goes to see not so much the plays as the players, whom they have come to know and admire." [127] In the mid-1920's dozens of such ingratiating survivals of the theater of Vincent Crummles and Charles Frohman still carried on.

On Broadway the theater seemed to get a marked, if temporary, lift as Hollywood relieved it of the cultural load of supplying melodramatic hokum and fourth road companies of *Turn to the Right*. An analogy may be the lively, if essentially morbid, blooming of a plant when its light and water are threateningly but not quite lethally skimped. In the post-War decade Broadway staged more dramatic scripts than ever before—the peak was 200-odd in 1927–28—in a range of idioms, purposes and techniques never seen before and certainly never tried since, showing, Macgowan said, "a technical perfection and list of distinguished plays that made it the capital of the theatrical world west of Germany and Russia." [128] Writers, producers and angels being what they are, take it for granted that in a rational world many of the weekly list of openings would never have seen production. But this readiness to gamble—possibly related to easy money from the boom in Wall Street—created an elastic, dynamic climate. In 1924 Benchley, keenest as well as most amusing of the day's play reviewers, actually apologized because he could not make his weekly Confidential Guide of thumbnail comments "smart-sounding this year. . . . There are too many good plays in town. You can't summarize a good play in anything but banal phrases." [129] He listed fourteen, "every one of which should be seen if the theatre means anything to you at all," and promised "plenty of others at which you will thoroughly enjoy yourself." Never since has a Broadway reviewer made—or had occasion to make—any such complaint.

It was the high tide between *The Emperor Jones* and *The Green Pastures*. Benchley's fourteen included *The Show-Off*, trig and tangy best work of vaudeville-reared George Kelly; *Sun-Up*, Lula Vollmer's model for regional-feeling plays; *Beggar on Horseback*, sparsely and admirably written, beautifully cast, admirably acted demonstration by George S. Kaufman and Marc Connelly of what Broadway's cleverest could do with Europe's Expressionism. . . . Emphasis was swinging away from the performer toward the script—a healthy thing, for, as Macgowan held, "a theatre lives by its playwrights more than its stars." [130] Hollywood did Broadway another favor in taking over star appeal and allowing the stage gradually to turn the matinee idol tradition out to grass. Too often in elder times it was CHAUNCEY GREENROOM in "Princes and Palaces" as flagrantly as on the musical stage it was FIFI FROUFROU in "The Pink Princess." Now Benchley's fourteen gems showed only one star—the veteran George M. Cohan in *The Song and Dance Man*—likely to attract a personal following whatever he played in. Not that certain names in the star slot no longer carried economic weight. After her triumph in *Rain* Jeanne Eagels, for instance, had that kind of draw. But it was growingly possible for a script as capable as Sutton Vane's *Outward Bound* to prosper greatly without being pulled all out of shape by starring John Barrymore as the drunk who discovers that he and his shipmates are all dead and for the glow and smother of the last few minutes of Karel Capek's *RUR* (which gave us the word robot) not to need Lionel Barrymore as the sententious scientist. That was good for acting—and better for playwriting, thus relieved of managers' clamor for a blatant star part in every script.

Those last three plays were imports, two British, one Czech. Much of the new effervescence behind American footlights came directly or indirectly from what genetics calls hybrid vigor. The adoption and adaptation of the emotional premises of the European theater culminated in the Theatre Guild, which did for Broadway what the Modern Library did for publishing—fostering a large body of customers self-consciously welcoming the unhappy endings, irregular personal relations, Tolstoyan profundities and radical protests hitherto scarce between Herald and Longacre Squares. In its first four seasons the Guild staged only two American scripts in a welter of work from the French, Russians, Germans and Hungarians. The results averaged better in the theater than in books. *RUR* and Ferenc Molnar's *Liliom* and various stagings of Shaw were a large part of why one gratefully recalls the texture of Broadway's 1920's. From Russia also in 1923 came the Moscow Art Players doing Chekhov, Gorki and so on in studiedly coordinated style that deeply impressed Manhattan's reviewers and audiences even though so few understood Russian.* Some of these Russians stayed on after their colleagues went home and strongly in-

---

* This miracle recurred in 1928, when the famous director-manager Max Reinhardt brought a company of picked Germans to dazzle Broadway with Old World drama in undiluted German. Old-timers recalled an earlier occasion when Sarah Bernhardt, playing here in a repertory of French dramas and *Hamlet*—all in French—skipped an entire scene one evening without any in the audience realizing it. (Atkinson, *Broadway*, 6.)

fluenced American acting, notably in the American Laboratory Theatre set up to train young performers hankering after Moscow Art; their practice productions were significantly admired.

Technically *Beggar on Horseback* (based—remotely by the time Kaufman and Connelly had finished—on a German original) was only one American manifestation of Europe's hope to make the stage as fluid as the movies. Lawson's quasi-morality play *Roger Bloomer* and his *Processional*, about coal strikes and lynching, Elmer Rice's *The Adding Machine*, Philip Barry's *White Wings* were borrowings happily interbred with the new styles of stage design. This Expressionism, however, was tricky to handle, often sought a life of its own—and was one of the several temptations that diverted O'Neill's talent into great dismal swamps. In his early bony realism and then in the wonderfully visceral pangs of *The Emperor Jones* and *The Hairy Ape* he had seemed well on the way. But a list toward badly digested psychiatry showed in *Desire Under the Elms*—the bare title is a warning— and the gimmicky masks of *The Great God Brown*, strongly reminding critics of German devices, presaged the cataleptic asides of *Strange Interlude*. Had Expressionism and the attitudinizings that it fostered never crossed the water, O'Neill might never have sponsored the love affair between hero and dynamo, shamelessly purring about it right there on the stage, that dismayed those seeing *Dynamo* as much as it did Claudette Colbert, third in the triangle. Soon the shadows of both versions of Oedipus—Sophocles' and Freud's, equally exotic though mutually incompatible—were too many for his crippled psyche. Once he had been a stripling actor supporting his perennial road-star father in that megalomanic romp *The Count of Monte Cristo*. In things like *Mourning Becomes Electra* he was clottily, murkily hoping to be American counterpart of Dostoevsky—a parable of the darker side, which need not obscure the brighter, of what the American theater did with new tools and freedoms.

A still brighter side of Broadway in the 1920's was also the one unimpeachable aspect of the *Follies/Scandals/Vanities* kind of thing. It gave high pay, long runs and stimulating exposure to a remarkable cluster of great comics: W. C. Fields, Joe Cook, Groucho and Harpo Marx, Ed Wynn, Bobby Clark. . . . The only woman comic of that rank whom Broadway saw in that period was an exotic, Beatrice Lillie. Suppose a supernal assayer weighing up the pure theatrical gold in the combined best three of those—choose your own three—and the combined *oeuvres* of O'Neill, Barry, Sidney Howard and Sherwood, one can hardly doubt which way the scale would tip. Think of a constellation so brilliant that among contemporaries it omits Chico Marx, Bert Lahr, Jimmy Durante, Eddie Cantor, Fannie Brice, Tom Howard.* A comparable baseball team (and all

* I omit Will Rogers because, though long a fixture in Ziegfeld shows, he was more journalist than comic, a newspaper wisecracker. At his untimely death, true, he was compared

at the top of their game at the same time, not a string of names in a Hall of Fame) would be Ty Cobb, Joe DiMaggio, Roberto Clemente, Hal Chase, Johnny Evers, Honus Wagner, Billy Cox, Mickey Cochrane, Babe Ruth and Satchel Paige. Here for once a theatergoer's recollections of vanished genius can be substantiated. The young, God pity them, can never see Joseph Schildkraut and Eva Le Gallienne in *Liliom*. But movies preserve generous samples of Fields and the Marxes in some of their best stage material so little distorted by camera and screen that one gets a fair gauge of their astounding qualities.

Gilbert Seldes, thinking back in 1957, called Fields "the greatest comedian of his time, on the stage and in the movies. He created laughter far beyond Chaplin's intention." [131] Only total agreement that Fields was *primus inter pares* keeps me from nominating Joe Cook, the round little One-Man Circus, the innocent-eyed man of principle who made a career of explaining why he would *not* imitate four Hywoyans, the chubbiest, wariest, most elliptically chatty of confidence men. About him nobody theorized. The mere memory of him makes coherent discourse impossible. His sense of verbal timing was awesomely winning, his physical skills almost equal to Fields'—who, remember, began as a witty juggler, witty without ever opening his mouth. Though a latter generation can hardly imagine Eustace McGargle without that querulously meditative false mutter, it was obscure until Fields first spoke lines in the *Follies* of 1921—and revealed to a national public the subtleties of which the human larynx is capable.

Like all that wondrous group, Fields was decanted, richly matured, on Broadway from big-time vaudeville. He—and they—struggled up from the three- and four-a-day small time, sometimes up to the small time from the proving ground of prestripper burlesque; Clark & McCullough began as comic tumblers in circuses. Long before the Four Marx Brothers graced Broadway first in *I'll Say She Is* in 1923—the same year Cook broke into the *Vanities*—Harpo's harp and Chico's finger-stabbing piano method had been familiar in vaudeville. Honed by trial and error competing with so many other hungry acts, their routines varied little from season to season. The customers disliked major changes. What the Marxes or Cook or Ed Wynn did—the way they did it—could not stale by repetition. My job once required me to visit a Marx Brothers show several nights a week for some months. Even after the fiftieth evening I still had hysterics as violently as ever when Groucho, seducing Madame du Barry, leered at her lan-

<hr />

to Lincoln by two men who had studied Lincoln closely: Sherwood and Sandburg (Brown, *The Worlds of Robert Sherwood*, 196–99). I doubt Lincoln would ever have said, "I never met a man I didn't like." Mark Sullivan's criticism of Rogers is just: "Rogers . . . commonly made the joke for the joke's sake . . . somewhere between humorist and clown." (*Over Here*, 553 n.) Lardner developed an unfavorable notion of Rogers' standards of humor from working with him on skits for Ziegfeld (Elder, *Ring Lardner*, 256–59). Homer Croy, who worked on several of Rogers' movies, recorded at some length how his misspellings and grammatical slips were deliberately cultivated stage decoration. (*Country Cured*, 224, 229.)

guishingly, saying, "May I call you Du?" and Chico and Zeppo marched on in lockstep singing, "Du, du liegst mir im Herzen. . . ."

The significance-and-symbolism boys brewed their flattering cup of hemlock for the Marxes fairly soon. For instance, William Bolitho, a dimly solemn South African-British journalist, saw the Groucho of *Animal Crackers* as a subliminal expression of Jews' peculiar ability to exteriorize laughing at themselves and Harpo as a "suppressed wish-complex." [132] Others breathed hard over Harpo as a modern Pan, a Pied Piper scored by Debussy, a satyr-minstrel (his harp was part of the temptation) escaped from a Grecian urn, a mute (his never speaking on stage was another part) leprechaun cavorting on the surface tension of the tears of things.* Groucho went scatheless, but in some of the later movies Harpo was clearly running a temperature. In the next generation the same thing happened to Danny Kaye. Fields' turn did not come till after his death, so no damage was done.

The vaudeville that licked those immortals into shape was part of the stage's post-War burst of glory. The big time—two-a-day, $2 top in New York City—filled some thirty first-class theaters coast to coast, some still flourishing where legitimate houses were already often dark. Manhattan's Palace was the largest brilliant in the necklace, but the Palace in Cleveland and the State-Lake in Chicago were also vaudeville heavens. Below them lay a maze of circuit-booked secondary and tertiary houses, in 2,000-odd of which three or four vaudeville turns supplemented feature movies, as previously noted. To supply them, booking agents advised, bullied and deployed upcoming acts, all eager for the big time, some with a chance to make it, and picked and chose among established acts that would never go higher but had three-a-day usefulness.

The Oriental acrobats or trained dogs that customarily opened and closed the best and the worst bills were usually, if one liked such at all, too good for their purpose—to quiet the newly arrived audience down and bow it out after the "next-to-closing" turn. The magic or mindreading acts, the ensembles of six gorgeously got-up dancing girls and a tenor in tails, the marimba band, the ladylike soprano coiffed within an inch of her life were agreeably professional. Up on the heights were, say, patter and lunacy from Clayton, Jackson & Durante; Marion Harris, angular, tubular, glittering, belting out "You Got to *See* Momma, *Ev*-ery Night" as if the *Aquitania*'s

---

* The same thing in local terms was going on in Britain, of course. Here is Clive Bell in 1924 spotting "those refined intellectual faces in the gallery of a Music Hall . . . trying so hard . . . to be amused by one fool knocking down another or by jokes about mothers in law and lodgers and coming home drunk . . . raving about a saxophone player or a tumbler in terms which to me would sound slightly hysterical were they leaving a perfect performance of *The Way of the World*. . . . I think a snob at a classical concert makes less of a fool of himself than a snob at a knockabout show." (Review of *The Seven Lively Arts*, in the *New Republic*, April 30, 1924.)

whistle were in her throat; Bill "Bojangles" Robinson, prince of Harlem tap dancers, rattling up and down his flight of steps with such gracious ease that one's eyes brimmed with tears of pure delight; Will Mahoney doing *his* taps on a xylophone. . . . That world of utter skill in achieving quick contact with an audience was what nurtured the likes of Fields and the Marxes.

Vaudeville, even small-time vaudeville, which could be dismal in an off week, deserved a better fate than the fission that came over it in the 1930's as various blights, particularly talking pictures and radio, sapped its vitality. One segment oozed toward the ordeal of drunk-infested nightclubs. The other was cannibalized by broadcasting. Simultaneously the legitimate theater's road continued to dwindle. Hence immediacy, the impact of the live, three-dimensional professional performer on an audience became occasional, something special—once a year at the circus, in the live theater for the Dayton businessman's wife "seeing a few shows" in New York City, in a nightclub for a special evening, and even there microphones stood among the orchestra and came between the audience's ears and the voluptuous blues shouter's tonsils. Shadows on a screen and artificially augmented sounds were taking over. This momentous thing was happening all over the Western world, of course, as the same technology led to the same effects—but soonest and most in America, as with the automobile and the telephone. Since the latter accustomed one to rely on ears alone, as if blind, it made straight the way for radio.

America's fifty years since the 1920's might almost be called the Age of the Mike—that shiny cylinder the entertainer points at his lips as though it were a valve emitting the sacred gas that makes him worth listening to, the gadget intervening distractingly between him and those paying to see and hear him. And whenever his connection with the loudspeaker fails, it is dismally clear that applied electronics has made the modern voice of show business as thin and weak as near beer. Is there such a word as microphony?

Mike and bullhorn combined in crude public address systems were soon making train calling and hotel paging less comprehensible than ever. But the first really wide effect was in politics. In 1919 President Wilson stumping the country for the League of Nations was heard through mikefed loudspeakers by 40,000 people at San Diego, California. The Democratic national convention of 1920 used them. Hence a subtle reorientation of leadership. It had been a great advantage to Bryan, say, that, as John Haynes Holmes, a gifted orator himself, reported, he could "stand at one end of the old Madison Square Garden and without any mechanical aid . . . be heard clearly . . . in the last row of the topmost balcony." [133] Such powers are rare, probably innate. After 1920, however, anybody but an abject mumbler could be clearly heard by large audiences. So the Democratic Party's next spellbinder could be Franklin D. Roosevelt, whose gentlemanly tenor was to Bryan's remarkable voice as the recorder is to the trombone. This breaking of the link between hog calling and statesmanship would have been great gain had it not applied to rabble-rouser as well as to statesman. More people could now hear what a new President said at his inauguration. But also more red-necks could now hear Huey Long at a colossal fish fry in Potlikker Parish, Louisiana. These new gadgets lacked built-in sense of the public weal.

The first wide application of "wireless"—America soon called it radio-telephony, then radio for short—was made by dewy innocents—hams, hobbyists building their own transmitters and receivers in order to revel in the miracle of ethereal gossip across many miles. The transmitting medium they called the ether, though, as was suspected then and is now known, no such stuff existed. Through it, in tireless delight with the possibility of such communication, they asked how's the weather out there in Michigan. But the War, necessarily raising interest in this means to messages without the clumsiness of dot and dash, set the Westinghouse Electric and Manufacturing Company of Pittsburgh on a crash program to develop it. And soon after the War entertainment fatefully got its muzzle into the tent. In Montreal the Canadian Marconi Company's CFCF,* in Detroit, the Detroit *News'* WWJ, in Pittsburgh Westinghouse's KDKA began experiments in broadcasting phonograph music interspersed with requests to hams hearing "Dardanella" or "Smiles" to write in where received, what time of day, how clearly . . . useful engineering data by which to learn what the new toy would do.

As the hams' hobby went musical, hence more diverting, integrity slackened. The active mood of cobbling up one's own equipment and sifting the ether for stranger voices slipped toward the passive mood of using a receiver assembled from mass-produced components bought from a supplier merely to enjoy an unidentified pianist playing "Margie." Soon ready-made sets were procurable by those content merely to listen. Powel Crosley, Jr., founder of Cincinnati's WLW, was selling thousands of them at only $20 each, and copper wire aerials to string from chimney to tree cost little. How clear Omaha came in began to replace flat tires and valve-in-head engines in smoking car chat. Then the loudspeaker superseded headphones, and roomfuls of people could share programs put on the air by stations subsidized by makers of receiving sets. At this point radio was becoming a national institution, exploiting public leisure, hence seeking to interest the public—whether or not in the public interest is another matter. A stalwart clan of do-it-yourself hams carried on. International shortwave broadcasting created a cult of listening for Bangkok and Valparaiso.

---

* Call letters in this section are not necessarily those that the same or successor stations now use. Note too that the question which American station first "broadcast" in the modern sense is and doubtless will stay hopelessly obscure. White (*The American Radio,* 12 n.) also mentions WHA, Madison; KQW, San Jose. . . . Other candidates could readily be brought in.

Workaday radio persisted at sea, in military use and other situations where it was impractical to string telephone or telegraph wires. But once broadcasting was linked to sales of living-room receiving sets, American radio was hogtied to advertising.

In November, 1920, KDKA had broken new ground by broadcasting the returns of the Presidential election. So did the Detroit *News'* WWJ but without the deliberate publicity causing so much talk round Pittsburgh that a vice-president of Westinghouse persuaded the company to manufacture home radios promoted by broadcasting. At first politicians were curiously sluggish about this new tool—a mammoth public address system with a loudspeaker in each of millions of homes. But the lesson began to clarify late in 1923, when ex-President Wilson's halting remarks on the fifth anniversary of the Armistice drew 3,000,000 listeners, many of whom wrote in about the gratification of hearing him right there in the sitting room. Later that year President Coolidge broadcast his message to Congress, and the microphone took the wire edge off his Yankee twang and made him something of a radio personality. The following summer the deadlocked national Democratic convention in New York City was broadcast blow by blow—literally, for it included a description by Norman Brokenshire of a toe-to-toe slugging match between two factions of delegates. For a while the nation's best-known voice was that of the head of the Alabama delegation answering still another roll call: "Ala-bama! Ala-bama casts twenty-four votes for Oscar W. Underwood!" Those broadcasts caused many to ask for the first time whether such clumsy and sordid charades were really the best way to choose Presidential candidates. By 1929 radio was so widely used in politics as to cause alarm lest the expense—Herbert Hoover and Alfred H. Smith were spending $35,000 to 40,000 a night on radio time—drive the cost of campaigning too high for the nation's good.

"Everywhere people are talking about the radio," said the 1922 Montgomery Ward catalogue offering for $49.50 assembly kits complete with headphones, A and B batteries and a 125-foot aerial. "It entertains . . . it fascinates . . . not only concerts, sport records, sermons and lectures but also Board of Trade [grain market] reports, news items and weather forecasts." The Detroit *News* and the New York *Globe* found that radio departments were good reader bait. The Dempsey-Carpentier fight in 1921 was the first thing broadcast over WJZ-Hoboken, maiden venture of the new Radio Corporation of America in the public-attracting sweepstakes. That fall Westinghouse put World Series baseball on the air for the first time. The next fall long-line telephone-and-broadcast hookups through the American Telegraph & Telephone Company's WEAF-New York gave listeners the 1922 Princeton-Chicago game at Chicago, then the Harvard-Yale game from New Haven. When Mary Garden, astute prima donna fixture of the Chicago Grand Opera, allowed Westinghouse's KYW-Chicago to broadcast a whole season in 1922, the number of receiving sets in local use rose from 1,300 at the beginning to 20,000 at the end.

In those early years the average level of material broadcast was watery. When WOR-Newark went on the air in 1922 to promote sale of radio sets (from $50 to $700) in the sporting goods department of the L. Bamberger store, the usual routine was an Irish tenor ("Mother Machree"), a basso ("Rocked in the Cradle of the Deep"), a close harmony quartet ("That Old Gang of Mine") and an astrologer or numerologist—none paid, everybody going it for publicity. Better-established stations favored the ether with what Erik Barnouw, conscientious historian of American broadcasting, calls " 'potted palm music' . . . the music played at tea time by hotel orchestras. . . . European in origin, it was culture to many Americans. . . ." [134] Yet new things were stirring among fast workers skilled in manipulating grass-roots audiences. Ahead of politicians the American Legion was broadcasting its tunnel-vision God-home-mother-and-flaggery over its own WTAS-Elgin, Illinois, and pumping millions of other such words into local stations pressured by state headquarters staffs. The Illinois Committee on Public Utility Information, propaganda arm of Samuel Insull's electric power empire, was also feeding program managers material for broadcast. And hot-gospel preachers, crank crusaders, nostrum peddlers of many kinds rode high on this wild new thing. Some set up their own transmitters; more secured use of the facilities of existing stations needing material to vary the phonograph records and news lifted from the afternoon papers. As number of sets and listeners snowballed without public control, in some areas the tone of the airwaves resembled that of skid row on Saturday night as savers of souls vied with raucous vendors of hate, corn cures and virility restorers. Suppose Johann Gutenberg had launched his press not with stately great Bibles but with the works of Kahlil Gibran, the works of Billy Sunday and Aunt Cindy's Dream Book.

Several kinds of religion staked airwave claims almost from the beginning. The publicity-minded urban pastor offered local radio his services—in both senses—like Sinclair Lewis' Elmer Gantry, "first clergyman in the state of Winnemac . . . to have his sermons broadcast" at a time when the town's sole radio station was carrying "only jazz orchestras and retired sopranos." [135] Or the suggestion could come the other way, as in the short church service for shut-ins, a different parson invited each Sunday morning, that Louisville's WHAS began to broadcast in 1922. Digging deeper were the cult-mongers pouncing on radio as far more effective than direct mail and the Bible-thumping tent-and-tabernacle brethren discovering that breathing hellfire and love into a microphone in a studio was less tiring than devil baiting on a revival platform and, when pleas for contributions were cleverly made, paid better, overhead being lower.

Early in 1922 shoppers in downtown Kansas City, Missouri, crowded around a store window displaying Francis J. Gable of the nearby Unity headquarters most audibly broadcasting the Truth into a mike for transmission to all mankind over local station WOQ. In 1924 Unity bought WOQ for exclusive use in urging listeners to seek prayer help—no charge, just send whatever gratitude suggests. California's Reverend Bob Shuler was not far behind Sister McPherson in tearing up the ether; his hate-spiked broadcasts anticipated those of the next decades' Gerald L. K. Smith. Presently Jehovah's Witnesses bought the most extensive radio hookup of 1927 to enable Judge Rutherford, long since sprung from the federal penitentiary, adequately to denounce orthodox Christianity as contrary to Christ's ideas. The public supporting such broadcasts were the millions of fortyish-to-elderly WASP-Fundamentalists pleased not to have to stir from their chairs to hear rousing sermons on the old-time religion and red-hot gospel hymns sung by nasally harmonious choirs. Then, after the closing prayer, Reverend Joe Bobby Backwater besought "love offerings to keep up this ministry of the air," just put a dollar in an envelope addressed care of this station. . . .

Top billing in early radio cheapjackery goes to "Dr." John Romulus Brinkley, a Carolina hillbilly who brought out most of what smelled worst about pioneer broadcasting. His doctorate came from an eclectic-medicine diploma mill in Kansas City, Missouri. The genuine things about him were his diamonds, as real as they were blinding; his silky mustache and chin tuft that made him look professional; and his cast-iron paranoid nerve. Several states—Kansas, Missouri, Texas, Arkansas, Connecticut—then still recognized eclectic medicine, a vestigial, racket-ridden survival of our forebears' herb doctoring, so he was only one of many such preying on the credulous. Soon after the War, however, he outdistanced the field with a gaudy claim that he could revive men's failing sexual powers by engrafting goat glands (meaning testicles) into their groins. It got him a priceless harvest of half-wishful, half-jeering publicity, for endocrinology was then new and extravagant notions about it were rife.

In a crossroads village, Milford, near Manhattan, Kansas, Doctor, as his wife, also an eclectic MD, respectfully called him, set up a rejuvenation clinic that at its height attracted some 500 people a day. Out of its profits he gave the place water and electric systems. His brick potency factory and herd of Toggenburg goats—he used only Toggenburgs, he gravely explained, because though the testicles of other breeds gave good results too, the patient might smell permanently goatish—were the sights of the neighborhood. Haldeman-Julius carried Doctor's propaganda in his magazine and had him write a Little Blue Book too. Newspapers kept the ball rolling. But the key to Doctor's fame and fortune was the radio station he set up in Milford in 1923—KFKB (for "Kansas First, Kansas Best") alias "The Sunshine Station in the Heart of the Nation," with the then relatively powerful signal of 1,000 watts. In 1930 KFKB got *Radio Digest*'s annual gold microphone award as most popular station in the country.

Most of his potential patients were elderly rural types eager to believe and lacking the unbecoming wariness that urban life may induce. Doctor swathed his radio personality in a trust-fostering just-folks idiom. Twice daily (except Sundays, remember the Sabbath day to keep it holy) he was on the air with unctuous half hours selling his bill of goods. The rest of the time KFKB spread secondary bait—kiver-to-kiver Bible preaching; old-time fiddlers, guitarists and banjoists with the good old tunes; market quotations on corn, wheat, hogs and cattle. Local contacts were tactfully exploited. A student at Kansas State College in Manhattan, who later became a power in the Federal Radio Commission, arranged for KFKB to carry college extension courses leading to academic credit. The Ninth Cavalry Band from nearby Fort Riley was frequently invited to perform. A local banker's wife was KFKB's "Tell-Me-a-Story Lady." In that reassuringly homey context, Doctor's earthily jocose patter about "the male change of life" and what to do about it prospered. Just come on down here and visit us in Milford and we'll talk it over. Why, this fellow from Madison County, Tennessee, last year, he come dragging himself in just plumb discouraged, and finally he said, well, he'd let us have a try—so we did, and sent him home, and just last week he wrote he had a new young wife and twins born nine months to the day—yes, sir, you might not think anything in creation would work that good, but maybe that's what the good Lord made goats for. Now you get to Milford by taking the Union Pacific to Junction City. . . .

As for what rejuvenation cost, Doctor and the staff knew how to determine at the time what the traffic would bear. Once a prospect reached Milford, his savings account, if he had one, was a gone goose; a mortgage on the old place would cover the balance. (Only a special printed offer sent to men of known affluence suggesting a transplant from a healthy young man who presumably needed money badly carried a definite price— $5,000.) Whether the surgery performed by Doctor—likelier his staff surgeons, usually genuine MD's in trouble with medical authorities in other states—actually inserted goat glands is not known. Physiological rejection of alien tissue might well have resulted. But there were the goats, the operating room, the congratulations afterward. . . . The mouth-watering testimonials that Doctor cited on the air need not all have been fabrications. Psychogenic impotence being common, some of the patients doubtless experienced improvement. Anyway the financial transplant was almost invariably successful. No source tells just when Doctor began to sport diamonds, but as KFKB and the Milford clinic passed the five-year mark, he could certainly afford them. By the time I interviewed him in 1940, he not only looked like Diamond Jim Brady's personal physician, he also boasted—and that is no figure of speech—four Cadillacs and eight other automobiles, four giant tortoises from the Galápagos Islands, acquired during a cruise in his seagoing yacht, and the largest swimming pool in

West Texas with DR. BRINKLEY in tiled letters a foot high on its upper rim.

Diamonds came even more easily after he invented his original money-making machine. In 1928 he began to give radio talks on children's ailments. Anxious parents lacking or mistrusting family doctors wrote in: "Johnny just picks at his vittles and has this scabby place on the nape of his neck. . . ." Diagnosing sight unseen, Doctor prescribed over the air first for children, then come one, come all. On request he sent medicines mail order—then the inspiration! He drew up a list of standard remedies, numbered them and arranged with distant drugstores to dispense by number, paying royalties on orders thus filled. Thenceforth the lady in Waterloo, Iowa, with a misery in her back was told she had elliptical epizootia and should ask her druggist for Dr. Brinkley's prescriptions Nos. 3 and 50. If no cooperating druggist was near, send $7 to the Milford Drug Company, Milford, Kansas, owned by guess who. The slogan of KFKB's Question Box Hour was "Don't let your doctor two-dollar you to death!" The Depression was beginning, but Doctor never felt it. Radio had turned this impudent pitchman into one of the best-known personalities between the middle Mississippi and the Rockies.

The political uses of radio being obvious by 1930, Doctor exploited his pose as folksy friend of the man in the furrow by running for governor of Kansas as write-in independent, crying, "Let's pasture the goats on the Statehouse lawn!" He promised free schoolbooks, free automobile licenses and for every county an artificial lake to provide not only boating and fishing but also evaporation to fall as rain on Kansas' often-droughty fields. The KFKB astrologer found the date of the election auspicious to Doctor. Radio was core of his campaign but he also worked in the other new wonder, the airplane. Each Sunday he hedgehopped to a strategic town to preach an open-air lay sermon to the multitude about his recent visit to the Holy Land; he had walked into the Holy Sepulcher and instantly "I knew how Jesus felt." His faithful wife and small son, Johnny Boy, helped on both airwaves and platform.

The returns proved the astrologer wrong but by a hairbreadth margin. Thousands of spoiled write-in ballots were duly disqualified, but even so, Doctor, third, but breathing down the necks of both regular candidates, got 30 percent of the total. It meant even more dismaying things about the electorates of the Southwest that he carried four counties in neighboring Oklahoma, where he was not a candidate. In 1932 he tried again, getting 244,000 votes, again only a nose behind his rivals. Both times he was hampered by opprobrium that few could have survived. The AMA had finally persuaded the medical authorities of Kansas to move against him. Well before he announced for the governorship in 1930, his license to practice had been revoked after hearings mobbed by his hay-shaking admirers and politicians deep in his debt for free time on KFKB. The very same day the Federal Radio Commission had closed KFKB on the grounds that its antics neglected the "public interest, convenience and necessity" that federal law required. Court appeals and leverage exerted by Doctor's allies, including Charles Curtis, part-Indian and all-Kansan Vice President, postponed the fatal day until early 1931—but then Doctor's command of the nation's most popular radio transmitter came to an end.

He had only begun to fight. Emotionally as well as economically, radio had become his life's blood. He leased a telephone line to take his voice into Mexico for broadcast back into the United States. When the FRC stopped that, he recorded his talks on discs and sent them over the border to be put on the air. Then he bought control of a Mexican station just across the Rio Grande, augmented its signal to the greatest power put out in North America—nominally 180 kilowatts, actually often 350—and advertised his goaty miracles as far north and northeastward as Hudson's Bay and Bangor, Maine, barreling in irresistibly everywhere between. When told that the specially made giant tubes that such a signal required would cost $36,000, he paid cash from a roll that was still thick as it returned to his pocket.* Previously he had bought a large hotel in Del Rio, Texas, across the river from his radio station, moved his rejuvenation hospital down from Milford into its upper floors and become first citizen of the town—president of the local Rotary, chief support of its library. His money kept Mexican radio authorities on his side when the FRC protested bitterly against what XERA's power and habit of wandering off the permitted frequency into others' wave bands was doing to American broadcasting. Shaking more Kansas dust from his feet, he moved the prescription mill to Little Rock, Arkansas, and bought a nearby bankrupt country club for a second hospital staffed by the same kind of under-a-cloud doctors. In his two-engine private plane with a huge "Dr. Brinkley" painted on its fuselage he was riding high until overtaken by twin calamities—death and bankruptcy—in the early 1940's.

Meanwhile, his drift toward paranoia had set him espousing certain quasi-Fascist causes of that time and making baseless complaints about persecution. He called the AMA the American Meatcutters' Association and Dr. Morris Fishbein, its doughty guiding spirit, "Fishy." His futile libel suit against Dr. Fishbein and the AMA *Journal* made lively legal history but was an ignominious defeat for him. He need not have taken the AMA's actions so personally. At the same time it and the FRC were doing the same things to "Dr." Norman Baker of Muscatine, Iowa, who, following Brinkley's lead, had promoted his cancer cure over his own radio station and then moved to Laredo, Texas, with control of a Mexican station just across the Rio Grande. Baker's shirts and Cadillacs were purple. When Laredo could stand him no longer, he persuaded the moribund resort of

* Much of the material in this section comes from my "Country Doctor Goes to Town," *Saturday Evening Post*, April 20, 1940; a good deal from Gerald Carson, *The Roguish World of Dr. Brinkley* (1960).

Eureka Springs, Arkansas, to welcome him—until the federals jailed him for mail fraud. Foulmouthed Reverend Bob Shuler was another of the FRC's victims.

The FRC had taken three years to embark on this cleanup of the most noisome broadcasters. Better late than never it raised issues that made Brinkley permanently significant. His effrontery did much, for instance, to set off long-needed improvement of public control of medical practice in the states whose laxness he exploited. His broadcasts from Mexico furthered the use of transcriptions on the air. Barnouw thought it important that he "swept aside the potted palms and spoke to a rural audience in its idiom. The radio careers of many a later figure, including . . . Huey Long, were to follow [his] trail." [136] And the leverage that he exerted on Kansas politicians presaged the great power over legislators now wielded by TV's news and talk programs. On the whole, Doctor's imaginative capers made it impossible further to avoid the public aspects of the new medium. Something had to be done about it. Done it was, with confusing consequences from which broadcasting—and the nation it serves—still ails.

The basic decision—nominal federal licensing of radio transmitters began in the dot-and-dash days of 1912—had already been made but drew little notice. The implied presumption that Uncle Sam had power over and consequent responsibility for broadcasting was strengthened in the War when he shut down all private transmitting equipment. The post-War question was whether to return the air waves to the hams and the government-fostered dot-and-dash radio-telegraphy systems. Some hoped for a permanent federal monopoly—the solution that most other advanced countries adopted and variously modified. What to do with America's railroads, similarly taken over in the War, was a parallel problem. In both cases the strong tradition of private enterprise prevailed. Post-War regulation of radio reverted to little more than licensing about as easy to arrange as a passport and revocable, if at all, on grounds nobody had yet thought through. As yet those weak little stations dabbling primitively in music, news, sermons, bigotry and soon advertising were concentrated on only two wavelengths. As they grew in number and wattage, however, the air was bound to become a caterwauling, backbiting chaos.

For some years Secretary of Commerce Hoover, who was in charge so far as anybody was, besought his annual conference of broadcasters to work out among themselves signal strengths, hours of transmission, ethics and so on—a self-policing about as promising, in both senses, as the Hays Office. Neither he nor the broadcasters bothered properly to explore the implications of federal license to use the air, a matter about as hard to make sense of then as it still is today. The stubborn difficulty is that the technological facts impose an inexorable upper limit on the number of broadcasters able to use the air without hopelessly fouling up one another's broadcasts. Hence some dominant agency—government or a private monopoly—must assign duly separated wavelengths and signal wattages. Suppose Uncle Sam had kept hands off radio, a private broadcasting company filling the vacuum might eventually have absorbed all transmitters and imposed its own kind of order. But that would have required decades of horribly confusing shakedown and doomed broadcasting to a tawdrily embroidered strait-jacket. Society could never tolerate so powerful a propaganda agency in uncontrolled private hands. Liberal Bruce Bliven sketching "How Radio Is Remaking Our World" in 1924 thought that possibility repugnant enough to justify making radio broadcasting "a public utility under strict [federal] regulation . . . it may be necessary to have the government condemn and buy the whole industry, operating it either nationally or locally on the analogy of the post-office and the public school system." [137] Maybe a faint premonition of that underlay the pre-War imposition of licensing, implying not only that the airwaves had better be inalienable public property but also that government, the only eligible custodian of the public's interest, should determine who may use them to broadcast what.

Britain's government monopoly created a public agency, the British Broadcasting Corporation, financed by use taxes on radio sets, with an august board hiring cultivated management to give the nation wholesome entertainment, education and reliable news. For some thirty years it worked much better than it probably would have in the more diffuse and variegated United States. America was probably wise to fight shy of such a system. But the alternative adopted was born to trouble—in effect a nonsystem depriving government and the public it represents of the leverage afforded by monopoly, leaving only the miseries of theoretical power without effective control, not even cutting the public in on the profits made by the use of its airwave property. Lumbermen pay adequately for the privilege of selling trees that foresters mark for harvesting in National Forests. But to this day broadcasters pay only nominal license fees for their highly lucrative exploitation of the public air.

Worse tangles lurked in the issue of *what* is broadcast. Constitutional protection of freedom of speech offers no easy answers. The authors of the Constitution necessarily had in mind only press, pulpit and platform—at that time probably not even the theater. Such means of communication lack the limitations built into broadcasting. Any number of people willing to pay for press and paper can use them and try to persuade others to read the results. But if more than a small number of politicians, parsons or press agents take to broadcasting at the same time, nobody can use the air at all. Or suppose some manage to bully the others into silence, the public property—the airwaves—is exploited by less-than-public and almost inevitably self-serving interests. Brinkley's capers were only the gaudiest example of what that led to.

By 1927 the problem was so inflamed that exorcism was attempted—a

Federal Radio Commission like agencies previously applied to railroads (Interstate Commerce Commission) and power companies (Federal Power Commission). The new FRC was gamely to try to square the circle—allocate frequencies and wattages and license transmitters on condition that the licensee observe "public interest, convenience and necessity" as prime purposes in choosing materials broadcast. It was specifically forbidden to censor—that is, bar materials *before* broadcast. Licensees were not to discriminate in favor of one political candidate over a rival in allotting air time or to create monopoly situations. All proper; but the wisest provisions spelled out the purpose of the act as "to maintain the control of the United States over all channels," to give licensees "use of them but not the ownership thereof," nor did licensing create "any right beyond the terms, conditions and periods of the license," and each licensee had to sign "a waiver of any claim to the use of any particular . . . wave length or of the ether [still assumed to exist] as against the regulatory power of the United States."

The FRC had early success in forcing sloppy broadcasters to stop "wandering"—letting the signal stray outside the allotted wavelength and interfere with broadcasts on nearby ones. Such a crackdown got the FRC this telegram from Sister McPherson: PLEASE ORDER YOUR MINIONS OF SATAN TO LEAVE MY STATION ALONE STOP YOU CANNOT EXPECT THE ALMIGHTY TO ABIDE BY YOUR WAVE LENGTH. [136] Then, after some years of chaos showed that the mere existence of the FRC would not rid the air of garbage, it made such striking examples of Brinkley, Baker, Shuler *et al.* that the average tone of American broadcasting has been slightly better ever since. In 1934 Congress expanded the FRC into a Federal Communications Commission also supervising the nation's telegraph and telephone systems. But this was not the good servant faithful in small things entrusted with greater. Firm as the law sounded, big broadcasters had already been treating their allotted wavelengths as if granted in perpetuity, and commission supervision of broadcasting was going the usual way. That is, an industry being newly regulated applies economic and personal pressures on appointments, decisions and attitudes until, in due time, it and its watchdogs are pretty cozy, with only occasional flurries of snarling over minor issues that are part window dressing, part results of indiscretions from new commissioners not yet completely aware of the score. It surprises nobody when, for instance, successive retiring chairmen of the Federal Aviation Commission retire into highly paid executive posts in the airlines on which they have been riding herd.* A poacher, as the Reverend Charles

---

* This was recently spelled out again by J. K. Galbraith: ". . . regulatory bodies . . . have a marked life cycle. In youth . . . vigorous, aggressive, evangelical, and even intolerant. Later they mellow, and in old age . . . ten or fifteen years—they become, with some exceptions, either an arm of the industry they are regulating or senile." (*The Great Crash*, 171.) Indeed on this basis the FRC/FCC was born at least middle-aged.

Kingsley said, is just a gamekeeper turned inside out.

So there are two reasons why unedifying usurpations will plague American broadcasting until ESP replaces it: one, the congenital difficulties of squaring any such medium with Western notions of freedom; the other, the high unlikelihood that agencies assigned to supervise it will do their job. All that was far in the future in the one-horse early 1920's, when Denver's KLF was founded by a ham broadcasting his own solos on the saxophone accompanied by his wife's piano. Note, however, that he did it to promote the small shop from which he sold radio components to other hams. He can have had no notion of the moral/social/constitutional breakers ahead, but he did recognize that advertising over the air paid. Once people outside the radio-set industry learned that, as they soon did, broadcasting was well on the road to the economic and public relations power that still dooms the FCC or any such agency to something near impotence.

In 1922 Secretary of Commerce Hoover told his convention of broadcasters: ". . . it is inconceivable that we should allow so great a possibility of service [as radio] to be drowned in advertising chatter." In 1924: ". . . the quickest way to kill broadcasting would be to use it for direct advertising." [138] Bliven believed that not only should radio advertising "be prohibited by legislation" but that even "incidental advertising . . . the motive behind a great deal of broadcasting, if unwanted by the listening public, will probably die of itself." [137] Exclamation points ad lib. Within a few years overt radio advertising was as well established an American thing as chewing gum. The permanent drop curtain of the small-time vaudeville house had long been a patchwork of advertisements of the local livery stable, barbershop, ice-cream parlor, hardware store and, as the marcel wave came in, beauty shop. At the movies magic-lantern slides of the same import flashed on the screen after LADIES WILL PLEASE REMOVE THEIR HATS. The American press, notably newspapers and popular weeklies, had long been more dependent even than Britain's on advertising revenue. The big-city daily selling for two cents cost several times as much to print. The *Saturday Evening Post* retailed for a nickel but cost about a quarter. The difference was more than made up, of course, by the whacking sums that department stores paid newspapers and the motor industry paid magazines for access to their readers.

Soon enough the shoe tried to get on the other foot. Once advertisers knew themselves essential to the mass press, they tried putting pressure on editorial policy, with considerable success at first. But after 1890 some independence resumed, else Joseph Pulitzer's proto-muckraking papers and the muckraking magazines could never have flourished. A sort of symbiosis emerged. In the press fairly frank entertainment—financial, political or erotic scandals; gaudily described crime; gossip about celebrities of stage or drawing room (the press agent's particular kingdom); comic strips; advice to the lovelorn—were essential at once to the advertiser as bait for his ads and to the publisher as bait for the advertiser. "The influence of an individual advertiser upon newspaper policy is only of incidental importance," O. W. Riegel wrote in 1934, "but . . . the whole tone of the American press is determined by the necessity to produce newspapers . . . of the greatest possible usefulness as advertising vehicles." [139] Almost as much as the magazine with its expensively illustrated serial stories, the newspaper had become a verbal/print branch of show business.

Solemn minds pondering the impact of radio saw it as a boon to shut-ins, invaluable as teacher. "Will the classroom be abolished," Bliven wondered, "and the child . . . be stuffed with facts as he sits at home or even [a wrong guess only in the nature of what he hears] as he walks about the streets with his portable receiving set?" [137] And for political education: "For the first time in history," said the *New Republic* in 1924, "a presidential candiate will . . . be judged out of his own mouth by any large portion of the electorate . . . when it is actually easier to listen in than to read and often more exciting . . . see grandmother being converted to socialism as she knits of an evening with her earphones on. . . ." [140] As for international comity, General J. G. Harbord, president of the new Radio Corporation of America, child of General Electric, parent of the National Broadcasting Company, intoned in 1928: "More than all the peace conferences of history [American radio] has served to make . . . 'Peace on Earth, Good Will Toward Men' a reality, and taking the world by the hand, has led it one big step farther down that shadowy trail that ends in Utopia." [141] Much that same list of windy hopes appeared when the wraps came off TV after World War II.

In the lee of those innocent predictions, advertising was unostentatiously taking over radio. WEAF-New York, arm of the American Telephone & Telegraph Company, began canvassing for advertising as soon as it was born. Its first client was an agency selling garden apartments in Jackson Heights, Queens. By the holiday season three department stores were in; soon the Metropolitan Life Insurance Company, Mineralava Soap. . . . And strange as it sounds now, for some years what amounted to institutional advertising for highly solvent companies went on the air without charge. Free time was swapped for free attention-securing material. WLW-Cincinnati, for instance, broadcast stock quotations credited to a local broker and piano music credited to the local Baldwin agency. WFAA-Dallas called its department store suppliers of entertainment "chaperones." In that spirit they used the mild disguise of chatty talks in which the store's name frequently cropped up—the "indirect advertising" of Hoover *et al.*—or the firm or brand name was hung on the performers: the Clicquot Club (ginger ale) Eskimos; the Gold Dust (scouring powder) Twins, a singing duo. . . . Sears, Roebuck was intensely identified with its WLS-Chicago (for "World's Largest Store"), broadcasting not only old-timey music—Chubby Parker's voice and banjo in "Whoa Mule!" and "The Little Brown Jug"; Ralph Waldo Emerson (not the philosopher) pealing out "Old Folks at Home" on the organ—but also "The Home-maker's Broadcast" about farmwives' canning and cleaning problems and for their husbands those invaluable market quotations on grain and livestock. A farmer following those cleverly, Sears claimed, could make enough extra to pay for one of Sears' Silvertone radio receivers.

As the 1920's passed midpoint, there was no more question of locking the door. The horse was gone. Irrevocably American broadcasting had become a monstrous expansion of the old courthouse-square medicine show. It had the medicine show's great advantage—like the performance of Little Doe Eyes, the Indian maid from the Land of the Skyblue Water selling Chief Uncompahgre's Swampy Snakeroot Tonic, radio cost the spectator nothing. And it could hold the sucker to the pitch better than the press. One might read a serial by Kathleen Norris in the *Ladies' Home Journal* without heeding the adjacent advertisements for face creams and fireless cookers. But the listener who liked the selections rendered by the A&P Gypsies risked missing something if he tuned out the interspersed announcements, which were rapidly becoming the modern commercial. The National Broadcasting Company, based on national networks, was organized in 1927 deliberately to reap the juicy profits to be made by slaking the public thirst for this highly aerated entertainment. The next year the Columbia Broadcasting System was strung together on a shoestring to begin an upward climb as steep as NBC's. Within two years a vast new quota of listeners' time was added as automobile radios, until then custom-made and costly, came on the market mass-produced and cheap from Chicago's Galvin Manufacturing Company under the brand "Motorola."

Many newspapers, unhappy over radio's growing share of the local advertising budget, refused to carry listings of radio programs—a logical policy but dependent on unanimity, and it raveled away when papers boycotting the boycott got increased circulation from radio fans. Those fans were spending half a billion dollars a year on radio sets. Advertisers were already paying broadcasters $5,000,000 a year. In 1932, in spite of the gnawing Depression, the sum was thirteen times greater. The year before, grim 1931, when so many established businesses went bankrupt, NBC and CBS each netted some $2,500,000. By 1939 the gross intake had tripled again, having risen every year but 1933, the season of bank closings. Simultaneously the opening of the Rockefellers' Radio City, named for its chief tenants, RCA and NBC, in midtown Manhattan loomingly symbol-ized the overshadowing position that radio had taken in the middle of American life.

More efficient and more reliable receivers studded the radiomakers' commercials with words like "heterodyne," "variometer" and "amplitron." Commercials as well as entertainment were less and less plagued by hoots, snarls, howls, squeaks, squawks, gurgles and cracklings as of thorns under a pot. In parallel refinement the speaker had retreated behind a cloth-filled grill of varnished slats in vaguely Gothic or baroque patterns set into the elaborate "console" cabinet housing the mysterious innards of the receiving set. Dial twiddling no longer required the slightest inkling of how "the miracle of radio" worked. As temptation to recreational passivity the radio far outdid the Sunday paper, which required page turning; the player piano, which required pedaling; the phonograph, for which one had at least to choose selections. In that respect it still exceeds TV because it does not interfere at all with housework and is consistent with driving a car.

What came out of it in its great pre-TV days was reliably predicted in 1916 by precocious David Sarnoff when assuring his boss that it could be "a household utility . . . a simple 'Radio Music Box' . . . arranged for several different wave lengths . . . with . . . a loudspeaking telephone . . . [giving out] events of national importance . . . lectures at home . . . baseball. . . ." Regular newscasting—five minutes daily from the Newark *Call* over WJZ—began in 1921. Until stations acquired their own news-gathering staffs, wire-service ticker bulletins were rewritten from the local papers with no regard to copyright. Soon show business had a new specialist, the radio newscaster. The color of his voice, the tenor of his vocabulary, the vividness of the personality projected sight unseen became crucial like a clown's makeup or the shape of a soubrette's legs. Hoping to keep the station's image paramount, management long tried to keep listener-inners from knowing the announcers' names. But under floods of fan mail they broke down, allowing these new public idols to identify themselves by initials, then in full: "This is your good friend, Marshall O. Armpit, saying good night to you, ladies and gentlemen of the radio audience, for the Trinitrotoluol Troubadours. . . ."

Rothafel, once industriously shaking hands in the lobby of whatever theater he was managing at the moment, was now busy as invisible focus of "Roxy and His Gang" on the air promoting New York City's Capitol Theater. One of the general press' first radio reviewers marveled in 1928 over the ability of a glib and weedy Dane, Nils T. Granlund—"NTG" to his fans, dead name and fame!—to keep WHN-New York's listeners happy "merely by the strength of his own personality" when the performances that he introduced were "pretty much tripe." Yet she missed the point when complaining that Graham McNamee, first of the nationally famous sportscasters, sought to be "a cross between a movie-star and an after-dinner speaker . . . sets his personality between the audience and the game." [142] That was what the unseen audience, individually isolated in kitchen, garage or sickroom, most wanted—the ebullient personality riding the ups and downs of doings in the faraway ball park. Though women had long been admitted to ball games if they wanted very much to go or somebody wanted very much to take them, the intense interest they developed in baseball in the 1930's came of radio's filtering the game and all its complex lore through McNamee, Ted Husing *et al.* Nor might the Democrats' rowdy convention of 1924 have so taken the public ear had its chief radio observers not been McNamee and J. Andrew White, another early sportscaster. It was then astonishing—now taken utterly for granted—that so close an illusion of personal contact came from what amounted to a one-way telephone call.

Children were fished for and usually caught by advertisers of not only breakfast cereals and candy bars but also of toothpaste and sneakers. When Johnny promised to brush his teeth if mother bought him Dentapearl toothpaste recommended by the Dentapearl Big Brothers, she had reason to comply. "Clubs" stiff with badges, rings and secret codes made small fry loyal to this or that radio-sticky product. Presently an invisible "Uncle Don" was notorious for the unction with which he advised little Shirley Lightfinger of Dover, Delaware, that if she didn't steal candy for a week, she'd find a nice present behind the vacuum cleaner in the broom closet. Educators and devotees of Child Study had good cause to lodge protests with the FRC, but the cartilaginous code of standards drawn up in 1929 by the National Association of Broadcasters in dim emulation of the Hays Code said nothing about improved airwaves diet for the nation's children. Indeed the NAB was set up in 1923 not so much to improve anything as to oppose efforts of the American Society of Composers, Authors and Publishers to make broadcasters pay for using words and music. Not for another ten years would the NAB loftily recommend that broadcasts for children should "be based upon sound moral concepts . . . with a superior degree of craftsmanship . . . reflect respect for parents, adult authority, law and order, clean living, high morals, fair play and honorable behavior" and renounce auditory enactments of torture likely to "overstimulate" [143] a child. That was nearer the Hays style—sounding great but easy to file and forget before reverting to business as usual.

Today a chief interest of the 1929 code lies in its showing how broadcasting has changed in forty-odd years. It recommended suppressing commercials between 7 and 11 P.M. Few stations cut their financial throats by complying, of course, but it actually was proposed thus to sterilize the economic function of prime time. The code also warned broadcasters to check the credit standing of new clients; to observe the federal rule of 1927 against presenting paid-for material as if originating with the station; to avoid things already barred from the mails as "fraudulent, deceptive or obscene"—all reminders that Brinkley-like high and low jinks were still lively. Some years later the Federal Communications Commission still had to disqualify as "not in the public interest" fortune-telling, astrology, fund-soliciting (had that taboo ever taken hold, many jackleg Fundamentalist preachers would have starved), defamatory statements, matter offending religious sensibilities and "programs in which a concert is interrupted for advertising announcements." That was what it said right there in print.

It all sounds as far away and long ago as nainsook BVD's. But many side effects already discernible c. 1930 persist—only on the wider scale of TV backed up by radio—as in the abject dependence of politicians on broadcasting. It was also important that radio supplied so much entertainment and contact with the nation in general to wide places in the road. That probably did not, as Walter White seriously hoped, reduce the likelihood of lynchings in stagnant Southern county seats, but it did shape the isolated farm family nearer congruence with their city cousins—which, whether or not it was desirable, most country folks liked. Hiram Corntossel's table model radio brought in at exactly the same time as radio-phonograph consoles on Lake Shore Drive the same rendition of "Carry Me Back to Old Virginny" on WLS. Broadcasts of "Everybody Step" from the same record took to young folks in Malone, New York, the same commercial jazz that one heard in Park Avenue penthouses. And once national networks were piping live broadcasts by wire into their multiple major outlets, Joe Penner's "Wanna buy a duck?" would be as much a byword in Manhattan, Kansas, as on Manhattan Island.

Some lasting side effects came of the impact of those national networks on local traits. The vocal habits of New York City announcers soon eroded the hush-ma-mouf talk that came natural among Southern announcers— and among young folks listening to them. The proliferation of radios in college dorms and high school pupils' bedrooms gave the rising generation an extraordinary indifference to extraneous noise. Incessant broadcasting of Tin Pan Alley's latest successes fattened ASCAP's royalties—once broadcasters were beaten into acceptable payments—but poisoned songwriting in general, for daily hammering on "Valencia," say, "made people hate this week what they had loved last week," [144] as Robert J. Landry, radio sage of *Variety*, once noted. It was also deleterious to force attention on performers' skills and away from what individual merits the number performed might have—the reverse of the theater's shift of attention away from the actor, toward the playwright. Then radio was a stay-at-home, centripetal new thing modifying the centrifugal interactions fostered by trolley cars and movies and most of all by the automobile. Probably the deepest marks, however, were left by the impact of radio advertising on consumer demand. That set radio alongside the tourist court as a new industry gathering momentum against the trend of the times all through the Depression. "Everywhere out of its dusty box the radio forms air into voices," Dos Passos wrote, "voices that lull, insinuate, incite the mind to grow new tendrils of appetite . . . stir in somebody embers of half extinguished wants, old needs rancid under the deep lid of everyday." [145,] Only TV could concoct such stimuli more effectively as, in due season, TV took over and did.

Yet never blame radio for all new appetites developed during its geometrically progressive growth. It barely existed in 1916 when Billy Sunday assumed that readers of his *Great Love Stories of the Bible* would know what he was talking about in referring to "six hamburger and hot-dog wagons in every block." [146] The order of precedence was prophetic. Within the 1920's the hamburger came seriously to rival the hot dog as America's favorite bought-in-public snack, and in the 1930's it swept on to become the nation's gastronomic trademark and a chief prop of its cattle industry.

The German enclaves of the Middle West distinguished between the Frankfurter (soon contracted to "frank") and the Wienerwurst (contracted to "weenie"). But in the amusement park and carnival trade the two blended into a bland, slender sausage boiled or grilled and eaten tucked into a long roll with mustard. Or the condiment might be piccalilli or, in the Southwest, a chili-flavored sauce. It seems to have been T. A. "Tad" Dorgan, the harshly wisecracking cartoonist of the Hearst papers, who, building on the vendor's "Get 'em *red*-hot, *red*-hot!" and the popular legend that their content might once have barked instead of grunting or bellowing, invented "hot dog." During the War the dog reference was strengthened by the affinity of the thing's shape and color to those of the dachshund that had become one symbol of Germany. By Joe College's time "Hot dog!" or even "Hot diggety dog!" expressed minor exultation. Sinclair Lewis correctly limited use of the term to the combination of sausage with roll—the form in which the Pim Pam chain of snackeries introduced it to Frenchmen as well as homesick Americans on the Rue de la Paix in the early 1930's and in which, to the joy of headline writers, the King and Queen of Great Britain met it *chez* Roosevelt in 1939.

Starting later, the hamburger took longer to make the eastward Atlantic crossing. This term too must be used carefully. "Hamburger steak"— chopped lean beef broiled in a thick cake, eaten with knife and fork—was a staple in German-American restaurants; in the pre-War decade a certain Dr. James Henry Salisbury based a whole alimentary hygiene on its virtues, hence some menus today still offer "Salisbury steak." But the hamburger-as-such—a thin patty of ground beef broiled (typically on the sizzling steel sheet of an all-night lunchroom), served in a squashy bun and eaten by hand, for not even a Briton ever ate a hamburger with knife and fork—has a confusingly mixed, dim and relatively recent provenance. *C.* 1900 the basic step seems to have been taken at Louis' Lunch in New Haven, Connecticut, when Louis Lassen, its proprietor, known for his excellent hamburger steaks, improvised it for a customer who was in too much of a hurry for the regular serving. The New Haven Preservation Trust has duly recognized the establishment's sound claim to be the holy spot where the hamburger was born. But that was, as Louis' still serves it, a two-slices-of-toast version with condiments discouraged. How the bun got into the act I cannot determine. There is no corroboration for the legend that the bun-hamburger was invented and popularized at St. Louis' Louisiana Purchase Exposition in 1904, though the Germanness of that city makes it a plausible story.* But the bun was the same as that used by some Midwestern lunchrooms and presently drugstore fountain lunches as vehicle for boiled ham and fried pork tenderloin.

By 1912, anyway, the hamburger, whether migrated westward from New Haven and marrying the bun along the way or independently invented complete with bun somewhere west of Pittsburgh—which is quite possible —was at home in the circus-lot context of one of Irvin Cobb's stories of pre-War Kentucky. The next year one finds it well established in Fort Lauderdale, Florida, doubtless through Midwestern influence. By 1923 condiments were bulking large in the picture to judge from the street carnival of Harry Leon Wilson's *Professor, How Could You!* which included a garish booth operated by an outsize lady: "SEE THAT FAT WOMAN! THE HAMBURGER QUEEN! Boys, We Make 'Em Big! Mustard and Onions Extra!" [147] The last line disappeared as competition made it inadvisable to charge extra no matter how generously the customer combined items from a growing list of accepted supplements—thin slabs of raw onion; dabs of fried onion; chopped raw onion; tomato ketchup; piccalilli; mustard. . . . In many places to respond "Everything!" to the counterman's "How'll you have it?" was code for ketchup, piccalilli *and* mustard all at once. In New York City a toasted English muffin became an admirable replacement for the bun.

The simple but sound virtues of the early hamburger go far to account for the generation of youngsters—now pushing middle age, but their progeny retain their folkways—willing and able to live on hamburgers, French fries (daubed into ketchup) and milk exclusively. Their folk hero was, of course, J. Wellington Wimpy, born full-blown late in the Hoover administration in Elzie Segar's comic strip *Thimble Theater.* Unfortunately the cult outlived the virtues that created it. Penny-pinchers put more and more fat into the beef or so stretched it with dubious ground pork that trichina-wary consumers' organizations warned against any hamburgers publicly obtainable in certain states. Then, as the economy straitened in the 1930's, a wild diversification distracted the customer from the shortcomings of the basic ground beef—if that's what it was. A slab of gluily melted process cheese on the patty made a cheeseburger, the only point to which was widening the range of proteins ingested. Flocking after came pickleburgers, tomato-burgers, pizzaburgers, bananaburgers, Texasburgers (with chili), occasion-

* That is, materials about the exposition surviving in St. Louis fail to mention hamburgers as they probably would if they had been a popular novelty at the time. One cannot prove a negative, but I came near it when taking the matter up with Thomas Hart Benton, who was fourteen years old at the time and saw a great deal of the exposition; he said that he had always been a particularly hungry kid and would certainly have remembered meeting his first hamburger there had any such thing been available.

ally wineburgers—an imbecility created by somebody who, hearing that red wine goes with beef, sloshed a glass of tepid, uncooked "red ink" over an otherwise passable hamburger. As the first syllable sloughed off, the trade launched on fishburgers, soyburgers (presumably for vegetarians), chickenburgers, recently eggburgers. Any day now highway eateries down the Peninsula from Richmond, Virginia, will be offering Williamsburgers. Less elaborately but calamitously, the British have expressed their fondness for Mr. Wimpy with a chain of hamburger lunchrooms named for him. Nothing as bad as London's "Wimpies" yet occurs in America even when, as denounced by Calvin Trillin, the nation's great student of the white-topped table cuisine, the counterman peels "some morbid looking patty from waxed paper and [tosses] it on some grease-caked grill." [148] Nevertheless, hamburgers are now almost like what fried chicken became forty years ago—a traditional American dish of merit and repute seldom commercially obtainable in worthy form.

In the 1920's the hot dog also came under pressure from the so-called barbecue sandwich of shredded overdone beef or underdone pork sloshed with a thin, reddish, spicy beef sauce only faintly reminiscent of the genuine down-home barbecues of the lower Mississippi basin. "Bar-B-Q" proclaimed its presence on roadside signs that still linger here and there, so it must still have friends. There was more style to the hot dog's third rival in wrong-side-of-the-tracks gastronomy, the various versions of chili con carne that, originating along the Mexican border, gradually infiltrated the nation. It combined most of the scanty comestible resources of the area, barring corn—beef, onions, dried beans, sometimes tomatoes, sometimes garlic and the hell-hot peppers handed down from pre-Columbian times. Even when commercial chili powder is substituted for the actual chopped peppers a well conceived "bowl of red" provides first a harmonious choir of robust flavors, then an intimate glow as of an incipient high fever, finally a strong awareness of having been most durably nourished. Some of the many variations use oregano and cummin for subtlety. Those reinforcing the peppers with cayenne are not for beginners.

The Southwest affectionately considers chili (for short) a proper part of its culture, not elegant but eligible like clam chowder in New England. For years, the rest of the nation tended to look down on it. The reason probably is that fifty years ago, when all its ingredients, even the beef ground from the coarsest cuts, were inexpensive, chili became associated with skid row, or at best Railroad Avenue, frequenters of which much appreciated such rib-sticking provender at 10 cents a throw, crackers included. In a gradual spread coast to coast about simultaneous with that of the boll weevil, the American town large enough to support a pawnshop developed in the same block an all-night eatery labeled JOE'S CHILI PARLOR in raised white letters on the glass of the dirty front window, and the dish appeared nowhere else.

Only in Cincinnati, however, a highly idiosyncratic version took a strikingly upward swerve in the early 1920's. There an immigrant Bulgarian lunch-room owner added traditional Balkan spices to the basic concept, stepped down the heat, served it with spaghetti and sometimes chopped onions and grated cheese. The result, rather like something you might greatly enjoy in Thessaloniki, so pleased the local palate that the innovator founded on it a whole chain of local parlors that served practically nothing else. A rival chain is just as successful under one of his former cooks, a Greek who added his own variations. For the nation at large this blend of Border Mexican, Southwest Gringo, Bulgarian, Greek and Italian motifs in one admirable dish is one of the Melting Pot's rare triumphs. Cincinnati is just happily parochial about it.

Pre-War nutritional theory had been first wrongheaded, then, for lack of knowledge of vitamins, too crude. The fashionable hygiene *c.* 1910 had been Swat-the-Fly and Fresh Air. Now it was lucky that just when hamburgers—not negligible nutritionally but no ideal diet—came along seducing the palate of the Jazz Age, the new nutrition was persuading parents that orange juice, milk and leafy garden truck were indispensable. The consequent panic of parental interest in the subtleties of these mysteriously alphabetized vitamins really did benefit children as well as the grove owners growing the oranges and the dairymen whose cows gave the milk.

"We Feed the World and Starve Our Children" was the *Ladies' Home Journal*'s eye-stopping headline on an article by U.S. Surgeon General Hugh S. Cummings in 1921. Many American children, it said, were about as badly off nutritionally as the Russians then being saved from famine by the American Red Cross. ". . . too little milk, too little [*sic*] fresh vegetables and . . . fruit, especially of the citrus variety . . . millions . . . still regard the orange as a Christmas luxury. . . . One quart of milk daily should be consumed by a growing child. . . . Illinois, Utah, Massachusetts and New Mexico report that one-half . . . of their school-children do not drink milk at all . . . by no means exclusively the children of the sub-merged tenth." [149]

Other women's magazines bayed on the same trail, and Dr. Lulu H. Peters' *Diet and Health*, so valued as a slimming handbook, also preached the new nutrition. Mothers taking it seriously made orange juice a national institution now stronger than ever thanks to the condensing and quick freezing developed during World War II. Few children objected when its tart freshness replaced the stewed prunes or baked apple previously served as first breakfast course because fruit was vaguely recommended. Until the mid-1920's, when tomato juice weighed in as the tomato juice cocktail for timid partygoers—nobody had yet thought of the Bloody Mary—orange juice had no serious rival on America's breakfast table. And its use in the Orange Blossom cocktail favored by Prohibition drinkers did much to keep the average level of vitamin C high in the American bloodstream.

As for milk, by 1925 Dr. E. V. McCollum, the nutritionist at Johns Hopkins whose handbook for the public was backbone of the movement, recommended a quart a day for adults wishing to stay healthy as well as for growing children. The *Woman's Home Companion* preached that "Any woman who does not appreciate the importance of milk in the diet should be prohibited by law from planning meals." [150] Many youngsters reared to swig down ten ounces three times a day acquired a sort of emotional addiction to the stuff. When they entered the armed forces in World War II, they were still drinking it as if inducted to fight for God, country and Elsie the Borden Cow. Their dismay when military exigencies deprived them of milk in the field—training camps were awash with it—suggested that in a psychometabolic sense they had never been weaned. One of the nation's tourist sights was the Walker-Gordon "rotolactor" in New Jersey—a slowly revolving milking stand accommodating sixty cows standing tails out so the public could study their behinds and agree with the laboratory that they were so clean their milk could be sold as bacteria-free without pasteurization. Such "certified" milk was for infants or adults unable to cope with the heavy curd of pasteurized cows' milk and for a dwindling number who thought pasteurizing immoral because unnatural. The rest of the nation, long warned against "bugs," poured pasteurized milk down its progeny without doubting its being, as advertised, "the perfect food." "Almost perfect" would have done better. Milk is low in iron, and pasteurization spoils its vitamin C and its normal content of the antirickets factor (vitamin D so called) important in growing children's bone structure. In the mid-1920's Dr. Harry Steenbock of the University of Wisconsin worked out a process that restored vitamin D by exposing pasteurized milk to ultraviolet rays, the critical metabolic frequency of sunshine.*

A possible drawback to this milk addiction was that it dulled children's appetites for other foods. A creature weighing some sixty pounds that swigs down a glass of milk soon after coming to table is less likely to crave boiled eggs or lima beans, and it might be shown that the first great wave of children having to be bullied into eating what was on their plates coincided with the glorification of milk. Yet the risk of permanent infantilization of the palate and of traumatic family frictions was doubtless made up for by the resulting millions of taller, well-moving, big-footed adolescents far superior to those born *c.* 1900 from the same gene pool. Maybe they hated

---

* Steenbock patented this and ascribed the soon handsome royalties from the food industry's use of it to the university to be used for further research. I was taken aback some years ago to learn that many milk processors and others are now neglecting thus to "irradiate" milk etc. because rickets had practically disappeared and that in consequence it is now reappearing in serious numbers of cases.

their mothers and had the gastronomic values of retarded puppies, but milk gave them a fine money's worth in achieved somatic potential. Their robustness made it the sadder to see the persisting results of malnutrition—some of cultural origin but mostly of economic—among the South's poor whites, the Indians on reservations, the slum dwellers not reoriented on nutrition and the masses of underprivileged blacks.

The parent/child rift was deepened by the third part of the new nutrition: ". . . fresh vegetables," Cummings said firmly, "[are] most greatly needed . . . the leafy sorts used as greens; carrots, rutabaga turnips, cabbage, and all salads." [149] Americans were never too fond of what many of their forebears called "garden sass." What they did eat in season or from winter storage—tomatoes, green beans, cabbage, carrots, squash and so on—were often cooked to death, reducing the vitamin content and sending valuable minerals down the drain. Only in the coleslaw that the Dutch brought in to fan out over the rest of the country were average Americans named Smith or McSomething well broken to raw green stuff. In those respects the Italian immigrant family shopping on Bleecker Street for things valued in a culture too poor to afford much meat were better off.

Her reading did shame Mrs. McSomething, however, into adding cooked greens and salads of lettuce or raw tomatoes to her family's long-standing meat-potatoes-and-pie, and the going rapidly grew rough—bad enough with her husband, far worse with the children who, gorged with milk, were even less inclined to rabbit food than to the fried round steak that probably dominated the chief meal. Inexplicably spinach, the most delicate of cooking greens, became the special symbol of this war over "Eat your vegetables, dear!" No, that improvement in the size and to some extent the shape of the new generation now reaching its fifties probably cannot be attributed substantially to the beneficial effects of more green stuff. Doubtless whatever was forced or cajoled past the child's resistance did him some good. But the amount was scanty while the scars were as deep and lasting as those of the great glaciers in the bedrock of New England.

Echoes of the new biochemistry took an even stranger turn in the sun cult that suffused the latter 1920's with unprecedented swarthiness. It came from Europe. For once Old Worldlings outdid Americans in overdoing something new and romantic in therapeutics.

European physicians, soon imitated by American colleagues, had long been sending cases of tuberculosis to warmer climates; then, as theory altered, to higher altitudes, in the belief—often shared by the patient, which fostered favorable results—that warmer or thinner air was specific for the disease. Madeira, the French Riviera and the Swiss Alps, successive best-known loci of this climate therapy, had more winter sunshine than the home environments of most of the patients. So *post hoc* reasoning linked sunshine and improved health as cause and effect. Such logic usually hinders but sometimes advances medicine. Certain sun-minded physicians, most notably Dr. Auguste Rollier of Switzerland, observing turns for the better in cases of bone tuberculosis tanning up in unwonted sunshine, had some success with deliberate sunbathing—nor was it all nonsense. Sunshine does check tuberculosis of the skin and skeleton, promotes healing of wounds and combats superficial microorganisms. Sanguine doctors went on to surmise that it might be good for many other ailments. Their hopes grew when, not long before the War, sunlight direct on the body was found to prevent rickets—the bone-deforming disease of growing animals and children. In 1919 a German doctor cured rickets indoors with artificial light from a quartz lamp, no natural sunshine involved. Then it was found that ordinary window glass cuts out the ultraviolet rays, so sunshine prevents rickets only when absorbed outdoors. Mothers putting baby outdoors for "air and sunshine" had been right all along. Even when he was all bundled up, exposed cheek and forehead afforded some rickets insurance. In 1922 a "vitamin D" created in the system to account for this biochemical quirk was postulated.

It proved to be a will-of-the-wisp. The antirachitic factor is now known to be calciferol, a hormone dependent on the invisible ultraviolet rays at one end of the sun spectrum. But since vitamins C and A, and sometimes B, were becoming household words, early talk of a sunshine vitamin furthered lay acceptance of a sunbath hygiene that soon became a runaway heliophilia. Sunshine specifically began to replace generalized "change of climate" as fashionable doctors sent to sunnier places not only those with upper respiratory ills but even those who had nothing identifiably wrong, just seemed to need better health. "Go soak up sunshine," they were told and, as the cult grew, were warned that to secure the optimum magical effect proportionately large areas of skin had to be exposed.

Actually the normal adult needs for health only a trace of sun-dependent biochemicals, particularly if he occasionally eats egg yolk and fish, which supply calciferol ready-made. Only the immature, growing organism— puppy or child—must have precautionary exposure to sun or, failing that, ingestion of cod-liver oil or irradiated milk. But fifty years ago enthusiastic doctors were hazy about that, and the beach-minded public welcomed a doctrine of massive exposure encouraging the already shrinking bathing suit to shrink farther. What might otherwise have been exhibitionism was now set down to doctor's orders. And among the gilt-edged idlers and bright young things whose bronzing bodies paved the beaches of the mid-1920's in Florida and California II what had once looked like bone laziness could now be called bone hygiene.

Even the terminology was attractive. "Ultraviolet" sounded like a blend of Shaw and Maxfield Parrish. Veblen might have invented the consequent tangle of cosmetic, economic, chronologic and pseudo-mystical confusions. Since, other things being equal, the sunshine seekers of Palm Beach or

Cannes were well off, a tanned face in winter, which had once meant farmer or seaman, now implied elegance and prestige. So in order to look as though just back from Florida, young bank tellers in Cleveland sought cheap tans by lying blindfold under ultraviolet "sun lamps." So did their women—in whose case the new value set on tanning was revolutionary. Previously picture hat, parasol, beach umbrella and the farmwife's sunbonnet had kept the female complexion as near as possible to ideal peaches-and-cream. A girl with a skim of tan on her cheekbones got told she looked like a veritable gypsy, my dear. Elizabeth Arden *et al.* heavily advertised special creams for post-summer use to erase "brown, coarsened skin . . . incongruously mannish . . . and obliterate the lines caused by exposure to sun and wind." Very soon, however, delicately reared young things would glory in turning into nut-brown maidens, and by no means only in the face. Yearly the trunks of bathing suits climbed higher, backs shrank down to the waist, stockings vanished from the beach. There sat Iris March or Betty Co-ed, bare legs uncomfortably stuck out to brown deeply, evenly and quickly. Then, to toast back and backs of legs, she lay prone—sand in her ears, oven-hot, basted with a salad-dressingish mixture of coconut oil and vinegar alleged to let her tan without burning, though its odor was troublesomely unattractive.

Sunning eventually ruined the men's hat trade. The cosmetics trade, however, exploited Betty's disappointment in her basting mixture by brewing up for the credulous specialized oils and goops for surefire brown without burn. The same counter offered salves to use when such preparations failed. The skins of most Americans tan readily as the middle layer develops a darkening substance to guard the inmost layers from sun damage. In a sun-addicted culture those with such skins have an advantage over the large minority, usually fair- or red-haired, who repeatedly burn and peel or, in the unluckiest cases, never tan at all. Darwin's sexual selection gained a new criterion as the bronzed lifeguard and the saddle-colored bathing beauty became archetypes of summer beaches. They puzzled Hawaii's surviving Polynesians, who, though swarthier than most whites, can tan. In the old days Hawaiian nobility stayed in the shade to avoid the darkened skin associated with common folks whose menial chores kept them out in the sun. Hawaiians of 1925, seeing *haole* tourists broiling themselves at Waikiki, said, "These people are born white—why do they want to brown?" [151]

The quick answer "Because they want to look as if they belonged to the Everglades Club" would have been partial and already obsolescent. For by then sunning was a hygienic fad founded on the fallacy that if a little sun is good, an awful lot more is better. Many were carried away into romantically persuading themselves that sunlight has a special soul-expanding, body-invigorating virtue, contains a close-to-nature essence of ineffable and inscrutable life-force—or words to that effect. Stuart Chase, who had been sunbathing naked before the cult of ultraviolet arose, told readers of the *Nation* in 1929 that he and his fellow gymnosophs knew "with a profundity which mocks science, that it was good for our bodies and good for our souls . . . the after-effects are a sense of well being, of calmed nerves, of inner vitality." [152] Millions were exposed to the actinic rays of such doctrine when the *Reader's Digest* reprinted that piece. Actually it closely followed the patter of the pre-War German cult of *Nacktkultur* that founded dogmatic Nudism. It reached its rhetorical height for the American public when Paul de Kruif, the outstanding popularizer of medical history of the 1920's, postulating a special "death-fighting energy" in sunlight, put the capsheaf on fashionable gurglings about it by telling the *Ladies' Home Journal*'s millions of readers: "Old Doctor Sun is the best physician I know. . . . On the sand by Lake Michigan's shore from March to October [he] burns me brown and keeps me strong. He's all the doctor I need." [153]

A sunbathing dermatologist with whom I once discussed these matters admitted that the sunbather's subsequent sense of well-being might be got just as well by "lying down . . . before a warm fire . . . if few clothes were worn, a brisk shower taken, and one's friends thereupon congratulated one on looking so healthy." [151] So psychologists may be the right ones to evaluate sunbathing. Or botanists—for sunbathers' rhapsodies sound like what a green plant might say of the crucial role of sunlight in the photosynthesis on which all vegetable life is founded. Man, biologically parasitic on the vegetable kingdom like other animals, has a far less direct relation to the sun and small excuse for trying to act like a two-legged heliotrope. But for the back-to-nature type of mind the will to believe is firm, and by the mid-1920's sun happiness was so prevalent that makers of quartz sun lamps used back-to-nature as come-on: ". . . throw off the restraints of social conformity . . . satisfy that inborn craving for ultra-violet . . . discard the trappings of civilization to spend strenuous, health-brimmed days in the beneficent sunshine . . . the vital ultra-violet portion of the sunlight can be brought into the home by . . . the justly famous Alpine Sun Lamp . . . a robust tan throughout the year."

Europe's heliophilia has not slackened yet. America's began to only in the last decade, though for a generation the alarm had been sounded by doctors who treat the heavy damage that prolonged sunning does to those who tan readily, let alone those whose hides are less tough. For sun unquestionably ages human skin prematurely. Broken capillaries in the cheeks, the roughened "golfer's neck" effect on the most exposed areas— years of persistent sunning can make an otherwise attractive woman in her forties look like her farmer grandfather. Such public warnings from doctors should have sent women wailing back to sunshades. But the presumptions that tan is "a status symbol," [154] as the New York *Daily News* still had it in 1972, and that sunshine is intrinsically healthy persist. And Woman, barring a few professional beauties, models and actresses, still largely ignores warnings that the same sunshine that keeps half-naked children from rickets will do more than Father Time to age her own half-naked self, especially in the face. Pressures from the tanning goop, resort and cruise industries and the new youth cult of "the natural," which equates sunlight with organically grown prunes, probably have dermatology beaten. Conscientiously sunburned faces will continue gradually to come to resemble those prunes.

The new biochemistry got into the comic strips in 1929, when the *Thimble Theater* acquired Popeye the Sailor, who prepared for rough-and-tumble fights by downing a can of spinach. The consequent demand for spinach—truck farmers in Texas erected a monument to Popeye—showed how this branch of journalism had saturated American culture, outdoing even the movies. Few saw a picture show daily, whereas most of the nation read several comics seven days a week. Even before the War *Mutt and Jeff, Bringing Up Father* and so on were as universal as proverbs, as familiar as Uneeda Biscuits. Their impact expanded farther when, soon after the Armistice, a revolution, usually dated from the start of Frank King's *Gasoline Alley*, brought a new ball game without superseding the old one.

The typical pre-War strip employed self-contained episodes and a few stock characters with stereotyped traits that so amused the public that it kept looking day after day to see what happened to Andy Gump this time. *Blondie, Peanuts, B.C.* are examples of more recent origin. Dagwood's sleepiness, Blondie's extravagance, Mr. Dithers' tantrums belong with Jiggs' craving for corned beef and cabbage and Maggie's voice lessons. Another kind of continuing interest came of one-panel drawings cramming a situation into a single tableau ringing daily changes on a basic theme with or without continuing characters—Clare Briggs' *When a Feller Needs a Friend*, Dorgan's *Favorite Indoor Sports*. Jimmy Hatlo's *They'll Do It Every Time* still follows that method. There is also the one-column single panel with a single unvarying character whose comments on the follies of the time or on basic human nature seek to create a public loyally eager to see what Ching Chow or Aunt Em has to say today.

King of those in the 1920's was Abe Martin, oracle of Brown County, Indiana (the Hoosier Ozarks), creation of Frank McKinney "Kin" Hubbard of the Indianapolis *News*. Abe was no ingratiating rustic, instead a sort of hillbilly hobgoblin lounging against a background of grotesque farm animals and skewed, tumbledown shacks—and a one-gallus master of sardonic concision. Will Rogers, the nation's chosen homespun wisecracker when Hubbard died in 1930, said accurately and generously, "No man in our generation was within a mile of him." [155] Franklin P. Adams, New York City's most demanding newspaper columnist, called him "my favorite humorist because he puts a whole novel into a sentence . . . malicious, critical, scornful, bunk-hating and tolerant." [156]

FPA might have added "occasionally ferocious." " 'I think I know who shot my wife, but I'm afraid t' say anything fer fear he'll poison my cow,' said Iry Bently t'day." Or, after Hubbard had taken a world cruise that included the exposure of Parsee corpses to vultures in India—a tourist attraction resulting in the only Hubbardism that his paper refused to print: "Nothing annoys a vulture like biting into a glass eye." [157] Abe Martin's specific virtue was a bleak wonder at the disconcerting feel of life: "The blamedest sensation is havin' a door knob come off in your hand." [158] "Men git ole before they know it but women don't." "Nothin' a little man says ever sounds probable." "Some girls are born with big feet and others wear white shoes." [159] "It's no disgrace to be poor but it might as well be." [160] His supporting cast of butts and alter egos was never depicted but became subliminally familiar to the nation's newspaper public as Abe Martin reached wide syndication in 200-odd newspapers by the mid-1920's: Ike Lark, Ez Pash, the Hon. Ex-Editor Cale Fluhart, Tilford Moots and his wife Em, the Rev. Wiley Tanger, Squire Marsh Swallow, Miss Tawney Apple and the rather desperately up-to-date Miss Fawn Lippincutt, who "went t' th' city t'day t' match a goldfish." [161] (Hubbard's source of these eerie names, he said, was partly Bellefontaine, Ohio, his hometown, partly jury lists in Kentucky.) E. V. Lucas, who took home to England and published a compilation of Abe Martin's best, called him "the funniest man now living." [162]

The usual purpose of the newspaper comic artist in any style was to rouse a reaction ranging from a nostalgic smile to a savage belly laugh. "The funnies" * was, after all, the original term for what varied from the masterly fantasies of *Krazy Kat* through the homely pith of J. R. Williams' *Out Our Way* to the imbecilities of Sidney Smith's incredibly, disastrously successful *The Gumps.* In the 1920's this laugh-seeking flowered further and richly in H. T. Webster's *The Timid Soul* and Milt Gross' *Count Screwloose of Toulouse.* But as the decade moved on, fun was gradually overshadowed and in time almost overlain by what can only be described as a blight of low seriousness.

This coincided with an overlapping of episodes from day to day in long stories about stock characters rather like the cliff-hanger movie serials that drew customers back each Friday for the next two-reel installment. Grim earnest was not basic to this method. The *Wash Tubbs* strip using it after 1924 preferred to be chipperly amusing. Later Al Capp's Dogpatch wallowed in continued-story grotesqueries burlesquing the values of the

---

* Harold Gray's *Little Orphan Annie* was still saying "the funnies" in September, 1945, as she defended the comic strip industry against well-merited charges of lowdownness and crime-mindedness. Note that, as *Newsweek* pointed out (March 5, 1973), the process to be described in this section has reversed, with long-continued plots being dropped (*e.g.,* as in the disappearance of *Terry and the Pirates, Smilin' Jack,* etc.) and self-contained episodes on the upbeat, usually with humorous intent.

serious strips. But emotional involvement of the reader was the new key to success. The adopted baby, Skeezix, in *Gasoline Alley* was taken to the nation's heart as Snookums, the monster baby of the pre-War *The Newlyweds*, never was, nor wished to be. Whether in the whimsical everydayishness of the Wallet household or the snarly melodrama of Harold Gray's *Little Orphan Annie* or the good-vs.-evil gimmicks of Chester Gould's *Dick Tracy*, identification with or hero worship of the protagonists was the new fashion. The funnies had become the comics and ceased to be comic.

Millions now invested emotional capital in daily contact with the comics' transparently synthetic personalities, suffering, struggling or triumphing with them more intimately than if they had actually lived next door. This went on in spite of the crude, subrepresentational draftsmanship lasting over from *Old Doc Yak* and *Polly and Her Pals*. Dick Tracy's famous profile was no nearer human than that of the White Mountains' Great Stone Face, yet when Gould had him shot up by gangsters, thousands wrote get-well letters and a Brooklyn man seriously volunteered blood if transfusion were needed. Henry Ford discussed at staff meetings how Annie's kidnappers could be foiled, scolded an executive not well enough versed in her career and, when her faithful dog, Sandy, was missing, telegraphed to Captain J. M. Patterson of the Chicago *Tribune*, her godfather: DO ALL YOU CAN TO HELP ANNIE FIND SANDY.[163] The same frighteningly loose grasp of reality later caused housewives to send flowers and home remedies to the heroines of radio soap operas when they took sick on the air.

All those newspaper buyers addicted to daily doses of *Moon Mullins* or loyally following the ring career of sterling *Joe Palooka* were manna for circulation managers and gold mines for publishers. The strips admirably reinforced sports, gossip about society and movie publicity as ways to sell papers day in and day out regardless of news columns and editorial page. It was often said that a paper like the Chicago *Tribune* could abandon regular news and prosper by printing only its comics, excellent sports coverage and Wall Street prices. By the mid-1920's the New York *Times* and the Boston *Transcript* were about the only conspicuous standard dailies in the country running no comics. Most bought six, eight, a dozen from both the "funnies" and the dreary schools: *Abie the Agent*, rich in Jewish stereotypes; *Minute Movies*; *Fritzi Ritz* (ancestress of today's *Nancy*); *Barney Google*, celebrated in a Tin Pan Alley hit by Billy Rose; *Toots & Casper*; *Winnie Winkle*. . . . Some papers massed them on one clogged page; others scattered them through the pages to please advertisers. European and Latin-American papers began to buy *Bringing Up Father*,* translating the lettered dialogue,

---

* Treatises on the comics point out that Europe supplied some of the earliest efforts toward narrative-in-drawings-and-lettered-dialogue. So it did, yet clearly 99 percent of today's comic-strip tradition welled up in America, and Europeans employing it have usually borrowed American-developed methods. It may also mean something that though American

substantially supplementing the movies in propagating American attitudes abroad.

The wizards of circulation, Hearst and the chiefs of the Chicago *Tribune* group, took a large personal hand in fostering these impertinent but cogent circulation builders. Nor was it 100-proof crassness. The best thing I know about Hearst is that he insisted on King Features' continuing George Herriman's *Krazy Kat* even though it never sold widely. Probably the only common ground that Hearst and Woodrow Wilson had was their being *Krazy Kat* fans. Bolder admirers found in this strip esthetic virtues of a sort previously never expected out of Nazareth. An early portent was the *Krazy Kat* strips posted on the walls of E. E. Cummings' room at Harvard in 1914. The great *succès d'estime* came soon after the War when John Alden Carpenter, middle-aged Chicago millionaire and talented composer of modern bent, wrote and produced a Krazy Kat ballet. It failed but before doing so had stirred Gilbert Seldes, a Kat fan of long standing and high cultivation, to celebrate ballet and strip in *Vanity Fair* and then in his highly influential *The Seven Lively Arts*. Thenceforward Herriman and his daily creation were drenched in the same extravagant adulation lavished on Chaplin and burlesque.

Here out of the corny welter of the funny papers, presumed home of dim vulgarity, had sprung Art, fashionably ambiguous (to this day nobody is sure whether Krazy was male or female), loose-coupled, complexly addictive Art as spontaneous as Cro-Magnon cave drawing and as symbolically eloquent as William Blake. ". . . this wonderful compound of mysticism, whimsy and Charles-Lamb-like wistfulness," wrote Ernest Bennecke, a critic joining the chorus in the *Century*. He detected an affinity between the shorthand architecture of Coconino County,* the desert locale of most of the episodes, and Cubist and other radical schools of painting, thus: "In this uproarious, fantastic world, the birds, trees, houses, and heavenly bodies are endowed with a beauty and even a humanity that form a most illuminating commentary on the progress of modern decorative art." [164]

That overdrew an association that probably did not exist to begin with. But for once the enthusiasm underlying such palaver had solid justification. The cap fitted far better than it had on Chaplin. This jerkily but so immediately drawn world, laced with engaging verbiage, in which Krazy, Ignatz Mouse and Offisa Pupp played out their intertwined destinies was as idiosyncratic as Selma Lagerlöf's Värmland and so pellucidly noncerebral

---

strips girdle the world outside the Iron Curtain, few European strips have done well in America. The best probably is the recent *Andy Capp*, a single-episode strip with drawing, dialogue and continuity keen enough to prosper here in spite of the exotic British-local idiom.

* Had Frank Lloyd Wright's Taliesin West existed at the time, these far-fetching critics might have found a considerable affinity between it and the building style of Krazy's world. In some of the exteriors at Taliesin West the resemblance is so strong that one would not be surprised to see Ignatz Mouse peer around a corner with a brick ready to throw.

that once the customer had the hang of it, the primordial absurdity of something basic—the universe?—seemed to show through innocently, yet chewily and always most amusingly. The first visit might confuse as though one were encountering an alien musical tradition. But Krazy's way of talking—a gentle but heady mixture of Dixie, Baxter Street and rep-show ham—was immediately ingratiating and a bridge into other dimensions. After a few weeks the neophyte could step daily into Coconino County as if entrusting himself to an escalator sweeping him serenely through a cumulative experience of such charm and grain that it would be a shame to miss it even once. He felt no mere curiosity about what happened next. It always ended with Ignatz conking Krazy with a brick, the significance of which ritual elicited some of the vainest explanations ever printed. But the circumambient whole had highly valid connotations. That Herriman could do all that with ink, a drawing pen, a slab of bristol board and the twenty-six letters of the alphabet was surely a miracle. Another was his invulnerability to apotheosis. His response to public investiture as a neglected genius was to go right on drawing *Krazy Kat* as if nothing much had happened.

Since the lode of the comics might well yield more richness if eagerly explored, many minor flurries ensued. Segar's *Thimble Theater* had some of *Krazy Kat*'s traits: a bracingly lunatic internal consistency and a shifting cast of remarkable monsters to back up Popeye, his spinsterish Olive Oyl and baby Swee'pea. Into the language stalked the "goon"—a troll-like, looming horror whose name came to be applied to gangland's killers—and the "jeep," a cheerful little friend of man that lent its name to the indispensable four-wheel-drive quarter-ton truck of World War II. Esthetes neglecting *Thimble Theater*, however, quested farther to F. Opper's bowing and scraping Alphonse and Gaston, who could never reach determination of which entered the door first. This, Bennecke explained, symbolized "with a delicacy . . . peculiarly Gallic [Opper was born and reared in Madison, Ohio] . . . the havoc that the technique of civilization can wreak upon the proper living of life." [164] And for a while it looked as if criticism might find in R. L. "Rube" Goldberg another Herriman to clothe with purple. Only he proved both too wide and too narrow for the robes.

Like James Swinnerton, dean of funny paper artists, Dorgan and Bud Fisher, Goldberg learned the trade in San Francisco. (Most of the other pace-setting early ones came from the Midwest; this sweeping development had little Eastern about it.) In the 1940's he returned to editorial cartooning for the New York *Sun* and won a Pulitzer Prize. His special fame, however, came of thirty years of illustrated gags, puns, popular catchwords and current fads culminating in the many devices of Professor Lucifer Gorgonzola Butts—exhaustively cobbled up travesties of machine production of banal results from fantastic chains of cause and effect involving gadgets, processes and people arising from the ingenuity of Goldberg's fancy and, if you cared to be profound about it, the absurdity of mechanistic behaviorism. My generation of Americans called any device elaborated out of proportion to its purpose a "Rube Goldberg machine." Then he did a half-witted, good-natured antihero, Boob McNutt, blundering through strange vicissitudes also involving his lushly pretty wife, Pearl, and his twin gnome-henchmen, Mike and Ike. This managed to travesty sentimentally melodramatic strips without alienating readers who liked such things. When Boob was in danger of being "forced against his will into a bigamous marriage . . . [Goldberg] received letters every week imploring [him] for Pearl's sweet sake, not to let Boob commit bigamy." [165] Boob was so stupid and yet so widely followed that Paul V. McNutt, able and handsome Democratic politician of the 1930's, blamed him for ruining his chance of the Presidency; the public would have had too keen a subliminal sense that "a fellow named McNutt might . . . be a boob." [166]

Much of Goldberg's most talked-of work was embodied in what Seldes saw as the culmination of a refreshing "intense ugliness" in the comic strip tradition: ". . . alarming grotesques: the men . . . made of putty with floating whiskers and strange knobs on their foreheads . . . the women . . . inhumanly fat and ill favored; the children are little pests, the beautiful women a mockery . . . hideous lamps set in the middle flight of a balustrade, the tortured figures on which whole edifices rest, the furniture that lacks equilibrium. . . ." [167] Bennecke thought, or anyway wrote, that Goldberg's *oeuvre* was "unconsciously perhaps . . . saturated with the disillusioned spirit of Schopenhauer. . . . 'Boob McNutt' might . . . be . . . a perfect illustration of 'Die Welt als Will und Vorstellung' " and compared Goldberg with Thomas Hardy for what would now be called existentialist irony. Fortunately for clarity of thought the term did not yet exist.

A good try, but it was no use trying to make him sound like Hieronymus Bosch crossed with Nietzsche. The combustible ingredients were not there in the right proportions. Goldberg's grotesques had more ingenuity than style. His attitudes were, though often bitterly shrewd, clumpy. He slugged flat-footed. None of that bothered the vast public on which he counted. He had the well-earned good fortune to become a national institution of the same order as Babe Ruth and Will Rogers, triumphantly the old-pro graphic journalist completely at home at the drawing board and with the public, a phenomenon with its own validity and too lumpy-bulky for deep thoughts to apply.

With Herriman he shared mastery of one of the guild's skills too little appreciated—getting the very most out of each hand-lettered word of what the characters say in the dialogue balloons. Each compact bit must mesh with and advance the action while also conveying needed information and setting off what passes for characterization in strips. Such dialogue can keep a strip successful in spite of the prevalently dismal draftsmanship. The worst was probably that of *Smilin' Jack*, about dashing plane pilots, that took on well in the early 1930's. One should file exceptions for the work of Herriman, Milt Gross and Crockett Johnson. But consider the younger women in *Little Orphan Annie*, a roaring success, who all looked alike with pudgy, Japanesy faces, also curiously like Punjab, the turbaned giant of muscle and magic who guarded Annie and her Daddy Warbucks. Had Daddy not occasionally donned a hat he would have had only one expression; Sandy, the dog, was put together as if sired by a puma; everybody had round holes for eyes; yet the story, concentrated in the big Sunday page, and the weekday interactions flowed so commandingly that none of that mattered. Since graphic quality means so little, this American-developed medium of entertainment might be classed as primarily writing self-illustrated.

Technical merit in word handling implies no corresponding cultural merit in *Annie*. Even aside from Daddy Warbucks' reactionaryism, the strip's content had a perversely archaic streak. Well into the 1930's here were the old village-skinflint-holds-the-widow's-mortgage plot, the almost as old orphan-made-to-drudge-by-unscrupulous-guardian plot, the villainous-doctor-with-private-sanitarium plot. Punjab was a relic from vaudeville magic vintage of 1890. His habit of disposing of troublesome thugs by throwing a cloth over them and making them vanish was almost as sharp practice in plot juggling as the magic drug with which he brought Daddy back to life after he had died as wordily and even more self-righteously than King Arthur. No movie had dared such capers for a decade. A misanthrope denouncing the human race as hopelessly dim-witted would need no more evidence than the fact that this strip and *The Gumps* were among the most successful. Since Edmund Burke, however, ruled it impossible to indict a whole people, call the grand jury's attention to an individual—Captain Joseph Medill Patterson, a hereditary prince of the Chicago *Tribune* dynasty, who abetted Gray in bringing Annie into being and, it is said, took a large hand in plotting her monotonously cyclical adventures: Daddy goes away on mysterious big-shot mission, Annie gets into trouble, Daddy comes back and gets Annie out of trouble, Daddy goes away. . . . In any case it was undeniably Patterson who, as impresario of the *Tribune*'s troupe of strips, did more than any other to make "comics" a ghastly misnomer.

Since he also founded the first and most successful American post-War tabloid newspaper, Patterson affected his native land's journalism more deeply than anybody since Joseph Pulitzer. Here was one of those rare cases in which inherited power falls on heirs able to exploit it better than any of its paid henchmen. This grandson of the redoubtable founder of the Chicago *Tribune*, basis of a sizable newspaper fortune, was also grandson of Cyrus H. McCormick, inventor and manufacturer of the world's best wheat harvester, basis of a large farm-equipment fortune. His high-chinned cousin

Robert R. McCormick, though hating Britain and keeping the isolationist-reactionary faith, was Anglophile in speech, dress and horsey habits. Joe, however, at first seemed ill fitted for his lavish share of inherited assets. He came shambly and rumpled out of Groton and Yale in 1901 to work for the *Tribune* in such a frame of mind that presently he proclaimed himself a Socialist and announced that in seven years he would have amassed irresistible economic power and would throw it all into support of the IWW. Meanwhile, he wrote, among other things, *A Little Brother of the Rich*, one of the worst novels of the decade, about unattractive people enjoying large incomes. It sold well.

A second stretch on the *Tribune* calmed him and interested him more closely in the family enterprise. Just before the War he and Cousin Bertie effected a palace revolution that gave them complete charge of the Midwest's most prominent and, in many technical ways, best newspaper. Bertie, a brilliant administrator, ran the *Tribune* as well as Charles M. Schwab ran Bethlehem Steel. Joe was a genius at circulation gags, such as paying readers $1 each for "Bright Sayings of the Children" and "My Most Embarrassing Moment" and exploiting the immense new interest in movies with printed versions of popular movie serials and daily lists of what movie house was showing what where. And, as aforesaid, nobody knew better the virtue of comic strips as circulation builders.

Disparate as the cousins' temperaments were, they came out much the same on foreign affairs: Leery of Britain, respectful of Germany after, as correspondents, they had seen the Kaiser's army in 1914–15, but tough toward Mexico. In the border troubles of 1916 both went soldiering in the National Guard. Bertie, so military-minded that he gave his wife a funeral with full military honors, was a major in the cavalry. Joe, residually common-manly, was a private in the artillery and refused proffered commissions. When the United States finally floundered into the War, they went soldiering again. Bertie saw shooting at Cantigny and came out a colonel on Pershing's staff. After the War he named his inherited estate west of Chicago Cantigny and set up a small museum there celebrating the prowess of his old outfit as the first white American troops to come solidly up against the Germans. Joe, in as a private, coming out a captain, saw far more shooting and was gassed and wounded. He retained the "captain" the rest of his life, most unusual in America for a nonprofessional below field rank. But the most fertile part of his overseas experience was a leave in London during which he met Alfred Harmsworth, Viscount Northcliffe, British newspaper magnate and creator, in the London *Daily Mirror*, of the "tabloid" * (= half size) format for mass circulation.

---

* "Tabloid" is a Britishism originating with a great British drug firm, Burroughs, Wellcome & Company, as identifying name for its products, particularly compressed pills; in the public mind it gradually became associated with "a compressed form or dose of anything," as a learned judge said in a decision on its legal use (*Oxford English Dictionary*).

Ordered Stateside to set up a new training program for draftees, Bertie learned that Joe's battery was posted near his farmhouse quarters and had him over for a family council. The house was noisy with passing trucks, so the cousins climbed out the back window onto the farmer's manure pile to drink scotch and discuss mutual affairs. Joe's contribution was that Northcliffe had told him a tabloid paper in America would probably prosper—advice that few publishers would lightly disregard—and that New York City would be a good place to try it. Apparently it was partly the notion of a paper specially for the masses that attracted him. Bertie's rising interest came partly, it is said, of hope that the losses from creating a new paper in so rugged a market as New York City would reduce the *Tribune*'s federal taxes. Maybe one or both knew that Hearst, well aware of the pre-War success of Northcliffe's *Daily Mirror*, was even then putting a skeleton editorial and printing staff through dry runs for a New York City tabloid. Anyway, once the Armistice put him back in civilian clothes, Patterson rushed ahead with such zeal that the first issue of his New York *Daily News* was on the streets in June, 1919. After a few faltering months its circulation began to snowball and eventually outstripped every other American newspaper, daily or Sunday. McCormick kept up the *Tribune*'s corporate interest, and the consequent Tribune-Daily News Syndicate did so well with the new comics that it could pay Sidney Smith $120,000 a year for *The Gumps* even in the depth of the Depression. Within five years, however, an amicable fission had each cousin completely in charge of his own paper, following the weird of his own temperament. The high technical competence remained common to both papers.

The reputed point of the tabloid size was ease of handling in crowded streetcar, subway or bus. That virtue had not kept alive the Scripps' tabloid Chicago *Day Book* of fifteen years earlier. Staid observers of the new venture, which played up gilt-edged divorces, Hollywood scandals and underworld killings, reproached it with fattening on sensationalism. Actually it was only following where Hearst's standard-size papers had long led. As Hearst's New York *Daily Mirror*, launched once Patterson had broken trail, and Bernarr Macfadden's New York *Evening Graphic* came into competition, the *Daily News* proved slightly less lurid than these straining rivals. True, the basic smells were the same; only, as John Tebbel says, the *Graphic*'s capers showed that "There is a point beyond which tabloidism becomes paranoia." [168] The trade called it the *Pornographic*.

Obviously the format has nothing necessarily in common with pruriency, else the present New York *Post*, Chicago *Sun-Times* and Long Island *Newsday* would not share it with the *Daily News*. Then what was "tabloidism"? The answer is in Patterson's first name for his brainchild—the New York *Illustrated Daily News*. Today its subtitle is still "New York's Picture Newspaper" and between *Daily* and *News* appears an old-style boxy news camera of the 1920's. Tabloidism was picturism, working news photographs to the limit for sex, horror, scandal, pathos, fun. Patterson was leading a long-pending journalistic revolution based on the halftone and the flashgun, applying through photographs to the newspaper as a whole what comic strips had taught him—that for those with substandard minds or reading skills pictures come first and then lead attention to the associated text. He supplied a crisp editorial page, pungently succinct news stories, gossip columns as they came in style. But his detractors probably erred in attributing his choice of news content to a taste for the sexy, gamey or noisome. It was just that the gorgeous divorcée perched on a ship's rail, knees crossed high, or modeling the nightgown in which she was caught in a love nest utilized the photographic medium better than any conceivable shots of a most newsworthy international conference. That is more readily understood today as the skewed demands of television, also a visual medium, dictate selection of one topic and neglect of another.

Hence the strongest reason why *Daily News* photographers, with reporters as second wave, so played up the several sordid trials of the 1920's. Covered just as zealously for the same reason were the far less lurid visit of the Prince of Wales and the Lindbergh flight. The *Daily News* and its rivals never lacked shots of Easter bunnies, strayed children eating ice-cream cones in police stations and aged mothers hugging long-lost sons. Yet what Patterson's paper is most—and deservedly—remembered for is covering its front page with that ghoulish, blurrily enlarged shot of Ruth Snyder, murderess, in the electric chair. The *Graphic* eventually dropped out of the grueling pace that Patterson and Hearst set but meanwhile gained immortality with its front-page "composographs" of the Peaches Browning divorce story—her and her eccentric elderly husband's heads stuck on models posed in the bizarre situations described in court; I particularly remember one in which Daddy Browning's pet goose was shown joining the connubial conversation with a comment in a comic-strip balloon: "Honk, honk, it's the bonk!"

The British genes in the tabloid newspaper kept it from being the second major jewel that Patterson created for the crown of American journalism. In the 1920's native innovations in that field were magazines—and highly important. Did the *Reader's Digest, Time* or the *New Yorker* most affect the next fifty years? The order of their births (1922, 1923, 1925) coincides with the relative sizes of their eventual circulations. All three, like the *Daily News*, showed that in that decade the arbitrary chieftain with the right subliminal impulses was still the key to editorial success. But none of the inventors of these better, or anyway unprecedented, mousetraps began with Patterson's wide experience and personal command of resources. And the slenderest shoestring was the one that eventually ensnared the most readers. De Witt Wallace's *Reader's Digest* showed that though America's tradition of mousetrap designing was waning, it could still twitch to great purpose.

The geometric progression of the rise of "The Little Wonder"—as John Bainbridge's sardonic piece in the *New Yorker* called it—made that of the Ford Motor Company look jerky and banker-ridden.

Son of a Presbyterian parson-college president in Minnesota, footloose alumnus of the University of California, Wallace had pre-War spadework in minor publishing, then got into the overseas shooting with substantial damage to his tall, spare person. In the hospital he tinkered with a scheme that had long been on his mind—a publication condensing for busy readers noteworthy stuff from each month's crop of magazines. Experiments in cutting and compressing satisfied him that it could be done without damaging the gist of the articles selected. When the brief hard times in 1920-21 lost him his public relations job, he took a dummy of his idea to publishers. None wanted it, maybe because it seemed close to the *Literary Digest*, a weekly then immensely successful as a rambling summary of recent events interspersing quotations from newspapers and magazines with connective comment and a selection of editorial cartoons. The only person sharing Wallace's faith was Lila Bell Acheson, his fiancée, also child of a Presbyterian parson (this one Canadian), who worked with him. But he did persuade his father to lend him $1,000, and a brother to add $500. Throwing in the $300 that was his all, he mailed out some thousands of mail-order subscription solicitations. The response was lively enough to launch the first issue of the *Reader's Digest*—thirty-one boiled-down "Articles of Lasting Interest."

"We paid our bills from the first," Wallace recalls, "and without benefit of newsstand sales or advertising. Lila kept her [social service] job the first year and paid the rent on our apartment" [169]—in a Greenwich Village basement, but no project was ever less Villagey. The Wallaces floated on the genially wholesome, the civic-constructive, the inspiring individual of grass-roots goodwill, the commonsense application of religion, science or hygiene to neglected situations. The motto might have been: "Go thou and do likewise." A *Digest* editor proffering clues to what not to suggest as article subjects said, "We don't scoff." Yet the pocket-size newcomer was not relentlessly solemn. A humorous magazine piece or newspaper column that struck Wallace as funny got picked up. Departmentalized jokes and anecdotes filling in short pages were often good, sometimes what then seemed even a bit risqué. As already noted, Chase's panegyric of sun-kissed nakedness was reprinted in 1929. Otherwise the thing could have been issued without comment by the community affairs worker of a large, WASP-dominated church on the right side of the tracks in a big city. Norman Rockwell might have been the staff artist—only for two decades the *Digest*, as the trade called it, carried practically no artwork. For its first thirty-three years it also eschewed advertising and yet made money hand over fist—which awed and shocked the trade. Further defying the rules, Wallace kept it off newsstands, confining circulation for the first seven years to paid-up subscribers. What made him reverse this in 1929 was the proliferation on newsstands of the most flattering tokens of success—blatant imitations calling themselves something like *Everybody's Digest, Browser's Digest. . . .*

None could make a contest of it. In the first year after newsstands stocked it, they averaged sales of 100,000 a month while subscriptions too were multiplying like yeast cells. The handiness of the pocket-size format was probably one reason. Add the striking variety of the contents listed on the front cover tempting the scanning eye to pick up an irresistible title: "The Strange Life of the Salmon," "How to Keep Young Mentally," "Charley Ross, the Unforgotten Lost Boy." Add the customer's belief that his quarter gave him the cream of the magazines without the trouble and expense of seeing them all. Add the hope of painless self-education that the *Digest* began to appeal to long before it made direct plays for the school market—an appeal cognate to Haldeman-Julius' only with another sociopolitical content. Whereas the Little Blue Books were cracker-barrel or bull-session radical, from the start the *Digest* was Rotary-conservative, frequently reprinting pieces deploring collectivist ideas and trends, seldom much of countertendency.

The mounting readership built by these appeals made the publishers of some of the source magazines restless. Wallace then dipped into profits to pay each magazine a negotiated sum yearly for blanket permission to reprint, plus $50 to the author of each article chosen—a gratifying surprise and, particularly after this honorarium rose to $100, sometimes more than he had got in the first place from some struggling or specialized publication. For the largest magazines such payments were drops in the bucket; but few even fairly stable middle-circulation ones sneezed at them, and just about the whole trade came to accept such reprinting as a tolerable new custom.

In the early 1930's an obscure, though not exactly secret, policy tied marginal magazines more closely to the *Digest* as the Wallaces began to commission, sometimes from their own editors, sometimes from free-lancers, original articles on topics that, in their view, were neglected or inadequately handled. Insanity, cremation were early choices. Sometimes the consequent texts were farmed out free of charge to minor magazines and then reprinted in the *Digest*. This gave the editor of the client magazine a welcome addition, sometimes by a well-known name, to his table of contents and to the *Digest* an item for the front cover precisely tailored to the Wallaces' notion of their public's interests. In 1935 one of these self-originated pieces set off a rocket blast that boosted the already gloriously profitable enterprise into superstratospheric orbit as well as caused public relations earthquakes in Detroit. Wallace noticed outside a wayside garage a brutally battered automobile wreck, said to the garageman that it was a sickening sight, and was told, "You should have seen it before they got the bodies out." After further chat about nasty motor accidents Wallace thought it over and assigned a free lance to write as highway safety propaganda the most vividly gruesome possible article on the raw-head-and-bloody-bones aspect of such smashups. The article, midwifed by the *Digest*'s Charles W. Ferguson, blew up in journalism's face, becoming almost overnight what Bainbridge reckoned to be "the most widely read magazine article ever published." *[170]

Newspapers ran it on the front page. Reversing the usual procedure, *Esquire*—itself a clinically interesting new magazine—reprinted it among the pneumatically sexy artwork. Highway police departments, insurance companies, service clubs flooded the country with reprints. Traffic court judges sentenced speeders to copy it ten times or pay heavy fines. *Time* magazine's synthetic newsreel, *The March of Time*, gave it ten minutes. It had appeared just when public dismay about the rising highway mortality rate was nearing dire need of expression. Had the Wallaces not already shown such masterly awareness of what their immense, diffuse public wanted, this might have been set down to luck. As it was, one could refer only to back-of-the-neck editorial judgment, the sole reliable kind. After all, once Babe Ruth knocked so many out of the park, nobody called it luck when he sent another two country miles instead of just one. Think too of the professional courage needed to lay before an essentially Nice Nelly audience the oozy, screaming facts of the matter. In the middle of the babble about "—And Sudden Death!" Richard M. Berlin, chief of Hearst's magazine empire, said to one of his editors, "Why didn't you do something like that?" The editor replied, "If I'd bought a piece like that, you wouldn't have let me print it." "He was right too," Berlin told me. "I wouldn't have had the nerve."

The second innovator of the 1920's who made magazines count more than newspapers in the 1930's—a crucial change for both public and Fourth Estate—was Henry R. Luce, also a veteran of the War and a parson's son, born in China to missionary parents. (The progeny of American missionaries in China bulk curiously large—Pearl Buck, John Hersey, John R. Service. . . .) Equally instrumental in founding *Time* was Luce's fellow big man on campus at Yale, Briton Hadden, who died just as the scheme got airborne. Both had brief but obviously fruitful experience on major newspapers. Inner resemblances between *Time* and the *Digest* were so many that one might suspect relationship—only both projects were pre-War dreams of young men unaware of each other's existence. Both played up

* This can't be established by cold figures. It is definitely known that through 1972 the *Digest* itself sold (at cost) almost 7,000,000 reprints. But nobody kept track of how many further reprintings came of permissions granted to any reputable seekers—traffic authorities, insurance companies, school systems—requesting the privilege. The scale of distribution can hardly be exaggerated, however. An archaeologist told me that in a post office in a part of Anatolia too remote ever to have seen a wheeled vehicle, he found on the bulletin board "—And Sudden Death!" translated into Turkish.

compactness and the implicit claim of supplanting a confusing plethora of regular publications. Both superficially resembled the *Literary Digest* as summarizer of a wide range of sources. The early *Time*, like the early *Digest*, relied chiefly on cannibalizing other periodicals; only in this case the raw material was large daily newspapers, and *Time* carried things a step farther, leaving few overt vestiges of the texts going into the compost. Its format, 8″ x 11″ and folded and stapled, was magazinelike, but it was actually a weekly national newspaper all rewrite desk and no reporters. It took some ten years for it to turn to the apparatus of local part-time correspondents, usually moonlighting newspaper reporters, that eventually became its present elaborate domestic and foreign range of news-gathering offices.

Originally its small staff worked solely from clipping outstanding American and some European dailies for comprehensive accounts and pungent details. Toward the weekly deadline they boiled down and sugared off the clips accumulated on, say, a national coal strike into a concise rundown written as if by an omniscient reporter who had simultaneously been on the picket line and attended a meeting of President Coolidge's cabinet and another of John L. Lewis' high command of the United Mine Workers. Through hindsight and cross-checking among sources the result was often more compact, coherent, comprehensive and readable—though not necessarily as accurate—as anything a given daily had carried. As *Time* prospered and the editorial payroll grew, several-stage collaboration took over. A did a draft, B revised it, C took it apart for D to reorganize and finally E, boss of them all, produced the final draft. This journalism-by-attrition, impossible on a daily, worked better than there was reason to expect. The only fragmentary precedents for it had been in the concoction of politicians' speeches, movie scripts and advertising copy. It was, one sees from the perspective of the 1970's, Luce and Hadden's unique contribution to their craft.

Eventually it became journalism-by-committee based on elementary reports and data accumulated by eager she-beavers called researchers recruited from among recent alumnae of prestige-heavy women's colleges. The upper staff members processing these raw materials had to reconcile themselves to seeing their writing "turned into sausage meat . . . and then stuffed into the magazine," [171] as Winthrop Sargeant, an alumnus of *Time*, described it. That took a while to develop, whereas very soon the sharpening crotchets of *Time*'s writing style, with which Hadden is usually particularly credited, were rousing comment. Its obsession with crispness led to rhetorical virtues. Senator La Follette was "a fighter. He was pure. He was uncompromising. He was a lonely leader. He was loyal to ideals rather than to party . . . too fierce a warrior to be a great general. . . ." [172] But it quickly betrayed itself into the euphuistically baroque: ". . . the aesthetic, erratic, eremitic Gabriele d'Annunzio";[173] Mickey Walker "slashed and bashed, uppercutted, jabberwocked and jamboreed . . .";[174]

Red Grange, an "Eel-hipped runagade . . . writhed through seas of grasping moleskin-flints with a twiddle of his buttocks and a flirt of his shin-bone. . . ." [175] Strange inversions added to the grotesquery of thus using gaudy words with too little heed to their actual meaning. As verbal showmanship, however, it not only stimulated circulation but also had a wide, if shallow, influence on journalism. With it came a flippancy that, though maybe good for the stuffed shirts whom it caused to bristle, became a bad habit as *Time* grew into a national institution sounding, as W. A. Swanberg justly said, as though written "by one impudent man." [176] *Time* often swung as wildly as Hearst's editorial pages, if not always at the same punching bags. And some of the wild swings came of failing to resist the temptation to cut a verbal or diagnostic caper regardless of whether its content matched the full range of pertinent facts.

Time was two years old, its style forming well, when the *New Yorker* weighed in—a slower starter and more derivative than its newcomer predecessors. Harold W. Ross, its monarchic father genie, was no such tyro as Wallace and Luce. He had been a precocious, footloose newspaper reporter in his native West; a ranking editor (while a private) of the AEF's soldiers' newspaper, *Stars & Stripes*; after the War an editor for the Butterick Company, publisher of dress patterns, and a prosperous women's magazine, the *Delineator*; then editor of the American Legion's magazine; then of *Judge*, second to the old *Life* among America's humorous weeklies. Maybe these dizzying swings supplied the critical molecular storms that brought him his heart's desire in 1925—command of his own ship, an urbane weekly for Gothamites and other Americans sharing the attitudes that Ross found most winningly characteristic of the Big Town. Financing came from Raoul Fleischmann, whose money came from the company supplying most of the nation's yeast—a commodity it was then advertising extravagantly and successfully as a home remedy indispensable to enteric peace of mind and consequent health of spirit.

For some time Ross had frequented the famous Round Table luncheons at the Algonquin Hotel, New York City's Mermaid Tavern-backscratching parlor. Thence he recruited the group who signed his prospectus as adviser-sponsors of the *New Yorker*, names to conjure with then, some still weighty: Laurence Stallings, Dorothy Parker, Edna Ferber, Heywood Broun, George S. Kaufman, Marc Connelly, Alexander Woollcott, Alice Duer Miller, Rea Irvin, Ralph Barton. Of those among them contributing early to the new venture, most were frequent or occasional performers for *Vanity Fair* and *Life*. If the *Digest* was parasitic on magazines and *Time* on newspapers, the young *New Yorker* was parasitic on already-established styles and talents. Not until the mid-1930's did it blend fresh young talents into a unique style.

Meanwhile, it understandably read like an uneasy marriage of *Life* and

Vanity Fair. Eventually it was credited with smothering the wordy He/She dialogue captions then usual on humorous cartoons, but in the first years most of its captions were of the older type. Its theater reviews were diffuse, nothing like what Benchley would do when he came over from *Life*. Its book reviews lacked sparkle until Dorothy Parker took over as Constant Reader. The "Talk of the Town" and the strangely brief "Profiles" were almost unbearably sprightly; as James Thurber wrote long afterward, they specialized on "a frivolous and curiously small-town kind of joke . . . and a self-conscious, intra-mural urbanity." [177] His and E. B. White's initials soon appeared, but their early wing trials lacked their brilliance-to-come. The signatures Helen Hokinson, Alice Harvey, [Barbara] Shermund graced rather limp cartoon ideas. Peter Arno's were worse still; the persistence of his Whoops Sisters was a sore burden to the teething magazine. But within a couple of touch-and-go years the advertising and circulation were glowing with health, well in advance of the editorial content. In the absence of other possibilities one must assume that what Ross frequently spoke of as "snob appeal" [178] was what had young Fleischmann's investment turning into a minor Little Wonder.

Ross was, as is frequently pointed out, a curious chief for either the giggly-sniffy early *New Yorker* or the stylized haven of independent wit and sensitivity that his heavy hands shaped it into.* *Vanity Fair*'s Frank Crowninshield, suave-spoken, absurdly well groomed, looked like his ideal subscriber's uncle. Ross was spiky-haired, ungainly, brusque, still much the rough-and-tumble newspaperman. Yet here he was filling his pages with elaborate palterings about polo, tennis—then still a gentleman's game— squash rackets, horse shows, yachts, regular "letters" from Paris and London that he insisted should recount doings that neither he nor most of his readers had ever heard of, and so committed to the upper reaches of the Ivy League that a Martian reader would have thought Yale, Columbia and Princeton were the only institutions of higher learning between East Rock and Nassau Street. Some of that was presaged in Ross' † famous manifesto

---

* The more reminiscences of Ross pile up, the less outsiders can make of the question whether the rough diamond was set in a heart of gold. The way he ran his editorial staff, all agree, was a mixture of utter professional competence in textual matters with a disregard of common fairness that, had the magazine been HMS *Bounty*, would have sent him walking the plank instead of being sent off in a boat. To me he sounds like that other utterly competent curmudgeon genius, Henry Ford. Anyway there is no denying the genius. Here from the *Encyclopaedia Britannica* is E. B. White's judgment: ". . . a revolutionary figure in American journalism . . . quickly toppled many conventional literary forms . . . satire and parody flourished, reporting became lighthearted and searching . . . The short story enjoyed a reprieve from the heavy burden of plot, and social cartooning became less diagrammatic and more vigorous. . . ." All deserved but needs qualifying—it holds good of the *New Yorker* after 1930, say, but cannot be applied to the extensive seriousness pervading it after World War II.

† Thurber (*The Years with Ross*, 25, 84): "I don't know who wrote the prospectus, but [it] bears neither the stamp of Ross' hand, nor, read aloud, the sound of Ross' voice," yet he also says elsewhere that the terms of at least one paragraph smell "remarkably of Ross' old fashioned vocabulary." Kramer (*Ross of the New Yorker*, 61) who seems to have checked with

of editorial intent: ". . . a reflection in words and pictures of metropolitan life . . . gaiety, wit and satire, but . . . not what is commonly called sophisticated . . . [The *New Yorker*] will hate bunk . . . is not edited for the old lady in Dubuque . . . expects a considerable national circulation, but this will come from people who have a metropolitan interest."

Just so; as its advertisers grew happily aware, it soon lay between *Harper's Bazaar* and *Elmer Gantry* on every backed-up-to-the-davenport table in Grosse Pointe. Within ten years of birth it had shed its water wings and become a force in American life and an influence in world literature. But it never completely lost the unbecoming savor of that sneer at the old lady in Dubuque that so pleased its first admirers. The trouble was that, Ross included, the majority of those who made it what it was at its best—the majority of those signing its birth certificate, plus Miss Hokinson, Miss Harvey, Thurber, Miss Shermund, Morris Markey, Garrett Price, Janet Flanner—came from the old lady's country west of the Alleghenies.

The 1920's seemed bent on revising America's reading habits, a project of particular consequence before broadcasting outstripped the printed word in cultural leverage. That *Elmer Gantry* on the davenport table probably came from the Book-of-the-Month Club of which it was the twelfth (March, 1927) selection. That same month the Literary Guild, continuing chief rival of the BOMC, mailed out its first selection, the Broun-Leech biography of Comstock. In one aspect book clubs made a third with the Modern Library and Little Blue Books in richening the content of what America read. It was just as important, however, that besides raising the average quality of material absorbed, they vastly increased the number of Americans who bought—and often read—books of timely validity.

Harry Scherman, guiding spirit of the BOMC, was not only the greatest book salesman of all time, as publishers describe him, but also a shrewd economist. He saw book clubs as part of an ongoing revolution in distribution, cognate to self-service and supermarkets. Like Sears, Roebuck and Montgomery Ward (selling popular reprints mail order, along with kerosene lanterns and corsets) and Haldeman-Julius, he understood the unique usefulness of the nation's post offices as retail outlets serving customers most of whom would otherwise find book buying discouragingly difficult. In the BOMC's first forty years every post office in the *U.S. Postal Guide*, no matter how small or how remote, most of them a long way from a bookstore, had handled at least one of the 200,000,000 volumes that the club had sold. Culturally, of course, the bookclubs' emphasis on timeliness made them rivals of *Time* and the *Digest* in offering to help the individual keep up with what should interest him. The BOMC's first advertisement

---

several connected with the magazine before Thurber was, thinks it did indeed come "from Ross' typewriter."

said: "You can now subscribe to the best new books—just as you do to a magazine. . . ." The Literary Guild, half tongue-in-cheek but wholly persuasive, early told readers of the *New Yorker*: "Picture . . . *you* . . . lazily unwrapping a new package. And then you drink in culture and joy and everything. . . . Later you ring for your butler and tell him to lay the Right Book where all the guests will see. . . ."

No such development is ever rootless. Hearst's *International Magazine* had used the "book of the month" label for the featured book review in each issue. Certain German publishers had been offering discount below regular retail price to customers agreeing to buy a certain number of preselected books each year. The taproot of this new American version, however, was Scherman's shrewd faith in mail-order bookselling. Already an acknowledged expert in that field, first with the great J. Walter Thompson advertising agency, then in association with the Bonis selling some 40,000,000 of the Little Leather Library reprints, he was keenly aware of the hordes of potential buyers out there, vaguely book-hungry but seldom in contact with the conventional sequence of publisher-to-book jobber-to-retail bookseller. On that foundation he built a secondary publishing medium as original as the diesel engine and as salutary as a good bedside manner.

"A unique service," his prospectus-advertisement said, ". . . will deliver to you every month, without effort or trouble on your part, the best book of the   month . . . at . . . the   publisher's   retail   price . . . no   extra charges. . . ." Which was that month's best book? The choice had been made from advance copies by a distinguished committee of five: two well-known men of letters, Henry Seidel Canby and Christopher Morley; a sturdily popular novelist, Dorothy Canfield; a nationally famous editor and elder statesman, William Allen White; a renowned liberal columnist for the New York *World*, Heywood Broun. Obviously the judgment of such a panel would be skilled, well informed and as free of undue influence as the advertisements promised. If the member disliked the choice, however, he had only to return it and receive another book from a list of secondary recommendations.

Arrangements with publishers handled by Scherman and Robert K. Haas, another able principal in the BOMC's early phase, took some working out, of course. At the very first the scheme made publishers uneasy and booksellers more so. The terms eventually arrived at did give the publisher of the chosen item much less profit per copy than he would have got from a copy of a fast-moving novel sold by a bookstore, and even that was shared with the author, who was also taking a sharply reduced royalty. But that smaller return multiplied by the BOMC's thousands of members usually looked very good in an industry in which not one book in ten moves anything like fast. And as bookstores began to learn, it was excellent promotion for an item to be chosen Book-of-the-Month. Gradually the trade developed the impression that the BOMC gave publisher and author, and to some extent bookseller, the best of both worlds. Publishers began falling over themselves to get advance proofs into the BOMC's hands at the rate of some 2,500 items a year. By the mid-1930's some booksellers were actually acting as agents for book club memberships.

Time, trial and error modified the above basic structures. Heavy influence was soon exerted by the Literary Guild's different setup. Its period of gestation had been much the same, but Samuel W. Craig, its founder, did not get his financing together in time to win the race to the delivery room. His committee was equally august: a widely loved critic-professor, Carl Van Doren; a liberal university president-publicist, Glenn Frank; two highly regarded women writers, Zona Gale and Elinor Wylie; an immensely popular writer of synoptic histories, Hendrik Willem van Loon; a liberal journalist-critic, Joseph Wood Krutch.* And the Guild had a bargain appeal that the BOMC lacked, setting sail under the advertising headline THE STORY OF A GIGANTIC ECONOMY. For an $18 paid-in-advance membership ($19 on installments) it supplied twelve monthly-choice books—about half what they cost in bookstores. "Guild" in the name made the point that this resembled the season-ticket, bargain-rate memberships in the then newly successful Theatre Guild. The corresponding drawback was that the Guild allowed no rejection-plus-exchange. It was sight unseen, like it or lump it—and the BOMC's competitive advertising dwelt on that indirectly, politely but happily.

Even so, as their fifty-year race began, the Guild's recruiting ran the BOMC a close second. Maybe the low cost carried great weight. If so, it was compensation for the stubborn opposition that these discounts roused against the Guild among publishers and even more among booksellers sensitized by such Guild slogans as "Down with the Wall between Writer and Reader!" For a while many established publishers refused to deal with the Guild. Several large bookstores boycotted the regular editions of its selections. In time, however, as BOMC and Guild took leaves out of each other's books, they grew more alike, and pressures on the Guild lifted. The BOMC, for instance, began to give discounts varying from item to item. The Guild began to allow members to reject and exchange. Eventually both allowed members to stay enrolled even when rejecting two out of three selections. Thenceforward, though minor differences persisted, competition was largely in terms of quality of selections—probably healthy for both. Their expanding memberships stumbled in the years immediately after the Great Crash, and have always been plagued with high turnover, but toward the mid-1930's the book clubs joined radio, chain stores and the three new

---

* Interclub rivalry did not much affect the early book clubs' committees' selecting. The BOMC chose *The Orphan Angel*, an elegant fantasy by Guild board member, Miss Wylie, in December, 1926. The Guild's first selection was coauthored by Broun, a BOMC board member.

magazines in showing how brilliant innovations could flourish even in the teeth of the Depression.

For the nation at large, of course, the effect on taste and mind was a chief issue. The notion of a committee of wiseacres arbitrarily identifying the "best" book set alarmists crying standardization! conformity! and deploring anything encouraging Americans, who already wore the same hats, drove the same cars and ate the same breakfast foods—the usual overdrawing—also to read the same book each month. Individual taste and intellectual spontaneity, already scarce enough, would further atrophy. Rising young authors would be frozen out of a literary market dominated by likely candidates for book club selection. . . . As for hyperconformity, experience proved that barely one member in three bought the selection of the month, the other two choosing among a wide number of alternates. Obviously most of them used book clubs primarily as general guides to current reading combined with mail-order book buying. That this led to more book buyers was clear as sales of conspicuous books in bookstores also rose rapidly. Early in the tumult Howard Brubaker, aware of how few Americans ever patronized bookstores, pounced on "Booksellers [who] do not like the selecting committee idea. They sigh for the good old days when the public followed its own literary tastes and bought no books at all." [179]

To the extent that book clubs affected the quality level of what was read, their effect was certainly salutary. In their first five years both the BOMC and the Guild chose some unmitigated tripe, of course. The BOMC got burned by Joan Lowell's allegedly autobiographical *The Cradle of the Deep*, soon shown to be fictitious. The Guild had little reason to boast of *Trader Horn*, an old Africa hand's autobiography almost as foolish and little more reliable. Of all titles selected in those years a good half are now meaningless even to those who, like me, were book-minded at the time. But anybody subscribing to both services and dutifully buying and reading what the committees chose in the first five years would have made the acquaintance of:

BOMC	GUILD

Fiction

BOMC	GUILD
Ellen Glasgow, *The Romantic Comedians*; O. E. Rölvaag, *Giants in the Earth*; Stephen Vincent Benét, *John Brown's Body* (verse-narrative); Erich Maria Remarque, *All Quiet on the Western Front*; Arnold Zweig, *The Case of Sergeant Grischa*.	Edwin Arlington Robinson, *Tristram* (verse-narrative); Ford Madox Ford, *The Last Post*; Aldous Huxley, *Point Counter Point*; Evelyn Scott, *The Wave*; Oliver La Farge, *Laughing Boy*.

Nonfiction

T. E. Lawrence, *Revolt in the Desert*; Carl Sandburg, *Abraham Lincoln*; Walter Lippmann, *A Preface to Morals*; Charles and Mary Beard, *The Rise of American Civilization*; Frederick Lewis Allen, *Only Yesterday.*

Claude G. Bowers, *The Tragic Era*; James Truslow Adams, *The Adams Family*; Robert M. Coates, *The Outlaw Years*; Walter Millis, *The Martial Spirit*; Lincoln Steffens, *The Autobiography of. . . .*

A backup list of another twenty titles chosen would be within a hair or two of as solid quality.

Many buying and in most cases reading those nourishing items came of parents who, if they read books at all, had made best sellers of Gene Stratton Porter's *Freckles* and the Reverend Harold Bell Wright's *The Winning of Barbara Worth.* Not that study of any year's publishers' lists did not remain depressing; it is still so today. But there was no denying an immense improvement between 1910 and 1930, and though that was well under way before the book clubs took a hand, their share in keeping it going was probably important. Note further the healthy high ratio of American writers in these lists. Even in fiction Americans had a majority in contrast to the Modern Library's heavy weighting toward the exotic. To confirm the point, contrast *Vanity Fair*'s previously noted Cheevyism with the origins of the book clubs' selections 1926–32:

	United States	Britain	Continental Europe
BOMC	48	20	18
Guild	48	11	10

Not bad for a nation still thick with cultural colonialism.

The book clubs had certain blemishes still to slough off. The committees began unduly fiction-minded; not till late in the 1930's did nonfiction, following the anxieties of the times, begin to dominate. And a far too large majority of the early members were women, a balance redressed since World War II. But it was a great day for the book trade and the nation when that first BOMC advertisement offered to send the best current hard-cover reading to any household the mailman could reach.

Demonstrably the early *Time* and the *New Yorker* smelled of the crypto-Cheevyite's need to show that Americans did not necessarily share the Old Lady in Dubuque's values. Actually, of course, the insecure hankerings that made them xenophiles to begin with were kin to hers. It was a question of terms. Theirs was the Cheevyism of place: "They order these things better in France"—or Greece, whither George Cram Cook out of Davenport, Iowa, by Greenwich Village betook himself to show local shepherds how to live the good life. The Old Lady's hankerings were in terms of time—after her own forebears dead too long for her to have known them personally. For their sake she cherished the shiny dining table that Grandpa had fetched up from New Orleans to Dubuque and read "historical" novels about *Richard Carvel* and *Alice of Old Vincennes* and coated-paper magazines extolling Duncan Phyfe and Charles Bulfinch. She was sure that her forebears had been more dignified, disported themselves more gracefully, cooked better, made better things and deserved better of posterity than her neighbors—let alone the rowdy Younger Generation that, she saw as well as read, her grandchildren were turning into.

Ah, that brave old world of hoopskirts, warming pans and minuets! Or, in a frontier mood, how deftly she would have plied the loom to weave lovely old woolen coverlets while rocking the cradle with her other hand and then, slim and rosy in a calico gown, danced everybody down to "Turkey in the Straw" at the infare. By the mid-1920's she valued one grandmother's bread trough almost as much as the other's ivory miniature of Great-uncle Cuthbert. And when she had not come by such heirlooms directly she was prepared to buy others' heirlooms and cherish them as if they were her own. Hence the glut of antique shops on Madison Avenue and in Pasadena and many places between. Nor were their customers necessarily middle-aged or worse. Numbers of the Old Lady's grandchildren sloughed off the hey-hey idiom to take a job in the family bank and marry a girl who had come around to shoemaker's benches and trivets.

More frivolous grandchildren, nevertheless capable of a *native* Cheevyism, found a homegrown nostalgic cult in the rising folk song movement. It was already so vigorous in 1916 that Dell complained about Villagers prone to break into "Franky and Johnny." That character in Edmund Wilson's *A Winter in Beech Street* went in for "Careless Love" and the cocaine song about have-a-little-whiff-on-me-baby. The sources were hillbilly cabin, bunkhouse, roundhouse, whorehouse, jailhouse, hobo jungle in about that order of volume. But the conduits carrying all that to a growing fandom had a strong academic-*cum*-settlement house feeling. For a generation social workers, regional novelists and others of some literacy whose work took them into southern Appalachia and the Ozarks had been discovering that the otherwise-underprivileged whites of those parts had a solid tradition of songs based on archaic British models. It understandably amazed a worthy young woman who had last dipped into Percy's *Reliques of Ancient English Poetry* at Bryn Mawr to find shoeless cabin dwellers along Dirtyface Creek singing the ballad of Lord Lovell. She and others, particularly professionals from folklore societies, began to collect and collate. In 1910 John Lomax, a Texan instructor in English with tastes unusually earthy for that walk of life, published the collection of cowboy songs, cousins of the hillbilly's with a wide streak of Yankee balladry, that became nucleus of the folk song archives of the Library of Congress. Others stalked the minstrelry of lumber camp and skid row.

As these several streams of interest deepened, minor faculty people at Limbo U spent Saturday evenings with banjo or guitar trying to sound authentic in "Git Along, Little Dogies" or "The Frog Went A-Courtin'." They often acquired undergraduate disciples. The germ took more readily because College boys had long sung over their beer a shifting repertory of obscure origin but with strong tokens of folk song ancestry, some of it, say "Casey Jones," familiar around the piano at home but mostly taboo in the presence of Mom and the girls, for it was about whoring, like "Franky and Johnny," or buggery, like "Christopher Colombo," or stiff with profanity like "Samuel Hall" or with obscenity like "The Eagles They Fly High." This taste for tuneful raffishness aided the rapid post-War spread of "The Foggy Foggy Dew," "When I Was Young and Foolish," "My God, How the Money Rolls In!" . . . Though in those bland times nobody was likely to do an unexpurgated "Derby Ram" in mixed company, he and she Bohemians felt a certain defiant naughtiness in singing together about never letting a fellow go an inch above your knee. Then as research, publication and soon phonograph records got into sea chanteys and hobo and high iron songs the self-impressed economics instructor might daringly strike up "Hallelujah, I'm a Bum," notoriously a Wobbly anthem, or the Waverly Place poet, whose only acquaintance with salt water was its taste when one swam at Provincetown, might plunk and troll his way through the whalerman's grievances in "Blow the Wind in the Morning."

The presiding genius was Carl Sandburg, guitar throbbing, cowlick ingenuously low on the forehead, patter chuckly, making a second career of folk song recitals in college towns—and a best seller of his *American Songbag* (1927). Its rich and valid contents contrast damagingly with the sticky palaver of his editorial comment promising: "Tarnished Love Tales Told in Song. . . . Picnic and Hayrack Follies. . . . Darn Fool Ditties. . . . Lovely People. . . . A big handsome bundle of bully ballads for big boys and their best girls. . . ." [180] The same pumped-upness marred other compilations popular at the time: *My Pious Friends and Drunken Companions; Songs My Mother Never Taught Me.* . . .

Another irritant was the dim-wittedness of many of the lyrics, particularly those in the hillbilly and self-pitying jailhouse idioms. Not the pulsing simplicity of "Careless Love" pouring along with the air like body and soul singing together, but the imbecile flabbiness that exasperated Benchley to the point of creating Joe McGee, the Baggage Man:

> 'Twas in the gay December,
> And the snow was up to your knees,

When Number 34 pulled round the bend
As pretty as you please,
Lord, Lord, as pretty as you please.

Now Joe McGee was the baggage man,
    On Number 34,
And he sat right down on the baggagestep
And killed that Sam Bassinette. . . .[181]

There was so much more to come. The country music industry was getting its feet under it with "The Prisoner's Song" on the flip side of "The Wreck of the Old 97" and the rise of radio to exploit gittar and squalling in the southern half of the country. Late in the 1930's the invasion of minor nightclubs in the wake of Burl Ives' well-earned success approached epidemic proportions. And in spite of the performances of the Sandburgs and the speakeasy minstrels, it would be churlish to deny that the movement had value on balance. Without this self-conscious cult large segments of the nation would never have known of Sweet Betsy from Pike. Children of my generation, growing up without "Lolly Toodum," were certainly deprived; never mind the didactic artificiality of the way today's child has access to it. It was healthy too that much of the folk song canon reminds the well-fed that in certain strata of society going to jail is an experience nearer normal than going to the dentist. Further, Lomax's running the Streets of Laredo right through the campus did tilt youngsters toward self-entertainment. They got sore fingers from guitar strings, sang songs themselves instead of leaning on boughten talent, genially tolerated the less-than-proficient because the performer was enjoying himself moaning "Down in the Valley." As the Reverend Charles Kingsley wisely said, anything's fun in the country.

Late medieval ballads with zither accompaniment wailing out of the automobile radio for fifteen minutes followed by Tin Pan Alley jazz from a phonograph record—the 1920's specialized in such anomalous contrasts between up-to-the-minute technology and self-conscious gropings after traditions exotic in time or space. That was never clearer than in the decade's dubious architectural habits. For America's unique contribution to mankind's ways of building—the curtain-walled, elevator-fitted, steel grid cage of practically unlimited height, alias the skyscraper—had been going not only technically sluggish after a brilliant start but also Cheevishly showy. Diffident about the merits of clean structure, subservient to the tradition-mindedness of clients, architects kept borrowing decoration and to some extent silhouette from past ages and other climes. The essential shape was a tall shaft of emphasized perpendicularity. But the base was a Hollywood-like Babylonian fortress and the upper end was crowned by a Romanesque arcade masking the water tank, or it might be a revised version of St. Peter's for the base and the Moorish Giralda for the crown. The clump of such examples of split personality on the lower end of Manhattan Island, the incoming European's first experience of the astonishingly distinctive New World that he expected, was properly considered one of the world's great spectacles. Its scale was overwhelming, its success as an accidental grouping admirably dramatized by the wild variety of its individual pinnacles; it was a kind of synthetic Alps. Returning grumpy from the War, Irvin S. Cobb saw it as "rising jaggedly like long dog teeth in Manhattan's lower jaw." [182] That came of looking too closely at its components, and would have fitted better still had it included Minneapolis' Foshay Tower, just finished in time for the Great Crash, an Egyptian obelisk with window holes up its sides instead of hieroglyphs.

Cobb's Manhattan c. 1919 was already showing the effect of a New York City ordinance of 1916 that, for a while, looked like a valuable stimulus. To preserve what light and air were left, it required new buildings above a given height to have setbacks narrowing the structure as height increased. An incidental virtue was that, applied to apartment houses, this afforded tenants on certain floors pleasant terraces. Some of the consequences, as in the Paramount Building on Times Square, looked like gargantuan versions of the traditional stepped front gable of the Low Countries. Others suffered from architects' inability to refrain from gussying up the new silhouette by borrowing from Tower of Babel ziggurats or Aztec pyramids or from diffuse ornament too far above street level to be any good to anybody except passengers in helicopters—which did not yet exist—or a few tenants in office buildings across the way. The Sherry-Netherlands Hotel on New York City's Grand Army Plaza—so elegantly new and green-and-gold in the mid-1920's, so inexorably torn down thirty years later—began with a Baths of Caracalla base, jagged upward as blockily as the law required and had as crowning glory on its culminating tower a Germanistic medieval mansion. Raymond Hood's American Radiator Building, all black and gold and blurred Gothic topping, was a much talked-of version of the terminal truncated pyramid.

The ever-growing cultural hegemony of Manhattan in American life was particularly evident in this context because that was where setbacks were first mandatory. In time cities with smaller or no congestion problems went in for setbacks in order to be in the swim. Manhattan's collection of them soon took the play away from their elders in the Wall Street area as the foreign visitor's delight. A pair of French architecture-buff brothers, for instance, giving *Harper's Bazaar* their impressions of America in 1926: ". . . each new building terminates in the manner of a gigantic stairway . . . monumental terraces . . . recall the palaces of Egypt [their archaeology was shaky] or the hanging gardens of Queen Semiramis . . . very American and very modern . . . in harmony with aesthetics peculiar to our

time . . . an architecture that really promises . . . to be classified as that of
the twentieth century. . . ." [183]

They certainly had half a point. Nobody could mistake the Chicago
Tribune Tower, the hyperdevelopment of skyscraper Gothic with which
Hood won a contest for the appropriate shrine for the World's Greatest
Newspaper, for anything that could have been built before 1900. And when
Coolidge was in the White House, too many new American buildings were
earnestly dedicated to looking as like as possible to Ye Goode Olde Dayes.
Half-timbered Tudor manor houses were still sprouting in affluent suburbs,
and even more flagrantly Limbo U's benefactors kept on insisting that the
campus's new bricks-and-mortar should follow archaic prototypes. Much of
the great Harkness fortune, another of those piled up by satraps of the
Rockefeller oil empire, went to the potent Commonwealth Fund for good
works. But several of its millions also built for Yale elaborate masses of
ornate pseudo-Gothic so bent on looking genuine that the quaint window-
panes were deliberately cracked and mended and the roof tiles shaped to
encourage accumulation of moss. Another such welter of gargoyles, ogives
and misbegotten purposes resulted when some of the Duke millions (from
tobacco originally) made Trinity College in Durham, North Carolina, into
Duke University.

On many another campus building money from the prestige-hungry
added Gothic town halls and abbey churches to an already dizzying—and
often entertainingly so—mixture of pseudo-Egyptian library, pseudo-Palla-
dian gymnasium, pseudo-Romanesque lecture hall, Second Empire Renaissance mansion for the president and pseudo-Jacobean student union. Or
suppose the place built all of a piece, it led to the Hispanicistics of Stanford
or, at what is now the University of Texas at El Paso, an ensemble
altogether Bhutanese—Bhutan being, you recall, a sort of geographical
suburb of Tibet. That style was chosen because the college dean's wife
admired the *National Geographic*'s photographs of the broad-roofed,
high-shouldered lamaseries of Bhutan and thought she detected resemblances between the landscape around El Paso and the foothills of the
Himalayas; hence the ornamental urns shaped like prayer wheels that stand
on the college's terraces. There was better logic in Harvard's new
dormitories of a defiantly Georgian style harmonizing with the revered
oldest buildings in the Yard, but even those were, after all, applications of
traditional peacock feathers over jackdaw steel frames and should all have
been named Cheevy Hall.

The cultivated French brothers' "aesthetics peculiar to our time"
appeared to take a firmer hold on Manhattan's architecture, hence on the
nation's, in 1929, when all the hardware finally got mounted on the
insistently new Chrysler Building. From a sheaf of ribbed half haloes in
shiny white metal, like stacked-up cooking aluminum, jutted heavenward a
spiky spire that a glib young Briton likened to "a comic needle . . . the

horn of a narwhal . . . suffering from elephantiasis." [184] Its purpose—to be as untraditionally modern as possible—was fully realized. The method was to pour over a magniloquently expensive and deliberately conspicuous building what is now called Art Deco,* then "vilely referred to," Deems Taylor told readers of *Vanity Fair* that very year, "as 'modernistic,' 'cubistic' and 'futuristic.' " [185] The French brothers would have known all about that idiom. Its source was Paris' Exposition Internationale des Arts Décoratifs et Industriels Modernes held in 1925 and revived in 1927. From its exhibits the effervescent talk of the cultivated took new notions of design spreading and sprouting all over the Western world. To judge from photographs and color renderings, the exposition's buildings exemplifying these new ideas were, inside and out, hideous to a degree never matched elsewhere—not even in the interiors of the triumphantly "modernistic" North German Lloyd liners *Bremen* and *Europa* and the decor of the Radio City Music Hall. But in America Art Deco's chief damage was done in smaller applications such as the Murray Hill apartment queasily catalogued by Van Vechten in 1928: ". . . electric lights imbedded in Lalique vases, Circassian walnut shelves on various levels tricked out with puppets from Copenhagen . . . divans and chairs upholstered with materials that bore some faint, meretricious resemblance to paintings in the manner of Picasso. . . ." [186] Or in the fat-cat speakeasy preserved by Sinclair Lewis: ". . . a circular bar of black glass edged with a silver band, bright aluminum bar stools with red-leather seats, pictures made with outlines of silver wire . . . walls splashed with sunbursts and torch flames of aluminum. . . ." [187] One misses only the etched glass panel of a Scandinavian female in profile striding leanly into a wind so high that her long hair streams out behind in ropy parallel lines like a musical staff; she was likely to have a greyhound alongside. Her male equivalent survives today in the Prometheus figure over the skating rink at Radio City. Modernistic meant Bauhaus furniture of shiny metal pipe and plate glass laboratory-style; the only furniture in the whole movement that proved livable was the blond-wood stuff from Sweden and Denmark. Modernistic meant angle-topped screens and random cylinders or prismatic pedestals, pointy-shiny effects like windowpane frosting done with a protractor, bookcases imitating skyscraper setbacks, lines professing to seek cleanness and achieving only brittleness. It meant, as Deems Taylor bitterly complained, "expressionistic cocktail shakers, cubist goldfish bowls, ultra-modern grandfathers' clocks, stylized hooked rugs . . . Grand Rapids futurism. . . ." [185] And it soon meant—or was soon indissolubly associated in the public mind with—a new profession born in the mid-1920's, that of industrial design.

---

* It used to take a hundred years for an artifact to become an antique. The cult of Victorian rococo in the 1920's narrowed that to fifty years. Today's cult of Art Deco has it down to forty. Designers will soon create items intended to become instantly obsolete for the antiques market.

The American pioneers in the field were Donald Deskey, Russel Wright, Norman Bel Geddes, Walter Dorwin Teague, Henry Dreyfuss. . . . Most of them had been more or less well-established graphic artists before they turned to putting their grasp of line, mass and proportion at the service of makers of household appliances, tableware, radios, cameras and so on. Geddes had also been a renowned stage designer in the tradition of Gordon Craig and Robert Edmond Jones. French-born and engineering-educated Raymond Loewy began his American career drawing women's fashions for *Harper's Bazaar* and the like. Industrial designers or their staffs had to have engineering sense enough not to design anything hampering the operation of the artifacts they dealt with and to avoid impossible or too costly architectural problems. By World War II, indeed, outstanding industrial designers had technical staffs able to make substantial innovative contributions to the war effort. But in the early days, as Loewy has recorded, the new profession was "nearly killed in the nest [by] . . . crackpot commercial artists, decorators, etc., without experience, taste, talent, or integrity, who called themselves industrial designers." [188] And it remains true that the prime contribution has been cosmetic—to make a given object look fashionably attractive. *C.* 1928 that meant looking functional whether or not the function hinted at had much to do with the actual one. From ten feet away the butcher's scale and the electric mixer became remarkably alike.

The typewriter I used in college was a foursquare standard with exposed works, conceding to looks only nickel plate on a few levers and black enamel on its right-angled frame. The recent, nonelectric model I write this on is, though too gadgeted up, about as good a machine, no better, shrouded in pale-gray steel of swanlike curves set in a dark-gray tray with space bar, platen knobs and such picked out in blue-green plastic—eloquent of the industrial designer's love for sleek disguise responding to the client's instructions to come up with something that will attract women secretaries. The shroud probably adds a few extra dollars to the sales price and must be dismounted to change ribbons; its one usefulness, as a ledge to hold a beer glass, is inadvertent. The electric toaster we used when first married neglected to disguise its slots and heating wires. Its successor, which toasts bread as well, no better, is encased in a double-bulging shiny metal shell giving no hint of what the device thus masked may be and making it harder to clean. I once voyaged in a ship the staterooms of which were drawn up by a fine industrial design firm—whose careful measurements fitted the depth of the door to the length of a coat hanger so neatly that the door wouldn't close when an overcoat was draped on a hanger. . . . Yet sensible results can be obtained. When Loewy, for instance, transformed refrigerators and kitchen stoves into rectangular spooks of white enamel, not only did he make them more attractive to housewives, but they were commendably easier to keep clean. The basic bed that Geddes designed for the Simmons Company early in this new game—plain rectangular headboard, single curve footboard, in between only box spring, mattress and basic frame made of salvage railroad rail—was an esthetic good example and its lack of gimcrackery made it cheap to produce.

Industrial design was not brand-new, of course. Special draftsmen egged on by the sales manager had drawn up those Art Nouveau lock escutcheons and window latches made as building hardware c. 1905. What got this function set apart in the 1920's as something obtainable from self-elected expert consultants was squeamish esthetic theory infiltrating public taste. The experts' designs were naturally no better than those in any other field employing a wide range of skill and taste. Geddes was soon deploring "senseless . . . geometrical . . . forms . . . of the cheapest and most vulgar sort." [189] Yet a generation later Loewy could write: "Today no manufacturer, from General Motors to the Little Lulu Novelty Company, would think of putting a product on the market without benefit of a designer . . . vindication of my early theory that . . . correct visual presentation would become an integral part of merchandising . . . industrial design is just as important as advertising." [190] Call it the pretentious aspect of packaging. Indeed a striking number of firms listed in classified directories under "Industrial Design" mention packaging first among services offered.

As industry learned that such services were worth paying for—at best they drew shoppers and publicity; at worst they kept salesmen feeling that the company was abreast of the times—industrial design was invited to go beyond soda-fountain equipment, cream separators, automobile batteries and so on into collective contexts: department store displays (and world's fair exhibits), automobile bodies, ships, locomotives. . . . Out of such fields came the ubiquitous thing called streamlining. That originally meant the teardrop shape that enables a solid object to go through a liquid or gas meeting least resistance. Knowledge of it was highly useful in shaping the fuselages and motor housings of airplanes to reduce resistance at the relatively high speeds being attained in the 1920's; as such, streamlining was vital to aviation. All through the period when industrial design was cutting its teeth, public enthusiasm about airplanes was so glowing that it hardly needed Charles A. Lindbergh to bring it to white heat. As explanation of why planes looked more and more like huge flying fish shimmering with speed, "streamlining" became part of the language of knowing persons. One no longer coordinated or reorganized an industry or a football team's strategy or a magazine's format; one streamlined it. Nor was it an accident that the airplane's sleekly eccentric curves and simple shapes chimed in with Art Deco as expression of modernity. It was probably inevitable that industrial designers would apply streamlining where it by no means belonged but where with-itness was important, often in versions so modified as to lose all engineering significance.

Actually reduction of air resistance has small practical importance at speeds below 50–55 mph, depending to some extent on mass and length of the moving object. Yet new ships unable to move much faster than 35 mph were voluptuously streamlined around the bridge. Loewy even streamlined the engine housings of farm tractors built to dash along at say 20 mph top when cruising to the job on the highway. But then it made even less sense to streamline bed lamps, vacuum bottles, radios. . . . Automobiles were a special case. The principle was highly pertinent to racing cars and soon applied, but did not seriously affect the family sedan until late in the 1930's. The delay did not imply commonsense recognition that a vehicle seldom traveling faster than 50 mph—on the highway of forty years ago 60 mph was unusual because unduly hazardous—had small need for streamlining. Instead, the cause was the curious failure of the first striking effort to apply it—on Chrysler's Airflow model of 1934. Whatever was wrong—the car was one of the best the company ever made, but it did look as if it had tried and failed to run under a truck—it soured Detroit on streamlining for years. Gradually, however, the modish *Zeitgeist* sneaked in, curves began to modify the jaunty old perpendiculars and right angles, wheels were shrouded in pseudo-streamlined fenders that made it hard to change a flat—and Detroit was on its way to that miracle of engineering false effrontery, the fastback of the late 1960's that, when standing still, looks as if it were hitting 70.

Twin of industrial design was another kind of professional packaging climbing up hand over fist in the 1920's—public relations counseling. The PR man is now as familiar as the personnel director and the security chief. The direct ancestor of the PR expert, the show business press agent, ally-hairshirt of newspapers bent on entertaining readers, was as old as Barnum's first capers. But only after 1900 did industry and propaganda-based movements employ specialists, often engagingly self-recommended, to help them put that best foot forward.

The term "public relations" was not coined until about the time of Theodore Roosevelt's "malefactors of great wealth" *c.* 1907. It described such lubricating devices as those first worked out by the John Gutenberg of the field, Ivy Ledbetter Lee, for those notorious MOGW's, the anthracite coal owners of Pennsylvania. During the harsh anthracite strike of 1902 John Mitchell, head of the United Mine Workers, gained useful public sympathy for his men by not only making a good case for them but also going courteously out of his way to make sure the press heard all about it. For a wonder the owners took this as valuable hint. Three years later, when another strike seemed to be heating up, they astonished the Fourth Estate by hiring Lee away from his reporter's job on the New York *Times* to represent them in keeping the press filled in on their version of what went on and why. Lee's inaugural manifesto stated for all time the fundamentals of sound PR work: "This is not a secret press bureau. All our work is done in the open . . . to supply news . . . not an advertising agency; if you think any of our matter ought to go to your business office, do not use any of it . . . any editor will be assisted most cheerfully in verifying directly any statement of fact. . . ." [191]

It worked so well that in a few months New York City's Consolidated Gas Company, the Equitable Life Assurance Company and that most unpopular of trusts the Rockefellers' Standard Oil Company had all hired experienced newspapermen to go and do likewise. Then the giant Pennsylvania Railroad retained Lee as a chronic litigant retains a lawyer. Though such consultants were still likely to be called press agents—"public relations" did not gain wide currency until after the War—their place in American life was thenceforth firm and expanding. Soon the Rockefellers turned to Lee to repair the wounds left in their reputations by the bloody war that their Colorado Fuel and Iron Company had been waging with its miners. Lee eventually became celebrated for having changed John D. Rockefeller, Sr.'s public image from the national Scrooge to the cadaverous but genial old gentleman cacklingly handing dimes to all and sundry. Such window dressing, seldom absent from skilled PR activity, is one of its strongest links to industrial design packaging. But this assignment also gave Lee opportunity to try his new principle of "shaping the affairs of the corporation so that when placed before the public they will be approved" [192] —in this case recommending drastic modification of Colorado Iron and Fuel's policies.

Thus "The public be damned!," which—whether or not W. K. Vanderbilt ever said it—had been the great corporations' policy began to shift toward "The public be heeded" or anyway "The public be taken into account." No longer need the press rely altogether on keyholes, employees' loose tongues, none-of-your-business encounters with company brass and occasional clumsy but sometimes successful bribery. Many of the devices that Lee *et al.* employed in the interests of big business proved also useful in spreading and supporting ideas. Before the War the formidable she-chiefs of the Women's Christian Temperance Union had shown the way there, and during the War, of course, Creel's committee did so on a gigantic scale and on many more levels. From these examples grew the Hays Office and the Klan, true, and the much abused trick of hiding a dubious or unwelcome purpose behind an ostensibly high-minded Committee for Something-Sounding-Unimpeachable headed by eminent people not necessarily aware of all its underlying ends. In the 1930's the Communist Party borrowed that ploy from capitalism's hirelings to form such Popular Front-Trojan Horses as the League Against War and Fascism and the American Writers' Congress. But the new art of public relations could also put the nation in its debt with such constructive successes as the March of Dimes (against poliomyelitis) and the revolutionarily candid campaign against syphilis in the late 1930's.

Behind Lee came other PR giants—Edward L. Bernays (who, as Dr. Freud's nephew, sometimes lent his talents gratis to the cause of psychoanalysis), Carl Byoir, Earl Newsom . . . the Murderers' Row of the PR big leagues. The powerful and well-barberedly sinister PR counselor conspicuous in Dos Passos' *USA* showed how seriously intellectuals took the new profession. It sometimes sat high in the client's councils seeking to keep policies defensible, even maybe so obviously good for public and company alike that they needed no defense. The capsheaf was put on late in the 1930's when the A&P's Hartford brothers dropped their archaic neglect of such matters and brought in Carl Byoir to loosen up the great chain's public image.

Down from those heights graded many minor opportunists, usually former newspapermen, diving into this opening in the same spirit as their counterparts of the drawing board entering industrial design. Some got jobs with the leading PR offices, which chronically needed canny recruits broken to the typewriter. Indeed one of the best reasons for seeking a reporter's notoriously ill-paid career became the chance that it would eventually lead to a good salary in PR work. Others set up their own offices and secured clients through influential connections made while covering City Hall or the financial district. A company in a vulnerable position might hire a PR firm tactfully to keep its name and doings *out* of print. That required special skills and was well rewarded to match. But on the whole it was true of large and small operations that the basic job was, as Silas Bent biliously defined it in 1931, "to graft for the client free space in the news columns . . . in magazine articles. One-half of the news-items are of this interested origin . . . a large share . . . sheer advertising, which properly belongs in the revenue-producing columns." [193] After all, a thick stack of clippings of neutral-to-approving tone was the PR man's best way to keep his profession's first commandment: THOU SHALT KEEP THE CLIENT PERSUADED HE IS GETTING HIS MONEY'S WORTH.

Most reporters are aware that an able PR man knowing what makes good raw material for a story, reasonably honest about carrying water on both shoulders, pushy at the right times only, is a useful adjunct to the Fourth Estate. But, as Bent hinted above, Lee's stipulation that a PR office must not be an advertising agency came to be much honored in the breach—most flagrantly and traditionally in sports and entertainment but by no means only there. It was an eloquent mistake when, in the 1920's, the large advertising agencies began to set up public relations departments. Space & Billings' PR chief could not possibly suggest to *Onceoverlightly Magazine* a piece on the new widget industry without both parties being tacitly aware that S&B handled advertising for the Hexagonal Corporation, new and big in widgets . . . and that Hexagonal's land-procurement policies out West had recently come under fire. . . .

Consulted by the American Tobacco Company about its advertising for

Lucky Strike cigarettes, Bernays studied a layout showing a woman offering Luckies to two men and turned for advice to his Uncle Sigmund's first apostle. Emotionally jarring, said Dr. Brill: "Two people should appear, one man and one woman. That is life. Nor should a woman . . . offer cigarettes. The cigarette is a phallic symbol to be offered by a man to a woman." Bernays believed that "brilliant piece of psychoanalytic thinking" to have been "the first instance of [the] application of psychoanalysis to advertising." [194] Very likely; but John B. Watson was already hard at work in the J. Walter Thompson advertising agency and already infamous among aspirants to its payroll for having drawn up the complex resumé-application-questionnaire to which they were subjected—a document that, like being tied neck and heels, grew more smothering the more one struggled with it. Here and there personnel departments were toying with modified Stanford-Binet and proto-aptitude tests. The meaning of these fragments would soon be clear. The American business administrator was adding to the efficiency expert, the PR man and the industrial designer a fourth outside consultant—the academically trained psychologist. Watson thought poorly of this new fashion, questioning the judgment of "expecting the psychologist to come in and, by some offhand pronunciamento, . . . settle [personnel, efficiency and other problems] which business men have not been able to settle by other means" and saying flatly that "the psychologists have been too ambitious." [195] But the tide rose rapidly. One wonders whether any such consulting psychologist ever suggested to a client that when a big shot in the widget business falls into this fashion of calling in outsiders to advise him what to do, it might mean he and his likes were losing their grip.

The uncomfortable notion that even the most formidable big shots can lose their grips was brought home to the nation in the Coolidge administration by the mercy killing of the Model T. One can no more keep Henry Ford from popping up constantly in this book than Dickens' Mr. Dick could keep Charles I's head from popping up in his. This time, however, Henry is object, not subject, significant in what he brought down on himself rather than in what he did for his own cranky purposes.

For fifteen years since the Model T was born, other automobile manufacturers had been seeking competitive advantage by going into new body styles enticingly christened Jackrabbit, Bearcat, Bulldog, Playboy; catered to the prestige market with six, eight, twelve cylinders; tinkered, guessed wrong and adjusted for the improving performance and reliability that were turning the automobile into something nearer the convenience and comfort of what one buys today. Some makers—Studebaker, Hudson, the General Motors combine (as a whole) et al.—made money out of this flexibility, but for a good while much more precariously than Ford's assembly lines turning out knee-deep profits with the same monotonous regularity as that basic car, choose any color just so it's black. Henry's dearly beloved and momentous Tin Lizzie, her design only occasionally refined in minor details, was Detroit's eternal verity. On May 26, 1927, Henry and his able but submerged son, Edsel, made the papers by driving the fifteen millionth Ford—still Tin Lizzie albeit with a spare tire and electric headlights.

Five days later with no warning at all Henry got off another of his grandstand plays—announced that he was deposing Tin Lizzie and shutting down his entire operation to retool for a completely new Ford. At the time nobody, not Henry himself, had the slightest idea what it would be like. This was just his abrupt, arbitrary reaction to having finally to admit that changing economics and customer attitudes had undermined Lizzie's throne.

Her crowned head had been lying uneasy for some years. The Dodge case might have warned her viceroy. Once large stockholders in the Ford Motor Company and chief suppliers of its component parts, John and Horace Dodge had done well since 1914 making their own cars with a Fordish approach to the market—reliable, cheap (though not quite as cheap) and basic (though rather more complex with, for instance, a hand gearshift), less grotesque-looking but changing lines little from year to year. The brothers died in 1919. By 1923 their heirs, under pressure from dealers reflecting the public's shifting demands, veered away from Fordishness and toward the rest of the industry—juggled outside appearance, tinkered up the insides, hung on more gadgets—and kept on doing well. But it took the Chevrolet case to cure Henry's mulishness. In 1923 General Motors (Cadillac, Oldsmobile, Oakland, Buick, Chevrolet) acquired a new chief, Alfred P. Sloan, who, had Henry never entered American automobile history, would have been its outstanding figure. He jacked up the Chevrolet nameplate and put under it a redesigned vehicle that he defined as a "mass-class" car to conquer Ford's mere mass car—"a bigger package of accessories and improvements beyond basic transportation . . . at a higher price [yet] so compellingly attractive as to draw buyers away from the Model T." [196]

The new Chevy—as it was soon affectionately called, a propitious sign—had more legroom, was longer and looked lower than the bunty Ford; offered economical color options thanks to GM's new Duco finish; automatic wipers, a great selling point, for the old hand-powered wipers were a murderous nuisance; dome lights in all closed models. . . . As for cost, by 1927 growing volume justified successive cuts deeper than Ford could match, taking Chevy down within $100 of the humdrum, funereal Model T. In 1926 Chevy's sales were already up by 40 percent, Ford's down by 25 percent. The revolt was about to turn into revolution.

As usual in revolutions the several causes were mostly economic. Chevrolet gave dealers 24 percent discount to make deals within; Ford dealers got only 17 percent. They were further hampered by Henry's reluctance to help facilitate time payments, whereas GM's Acceptance Corporation had led the industry in that growingly important respect since 1919. And for a major factor, since 1921 or so booming production and sales had made the secondhand market a major drag on distribution. By 1924 or so most families had owned a car for a few years and, as income expectation rose with good times, hankered after turning it in on a fancier replacement likely to impress the Joneses—an impulse in itself bad for Ford. So the dealers with whom they traded were accumulating back lots full of still serviceable, not too ratty-looking transportation to be worked off at prices well below what a new Ford cost somebody buying for the first time. The pileup grew so awkward that Chevrolet gave its dealers a bonus of $25 for every trade-in certified to have been junked; from 1927 to 1930 650,000 jalopies went that road to the scrap heap. And for a cultural-emotional factor maybe the Ford jokes, once good publicity for a product becoming a national legend while filling a national need, now came home to roost in a hazy but damaging impression that the old Model T was faintly ridiculous, discreditably archaic—who would put up with that old-timey makeshift if he could afford anything better?

Back to Sloan's mass-class notion, guiding symptom of this world of easy financing and glutted secondhand market—factors that have fouled up the economy ever since, good times or bad. This hunger for the shinier and larger even if it cost more was what moved the average first-car owner to send it to the used-car lot well before it was worn out as part of a deal for something he could pay for only by mortgaging a large segment of his future. In view of the typical American's taste for conspicuous consumption that had probably always been latent. Once he assumed that he would always own some kind of car, just as he would always use some kind of soap, this economic absurdity could surface. Its rapid rise after the Armistice explains why, though Ford had been on the right sales track in the inchoate conditions of 1916, when mere ownership of gasoline-powered wheels was joy as well as convenience, Sloan was right ten years later and rubbing Henry's nose in it.

The Ford shutdown lasted months and months, a period of gestation suitable to anything so important as the kind of car that would come out of the gesture—Model A, beginning a new series to betoken the dawn of a totally new motoring day. When the unveiling finally came in December with the fanfare of a coronation, America took it about as big as the approaching Christmas celebrating another momentous birth. What the public was finally allowed to see was a very nice little car, though its only miraculous aspect was that so well conceived a thing could have been engineered in so short a time. Tin Pan Alley came out with "Henry's Made a Lady Out of Lizzie." Model A stuck to a four-cylinder motor where engineering counted most. Where style counted most, it fielded an ingratiatingly chubby body gleaming in (at last!) a choice of four colors. Its wheels were of the then dashing bicycle-wire design; the closed coupe had a rumble seat. For gadgetry its standard equipment included four wheel brakes, standard shift, foot throttle, speedometer, battery ignition—a list making one recall how primitive Model T had been—and for *pièce de résistance* the new shatterproof glass in the windshield . . . altogether well able to stand up to Chevy and the new Plymouth with which Walter P. Chrysler's ambitious company was competing. Indeed Model A outsold Chevy in 1929, after which, of course, the shadow of Depression fell on normal comparisons of economic impact. But the Fords never regained their hegemony in the minimum price field.

Sloan could rightly boast that by hanging on too long and then taking such abruptly traumatic corrective measures, Ford had "lost the lead to General Motors." [197] Worse, having let Model T lose its virginity, Ford now had to follow most of the industry and play the game GM's way. Superficial changes for salesmen to flash; growing list of gadgets included standard instead of being ordered ad lib from the Sears catalogue; sturdiness and gas economy neglected for a range of color options that eventually made parking lots seen from above look like displays of mixed penny candies. Within a year the Fords were even tempting the family living between the Joneses and Mrs. Grundy in Colonial Heights with a style of car previously confined to estate owners ordering it special from a fat-cat manufacturer—a wooden station wagon on a Model A chassis. Thus began the evolution of today's widely favored metal-clad monster used as day nursery or kennel on wheels.

More broadly the Fords' knuckling under completed Detroit's abject submission to the advertising and sales departments. Hence the emergence of the merchandising strategy on which the motor industry has ever since anchored as the patent medicine industry anchors on hypochondria—the annual model change. Sloan's memoirs (1964) seem reluctant to claim this practice for his company: ". . . not a declared policy of General Motors, or of any one . . . in the 1920s . . . [but] inherent in the policy of bigger and better packages each year." [197] Indeed it was. John B. Rae's authoritative *The American Automobile* says that well before Henry had put away Tin Lizzie like a Biblical patriarch putting away a wife, "General Motors made the annual model change a definite sales technique . . . meeting competition not only from the ageing Model T but also from the secondhand car." [198] Packard alone stood with Ford in trying to resist this trend. Sloan's diffidence may mean that several decades later he was uncertain how commendable it had been to lead Detroit in conditioning the nation to an annual spree of new gimmicks meant to make owners of elder models feel they were driving last year's bird's nests.

One probable source of the practice was annual automobile shows, going back two decades, that needed novelty to display each year. At first, however, their public came to see *new makes* of cars rather than new wrinkles on familiar makes. Every year brought two dozen more mushroom companies cobbling up new brands out of suppliers' parts, motors included, and thirty others going bankrupt or merging with rivals. As the number of makes dwindled, the shows to some extent encouraged the industry consciously or unconsciously to act like the world of women's fashions with an annual creation of deliberate obsolescence. The style laboratories that all automobile makers set up in the 1930's operated just like Potash & Perlmutter on Seventh Avenue—blueprinting a year or two in advance what would be competitively just far enough ahead of the general trend meant to make garments bought the previous season look dowdy. Here is the explanation for the otherwise curious distinction between selling a horse after riding it a few months and selling a car after driving it a few months. Who ever heard of a secondhand horse? Or house? But every car turns secondhand, with an immediate drop of several hundred dollars in sale value, the moment its new owner drives it away.

Psychologist Ernest Dichter had not yet come out of the wilderness to persuade openmouthed Detroit that to Americans an automobile is primarily a sex object to be pimped for as such. Before World War II to mention a sex angle in automobile merchandising would have meant refined shape, color and upholstery to appeal to women; the appeal to men was assumed to lie in steady increase in horsepower. The analogy with the garment trade is all the closer because Woman came to have more to do with when a new car was bought and which was chosen. Fortunately her lack of interest in what was under that long, sleek beige hood mattered less each year because progress in engineering was raising most makes of car to much the same level of reliability. By 1935 both GM's Cadillac and GM's Chevrolet started readily on cold mornings and could go faster than was safe for most drivers on most highways. The advantages one had over the other were that it was somewhat quieter, rode a little better—but chiefly that it cost several thousands more and everybody knew it. The annual-model sales revolution culminated in the doctrine, doubtless originated by dealers but popularized by cliché swappers in locker rooms and on commuter trains, that it made economic sense to turn in for the new model every fall—in spite of the notorious fact that a car's loss in resale value is proportionally highest the first year. No matter what the state of the secondhand market, the resulting steady flow of changes in ownership kept the finance companies fairly happy.

"Why do you buy one make of automobile rather than another?" was the first sentence of an article in the *New Republic*, late in 1925. It was not another panegyric of the cleverness of Madison Avenue or the unfailing prowess of Detroit's engineers, for it went on: "Why do you buy the toothpaste you are using? . . . do you know if it has, beyond a pleasant

taste, any merits at all? . . . Is this cake of soap really going to give you a
school girl complexion? . . . How many washings will these shirts
survive?" [199] Eighteen months later this and a subsequent article went far
beyond the *New Republic*'s small and specialized readership as basis for an
early Book-of-the-Month—*Your Money's Worth* by Stuart Chase and F. J.
Schlink. Thus was born an American consumers' self-protective movement
as at least potential antidote to what had undermined Henry Ford's Model
T. Not that that made Henry a tragic hero or any other kind. His basic
drives were in their own way as uncivilized as Hearst's. But Model T did
represent much of what made sense about mass production while the
devices with which GM beat it down were perversions of it that, in the view
of the consumers rallying to Chase and Schlink, were unnecessary as well as
toxic.

In name and in some ways in fact the consumers' movement goes back to
c. 1900, when groups with settlement-house values, mostly in the Northeast,
organized to improve working conditions in garment, candy, food factories
and so on by pledging members and their friends to buy only brands
produced under approved conditions—a sort of converse boycott that labor
unions soon found useful. The consequent National Consumers' League
eventually concentrated on lobbying for strict laws against offensive factory
practices.* But the bare existence of the league's name and some of its
tactics contributed to a notion of "the consumer" not as an economist's
abstraction but as the man in the street—more to the purpose, his wife in
the department store—intimately concerned with what his and her money
buys. Simultaneously that issue had sharpened with the growth of the pure
food and drug movement—war-horse of the great Dr. Harvey W. Wiley.
This Hoosier professor of chemistry, also an MD, combined a muckraking
spirit with a strong scientific conscience. He fathered federal regulation of
patent medicines, meat-packing, canning and various other fields in which
rampant enterprise had been getting away with economic murder and
sometimes actual manslaughter. Credit an assist to Upton Sinclair, whose
novel *The Jungle* failed of its purpose to turn America Socialist but did
horrify a vast public by its well-founded charge that employees occasionally
fell into meat-packers' cooking vats and got processed, overalls and all, into
the lard that the nation fried most of its meals in.

Dr. Wiley's cogent propaganda further firmed up the outlines of the
consumer-as-individual whom he sought to protect. In 1912 manufacturing
interests on whose toes he kept treading finally worked up such hostile
pressures that he resigned as Uncle Sam's consultant on food and drugs.
That took him and consumerism into another phase, equivocal but
eventually fruitful. Hearst's *Good Housekeeping*, a magazine entertaining as

---

* In some ways the consumers' cooperatives, of British origin, that took root in America in
the 1890's were also ancestors of the consumerism here discussed. But their emphasis began
and remained primarily on dollars and cents, only secondarily on quality and relative values.

well as counseling housewives, hired him to create and manage a Good Housekeeping Bureau of Foods, Sanitation and Health to test for quality and, where he found it justified, endorse for its readers foods, drugstore stuff, household gadgets and so on advertised therein.

Women's magazines generally had supported Wiley's past agitations, giving suggestive pertinence to such a connection. The auspices were dubious, however. The mere name Hearst on a purportedly high-minded scheme jarred on many unaware that Hearst was inclined to let the magazine area of his empire pretty much alone so long as the balance sheets shaped up. Besides, the arrangement had the odor, commoner now but already known then, of an industry under attack hiring the chief attacker to turn false front. And though to advertise in *Good Housekeeping* did not automatically entitle a product to Dr. Wiley's Seal of Approval, the seal went only to products that did advertise, which might tend to flaw objectivity. Yet Dr. Wiley, working on criteria rather loose but well observed as far as they went, so managed that until he died in 1930 he could look himself in the face mornings. During his seventeen years the magazine had rejected on his say-so over a million dollars' worth of advertising. What was more important, as readers learned that the seal really meant something—if not all it might—the previously unheard-of possibility of giving the individual consumer reliable advice—if not in this case exactly disinterested—began to take on substance.

The crucial ingredient of disinterestedness was added in 1927 in, of all places, White Plains, capital of New York City's commuter-rich suburban satellite, Westchester County. There dwelt Schlink, a youngish, crisp-minded mechanical engineer on the staff of the American Standards Association, industry's clearinghouse for technical quality. He had previously worked in the U.S. Bureau of Standards, where Uncle Sam draws up specifications for and tests most of the things he buys. The dollars-and-cents aspect of this operation had delighted Schlink. The bureau cost $2,000,000 a year to run. By objectively determining which manufactured products were the best normally available and by insisting that purchases measure up to objective standards, it saved the government some $100,000,000 a year on baseballs, thumbtacks, concrete, paper and the thousands of other items it needed. As Schlink observed the rising tides of advertising for Listerine to cure halitosis (that began in 1916) and radios now for the first time *exactly* reproducing the sound fed into the studio microphone (a claim made every year), he wished that the confused, badgered and ever-more-flagrantly-lied-to consumer could, as purchasing agent for himself, have some of Uncle Sam's advantages. Among his fellow members of the White Plains Community Church (nondenominational) he organized a Consumers' Club, collecting down-to-earth data wherever available on the actual merits of various brands of razor blades, shoes, toothbrushes and so on; they even did some of their own testing. There, going far beyond Dr. Wiley, was the do-it-yourself germ of today's Consumers Research and its schismatic rival, Consumers Union. With Stuart Chase, Schlink wrote in the *New Republic*: "If the poor boobs—of whom we have the honor to be two—haven't the sense and intelligence to devise ways and means [to learn what they need to know about consumers' goods] . . . they must stew in their own juice. They will deserve to be taken by every cymbal-clanging salesman from here to Jericho." [200]

Much of the germ's culture medium was brewed by Chase—youngish, technology-minded alumnus of MIT and Harvard, accountant and amateur economist, former investigator of the meat industry for the Federal Trade Commission. His recent conspicuous book, *The Tragedy of Waste*, had shown him to be the most engagingly readable as well as clearest of the nation's writers for general audiences on socioeconomic matters. Expanding their *New Republic* manifesto, Schlink and he made *Your Money's Worth* brilliantly amusing with hilariously apt chapter mottoes from *Alice in Wonderland*. Not least because it remained good-natured, what the book said stuck and stung. The reader was at once diverted, educated and outraged by learning that for both hygienic and cosmetic purposes prepared chalk obtainable at the drugstore was as efficient as toothpaste bought in a tube at ten times the cost per brushing; that Shredded Wheat was practically alone among dry breakfast cereals in affording substantial nourishment per serving; that fancy lipsticks sold for a dollar came out of the same factory, nay, out of the same batch of goop, as those that dime stores sold for a quarter under another brand. Aunt Agatha's conviction that high cost meant high quality was badly damaged. Obviously when the same quality of mattress came out of the same factory under six different brand names commanding six different retail prices, only one out of six groups of purchasers escaped being swindled. Yet shoddy and gouging were not inevitable. Ivory soap was inexpensive and of unimpeachable quality, even though not smelling like a Persian garden. The Underwriters Laboratory tag on an electric gadget really did mean it met exacting engineering standards. Thanks to amateur volunteer fire companies' insistence on quality, their fire-fighting equipment was a shining (in both senses) example of a first-class money's worth. The book asked only that "the run of the goods in the shops and houses and factories of Main Street [be] as dependable as the [local] fire truck." [201]

It attacked neither mass production nor advertising as such. Mass production, it admitted, often made things better than elder methods could and at prices lower in real wages—Model T's, for instance, and Waltham watches. Indeed advertising that reliably set forth the good points of well-made and responsibly designed things could be valuable to society, and a few advertisers actually acted on that principle. The trouble was that (quoting W. T. Grant of the great variety-store chain) ". . . not quality but salesmanship . . . makes or breaks a business . . . to-day. Fads and fancies

. . . are jammed down the throats of consumers by hollow-bottomed advertising. . . . Competing companies . . . become so concerned about . . . 'putting it over' that they forget the first duty to the consumer." [202]

Today most people with IQ's above 90 are at least aware of that tension between consumer and manufacturer/advertiser/retailer and keep it somewhat in mind in drugstore, supermarket and so on. Much of that healthy wariness one owes to Schlink and Chase. Until they achieved a wide public in 1927 even most people uneasy about or contemptuous of advertising— then riding higher every year—lacked enough specifics to crystallize suspicions on. Now here were 200-odd pages of specifics—short weight loaves of bread cost the nation $100,000,000 a year!—and several final pages of such pithy advice as: "Read labels carefully; compare them with the advertising. . . . Look for weights on package goods; figure out how much you are paying *per pound*. . . . When you hear the word *guarantee* laugh heartily." [203] Such doctrine appealed greatly to those valuing an opportunity to exercise thrifty common sense, or who resented being taken, or who felt the wise guy's pleasure in knowing the score, or who had to cover exacting demands with low incomes, or who held a grudge against the System and were delighted with all these new reasons why.

With all these groups stirred up, no wonder the authors were overwhelmed with mail. Schlink tried to handle it evenings and weekends but ended by creating what was obviously needed—M. C. Phillips, one of its earliest pillars, described it as "a clearing-house where information of importance to consumers may be assembled, edited, and promulgated [to develop] an art and a science of consumption by . . . which ultimate consumers may defend themselves against the aggressions of, advertising and salesmanship." [204] Name: Consumers Research. The original financing was a $10,000 line of credit from Mrs. Dorothy Payne Whitney Straight Elmhirst, another of William C. Whitney's open-minded children, whose fortune had already helped the *New Republic*, women's suffrage, Progressive Education. . . . In due time CR, as it still jauntily calls itself, managed to float itself on memberships sold magazine-fashion to those letter writers and their acquaintance. The membership list tripled in 1931, doubled in 1932, reaching 50,000-odd. That meant probably 200,000 people sipping this heady cocktail made of two parts Benjamin Franklin, one part Henry David Thoreau, one part Thorstein Veblen, a heavy dash of Frederick Winslow Taylor. Its board of sponsors included Judge Mack, Melville Herskovits (influential anthropologist), Harry Elmer Barnes, George S. Counts and Agnes de Lima (Progressive Educationists), liberal lawyers like Morris Ernst, distinguished liberal economists like Harvard's Sumner H. Slichter, Chicago's Paul H. Douglas, Columbia's Rexford G. Tugwell . . . a cross-section of the cream of subscribers to the *New Republic*.

Only CR's subscribers received its publications in which were promulgated its realistic ratings of available electric irons, soap powders, automo-

bile jacks, towels or whatever for relative quality on the basis of data from
the U.S. Bureau of Standards, the AMA, technician members volunteering
in their fields of competence and gradually, as resources grew, CR's own
laboratories. Yearly the latest findings on testable products that would
interest most households were compiled into a thickish handbook to which
CR's kind of family looked forward as eagerly as a remote farm family to
the Sears catalogue. Previously only Dr. Arthur Cramp of the AMA's
Bureau of Investigation had ever thus invidiously named trademarks—and
then only of patent medicines, cosmetics and medical gadgets. CR was
proud of taking "the risks of controversy and antagonism involved in
dealing with inferior products in terms which anyone can understand and
apply. . . . If we believe a thing to be true we will say it even if it ruins our
grandmother's silk-dying business or your Uncle Harry's trade in canned
asparagus." [205]

It did not go into the risk of Uncle Harry's suing. CR guarded against
that by imposing confidentiality on subscribers, who signed a pledge never
to divulge CR's findings outside the immediate family. Materials mailed to
them included follow-up warnings. Otherwise, it might well have been
legally disastrous thus to circulate CR's expert, disinterested judgment that
Heelantoe's fancy grade of wool socks gave only 80 percent as good wear as
its chief competitor's, no matter what the Heelantoe Boys, formerly Bibb &
Tucker on the Pantages time, sang about them on the radio. When tested in
court by irate manufacturers, this shield of confidentiality held good even
though the members' private indiscretions very probably kept it full of
small holes. By the end of the 1930's in any case judges had so liberalized
decisions in this ticklish field that both CR and CU—Consumers Union, by
then firmly on its way—could scrap the shield and widen their influence by
newsstand sales of periodicals publicly calling such-and-such a spade poor
value. The consequent loosening up has now gone so far that advertisers
who once owlishly disparaged the competition only as "Brand X" now
come right out and say our compact costs $100 less than Volkswagen and
gives more gadgets for the money.

However gingerly about attacking the competition by brand name, the
advertising industry of the 1920's otherwise threw its weight about quite
heedlessly and was well cast as Goliath to CR's David—that is, as an
overgrown menace that needed cutting down to size. The section on
"Advertising" in *Civilization in the United States* was done by J. Thorne
Smith, an experienced writer of advertising copy who presently kicked over
the traces to write ribald—as the 1920's understood ribaldry—fantasies that
became a small cult. After an intimately well-founded attack on his bread
and butter, Smith needed some on-the-other-hand. The best he could come
up with was: Advertising's popularization of soap, toothpaste, deodorants
and such had gratifyingly raised the average level of personal cleanliness in

America. Its methods sometimes promoted good causes. It had greatly improved America's typography. And it afforded a living to many graphic artists who might otherwise have had to drop the habit of eating. He could have added that it had developed electric outdoor display so magnificently that for out-of-towners and wonder-struck visitors from Europe Times Square after dark ranked with the Grand Canyon as something to see. All true as far as they went, but obviously amounting to only drops of mitigation in a vast bucket of reproach against advertising there and then. As one looks back through it today, it looks rather less raucous and unscrupulous than memory recalls. But it was a limited period. Madison Avenue was just feeling its way into broadcasting; TV did not exist. With mere printed words and pictures how could it be as blatant as we have come to expect?

Advertising's own plea in mitigation then as now would have been a blast of prideful economics—and by no means altogether nonsense. The mass demand supporting mass production, the backbone of the American economy, was to an important extent—just how much depended on the taste and fancy of the speller—the advertisers' creation. Cut back its impact on automobiles, silk stockings, breakfast foods, winter sunshine and so on, said Madison Avenue, and grass would grow in the streets of Detroit, Indianapolis, Battle Creek and Santa Barbara. And since that impact depended on two things—volume of insertions and extravagance of emotional appeal—to modify either would be extremely dangerous. The argument had flaws. Much of advertisers' money went not into widening their industry's market but into trying to increase the individual firm's share of it. Another large fraction went not into stimulating the gross national product but into competition among industries for the consumer's dollar—persuading him to spend it on the movies instead of a quart of ice cream. Anyway, nobody knew how much the rising demand for which advertising took credit came not of its well-applied skills but of continuing rise in population plus shifts in buying habits among people shifting from country to city. Worse, a few highly solvent, impressively large businesses with sharp competition, such as Hershey's Chocolate, advertised hardly at all. Yet the stubborn residue of value under all Madison Avenue's defensive bluster persisted. It might have been interesting as semiscientific experiment to close down all the agencies for a few years and see what happened. But the trial was no likelier than the adoption of the Golden Rule among jockeys. In good times advertise to keep your ball rolling and your competition's stymied. In bad times advertise to start yours rolling again. Those were principles pretty well taken for granted.

How far the advertising dollar called the tune on editorial policy has been touched on. That it may have been less than liberals suspected does not mean that the extent to which it obtained was not pernicious. "He won't play straight for an advertiser," a man close to a very great editor once told me, "but he won't go out of his way to spit in his eye either." From the economist's point of view a more serious charge was that advertising fattened on the pyramiding national bad habit of wanting a wider variety of things or fancier versions of things already possessed—and buying them on time. Computerized bookkeeping had not yet come along to make available interest-bearing credit cards and bank loans for go-now-pay-later vacations. But a distinct and growing hazard had nevertheless been created by the snowballing amount of simpler consumer credit that represented sales of automobiles, radios, furniture . . . all a tribute to the advertisers' skill at persuading too many Americans that they could no longer—why should they?—do without some kind of car. Or a larger, shinier car. Or a second car for suburban convenience. The temptation content of it all led many to agree with the cliché that the advertisements in the *Saturday Evening Post* were as entertaining as the stories and articles in between. Actually no advertisement ever written lived in the same world as what Lardner, Harry Leon Wilson *et al.* wrote for the *Post.* But the cliché did reflect the waves of simpleminded daydreaming profitable for advertisers occasioned by the picture of the beautiful young people zooming through Arcady in their Jordan Playboy or the dewy young housewife's beaming pride in her new kitchen of matching stove, refrigerator and counters.

Hard goods represented the bulk of consumer credit dollars, but they had help indirectly from other effects of advertising on consumption. Few automobile ads carried the sleekly voluptuous persuasiveness of the Coles Phillips girl purring over her silk-to-the-top stockings. As they became absolute necessity for schoolteacher and stenographer alike, their fragility and high price so nibbled away salaries that when a girl had to have a new winter coat—not of fur, just something becoming to keep out the cold—the installment plan at high interest was also an absolute necessity. CR's M. C. Phillips wrote a book *Skin Deep*, about the further inroads on a girl's paycheck made by insidiously advertised lotions, creams, astringents, eyewashes and such doing little or nothing for her—some were actually harmful—and sold at exorbitant markup to make them sound magically important. The book sold gorgeously well. But when Miss Phillips, talking to working girl groups, said that that lipstick from Woolworth's was the same as the one sold at several times the price under the brand name of the Marquise de Carabas, they sometimes objected resentfully that they had as much right to expensive lipsticks as any girl on Park Avenue.

At least the thing did redden lips, the absurdly expensive soaps did lather, whereas most cosmetics, drugstore stuff for self-medication, hosiery, underwear and gadgetry were extravagantly extolled in advertisements with little or no concern with whether the claims the copy made had any substance. Too often the customer's money bought him only a psychological lift from half-witted intangibles. And on worthy and unworthy items alike the cost of advertising was loaded pro rata. So was the wholesale salesman's commission. The consumer did get a certain advantage from the mass market thus created and sustained. But the excessive lengths to which sales effort and advertising were carried probably canceled most of it in the long run.

Not that the 1920's invented irresponsible misrepresentation; in some fields they had reformed the swindles of previous decades. Until Dr. Wiley camped on their trail, followed by a posse of magazine reporters, patent medicine advertisers had for generations filled the back pages of newspapers with Grandma's Old Homestead Swamp Bitters for everything from botulinus to bots. After the Armistice that sort of thing dwindled. But the technique had an elegant new future in slick-paper magazines. Mellifluously worded, masterfully illustrated full-page advertisements came insisting that to eat Fleischmann's yeast made one beautiful, emotionally serene and winsomely happy—it's really intestinal flora that account for one's charm. Use Listerine and not only cure your halitosis*—a neologism coined by advertising—but also "avoid sore throat and those more serious illnesses that start with throat infections." Actually Listerine masks foul breath only while its own distinctive bouquet persists and is no less—but no more— effective than warm water against throat infections, but that had no bearing on the blazing success of the halitosis campaign. It set a fashion of fear-appeal ads and put "Even Your Best Friend Won't Tell You" in the same Hall of Fame for slogans as "His Master's Voice," "99 44/100% Pure," "That Schoolgirl Complexion," "Time to Re-Tire," "You Just KNOW She Wears Them," "Ask the Man Who Owns One," "The Ham What Am." . . . Few under the age of forty could now match all those to the products they represented. But in their day they were the universally recognized predecessors of the singing commercial. The purely visual equivalents were the Campbell [soup] Kids, Rose O'Neill's rubicund national symbols of well-nourished health, and J. C. Leyendecker's shinily clean-cut Arrow Collar Man, now as dead as *Homo neanderthalensis,* so many of whose incarnations looked like a somewhat sterner version of F. Scott Fitzgerald.

Another standby of the old patent-medicine racket—the testimonial advertisement—also came to elegantly impudent flower on Madison Avenue in the 1920's. In its elder form it was mussy linecuts of hard-favored housewives from Oolitic, Indiana, or Level, Maryland, testifying that that misery in the back had let up after they took two bottles of the green label Swamproot. Now it was beautiful actresses and patrician young matrons in achingly fashionable dinner gowns ascribing their ravishing complexions to their exclusive devotion to Thistledown Soap. The presumption was that the cash fees, said to be substantial, paid to former debutantes for the use of

---

* The word is now firmly fixed in the language. It could have been worse. In the early Listerine campaign it had a running mate, "halitoxic," mercifully long since forgotten.

their faces on full pages in *Vanity Fair* and the top mass-circulation women's magazines went to one's favorite charity. In the arrangements I made for Broadway leading ladies no sordid cash changed hands. The economic consideration was one case of soap delivered at the stage door, and the main point was the appearance of one's most charming recent photograph in millions on millions of copies of magazines. Obviously the other presumption was that millions on millions of American women would be stirred to go clamoring for Thistledown or, less crudely, that the combination of those prestige-rich names, lovely faces and hard-sell copy would create a subliminal association that would guide choice at the drugstore counter.

Apparently accumulating years of experience demonstrated the effectiveness of the device to the satisfaction of Madison Avenue and clients. It went onward and upward into the sprightly "She's engaged—she's lovely—she uses Ponds!" campaign and the remarkable fatuity of the "Man of Distinction" series etc. etc. But testimonials from a man had already reached the peak of effrontery late in the 1920's. The ship's company of the U.S. Lines' *America* (Captain George Fried commanding) deservedly became overnight heroes for rescuing the crew of a sinking freighter in mid-Atlantic in impossibly wild weather. Madison Avenue and the American Tobacco Company took to the radio. Even before the *America* made New York City, huge advertisements had Captain Fried telling the nation in the first person over his signature how Lucky Strikes had put new life into the freighter's exhausted deckhands and that Luckies were indispensable to his personal well being as nerve settlers and insurance against gaining weight—whenever he craved something fattening, he obeyed Luckies' current slogan: "Reach for a Lucky instead of a sweet!" The evening after the *America* docked, her officers were guests of the management in a stage box at the Marx Brothers' *Animal Crackers*, arriving after the show had begun. Groucho Marx was onstage. The show stopped, a spotlight picked out the box, Fried in front center, the orchestra played "The Star-Spangled Banner," everybody rose and cheered. . . . When the house was finally quiet again and the spotlight turned off, one expected Groucho to pick up lines and business where he had left off. Instead, he went over to the box, offering a pack of cigarettes from his pocket. "Have a Lucky, Cap?" he said.

Some years earlier the advertising mind of the 1920's had done itself even prouder in a book—the roaring best seller *The Man Nobody Knows*, by Bruce Barton of the great Madison Avenue agency Batten, Barton, Durstine & Osborn. The Man was Christ. The handsome, genial author had worked for grass-roots publishing enterprises before becoming one of the kings and councillors of the advertising earth. He came legitimately by the earnest respect with which—in spite of his consequent grotesquery—he regarded his subject and the Scriptures that told His story. Barton's father was a Presbyterian parson down in Tennessee who helped son with the book and its sequel, *The Book Nobody Knows*, and doubtless had something to do with son's telling use of the old hot-gospel pulpit trick of taking a tiny hint from the Bible and inflating it into a familiarly detailed parallel to the congregation's experiences and proclivities. Run-of-mine preachers shared that with Billy Sunday bringing Salome on as a carnival cooch dancer and Bouck White wishfully seeing Christ as a Wobbly agitator.

The successful, powerful, affluent, enterprising, manipulative leaders of American business—and their henchmen and those emulous of their prestige—were the targets of Barton's study of Christ. As a boy in Sunday school, he wrote, he had been put off by the conventional pictures of Christ, the all-powerful Saviour of mankind, as resembling an insipid woman with a beard. When, come to man's estate, he searched the Gospels himself, he found a man who wrought vigorously with plane and adze as a "successful carpenter," often slept outdoors, took long walks and was so muscular that no money changer dared resist Him in the Temple. Far from being a milk-and-water "killjoy," He was "the most popular dinner guest in Jerusalem" and—here the flattery of the business world began to brown nicely on top—far from being a passive sufferer, He "picked up twelve men from the bottom ranks of business and forged them into an organization that conquered the world. . . . Surely no one will consider us lacking in reverence if we say that every one of the 'principles of modern salesman-ship' on which business men so pride themselves, are brilliantly exemplified in Jesus' talk and work. . . ." * [206]

Here was the former assistant sales manager of the P. F. Collier Company, publishers, making the key speech at a convention of Rotary and Kiwanis chaplains and overdoing it—again America's besetting sin, one of the few generalized reproaches against that much commented-on nation that holds water. On he swirled from salesmanship to advertising: "As a profession . . . young . . . as a force . . . old as the world. The first four words ever uttered, 'Let there be light,' constitute its charter. All nature is vibrant with its impulse. The brilliant plumage of the bird is color advertising directed to the emotions of its mate"; the stars that (the Psalmist said) "Thou hast ordained" were "the first and greatest electric sign." [207] Yet nobody getting that far could complain of the growing odor of blasphemy. There had been fair warning. The epigraph of the book, the first

---

* Actually the Gospels, Barton's stated sources, call Christ a carpenter only once (*Mark* 6:3) and this, according to St. Origen, the greatest early Christian expert on these texts, is a mistake owing to misreading (*cf. The Interpreter's Bible*); in any case nothing is said of His success. For the rest, Christ often slept outdoors because His mission made Him much of a vagrant; He walked much because persons who could not afford beasts of burden had no other way to get about in the Holy Land then—no buses. Barton deduced His popularity as dinner guest from a few minor instances in which those interested in His teaching asked Him to come and eat. Whether Barton owed this to Unity's aforementioned ideas of His social standing I do not know.

thing catching a reader's eye, is Christ's words to His troubled parents in the Temple: "Wist ye not that I must be about my Father's *business?*" (Luke 2:49. Italics Barton's.)

It sounds like a passage excised from the manuscript of *Babbitt* because an editor thought it too overdrawn. In 1925–26, President Coolidge's first years in his own right, with the stock market lengthening its stride to take the ache out of the collapse of the Florida boom, *The Man Nobody Knows* sold hundreds of thousands in the same bookstores, if not necessarily to the same people, in which *Babbitt* had been a runaway best seller three years earlier. For advertising's swooning self-admiration was not likely to disconcert the equally self-admiring build-up-the-area real estate developer, the omniscient stockbroker, the omnipotent widget manufacturer, the statesmanlike investment banker midwifing Peruvian bonds—all the large and middle-sized economic nobility in stiff collars whose pictures appeared in the *American* magazine month after month on featured interviews about the Secret of My Success and how it exemplified the importance of Vision and Service in the Religion of Business. All those narcissistic egos converged on the doctrine, sometimes tacit, sometimes condescendingly spelled out, that they knew exactly what they were doing and what they were doing was exactly the right thing for God's country. The only difference between them and the president of Space & Billings—on whom, directly or indirectly, most of them believed they depended to keep the inflationary hot air pumping into their profit and loss statements—was that no matter how windily they blew their own horns, he was a professional making a good thing out of knowing how to blow even more so. As the end of the 1920's approached, advertising and its handmaiden, public relations, had permeated the national economy with exhilarating extravagances, and their dazzled clients had come to believe in their own wishful nonsense.

A great many others contributed to the big-shot community's psychological delinquency by taking them as seriously as they did themselves. Their aura of economic statesmanship impressed even André Siegfried, an exceedingly hardheaded French economist who wrote a condescendingly astringent best seller about America in the mid-1920's. Among the few things he admired in his six months' tour was the way "The Wall Street banker, the director of a Chicago department store, and the Los Angeles real estate agent [study] charts . . . showing wholesale and retail prices, wages and rates of discount. In periods of calm they endeavour to foresee business storms and depressions . . . like meteorologists, observe the . . . barometer and wind-gauge of business . . . they believe implicitly in economic science. . . ." [208] But three years after his approving visit to their instrument boards it was shatteringly clear that they had been doing precious little dial interpreting—instead, they had been concentrating on the economic equivalent of the *Racing Form*.

There is no intersection of Madison Avenue and Wall Street. If there were, the 1920's would have erected there a monument to the New Era crowned with a statue of Calvin Coolidge. Apparently it was he who so named the skewedly exuberant American economy in the course of a speech extolling a "new era of prosperity" [209]—"an era of high wages and prices, 'easy' credit and satisfactory profits . . . [continuing] indefinitely," [210] as Erik Erikson later defined it from the vantage point of the 1930's. "Silent Cal" had been doing a good deal of talking to encourage that sort of illusion and congratulate his countrymen on the rewards of their virtues. "The requirements of [American] existence have passed beyond the standard of necessity into the region of luxury," he told them at the end of 1928. "The main source of these unexampled blessings is the integrity and character of the American people." [211]

Andrew Mellon, who, as industrial emperor of oil, aluminum and so on and member of the Harding-Coolidge Cabinets as Secretary of the Treasury, was in a position to know, also seemed convinced that America had found the economic equivalent of the philosopher's stone. In the press and sometimes over the radio dozens and scores of sententious big shots were claiming personal credit for their alleged part in this miracle. They took their tone not only from Coolidge and Mellon but also from Herbert Hoover, who, though he had private misgivings about some of the financial symptoms of the New Era, spoke ringingly in 1928 of the glory of "rugged individualism" and described the American notion of progress as recently changing from the mere "full dinnerpail to the full garage." * [212] To share this euphoria had become the responsible citizen's duty and virtue; to question it was a civic sin. And the outward and visible sign of it all was the Great Bull Market.

What was happening on Wall Street did bear embarrassing resemblance to what had so devastatingly waxed and waned in Florida a few years earlier. Its raw materials were, however, securities rather than land—which from the point of view of a savage unaccustomed to pieces of paper would have made it seem even less substantial—and its scale was far less regional, nearer national. Symptoms grew unmistakably grave by 1924, when the New York Stock Exchange began ebulliently to reflect industry's buoyant recovery from post-War hard times. As volume of business and the profits of many industries continued to rise, stocks of more companies began to look brilliantly attractive. Lively buying of them nudged quotations on the Big Board higher and higher until—just as had happened in Florida—the economic facts lying beneath projected values began to be lost sight of. Stocks were, as Colonel Leonard Ayres of the Cleveland Trust Company told the American Bankers Association in 1928, selling "on expectation

---

* George Seldes' highly conscientious *The Great Quotations* rejects the "chicken in every pot and two cars in every garage" usually attributed to Hoover. It does allow the above quotations and points out that the chicken in the pot is somehow a borrowing from Henry IV of France.

rather than realization" [213]—that is, because of their developing habit of going up, up, up in the morning paper with small heed to situations more than half a mile from the corner of Broad and Wall. For instance, Radio Corporation of America was a flashy favorite throughout the entire sleigh ride without ever paying a single dividend.

Now and again during the golden five or six years the upward rush of stock quotations faltered, even slipped back temporarily, while professional traders stroked their beards and spoke of "technical corrections" to impress the financial reporters without cooling the amateurs off too long. When an individual stock swooped downward, it might mean the climax of a "pool"—jugglery now frowned on but accepted then, a contrived show of frantic buy-and-sell activity to attract attention to Amalgamated Widgets to tempt buyers not in the know; then, once their buying had pushed the price high enough, the insiders "pulled the plug" and unloaded, making whacking profits at the outsiders' cost. Several times—particularly in 1926 and 1928—inadvertent misfires of more complicated origin caused many leading issues to sputter and cough at the same time in a "shake-out" causing widespread nervousness. But moneymen spoke reassuringly, Mellon setting the tone: ". . . no cause for worry. The high tide of prosperity will continue," [214] and the roar of the self-feeding fire storm picked up again.

Just as the option-to-buy replaced actual titles to Florida lots as fuel when speculation really got airborne, so did stock buying on margin—in effect borrowing from one's broker most of the funds for a speculative purchase—dominate Wall Street. The device had long existed to enable professional speculators, whose educated guesses and inside tips were warp and woof of normal stock exchange activity, better to carry out their useful function of maintaining a day-in-and-day-out securities market—with considerable (if chancy) profit to themselves and fatter (and certain) commission to brokers. For the nibbler drawn by the market's growing glitter, the amateur going on rumor and hope, this buying on margin became treacherously attractive. It let him deal in thousands by committing only hundreds, which felt important. It set him frequenting the "customers' rooms" of brokers' offices crowded by fellow addicts gossiping about stocks, which was exciting. He might get nipped in a pool or a general temporary deceleration and be sold out because he couldn't raise enough additional margin. But while the Great Bull Market lasted, he was likelier to win than to lose—a thing true of no other form of gambling in which the house takes a steady percentage off the top—and that made him think he was clever.

So Wall Street in the latter 1920's was about as implausible a spectacle as Miami in 1925. While enough participants kept on acting on the belief that everything was always going up and up, it was true. Least likely to lose was the bank that charged the broker high interest for the money he lent to his margin customers on the security of the stocks they bought. Before the party was over, large corporations making high profits found it paid better to put them into such call loans than into more efficient plant or raising the hands' wages or the stockholders' dividends or—as 'the great Taylor had advised—lowering the price of products to widen their market. That made it more difficult for the banking system to control stock speculation when that unpopular possibility was broached. And the more it developed, the greater the Wall Street tumor swelled at the expense of healthier tissues.

People worth millions or a hundred thousand, people with sizable cash savings, people with small salaries got in. Significantly the characters in Philip Barry's comedy *Holiday* (1928) took it for granted that the hero, wanting a competence to retire on young, had only to know the right people and play Wall Street for a few years. In large cities, where financial gossip seethed, particularly in New York City, where Broadway actually stopped talking angels and grosses to talk RCA and United Corporation, bellhops, barbers, elevator starters listened sharp for rumors and had miniature accounts at a nearby branch of Wisenheimer and Company, Members New York Stock Exchange. Prowling the Street in 1928, Morris Markey found that though brokers' office help seldom got around rules against their playing the market, the district's bootblacks and office scrubwomen were often addicted. So were newspapermen covering the Street. With his noted scientific caution in matters of mass psychology John B. Watson linked this to the much discussed erotic laxity of the Jazz Age: ". . . sex has become so free and abundant . . . that it no longer provides the thrill it once did . . . gambling in Wall Street is about the only thrill we have left." [215] At least that overingenious suggestion hinted at a probable affinity between the movies' Jazz Age and the simultaneous cult of speculation. Playing the market was the Younger Generation's elders' cognate to necking? Flaming Middle Age. . . .

Subsequent folklore made too much of all that, of course. "Everybody was in the market . . . the whole nation on a stock gambling spree. . . ." In certain circles it did seem so. Yet the most liberal estimates of the number of brokers' customers involved throughout never exceed 1,500,000. It is probably high to postulate 500,000 to 600,000 buying on margin in a given year—that is, little more than 1 American in 200, which is no cultural epidemic. Nor was participation of people with anomalously slim resources altogether new. In the wild days of the early 1870's, the era of Black Friday and the railroad wars, New Yorkers noted with amused dismay that hack drivers and barkeeps were taking fliers in gold and trying to ride Jay Gould's coattails. The notorious bucket shops (fly-by-night brokers' offices) of the turn of the century fed on gullible small potatoes. This time, though, the number of moths was far larger to match the unprecedented size and brightness of the flame that through radio as well as the press cast its distorting shadows and stultifying fumes coast to coast. Yet in today's terms it was no big market. The daily listing of issues traded on the Big Board hardly covered a full newspaper page. A 6,000,000-share day meant either extreme bullishness or a sharp temporary drop.

The aspect difficult to exaggerate is the adenoidal imbecility of so many of the players, as in the speculative consequences of Charles A. Lindbergh's solo flight across the Atlantic in May, 1927. With the possible exception of Babe Ruth's home run records, that was *the* event of the decade up to then. Here was a lanky, shy but formidably capable lad with an old-swimming-hole grin accomplishing with an extremely photogenic and human-interest-rich modesty what man had never done before. In the narcissistically morbid Jazz Age his diffident wholesomeness and hygienic good looks pushed gangsters and love nests off the front page. Suddenly the public realized it was tired of speakeasy fetor and got a little high on the unwonted stimulus of a breath of fresh air. Overseas the Lone Eagle was taken just as big, doubtless because he contrasted so favorably with the previous stereotype of the American tourist tipsy on champagne and talking too loudly while plastering his suitcase with devalued francs. Indeed what the newspapers did with Lindbergh was so well calculated to improve the American image that one almost suspected Ivy Lee of having had a hand in it.

It was also fine promotion for flying. Most appropriately the impromptu confetti showered on Lucky Lindy, once just another airmail pilot called Slim, as he was paraded through the financial district contained much paper tape from stock tickers. For stocks connected with aviation rose sharply for no better reason than that his feat had drawn simple minds' attention to potentialities on which the air-minded had been working for years. This emotional pressure increased steadily as Lindbergh went to work prospecting air-service routes in Latin America for the nascent airlines—and in the process met, wooed and married a daughter of the Morgan partner, Dwight Morrow, who was then U.S. ambassador in Mexico City. Maybe there was at least some half-superstitious sense in taking the young man's obviously promising future as a good financial omen for the flying industry. But there was none whatever in the ensuing high point of Wall Street daffiness—a rush to buy the stock of Seaboard Airline among people too little acquainted with business affairs to know it was a railroad.

In the summer of 1925 the Florida boom had spiraled upward unabated. In the summer of 1929 Wall Street, usually less active in the vacation season, continued to seethe, and John J. Raskob, recently finance chairman of General Motors, national chairman of the Democratic Party and head of the company then planning the Empire State Building to ornament the New Era, gave an interview to Samuel Crowther, veteran interpreter of big shots for slick magazines. The title that the *Ladies' Home Journal* put on it was "Everybody Ought to Be Rich." It deplored savings banks as mere interest-bearing dead ends for dollars one might have to spare. Keeping money withdrawable like that tempted one's brother-in-law to tap it for a loan to pay for his wife's operation. . . . Anybody who had put $10,000 into General Motors in 1919 would now be worth more than $1,500,000. "And General Motors is only one of many first-class industrial corporations. . . . In my opinion the wealth of the country is bound to increase at a very rapid rate. . . ." [216] A man saving $15 a month invested in one of the new investment trusts that Raskob and many others had been creating—companies owning stock in other companies—and letting income and rights accumulate could expect to be worth at least $80,000 in twenty years. . . .

That came on the newsstands in late September, when, in spite of what can now be seen as significant storm warnings, the consensus was still as bullish as Raskob's public utterances. The investment trusts that he recommended were gloriously conspicuous among stocks leading the pack. The plush transatlantic liners had installed brokers' offices so fat-cat passengers could keep up the game by radio during their five-day crossings. In *The Gumps* comic strip chinless Andy Gump had been making killings in the market—which could have been but probably was not a sardonic hint that in that kind of Wall Street any fool could clean up.

Caution again, however—subsequent legend about "Nobody saw it coming," the savvy old pros and the bleating amateurs all went over the falls together, is not too reliable. For months there had been isolated instances of cooler heads looking over the edge and growing dizzy enough to take unobtrusive safety measures. In 1928 Eugene Meyer, impeccably professional moneyman, was asking other moneymen, "What will happen when they forget to bid?" [217] Raskob himself had been selling many of his holdings because, he said, his political role made it advisable. Bernard Baruch had been uneasy ever since 1927, when the Federal Reserve Board, created to keep the economic ship trimmed, lowered its discount rate to oblige the Bank of England, which pumped still more brokers' loan money into Wall Street. Though still making New Era-ish public statements in the spring of 1929, he had long been following the old maxim that nobody ever went broke taking a profit and was gradually selling off his volatile stocks and putting the proceeds into gold and tax-exempt bonds. Joseph P. Kennedy, father of politicians, whose speculator's bloodstream ran as cool as Baruch's, was also getting out early in 1929, telling a crony, "Only a fool holds out for the top dollar." [218] Albert H. Wiggin, president of the Chase National Bank, was selling his own bank's stock short in the summer of 1929. In another context George Hartford, unable to "go along with all their big [that is, New Era-ish] talk," [219] was keeping the A&P out of any but very short leases after 1927.

Some amateurs with, of course, far smaller commitments also managed to get off the escalator before it left them pawing thin air at the top. Benjamin Cohen, soon to be a brilliant lawyer-planner for the New Deal, was one. Others were lucky enough to be warned in time—and follow the warning—

by a young, minor but brilliant Wall Streeter, John W. Pope, an early graduate of the Harvard Business School, whose steely analytical skills led him to unfashionable skepticism long before the bottom fell out. Bernays was among those benefiting by Pope's private insistence that hell was going to pop. Then there was the psychiatrist to whom a certain very highly considered veteran Wall Streeter was sent by anxious friends. He had been going around questioning the permanence of the New Era and the popular certainty that stocks would keep on going up forever. Such unorthodoxy seemed to augur ill for his mental and emotional health, it was felt, and he allowed himself to be persuaded to seek medical help. First he explained to the doctor why his friends had sent him; then why he held such iconoclastically deviant views. The psychiatrist considered, declared him one of the sanest men he had ever met and sold out his own stockholdings —just in time.

Actually as the 1920's wore thin, the Jazz Age was showing other signs of losing its grip along with Henry Ford and the industrialist seeking PR counsel. Its euphoria reached the high point not with the raucous advent of the Charleston but in 1927 with that totally unjazzy episode of the Lindbergh flight. The following fall Atlantic City's not exactly unsophisticated hotel men made the unjazzy decision, maybe cryptically significant, to suspend the Miss America contest because, if you please, it had suddenly occurred to them it was undignified. The very existence—and steady growth—of Consumers Research while times were allegedly so piping could be considered a breath of a new climate. Such symptoms fitted with the examples of the several impressive Big Frogs who, as above, sensed thundery line squalls in time and of the indeterminable number of tadpoles who acted on the judgment—or pure hunch—that the house of cards was built too high. Conceivably the GBM could have turned progressively soggy and gradually let the Jazz Age down into the economic dumps without the excitements of cataclysm. But that would not have suited the style of this self-dramatizing decade, specializing in self-proclaimed economic statesmen and self-pitying spiritual exiles, committed like the heroine of *The Green Hat* to never being let off anything. Gamely the GBM hung on until the last quarter of the last year of the decade, managing to give the Jazz Age the kind of bang it would have chosen—no matter how many whimpers were bound to ensue.

Portal to portal, Sarajevo to the Great Crash, it had taken no longer than the life of a healthy small dog. A boy child conceived in August, 1914, would have barely attained his first long trousers when the curtain rang down. But it was long enough to have cantilevered the glittering bridge between the War already capitalized as uniquely catastrophic and the Depression—capitalized for the same reason.

Appendix of Definitions

IN dealing with ideological groups significant in America during and after World War I this book uses the following labels and usually observes the following definitions. All these terms have been so misused by propagandists and public scolds, however, that accuracy in employing them is hardly possible.

LIBERAL: The writer's private definition is: Disposed to consider the preamble and amendments the most important parts of the Constitution. To square with customary recent usage, however, "liberal" must mean something like: Temperamentally inclined to welcome changes promising wider social and economic responsibilities usually but not necessarily of a sort tending toward collectivism (*q.v.*); usually also concerned with maintaining individuals' rights and interests particularly when threatened by property rights.

PROGRESSIVE: Used here only with a capital *P* to mean the kind of liberal once associated with Theodore Roosevelt's Bull Moose episode. Please distinguish from the specific meaning of Progressive Education worked out in the second section.

RADICAL: Should, of course, mean anybody inclined to get down to the roots of things to effect sweeping changes of whatever flavor. Recent usage confines it to the admittedly collectivist liberal become impatient of gradualism. Radicals tend to go doctrinaire in either the anarchist (*q.v.*) or the Socialist (*q.v.*) direction.

REACTIONARY: Emotionally committed to a Good Old Days of free enterprise, unlimited opportunity and 100 percent Americanism that never existed in any such terms. Often goes with some form of racism, sometimes with some form of religiosity. Shares certain psychopathological traits with extreme radicals. "Fascist" is often applied to the reactionary, but the terms are not congruent, and the context of Fascism is awkwardly European.

COLLECTIVIST: Temperamentally disposed to prefer cooperative to lone-hand enterprise and to believe that social justice is usually advanced in proportion to pooling of ownership of economic enterprises in public hands.

SOCIALIST: One who advocates public ownership and management of all—at the very least the chief—means of economic production. How to bring this about—immediately or gradually, peacefully or violently, whether for moral or economic reasons or both—depends on the kind of socialist. With a capital *S* means a member, avowed or secret, of an organized Socialist group. Since long before World War I Marxist Socialists have been the most conspicuous. They include Communists (*q.v.*), but only the Bolshevik (*q.v.*) segment of Marxist Socialism is now properly called Communist; it has numerous splinters.

RED: Emotionally committed to the Socialism of which a red flag has been the rallying symbol for the last century. Applies to a revolutionary frame of mind including much beyond specific Communism.

ANARCHIST: Emotionally committed to the theory developed in Europe in the last century that governments are the crucial enemies of social justice, and the way to it is by destruction of government and creation of voluntary cooperation. Anarchists vary widely in their notions of how much violence should be undertaken to bring this about.

COMMUNIST: Formally enrolled member of the worldwide Communist parties. In certain non-Communist countries at certain times all or many Communists make a secret of membership. All are presumably under complete party discipline as distinguished from the

FELLOW TRAVELER: A zealous proponent of Communist aims and ideas who, for reasons of expediency or individual unsuitability, is not formally enrolled but presumably follows party directives received directly or indirectly deduced. The Russian term is *popuchik,* which, Max Eastman said, "used to mean a man of independent judgment whose aims coincide with those of the party for a time. . . . Under Stalinization . . . came to mean one who without joining the party, surrenders his independent judgment and 'toes the party line.' " (*Love and Revolution,* 166.)

BOLSHEVIK: (= "majority" in Russian) pertaining to the "Majority" portion of the Russian Social Democrats (Marxist) who split away from the Menshevik (= "minority" in Russian) portion in 1903. On the whole the Bolsheviki were more militant and discipline-minded.

LEFT and RIGHT to mean opposite ends of a graduated political spectrum will be avoided wherever possible. They are imported from traditional European situations, and, though not always meaningless this side of the water, usually oversimplify or distort an American context.

Notes

Full information on the following references is given in the subsequent list of sources quoted; books only, periodicals self-explanatory. The run of *Life* used often has page numbers cropped away.

I. OLD TIMES THAT WERE BEFORE US

1. JOHN and EVELYN DEWEY, *Schools of To-morrow*, 246.
2. LINDSAY, *Selected Poems of* . . . , 32.
3. POST, *By Motor to the Golden Gate*, 246–47.
4. *Ibid.*, 23–24.
5. DREISER, *Hoosier Holiday*, 93.
6. NEVINS, *Ford: The Man* . . . , 138.
7. DOOLITTLE, *Romance* . . . , 137.
8. *Life*, Vol. 68, 877.
9. HARRISON, *Culture Under Canvas*, 108.
10. TARKINGTON, *Turmoil*, 1, 4, 82–85.
11. *American Cookery*, December, 1914.

II. ALL THE LITTLE ACORNS

1. FERBER, *Peculiar Treasure*, 219.
2. DELL, *Briary-Bush*, 250–52.
3. ROBERT PAUL SMITH, *Where Did You Go* . . . , 43.
4. HARRY LEON WILSON, "Ma Pettengill," *Saturday Evening Post*, August 28, 1915.
5. THOMPSON, *Eat and Grow Thin*, 13.
6. NASH, "Curl Up and Diet," in *Bed Riddance*, 79.
7. *Smart Set*, February, 1915.
8. *Life*, Vol. 67.
9. LIPSET, "Cyclical Trends . . . ," *Freedom at Issue*, September–October, 1970.
10. KOELSCH, "Freud Discovers America," *Virginia Quarterly*, Winter, 1970.
11. BRILL, introduction to *Basic Writings of Sigmund Freud*, 29.
12. FREUD, *Basic Writings of* . . . , 95.
13. HALE, *Freud and the Americans*, 392.
14. BRILL, *American Journal of Sociology*, November, 1939.
15. JONES, *Life and Works of Sigmund Freud*, Vol. I, 419.
16. HALE, *Freud and the Americans*, 378–79.
17. STEFFENS, *Autobiography of* . . . , 655.

18. *Forum*, Vol. XIV.
19. MAX EASTMAN, "Exploring the Soul . . . ," *Everybody's*, July, 1915.
20. HOFFMAN, *Freudianism* . . . , 30.
21. MARQUIS, *Hermione and Her Little Group* . . . , 581.
22. HUXLEY, *Jesting Pilate*, 309.
23. BOURNE, *History of a Literary Radical* . . . , 127.
24. McLOUGHLIN, *Billy Sunday* . . . , 147–48.
25. STRATTON PORTER, *Her Father's Daughter*, 149.
26. *Ibid.*, 151.
27. HIGHAM, *Strangers in the Land*, 156.
28. GRANT, *Passing of the Great Race*, 198–99, 57, 23, 35, 80–81.
29. PERKINS, *Yield of the Years*, 28.
30. STODDARD, *Rising Tide* . . . , 183, xxix.
31. *Ibid.*, 308.
32. *Nation*, Vol. III.
33. *Reader's Digest*, February, 1922; September, 1926.
34. LONDON, *Mutiny of the Elsinore*, 197–98.
35. WARE, "Immigration," *Encyclopedia of Social Sciences*, 1st ed.
36. *Life*, May 8, 1924.
37. POMEROY, *Pacific Slope*, 284.
38. WARE, *Greenwich Village*, 241.
39. ANDERSON, *Winesburg, Ohio*, 199.
40. DELL, *Homecoming*, 65, 272.
41. KUMMER, *Harry Leon Wilson*, 41.
42. SINCLAIR LEWIS, *Main Street*, 15, 426.
43. STEFFENS, *Autobiography* . . . , 656.
44. *Harper's Weekly*, October 10, 1914.
45. EASTMAN, *Venture*, 110.
46. SWANBERG, *Dreiser*, 181.
47. SCHORER, *Sinclair Lewis*, 385.
48. HEMINGWAY, *By-line*, 23–25.
49. HOTCHNER, *Papa Hemingway*, 53.
50. DOS PASSOS, introduction to *Three Soldiers* (Modern Library ed.), v.
51. DELL, *Briary-Bush*, 110.
52. DELL, *Homecoming*, 219.
53. Back matter of *Thus Spoke Zarathustra*, Modern Library ed.
54. COWLEY, *Exile's Return*, 17–18.
55. DOS PASSOS, "Against American Literature," *New Republic*, October 14, 1916.
56. EASTMAN, *Love and Revolution*, 71.
57. *New York Times Book Review*, August 22, 1971.
58. MADISON, *Critics & Crusaders*, 455.
59. HALDEMAN-JULIUS, *First Hundred Million*, 30.
60. *The Drama*, Spring, 1912.
61. *Ibid.*, May, 1912.
62. MACKAY, *Little Theater* . . . , 18.
63. HARRY LEON WILSON, *Ruggles of Red Gap*, 162–65.
64. KELLY, *Torch-Bearers*, 10.
65. MARQUIS, *archy and mehitabel*, 20.

66. PUTZEL, *Man in the Mirror*, 7.
67. FRANK, *Our America*, 128.
68. MASTERS, *Across Spoon River*, 410–11.
69. HOFFMAN, *Freudianism . . .* , 354–55.
70. Davis, *Show Window*, 39 n.
71. BOYD, introduction to Anderson, *Winesburg, Ohio* (Modern Library ed.), xv.
72. SINCLAIR LEWIS, *Main Street*, 257.
73. DEEMS TAYLOR, "Music," in Stearns, *Civilization . . .* , 204.
74. LIPPMANN, *Men of Destiny*, 71, 92.
75. SCHORER, *Sinclair Lewis*, 285.
76. BISHOP and WILSON, *Undertaker's Garland*, 18.
77. *Little Review Anthology*, 303.
80. BRITTEN, "School and College Life," in Stearns, *Civilization . . .* , 109.
81. VAN WYCK BROOKS, "The Literary Life," *ibid.*, 188.
82. *Nation*, April 15, 1925.
83. *Ibid.*, December 4, 1925.
84. *Ibid.*, June 10, 1925.
85. MARQUIS, *Best of . . .* , 609.
86. FRANK, *Our America*, 199–200.
87. COWLEY, *Exile's Return*, 118.
88. PARRY, *Garrets and Pretenders*, 343.
89. DOS PASSOS, *One Man's Initiation*, 156.
90. "Americans Are Boys," *Harper's*, July, 1928.
91. STEARNS, *Civilization . . .* , 289.
92. *New York Times Book Review*, August 12, 1973.
93. JOHN HAYNES HOLMES, *I Speak for Myself*, 31.
94. VAN DOREN, introduction to Wagner, *Prize Poems*, 4.
95. DAVIS, *By Elmer Davis*, 20.
96. NORMAN, *Ezra Pound*, 87.
97. MENCKEN, *Prejudices I*, 83–84.
98. GILBERT SELDES, *Seven Lively Arts*, 117.
99. MCFEE, introduction to *Ring Lardner's Best Stories*, vii.
100. ELDER, *Ring Lardner*, 119.
101. DOS PASSOS, *Best Times*, 129.
102. DAVIS, *Show Window*, 39.
103. GILBERT SELDES, *Seven Lively Arts*, 118.
104. *Portable Ring Lardner*, 726–56.
105. DOUGLAS, *Margaret Sanger*, 25.
106. COLE, *History of Fundamentalism*, 42–43.
107. LAKE, "The Real Divisions in Modern Christianity," *Atlantic Monthly*, June, 1925.
108. BERT LESTON TAYLOR, *So-Called Human Race*, 132.
109. HARTT, "The War in the Churches," *World's Work*, Vol. 46.
110. GEORGE SELDES, *Great Quotations*, 668.
111. COLE, *History of Fundamentalism*, 290.
112. DE CAMP, *Great Monkey Trial*, 33.
113. *Ibid.*, 124–25.
114. LIPPMANN, *American Inquisitors*, 10.

115. DE CAMP, *Great Monkey Trial*, 436.

116. BRUMBAUGH, *Six Trials*, 107.

117. COLE, "Fundamentalism," *Dictionary of American History*.

118. FERGUSON, *New Books* . . . , 173.

119. *Ibid.*, 179.

120. *Ibid.*, 215–16.

121. *Ibid.*, 217.

122. Signed pledge displayed at Unity headquarters, November, 1972.

123. FERGUSON, *New Books* . . . , 226.

124. R. K. JOHNSON, *Builder of Bridges*, 76.

125. HARRISON, *Culture Under Canvas*, 146.

126. *Anti-Prohibition Manual*, 18.

127. McLOUGHLIN, *Billy Sunday* . . . , 171.

128. *Ibid.*, 181.

129. GEORGE CREEL, "Salvation Circus," *Harper's Weekly*, June 19, 1915.

130. SANDBURG, *Complete Poems*, 29–30.

131. JOHN REED, "Back of Billy Sunday," *Metropolitan Magazine*, April, 1915.

132. R. K. JOHNSON, *Builder of Bridges*, 68.

133. *Ibid.*, 140.

134. *Ibid.*, 78–79.

135. ADAMIC, CAMPBELL, SCHNEIDER, MASON, *Truth About* . . . , 10.

136. LATELY THOMAS, *Storming Heaven*, 114.

137. LATELY THOMAS, *Vanishing Evangelist*, 176.

138. EASTMAN, *Enjoyment of Living*, 110–11.

139. COLE, *History of Fundamentalism*, 83.

140. JOHN HAYNES HOLMES, *I Speak for Myself*, 101.

141. *Life*, October 1, 1914.

142. GILBERT SELDES, *Seven Lively Arts*, 14.

143. RICHARD GRIFFITH, introduction to Hampton, *History of* . . . , vi.

144. LINDSAY, *Art of the Moving Picture*, 6–7.

145. TARKINGTON, *Penrod*, 39.

146. WAGENKNECHT, introduction to Mrs. Griffith, *When the Movies Were Young*, viii.

147. VAN LOAN, *Buck Parvin and the Movies*, 93.

148. *Motion Picture Story Magazine*, April 1912.

149. GIBBS, *People of Destiny*, 75–77.

150. FULTON, *Motion Pictures*, 22.

151. LINDSAY, *Art of the Moving Picture*, 224.

152. RUGGLES, *Westering Heart*, 239.

153. LINDSAY, *Art of the Moving Picture*, 27–28.

154. LINDSAY, *Selected Poems of* . . . , 34.

155. *Motion Picture Story Magazine*, July, 1912.

156. *Harper's Weekly*, December 19, 1914.

157. GISH, *Movies, Mr. Griffith and Me*, 161–62.

158. *St. Nicholas*, May, 1915.

159. *Ladies' Home Journal*, 1925.

160. *Life*, Vol. 70.

161. HOLT, *Care and Feeding* . . . , 29.

162. *Touchstone*, September, 1918.
163. MURRAY, *History of the Boy Scouts . . .* , 18.
164. LEVY, *Building a Popular Movement*, 24.
165. CAMP FIRE GIRLS, *Wo-He-Lo*, 15.
166. *Ibid.*, 43.
167. COLLIER, *From Every Zenith*, 97.
168. CAMP FIRE GIRLS, *Wo-He-Lo*, 22.
169. "Girl Scouts, Inc.," *Dictionary of American History*.
170. CROY, *Country Cured*, 101.
171. JOHN DEWEY, *Impressions of Soviet Russia*, 78.
172. KEATS, *Schools Without Scholars*, 142.
173. STREET, *Abroad at Home*, 226.
174. BOURNE, *The Gary Schools*, 28–29.
175. NEARING, *The New Education*, 74.
176. WHARTON, *Backward Glance*, 47.
177. CREMIN, *Transformation of the School*, 129.
178. *Ibid.*, 132–35.
179. *Ibid.*, 128.
180. HOOK, *John Dewey*, 16.
181. JOHN DEWEY, "My Pedagogic Creed," in Dworkin, *Dewey on Education*, 29.
182. JOHN DEWEY, "School and Society," *ibid.*, 69.
183. JOHN and EVELYN DEWEY, *Schools of To-Morrow*, 124–25.
184. JOHN DEWEY, "School and Society," in Dworkin, *Dewey on Education*, 55.
185. JOHN DEWEY, "My Pedagogic Creed," *ibid.*, 30, 32.
186. BARR, *Who Pushed Humpty Dumpty?*, 95.
187. CREMIN, *Transformation of the School*, ix.
188. STANWOOD COBB, "What Is Progressive Education?", *Parents' Magazine*, October, 1929.
189. MASSON, "Teaching Children to Teach Themselves," *World's Work*, August, 1922.
190. JOHN DEWEY, "Progressive Education . . . ," in Dworkin, *Dewey on Education*, 120.
191. PARKHURST, *Education on the Dalton Plan*, 18.
192. HUXLEY, *Tomorrow and Tomorrow*, 14–15.
193. KEATS, *Schools Without Scholars*, 115.
194. DE LIMA, *Little Red Schoolhouse*, 17–18.
195. *Ibid.*, 25.
196. STANWOOD COBB, "What Is Progressive Education," *Parents' Magazine*, October, 1929.
197. JOHN DEWEY, introduction to Clapp, "The Use of Resources in Education," in Dworkin, *Dewey on Education*, 127.
198. [HUBBARD], *Abe Martin's Almanac*, n.p.
199. BUNDESEN, *The Baby Book*, n.p.
200. DE LIMA, *Little Red Schoolhouse*, 12.
201. National Congress of Parents and Teachers, *Golden Jubilee History*, 16.
202. *Ibid.*, 19.
203. *Ibid.*, 20.
204. EVELYN DEWEY, *New Schools for Old*, 179–80.

205. NEARING, *The New Education*, 46.
206. WATSON, *Behaviorism*, 234–35.
207. WATSON, *Psychological Care* . . . , 182.
208. BIGELOW, *Sex-Education*, 109.
209. SINCLAIR LEWIS, *Dodsworth*, 236–37.
210. PINKEVITCH, *New Education in the Soviet Union*, 81–82, 336–37.
211. BIGELOW, "Sex-Education," *Encyclopedia of Social Sciences*, 1st ed.
212. WINTER, *Red Virtue*, 161.
213. BARR, *Who Pushed Humpty Dumpty?*, 106–7, 110.
214. WISTER, *Pentecost of Calamity*, 33.
215. PINCHOT, *Breaking New Ground*, 48.
216. SWARD, *Legend of Henry Ford*, 33–34 n.
217. "Frederick Winslow Taylor," *Dictionary of American Biography*.
218. FREDERICK WINSLOW TAYLOR, *Principles of Scientific Management*, 39.
219. New York *Times*, March 22, 1915.
220. FREDERICK WINSLOW TAYLOR, *Principles of Scientific Management*, 28–29:
221. *Ibid.*, 74.
222. *Ibid.*, 136.
223. "Scientific Management," *Encyclopedia of Social Sciences*, 1st ed.
224. TAYLOR SOCIETY, *Memorial Volume*, 76–79.
225. LEBHAR, *Chain Stores in America*, 82.
226. "Medicine . . . Medical Education," *Encyclopedia of Social Sciences*, 1st ed.
227. ROBERT H. EVERT, "The Medical School," *Scientific American*, September, 1973.
228. FLEXNER, *Medical Education* . . . , x.
229. *Ibid.*, 12.
230. *Ibid.*, 166.
231. *Ibid.*, 163–64.
232. FISHBEIN, *Medical Follies*, 54.
233. RALPH LEE SMITH, *At Your Own Risk*, 19–20.
234. FISHBEIN, *Medical Follies*, 86.
235. RALPH LEE SMITH, *At Your Own Risk*, 9.
236. GEORGE CREEL, "Making Doctors While You Wait," *Harper's Weekly*, April 3, 1915.
237. GEORGE CREEL, "Easy Money Doctor," *Harper's Weekly*, April 24, 1915.
238. POST, *By Motor to the Golden Gate*, 229.
239. DUFFUS, *Tower of Jewels*, 120.
240. TODD, *Story of the Exposition*, Vol. II, 318.
241. *Ibid.*, Vol. V, 250.
242. LIPPMANN, *Early Writings*, 4.
243. JAMES, *Exposition Memories*, 17.
244. San Diego *Union*, February 24, 1916.

III. 1914 AND ALL THAT

1. SULLIVAN, *Our Times*, Vol. V, 43.
2. *Life*, August 27, 1914.
3. WISTER, *Neighbors Henceforth*, 29.

4. HALL and NORDHOFF, *Lafayette Flying Corps*, Vol. II, 21.
5. *Hearst's Magazine*, December, 1915.
6. DOS PASSOS, introduction to *One Man's Initiation*, 25 n.
7. NORMAN, *E. E. Cummings*, 60.
8. DOS PASSOS, introduction to *One Man's Initiation*, 61.
9. MILLIS, *Road to War*, 210.
10. EDMUND WILSON, *Prelude*, 150.
11. *Harper's Weekly*, December 12, 1914.
12. LINN, *Jane Addams*, 339.
13. SULLIVAN, *Our Times*, Vol. V, 77.
14. VIERECK and CHESTERTON, *Debate* . . . , 4.
15. *World's Work*, June, 1915.
16. New York *Times*, August 6, 1915.
17. New York *Times*, September 23, 1915.
18. *Life*, February 4, 1915.
19. SWANBERG, *Dreiser*, 183.
20. MILLIS, *Road to War*, 132.
21. LIPPMANN, *Early Writings*, 152.
22. LINDBERGH, *Your Country* . . . , 90, 18, 34.
23. WOODWARD, *Tom Watson*, 453–56.
24. LASSWELL, *Propaganda Technique*, 107.
25. IRVIN COBB, *Paths of Glory*, 79.
26. *Ibid.*, 67. *Cf.* also DUNN, *Five Fronts*.
27. *Metropolitan Magazine*, November, 1914.
28. *Harper's Weekly*, January 30, 1915.
29. *Ibid.*, July 10, 1915.
30. DOS PASSOS, *One Man's Initiation*, 47–49.
31. CUMMINGS, *Enormous Room*, 16.
32. GRAVES, *Goodby to All That*, 234–35.
33. *Life*, September 24, 1914.
34. *Ibid.*, 1914-II, 527.
35. *Ibid.*, 1915-I, 909.
36. GIBBS, *Now It Can Be Told*, 456.
37. GIBBS, *People of Destiny*, 152.
38. Affaires Etrangères, *Violations* . . . , 116.
39. *Harper's Weekly*, November 14, 1914.
40. BRYCE, introduction to *Report* . . . , 39–40.
41. NEILSON, *How Diplomats Make War*, 366.
42. KELLOGG, *Headquarters Nights*, 84–85.
43. SULLIVAN, *Our Times*, Vol. V, 468.
44. JANIS, *So Far*, 157.
45. WISTER, *Neighbors Henceforth*, 13.
46. DUFFUS, *Tower of Jewels*, 117.
47. *Everybody's Magazine*, October, 1915.
48. LARSEN, *Good Fight*, 128.
49. *Life*, January 7, 1915.
50. New York *Sun*, May 7, 1915.
51. MILLIS, *Road to War*, 94.

52. *Survey*, December 30, 1916.
53. LINDSAY, *Collected Poems*, 380–81.
54. LINN, *Jane Addams*, 284, 292–93.
55. *Atlantic Monthly*, December, 1914.
56. WILLIAMS, *In the Claws . . .* , 8.
57. MILLIS, *Road to War*, 99.
58. WHARTON, *Marne*, 31–32.
59. *Life*, Vol. 69.
60. WOLFE, *Strange Communists . . .* , 38–39.
61. LOCHNER, *America's Don Quixote*, 18.
62. New York *Times*, September 9, 1915.
63. MERZ, *And Then Came Ford*, 150–72.
64. New York *Times*, August 5, 1916.
65. LOCHNER, *Always the Unexpected*, 60.
66. NEVINS, *Ford: Expansion . . .* , 53.
67. *Metropolitan Magazine*, October, 1916.
68. HAYWOOD, *Bill Haywood's Book*, 293.
69. DOS PASSOS, *Mr. Wilson's War*, 434.
70. SULLIVAN, *Our Times*, Vol. V.
71. MILLIS, *Road to War*, epigraph, n.p.
72. JOHN HAYNES HOLMES, *I Speak for Myself*, 168.
73. CHAFEE, *Free Speech*, 55–56.
74. HOFSTADTER and METZGER, *Development of Academic Freedom . . .* , 502.
75. *American Mercury*, June, 1927.
76. *Life*, October 18, 1917.
77. MILLIS, *Road to War*, 428–29.
78. JOHN DEWEY, *German Philosophy and Politics*, 35.
79. *American Mercury*, June, 1927.
80. HERSHEY, *Odyssey of Henry Ford*, 82.
81. WELLS, *Mr. Britling . . .* , 328.
82. SULLIVAN, *Our Times*, Vol. V, 339.
83. WISTER, *Pentecost of Calamity*, 87.
84. FITZGERALD, *Beautiful and Damned*, 270–72.
85. LASSWELL, *Propaganda Technique . . .* , 156–57.
86. DOS PASSOS, *One Man's Initiation*, 159.
87. EASTMAN, *Venture*, 43.
88. *Life*, Vol. 75.
89. DOS PASSOS, *Three Soldiers*, 34–35.
90. *American Mercury*, February, 1927.
91. *St. Nicholas*, July, 1917.
92. *St. Nicholas*, April, 1919.
93. SULLIVAN, *Our Times*, Vol. V, 376.
94. CLARKSON, *Industrial America . . .* , 65.
95. *Ibid.*, 73–74.
96. SULLIVAN, *Our Times*, Vol. V, 471.
97. BERT LESTON TAYLOR, *So-Called Human Race*, 230.
98. STALLINGS, *Doughboys*, 301–2.
99. NORMAN THOMAS, *Conscientious Objector . . .* , 23–24.

100. New York *Times*, June 7, 1918.
101. CHAFEE, *Free Speech*, 77.
102. *Ibid.*, 75–76.
103. MOCK and LARSON, *Words That Won the War*, 43–44.
104. New York *Times*, April 6, 7, 1919.
105. CARY, *Prisoner of Grace*, 43.
106. GRAVES, *Goodby to All That*, 88.
107. WEST, *Strange Necessity*, 255.
108. MASON, *Lafayette Escadrille*, 12.
109. JAMES NORMAN HALL, *Kitchener's Mob*, 98–99, 165–66.
110. GIBBS, *Now It Can Be Told*, 146.
111. DOS PASSOS, *1919*, 102.
112. DOS PASSOS, introduction to *One Man's Initiation*, 10.
113. HEMINGWAY, *Men at War*, xvi.
114. LATZKO, *Men in War*, 74.
115. *Ibid.*, 89.
116. HEMINGWAY, *Farewell to Arms*, 196.
117. DOS PASSOS, *1919*, 203.
118. CUMMINGS, *Enormous Room*, 36.
119. Streeter, *Dere Mable*, 24.
120. *Life*, Vol. 73.
121. *American Legion Magazine*, September 27, 1919.
122. WISTER, *Neighbors Henceforth*, 131.
123. *Life*, Vol. 75.
124. HEXAMER, *Address of* . . . , n.p.
125. LIPPMANN, *Early Writings*, 73.
126. WISTER, *Neighbors Henceforth*, 108–9.
127. *Life*, Vol. 75.
128. BENÉT, "Short Ode," *Selected Works*, Vol. I, 438.

IV. SYMPTOMS OF THE MORNING AFTER

1. SULLIVAN, *Our Times*, Vol. V, 6.
2. DOS PASSOS, *Big Money*, 110.
3. GIBBS, *People of Destiny*, 146–47.
4. *Harper's Bazaar*, March, 1919.
5. GISH, *Movies, Mr. Griffith* . . . , 245.
6. *Atlantic Monthly*, January, 1920.
7. *Review of Reviews*, January, 1920.
8. *Life*, September 4, 1919.
9. LIPPMANN, *Early Writings*, 166.
10. DRAPER, *Roots of American Communism*, 204.
11. *Life*, Vol. 75.
12. GENE SMITH, *When the Cheering Stopped*, 150.
13. *South Atlantic Quarterly*, January, 1949.
14. GITLOW, *Whole of Their Lives*, 62–63.
15. FERBER, *Peculiar Treasure*, 171.
16. HICKS, *John Reed*, 114.

17. LIPPMANN, *Early Writings*, 294.
18. O'CONNOR and WALKER, *The Lost Revolutionary*, 97.
19. PHYLLIS McGINLEY, "Public Journal," *Subtreasury of American Humor*, 570.
20. WOLFE, *Strange Communists . . .* , 45.
21. HICKS, *John Reed*, 341.
22. AUSTIN, *26 Jayne Street*, 350.
23. FELIX, *Protest*, 247.
24. RINGEL, *America as Americans See It*, 184.
25. RUSSELL, *Tragedy in Dedham*, 2.
26. JOLL, *Anarchists*, 111.
27. *Life*, Vol. 75.
28. DELL, *Homecoming*, 337.
29. ELDER, *Ring Lardner*, 131.
30. BRYAN, *In His Image*, 229.
31. *World's Work*, May, 1923.
32. WALTER F. WHITE, *Man Called White*, 8.
33. MYERS, *History of Bigotry . . .* , 273.
34. ARNOLD S. RICE, *Ku Klux Klan*, 5.
35. *Ibid.*, 7.
36. FERGUSON, *New Books . . .* , 264.
37. WOODWARD, *Tom Watson*, 450.
38. *World's Work*, June, 1923.
39. ARNOLD S. RICE, *Ku Klux Klan*, 8.
40. *Forum*, December, 1925.
41. McLOUGHLIN, *Billy Sunday . . .* , 274–76.
42. KOENIG, *Bryan*, 621–22.
43. *Forum*, September, 1925.
44. *World's Work*, August, 1923.
45. DAVIS, *Show Window*, 205.
46. New York *Times*, April 14, 1928.
47. TEBBEL, *Compact History . . .* , 257.
48. SANDBURG, *Chicago Race Riots*, 23.
49. *Ibid.*, 29.
50. *Journal of Negro History*, July 1919.
51. SANDBURG, *Chicago Race Riots*, 30.
52. *Ibid.*, iii.
53. *Ibid.*, 35–36.
54. *Ibid.*, 61–62.
55. WALTER F. WHITE, *Man Called White*, 72.
56. *World's Work*, July, 1925.
57. *World's Work*, May, 1924.
58. *Crisis*, February, 1918.
59. O'CONNOR, *Black Jack Pershing*, 43.
60. BRALEY, *Buddy Ballads*, 78.
61. *Crisis*, June, 1919.
62. New York *Times*, July 26, 1904.
63. JAMES WELDON JOHNSON, *Black Manhattan*, 152–53.
64. REID, *Negro Immigrant*, 115.

65. Cronon, *Black Moses*, 10.
66. *Century*, February, 1923.
67. Walter F. White, *Man Called White*, 61.
68. Draper, *Rediscovery* . . . , 13.
69. *Life*, Vol. 77.
70. Fax, *Garvey*, 161.
71. *Century*, February, 1923.
72. Bradford, *Ol' Man Adam* . . . , 263.
73. Fax, *Garvey*, 235.
74. Reid, *Negro Immigrant*, 152.
75. James Weldon Johnson, *Black Manhattan*, 256–59.
76. Wendt and Kogan, *Big Bill of Chicago*, 161–62.
77. *Ibid.*, 95.
78. *Ibid.*, 50–51.
79. Davis, *Show Window*, 231.
80. Wendt and Kogan, *Big Bill of Chicago*, 155.
81. Bright, *Hizzoner* . . . , 166.
82. Wendt and Kogan, *Big Bill of Chicago*, 228–29.
83. *Ibid.*, 326.
84. *Ibid.*, 302.
85. *Ibid.*, 333.
86. *Ibid.*, 357.
87. Loos, *A Girl Like I*, 190.
88. Sargeant, *Jazz* . . . , 200.
89. Sullivan, *Our Times*, Vol. VI, 482.
90. *New Yorker*, August 6, 1972.
91. Hale, *Freud* . . . , 416–17.
92. *Ladies' Home Journal*, August, 1921.
93. *Jazz Monthly*, June–July, 1958.
94. *Ladies' Home Journal*, December, 1921.
95. *Ladies' Home Journal*, January, 1922.
96. Labatut and Lane, *Highways* . . . , 224.
97. *Scientific American*, March, 1923.

V. SELF-MOVED REVOLUTION

1. Advertisement in *Life*, Vol. 86.
2. Johnston, *Legendary Mizners*, 37.
3. Hergesheimer, *Tropical Winter*, 3.
4. Johnston, *Legendary Mizners*, 32.
5. Birmingham, *Right People*, 248.
6. Ballinger, *Miami Millions*, 93.
7. Roberts, "Florida Diversions," *Saturday Evening Post*, February 20, 1926.
8. Davis, *White Pants Willie*, intro.
9. Quoted in Weidling and Burghard, *Checkered Sunshine*, 113.
10. Johnston, *Legendary Mizners*, 215.
11. Tebeau, *History of Florida*, 388.
12. Weidling and Burghard, *Checkered Sunshine*, 133.

13. ROBERTS, "Florida Fever," *Saturday Evening Post*, December 5, 1925.

14. ELDER, *Ring Lardner*, 106.

15. *Life*, Vol. 77.

16. Quoted in LABATUT and LANE, *Highways* . . . , 304.

17. *Life*, Vol. 79.

18. FLAGG, *Boulevards All the Way*, 36, 68.

19. R. L. DUFFUS, "Putting Wheels Under the Old Homestead," *Independent*, February 13, 1926.

20. JARDIM, *First Henry Ford*, 71–72.

21. MARKEY, *This Country of Yours*, 118.

22. Quoted in ASBURY, *Great Illusion*, 325.

23. HAYNES, *Prohibition Inside Out*, 87.

24. U.S. Senate, 71st Congress . . . *Enforcement of the Prohibition Laws*, II, 149.

25. New York *Times*, July 12, 1971.

26. HOWARD, *They Knew What They Wanted*, in Macgowan, *Famous American Plays of the 1920s*, 142.

27. MARKEY, *This Country of Yours*, 290.

28. U.S. Senate, 71st Congress . . . *Enforcement of the Prohibition Laws*, IV, 252.

29. *Ibid.*, V. 49.

30. *Ibid.*, IV, 408–10.

31. *Ibid.*, IV, 903.

32. DAVIS, *Show Window*, 199; 201.

33. U.S. Senate, 71st Congress . . . *Enforcement of the Prohibition Laws*, IV, 444.

34. *Ibid.*, 473–99.

35. PEGLER, *'Tain't Right*, 241.

36. PEGLER, *Dissenting Opinions of Mister Westbrook Pegler*, 128.

37. GLAZER and MOYNIHAN, *Beyond the Melting Pot*, 33.

38. SINCLAIR LEWIS, *Free Air*, 120.

39. SINCLAIR LEWIS, *Prodigal Parents*, 174–77.

40. J. EDGAR HOOVER, "Camps of Crime," *American Magazine*, February, 1940.

41. *Ibid.*

42. SAUL, *Hospitality Magazine*, April, 1967.

VI. OTHER SIDES OF PARADISE

1. FITZGERALD, *Tales of the Jazz Age*, "May Day."

2. [ADAMS, SAMUEL HOPKINS], pseud. WARNER FABIAN, *Flaming Youth*, 59.

3. MARKS, *Plastic Age*, 84.

4. DELL, *Homecoming*, 360.

5. *Ladies' Home Journal*, March, 1924.

6. *Ibid.*

7. SULLIVAN, *Our Times*, VI, 383–96.

8. DAVIS, *Show Window*, 37.

9. *Ladies' Home Journal*, November, 1921.

10. BEGBIE, *More Twice-Born Men*, 36.

11. DRIBERG, *Mystery of Moral Re-Armament*, 120.

12. BEGBIE, *More Twice-Born Men*, 146.

13. *Plain Talk*, December, 1927.

14. *Outlook*, January 7, 1925.
15. *Ibid.*
16. DRIBERG, *Mystery of Moral Re-Armament*, 33.
17. BEGBIE, *More Twice-Born Men*, 21.
18. *Plain Talk*, December, 1927.
19. *Outlook*, January 7, 1925.
20. BEGBIE, *More Twice-Born Men*, 126.
21. MARKEY, *This Country of Yours*, 127.
22. WATSON, *Behaviorism*, 224–25.
23. HOFSTADTER and METZGER, *Development of Academic Freedom . . .* , 380.
24. SHEEAN, *Personal History*, 9–10.
25. VEBLEN, *Higher Learning . . .* , 122–23, 119.
26. BOURNE, *History of a Literary Radical*, 149.
27. FLEXNER, *Universities*, 63, 175–76.
28. RINGEL, *America as Americans See It*, 226.
29. FLEXNER, *Universities*, 84–85.
30. *Life*, September 29, 1928.
31. GALLICO, *Farewell to Sport*, 218.
32. KROUT, *Annals of American Sport*, 257.
33. WEYAND, *Football*, 68.
34. RINGEL, *America as Americans See It*, 122.
35. MacIVER, *Academic Freedom . . .* , 1.
36. *American Association of University Professors Bulletin*, Summer, 1965.
37. *Ibid.*
38. CATTELL, *University Control*, 31.
39. YEOMANS, *Abbott Lawrence Lowell . . .* , 104.
40. HOFSTADTER and METZGER, *Development of Academic Freedom*, 389–90.
41. *Ibid.*, 489.
42. *Science*, May 28, 1971.
43. New York *Times*, April 4, 1971.
44. *Time*, May 10, 1971.
45. *Harper's Weekly*, April 8, 1916.
46. SEYMOUR, *Baseball*, 423.
47. ELDER, *Ring Lardner*, 170.
48. GRANTLAND RICE, *Tumult and the Shouting*, 105–6.
49. PEGLER, *'Tain't Right*, 235.
50. *Ibid.*, 234.
51. ELDER, *Ring Lardner*, 160.
52. GALLICO, *Farewell to Sport*, 33.
53. A. LAWRENCE HOLMES, *More Than a Game*, 132.
54. Indianapolis *News*, February 9, 1924.
55. *Life*, Vol. 83.
56. DELL, *Homecoming*, 278.
57. BROUN and LEECH, *Anthony Comstock . . .* , 15.
58. MYERS, *History of Bigotry . . .* , 253.
59. UPTON SINCLAIR, *Money Writes!*, 102–3.
60. *Life*, June 6, 1923.
61. BISHOP and WILSON, *Undertaker's Garland*, 18.

62. SWANBERG, *Dreiser*, 211.
63. New York *Times*, March 6, 1926.
64. New York *Times*, February 12, 1926.
65. LARSEN, *Good Fight*, 192.
66. LINDSEY and EVANS, *Revolt of Modern Youth*, 174.
67. *Ibid.*, 195.
68. *Ibid.*, 175–76.
69. LARSEN, *Good Fight*, 152.
70. LINDSEY and EVANS, *Revolt of Modern Youth*, 308–9.
71. *Ibid.*, 220.
72. *Ibid.*, 352.
73. LINDSEY and EVANS, *Companionate Marriage*, v.
74. LARSEN, *Good Fight*, 175.
75. *Ibid.*, 220–21.
76. *New Yorker*, February 14, 1928.
77. DAVIS, *Show Window*, 81–82.
78. BERNARD SOBEL, *Burleycue*, 205.
79. ZEIDMAN, *American Burlesque Show*, 11.
80. *Ibid.*, 207, 209–10.
81. *Life*, Vol. 77.
82. DELL, *Briary-Bush*, 218, 221.
83. *Vanity Fair*, December, 1925.
84. DOS PASSOS, *Best Times*, 85.
85. *Stage*, March, 1936.
86. ZEIDMAN, *American Burlesque Show*, 221–22.
87. *TV Guide*, September 1, 1973.
88. *Life*, November 10, 1921.
89. AUSTIN, *26 Jayne Street*, 292.
90. LARSEN, *Good Fight*, 96.
91. ANDREW SINCLAIR, *Better Half*, 337.
92. [HUBBARD], *Abe Martin: Hoss Sense . . .* , n.p.
93. *Ladies' Home Journal*, May, 1925.
94. *Life*, Vol. 82.
95. UPTON SINCLAIR, *Jungle*, 336.
96. SINCLAIR LEWIS, *Main Street*, 404–5.
97. *Ladies' Home Journal*, September, 1922.
98. *Life*, Vol. 75.
99. HARRY LEON WILSON, *Merton of the Movies*, 104–5.
100. *Ibid.*, 23–25.
101. *Ibid.*, 269–70.
102. LOOS, *Girl Like I*, 21.
103. *Ibid.*, 121.
104. *Ibid.*, 116–18.
105. New York *Times*, September 29, 1921.
106. *Literary Digest*, May 7, 1921.
107. *Life*, Vol. 80.
108. New York *Times*, September 22, 1921.
109. New York *Times*, January 1, 1922.

110. New York *Times*, January 8, 1922.
111. GILBERT SELDES, *Seven Lively Arts*, 287.
112. *Fortnightly Review*, January, 1935.
113. New York *Times*, September 29, 1921.
114. *Life*, Vol. 77.
115. *Literary Digest*, May 14, 1921.
116. GILBERT SELDES, *Seven Lively Arts*, 298.
117. MACGOWAN, *Behind the Screen*, 211.
118. NICHOLS, *Star-Spangled Manner*, 265.
119. *New Yorker*, February 18, 1928.
120. BEN W. HALL, *Best Remaining Seats*, 141.
121. *Life*, Vol. 90.
122. OSCAR LEWIS, *Fabulous San Simeon*, 15.
123. HUXLEY, *Tomorrow and Tomorrow . . .* , 178–79.
124. GISH, *Movies, Mr. Griffith . . .* , 152.
125. *Life*, Vol. 83.
126. *Life*, Vol. 77.
127. *Drama*, February, 1912.
128. MACGOWAN, *Footlights Across America*, 40.
129. *Life*, Vol. 83.
130. MACGOWAN, *Footlights Across America*, 40.
131. GILBERT SELDES, *Seven Lively Arts*, 192.
132. *Life*, Vol. 92.
133. JOHN HAYNES HOLMES, *I Speak for Myself*, 93–94.
134. BARNOUW, *Tower in Babel*, I, 126.
135. SINCLAIR LEWIS, *Elmer Gantry*, 384.
136. BARNOUW, *Tower in Babel*, Vol. I, 171–72.
137. *Century*, June, 1924.
138. LANDRY, *This Fascinating Radio Business*, 49.
139. RIEGEL, *Mobilizing for Chaos*, 94.
140. *New Republic*, March 19, 1924.
141. RIEGEL, *Mobilizing for Chaos*, 94.
142. *Life*, Vol. 91.
143. LLEWELLYN WHITE, *American Radio*, 242.
144. LANDRY, *This Fascinating Radio Business*, 205.
145. DOS PASSOS, *Number One*, 45–47.
146. SUNDAY, *Great Love Stories of the Bible*, 90.
147. HARRY LEON WILSON, *Professor, How Could You!*, 113.
148. *New Yorker*, December 4, 1970.
149. *Ladies' Home Journal*, December, 1921.
150. *Woman's Home Companion*, February, 1931.
151. *Saturday Evening Post*, July 31, 1948.
152. *Nation*, June 26, 1929.
153. *Ladies' Home Journal*, April, 1934.
154. New York *Daily News*, August 4, 1972.
155. Indianapolis *News*, December 27, 1930.
156. ADAMS, introduction to [Hubbard], *Abe Martin's Hoss Sense*, n.p.
157. FRED C. KELLY, *Life and Times of Kin Hubbard*, 144.

158. "Frank McKinney Hubbard," *Dictionary of American Biography*.
159. *American Magazine*, May, 1910.
160. FRED C. KELLY, *Life and Times of Kin Hubbard*, 64.
161. *American Magazine*, April, 1924.
162. FRED C. KELLY, *Life and Times of Kin Hubbard*, 104.
163. TEBBEL, *American Dynasty*, 168.
164. *Century*, June, 1924.
165. GOLDBERG, *Rube Goldberg vs. the Machine Age*, 140.
166. *Ibid.*, 212.
167. *New Republic*, XLIII.
168. TEBBEL, *American Dynasty*, 255.
169. Personal communication.
170. BAINBRIDGE, *Little Wonder*, 55.
171. SARGEANT, *In Spite of Myself*, 229.
172. *Time Capsule 1925*, 20.
173. *Ibid.*, 97.
174. *Ibid.*, 142.
175. *Ibid.*, 144.
176. SWANBERG, *Luce and His Empire*, 68.
177. THURBER, *Years with Ross*, 25.
178. KRAMER, *Ross and the New Yorker*, 78.
179. *New Yorker*, May 31, 1927.
180. SANDBURG, *American Songbag*, vii.
181. *Life*, Vol. 89.
182. IRVIN COBB, *Back Home*, 244.
183. *Harper's Bazaar*, February, 1927.
184. MACDONNELL, *Visit to America*, 18.
185. *Vanity Fair*, February, 1929.
186. VAN VECHTEN, *Parties*, 65.
187. SINCLAIR LEWIS, *Work of Art*, 371.
188. LOEWY, *Never Leave Well Enough Alone*, 128.
189. *Fortune*, July, 1930.
190. LOEWY, *Never Leave Well Enough Alone*, 187, 237.
191. *American Magazine*, September, 1906.
192. FLYNN, *God's Gold*, 460.
193. RINGEL, *America as Americans See It*, 285.
194. BERNAYS, *Biography of an Idea*, 395.
195. WATSON, *Behaviorism*, 226.
196. SLOAN, *My Years with General Motors*, 153.
197. *Ibid.*, 163.
198. RAE, *American Automobile*, 98–99.
199. CHASE and SCHLINK, *Your Money's Worth*, 1.
200. *New Republic*, January 26, 1926.
201. CHASE and SCHLINK, *Your Money's Worth*, 60.
202. *Ibid.*, 73–74.
203. *Ibid.*, 264–66.
204. PHILLIPS, *Skin Deep*, viii.
205. CONSUMERS RESEARCH, *Introduction to* . . . , 8.

206. BARTON, *Man Nobody Knows*, preface, n.p.
207. *Ibid.,* 124–25.
208. SIEGFRIED, *America Comes of Age,* 176.
209. BROOKS, *Once in Golconda,* 90.
210. "New Era," *American Dictionary of History.*
211. *Life,* December 28, 1928.
212. GEORGE SELDES, *Great Quotations,* 332.
213. *Life,* October 12, 1928.
214. ROBERT SOBEL, *Great Bull Market,* 54.
215. RINGEL, *America as Americans See It,* 310.
216. *Ladies' Home Journal,* August, 1929.
217. BARUCH, *Baruch,* 221.
218. WHALEN, *Founding Father,* 200.
219. *Saturday Evening Post,* December 31, 1938.

Non Periodical Sources Quoted

THIS list identifies where necessary books and pamphlets directly quoted in the foregoing text and distinguished by a number. A proper bibliography would be impossibly bulky. It may not be assumed that because a certain pertinent work is not mentioned here, it has not been consulted. The edition cited is always the one to which pages are referred.

ADAMIC, LOUIS; CAMPBELL, EDWARD; SCHNEIDER, MIKE; MASON, ROBERT M., *The Truth About Aimee Semple McPherson*. Girard, Kan. Haldeman-Julius Company, n.d.

[ADAMS, SAMUEL HOPKINS], pseud. Warner Fabian, *Flaming Youth*. New York, The Macaulay Co., [© 1934].

AFFAIRES ETRANGÈRES [FRANCE], Ministre de . . . , *Les Violations des Lois de la Guerre par l'Allemagne*. Paris, Librairie Berger-Levrault, 1915.

ANDERSON, SHERWOOD, *Winesburg, Ohio: A Group of Tales of Ohio Small-Town Life*. Introduction by Ernest Boyd. New York, The Modern Library, [© 1919].

The Anti-Prohibition Manual: A Summary of Facts and Figures Dealing with Prohibition. Cincinnati, National Wholesale Liquor Dealers Association, [© 1917].

ASBURY, HERBERT, *The Great Illusion: An Informal History of Prohibition*. New York, Doubleday & Company, 1950.

AUSTIN, MARY, *26 Jayne Street*. New York, Houghton Mifflin Company, 1920.

BAINBRIDGE, JOHN, *Little Wonder: or, The Reader's Digest and How It Grew*. New York, Reynal & Hitchcock, [© 1946].

BALLINGER, KENNETH, *Miami Millions: The Dance of the Dollars in the Great Florida Boom of 1925*. Miami, Florida, The Franklin Press, 1936.

BARNOUW, ERIK, *A Tower in Babel: A History of Broadcasting in the United States*, Volume I—to 1933. New York, Oxford University Press, 1966.

BARR, DONALD, *Who Pushed Humpty Dumpty?: Dilemmas in American Education Today*. New York, Atheneum, 1971.

BARTON, BRUCE, *The Man Nobody Knows: The Discovery of the Real Jesus*. Indianapolis, The Bobbs-Merrill Company, [© 1924].

BARUCH, BERNARD, *Baruch: My Own Story*. New York, Harper & Brothers, 1957.

BEGBIE, HAROLD, *More Twice-Born Men: Narratives of a Recent Movement in the Spirit of a Personal Religion*. New York, G. P. Putnam's Sons, 1923.

BENÉT, STEPHEN VINCENT, *Selected Works of*. . . . New York, Farrar & Rinehart, 1942.

BERNAYS, EDWARD L., *Biography of an Idea: Memoirs of Public Relations Counsel*. New York, Simon and Schuster, [© 1965].

BIGELOW, MAURICE A., *Sex-Education*. New York, The American Social Hygiene Association, 1936.

BIRMINGHAM, STEPHEN, *The Right People: A Portrait of the American Social Establishment*. [New York], A Dell Book, [1969].

BISHOP, JOHN PEALE, and WILSON, EDMUND, JR., *The Undertaker's Garland*. New York, Alfred A. Knopf, 1922.

BOURNE, RANDOLPH S., *The Gary Schools*. Boston, Houghton Mifflin Company, [© 1916].

——, *The History of a Literary Radical & Other Papers*. With an Introduction by Van Wyck Brooks. New York, S. A. Russell, 1956.

BRADFORD, ROARK, *Ol' Man Adam an' His Chillun: Being the Tales They Tell About the Time When the Lord Walked the Earth Like a Natural Man*. With Drawings by A. B. Walker. New York, Harper & Brothers, [© 1928].

BRALEY, BERTON, *Buddy Ballads: Songs of the A.E.F.* New York, George H. Doran Company, [© 1919].

BRIGHT, JOHN, *Hizzoner Big Bill Thompson: An Idyll of Chicago*. With an Introduction by Harry Elmer Barnes. New York, Jonathan Cape & Harrison Smith, [© 1930].

BRILL, DR. A. A., ed., *The Basic Writings of Sigmund Freud*. Translated and Edited with an Introduction by. . . . New York, The Modern Library, [© 1938].

BROOKS, JOHN, *Once in Golconda: A True Drama of Wall Street 1920–1938*. New York, Harper & Row, [© 1969].

BROUN, HEYWOOD, and LEECH, MARGARET, *Anthony Comstock: Roundsman of the Lord*. New York, Albert & Charles Boni, 1927.

BRUMBAUGH, ROBERT, *Six Trials*. New York. Crowell, [© 1969].

BRYAN, WILLIAM JENNINGS, *In His Image*. New York, Fleming H. Revell Co., [© 1922].

BRYCE, THE RIGHT HON. VISCOUNT, *Report of the Committee on Alleged German Outrages* . . . London, His Majesty's Stationery Office, 1915.

BUNDESEN, DR. HERMAN N., *The Baby Book: A Complete Health Guide in Three Parts* . . . Chicago, Published by Woman's World, [© 1927].

CAMP FIRE GIRLS, *Wo-He-Lo: The Story of . . . 1910–1960*. New York, Camp Fire Girls, Inc., [© 1961].

CARY, JOYCE, *Prisoner of Grace*. Carfax Edition. London, Michael Joseph, [© 1953].

CATTELL, J. McKEEN, *University Control*. New York, The Science Press, 1913.

CHAFEE, ZECHARIAH, JR., *Free Speech in the United States*. Cambridge, Massachusetts, Harvard University Press, 1964.

CHASE, STUART, and SCHLINK, F. J., *Your Money's Worth: A Study in the Waste of the Consumer's Dollar*. New York, The Macmillan Company, 1927.

CLARKSON, GROSVENOR E., *Industrial America in the World War: The Strategy Behind the Line 1917–1918*. With an Introduction by Georges Clémenceau. Boston, Houghton Mifflin Company, 1923.

COBB, IRVIN S., *Back Home*. New York, George H. Doran Company, [© 1911].

——, *Paths of Glory: Impressions of War Written at and Near the Front*. New York, George H. Doran Company, [© 1915].

COLE, STEWART G., *The History of Fundamentalism*. New York, Richard R. Smith, Inc., 1931.

COLLIER, JOHN, *From Every Zenith: A Memoir and Some Essays on Life and Thought.* Denver, Sage Books, [© 1963].

CONSUMERS RESEARCH, *Introduction to . . . , Not Confidential.* [New York], Consumers Research, 1932.

COWLEY, MALCOLM, *Exile's Return: A Narrative of Ideas.* New York, W. W. Norton & Company, [© 1934].

CREMIN, LAWRENCE A., *The Transformation of the School: Progressivism in American Education 1876–1957.* New York, Vintage Books, [© 1961].

CRONON, E. DAVID, *Black Moses: The Story of Marcus Garvey* . . . Foreword by John Hope Franklin. Madison, The University of Wisconsin Press, [© 1955].

CROY, HOMER, *Country Cured.* New York, Harper & Brothers, [© 1943].

CUMMINGS, E. E., *The Enormous Room.* New York, The Modern Library, 1934.

DAVIS, ELMER, *By Elmer Davis,* edited by Robert Lloyd Davis. Indianapolis, The Bobbs-Merrill Company, [© 1964].

———, *Show Window.* [New York], The John Day Company, 1927.

———, *White Pants Willie.* Indianapolis, The Bobbs-Merrill Company, [© 1924].

DECAMP, L. SPRAGUE, *The Great Monkey Trial.* Garden City, N.Y., Doubleday & Company, 1968.

DELIMA, AGNES, *The Little Red School House.* By . . . , and the staff . . . New York, The Macmillan Company, 1942.

DELL, FLOYD, *The Briary-Bush.* New York, Alfred A. Knopf, 1921.

———, *Homecoming: An Autobiography.* New York, Farrar & Rinehart, [© 1933].

DEWEY, EVELYN, *New Schools for Old.* New York, E. P. Dutton & Company, [© 1919].

DEWEY, JOHN, *German Philosophy and Politics.* New York, Henry Holt and Company, 1915.

———, *Impressions of Soviet Russia and the Revolutionary World Mexico-China-Turkey.* New York, New Republic, Inc., 1929.

———, and DEWEY, EVELYN, *Schools of To-Morrow.* New York, E. P. Dutton & Company, [© 1915].

DOOLITTLE, JAMES ROOD, *The Romance of the Automobile Industry.* New York, The Klebold Press, 1916.

DOS PASSOS, JOHN, *The Best Times: An Informal Memoir.* [New York], The New American Library, [© 1966].

———, *The Big Money.* Introduction by Maxwell Geismar. New York, Pocket Books, [1955].

———, *Mr. Wilson's War.* Mainstream of American History Series. Garden City, N.Y., Doubleday & Company, Inc., 1962.

——— *1919.* Introduction by Maxwell Geismar. New York, Pocket Books, [1954].

———, *Number One.* Boston, Houghton Mifflin Company, [© 1943].

———, *One Man's Initiation: 1917.* Authorized Edition, Complete and Unexpurgated. . . . Ithaca, New York, Cornell University Press, [1969].

———, *Three Soldiers.* With an Introduction by the Author. New York, The Modern Library, [1932].

DOUGLAS, EMILY TAFT, *Margaret Sanger: Pioneer of the Future.* New York, Holt, Rinehart and Winston, [© 1970].

DRAPER, THEODORE, *The Rediscovery of Black Nationalism.* New York, The Viking Press, [© 1969].

DRAPER, THEODORE, *The Roots of American Communism.* New York, Viking Press, 1957.

DREISER, THEODORE, *A Hoosier Holiday.* New York, John Lane Company, 1916.

DRIBERG, TOM, *The Mystery of Moral Re-Armament: A Study of Frank Buchman and His Movement.* New York, Alfred A. Knopf, 1965.

DUFFUS, R. L., *The Tower of Jewels: Memories of San Francisco.* New York, W. W. Norton Company, [© 1960].

DUNN, ROBERT, *Five Fronts: On the Firing-Line with English, French, Austrian, German and Russian Troops.* New York, Dodd, Mead and Company, 1915.

DWORKIN, MARTIN E., ed., *Dewey on Education:* Selected with an Introduction and Notes by. . . . New York, Teachers College Press, [© 1959].

EASTMAN, MAX, *Enjoyment of Living.* New York, Harper & Brothers, [© 1948].

———, *Love and Revolution: My Journey Through an Epoch.* New York, Random House, [© 1964].

———, *Venture.* New York, Albert & Charles Boni, 1927.

ELDER, DONALD, *Ring Lardner: A Biography.* Garden City, N. Y., Doubleday & Company, 1956.

FAX, ELTON C., *Garvey.* New York, Dodd, Mead & Company, 1972.

FELIX, DAVID, *Protest: Sacco-Vanzetti and the Intellectuals.* Bloomington, Indiana, Indiana University Press, [© 1965].

FERBER, EDNA, *A Peculiar Treasure.* New York, Lancer Books, [1960].

FERGUSON, CHARLES W., *The New Books of Revelations: The Inside Story of America's Astounding Religious Cults.* Garden City, N. Y., Doubleday, Doran & Company, [© 1928].

FISHBEIN, DR. MORRIS, *The Medical Follies: An Analysis of the Foibles of Some Healing Cults.* New York, Boni & Liveright, 1925.

FITZGERALD, F. SCOTT, *Tales of the Jazz Age.* New York, Charles Scribner's Sons, 1922.

———, *The Beautiful and Damned.* New York, Permabooks, 1951.

FLAGG, JAMES MONTGOMERY, *Boulevards All the Way—Maybe: Being an Artist's Truthful Impressions of the U.S.A. from New York to California and Return, by Motor.* New York, George H. Doran Company, [© 1925].

FLEXNER, ABRAHAM, *Medical Education in the United States and Canada,* A report to the Carnegie Foundation for the Advancement of Teaching. New York . . . , [© 1910].

———, *Universities: American, English, German.* New York, Oxford University Press, 1930.

FLYNN, JOHN T., *God's Gold: The Story of Rockefeller and His Times.* New York, Harcourt, Brace and Company, [© 1932].

FRANK, WALDO, *Our America.* New York, Boni and Liveright, [© 1919].

FULTON, A. R., *Motion Pictures: The Development of an Art from Silent Films to the Age of Television.* Norman, University of Oklahoma Press, [© 1960].

GALLICO, PAUL, *Farewell to Sport.* New York, Alfred A. Knopf, 1938.

GIBBS, PHILIP, *Now It Can Be Told.* New York, Harper & Brothers, [© 1920].

———, *People of Destiny: Americans as I Saw Them at Home and Abroad.* New York, Harper & Brothers, [© 1920].

GISH, LILLIAN, *The Movies, Mr. Griffith and Me.* [New York], Avon, [1970].

GITLOW, BENJAMIN, *The Whole of Their Lives: Communism in America* . . . New York, Charles Scribner's Sons, [© 1948].

GLAZER, NATHAN, and MOYNIHAN, DANIEL PATRICK, *Beyond the Melting Pot: The Negroes, Puerto Ricans, Jews, Italians and Irish of New York City.* Second Edition. Cambridge, Massachusetts, The M.I.T. Press, [© 1970].

GOLDBERG, R. L., *Rube Goldberg vs. the Machine Age* . . . Edited by Clark Kinnaird. New York, Hastings House, [© 1968].

GRANT, MADISON, *The Passing of the Great Race:* or, The Racial Basis of European History. New York, Charles Scribner's Sons, 1916.

GRAVES, ROBERT, *Good-Bye to All That: An Autobiography.* London, Jonathan Cape, [© 1929].

GRIFFITH, MRS. D. W. (Linda Arvidson), *When the Movies Were Young.* With a new Introduction by Edward Wagenknecht. New York, Dover Publications, [1969].

HALDEMAN-JULIUS, E., *The First Hundred Million.* New York, Simon and Schuster, 1928.

HALE, NATHAN G., JR., *Freud and the Americans: The Beginnings of Psychoanalysis in the United States 1876–1917.* New York, Oxford University Press, 1917.

HALL, BEN W., *The Best Remaining Seats: The Story of the Golden Age of the Movie Palace.* New York, Bramhall House, [© 1956].

HALL, JAMES NORMAN, *Kitchener's Mob: The Adventures of an American in the British Army.* Boston, Houghton Mifflin Company, [© 1916].

——, and NORDHOFF, CHARLES BERNARD, eds. *The Lafayette Flying Corps.* Port Washington, N.Y., Kennikat Press, [© 1920].

HAMPTON, BENJAMIN B., *History of the American Film Industry.* With a new Introduction by Richard Griffith . . . New York, Dover Publications, [1970].

HARRISON, HARRY P., *Culture Under Canvas: The Story of Tent Chautauqua.* New York, Hastings House, [© 1958].

HAYNES, ROY A., *Prohibition Inside Out.* New York, Doubleday, Page & Company, 1923.

HAYWOOD, WILLIAM D., *Bill Haywood's Book: The Autobiography of.* . . . New York, International Publishers, [© 1929].

HEMINGWAY, ERNEST, *By-Line: Ernest Hemingway.* Selected Articles and Despatches of Four Decades. Edited by William White. New York, Charles Scribner's Sons, [© 1967].

——, *A Farewell to Arms.* New York, Charles Scribner's Sons, 1929.

——, ed. *Men at War: The Best War Stories of All Time.* New York, Crown Publishers, [© 1942].

HERGESHEIMER, JOSEPH, *Tropical Winter.* New York, Alfred A. Knopf, 1933.

HERSHEY, BURNET, *The Odyssey of Henry Ford and the Great Peace Ship.* New York, Taplinger Publishers, [© 1967].

HEXAMER, C. J., *Address of* . . . , President of the National German-American Alliance, October 14, 1914. N.P., n.p.

HICKS, GRANVILLE, *John Reed: The Making of a Revolutionary.* New York, The Macmillan Company, 1936.

HIGHAM, JOHN, *Strangers in the Land: Patterns of American Nativism 1860–1925.* New York, Atheneum, 1963.

HOFFMAN, FREDERICK J., *Freudianism and the Literary Mind.* Baton Rouge, Louisiana State University Press, 1945.

HOFSTADTER, RICHARD, and METZGER, WALTER P. *The Development of Academic Freedom in the United States.* New York, Columbia University Press, 1955.

HOLMES, A. LAWRENCE, ed. *More Than a Game* . . . Introduction by Paul Gallico. New York, The Macmillan Company, [© 1967].

HOLMES, JOHN HAYNES, *I Speak for Myself: The Autobiography*. New York, Harper & Brothers, [© 1959].

HOLT, DR. L. EMMETT, *The Care and Feeding of Children*. Tenth Edition Revised and Enlarged. New York, D. Appleton and Company, 1920.

HOOK, SIDNEY, *John Dewey: An Intellectual Portrait*. Westport, Conn., Greenwood . Press. [© 1939].

HOTCHNER, A. E. *Papa Hemingway: A Personal Memoir*. New York, A Bantam Book, [1967].

HOWARD, SIDNEY, *They Knew What They Wanted*, in Kenneth Macgowan, *Famous American Plays of the 1920s*. The Laurel Drama Series. [New York, Dell Publishing Company, © 1959].

[HUBBARD, FRANK McKINNEY], *Abe Martin*: Hoss Sense and Nonsense, by Kin Hubbard. Indianapolis, The Bobbs-Merrill Company, [© 1926].

HUXLEY, ALDOUS, *Jesting Pilate: An Intellectual Holiday*. New York, George H. Doran Company [© 1926].

——, *Tomorrow and Tomorrow and Tomorrow and Other Essays*. A Signet Book [New York], The New American Library, [© 1964].

JAMES, GEORGE WHARTON, *Exposition Memories: Panama-California Exposition San Diego, 1916* . . . Pasadena, The Radiant Life Press, 1917.

JANIS, ELSIE, *So Far, So Good! An Autobiography*. New York, E. P. Dutton & Co., 1932.

JARDIM, ANNE, *The First Henry Ford: A Study in Personality and Business Leadership*. Cambridge, Mass, The MIT Press, [© 1970].

JOHNSON, JAMES WELDON, *Black Manhattan*. [New York], Arno Press and The New York Times, 1968.

JOHNSON, R. K., *Builder of Bridges: The Biography of Dr. Bob Jones, Sr.* Murfreesboro, Tenn. Sword of the Lord, [© 1929].

JOHNSTON, ALVA, *The Legendary Mizners*. Illustrated by Reginald Marsh. New York, Farrar, Straus and Young [© 1953].

JOLL, JAMES, *The Anarchists*. Boston, Little, Brown and Company, [© 1964].

JONES, DR. ERNEST, *The Life and Works of Sigmund Freud*. New York, Basic Books, [© 1953].

KEATS, JOHN, *Schools Without Scholars*. Boston, Houghton Mifflin Company, 1958.

KELLOGG, VERNON, *Headquarters Nights: A Record of Conversations and Experiences at the Headquarters of the German Army in France and Belgium*. Boston, The Atlantic Monthly Press, [© 1917].

KELLY, FRED C., *Life and Times of Kin Hubbard*. New York, Farrar, Straus and Young, [© 1952].

KELLY, GEORGE, *The Torch-Bearers: A satirical comedy in three acts*. New York, American Library Service, 1923.

KOENIG, LOUIS W., *Bryan: A Political Biography of William Jennings Bryan*. New York, G. P. Putnam's Sons, [© 1971].

KRAMER, DALE, *Ross and the New Yorker*. New York, Doubleday & Company, 1951.

KROUT, JOHN ALLEN, *Annals of American Sport*. The Pageant of America Series. New Haven, Yale University Press, 1929.

KUMMER, GEORGE NICHOLAS, *Harry Leon Wilson: Some Account of the Triumphs and*

Tribulations of an American Popular Writer. Cleveland, Press of Western Reserve University, 1963.

LABATUT, JEAN, and LANE, WHARTON J., eds., *Highways in Our National Life: A Symposium.* Princeton, Princeton University Press, 1950.

LANDRY, ROBERT J., *This Fascinating Radio Business.* Indianapolis, The Bobbs-Merrill Company, [© 1946].

LARDNER, RING, *The Portable Ring Lardner.:* Edited and with an Introduction by Gilbert Seldes. New York, The Viking Press, 1946.

———, *Ring Lardner's Best Stories.* With a Foreword by William McFee. New York, Garden City Publishing Company, [© 1938].

LARSEN, CHARLES, *The Good Fight: The Life and Times of Ben B. Lindsey.* Chicago, Quadrangle Books, 1972.

LASSWELL, HAROLD D., *Propaganda Technique in the World War.* London, Kegan Paul, Trench, Trubner & Co., 1927.

LATZKO, ANDREAS, *Men in War.* New York, Boni & Liveright, 1918.

LEBHAR, GODFREY M., *Chain Stores in America: 1859–1959.* New York, Chain Store Publishing Corporation, [© 1959].

LEVY, HAROLD P., *Building a Popular Movement: A Case Study of the Public Relations of the Boy Scouts of America.* New York, Russell Sage Foundation, 1944.

LEWIS, SINCLAIR, *Dodsworth.* New York, Pocket Books, [1941].

———, *Elmer Gantry.* A Signet Book. [New York], The New American Library, [1967].

———, *Free Air.* Harcourt, Brace and Company, [© 1919].

———, *Main Street.* With an afterword by Mark Schorer. A Signet Classic. [New York], The New American Library, [1961].

———, *The Prodigal Parents: A Novel.* New York, Doubleday, Doran & Company, 1938.

———, *Work of Art.* New York, Doubleday, Doran & Company, 1934.

LINDBERGH, CHARLES A. [Sr.], *Your Country at War and What Happens to You After a War.* Philadelphia, Dorrance & Company, [1934].

LINDSAY, VACHEL, *The Art of the Moving Picture.* New York, The Macmillan Company, 1915.

———, *Collected Poems of . . . ,* edited by Mark Harris. New York, The Macmillan Company, [1963].

LINDSEY, BEN B., and EVANS, WAINWRIGHT, *The Companionate Marriage.* New York, Boni & Liveright, 1927.

———, *The Revolt of Modern Youth.* New York, Boni & Liveright, 1925.

LINN, JAMES WEBBER, *Jane Addams: A Biography.* New York, D. Appleton-Century Company, 1935.

LIPPMANN, WALTER, *American Inquisitors: A Commentary on Dayton and Chicago.* New York, The Macmillan Company, 1928.

———, *Early Writings.* Introduction and annotations by Arthur Schlesinger, Jr., New York, Liveright, [© 1970].

———, *Men of Destiny.* New York, The Macmillan Company, 1927.

The Little Review Anthology, edited by Margaret Anderson. New York, Hermitage House, 1953.

LOCHNER, LOUIS P., *Always the Unexpected.* New York, The Macmillan Company, 1956.

LOCHNER, LOUIS P., *America's Don Quixote: Henry Ford's Attempt to Save Europe.* With a preface by Maxim Gorki. London, Kegan Paul, Trench, Trubner & Co., 1924.

LOEWY, RAYMOND, *Never Leave Well Enough Alone.* New York, Simon and Schuster, 1951.

LONDON, JACK, *The Mutiny of the Elsinore.* New York, The Macmillan Company, 1914.

LOOS, ANITA, *A Girl Like I.* New York, The Viking Press, [© 1966].

MACDONNELL, A. G., *A Visit to America.* New York, The Macmillan Company, 1935.

MACGOWAN, KENNETH, *Behind the Screen: The History and Techniques of the Motion Picture.* New York, Delacorte Press, [© 1965].

————, *Footlights Across America: Towards a National Theater.* New York, Harcourt, Brace and Company, [© 1929].

MACIVER, ROBERT, *Academic Freedom in Our Time.* New York, Columbia University Press, 1955.

MACKAY, CONSTANCE D'ARCY, *The Little Theatre in the United States.* [Titlepage missing in copy consulted.]

MADISON, CHARLES A., *Critics & Crusaders: A Century of American Protest.* Second Edition. New York, Frederick Ungar Publishing Co., [© 1959].

MARKEY, MORRIS, *This Country of Yours.* Boston, Little, Brown and Company, 1932.

MARKS, PERCY, *The Plastic Age.* New York, Century, [© 1924].

MARQUIS, DON, *The Best of. . . .* With an introduction by Christopher Morley. Garden City, N.Y., Doubleday, 1946.

————, *Hermione and Her Little Group of Serious Thinkers.* New York, D. Appleton and Company, 1916.

————, *The lives and times of archy and mehitabel.* New York, Doubleday & Company, [© 1934].

MASON, HERBERT MOLLOY, JR., *The Lafayette Escadrille.* New York, Random House, [© 1964].

MASTERS, EDGAR LEE, *Across Spoon River; An Autobiography.* New York, Farrar & Rinehart, [© 1936].

MCLOUGHLIN, WILLIAM G., JR., *Billy Sunday Was His Real Name.* [Chicago], University of Chicago Press, [© 1955].

MENCKEN, H. L., *Prejudices, First Series.* Borzoi Pocket Books. New York, Alfred A. Knopf, 1929.

MERZ, CHARLES, *And Then Came Ford.* Garden City, N.Y., Doubleday, Doran & Company, 1929.

MILLIS, WALTER, *Road to War: America 1914–1917.* Boston, Houghton Mifflin Company, 1935.

MOCK, JAMES R., and LARSON, CEDRIC, *Words That Won The War: The Story of the Committee on Public Information 1917–1919.* Princeton, Princeton University Press, 1939.

MURRAY, WILLIAM D., *The History of the Boy Scouts of America.* New York, Boy Scouts of America. [© 1937].

MYERS, GUSTAVUS, *History of Bigotry in the United States.* New York, Random House, [© 1943].

NASH, OGDEN, *Bed Riddance:* A Posy for the Indisposed. Boston, Little Brown and Company, [© 1969].

NEARING, SCOTT, *The New Education: A Review of Progressive Educational Movements of the Day.* Chicago, Row, Peterson & Company, [© 1915].

NEILSON, FRANCIS, *How Diplomats Make War.* New York, B. W. Huebsch, 1916.

NEVINS, ALLAN, *Ford: The Man, the Company* . . . With the collaboration of Frank Ernest Hill. New York, Charles Scribner's Sons, 1954.

———, *Ford: Expansion and Challenge* . . . New York, Charles Scribner's Sons, [© 1957].

NICHOLS, BEVERLEY, *The Star-Spangled Manner.* London, Jonathan Cape, [© 1928].

NORMAN, CHARLES, *E. E. Cummings: The Magic-Maker.* New York, Duell, Sloan and Pearce, [© 1964].

———, *Ezra Pound.* New York, The Macmillan Company, 1960.

O'CONNOR, RICHARD, *Black Jack Pershing.* Garden City, N.Y., Doubleday, 1961.

———, and WALKER, DALE L., *The Lost Revolutionary: A Biography of John Reed.* New York, Harcourt, Brace & World, [© 1967].

PARENTS AND TEACHERS, NATIONAL CONGRESS OF . . . , *Golden Jubilee History,* Chicago, . . . [© 1947].

PARKHURST, HELEN, *Education on the Dalton Plan* . . . New York, E. P. Dutton & Company, [© 1922].

PARRY, ALBERT, *Garrets and Pretenders: A History of Bohemianism in America.* New York, Covici-Friede, 1933.

PEGLER, WESTBROOK, *The Dissenting Opinions of Mister Westbrook Pegler.* New York, Charles Scribner's Sons, 1938.

———, *'Tain't Right,* New York, Doubleday, Doran & Co., 1936.

PERKINS, DEXTER, *Yield of the Years: An Autobiography.* Boston, Little, Brown and Company, [© 1969].

PHILLIPS, M. C., *Skin Deep: The Truth About Beauty Aids—Safe and Harmful.* New York, The Vanguard Press, [© 1934].

PINCHOT, GIFFORD, *Breaking New Ground.* New York, Harcourt, Brace and Company, [© 1947].

PINKEVITCH, ALBERT P., *The New Education in the Soviet Republic.* . . . edited by George S. Counts. New York, The John Day Company, [© 1929].

POMEROY, EARL SPENCE, *The Pacific Slope: A History of California, Oregon, Washington, Idaho, Utah and Nevada.* New York, A. A. Knopf, 1965.

POST, EMILY, *By Motor to the Golden Gate.* New York, D. Appleton & Co., 1916.

PUTZEL, MAX, *The Man in The Mirror: William Marion Reedy and His Magazine.* Cambridge, Harvard University Press, 1963.

RAE, JOHN B., *The American Automobile: A Brief History.* Chicago, University of Chicago Press, [© 1965].

REID, IRA DE AUGUSTINE, *The Negro Immigrant: His Background, Characteristics and Social Adjustment 1889–1937.* New York, [Columbia University Press], 1939.

RICE, ARNOLD S., *The Ku Klux Klan in American Politics.* Introduction by Harry Golden. Washington, D.C., Public Affairs Press, [© 1962].

RICE, GRANTLAND, *The Tumult and the Shouting: My Life in Sport.* New York, A. S. Barnes, Company, [© 1964].

RIEGEL, O. W., *Mobilizing for Chaos: The Story of the New Propaganda.* New Haven, Yale University Press, 1934.

RINGEL, FRED J., ed., *America as Americans See It*. New York, Harcourt, Brace and Company, [© 1932].

RUGGLES, ELEANOR, *The Westering Heart*. New York, W. W. Norton, [© 1959].

RUSSELL, FRANCIS, *Tragedy in Dedham: The Story of the Sacco-Vanzetti Case*. New York, McGraw-Hill Book Company, [© 1962].

SANDBURG, CARL, *The American Songbag*. New York, Harcourt, Brace & Company, [© 1927].

———, *The Chicago Race Riots*. With an introductory note by Walter Lippmann. New York, Harcourt, Brace and Howe 1919.

———, *Complete Poems*. New York, Harcourt, Brace and Company, [© 1950].

SARGEANT, WINTHROP, *In Spite of Myself; A Personal Memoir*. Garden City, N.Y., Doubleday & Company, 1970.

———, *Jazz, Hot and Hybrid*. New York, Arrow Editions, [© 1938].

SCHORER, MARK, *Sinclair Lewis: An American Life*. New York, McGraw-Hill Book Company, [© 1961].

SELDES, GEORGE, *The Great Quotations*. New York, Lyle Stuart, [© 1960].

SELDES, GILBERT, *The Seven Lively Arts*. New York, The Sagamore Press, [© 1957].

SEYMOUR, HAROLD, *Baseball: The Golden Age*. New York, Oxford University Press, 1971.

SHEEAN, VINCENT, *Personal History*. 1969 edition with a new introduction by the author. Boston, Houghton Mifflin Company, 1969.

SIEGFRIED, ANDRE, *America Comes of Age: A French Analysis*. New York, Harcourt, Brace and Company, [© 1927].

SINCLAIR, ANDREW, *The Better Half*. New York, Harper & Row, [© 1965].

SINCLAIR, UPTON, *The Jungle*. New York, New American Library, 1960.

———, *Money Writes!* New York, Boni & Liveright, 1927.

SLOAN, ALFRED P., JR., *My Years with General Motors*. New York, Doubleday & Company, 1964.

SMITH, GENE, *When the Cheering Stopped: The Last Years of Woodrow Wilson*. With an introduction by Allan Nevins. New York, Bantam Books, [1965].

SMITH, RALPH LEE, *At Your Own Risk: The Case Against Chiropractic*. New York, Trident Press, [© 1969].

SMITH, ROBERT PAUL, *"Where Did You Go?" "Out." "What Did You Do?" "Nothing."* New York, W. W. Norton, [© 1957].

SOBEL, BERNARD, *Burleycue*. New York, Farrar & Rinehart, [© 1931].

SOBEL, ROBERT, *The Great Bull Market*. New York, W. W. Norton & Company, [© 1968].

STALLINGS, LAURENCE, *The Doughboys: The Story of the AEF, 1917–1918*. New York, Harper & Row, [© 1963].

STEARNS, HAROLD E., ed., *Civilization in the United States: An Inquiry by Thirty Americans*. New York, Harcourt, Brace and Company, [© 1922].

STEFFENS, LINCOLN, *The Autobiography of. . . .* New York, Harcourt, Brace and Company, [© 1933].

STODDARD, LOTHROP, *The Rising Tide of Color Against White World-Supremacy*. With an introduction by Madison Grant. New York, Charles Scribner's Sons, 1920.

STRATTON PORTER, GENE, *Her Father's Daughter*. Garden City, Doubleday, Page & Company, 1921.

STREET, JULIAN, *Abroad at Home.* New York, Century Company, 1914.

STREETER, EDWARD, *Dere Mable—Love Letters of a Rookie* . . . New York, Frederick A Stokes Company, [© 1918].

SULLIVAN, MARK, *Our Times,* Vol. V, Vol. VI. New York, Charles Scribner's Sons, 1933, 1935.

SUNDAY, BILLY, *Great Love Stories of the Bible and Their Lessons for Today.* New York, G. P. Putnam's Sons, 1917.

SWANBERG, W. A., *Dreiser.* New York, Charles Scribner's Sons, [© 1965].

———, *Luce and His Empire.* New York, Charles Scribner's Sons, [© 1972].

SWARD, KEITH, *The Legend of Henry Ford.* New York, Rinehart & Company, 1948.

TARKINGTON, BOOTH, *Penrod: His Complete Story.* New York, Doubleday & Co., n.d.

———, *The Turmoil.* New York, Harper & Brothers, 1915.

TAYLOR, BERT LESTON, *The So-Called Human Race.* Arranged, with an introduction, by Henry B. Fuller. New York, Alfred A. Knopf, 1922.

TAYLOR, FREDERICK WINSLOW, *The Principles of Scientific Management.* New York, Harper & Brothers, 1916.

TAYLOR SOCIETY, *Frederick Winslow Taylor: A Memorial Volume.* New York, Taylor Society, [© 1920].

TEBBEL, JOHN, *An American Dynasty: The Story of the McCormicks, Medills and Pattersons.* New York, Doubleday & Company, 1947.

TEBEAU, CHARLTON W., *A History of Florida.* Coral Gables, University of Miami Press, [© 1971].

THOMAS, LATELY, *Storming Heaven: The Lives and Turmoils of Minnie Kennedy and Aimee Semple McPherson.* New York, William Morrow and Company, 1970.

———, *The Vanishing Evangelist (The Aimee Semple McPherson Kidnap Case).* New York, The Viking Press, 1959.

THOMAS, NORMAN, *The Conscientious Objector in America.* Introduction by Robert M. La Follette. New York, B. M. Huebsch, 1923.

[THOMPSON, VANCE], *Eat and Grow Thin: The Mahdah Menus.* New York, E. P. Dutton & Company, [© 1914].

THURBER, JAMES. *The Years with Ross.* Boston, Little, Brown and Company, [© 1957].

TODD, FRANK MORTON, *The Story of the Exposition, Being the Official History* . . . New York, G. P. Putnam's Sons, 1921.

VAN LOAN, CHARLES E., *Buck Parvin and the Movies.* New York, George H. Doran Company, [© 1915].

VAN VECHTEN, CARL, *Parties: Scenes from Contemporary New York Life.* New York, Alfred A. Knopf, 1930.

VEBLEN, THORSTEIN, *The Higher Learning in America: A Memorandum on the Conduct of Universities by Business Men.* New York, B. W. Huebsch, 1918.

VIERECK, GEORGE SYLVESTER, and CHESTERTON, CECIL, *Debate Between.* . . . Cort Theatre, January 17th, 1915. Published by the Fatherland Corporation, 1123 Broadway, New York City.

WAGNER, CHARLES A., ed., *Prize Poems.* With an introduction by Mark Van Doren. New York, Albert and Charles Boni, 1930.

WARE, CAROLINE F., *Greenwich Village 1920–1930: A Comment on American Civilization in the Post-War Years.* New York, Harper & Row, [© 1935].

WATSON, JOHN B., *Behaviorism*. New York, W. W. Norton & Company, [© 1924].

———, *Psychological Care of Infant and Child*. New York, W. W. Norton & Company, [© 1928].

WEIDLING, PHILIP, and BURGHARD, AUGUST, *Checkered Sunshine: The History of Fort Lauderdale*. Gainesville, University of Florida Press, 1966.

WELLS, H. G., *Mr. Britling Sees It Through*. New York, The Macmillan Company, 1916.

WENDT, LLOYD, and KOGAN, HERMAN, *Big Bill of Chicago*. Indianapolis, The Bobbs-Merrill Company, [© 1953].

WEST, REBECCA, *The Strange Necessity*. London, J. Cape, 1928.

WEYAND, ALEXANDER M., *Football*. Foreword by Grantland Rice. New York, The Macmillan Company, [© 1955].

WHALEN, RICHARD J., *The Founding Father: The Story of Joseph P. Kennedy*. [New York] The New American Library, [© 1964].

WHARTON, EDITH, *A Backward Glance*. New York, D. Appleton-Century Company, 1934.

———, *The Marne*. New York, D. Appleton & Company, 1918.

WHITE, LLEWELLYN, *The American Radio: A Report on the Broadcasting Industry in the United States from the Commission on Freedom of the Press*. Chicago, the University of Chicago Press, [© 1947.]

WHITE, WALTER F., *A Man Called White: The Autobiography of. . . .* New York, The Viking Press, 1948.

WILLIAMS, ALBERT RHYS, *In the Claws of the German Eagle*. New York, E. P. Dutton & Co., [© 1917.]

WILSON, EDMUND, *A Prelude: Landscapes, Characters and Conversations from the Earlier Years of My Life*. New York, Farrar, Straus and Giroux, [© 1967].

WILSON, HARRY LEON, *Merton of the Movies* (in *Ruggles, Bunker & Merton: Three Masterpieces of Humor*). Garden City, Doubleday, Doran & Co., 1935.

———, *Professor, How Could You!* New York, Cosmopolitan Book Corp,. 1924.

WINTER, ELLA, *Red Virtue: Human Relationships in the New Russia*. New York, Harcourt, Brace and Company, [© 1933].

WISTER, OWEN, *Neighbors Henceforth*. New York, The Macmillan Company, 1928.

———, *The Pentecost of Calamity*. New York, The Macmillan Company, 1915.

WOLFE, BERTRAM D., *Strange Communists I Have Known*. New York, Stein and Day, [© 1965].

WOODWARD, C. VANN, *Tom Watson: Agrarian Rebel*. New York, The Macmillan Company, 1938.

YEOMANS, HENRY AARON, *Abbott Lawrence Lowell 1856–1943*. Cambridge, Mass., Harvard University Press, 1948.

ZEIDMAN, IRVING, *The American Burlesque Show*. New York, Hawthorn Books, [© 1957].

Index